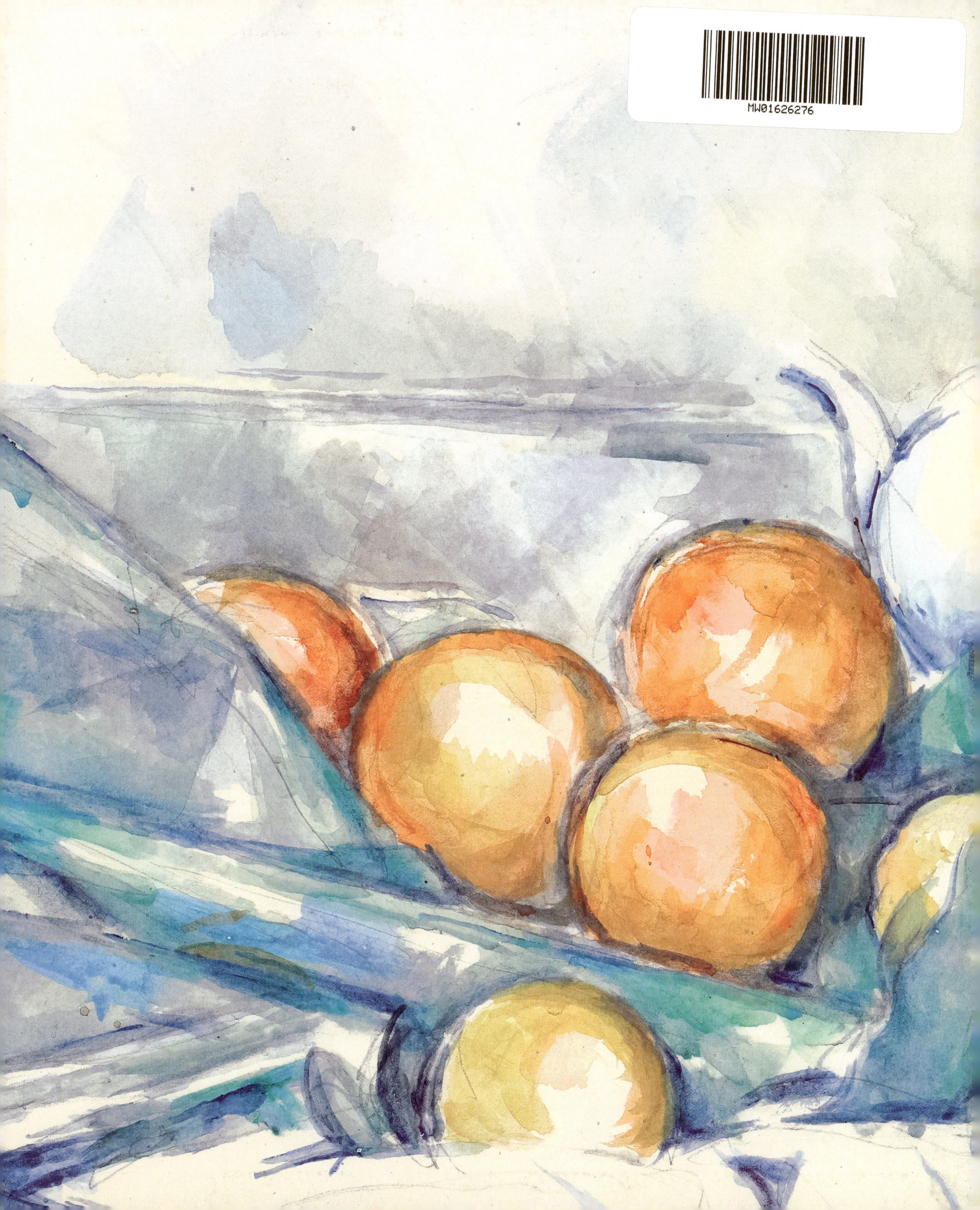

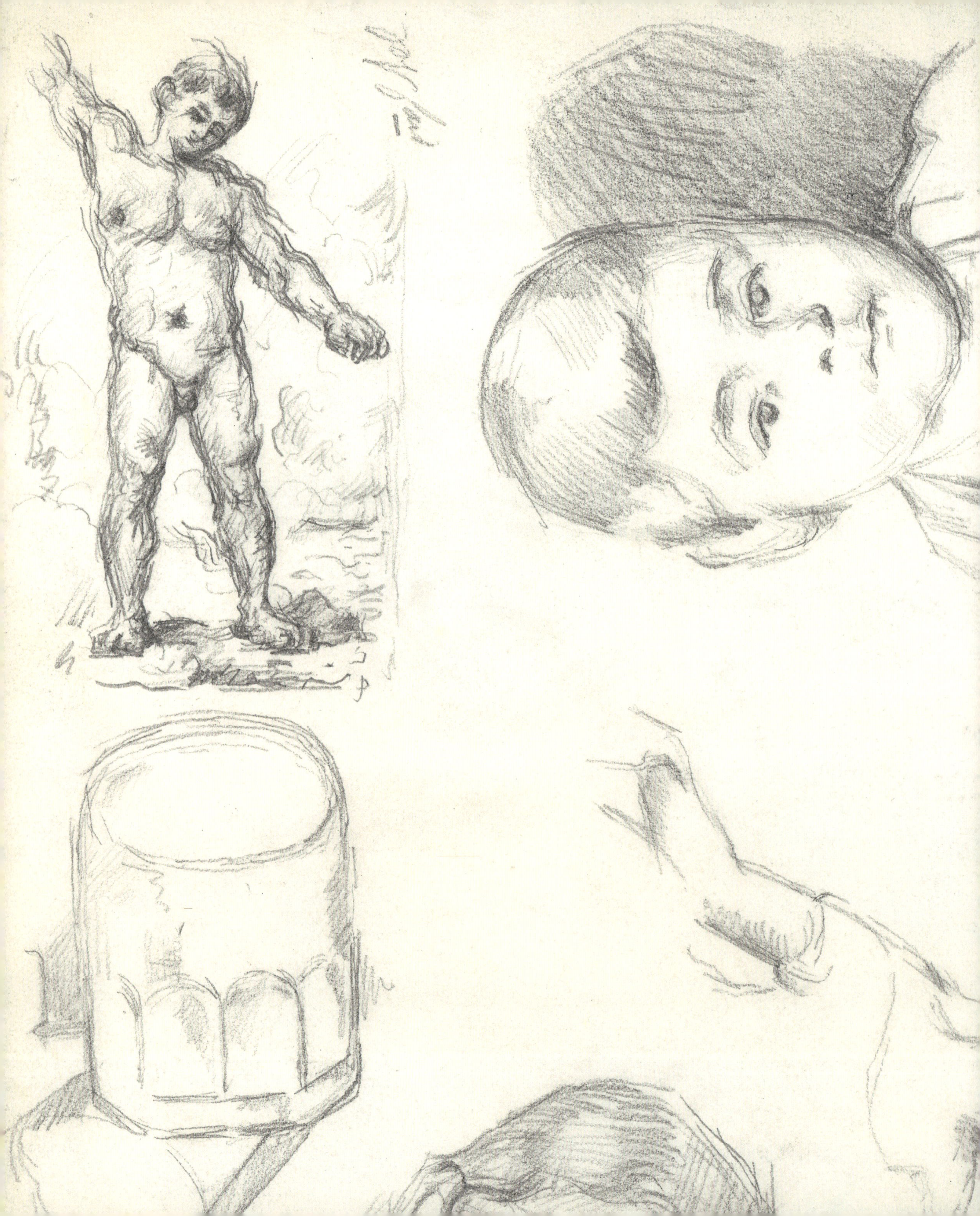

CÉZANNE DRAWING

CÉZANNE DRAWING

Edited by Jodi Hauptman
and Samantha Friedman

With essays by
Kiko Aebi
Samantha Friedman
Jodi Hauptman
Annemarie Iker
Laura Neufeld

The Museum of Modern Art, New York

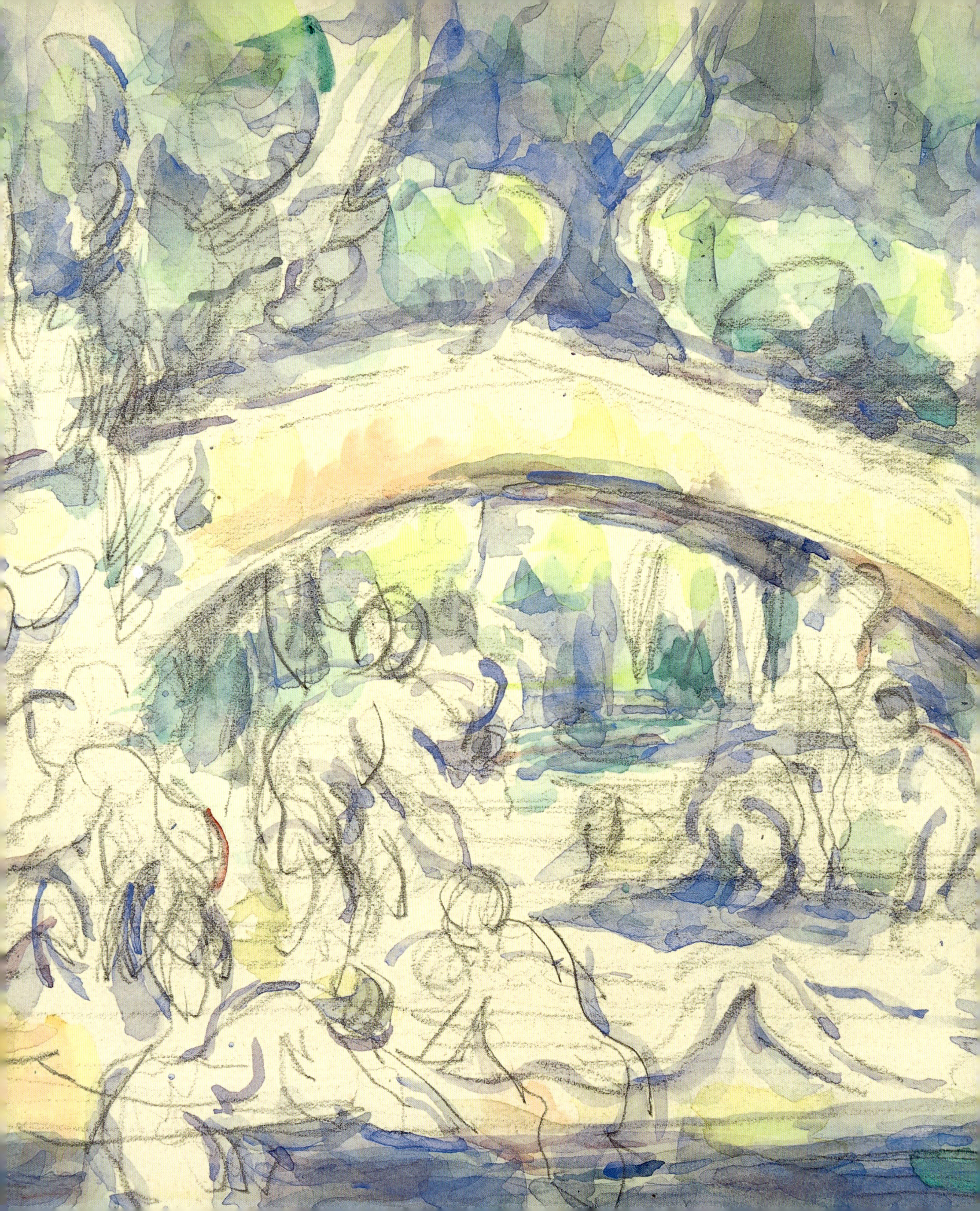

Foreword

The Museum of Modern Art made its debut on November 7, 1929, with an exhibition of work by Paul Cézanne, Paul Gauguin, Georges Seurat, and Vincent van Gogh—just nine days after the stock market crash that became known as Black Tuesday saw the loss of billions of dollars and initiated an economic downturn and depression that would last until 1939. "Wall Street was a street of vanished hopes," the *New York Times* reported the day after the crash, "of curiously silent apprehension and a sort of paralyzed hypnosis."

Over the course of the 1930s, Cézanne's work would be central to at least five exhibitions, including two honoring Lillie P. Bliss, whose collection, with its eleven paintings, thirteen drawings and watercolors, and two lithographs by Cézanne, was the cornerstone of MoMA's holdings. Given the way the Museum's founding director, Alfred H. Barr, Jr., understood Cézanne's importance for modern art (as a pioneer who "founded new traditions," an artist who "changed the direction of the history of art," "a bridge between the art of his predecessors and the art of his successors") and the artist's place in Bliss's holdings (Barr wrote that "without question the twenty-six works by Cézanne . . . are the most important section of the collection"), it is not surprising that this "prodigiously ambitious but abnormally sensitive" artist would show up again and again as the Museum's curators created a program to introduce and explicate modern art in New York. What we can't fully comprehend, even from reading contemporaneous reviews of these exhibitions and installations, is what Cézanne's work meant to the Museum's early visitors, who were facing an unprecedented and turbulent decade. Did Cézanne's attempts to give shape to form help viewers to make sense of their own moment? Did what Barr called Cézanne's "crudely powerful" approach speak to the experience of everyday life? In 1934 the Museum's president, A. Conger Goodyear, described the challenges of collection building and exhibition making in this era, acknowledging the "troubled times" and the "years of discouragement and depression." He called for "courage and determination" as the Museum sought to meet its mandate as a permanent institution. Lloyd Goodrich, writing in the *Nation*, praised the Museum at its opening for helping audiences feel their way "through difficult and uncharted seas" and called for courage and farsightedness.

Now, as we present another exhibition of Cézanne's work, we find ourselves again in troubled times, in an epoch likewise marked by discouragement and inflected by uncertainty, mourning, and turmoil, and one also braced by hope, courage, and foresight. As much as Cézanne's works are of his own day, and may have taken on meaning for those Depression-era audiences, we are especially conscious of the way his works—especially his drawings, the subject of this project—resonate in our pandemic moment. We see this particularly in the artist's repeated, searching pencil lines that visualize precariousness; in his distorted figures that reveal the body in process; in his multihued, layered veils of pigment that push the bounds of color. His subjects, too, are resonant: from the narrow range of objects and people that surrounded him at home or in his studio, which reminds us of the creative possibilities present even when sheltering in relative isolation, to the prismatic landscapes that induce wonder at our relations with the natural world.

Cézanne Drawing is the first major exhibition in the United States to unite drawings from across the artist's career, bringing together an unprecedented number of works on paper from public and private collections around the world. We are excited to imagine what our audiences will take from, and do with, the experience of seeing these drawings together.

At any time, an exhibition of this scale is an ambitious undertaking, requiring contributions from the entire Museum staff and the close collaboration of friends and colleagues across the globe. Bringing this project to completion during a pandemic was exceptionally challenging. It would not have been possible without the leadership support provided by The International Council of The Museum of Modern Art, Ronald S. and Jo Carole Lauder, the Kate W. Cassidy Foundation, the Steven & Alexandra Cohen Foundation, The Halvorsen Family Foundation, and Monique M. Schoen Warshaw. Generous funding is provided by the Eyal and Marilyn Ofer Family Foundation, the Robert Lehman Foundation, the Dian Woodner Exhibition Endowment Fund, and Emily Rauh Pulitzer. Special thanks to William L. Bernhard and the late Catherine Cahill, Andreas Dracopoulos, Jack Shear, Anne Hendricks Bass Foundation, Ann R. Kinney in Memory of Gilbert H. Kinney, John Wilmerding, Thierry Barbier-Mueller, Pontus Bonnier, H.R.H. Duke Franz of Bavaria, Brigitte Oetker, and Eleanor Ford Sullivan for their gifts to The International Council in support of the exhibition. We are tremendously grateful for the essential indemnity support granted by the Federal Council on the Arts and Humanities.

Again and again, we have been most heartened and encouraged by the enthusiasm of the custodians of these works, private collectors and our counterparts at other museums. Their willingness to share precious drawings and paintings from their collections, even in the midst of their own challenges and heartbreak, is nothing short of awe inspiring. Like us, they believe in the transformative power of art, the potential it sparks in our audiences.

Even as our far-flung friends shared their expertise and readied their works for travel, much was happening here at home. We are indebted to the efforts of the Museum's senior staff, including Ramona Bannayan, Todd Bishop, James Gara, James Grooms, and Sarah Suzuki, and their dedicated staffs. This project is grounded in close looking, and I am grateful to the Cézanne team in the Museum's Department of Drawings and Prints—Jodi Hauptman, Senior Curator; Samantha Friedman, Associate Curator; and Kiko Aebi, Curatorial Assistant—for training their eyes and minds on Cézanne's ever-thrilling practice. They partnered with Laura Neufeld, Associate Paper Conservator, in creating an enriching curatorial/conservation collaboration, together illuminating the way Cézanne used pencil, ink, and watercolor to transform vision.

Glenn D. Lowry
The David Rockefeller Director
The Museum of Modern Art

Acknowledgments

Even the unsociable Cézanne depended on the goodwill of his intimates–his wife Hortense, his son Paul, his gardener Vallier, his dealer Vollard–to achieve his vision. And we, too, have relied tremendously (indeed, in the midst of a pandemic, all the more) on the unstinting support and cooperation of dear colleagues both at home and abroad, all of whom have believed unwaveringly in the importance of this project.

We extend our deepest gratitude to the many lenders who entrusted these precious works to our care at a moment of great uncertainty. From institutions, we would like to thank: at the Albertina, Vienna, Klaus Albrecht Schröder (Director General), Heinz Widauer (Curator of French Art), and Jasha Greenberg (Exhibition and Loan Management); at the Arkansas Museum of Fine Arts, Little Rock, Victoria Ramirez (Executive Director), Ann Prentice Wagner (Jackye and Curtis Finch, Jr. Curator of Drawings), and Katharine Hall (Collections Manager and Head Registrar); at the Art Institute of Chicago, James Rondeau (President and Eloise W. Martin Director), Jay A. Clarke (Rothman Family Curator of Prints and Drawings), Gloria Groom (Chair of European Painting and Sculpture and David and Mary Winton Green Curator of 19th Century Painting and Sculpture), and Natasha Derrickson (Associate Director, Collections); at the Baltimore Museum of Art, Christopher Bedford (Dorothy Wagner Wallis Director), Andaleeb Banta (Senior Curator and Department Head of Prints, Drawings, and Photographs), and Giselle Piqué (Assistant Registrar); at Museum Berggruen, Nationalgalerie, Staatliche Museen zu Berlin, Udo Kittelmann (former Director) and Gabriel Montua (Curator of the Collection); at Fondation Beyeler, Riehen/Basel, Sam Keller (Director), Ulf Küster (Curator), Simon Crameri (Library and Provenance), Tanja Narr (Registrar), and Svenja Eckell (Assistant Registrar); at the Museum Boijmans Van Beuningen, Rotterdam, Sjarel Ex (Director), Albert J. Elen (Senior Curator of Prints and Drawings), Mieke Fransen (Registrar), and Lindy de Heij (Loan Coordinator); at Kunsthalle Bremen, Christoph Grunenberg (Director) and Tanja Borghardt (Registrar); at the British Museum, London, Hartwig Fischer (Director), Hugo Chapman (Simon Sainsbury Keeper of Prints and Drawings), Stephen Coppel (Curator of the Modern Collection), Rocío Mayol (Loans Coordinator), Carlota Iris (Loans Coordinator), and Christopher Stewart (Registrar); at the Brooklyn Museum, Anne Pasternak (Shelby White and Leon Levy Director), Shea Spiller (Curatorial Assistant), Elizabeth Largi (Assistant Registrar), and Erika Umali (Assistant Curator of Collections); at the Canadian Centre for Architecture, Montreal, Catherine LaRivière (Coordinator of Loans); at the Cincinnati Art Museum, Cameron Kitchin (Louis and Louise Dieterle Nippert Director) and Carola Bell (Registrar); at the Cleveland Museum of Art, William M. Griswold (Director and President), Heather Lemonedes Brown (Virginia N. and Randall J. Barbato Deputy Director and Chief Curator), Britany Salsbury (Associate Curator of Prints and Drawings), and Gretchen Shie Miller (Registrar); at the Courtauld Gallery, London, Ernst Vegelin Van Claerbergen (Head), Ketty Gottardo (Martin Halusa Curator of Drawings), Rachel Sloan (Assistant Curator), and Julia Blanks (Registrar); at the Dallas Museum of Art, Agustín Arteaga (Eugene McDermott Director), Nicole R. Myers (Barbara Thomas Lemmon Senior Curator of European Art), and Tricia Taylor Dixon (Associate Registrar); at the Detroit Institute of Arts, Salvador Salort-Pons (Director), Clare I. Rogan (Curator of Prints and Drawings), and Michelle Smith (Registrar); at the Fitzwilliam Museum, University of Cambridge, Luke Syson (Director and Marlay Curator), Jane Munro (Keeper of Paintings, Drawings, and Prints), David Packer (Registrar), and Elena Saggers (Assistant Registrar); at Fondazione Magnani-Rocca, Parma, Stefano Roffi (Scientific Director); at the Galleria Nazionale d'Arte Moderna e Contemporanea, Rome, Cristiana Collu (Director) and Stefano Marson (Registrar); at the J. Paul Getty Museum, Los Angeles, Timothy Potts (Maria Hummer-Tuttle and Robert Tuttle Director), Emily A. Beeny (Associate Curator of Drawings), and Jennifer Garpner (Associate Registrar); at the Musée Granet, Aix-en-Provence, Bruno Ely (Chief Curator) and Stéphanie Lardez (Registrar); at the Solomon R. Guggenheim Museum, New York, Richard Armstrong (Director), Vivien Greene (Senior Curator of 19th and Early 20th Century Art), Megan Fontanella (Curator of Modern Art and Provenance), and Carol Nesemann Klebanoff (Registrar); at Hamburger Kunsthalle, Alexander Klar (Director), Andreas Stolzenburg (Head of Department of Prints and Drawings), and Kazusa Haii (Registrar); at Harvard Art Museums, Martha Tedeschi (Elizabeth and John Moors Cabot Director), Soyoung Lee (Landon and Lavinia Clay Chief Curator), Joachim Homann (Maida and George Abrams Curator of Drawings), Elizabeth Rudy (Carl A. Weyerhaeuser Associate Curator of Prints), and Nicole Linderman-Moss (Associate Registrar); at Kunsthaus Zürich, Christoph Becker (Director), Philippe Büttner (Curator), Jonas Beyer (Curator), and Karin Marti (former Registrar); at Kunstmuseum Basel, Josef Helfenstein (Director), Anita Haldemann (Head of Department of Prints and Drawings and Deputy Director), Irène Tschopp (Assistant Exhibitions and Collections), and Maya Urich (Registrar); at the Los Angeles County Museum of Art, Michael Govan (CEO and Wallis Annenberg Director), Leslie Jones (Curator of Prints and Drawings), Jayne Manuel (Registration Administrator), and Megan Smith (Associate Registrar); at the Metropolitan Museum of Art, New York, Max Hollein (Marina Kellen French Director), Nadine M. Orenstein (Drue Heinz Curator in Charge, Drawings and Prints), Dita Amory (Curator in Charge and Administrator of the Robert Lehman Collection), Allison Rudnick (Associate Curator of Drawings and Prints), and Emily Foss (Senior Associate Registrar); at the Morgan Library and Museum, New York, Colin B. Bailey (Director), Jennifer Tonkovich (Eugene and Clare Thaw Curator of Drawings and Prints), John Alexander (Senior Manager of Exhibition and Collection Administration), and Sophie Worley (former Assistant Registrar); at the Museum of Fine Arts, Budapest, László Baán (General Director), Judit Geskó (Chief Curator), and Katalin Borbély and Judit Kata Virág (Registrars); at the National Gallery of Art, Washington, D.C., Kaywin Feldman (Director), Jonathan Bober (Andrew W. Mellon Senior Curator of Prints and Drawings), Kimberly A. Jones (Curator of Nineteenth-Century French Paintings), Paula Binari (Loan Officer), and Ginger Crockett Hammer (Print Room Specialist); at the National Gallery of Ireland, Dublin, Sean Rainbird (Director) and Caroline Clarke (Collection Registrar); at the National Museum of Western Art, Tokyo, Akiko Mabuchi (Director General), Takashi Iizuka (Curator), and Naoko Asano and Azu Kubota (Associate Curators); at the Nationalmuseum, Stockholm, Susanna Pettersson (Director General) and Audrey Lebioda (Loans Administrator); at the Philadelphia Museum of Art, Timothy Rub (George D. Widener Director and CEO), Alice Beamesderfer (Pappas-Sarbanes Deputy Director for Collections and Programs), Louis Marchesano (Audrey and William H. Helfand Senior Curator of Prints, Drawings, and Photographs), Sharon Hildebrand (Head Preparator), Clare Kobasa (former Suzanne Andrée Curatorial Fellow of Prints, Drawings, and Photographs), Morgan Webb (Interim Head of Registration for Collections), and Lisa Morra (Collections Assistant of Prints, Drawings, and Photographs); at the Musée d'Orsay, Paris, Laurence des Cars (President), Sylvie Patry (Deputy Director for Curatorial Affairs and Collections), Stéphane Bayard (Deputy Head of Exhibitions), Elise Dubreuil (Curator of Decorative Arts), Leïla Jarbouai (Curator of Graphic Arts), and Isabelle Gaëtan (Documentation des Dessins); at the Musée Picasso Paris, Laurent Le Bon (President), Sophie Daynes-Diallo (Head of Production), and Juliette Pozzo (Collection Specialist); at the Picker Art Gallery, Colgate University, Nick West (Co-Director of University Museums and Curator) and Susanna White (Registrar and Collections Manager); at Princeton University Art Museum, James Steward (Nancy A. Nasher–David J. Haemisegger, Class of 1976, Director), Laura Giles (Heather and Paul G. Haaga Jr., Class of 1970, Curator of Prints and Drawings), Caroline I. Harris (Diane W. and James E. Burke Associate Director for Education), Alexia Hughes (Chief Registrar and Manager of Collections Services), and Carol Rossi (Associate Registrar); at Smith College Museum of Art, Jessica Nicoll (Director and Louise Ines Doyle '34 Chief Curator), Aprile Gallant (Associate Director of Curatorial Affairs and Senior Curator of Prints, Drawings, and Photographs), and Deborah Diemente (Collection Manager and Registrar); at the Snite Museum of Art at the University of Notre Dame, Joseph A. Becherer (Director and Curator of Sculpture) and Victoria Perdomo (Registrar); at Staatsgalerie Stuttgart, Christiane Lange (Director), Annette Blattmacher and Kathrin Wrona (Registrars), and Anne-Katrin Koch (Head of Library and Digital Image Archive); at the Städel Museum, Frankfurt, Philipp Demandt (Director), Alexander Eiling (Head of Modern Art), and Beatrice Drengwitz (Registrar); at Tate, Maria Balshaw (Director of the Tate Art Museums), Frances Morris (Director, Tate Modern), Achim Borchardt-Hume (Director of Exhibitions, Tate Modern), and Hannah Murray and Sarah-Jane Stockings (Registrars); at the Museo Nacional Thyssen-Bornemisza, Madrid, Guillermo Solana (Artistic Director), Marián Aparicio (Head Registrar), and Beatriz Blanco (Senior Registrar); at the Virginia Museum of Fine Arts, Richmond, Alex Nyerges (Director) and Nancy T. Nichols (Senior Registrar); at the Wadsworth Atheneum Museum of Art, Hartford, Thomas J. Loughman (Director and CEO) and Mary Busick (Registrar); and at the Whitworth, University of Manchester, Alistair Hudson (Director), Leanne Green (Curator of Modern and Contemporary), and Gillian Smithson (Registrar).

We are extraordinarily grateful to the following individuals and private collections that shared their treasured objects: Adriani Foundation; Collezione Marco Brunelli, Milan, with Giovanni Renzi (Curator); Bruce Barnes and Joseph Cunningham; the Callimanopulos Collection, with Florence Carrie (Curator and Art Collection Manager); Mr. and Mrs. Carroll L. Cartwright; Fondation Marie Anne Krugier Poniatowski, with Evelyne Ferlay (Curator); Fondation Socindec, with David Ryser; Kate Ganz Collection; Esther Grether Family Collection, with Oliver Wick (Curator); Rita and Alex Hillman Foundation, with Ahrin Mishan (Executive Director) and Emily Braun (Curator of the Collection); Jasper Johns, with Maureen Pskowski; R. Stanley and Ursula M. Johnson; Mr. and Mrs. Barron U. Kidd; the Kravis Collection, with Gary Owen; David Lachenmann, with Beatrice Reymond; Phyllis Lambert Collection; Claudio and Doriana Marzocco Collection, with Matthew Stephenson; Stephen Mazoh and Martin Kline; the Phillips Family Collection; Véronique and Louis-Antoine Prat; Galerie Rosengart, Lucerne; at Karsten Schubert Ltd., London, Caroline Manganaro (Exhibitions Director); Rudolf Staechelin Family Collection; and Keith D. Stoltz, with Lorraine Parker; and at the Henry and Rose Pearlman Foundation, Daniel Edelman (President), who not only granted us additional time for close study, but also engaged us in a lively dialogue around the presentation and preservation of the works. We remain deeply indebted as well to the generous lenders who wish to remain anonymous.

For guidance crucial to our project's success, we appreciate the graceful and determined efforts of: Nicholas and William Acquavella, with Jean Edmonson; Fred Bancroft; Olivier Berggruen; Mark Brady; Carrie Bray; James Butterwick; Thomas Colville; David Cusin and Marielle Chatelain, Simon Studer Art, Geneva; Tatyana Franck; Peter Galassi; Léonard Gianadda, President of Fondation Pierre Gianadda; Franck Giraud; Markus Krause, Grisebach, Berlin; Susan Hirschfeld; Jesse Jacobson; Elise Johnson; Jennifer Jones; Julie Kennedy, Hans Purrmann Archive; Alice Lamarre-Bourgoin; Daniella and Alma Luxembourg and Inès Leynaud; Maura Lynch; Marsha Malinowski; Georges Matisse; Laura Mattioli; Kaoru Murakami; Jill Newhouse and Christa Savino; Annalisa Powers; Kadee Robbins and Tobias Bäume, Michael Werner Gallery; Laurie Rubin; Flor Souto; Wendy Wang, Nukaga Gallery, Tokyo; Ully Wille; and Matthew Wolfson. We also thank Emma Boyd, Cyanne Chutkow, Katherine S. Drake, Keith Gill, Sharon Kim, Conor Jordan, and María García Yelo, all currently or formerly of Christie's; and Arielle Amzallag, Brooke Lampley, Skye Marigold, and Alexis Wells, all of Sotheby's, for their generous support at multiple stages of this project. We would also like to thank Rebecca Rabinow, Director, the Menil Collection; Bronwen Colquhoun, Senior Curator of Photography, and Melanie Polledri, Curator of Art Collections Management and Access, both at the National Museum Wales, Cardiff; Jan Howard, Chief Curator and Houghton P. Metcalf Jr. Curator of Prints, Drawings, and Photographs, RISD Museum, Providence; Elisabeth Hodermarsky, Sutphin Family

Senior Associate Curator of Prints and Drawings, Yale University Art Gallery; and Achim Moeller and Tamara Vassilidze, Moeller Fine Art, New York.

This exhibition is supported by an indemnity from the Federal Council on the Arts and the Humanities. For their faithful advice during that process, we are extremely grateful to Patricia Loiko, Indemnity Administrator, and Daniel Hoffman, Assistant Indemnity Administrator, Visual Arts Division, National Endowment for the Arts.

The community of scholars committed to and interested in plumbing Cézanne's methods and meanings is vast, and while our footnotes acknowledge our debt to many of them, and our list of lenders includes many others, we would like to extend our special appreciation as well to Matthew Affron, S. Hollis Clayson, André Dombrowski, Aruna D'Souza, Noam Elcott, John Elderfield, Maria Gough, Nancy Ireson, Edouard Kopp, Ewa Lajer-Burcharth, Martha Lucy, Fabienne Ruppen, and Jeffrey Weiss, all of whom gamely dialogued with us, and their insights shaped our work in ways both evident and less so. It is no exaggeration to say that this exhibition and publication would not have been possible without Jayne Warman, Walter Feilchenfeldt, and David Nash, whose indispensable online catalogue raisonné of Cézanne's paintings, watercolors, and drawings was a godsend during a period of remote work, and who supplemented its contents by attending to our innumerable questions with patience and generosity.

Even throughout a challenging period, our colleagues at MoMA never wavered in their commitment to realizing this project's ambitions. Glenn D. Lowry, The David Rockefeller Director, championed the effort with characteristically unfailing support, aided by the vital efforts of Diana Pulling, Chief of Staff, and Madeleine Casella, Assistant to the Director. Equally enthusiastic backing came from Ramona Bannayan, former Senior Deputy Director, Exhibitions and Collections; Peter Reed, former Senior Deputy Director, Curatorial Affairs; Sarah Suzuki, Deputy Director, Curatorial Affairs; James Gara, Chief Operating Officer; Todd Bishop, former Senior Deputy Director, External Affairs; Jay Levenson, Director, International Program; Carol Coffin, Executive Director, International Council; James Grooms, General Counsel; Nancy Adelson, former Deputy General Counsel; Ava Childers, Assistant General Counsel; and James DeLeon, Paralegal and Department Manager, General Counsel.

Our colleagues in other curatorial departments contributed both their works and their expertise to this exhibition, allowing us to showcase Cézanne's achievements in multiple mediums. In the Department of Painting and Sculpture, we are grateful to Ann Temkin, The Marie-Josée and Henry Kravis Chief Curator; Anne Umland, The Blanchette Hooker Rockefeller Senior Curator; and Lily Goldberg and Kayla Dalle Molle, Collection Specialists. In the Department of Photography, we are similarly indebted to Clément Chéroux, The Joel and Anne Ehrenkranz Chief Curator; Sarah Meister, former Curator; and Tasha Lutek, Collection Specialist.

Despite uncustomary distance, our colleagues in the Department of Drawings and Prints nonetheless found ways to sustain us with their incisive advice and always-available ears. In particular, Christophe Cherix, The Robert Lehman Foundation Chief Curator, buoyed our endeavor with steadfast wisdom and warmth. John Prochilo, Department Manager, served, as always, as sounding board par excellence and was ably supported by Margaret Birnbaum, Assistant to the Chief Curator, and Bernadette Fitzgerald and Alicia Russo, former Department Assistants. Starr Figura, Lanka Tattersall, and Inés Katzenstein, Curators; Esther Adler, Associate Curator; Emily Cushman and Kunbi Oni, Collection Specialists; David Moreno and Jeff White, Preparators; and Jane Cavalier, Curatorial Assistant, all supported this exhibition and its curatorial team in a multitude of ways. And during their time as Louise Bourgeois Interns, Sarah Rapoport and Kathleen Maher made vital contributions to shaping our story about Cézanne.

Every aspect of exhibition-making becomes more challenging in a pandemic, so we are superbly fortunate that our colleagues across MoMA are the absolute best at their respective roles. For securing support in the most difficult of landscapes, we thank Caralynn Sandorf, former Director, Major Gifts and Campaign Operations; Nicky Combs, Assistant Director, Major Gifts; Meagan Johnson, Director of Institutional Giving and Development Operations; Jessica Smith, Assistant Director of Institutional Giving, Global Partnerships; Nora Webb, Assistant Director of Institutional Giving, Foundation Relations; Meredith Dean, Development Associate; and Jocelyn Packman, Development Assistant, Institutional Giving, Foundation Relations. For engaging audiences in the press, virtually, and in our stores, we appreciate the partnership of Amanda Hicks, Director, Communications and Public Affairs; Sara Beth Walsh, Communications Manager; Rob Baker, Director, Marketing and Creative Strategy; Leah Dickerman, Director, Editorial and Content Strategy; Prudence Peiffer, Managing Editor; Rebecca Stokes, Director, Marketing Campaigns and Audience Development; Emily Bahret, Production Assistant; Alex Halberstadt, Senior Writer; Jason Persse, Editorial Manager; Carolyn Kelly, Writer and Editor; Isabel Custodio, Content Producer; Jacqueline Cruz, Department Manager, Digital Media; Derek Flynn, Retail Art Director; and Karen Hernandez, Senior Product Manager. For welcoming our in-person visitors with warmth and safety, we recognize the commitment of Sonya Shrier, Director, Visitor Engagement, and her entire team of frontline staff; and Daniel Platt, Director, Security, and Tunji Adeniji, Chief Facilities and Safety Officer, and the unparalleled security officers who keep both our visitors and our artworks safe. And for making Cézanne's lessons accessible to everyone, we are grateful to Sara Bodinson, Director, Interpretation, Research, and Digital Learning; Sarah Kennedy, Assistant Director, Learning Programs and Partnerships; and Adelia Gregory, Associate Educator, Public Programs and Gallery Initiatives, with whom collaborating is always a pleasure.

Accessing mountains of Cézanne-related resources became extra daunting during the span of this project. We are therefore especially thankful to have leaned on Michelle Elligott, Chief of Archives,

Library, and Research Collections; Jillian Suarez, Head of Library Services; Jennifer Tobias, former Librarian; Michelle Harvey, The Rona Roob Head of Archives Services; and Ana Marie, Archivist. In Collection and Exhibition Information, Ian Eckert, Associate Director; Kathryn Ryan, Senior CEMS Coordinator; Hannah Hoose, Coordinator; and Jaye Melino, Assistant, helped us organize forests of data. And in Imaging and Visual Resources, Robert Kastler, Director; Jennifer Sellar, Digital Assets Manager; Kurt Heumiller, Studio Production Manager; and Roberto Rivera, former Production Assistant, furnished images of superior quality.

Bringing together a vast number of delicate objects during a time when travel has been dramatically curtailed posed new trials to our seasoned colleagues Susan Palamara, Registrar; Victoria Manning, Assistant Registrar; and Jennifer Wolfe, former Associate Registrar, which they met with incomparable grace, under the capable leadership of Stefanii Ruta-Atkins, Head Registrar. Similarly, Margaret Aldredge, Exhibition Manager, negotiated the logistics of these many loans with meticulous persistence, ably assisted by Maya Taylor, Exhibition and Budget Assistant, and expertly guided by Jennifer Cohen, Associate Director, and Erik Patton, Director, both of Exhibition Planning and Administration.

The intimate scale and infinite subtlety of Cézanne's drawings requires special sensitivity, a quality Lana Hum, Director, and LJ McNerney, Assistant Production Manager, both in Exhibition Design and Production, displayed in abundance when tailoring our galleries to receive these treasures. As ever, Peter Perez, Foreman, Frame Shop, and his talented team fashioned the handsomest of frames for these works, which Rob Jung, Manager, and Tom Krueger, Assistant Manager, and their crew in Art Handling and Preparation installed with expert eyes and hands. Also making indispensable contributions to the exhibition's design were Claire Corey, Production Manager; Elle Kim, Associate Creative Director; Ashley Edwards, Design Operations Manager; Aaron Louis, Director, Audio Visual; and Aaron Harrow, Design Manager, Audio Visual.

Enabling a seamless relationship between the space of the exhibition and the pages of this book were Damien Saatdjian, Art Director, and Prin Limphongpand, Senior Designer, Creative Team, who lent their exquisite aesthetics to both aspects of this project. Marc Sapir, Production Director, and Matthew Pimm, Production Manager, steered the catalogue's creation with unflappable dedication; Hannah Kim, Business and Marketing Director, and Curtis Scott, Associate Publisher, skillfully attended to the business of the book; and Naomi Falk, Rights Coordinator, and Sophie Golub, Department Manager, oversaw some of its finer points. The clear-eyed intelligence of Rebecca Roberts, Editor, immeasurably bettered our prose, as did the insightful contributions of Don McMahon, Editorial Director—qualities that Maria Marchenkova, Senior Assistant Editor, and Jackie Neudorf, Assistant Editor, also brought to our wall texts and labels.

Few bodies of work reward close looking as generously as Cézanne's oeuvre on paper, and looking along with our conservator colleagues has incalculably sharpened our perceptions. At partner institutions, we appreciate the collegial expertise of Barbara Buckley, Senior Director of Conservation and Chief Conservator of Paintings, the Barnes Foundation, Philadelphia; Markus Gross, Chief Conservator, and Friederike Steckling, Conservator, Fondation Beyeler; Gillian McMillan, Associate Chief Conservator for the Collection, and Jeffrey Warda, Senior Conservator of Paper and Photographs, the Solomon R. Guggenheim Museum; Rupert Featherstone, Director, and Rowan Frame, Postgraduate Student in the Conservation of Easel Paintings, the Hamilton Kerr Institute, Cambridge, U.K.; Penley Knipe, Philip and Lynn Straus Senior Conservator of Works of Art on Paper and Head of Paper Lab, Harvard Art Museums; Jay Krueger, Head of Painting Conservation, and Kimberly Schenck, Head of Paper Conservation, National Gallery of Art, Washington, D.C.; Thomas Primeau, Conservator of Works of Art on Paper, the Philadelphia Museum of Art; Bart Devolder, Chief Conservator, the Princeton University Art Museum; and Kateryna Kostiuchenko, Researcher, Von der Heydt-Museum, Wuppertal. At our own Museum's David Booth Conservation Center and Department, we salute Kate Lewis, The Agnes Gund Chief Conservator, for enthusiastically encouraging our collaborations with Lee Ann Daffner, Photography Conservator; Anny Aviram, Senior Paintings Conservator; Michael Duffy, Paintings Conservator; Chris McGlinchey, former Sally and Michael Gordon Senior Conservation Scientist; and Ana Martins, former Conservation Scientist, all of whom enabled us to understand Cézanne's practice in new ways. Finally, we are indebted to Laura Neufeld, Associate Paper Conservator, a true companion on this project, whose astute observations transcend her excellent essay in this volume and color the project's entire scope.

Laura joins two other remarkable individuals whose contributions to this book represent only one aspect of the devotion they brought to realizing this ambitious endeavor at a most challenging moment. Annemarie Iker, former Mellon-Marron Research Consortium Fellow, supplied unimpeachable scholarship and invigorating enthusiasm in equal measure. And Kiko Aebi, Curatorial Assistant, displayed superhuman dedication to every aspect of this project, from its most stubborn administrative detail to its most revelatory discovery. We thank them—as well as the Hortenses and Pauls who were especially close to this undertaking, completed largely from home.

Jodi Hauptman, Senior Curator
Samantha Friedman, Associate Curator
Department of Drawings and Prints

Jodi Hauptman

CÉZANNE'S DRAWINGS: A GRAPHOLOGY

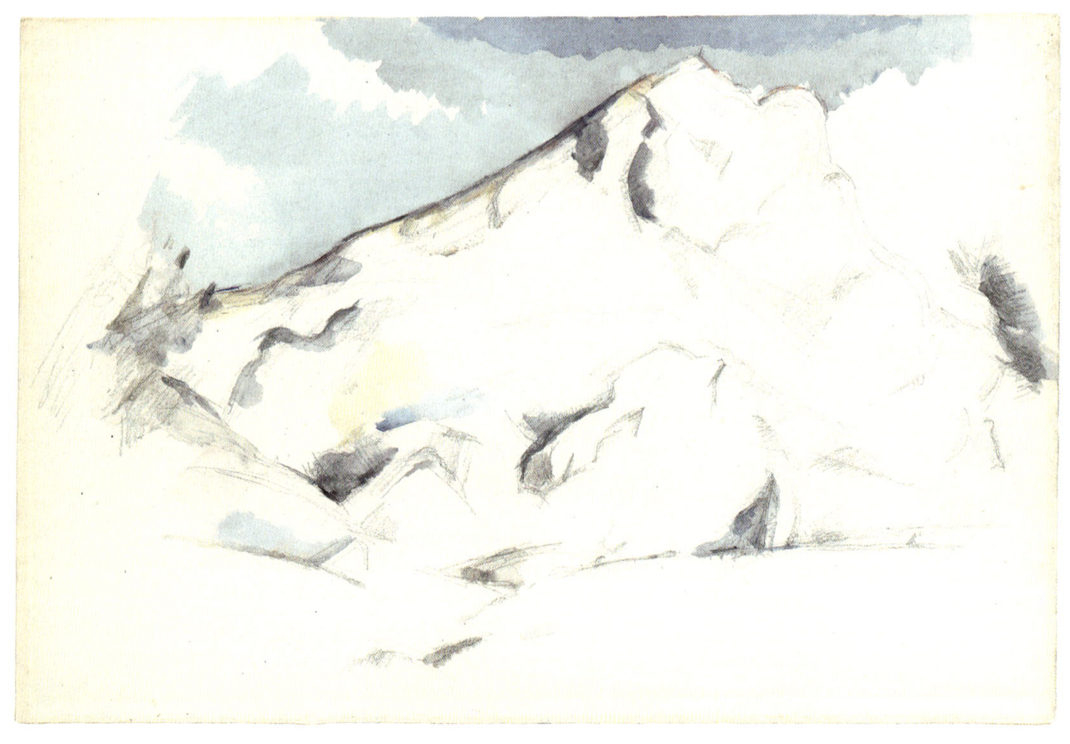

Paul Cézanne (French, 1839–1906). *Mont Sainte-Victoire* (*La Montagne Sainte-Victoire*). 1900–02. Pencil and watercolor on paper, 12 3⁄16 × 18 7⁄8" (31 × 48 cm). Private collection

A deep dive into Paul Cézanne's process in pencil, ink, and watercolor, on individual sheets and across the pages of sketchbooks, *Cézanne Drawing* traces the development of the artist's practice on paper and explores his working methods, from his student days to his final years at the start of the twentieth century. Cézanne's means—his materials, methods, and techniques; his hand and eye—emerge with greatest clarity, we hope to demonstrate, when his works are viewed in concert. And even as we acknowledge the artist's development over time—"a more personal character" to his mark-making in the 1860s; his dialogue with Pissarro that intensified in the 1870s when they painted together; and the deepening of his skill and ambition with watercolor toward the turn of the twentieth century, to just name a few milestones[1]—our focus here is on close looking, an investigation of the qualities that persist, the strategies to which Cézanne returned again and again. *Cézanne Drawing* makes the case that this foundational figure of modern art, more often recognized as a painter, produced his most radical work on paper.

From the late 1850s until his death in 1906, Cézanne drew almost daily. Drawing was for him an activity of interest and importance in its own right, part of his effort to give "concrete expression to his *sensations*, his perceptions."[2] The sheer numbers attest to drawing's role in what he called his "research": more than two thousand extant works on paper, with more than twelve hundred in pencil and almost seven hundred watercolors. Cézanne also occasionally used ink, pastel, and crayon. He preferred standard materials that were easily prepared, widely available, and relatively inexpensive: industrially produced pencils, watercolors, and papers, purchased from art suppliers in Paris and Aix-en-Provence, where he spent most of his time. While he made many of his drawings on individual sheets of wove or laid papers, the majority were created in linen-covered, flexibly bound sketchbooks, most of which have been taken apart so that sheets could be individually sold.[3] Of the nineteen known, eight remain largely intact. These extant books and the reconstruction of others reveal that Cézanne reliably returned to certain subjects: drawings after the work of other artists, particularly sculpture; intimate moments with his wife and young son; aspects of the natural world, both long views and close details; bathers, on their own or in groupings; kitchen items composed into still lifes. In using these books, he was not restricted by sequence, which makes dating these drawings difficult but thrillingly deepens their complexities.

Though Cézanne was rejected by the École des Beaux-Arts, he briefly studied at the École Gratuite de Dessin in Aix-en-Provence and drew from live models at the Académie Suisse in Paris.[4] A lifelong and avid correspondent, Cézanne often referred to drawing in his letters, from mentions of specific draftsmen he admired (Delacroix) or critiqued (Ingres) to theoretical exegeses; from descriptions of technique to connections between mediums. Sometimes he included an intimate sketch, especially in his youthful missives to his boyhood friend Émile Zola. To Charles Camoin he boiled down the medium's purpose: "Drawing is merely the configuration of what you see."[5] He walked his protégé Émile Bernard through drawing's functions: "Lines parallel to the horizon give breadth. . . . Lines perpendicular to this horizon give depth."[6] Apprising his Paris-based son, Paul, of his activities in the country, he wrote of abandoning the banks of the river in favor of steep paths, hiking "with just a bag of watercolors," committed, as always, to "the methods, *sensations* and developments suggested by the model."[7] Aside from such first-person commentary, much of what we know of Cézanne's approach to drawing (and everything else) is based on retrospective accounts. And while narrators Maurice Denis, Bernard, Joachim Gasquet, R. P. Rivière and Jacques Schnerb, and Léo Larguier are not always the most reliable, overlap among their reports and the artist's letters allows us to accept much of what they said (taken with a grain of salt). Bernard, for example, shared Cézanne's recognition of the enigma at the heart of the medium: "The secret of drawing and modeling lies in the contrasts and affinities of color."[8] Similarly, Larguier quoted Cézanne: "Drawing is the relationship of contrasts or, simply, the rapport of two tones, white and black."[9] Likewise, Gasquet reported that Cézanne declared, "Drawing can never be separated from color. It's as if you wanted to think without words."[10]

Denis's description of Cézanne's daily approach to drawing is particularly instructive. The artist's afternoon routine, Denis wrote in his journal, consisted of two options: going "to the Louvre or the Trocadéro in order to draw the statues—either the antiques or the Pugets" or venturing outdoors to "make a watercolor." "He believes," Denis continued, "that this prepares him to see well the following day."[11] In these few sentences we understand that drawing was a daily practice; that one of Cézanne's preferred mediums was watercolor (the other, specifically used

1. Adrien Chappuis, *The Drawings of Paul Cézanne: A Catalogue Raisonné* (Greenwich, Conn.: New York Graphic Society, 1973), 1:16, and, for example, T. J. Clark, "Strange Apprentice," *London Review of Books* 42, no. 19 (October 8, 2020).
2. Cézanne, letter to Émile Bernard, May 26, 1904, in *The Letters of Paul Cézanne*, ed. and trans. Alex Danchev (Los Angeles: J. Paul Getty Museum, 2013), no. 235.
3. For a discussion of Cézanne's materials and techniques, see the essay by Laura Neufeld in this volume. For an extensive and illuminating treatment of the artist's sketchbooks, see Marjorie Shelley, "Cézanne as Draftsman," in Dita Amory, ed., *Madame Cézanne* (New York: Metropolitan Museum of Art, 2014), 107–27.
4. On the artist's biography, see Danchev, *Cézanne: A Life* (New York: Pantheon, 2012).
5. Cézanne, letter to Charles Camoin, December 9, 1904, no. 242.
6. Cézanne, letter to Bernard, April 15, 1904, no. 233.
7. Cézanne, letter to his son, October 13, 1906, no. 274.
8. Cézanne, in Bernard, "Paul Cézanne," *L'Occident* 6 (July 1904): 24. Trans. in Michael Doran, ed., *Conversations with Cézanne*, trans. Julie Lawrence Cochran (Berkeley: University of California Press, 2001), 39.
9. Cézanne, in Léo Larguier, *Le Dimanche avec Paul Cézanne* (Paris: L'Édition, 1925 [1902]). Trans. in Doran, *Conversations*, 17.
10. Cézanne, in Joachim Gasquet, *Cézanne* (Paris: Les Éditions Bernheim-Jeune, 1921 [1912–13]), 91. Trans. in Doran, *Conversations*, 124.
11. Maurice Denis, *Journal*, vol. 1, *1884–1904* (Paris: La Colombe, 1957), 157: October 21, 1899. Quoted and discussed in Matthew Simms, *Cézanne's Watercolors: Between Drawing and Painting* (New Haven, Conn.: Yale University Press, 2008), 146–47.

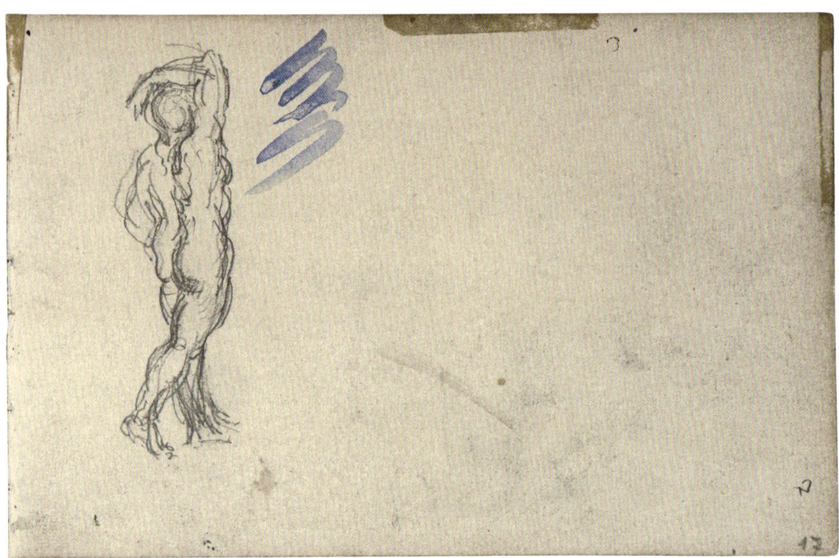

fig. 1

to render sculpture, was pencil); and that drawing from sculpture, translating a three-dimensional medium into a two-dimensional picture, was of particular importance. We understand, and elsewhere find confirmed, that his dedication to the past ("The Louvre is the book from which we learn to read"[12]) only intensified when in tandem with attention to the present, particularly to the wonders of nature (Cézanne, wrote his contemporary Gustave Geffroy, "is a man who looks everywhere around him, who experiences an intoxication in the spectacle unfurled before him, and who wishes to transfer the feeling of this intoxication to the restricted space of his art"[13]); and that the benefits of such attention could emerge only over time. We learn that the manual, tactile act of drawing—moving an implement across a sheet of paper—was also a method of deepening and expanding vision, of "seeing well," and that the work of the hand was inextricably connected to that of the eye. Drawing for Cézanne was thus preparatory in the best sense—not a step that ends with a finished painting, but a training ground for vision, instruction that, given Cézanne's indefatigable commitment, would never end.

It is in his drawings that this curriculum—materials, methods, techniques—is most fully on display. The pressured mark of a pencil, the brush of liquid watercolor, maintain a kind of integrity as marks, as strokes, without obfuscation (there is no smoothing out, no obscuring of process here), allowing us to follow along. Acknowledging this revelation of process in the result, Bernard referred to Cézanne's drawings as "documents without artifice." They are, he wrote, "captivating for anyone who attempts to seize the quality of his thought, his preoccupations, and his objectives."[14] For Carol Armstrong, his drawing is a "repeated demonstration of the 'how' of its own making."[15] And the result of grasping these "hows"? Cézanne's drawings allow us to see as he does.

"Shall we do a graphology of Cézanne?" Denis asked almost a century ago.[16] A question and a challenge, this query proposes a systematic investigation of Cézanne's means. Taking up Denis's challenge, we examine four key elements of the artist's work on paper.

fig. 1 Paul Cézanne (French, 1839–1906). *Standing Female Bather (Baigneuse debout)*. n.d. Page 17 from Sketchbook Philadelphia I. Pencil and watercolor on wove paper, 4 9/16 × 7 3/16" (11.6 × 18.3 cm). Philadelphia Museum of Art. Gift of Mr. and Mrs. Walter H. Annenberg

12. Cézanne, letter to Bernard, Friday [1905], no. 253.
13. Gustave Geffroy, in Simms, *Cézanne's Watercolors*, 3. Shelley discusses contemporary drawing reforms about which Cézanne would have been aware as well as the impact of Thomas Couture, who, she writes, "urged the student to go outside the studio, always with a small carnet in hand, and record in a few lines whatever beauty caught the eye." See "Cézanne as Draftsman," 112–13.
14. Bernard, "Les Aquarelles de Cézanne," *L'Amour de l'art* 5, no. 2 (February 1924): 35.
15. Carol Armstrong, *Cézanne in the Studio: Still Life in Watercolor* (Los Angeles: J. Paul Getty Museum, 2004), 129.
16. Denis, "Le Dessin de Cézanne," *L'Amour de l'art* 5, no. 2 (February 1924): 37.
17. Cézanne, in Bernard, "Paul Cézanne," 24. Trans. in Doran, *Conversations*, 38.
18. Cézanne, in Gasquet, *Cézanne*, 100. Trans. in Doran, *Conversations*, 131.
19. R. P. Rivière and Jacques Schnerb, "L'Atelier de Cézanne," *La Grande Revue* (December 25, 1907 [January 1905]): 813. Trans. in Doran, *Conversations*, 86. Roger Fry referred to Cézanne's "tentatives" that "prove his desperate courage in face of the elusive theme." See *Cézanne: A Study of His Development* (New York: Macmillan, 1927), 2.
20. Cézanne, in Gasquet, *Cézanne*, 100. Trans. in Doran, *Conversations*, 131. The original French is "Mais il y a là un écueil."
21. This pose can be found in Cézanne's work as

LINE

While Cézanne provocatively declared "There is no line," what is most distinct about his drawing is the profusion of line—the way it multiplies, repeats, twists, trembles, searches.[17] Wary of singularity, definition, purity, Cézanne warned, according to Gasquet, that, however beautiful, a precise "bloodless" contour should not be trusted.[18] Similarly, Rivière and Schnerb described Cézanne vigorously "declar[ing] his horror of the photographic eye, of the precise and automatic drawing taught in the École des Beaux-Arts."[19] The almost mechanical wirelike line of Ingres, Holbein, or Clouet is a trap; that line, he said, "can be a hazard."[20] Cézanne instead used line to doubt line, used it to displace contour.

On a sheet now detached from its sketchbook, a blue scrawl of watercolor ricochets dangerously close to the twisted arm of a bather, an image of an abstracted, unmoored threat (fig. 1). As much as that luminous, unreadable ultramarine puts this figure in jeopardy, the lines that form the body, that should define it, may be a deeper menace. The position of this figure, seen from behind, though at a slight rightward angle here, is a favorite of Cézanne's, drawn again and again, on its own or as a member of a group of bathers, often in a waterside glen.[21] No matter how well Cézanne knew this pose, he could not—or would not—commit to its form. What we comprehend in these multiplied, repeated, crossed, and aligned strokes is the material equivalent of seeing, whether that seeing is wholly contingent, uncertain, and precarious; on the verge of coming to terms with its subject or an allowance that something may be more than one thing;[22] or a demonstration of how vision fails as it rounds an edge, the limits of sight.[23] Rainer Maria Rilke described this coming to terms with the subject as the "conflict" at the heart of Cézanne's work: "A mutual struggle between the two procedures of, first, looking and confidently perceiving, and then of appropriating and making personal use of what has been perceived; . . . perhaps as a result of becoming conscious, [the two] would immediately start opposing the other, talking out loud, as it were, and go on perpetually interrupting and contradicting each other."[24]

Repeating short and longer strokes tell us something about this figure, too, although the results also interrupt each other: contradictory senses that the bather is in motion; that the body is planted in place; that it lacks borders, energizing the surrounding space; that it transforms into something else—a nest of twigs, a tangle of threads, a twisted tree. Look closely at the left arm. To find it, first locate one of the elongated *S*'s that define the shape of upper back to waist on the body's left side. A step further left are four wobbly braided lines that stretch down from the shoulder, out to the left and back toward the behind, forming a soft angle and hinting at a left arm, elbow slightly bent. Multiplied, these lines may imply that the arm or the figure is in motion: first close to the body, then further away. Similarly, the right forearm is composed of a series of horizontals, tacked at right to the little mound of right elbow. These vectors start at different locations but then come together near the strangely elongated hand, another suggestion that Cézanne considered the position of the figure from slightly varying angles. The left leg, meanwhile, is a thicket of repeated overlapping verticals with a strong *X*. So dense, the calf leads to no foot at all: the lines spread out at the very bottom of the "leg" make the limb appear planted and fused with the ground, like the trunk of a tree emerging from soil, or, in an opposite take, repeating overlaps that express movement. In other moments—the rounded bottom of the right buttock, the right thigh, and the space between head and right arm—firmer and darker lines, including some hatching, offer a sense of shadow, and with it dimension.[25]

Such a refusal of contour, of borders, of finality, of commitment is found throughout Cézanne's pencil drawings (and his far fewer ink ones, as well—jagged strokes at times resemble a pile of pins [plate 28]). But it can also be seen in his watercolors, specifically in broken lines, most often in blue pigment. That broken line tracks the prominent peak of Mont Sainte-Victoire (plate 180), vessels in his late still lifes (plate 217), slender trees in a forest (plate 189), and cavorting bathers (plate 105). In these examples, whether in the studio interior or out in the landscape, Cézanne implies the skips and pauses of vision and in particular the impact of light, reflections off shiny glass, dappled sunlight through foliage, bright patches on exposed earth, so dazzling they make us squint.[26]

early as 1870, in the painting *The Temptation of Saint Anthony* (*La Tentation de saint Antoine*), now in the Emil Bührle Collection, Zurich.

22. Lawrence Gowing has described how "successive contours narrowed down the zone of uncertainty." See *Watercolour and Pencil Drawings by Cézanne* (London: Lund Humphries, 1973), 18. John Elderfield, in correspondence with the author, has suggested that, in addition to the ongoing questioning these multiple lines reveal, Cézanne might also have been opening up the possibility of the artist showing us more than one thing. Likewise, Kathryn Tuma has written, "In vision, we are not asked to decide between one thing and another. When we look, we see in permissive coincidence and contradiction, and this truth about the nature of vision Cézanne works to preserve." See "Cézanne and Lucretius at the Red Rock," *Representations* 78, no. 1 (Spring 2002): 73.
23. Richard Shiff has described Cézanne's edges as where the eye turns away; the edges are "axes of sensory stress." See "Sensation, Cézanne," in Judit Geskó, ed., *Cézanne and the Past: Tradition and Creativity* (Budapest: Museum of Fine Arts, 2012), 46. Elsewhere, Shiff has identified the reactive propensity in Cézanne's repeated mark-making. That "mark to mark"—"discrete moments in transience"—as he describes it, "connotes temporal passage." See "Cézanne Photographic," *nonsite.org*, no. 26 (November 11, 2018).
24. Rainer Maria Rilke, *Letters on Cézanne*, ed. Clara Rilke, trans. Joel Agee (New York: North Point, 1985, 2002), 33–34. Letter dated October 9, 1907.
25. For an illuminating and in-depth look at the bather paintings, with a particular emphasis on their materiality, see Aruna D'Souza, *Cézanne's Bathers: Biography and the Erotics of Paint* (University Park: Pennsylvania State University Press, 2008).
26. In response to Gasquet's assertion that "Provence is often gray," Cézanne described Provençal light as "flashy, like confetti." Cézanne, in Gasquet, *Cézanne*, 86–87. Trans. in Doran, *Conversations*, 118.

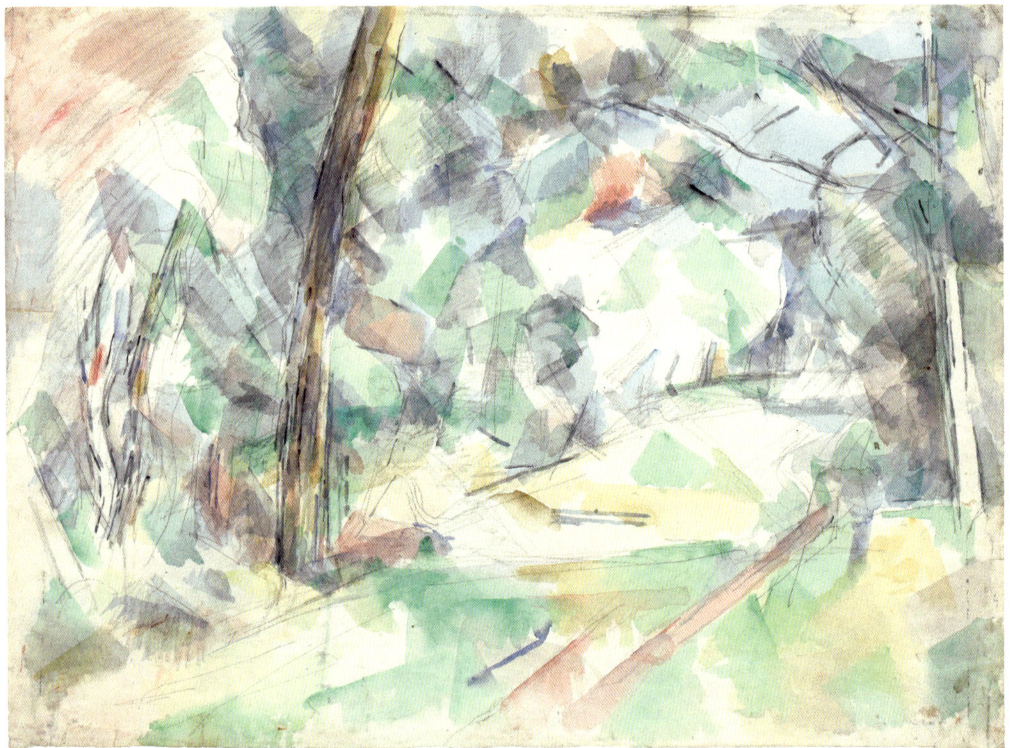

fig. 2

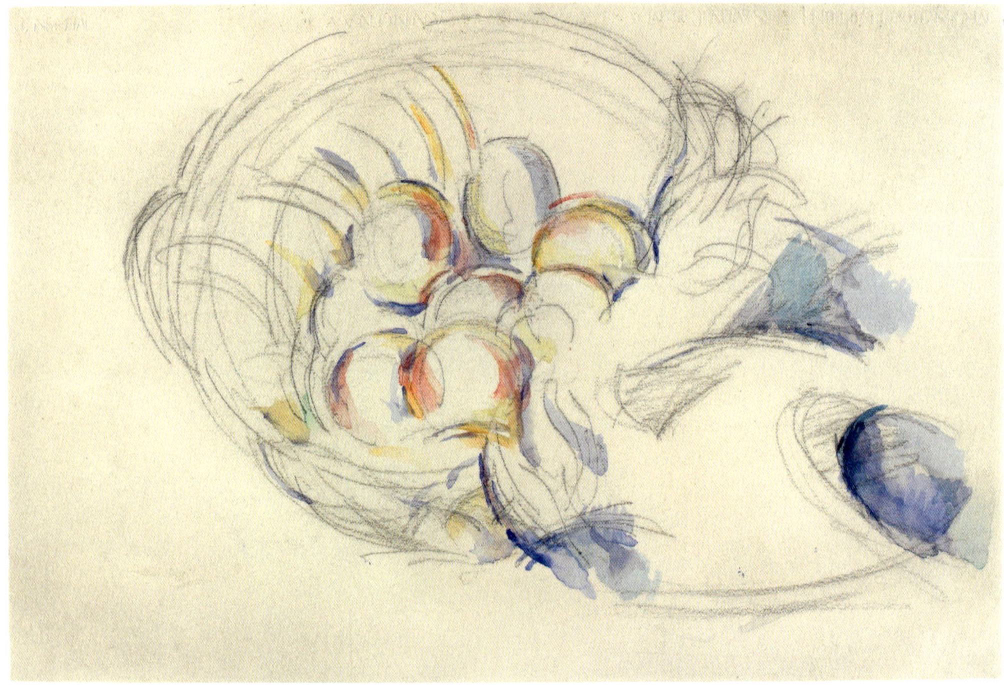

fig. 3

fig. 2 Paul Cézanne (French, 1839–1906). *Forest Path* (*Chemin sous bois*). 1904–06. Pencil and watercolor on paper, 17 15⁄16 × 24 13⁄16" (45.5 × 63 cm). Henry and Rose Pearlman Foundation (on extended loan to the Princeton University Art Museum)

fig. 3 Paul Cézanne (French, 1839–1906). *Basket of Fruit* (*Corbeille de fruits*). c. 1890 (possibly later). Pencil and watercolor on paper, 11 13⁄16 × 17 11⁄16" (30 × 45 cm). Fondazione Magnani-Rocca, Mamiano di Traversetolo, Parma

TRANSPARENCY

"In water-colour we never can lose the sense of the material, which is a wash upon the paper," cautioned Roger Fry, one of Cézanne's earliest interpreters.[27] Watery color on creamy white paper: a partnership of transparent pigment and opaque ground, carefully calibrated so that the paper's brightness is seen through the paint. Cézanne's watercolors shift and shimmer, appear to be in motion, conjuring a sense of the aliveness of the natural world.

Consider, for example, a green patch just to the right of the left-hand tree in *Forest Path* (1904–06; fig. 2). Rotating his wrist slightly so that the longer side of the brush was at an angle, Cézanne created a rectangle with its corner pointing up, like a diamond. He then repeated that gesture across the sheet, suggesting the density, texture, and hue of the forest's foliage and mossy ground, and the trajectory of a path. To those patches of green, Cézanne added blue, yellow, and rose. Together, in the upper half of the picture, the overlapping patches form an arched canopy. One of the branches from the right-hand tree—its thickest section precariously attached to the trunk by a single thread of pencil—reaches up and across toward the middle of the composition. Its angle is mirrored on the left by the tide lines of a sequence of colorful patches. Branch and colored line meet in the center, at a triangular blue apex. This patch forms a hinge: each side of the composition gives the illusion of reflecting the other. As evanescent as these colors are, they provide a sense of space, as if we might walk down that path and underneath the canopy. "Form is at its fullest," Cézanne is quoted as saying, "when color is at its richest."[28]

Bernard described the way these patches of color "produced screens," as if they are akin to see-through material in front of a light source, like a lamp or roaring fire.[29] While we cannot know the order in which they were placed on the page, we do know—because there is very limited bleeding of one color into another or color mixing—that Cézanne let each patch dry before he laid down the next. Even when the patches—these screens—overlap, we still understand the green or the blue as individual areas of color. Cézanne emphasized this individuality even in their layering by extending the second patch "beyond the first," according to Bernard, who watched his friend at work on his watercolors.[30] By extending one beyond the other, by not lining up exactly, the colored patches reveal the "how" of making. This process, Yve-Alain Bois has observed, "is not simply additive, but multiplying . . . each skein responding to both the one that precedes it and to the whiteness of the support."[31]

Here and in other watercolors, Cézanne left spaces between his patches, and the white in-between crackles through the composition. This air, Armstrong has argued, is "a palpable medium,"[32] which brings us to the next entry in our graphology.

UNFINISH

In Cézanne's drawings, as in his paintings, what is unmarked and unrendered—what defines their status as "non finito," their condition of "unfinish"—is just as important as what is marked (fig. 3). In some cases, areas of blank paper lend dimension to the forms depicted, providing their "culminating point," the spot on a subject closest to the viewer, most clearly seen as a highlight on a spherical fruit as it rounds outward (plate 208).[33] Cézanne also exploited the creaminess of unmarked paper to signify elements in a composition: a crisp tablecloth (plate 212), a jagged boulder (plate 153), a skull's polished cranium (plate 53), to offer a few examples. Often Cézanne laid pigment down adjacent to an object or used color or line to define an edge, leaving the main event—the bark of a tree, the wall of a structure—undrawn (plate 150). The context provides enough visual evidence for us to identify the undescribed object.

In other moments, elements of a subject were left completely unfinished, as in the void at the center of a large-scale portrait of Madame Cézanne (plate 64). Cézanne rendered his wife, Hortense, with a combination of dark pencil lines and delicate diagonal hatches. With her concentrated expression and downturned head, Hortense is absorbed in her needlework—and yet no needle appears between her fingers. With myriad details here—the curves of her coiffure; the silhouette of her jacket; the shape of the wooden chair, and the bit of the bedpost behind her; the pile of books on an adjacent nightstand—the lacuna at the center of the action is all the more striking, whether we interpret it as an element in the composition (a bright highlight, for example), an analogy between the paper of a draftsman and the fabric of a needleworker, or an invitation to the viewer to sketch (or

27. Fry, *A Study*, 64.
28. Cézanne, in Bernard, "Paul Cézanne," 24. Trans. in Doran, *Conversations*, 39.
29. Bernard, "Souvenirs sur Paul Cézanne et lettres inédites," *Mercure de France* 248 (October 15, 1907): 396 (published 1907, observed 1904–06). Trans. in Doran, *Conversations*, 60. The translation there is "folding screens," but the French word Bernard used is *écran*, which at that time would have indicated a lampshade or fire screen as opposed to a decorative folding screen (later *écran* would be used for projection screens). My thanks to Noam Elcott for sharing his research on *écran*, part of his forthcoming book project *Art in the First Screen Age*.
30. Ibid.
31. Yve-Alain Bois, "Cézanne: Words and Deeds," trans. Rosalind Krauss, *October* 84 (Spring 1998): 39. Bois summarized Maurice Merleau-Ponty: "To look at a Cézanne, particularly a late watercolor, is to see simultaneously its molecular surface and the depicted object in the act of germinating under our very eyes."
32. Armstrong, *Cézanne in the Studio*, 122. See also Simms, *Cézanne's Watercolors*, 162: he describes "an insertion of filaments of bright light into the intervals between colors."
33. In a letter to Bernard, Cézanne wrote, "I mean that in an orange, an apple, a ball, a head, there is a culminating point, and this point is always the closest to our eye, the edges of objects recede towards a centre placed at eye level." July 25, 1904, no. 237. The culminating point is often, but not only, this area of unpainted paper. See Gowing, "The Logic of Organized Sensations," in William Rubin, ed., *Cézanne: The Late Work* (New York: The Museum of Modern Art, 1977), esp. 57–59. Unfinish is discussed throughout the scholarship on Cézanne.

stitch) the missing information. For Geffroy, the "unfinished quality" reflected the uncertainty of Cézanne's times: "Art does not proceed without a certain incompletion, because the life it reproduces is in perpetual transformation."[34] Cézanne himself, even early in his career, derided conventional finish as superficial. "I have to work all the time, but not to achieve the finish that earns the admiration of imbeciles," he wrote to his mother. "And that thing that is so widely valued is nothing more than a workman's craft, and makes all the resulting work inartistic and common."[35]

VOID

Cézanne's "unfinish"—conjuring something using nothing—is often cited as a marker of his modernity. But what if we reverse that equation and consider how Cézanne made nothing into something? Cézanne's drawings are filled—contradiction is unavoidable when describing his work—with voids, holes, and gaps: spaces around and within sculpture; architectural apertures like windows and arches; nature's caverns and canyons; eye sockets in skulls. It can seem that he was more interested in describing the space around his subjects than in the subjects themselves.[36]

Standing out in Cézanne's pencil drawing of an écorché (fig. 4)—his fine pencil lines emphasizing the torso's stretched musculature, revealed by the flayed skin—is a dark shape at the sheet's center. This triangular form has one relatively straight edge, one curved, and one undulating. The straight and the wavy edges are reinforced by darker and thicker lines, while the interior of the triangle is dense with hatches, in groupings with marks lined up and repeated, aimed in different directions. Those groups abut each other, creating multiple seams. Depending on how close together the hatched lines are placed, the paper support is revealed and light seems to flow in. The edge of the triangle also defines the body—in other words, they share a common boundary. The effect created is an oscillation between sculpture and space. Is Cézanne's subject the écorché or the spaces created by its gestures? Instead of clarifying that relationship, Cézanne forces us into a never-ending back-and-forth, a perceptual tension between projection and recession, near and far. What is so richly textured, dense, material, and substantial is actually nothing at all: the triangle of empty space created between torso and arm, when the elbow is folded in as hand cradles head.[37]

Cézanne's focus on the voids in drawings after the écorché and other sculptures, including Pierre Puget's 1661 *Hercules at Rest* (plates 106–09), derived from close study of this Baroque sculptor's approach. Puget, he told Gasquet, "used surrounding shadows in the same spirit as his contemporaries used dark underpainting."[38] The darkness of these "shadowy holes . . . makes highlights and put everything into relief, into color, as in Rembrandt's drawings where the quality of black alone creates all the vertigo of the prism."[39] Cézanne found similar materiality in the outside world, describing the shadows on Mont Sainte-Victoire as "convex, bulbous."[40] And there are other examples in which pencil or watercolor materializes shadow and darkness. See, for example, the yawning mouth created by the open end of the left sleeve in *Coat on a Chair* (1890–92; plate 68). By interweaving scrawled pencil and multiple campaigns of watercolor, he transformed murky interiority into a bulbous growth.

These Rembrandtesque shadows, an "intertwining of visibility and invisibility, of substantiality and insubstantiality," are, Kathryn Tuma has written, a "final horizon," a "point at which vision is lost."[41] Taking drawing to its limits, this play between what can be seen and what is not seen at all is most poignant in Cézanne's rendering of a skull's eyeless sockets, whether in conveying haunting darkness with layers of deep black pigment (plate 75); time's polish, through unpainted paper and watercolor wash (plate 74); or vacancy, as background fabric shows through. In a single skull perfectly centered on the sheet and nestled into a patterned tapestry, the sockets' shadowy voids are complex layers of soft pencil, blue and green pigment, and darker blue and blue-black lines, with traces of white paper (plate 53)—at once an enter-able nowhere and an impenetrable solid. In orchestrating this affecting one-to-one of viewer and cranium, eyes and voids, was Cézanne revealing mortality at the boundary of pictorial legibility and the threshold of sight?[42]

In a letter to his son, at the very end of his life, Cézanne wrote, "I live a little as if in a void."[43] Tuma reminds us that this was written in a melancholic and even resigned spirit. But as we see here, to live in

34. Geffroy, in Shiff, "Sensation, Cézanne," 45.
35. Cézanne, letter to his mother, November 26, 1874, no. 54.
36. Similar examples can be found in his paintings.
37. This and other drawings were made after a plaster cast Cézanne kept in his studio, itself made after a work by Michelangelo. See Mary Tompkins Lewis, "Flayed Figures and Plaster Casts: Cézanne's Écorchés, Their Origins and Progeny," in Geskó and Anna Zsófia Kovács, eds., *Cézanne and the Past: Tradition and Creativity* [symposium proceedings] (Budapest: Museum of Fine Arts, 2016), 40–61, for a fascinating look at the artist's engagement with the écorché. Lewis quotes Gasquet: "To the last day of his life, every morning as a priest reads his breviary, he spent an hour drawing Michelangelo's plaster figure from every angle"(49). She notes that Cézanne also drew from Jean-Antoine Houdon's écorché (48). See also Tuma, "La Peau de chagrin," in Jeffrey Weiss, ed., *Picasso: The Cubist Portraits of Fernande Olivier* (Washington, D.C.: National Gallery of Art, 2003), 127–63.
38. Cézanne, in Gowing, *Paul Cézanne: The Basel Sketchbooks* (New York: The Museum of Modern Art, 1988), 26.
39. Cézanne, in Gasquet, *Cézanne*, 116. Trans. in Doran, *Conversations*, 149–50. See also Klaus Herding, "A Dramatic Interplay in Form and Expression: Cézanne and Puget," in Geskó, *Cézanne and the Past*, 82–93.
40. Cézanne, in Gasquet, *Cézanne*. Trans. in Doran, *Conversations*, 123.
41. Tuma, "Cézanne and Lucretius," 73.
42. The very intriguing topic of blindness in Cézanne's drawings and paintings is for another essay. Further, T. J. Clark finds that "death is this painter's ultimate subject." See "Phenomenality and Materiality in Cézanne," in Tom Cohen et al., eds., *Material Events: Paul de Man and the Afterlife of Theory* (Minneapolis: University of Minnesota Press, 2000), 111. Tuma has written, "I believe that the ultimate object of the late Bibémus paintings . . . is death." See "Cézanne and Lucretius," 74.
43. This is Tuma's translation, in ibid., of "Je vis un peu comme dans un vide." Danchev, in *Letters of Paul Cézanne* (August [26], 1906, no. 265), translates it as "I live as if in a dream."
44. Cézanne, letter to Roger Marx, January 23, 1905, no. 248.
45. Cézanne, letter to his son, September 8, 1906, no. 267.

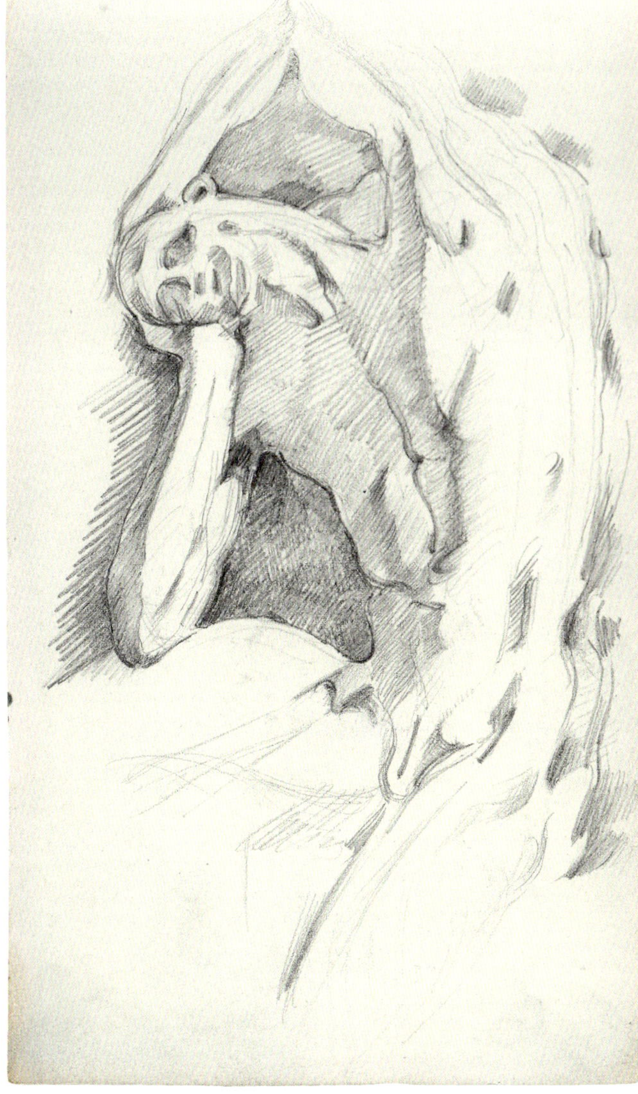

fig. 4

the void is not to surrender but to see the meeting of visibility and invisibility, to push perception to the very edge.

In a 1905 letter to Roger Marx, Cézanne wrote, "In my opinion, one does not replace the past, one only adds a new link."[44] The conception of art history as an ever-growing chain is fitting for Cézanne's approach to his forebears, as the metaphor captures the way he built on, but did not seek to stamp out, the art of the past: Chardin, Courbet, Delacroix, Manet–all significant touchstones. The chain and, specifically, the idea of iteration that it implies–one link, then the other, together yet apart, the same yet varied, on and on–is also a useful construct in thinking about Cézanne's approach to drawing. There are certain motifs that persist across his career–his incessant return to Mont Sainte-Victoire, his ongoing analysis of his seated wife, to name just two–but that persistence is deeper in his drawings, both in the sheer numbers of the same subject, in presentation sheets and sketchbooks, and in the variations to which each subject is put: enlarged, reduced, reversed, isolated or grouped, placed in a setting or not. Cézanne himself evocatively called out the possibilities before him in a letter to his son: "Here on the riverbank the motifs multiply, the same subject from a different angle provides a fascinating subject for study, and so varied that I think I could occupy myself for months without moving, leaning now more to the right, now more to the left."[45] Likewise, Cézanne continually reaffirmed his aspiration to realize his sensations, and that effort, the linkage of seeing and making, eye and hand, that insistence on close study remains a model and a spark. While of his time, his drawings speak eloquently and movingly to the present.

What is most striking in his works on paper is what they make possible. Even as they engage the past, Cézanne's drawings reproach the authority of convention. Close looking at this body of work reveals how his approaches to the bounds and permeability of the human figure, his visualization of precarity, his expansion of the function and meanings of color, and his engagement with the evolving natural world open up the parameters of sight.

fig. 4 Paul Cézanne (French, 1839–1906). *After the Écorché (D'après l'écorché)*. 1879–82. Page XXIII verso from Sketchbook Chicago. Pencil on wove paper, 8 9/16 × 4 7/8" (21.7 × 12.5 cm). The Art Institute of Chicago. Arthur Heun Purchase Fund

Samantha Friedman

CONDENSATION: CÉZANNE'S STUDY SHEETS

fig. 1

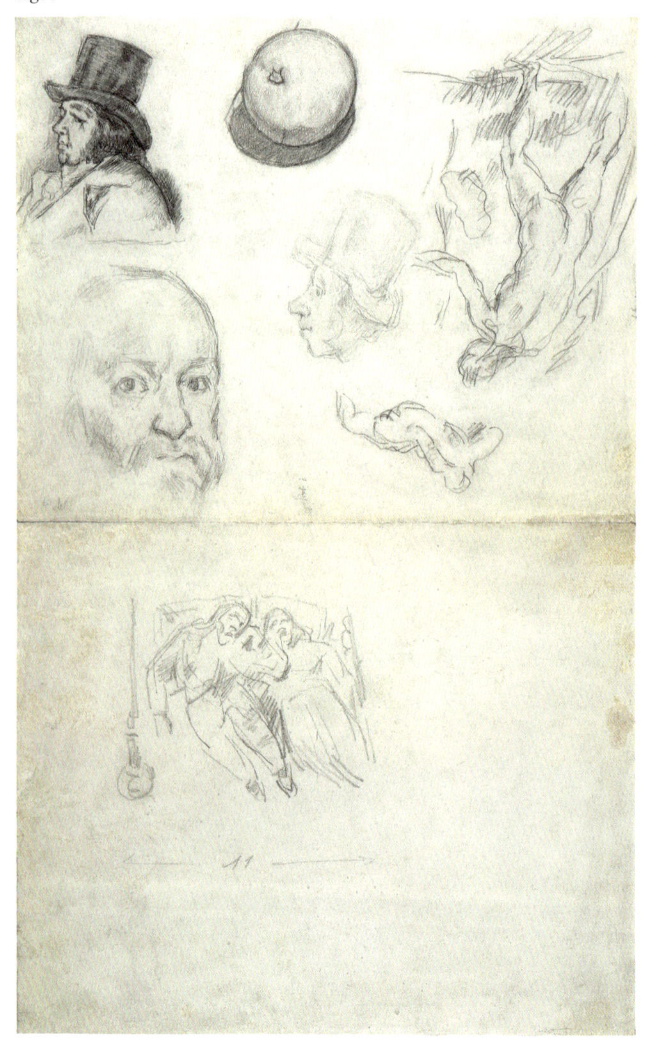

figs. 1, 2 Paul Cézanne (French, 1839–1906). *Page of Studies, Including a Portrait of Goya (Feuille d'études dont un portrait de Goya)* (recto); *Page of Studies (Feuille d'études)* (verso). 1877–80 (recto); 1880–81 (verso). Pencil on paper, 19 11/16 × 11 13/16" (50 × 30 cm). Private collection, New York

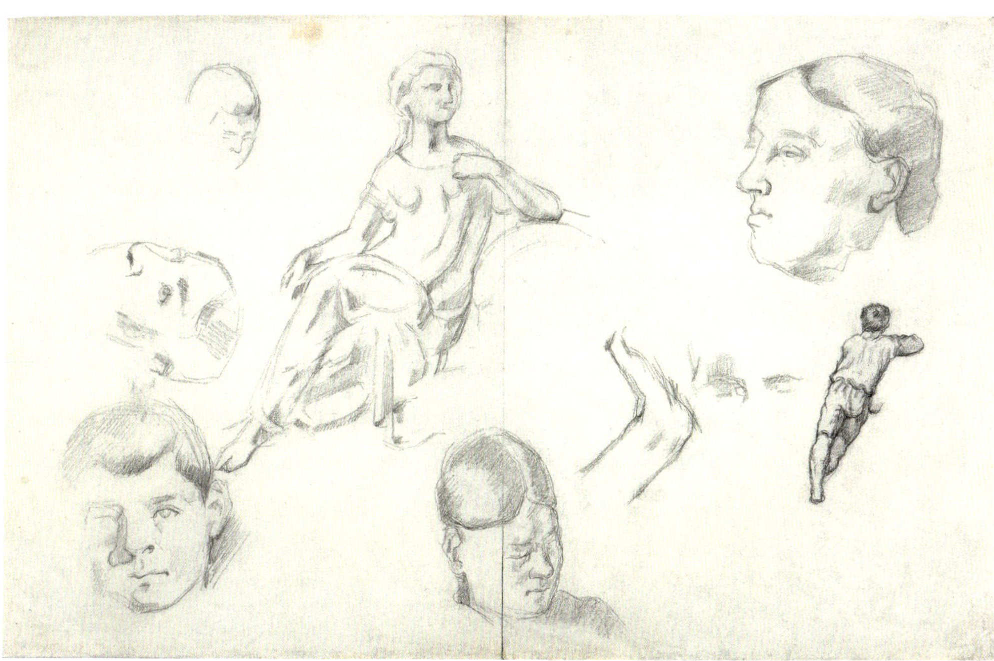

fig. 2

Sixteen motifs fill the two sides of a sheet of studies drawn between 1877 and 1881 (figs. 1, 2). On the recto, pinwheeling around the sheet in various orientations, are two copies after a Goya self-portrait surrounding a self-portrait of the present artist, Cézanne; an apple, dimensional enough, despite its dislocation from any surface, to warrant a cast shadow; a striding bather; a reclining nude; and, across a fold halfway down the sheet, an aerial view of a couple in bed. On the verso, six portrait heads in varying degrees of finish—some of which are recognizable as the artist's wife and son—look this way and that, joined by two other visitors: a seated female, who happens to be the decorative element from a late-eighteenth-century clock, and a male youth, a copy after Pedro de Moya from the very book of engravings in which Cézanne found the Goya. Though the bodies of these last two figures share the same, elbow-propped lean, she faces forward while he faces away, into the sheet, as if toward his top-hatted source-mate on the other side.

Considered together, the disparate motifs that populate this drawing—just one of some 320 known study sheets[1]—effectively summarize the subjects for which Cézanne is best known.[2] Portraits, still life objects, a bather sited in a hint of landscape: this content, keyed to the academy's categories, often shapes our understanding of this artist, as considerations of his work concentrate on one genre at a time. But what happens when all of these subjects are condensed onto a single support? And what connections—formal, material, conceptual—between works of different subjects do we miss when studying them in isolation?

An investigation of the artist's works on paper reveals the boundaries between genres to be more porous than often acknowledged.[3] Indeed, the strategies that constitute a drawing like the one described above—proximity, juxtaposition, superimposition, rhyme, repetition, and reversal—are the same that structure Cézanne's work on paper as a whole. The associative linkages between isolated motifs on the same sheet extend equally to motifs across multiple sheets—many of which, after all, were once bound together in now-separated sketchbooks. In this way, the study sheets, with their logic of condensation—the dense compression of disparate visual ideas into significatively rich adjacency—can serve as a key to the larger practice. These study sheets relate to two traditions—one academic, one popular—in which Cézanne was simultaneously immersed. It is the combination of these two modes, each explored here through a singular example of one of the artist's very early drawings, that results in the unique modernity of the artist's study sheets and of the larger body of work that follows their generative model.

1. This count includes approximately eighty single-sided loose sheets, twenty double-sided loose sheets, 160 single-sided sketchbook pages, and sixty double-sided sketchbook pages; it does not account for the additional study sheets that were cut into fragments after Cézanne's time.
2. For a detailed reading of this sheet's motifs and sources, as well as the observation that it encapsulates the spectrum of genres, see Ann Dumas et al., *Woodner Collection: Master Drawings* (New York: Metropolitan Museum of Art, 1990), 300–01.
3. This belief builds on the important work of Fabienne Ruppen, who has asserted, "More so than Cézanne's paintings, his works on paper demonstrate the potential arbitrariness not just as concerns medial subdivisions of his oeuvre, but of the isolated consideration of a single subject or genre, as well." Ruppen, "On Margins and Versos: The Hidden Interrelationships among Cézanne's Works on Paper," in Alexander Eiling, ed., *Cézanne: Metamorphoses* (Munich: Prestel/Staatliche Kunsthalle Karlsruhe, 2017), 85.

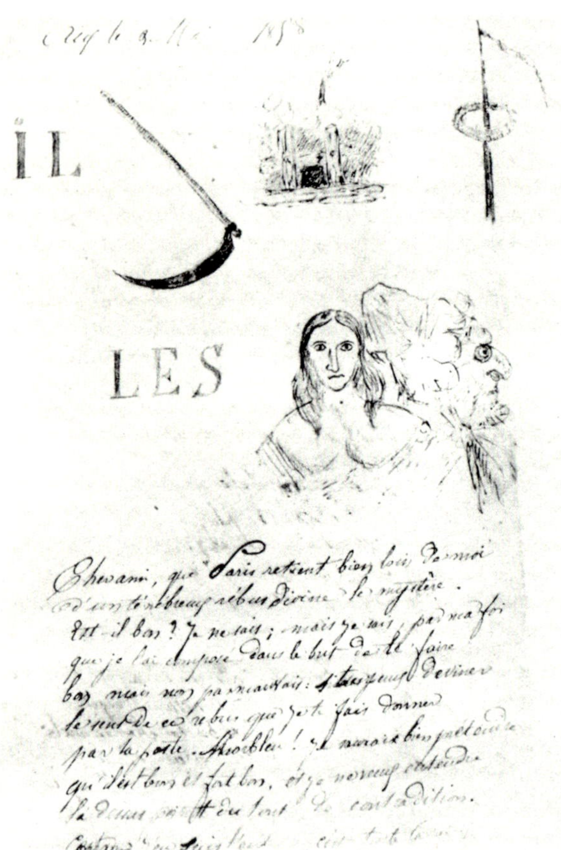

fig. 3

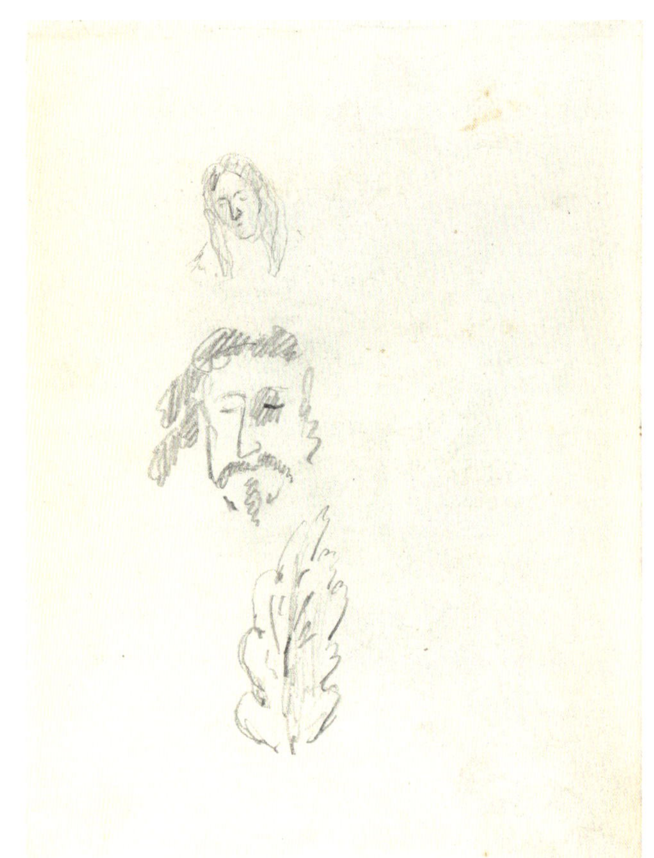

fig. 4

fig. 5

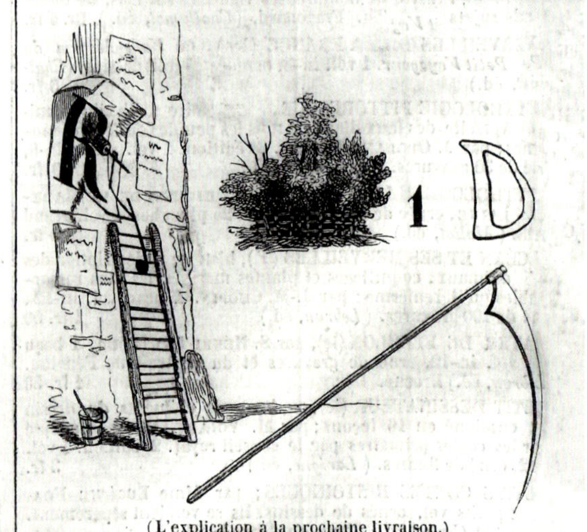

fig. 6

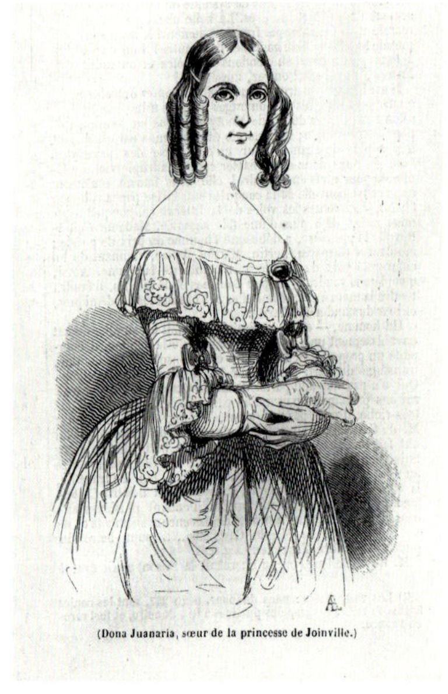

fig. 3 Paul Cézanne (French, 1839–1906). *Drawings Composing a Rebus* (*Dessins composant un rébus*). Ink on a letter from Cézanne to Émile Zola, May 3, 1858, dimensions unknown. Private collection, France

fig. 4 Paul Cézanne (French, 1839–1906). *Two Faces and a Leaf* (*Deux visages et une feuille*). 1856–57. Page V verso from Sketchbook Jerusalem. Pencil on wove paper, 9 ⅝ × 6 ⅞" (24.4 × 17.5 cm). The Israel Museum. Gift of Henry Pearlman, New York

fig. 5 Rebus in *L'Illustration* 1, no. 2 (March 11, 1843): 32

fig. 6 "Dona Junaria, soeur de la princesse de Joinville" (Dona Junaria, sister of the Princess of Joinville), *L'Illustration* 1, no. 17 (June 24, 1843): 257

In his late twenties, following stints at the École Gratuite de Dessin in Aix-en-Provence and the Académie Suisse in Paris, and during a period of repeated submissions to—and rejections from—the Salon, Cézanne executed *Studies of a Rower* (1867–69; plate 3). Three studies of an oarsman sweep across the page. The central figure, heavily shaded, with indications of facial features, is the most fully realized, while the other two reverberate around him, like ripples in the water through which he rows. The sheet's trio of drawings—made from a studio model—are stabs: three attempts to get the musculature just right.[4] At the same time, its subject justifies the composition's implication of motion—specifically, a repeated motion: an unbroken rhythm of strokes not unlike the act of drawing.

The presence of multiple motifs on a page is not in itself modern but part of a tradition—from at least the fifteenth through the nineteenth century—that Cézanne would have known well from his visits to the Louvre's Cabinet des Dessins.[5] Although the Old Master drawings—by Raphael, Michelangelo, Signorelli, et al.—that Cézanne is known to have copied there are all individual compositions,[6] the Cabinet's collection does hold study sheets by these artists, making it possible that Cézanne would have seen them. Exhibiting a "brainstorm technique" in which "one set of ideas often led to another,"[7] such Renaissance precedents—as well as subsequent examples from Watteau in the eighteenth century to Delacroix in the nineteenth—provide an evident lineage for Cézanne's own aggregations. Yet in a characteristic infusion of a convention from the past with the spirit of modernity, Cézanne—in a work like *Studies of a Rower*, or in the related *Male Nude, Back View* (1863–65; plate 1)—updated the convention of the study sheet by animating it with time and motion. The effect is similar to what Ewa Lajer-Burcharth has located in Watteau's study sheets—"a descending sequence of slowly rotating 'takes' [that] creates a quasi-cinematic effect of movement"—and to which she attributes drawing's reinvention "as a modern medium."[8]

The popular tradition to which we might productively refer in considering Cézanne's study sheets is perhaps less obvious. In 1858, when he was just nineteen, Cézanne included a drawing—or rather, a group of small drawings (fig. 3)—in a letter to Émile Zola, along with the exhortation to "divine the mystery of a shadowy rebus."[9] In its combination of words and images—a scythe (*une faux*), a hedge (*une haie*), a May tree (for *mai*), and two women (*les femmes*)—this rebus spells out the adolescent dictum *Il faut aimer les femmes*, or "We must love women."[10] Like the study-sheet drawings, this form of picture puzzle comprises multiple "seemingly unrelated motifs,"[11] whose potential interrelationships are awakened through the active interpretation of the viewer. Cézanne is only known to have produced this one rebus; the sketchbook page *Two Faces and a Leaf* (1856–57; fig. 4), with its vertical stack of three unrelated images, has something of the composition, but not the official character, of the form. Yet the rebus was a prevalent part of the late-nineteenth-century image culture in which he was immersed.

Like the crosswords and sudoku puzzles in today's periodicals, rebuses appeared in several of the publications that Cézanne and his friends were known to have encountered. André Dombrowski has illuminated Cézanne's reliance on popular reproductions, highlighting how he drew on the verso of two plates from the fashion magazine *La Mode illustrée* (plates 16, 29) and appropriated the compositions of others.[12] *La Mode illustrée* published rebuses, as did the similarly titled but more general-interest *Le Monde illustré* and *L'Univers illustré*, as well as the sister fashion periodical *Le Magasin des demoiselles*, with which we know Cézanne's intimate Zola was familiar.[13] (One of the latter publication's rebuses would later be invoked in philosopher Jean-François Lyotard's reminder, relevant here, that the etymology of *rebus* reflects a "speaking 'through things.'"[14]) The weekly *L'Illustration* featured a back-page rebus whose specific repertory of images—the scythes and hedges—is so close to Cézanne's own epistolary attempt as to suggest a direct debt (fig. 5); his rebus's young lady seems similarly correlated to other reproductions in *L'Illustration* (fig. 6).[15] And in a further

4. Adrien Chappuis has described this drawing as "three studies of a model posed as an oarsman," noting that "movement is expressed in these studies, which is rare in the academy nudes." Chappuis, *The Drawings of Paul Cézanne: A Catalogue Raisonné* (Greenwich, Conn.: New York Graphic Society, 1973), 1:94, no. 205.
5. For a discussion of late medieval modelbooks as early examples of various drawings "preserved in isolation from their iconographical and spatial-pictorial surrounding," see Ulrike Jenni, "The Phenomena of Change in the Modelbook Tradition around 1400," in Walter Strauss and Tracie Felker, eds., *Drawings Defined* (New York: Abaris, 1987), 35–47.
6. See Mary Tompkins Lewis, "Cézanne and the Louvre," in Judit Geskó, ed., *Cézanne and the Past: Tradition and Creativity* (Budapest: Museum of Fine Arts Budapest, 2012), 102–03.
7. This technique is discussed in conjunction with Leonardo da Vinci. See Carmen C. Bambach, *Leonardo da Vinci: Master Draftsman* (New York: Metropolitan Museum of Art, 2003), 293.
8. Ewa Lajer-Burcharth, "Drawing Time," *October* 151 (Winter 2015): 3, 7.
9. Cézanne, letter to Émile Zola, May 3, 1858, in *The Letters of Paul Cézanne*, ed. and trans. Alex Danchev (Los Angeles: J. Paul Getty Museum, 2013), no. 2.
10. See Chappuis, *Drawings of Paul Cézanne*, 1:59, no. 17.
11. This phrase, used by Susan Sidlauskas in *Cézanne's Other: The Portraits of Hortense* (Berkeley: University of California Press, 2009), 162, echoes Nicholas Turner and Jane Shoaf Turner's description of an "apparently random accumulation of images" in figs. 1 and 2. Turner and Turner, *Woodner Collection: Master Drawings*, 300.
12. André Dombrowski, "The Emperor's Last Clothes: Cézanne, Fashion, and 'l'année terrible,'" in *Cézanne, Murder, and Modern Life* (Berkeley: University of California Press, 2013), 189–231.
13. Indeed, the names of *La Mode illustrée* and *Le Monde illustré* are so close that they were apparently confused by Wayne Andersen in *Cézanne's Portrait Drawings* (Cambridge, Mass.: MIT Press, 1970), when, on p. 116, he mistakenly refers to the latter when referencing the former. Anna Zsófia Kovács lists *L'Univers illustré* among the "illustrated journals" Cézanne "kept at home" in "Cézanne's Use of Reproductive Prints," in Geskó, *Cézanne and the Past*, 137. Zola's reference to *Le Magasin des demoiselles* provides the epigraph for Dombrowski's article "The Emperor's Last Clothes: Cézanne, Fashion and 'l'année terrible,'" *Burlington Magazine* 148, no. 1242 (September 2006): 586–94 (epigraph on p. 586), which would later become the book chapter cited above.
14. Jean-François Lyotard, *Discourse, Figure*, trans. Mary Lydon (Minneapolis: University of Minnesota Press, 2011), 297–98. Lyotard cited this rebus's later publication in Roland Topor's *Rébus* (Paris: Horay, 1964), but Tom Conley attributed it to its original publication in an 1844 issue of *Le Magasin des demoiselles* in "From *Rebut* to *Rébus*," *Yale French Studies*, no. 99 (2001): 34.

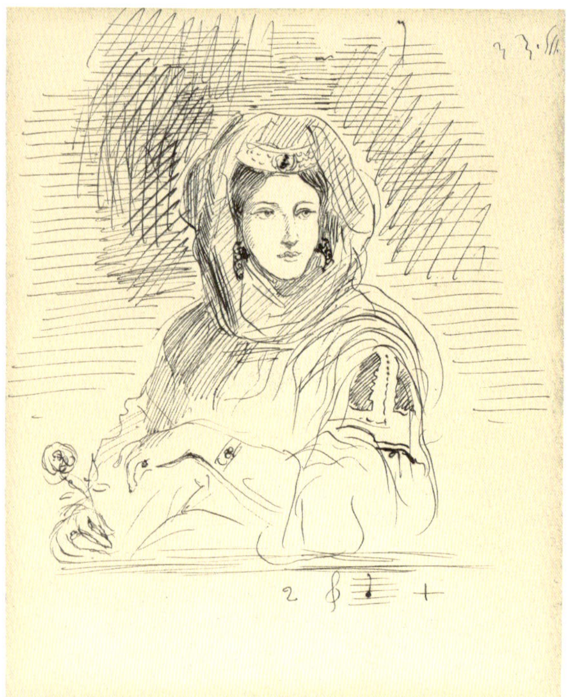

fig. 7

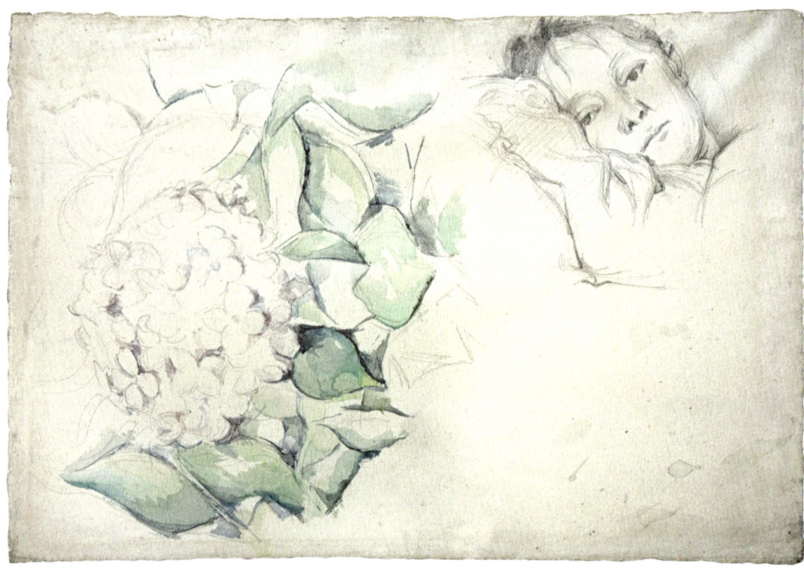

fig. 8

testament to the rebus's place in the nineteenth-century visual imagination, Eugène Delacroix, whom Cézanne esteemed above all other predecessors, used the combination of the numeral 2 (*deux*), the note on the scale la, and a cross (*croix*) to sign at least one letter and one drawing (fig. 7), the latter belonging to Victor Chocquet, the collector who also championed Cézanne.[16]

This is not to suggest that Cézanne's drawings function like riddles whose solution is to be found in next week's answer key.[17] Rather, approaching these drawings through the lens of the rebus reminds us that these images are potential ones, thick with meaning, and how reliant they are on the beholder for these significations to unfold.[18] The copresence of images on a single study sheet yields rich correspondences that point toward similar connections across drawings, compelling our attention more deeply than would a puzzle with a unique solution. Rather than suggesting that Cézanne's study sheets can be solved, the device of the rebus serves to emphasize their infinite interpretability—which ultimately stems from their very *unsolvability*.

In her insightful article about the "graphic unconscious" of the nineteenth-century rebus, Julia Louise Langbein has cited the frequent observation that "a puzzle solved exhausts itself."[19] Yet she notes that Freud—who, during the same period in which Cézanne was working,[20] found the rebus a useful metaphor for the condensation of images in a dream—"does not consider the rebus self-exhausted or spent when solved." Rather, Langbein continues,

> he believes that the solution itself has an aesthetic remainder . . . and the possibility of yet future meaning. . . . Freud describes not the solution of rebuses but their 'interpretation,' as if the technique required were that of the sensitive connoisseur or the experienced analyst.[21]

Or, we might add, the attentive art historian. For, lacking solutions, the potential meanings of Cézanne's study sheets are never exhausted.

Among the most straightforward compositionally, the study sheets in which Cézanne proposed parallels between a person and a corresponding object are also among the richest in their significations. Tellingly, these center on the family trio—the artist;

fig. 7 Eugène Delacroix (French, 1798–1863). *Pauline Villot in Algerian Costume*. c. 1833. Pen and ink, 7 3/8 × 6 1/16" (18.7 × 15.4 cm). The Morgan Library and Museum, New York. Thaw Collection

fig. 8 Paul Cézanne (French, 1839–1906). *Madame Cézanne with Hortensias* (*Madame Cézanne aux hortensias*). c. 1885. Pencil and watercolor on paper, 12 1/2 × 19" (31.8 × 48.3 cm). Private collection

15. Though I have not found evidence of Cézanne's having read *L'Illustration*, the periodical's wide circulation makes it likely.
16. The same rebus signature appears on a June 1838 letter from Delacroix to George Sand, now in the Bibliothèque de l'INHA, collections Jacques Doucet.
17. This is the approach taken by Sidney Geist in the "Cézanne the Francophone" chapter of his *Interpreting Cézanne* (Cambridge, Mass.: Harvard University Press, 1988), 1–29. Although Geist's cryptomorphic trouser folds and overzealous word play remain unconvincing, his case for the pervasiveness of the rebus in late-nineteenth-century culture—from *L'Illustration* to Delacroix (including the drawing that appears here as fig. 7); see esp. p. 28—is extremely useful.
18. I use "potential images" in the sense defined by Dario Gamboni as "those established . . . by the artist but dependent on the beholder for their realization." Gamboni, *Potential Images: Ambiguity and Indeterminacy in Modern Art* (London: Reaktion, 2002), 18. I am indebted to Juliane Betz's helpful invocation of Gamboni in her essay "*Hineinsehen* or 'Seeing-In': Some Basics on Formal Ambiguities in the Works of Paul Cézanne," in Eiling, *Cézanne: Metamorphoses*, 71, 74.
19. Julia Louise Langbein, "The Nineteenth-Century Rebus: Picture Puzzles and Dream Work in the Illustrated Journal," *Notes in the History of Art* 38, no. 1 (Fall 2018): 49.
20. T. J. Clark has wondered "why writers about Cézanne shy away from the strict coincidence" of their respective contributions' overlapping

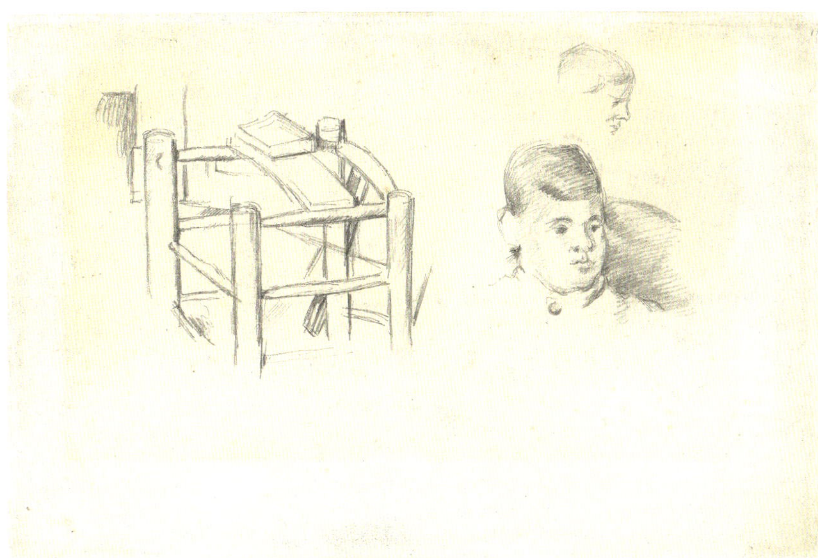

fig. 9

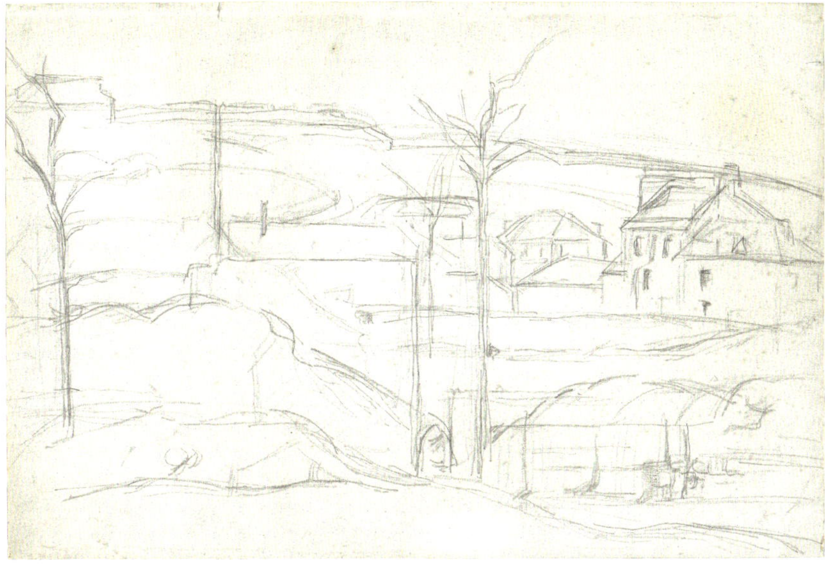

fig. 10

his wife, Hortense; and his son, Paul Jr.—each matched, as if a Greek or Roman god, with an attribute as fitting in form as it is in character.[22] The artist's unusually spherical skull matches the volume of the apple with which he wished to "astonish Paris" (plate 21).[23] Hortense is sometimes paired with the hortensia for which she is named (fig. 8), or with whichever flower's form echoes the vector of her recumbent figure (plate 18).[24] Other times, her own round head repeats the curves of a pail (plate 20), or a spherical fruit (plate 19)—the latter introducing a verbal-visual pun on her unfortunate nickname, La Boule.[25] But in this case, the formal rhyme seems to extend to a relationship between the drawing's two sides as well, for the round fruit occupies the same position on the recto as a bridge's curved arch on its verso. A similar triangulation exists in *Piece of Furniture Made of Chair Rungs and Uprights, and Portrait of the Artist's Son* (1880–81; fig. 9), in which the structure of Paul Jr.'s assigned attribute—an appropriately domestic chair—is extrapolated onto the rectilinear organization of the landscape on the other side of the sheet (fig. 10). If both wife and son are aligned with interior objects, these surrogates are nonetheless projected onto the outside world, suggesting a permeability between realms. Access to the potential meanings of Cézanne's drawings, it becomes clear, is dependent on acknowledging their material reality as dimensional objects, with conversations between images straddling both sides of the support.

If these portrait-attribute pairings propose one-to-one relationships, the analogies between motifs only multiply as the study sheets become more populated. The three elements of *Studies* (1869–72; plate 10) could not be more disparate in terms of their origins: the Venus figure extracted from Delacroix's Apollo ceiling at the Louvre, a study for Cézanne's own *Afternoon in Naples* (*L'Après-midi à Naples*, 1873–77), and a rangy dog of uncertain provenance. Yet they share not only the page but also the arabesques of their bodies. And while their placement may seem haphazard, with multiple orientations and the bacchanalian bedroom scene set off in a makeshift frame, each figure in fact reaches toward the other—hand to paw, paw to backside, elbow to heel—in a compositional eddy that activates the entire page.

figs. 9, 10 Paul Cézanne (French, 1839–1906). *Piece of Furniture Made of Chair Rungs and Uprights, and Portrait of the Artist's Son* (*Meuble en bâtons de chaise et portrait du fils*) (verso); *Hills, with Houses and Trees* (*Collines avec maisons et arbres*) (recto). 1880–81 (verso); 1880–83 (recto). Pencil on laid paper, 12 5/16 × 18 5/8" (31.3 × 47.3 cm). Kunstmuseum Basel, Kupferstichkabinett

dates," and has read Cézanne's *Bathers at Rest* (*Baigneurs au repos*, 1875–77; Barnes Foundation, Philadelphia)—relevantly to this essay—as "paratactic" or "a compound of separate images." Clark, "Freud's Cézanne," *Representations*, no. 52 (Fall 1995): 96–97.

21. Langbein, "Nineteenth-Century Rebus," 49.
22. Such relationships engage not only the metaphoric mode—what Richard Shiff has defined as "resemblance in form"—but also the metonymic one, "an analogous structural and compositional function, exchangeable from one pictorial environment to the other." Shiff, "Risible Cézanne," in Eik Kahng, ed., *The Repeating Image: Multiples in French Painting from David to Matisse* (Baltimore: Walters Art Museum, 2007), 156.
23. For the mythical resonance of this pun, see Danchev, *Cézanne: A Life* (New York: Pantheon, 2012), 11–12 and 382n27.
24. In Walter Feilchenfeldt, Jayne Warman, and David Nash, *The Paintings, Watercolors and Drawings of Paul Cézanne: An Online Catalogue Raisonné*, the sleeping figure in plate 18 is identified as the artist's son. Theodore Reff and Innis Howe Shoemaker offer the more ambiguous designation *Person Asleep*, suggesting that "the sleeping figure, previously identified as the artist's son, may well be his wife," an assessment with which I agree. Reff and Shoemaker, *Paul Cézanne: Two Sketchbooks* (Philadelphia: Philadelphia Museum of Art, 1989), 53.
25. "Among his friends, particularly his literary friends, her nickname was La Boule (the Ball, or the Dumpling)." Danchev, *Cézanne: A Life*, 157.

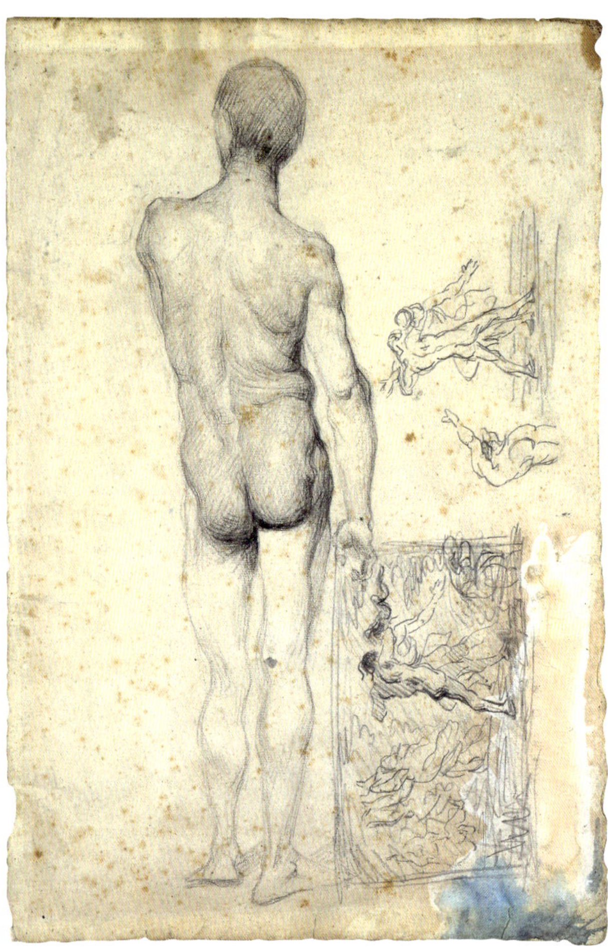

fig. 11

Ultimately, it seems that Cézanne took particular pleasure in inviting associations between motifs of different registers, linking the animate with the inanimate, the everyday with the exalted, the flat with the dimensional, or the observed with the imagined.[26] In *Studies and Portraits of the Artist's Son* (1877–78; plate 22), the arm of the same decorative figure on the Louis XVI clock from *Page of Studies, Including a Portrait of Goya* (presumably sketched from dimensional life; see fig. 1) reaches out toward a bather with arms outstretched (presumably conjured by the artist), while, on the verso, the lip of an inanimate casserole lid repeats the curves of hair on the foreheads of several figures who are very much alive. Similar links between motifs of different character are rife in a study sheet dating to 1873–77 (plate 13)—with its hunched workers providing mirrored reversals of a bending bather (labor pictured as the inverse of leisure)—and another dating to 1879–80 (plate 14), in which a young woman's head from an engraving after Tintoretto (who will never age beyond this representation) offers an improbable yet fitting companion for the artist's son (who must). In these examples, and others, the unlikeliness of the correspondence makes it all the more delectable.

In other study sheets, these parallels become intersections, in which the interactions between motifs produce little dramas—or, thanks to the humor of strange juxtapositions and unlikely shifts in scale—comedies.[27] Cézanne embellished a decorative engraving with his own drawings, for example, so that a sketched stand-in for the artist with an outstretched implement seems to be adding the finishing touches to the printed vase (plate 4). Crouched alongside a goblet, a diminutive Saint Anthony becomes an action figure poised to take on an unlikely adversary (plate 5), while, on another study sheet, a bather extends her arm as if to quell two wrestlers' tussle (plate 16). And in perhaps the most realized of these playlets, *Studies after Passarotti, Domenichino, and an Unknown Master* (1867–70; plate 12), a woman balances Diana on her fingertip and a nymph upon her forehead, while two men lean in as if to gossip about the incongruity. "A boat has no business to be on the roof of a house, and a headless man cannot run," Freud cautioned of a rebus's lack of logic, going on to reference conflicts of scale: "Moreover, the man is bigger than the house." And yet, such nonsensical inconsistencies, he continued, "may form a poetical phrase of the greatest beauty and significance."[28]

26. Shiff has reflected on the pleasure inherent in making such drawings, "imagin[ing] the artist engaging in aesthetic play that he never actively sought but could not resist. Sketching, he indulged himself." Shiff, "Cézanne in a Sketchbook," *Master Drawings* 47, no. 4 (Winter 2009): 447.
27. While humor is a quality not often attributed to this artist, Nina Athanassoglou-Kallmyer has cited the rebus as an example of the vernacular forms of wit in which the Aixois artist indulged, while Shiff has theorized how Cézanne's repetitions become "risible." Athanassoglou-Kallmyer, *Cézanne and Provence: The Painter in His Culture* (Chicago: University of Chicago Press, 2003), 55–56. Shiff, "Risible Cézanne," 127–70.
28. Sigmund Freud, *The Interpretation of Dreams*, trans. and ed. James Strachey (New York: Basic, 2010), 296.
29. See Wayne Andersen, *Cézanne's Portrait Drawings* (Cambridge, Mass.: MIT Press, 1970), 53, no. 6. For the evolution of scholarship around the "TEL" inscription, which appears throughout Cézanne's drawings and is believed to be Vollard's annotation, see Chappuis, *Drawings of Paul Cézanne*, 1:29n25.
30. Shiff, "Risible Cézanne," 157. John Elderfield, "Excavations," in *Cézanne: The Rock and Quarry Paintings* (Princeton, N.J.: Princeton University Press, 2020), 16. Langbein, "The Nineteenth-Century Rebus," 49.
31. Cézanne, letter to Zola, May 3, 1858, no. 2.
32. Cézanne, letter to Zola, July 9, 1858, no. 3.

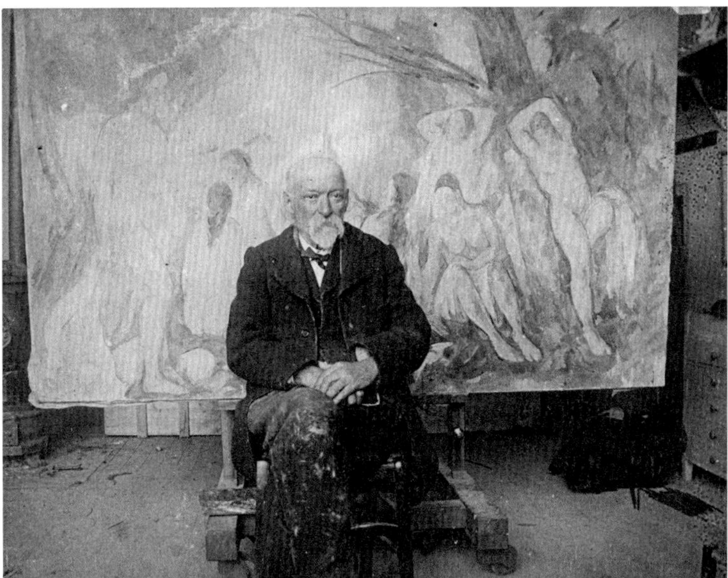

fig. 12

In other study-sheet drawings, Cézanne included frames around motifs only to subvert their delimiting role by self-consciously referencing—or trespassing—the boundary. In an example from 1865–75 (plate 9 verso), a series of these enclosures serve as platforms across which two unbounded figures gambol. In another, the artist returned years later to an earlier drawing—a habitual practice that contributes to these works' extended temporality—adding two studies of a violent encounter to the sheet (fig. 11). One of them he enclosed in a border and turned on its side, placing its corner squarely in the nude figure's palm, as if it were an object onto which he might, finally, rest the weight of his contrapposto stance. Meanwhile, in *Study for The Eternal Feminine* (c. 1870–75; plate 44), three escapees exceed the boundaries of a narrative scene, while a Cézanne surrogate peeks around the corner of the picture-within-the-picture, as if to monitor the getaway.

The study sheets in which Cézanne inserted himself into the chain of associations can't help but arouse compelling potential meanings. By presenting his own face alongside a portrait of Goya (see fig. 1), was Cézanne raising himself to his forerunner's ranks? Can the replacement of his wife with a sculpture of the beautiful, abandoned Psyche in a family portrait with father and son (plate 24) be mere coincidence? And what about the direct superimposition of a scene of bathers over the artist's face (plate 23)—a merging of artist and subject that anticipates the iconic photograph Émile Bernard took of Cézanne in front of his late monumental canvas (fig. 12)? To this sheet, a later hand added the instruction "DÉTACHER LES 3 SUJETS" and three corresponding inscriptions of "TEL"—indicating that one might reproduce each individual element "like so."[29] But how can you disentangle subjects that are so intimately interlinked? And why—when the artist drew them there, in a radically generative disregard for genre and scale and logic—would you want to?

Indeed, such attention to the relationships between the study sheets' motifs introduces the issue of the artist's intention. Both Richard Shiff and John Elderfield have addressed this question, the former intuiting the process to have been "a procedural tic," or "a habit of linking disparate images by their happenstance form," and the latter attributing the results to "instincts and intuitions of which the artist was not necessarily conscious"—related explanations that are not unlike the "graphic unconscious" Langbein associates with the rebus.[30] In the letter written to Zola, Cézanne, referring to some poetry he has penned alongside the rebus drawing, seems to undermine his purposefulness, warning, "These are rhymes without reason."[31] Yet in a subsequent letter, sent two months later, he betrays his excitement over conjuring still more eccentric pairings—of words, though he might just as easily be talking about images—and proposing himself as a kind of a condensation machine: "I'll get busy researching other rhymes, richer and more outlandish. I'm preparing them, I'm developing them, I'm distilling them in my alembic brain."[32]

fig. 11 Paul Cézanne (French, 1839–1906). *Standing Male Nude Seen from the Back and Two Studies for The Abduction* (*Nu debout vu de dos, deux études pour L'Énlèvement*). c. 1861, studies 1866–67. Pencil on paper, 16 15/16 × 11 7/16" (43 × 29 cm). Ohara Museum, Kurashiki

fig. 12 Cézanne in his studio at Les Lauves, in front of *The Large Bathers* (*Grandes baigneuses*, 1895–1906), 1905. Photograph by Émile Bernard. Musée d'Orsay, Paris

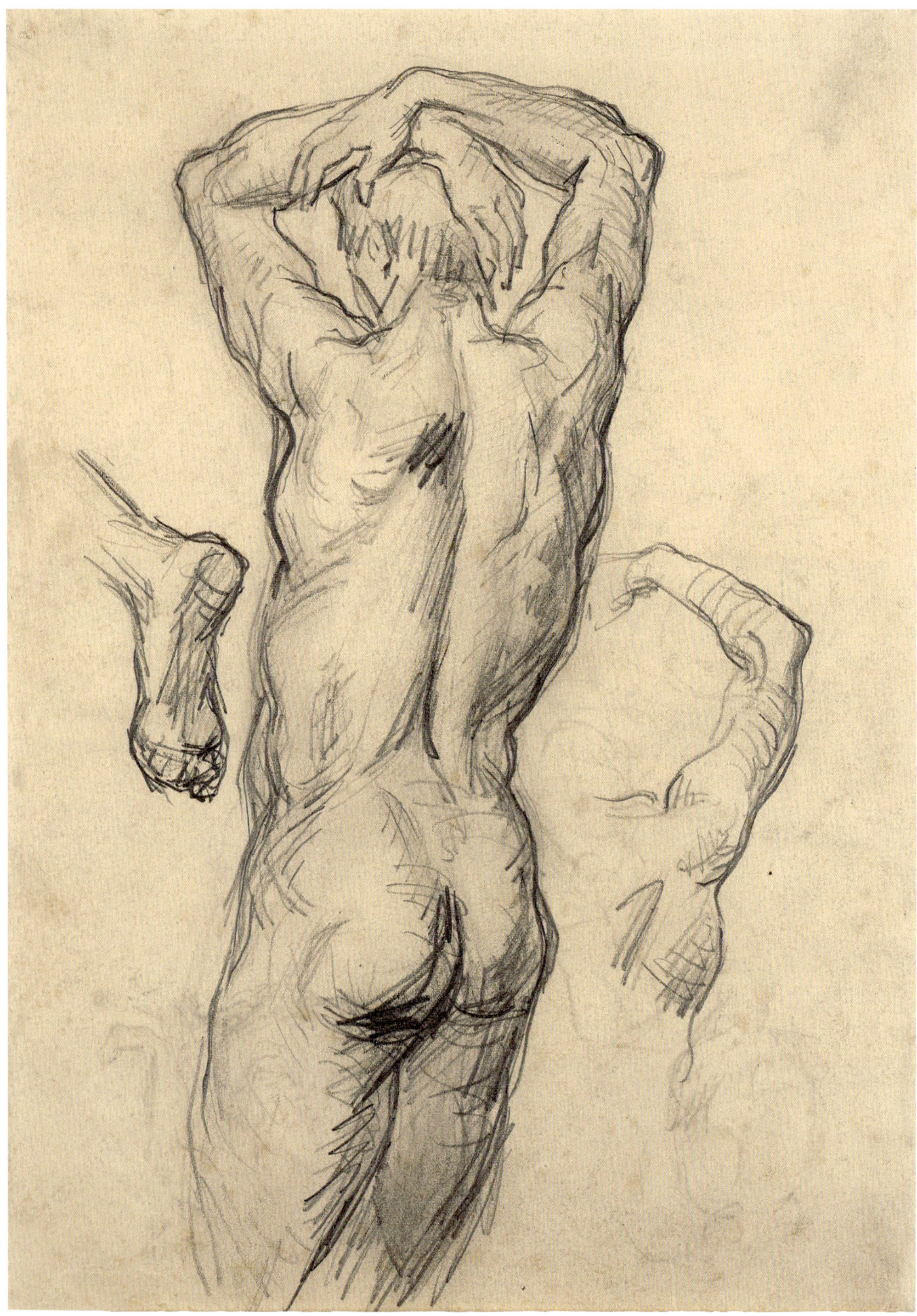

1. *Male Nude, Back View.* 1863–65. Pencil on wove paper, 9 ½ × 7" (24.1 × 17.8 cm)

2. *Study of Nudes Diving.* 1865–66. Pencil on paper, 7 ⅛ × 10 ⅝" (18.1 × 27 cm)

3. *Studies of a Rower.* 1867–69. Pencil on laid paper, 8 15/16 × 11 ¾" (22.7 × 29.9 cm)

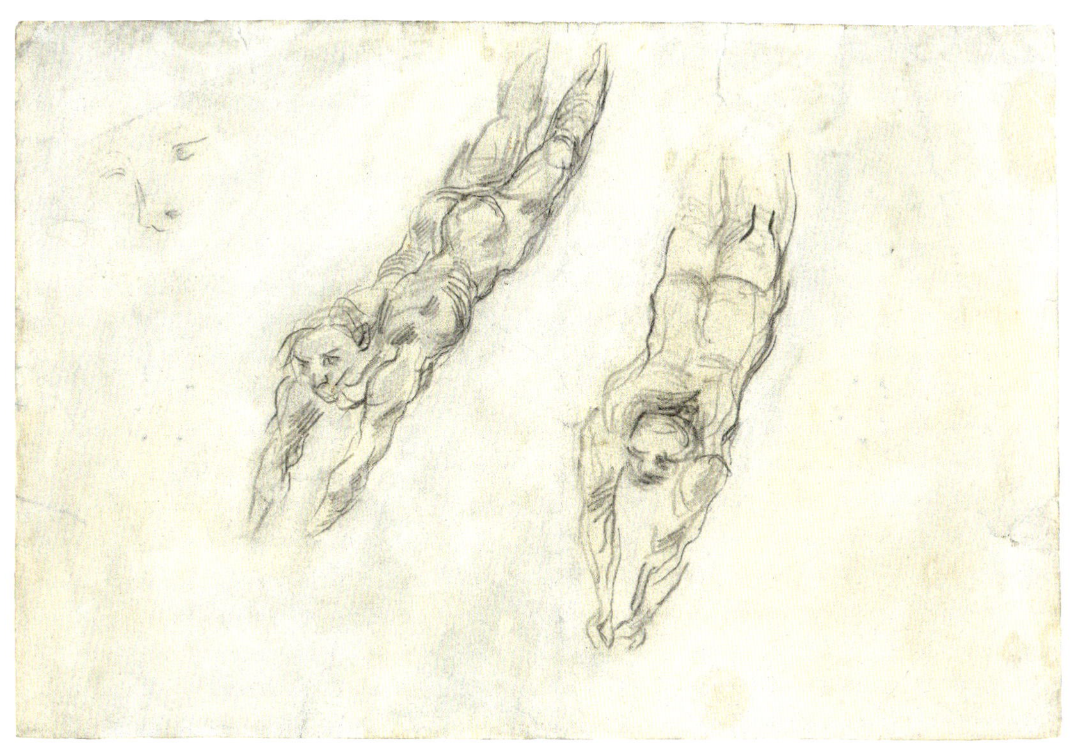

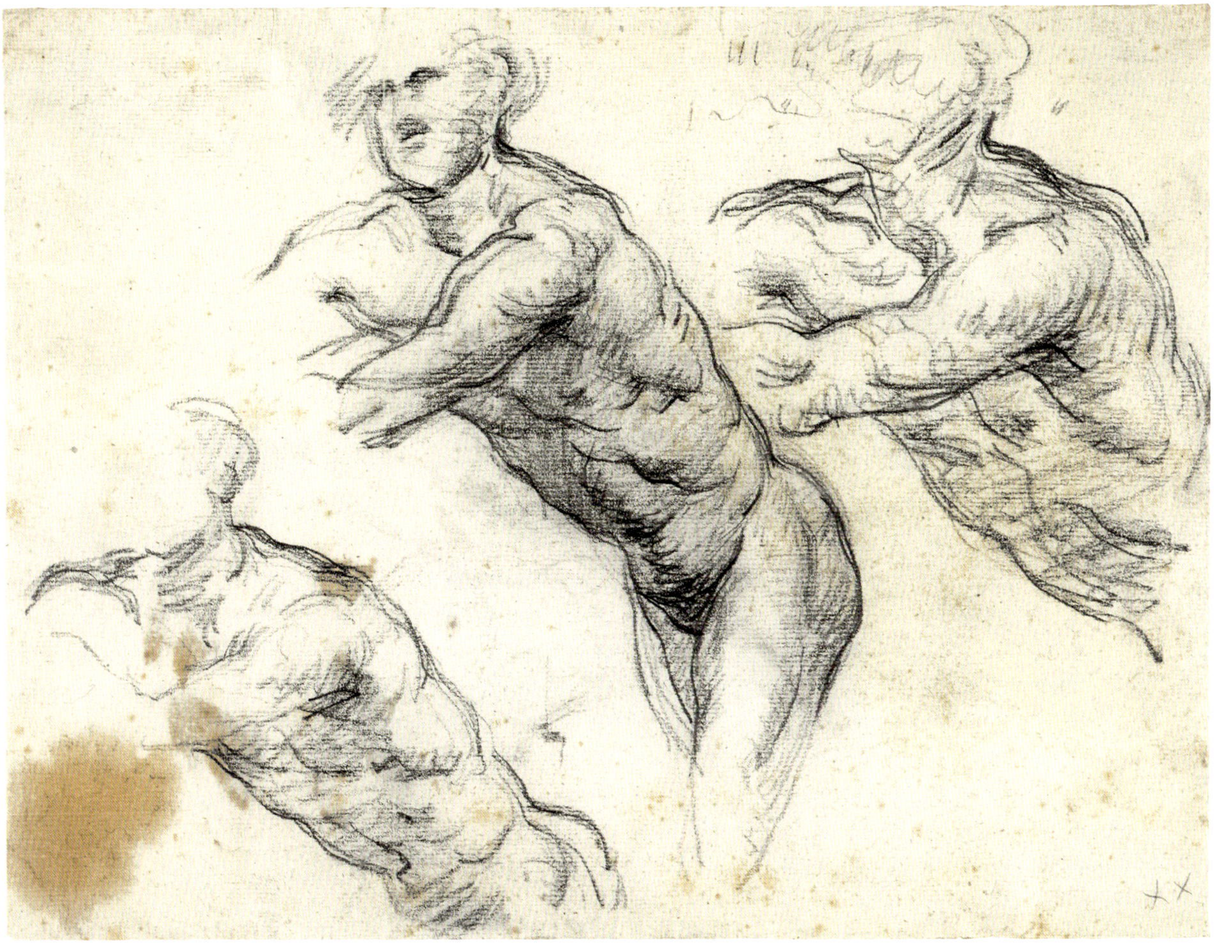

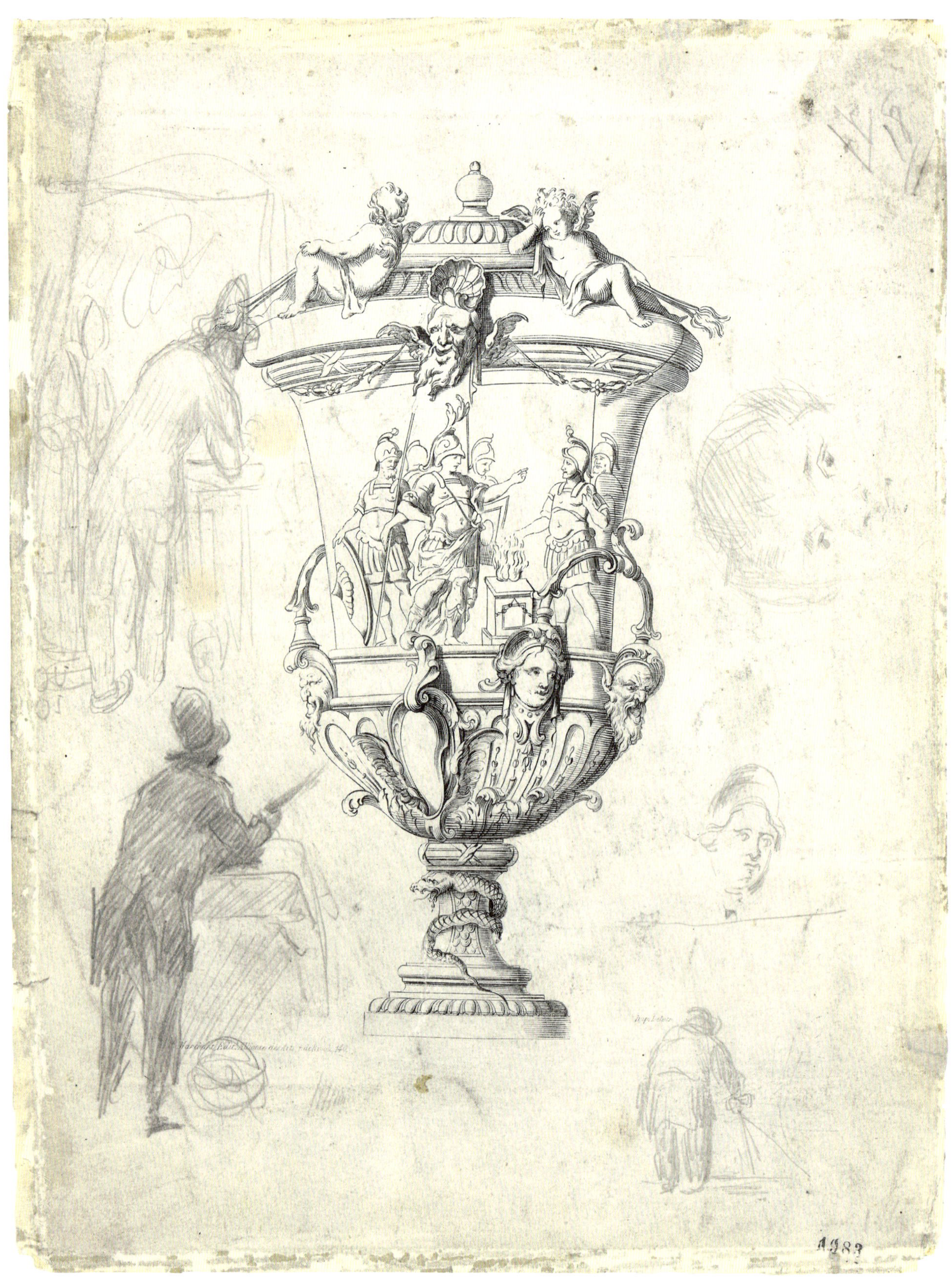

4. *Figure Studies around an Engraving of an Ornamental Vase.* c. 1878. Pencil on found etching, 12 7/16 × 9 9/16" (31.6 × 24.3 cm)

5. *Goblet, and Study for The Temptation of St. Anthony.* 1870–73. Pencil on paper, 6 × 8 3/8" (15.3 × 21.2 cm)

6. *Mother and Child, Ornamental Vase, Figure of a Woman.* 1866–71. Pencil on wove paper, 7 × 9 7/16" (17.8 × 23.9 cm)

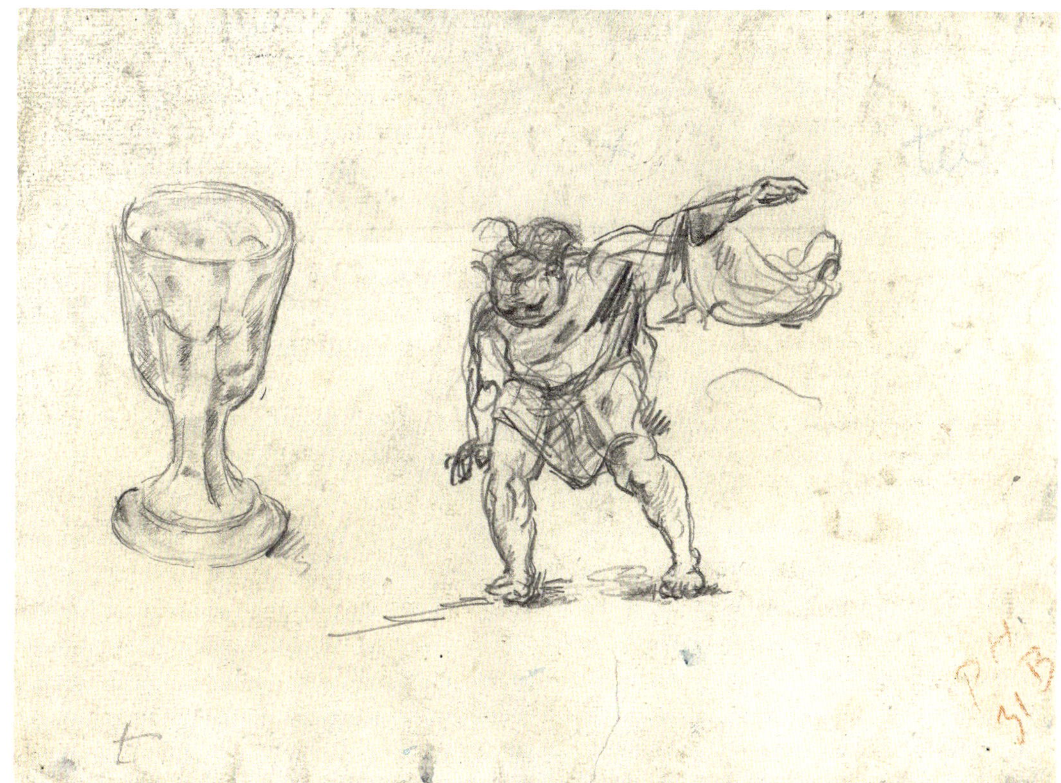

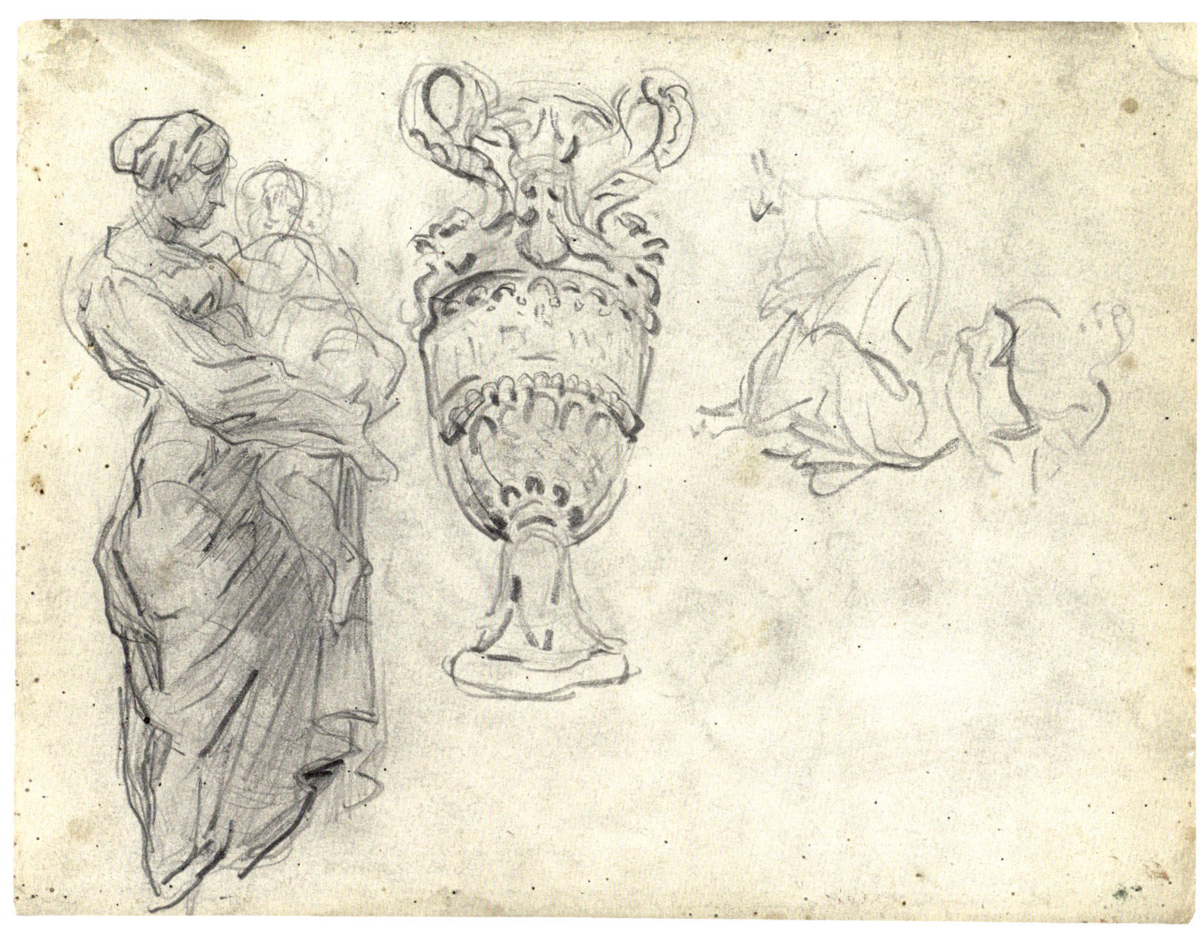

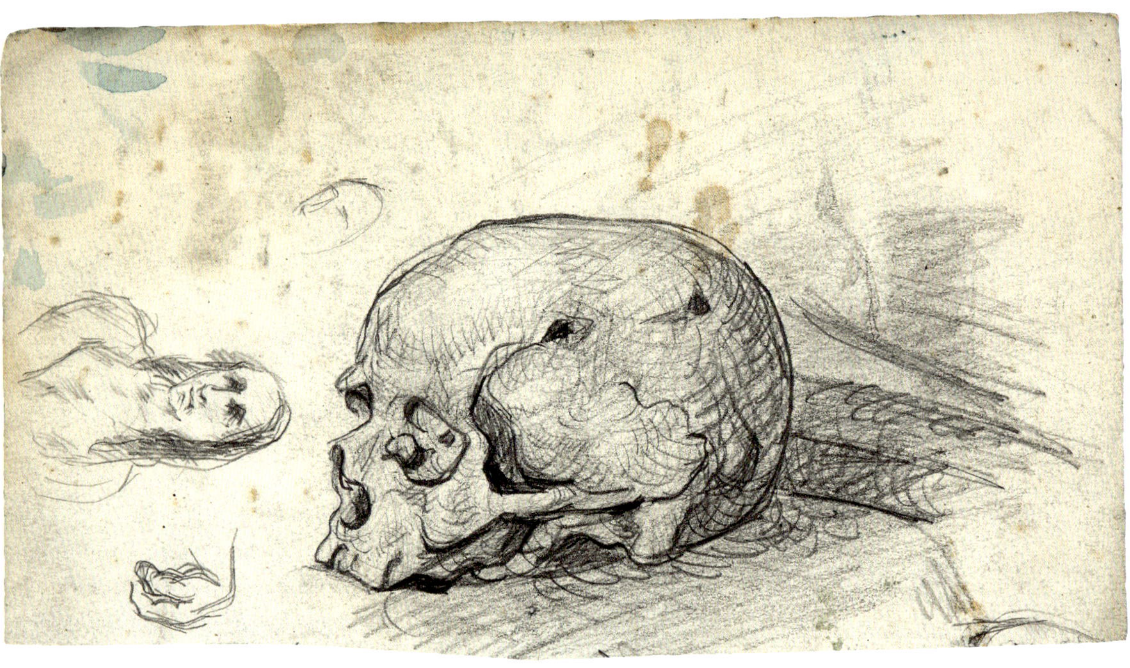

7. *Sheet of Studies, Including a Skull*. c. 1868. Pencil with splatters of watercolor on wove paper, 4 13⁄16 × 9 1⁄16" (12.2 × 23 cm)

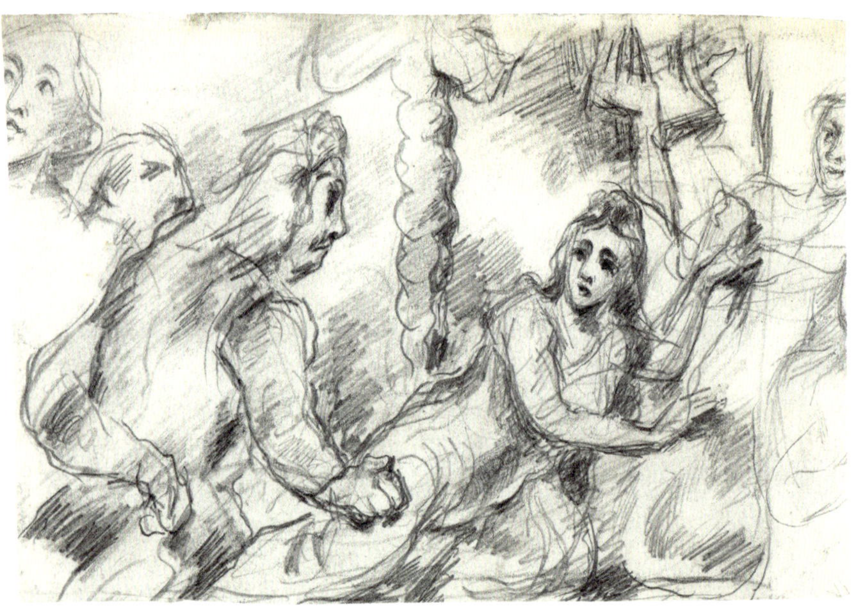

8. *A Historical or Biblical Scene (The Rape of Lucretia)*. 1865–69. Pencil and ink on paper, 4 5⁄8 × 6 7⁄8" (11.8 × 17.5 cm)

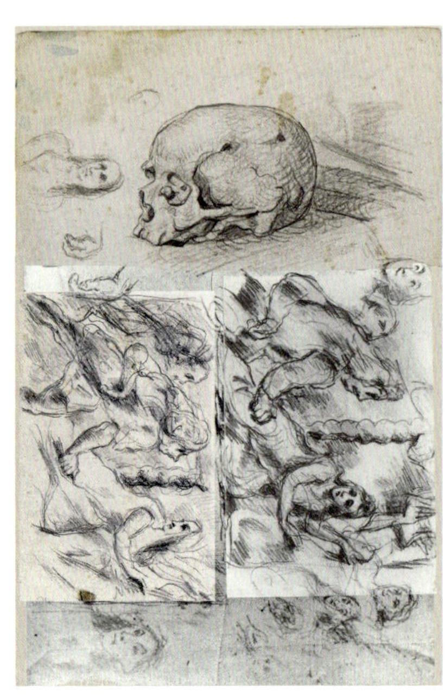

A. Reconstruction of plates 7–8, with *A Historical or Biblical Scene*, 1865–69 (private collection)

9. *Study after Pierre Puget's Sculpture the Milo of Croton, Composition Sketch of Figures in a Landscape around a Fire* (recto); *Sheet of Studies with Various Figures* (verso). 1866–69, 1870–73 (recto); 1874–75, 1865–68 (verso). Pencil on laid paper, 9 3/8 × 12 5/16" (23.8 × 31.3 cm)

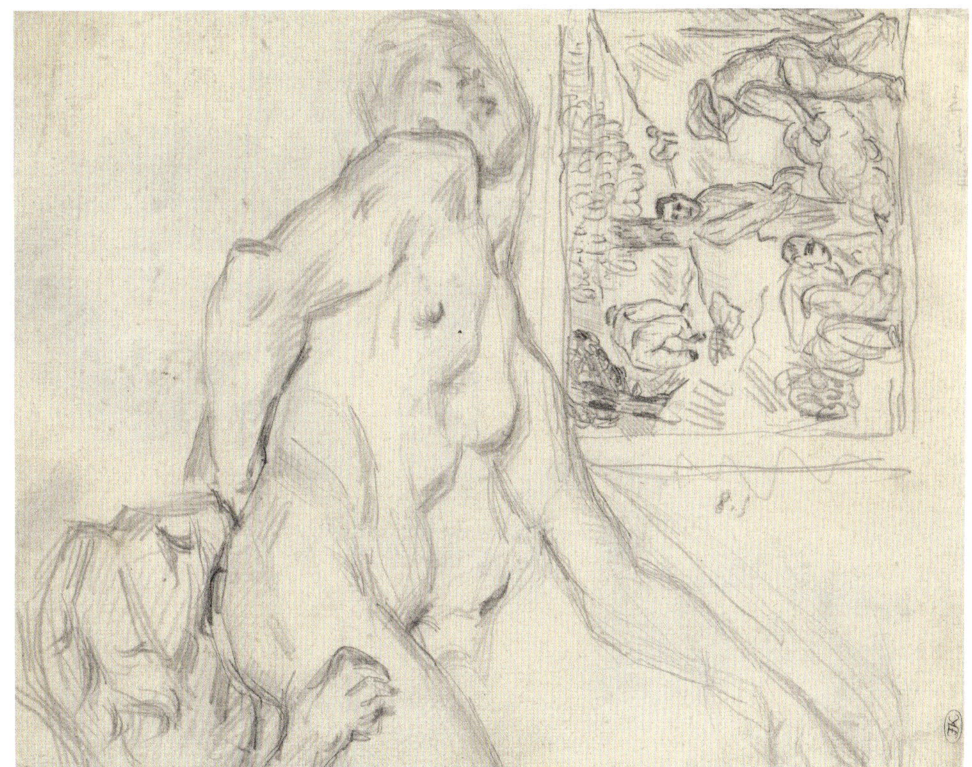

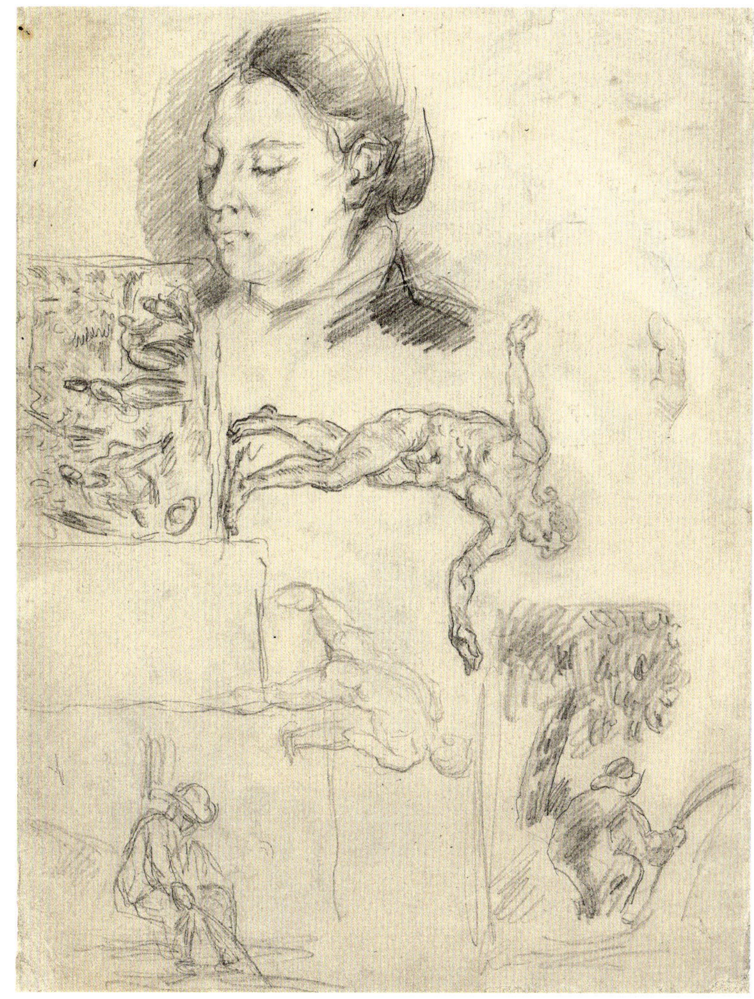

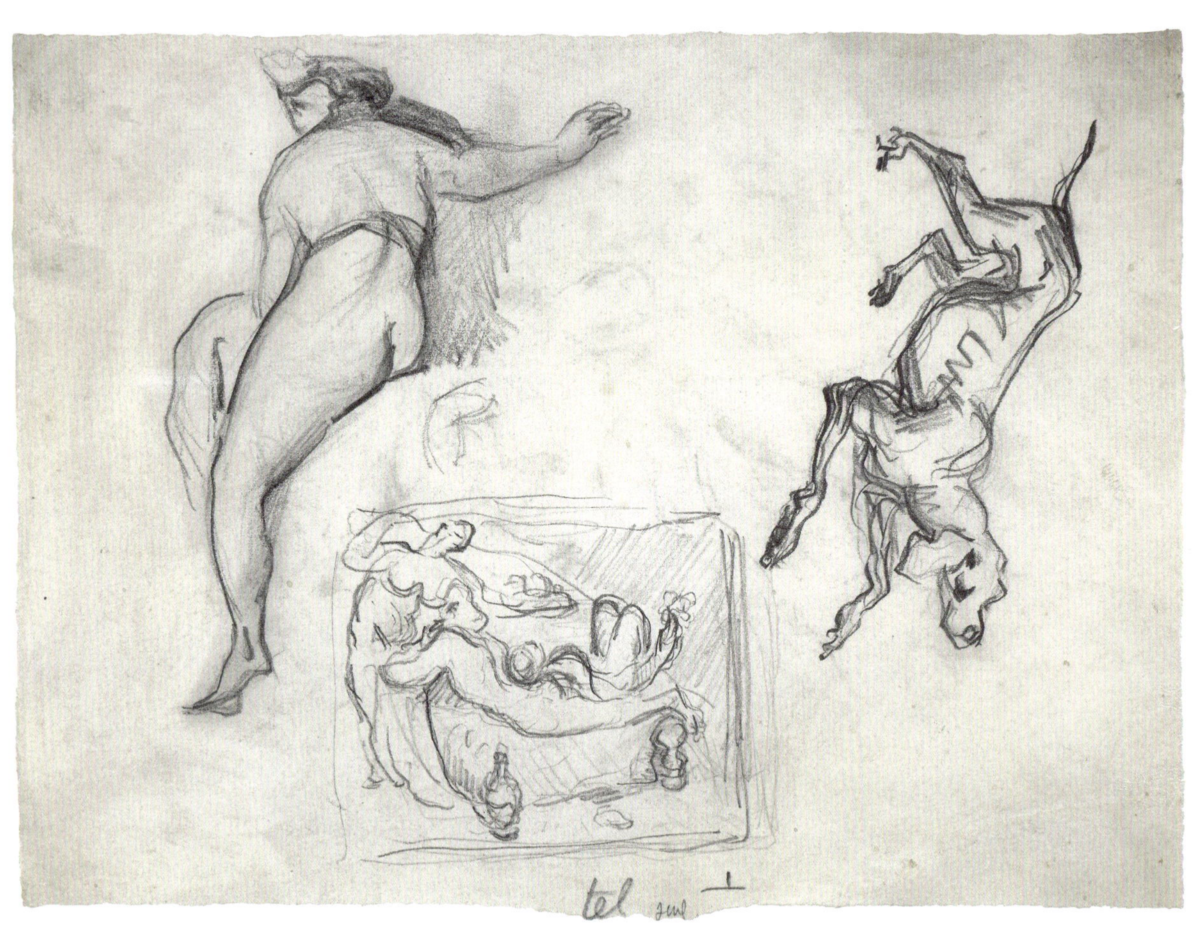

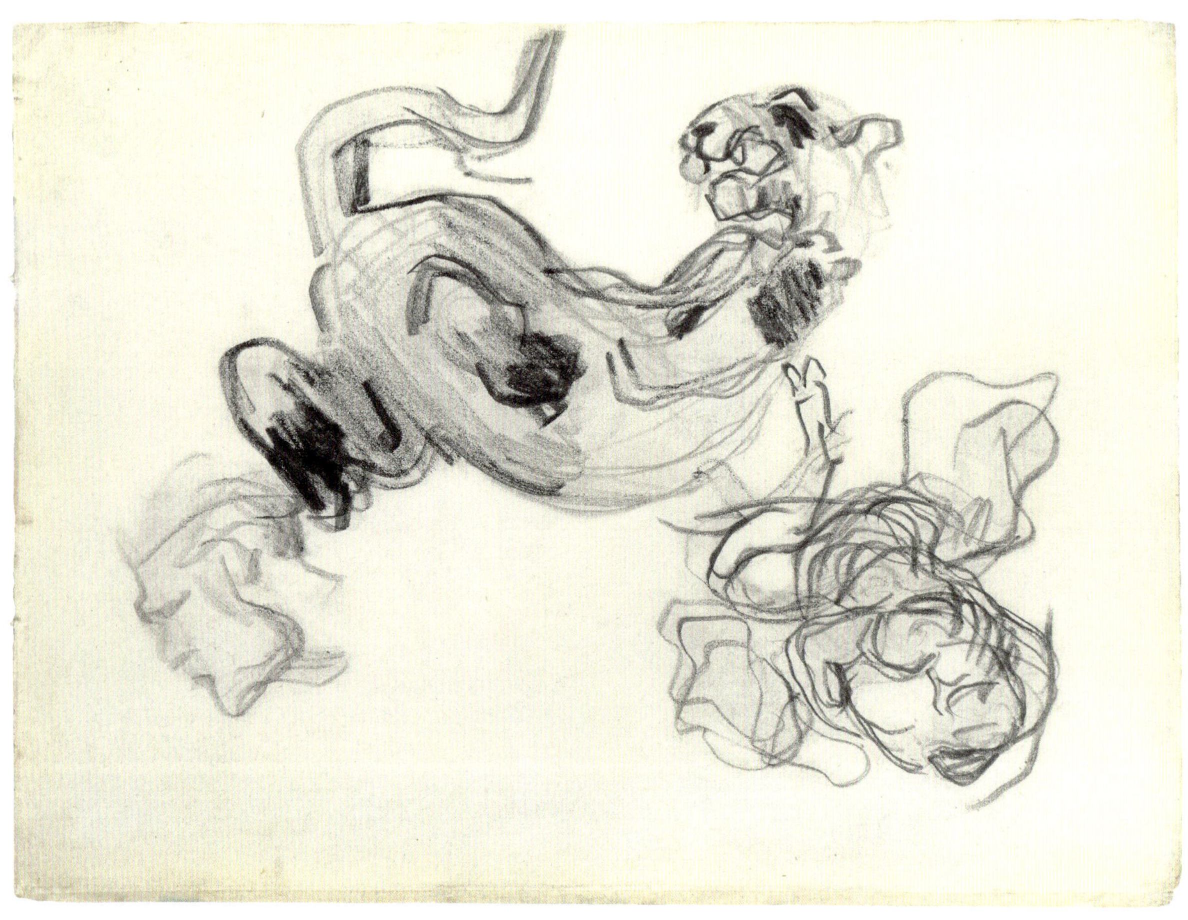

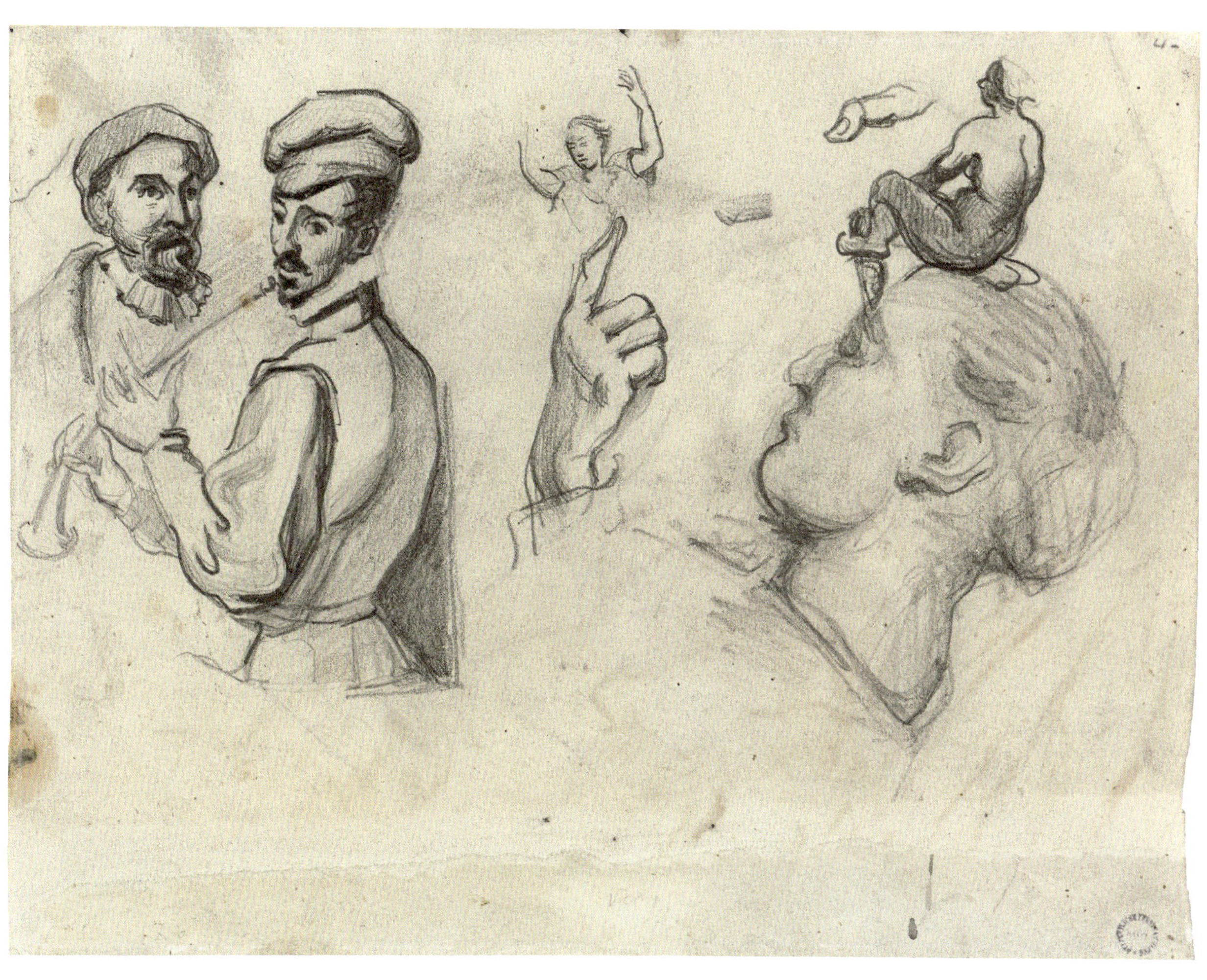

10. *Studies*. 1869–72. Pencil on wove paper, 7 1/16 × 9 7/16" (18 × 24 cm)

11. *After Delacroix: Wild Animal, and Figure in Movement*. 1865–68. Crayon on wove paper, 7 1/16 × 9 7/16" (18 × 24 cm)

12. *Studies after Passarotti, Domenichino, and an Unknown Master*. 1867–70. Pencil on wove paper, 7 1/16 × 9 1/2" (18 × 24.1 cm)

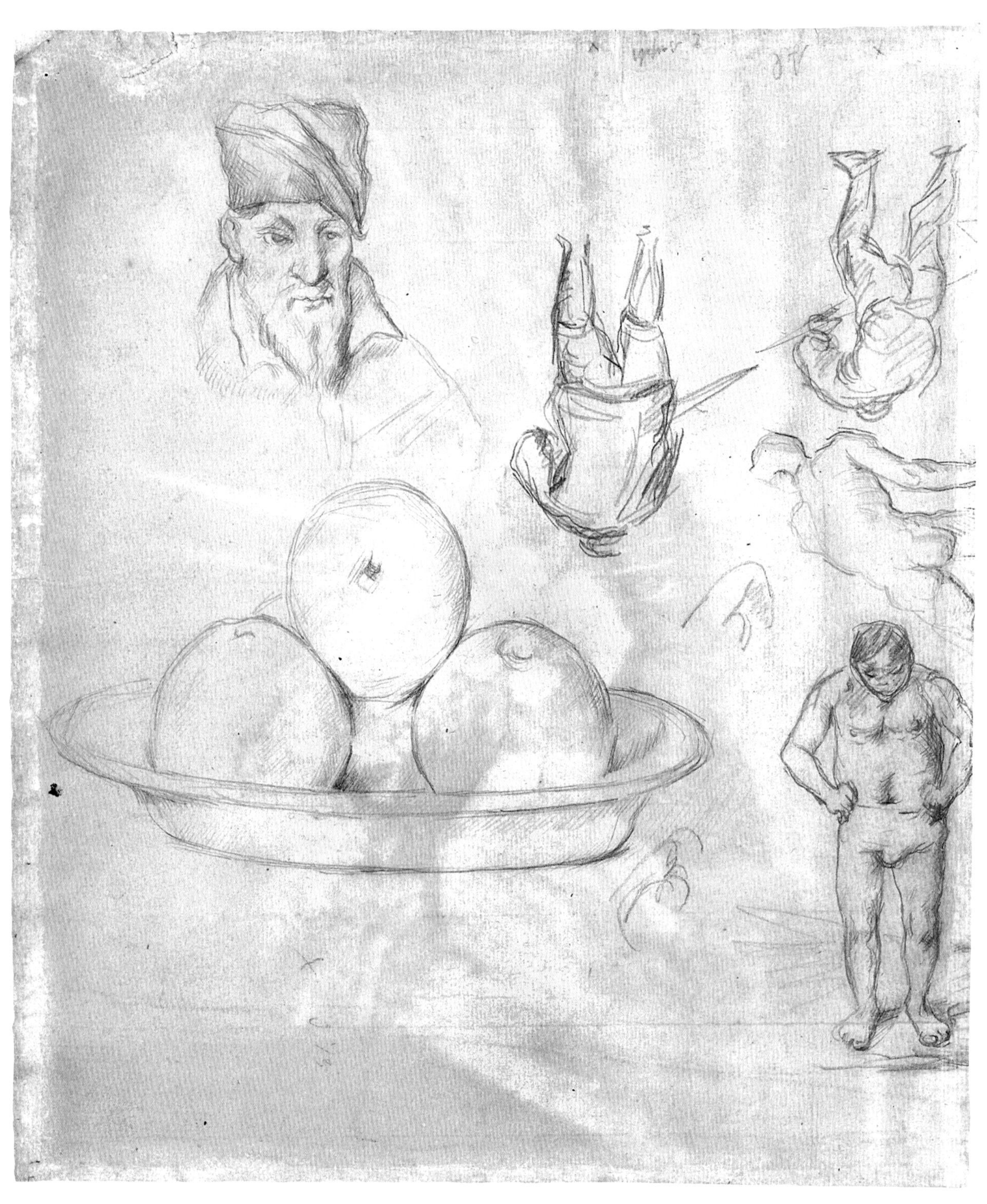

13. *Sheet of Studies: Still Life with Apples, Portrait of Fernand Navarrete, Bather, and Other Figures*. 1873–77. Pencil on laid paper, 12 1/16 × 10 3/8" (30.7 × 26.3 cm)

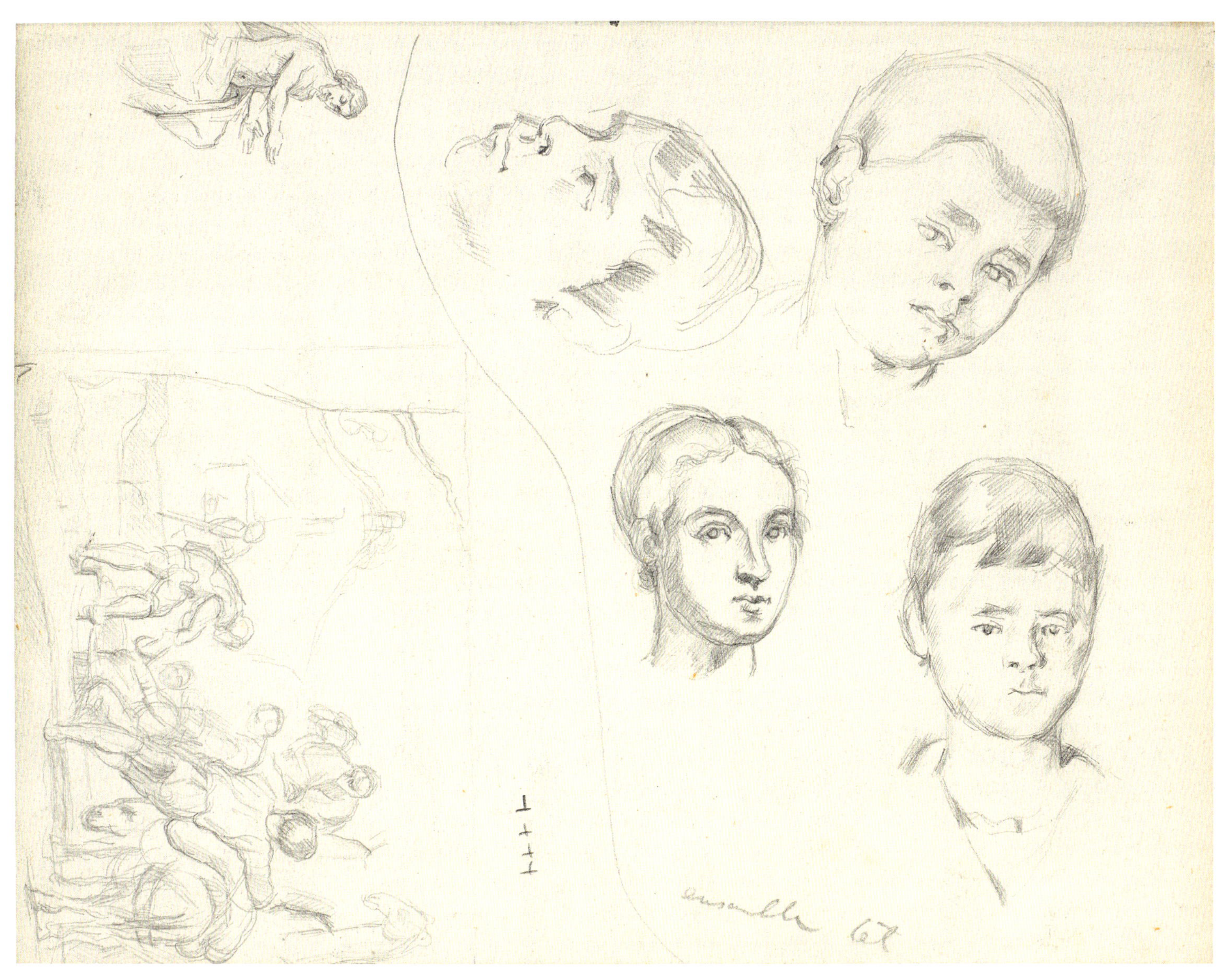

14. *Three Portraits of Paul and Studies after Pedro de Moya and Tintoretto.* 1879–80. Pencil on paper, 9 7/16 × 12 3/16" (24 × 31 cm)

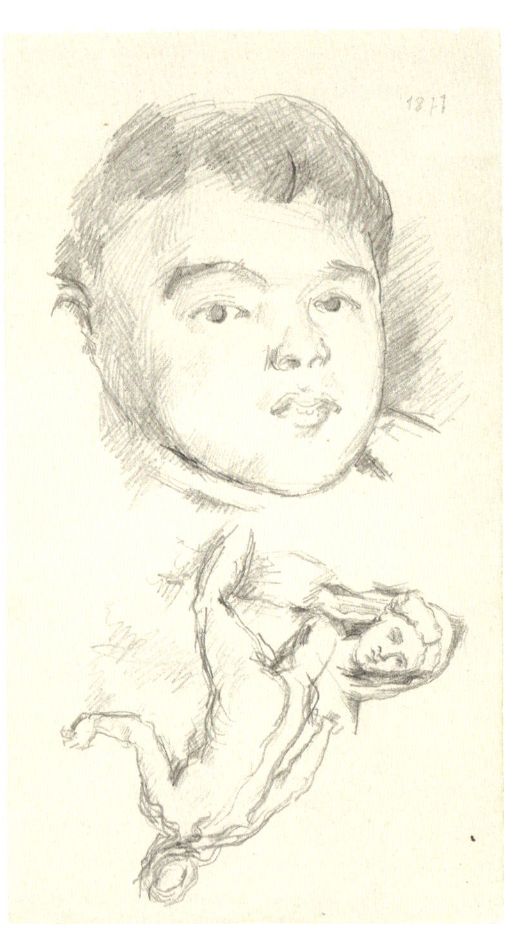

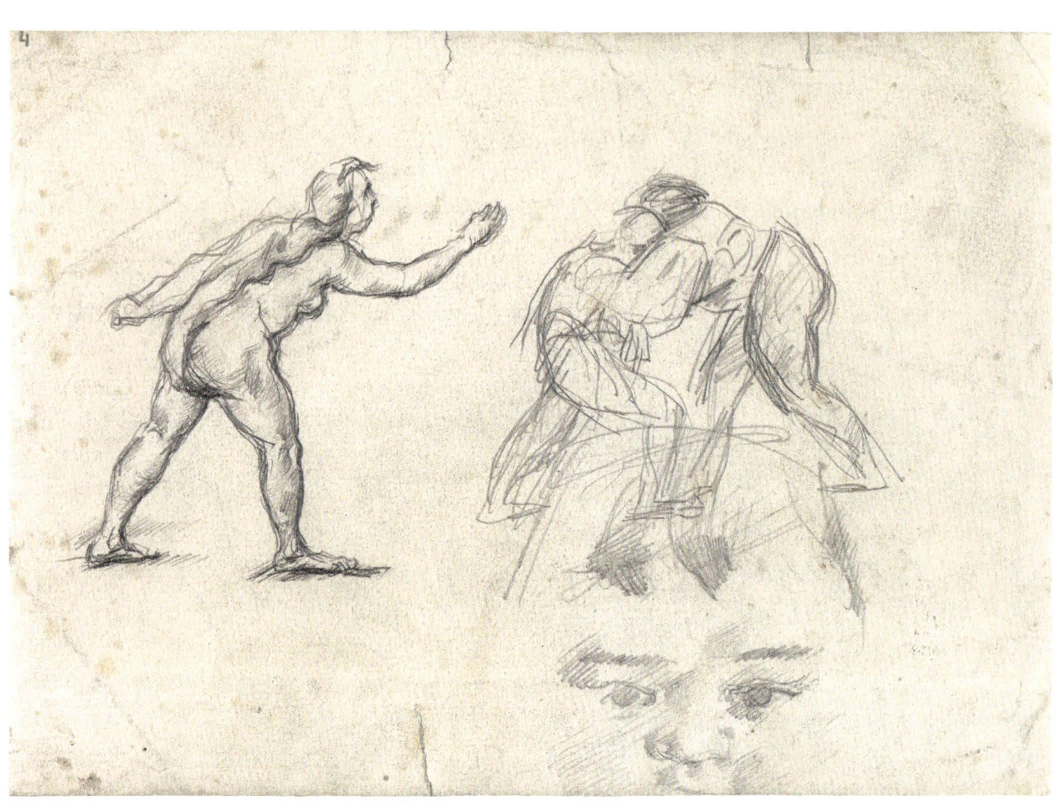

15. *Page of Studies: The Artist's Son; Head of Ceres (after Rubens); Female Bather*. c. 1879, 1882–83, 1880. Pencil on wove paper, 8 ¹¹⁄₁₆ × 4 ¹⁵⁄₁₆" (22 × 12.5 cm)

16. *Woman Bather, Two Men Wrestling, Boy's Head*. 1871–78. Pencil on paper, 7 ³⁄₁₆ × 10 ⁵⁄₁₆" (18.2 × 26.2 cm)

17. *Page of Studies, Including a Centaur after the Antique*. 1879–82. Pencil on laid paper, 14 ¹⁵⁄₁₆ × 12 ⁵⁄₁₆" (37.9 × 31.3 cm)

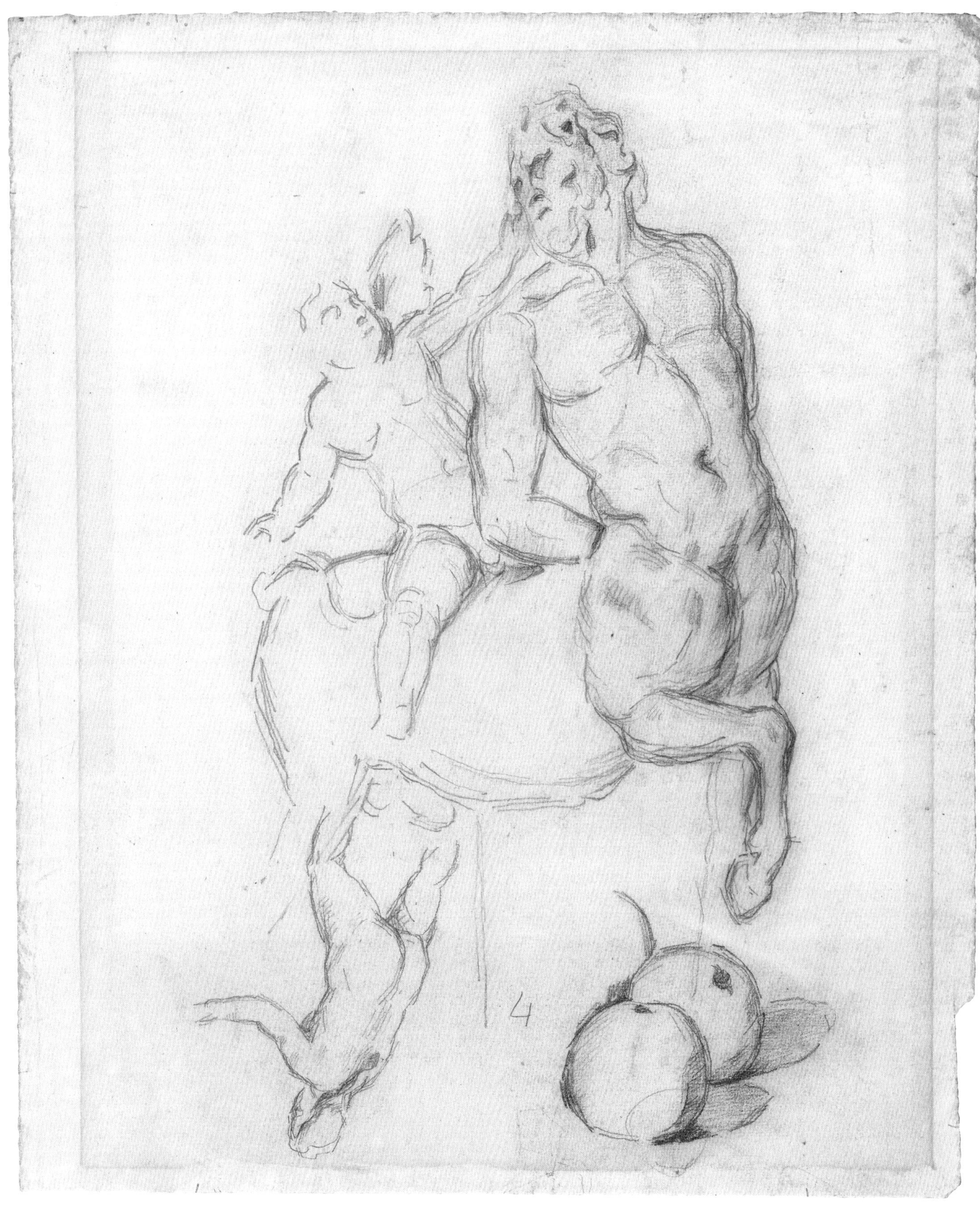

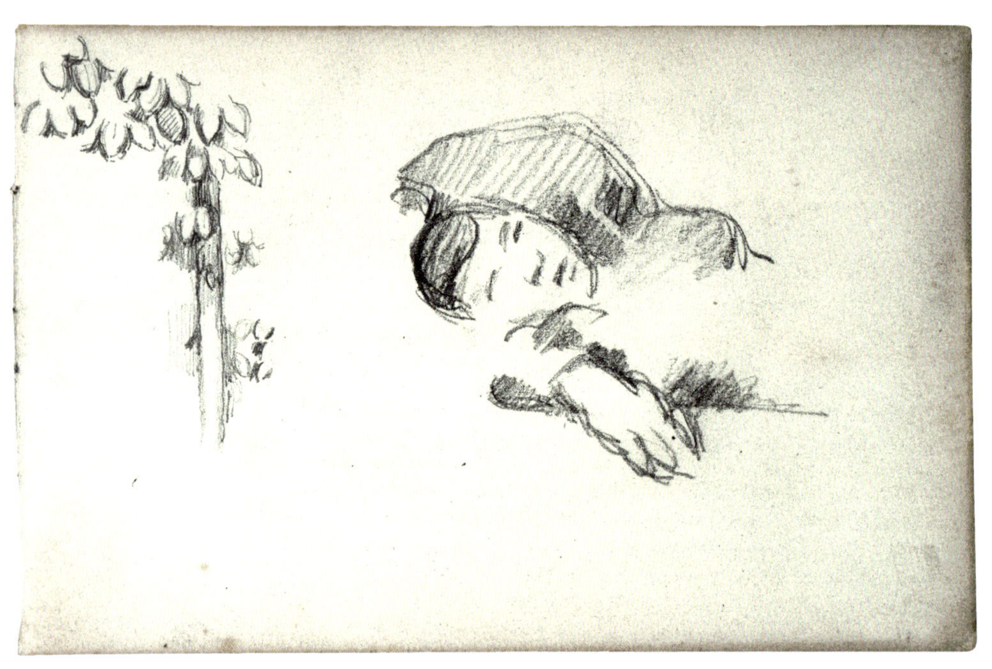

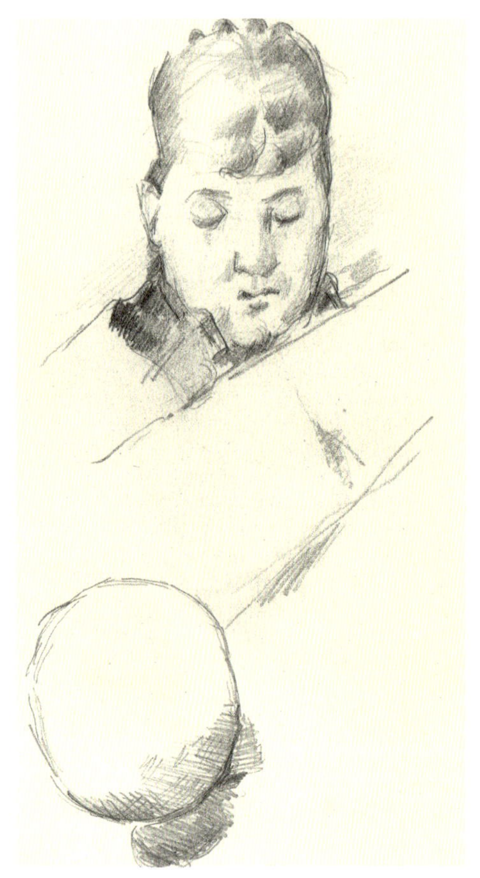

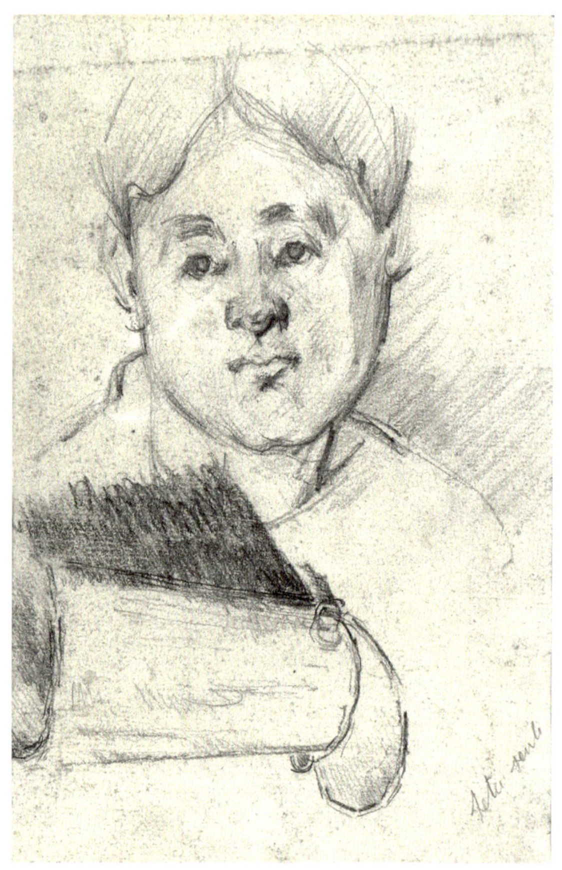

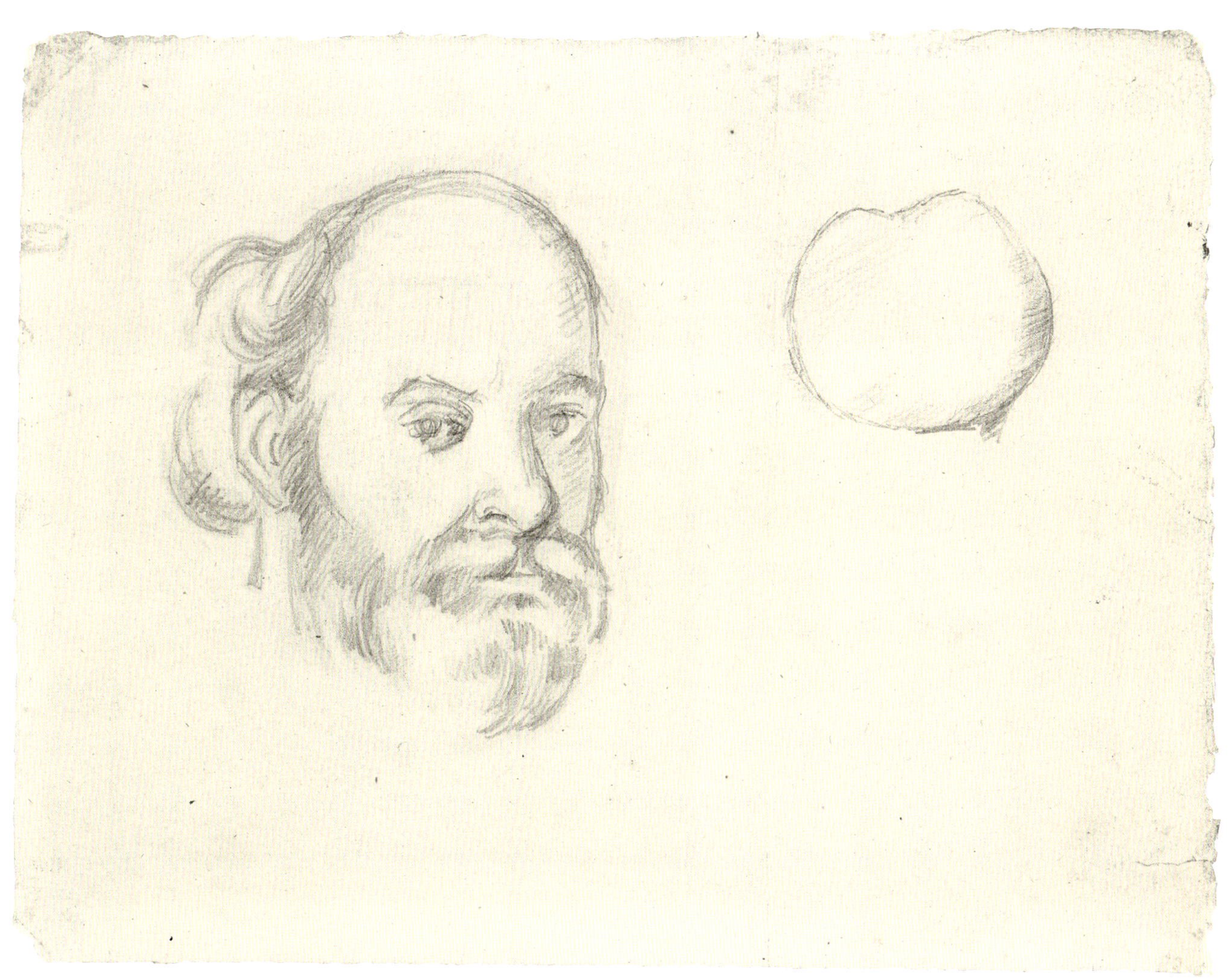

18. *Small Tree; Person Asleep.* After 1882. Pencil on wove paper, 4 ⁹⁄₁₆ × 7 ³⁄₁₆" (11.6 × 18.2 cm)

19. *Bust of Madame Cézanne.* c. 1880. Pencil on wove paper, 8 ⁹⁄₁₆ × 4 ⁷⁄₈" (21.8 × 12.4 cm)

20. *Madame Cézanne and a Milk Can.* 1877–80. Pencil on laid paper, 9 ¹⁄₁₆ × 5 ⁷⁄₈" (23 × 15 cm)

21. *Self-Portrait and Apple.* 1880–84. Pencil on paper, 6 ¹³⁄₁₆ × 9 ¹⁄₁₆" (17.3 × 23 cm)

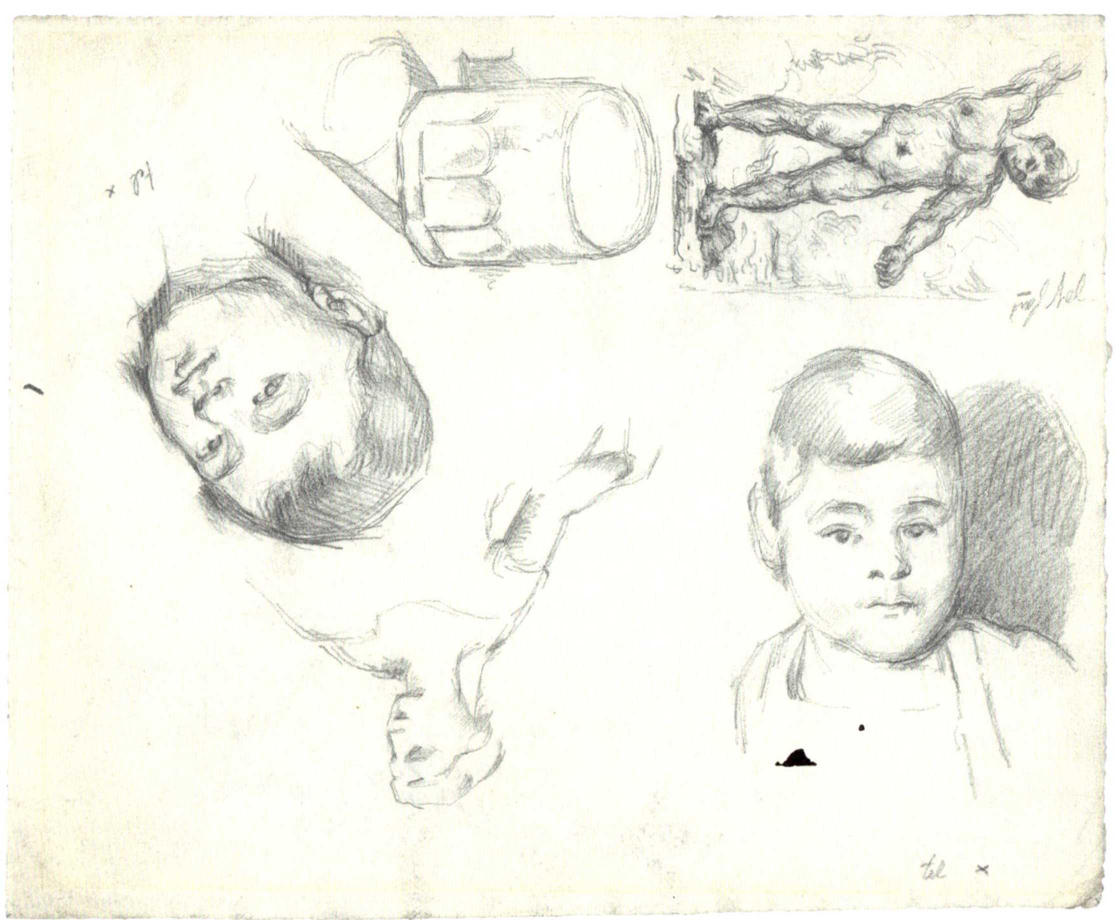

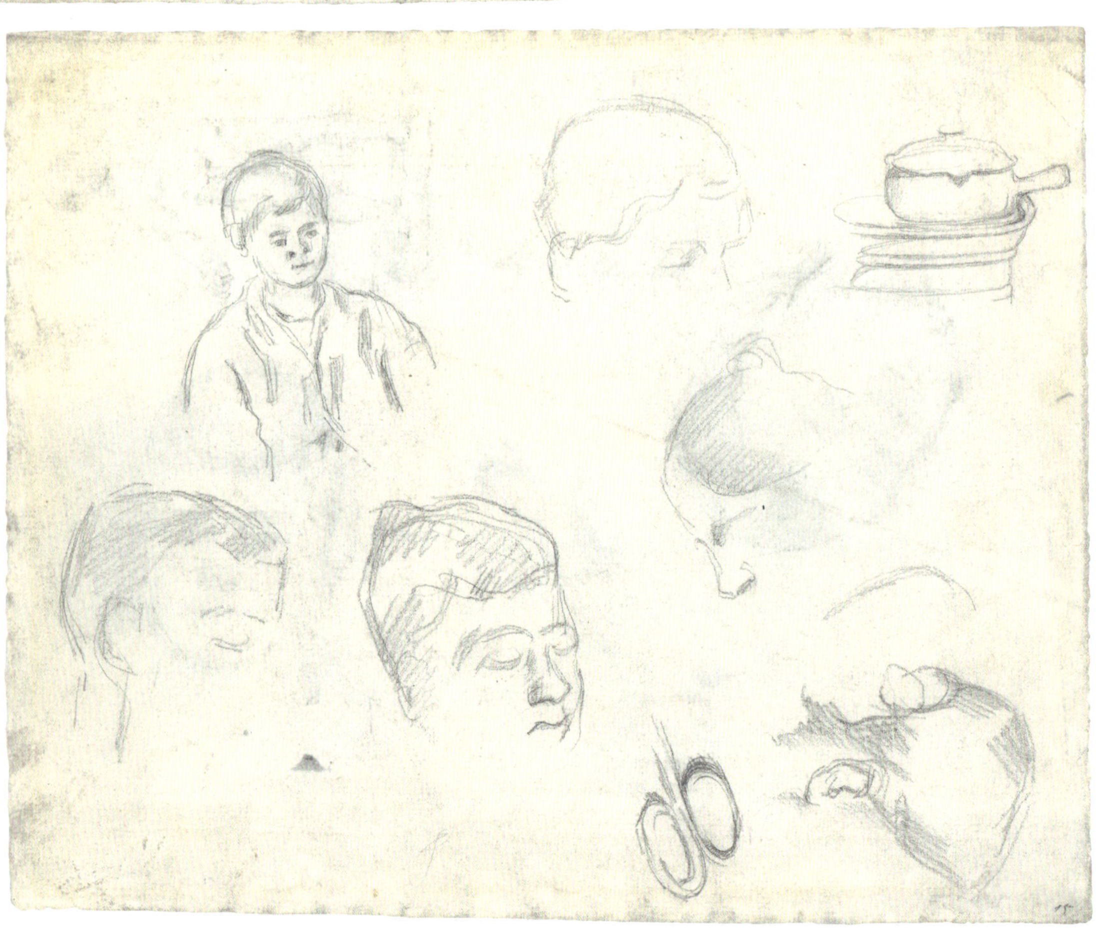

22. *Studies and Portraits of the Artist's Son* (recto); *Studies, Including a Head and a Small Casserole* (verso). 1877–78 (recto); c. 1878 (verso). Pencil on paper, 9 ¾ × 12 ⅛" (24.8 × 30.8 cm)

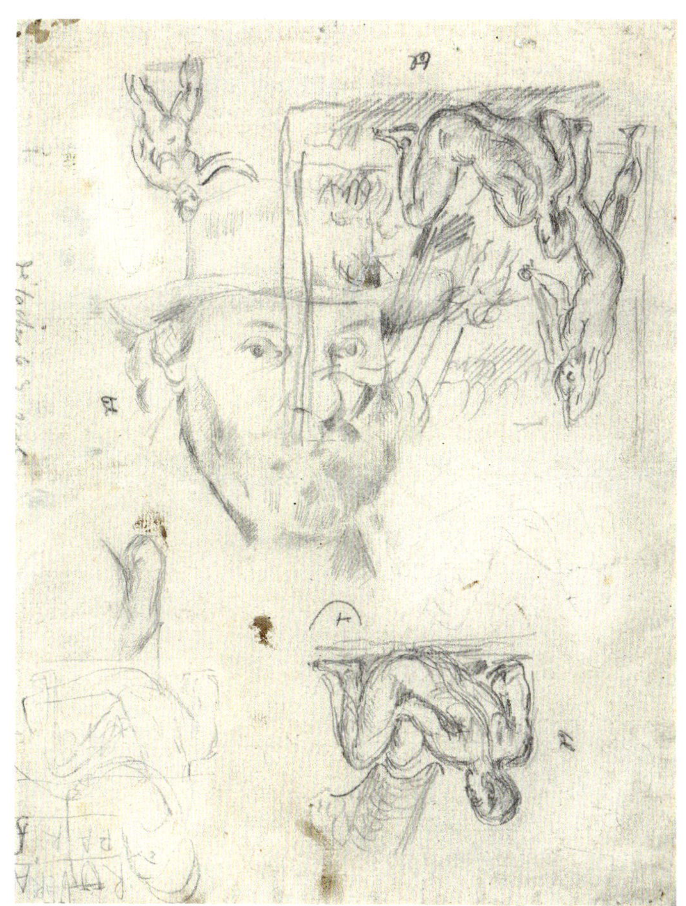

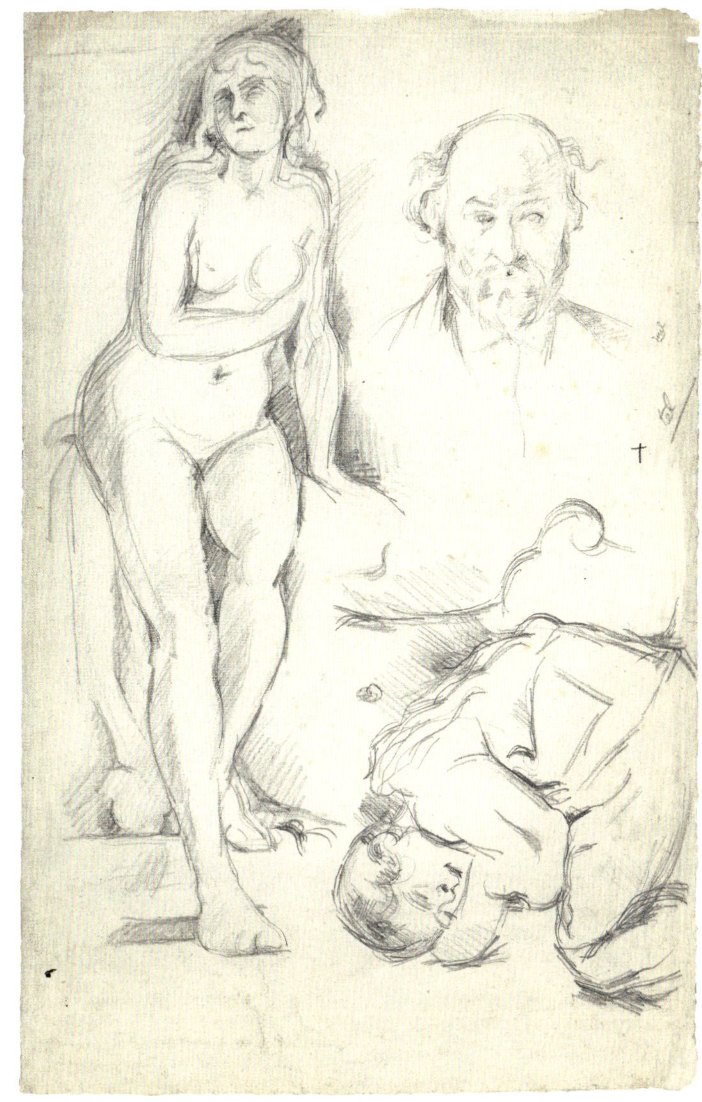

23. *Page of Studies, Including Bathers and a Self-Portrait*. 1875–78. Pencil on laid paper, 11 ⁵⁄₈ × 9 ¹⁄₈" (29.5 × 23.2 cm)

24. *Studies of Three Figures, Including a Self-Portrait*. c. 1876, 1883, 1885. Pencil on laid paper, 19 ¹⁄₈ × 12 ⁵⁄₈" (48.5 × 32 cm)

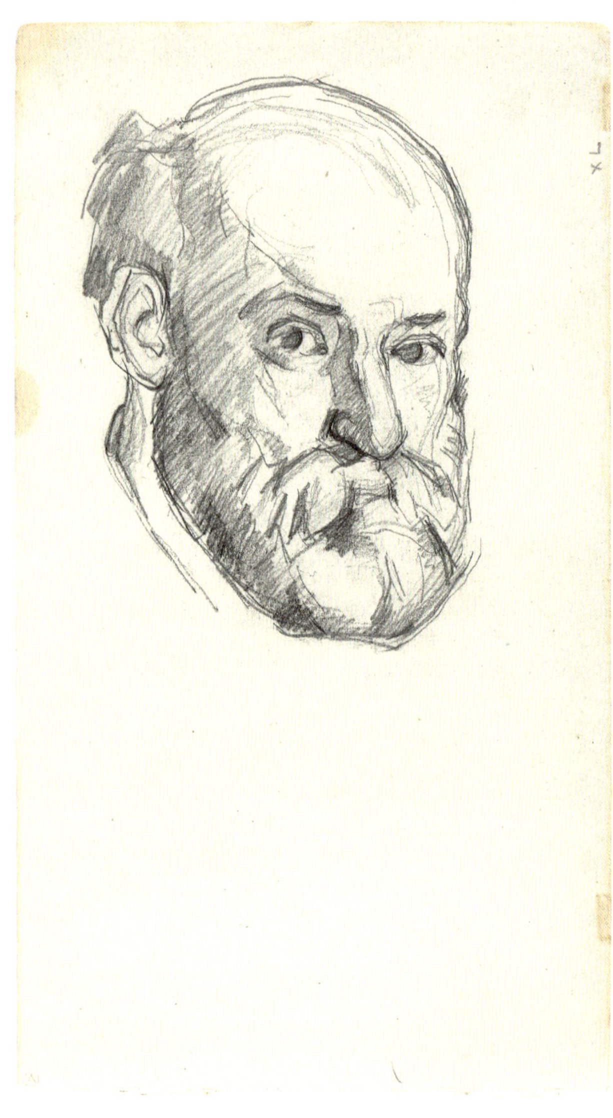

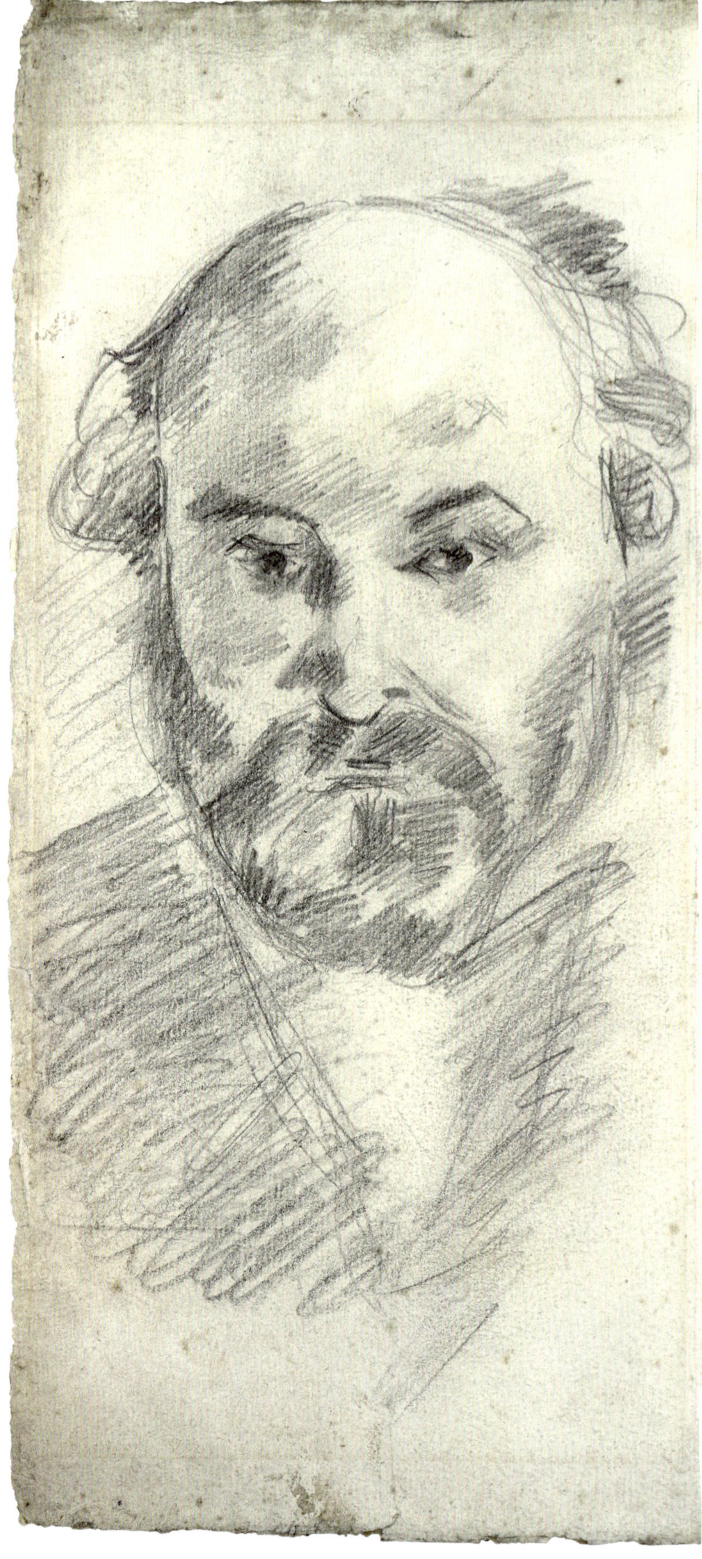

25. *Self-Portrait*. 1880–82. Pencil on wove paper, 8 11/16 × 4 15/16" (22 × 12.5 cm)

26. *Self-Portrait*. c. 1880. Pencil on laid paper, 12 5/8 × 5 3/4" (32.1 × 14.6 cm)

27. *Portrait of the Artist*. 1880. Pencil on laid paper, 13 7/16 × 11 3/16" (34.1 × 28.4 cm)

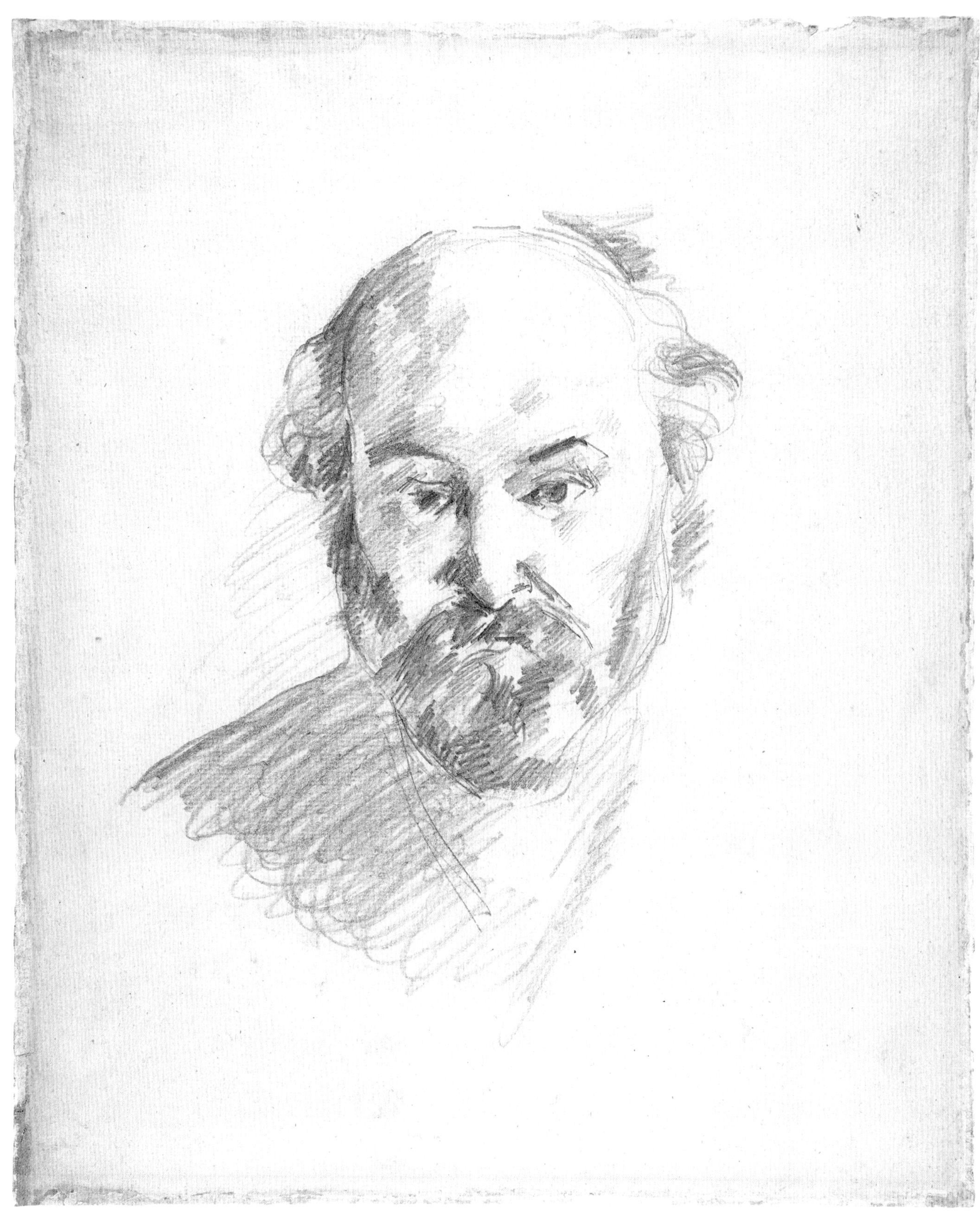

Annemarie Iker

"I have very strong sensations."
—Paul Cézanne, to a journalist (1870)

"The artist most attacked and most mistreated by the press and by the public over the last fifteen years is M. Cézanne."[1] So declared the critic Georges Rivière in 1877, on the occasion of the third Impressionist exhibition. "Those who have never held a brush or a pencil have said that he doesn't know how to draw," continued Rivière, "and they have reproached him for *imperfections* that are nothing other than refinement obtained through great skill."[2] But while reviewers largely scorned Cézanne's contributions to the exhibition, Rivière praised them for their authenticity. "All the artist's pictures are moving," the critic concluded, "because he himself experiences a violent emotion before nature that skill transmits to canvas."[3]

In linking the visual and material qualities of Cézanne's work to a presumed experience of "violent emotion" on the part of the artist, Rivière raised interpretive questions that would extend from the nineteenth century into the twenty-first. Among these questions is how to broach the roughly twenty grisly depictions of assault and murder that Cézanne made during the 1860s and '70s. Are these so-called *scènes de violence* best understood as expressions of the troubled psychology of the young artist, who claimed in 1870, "I paint as I see, as I feel—and I have very strong sensations"?[4] Do they attest to the misogyny of the literary and artistic tradition that he emulated (and at times advanced)? Or do they reflect the sensationalism of the mass media and popular science that emerged in France during his youth?[5] Most important, how does Cézanne, in the scènes de violence, transmit violence to paper?

Few works demonstrate the intractable nature of these questions more clearly than *The Abduction* (c. 1867; plate 28), a dense, diminutive drawing in ink, watercolor, and gouache. Over the decades, scholars have construed this work—and a larger, related canvas—as representing an invented rape, a mythological abduction, and a prehistoric conquest.[6] At issue is the source of its violence, variously perceived to be Cézanne's imagination, Ovid's *Metamorphoses*, or contemporary scientific illustrations of primeval Provence. Common to all three interpretations is an attentiveness to correspondences among subject, style, and facture—that is, between the violence pictured and the picturing of violence. Consider, for instance, the nude assailant, seen from the rear, whose muscled arms, back, and legs are described with repeated slashes of ink, and the spill of watercolor washes and gouache daubs that saturate the page—including, most conspicuously, crimson streaks evoking blood.

At the drawing's lower right, in white, is a signature: "P. Cezanne." Because Cézanne rarely signed his works on paper, this script—large in relation to the drawing as a whole—reads like an uncommon statement of identification between artist and artwork. As an invocation of Cézanne's hand, it points to a feature of the scènes de violence at large: the recurring conflation of touch and force, with the forceful touch of the artist used to convey forceful touch between figures. In another such work, titled *The Rape* (1868–70; plate 31), a perpetrator lunges toward a victim, their bodies defined by a welter of frenzied graphite lines. While the identity of each figure is unclear—male or female? old or young?—the two are connected by the fierce clutch of the attacker, whose left arm culminates in a scrambled fist and whose right arm, extended ominously beyond the uppermost edge of the composition, appears poised to strike a blow. Moreover, the bodies are linked by the agitated lines defining them, lines that visualize the controlling grasp of the attacker and materialize the intensity with which they were rendered.

The convergence of touch and force is deepened on a page of studies torn from an early sketchbook, where an outstretched, oversize hand has been drawn in ink beside the image of a vicious attack (plate 34). In the lower-left corner of the sheet, a victim or victims sprawl in a tangle of limbs beneath an aggressor who is wielding a knife in a raised fist; to the right, the large hand's inky fingertips nearly graze what appears to be a knee. As in the 1868–70 work, the frenetic handling of the medium makes the gender, age, and setting of the figures difficult to discern. André Dombrowski has argued that Cézanne deliberately cultivated this outwardly crude technique, considering it suited, stylistically, to his representations of stabbings and strangulations. "Equating the breaking of the law with the breaking of artistic rules," Dombrowski has written, the artist sought to contravene both social and aesthetic conventions.[7]

Given the small size and brutal subject matter of these scènes de violence, it might be presumed that Cézanne kept them to himself. Yet one such work, *The Murder* (1874–75; plate 29), was included in an exhibition of his drawings and paintings organized by the dealer Ambroise Vollard in 1895. This watercolor portrayal of a brazen attack in a picturesque cove was displayed in Vollard's Paris gallery among portraits, landscapes, still lifes, and bathers that many critics regarded, like Rivière nearly twenty years earlier, as products of Cézanne's artistic and personal fervor. Thadée Natanson, in the pages of *La Revue blanche*, emphasized "the intensity, the violence" of the color, form, and facture of works on view, concluding that Cézanne "dares to be rough as well as savage."[8] Similarly, Camille Mauclair, in *Gil Blas*, deemed the artist a "violent colorist" and characterized his style, more broadly, as "heavy, thick, and powerful." "Go to see him," advised Mauclair. "You will be reluctant or enthusiastic, but you will not be left cold."[9]

Notably, it was the still lifes at Galerie Vollard that led Mauclair to characterize Cézanne's work in this way (plates 197, 199, 243, 244). In the last decade of the artist's life, suggestions of violence continued to suffuse such works in ways that include—and exceed—color. In *Still Life with Apples, Pears, and a Pot* (1900–04; plate 205), for instance, a pot handle looms above a cluster of fruit on a kitchen table. Its cool hue contrasts with the warm reds and yellows of the apples and pears below, but its knifelike thrust, so close to what Carol Armstrong has described as the "exaggeratedly corporeal" curves of the fruit, poses the real threat.[10] Did Cézanne, one might ask, ever truly abandon his youthful scenes of violence?

1.
Georges Rivière, "L'Exposition des impressionnistes," *L'Impressionniste*, April 14, 1877, 1. Translations in this essay are by the author.

2.
Ibid., 2.

3.
Ibid.

4.
Cézanne, in John Rewald, *The History of Impressionism* (New York: The Museum of Modern Art, 1973), 246. Rewald describes the context of the quotation, an encounter between the artist and a journalist in 1870. On Cézanne and sensation, see Richard Shiff, "Sensation, Cézanne," in Judit Geskó, ed., *Cézanne and the Past: Tradition and Creativity* (Budapest: Museum of Fine Arts, 2012), 33–47.

5.
For two indispensable studies of Cézanne's scènes de violence, see Robert Simon, "Cézanne and the Subject of Violence," *Art in America* 79, no. 5 (May 1991): 120–35, 185–86; and André Dombrowski, *Cézanne, Murder, and Modern Life* (Berkeley: University of California Press, 2012).

6.
See, respectively, Rewald, *Cézanne: A Biography* (New York: Abrams, 1986), 79; Mary Tomkins Lewis, "Savagery Redeemed," in *Cézanne's Early Imagery* (Berkeley: University of California Press, 1989), 159–62; and Richard Kendall, "Monet and the Monkeys: The Impressionist Encounter with Darwinism," in Diana Donald and Jane Munro, eds., *Endless Forms: Charles Darwin, Natural Science, and the Visual Arts* (New Haven, Conn.: Yale University Press, 2009), 295–97. The oil painting is *The Abduction* (*L'Enlèvement*, 1867; Fitzwilliam Museum, Cambridge, UK).

7.
Dombrowski, *Cézanne, Murder, and Modern Life*, 4.

8.
Thadée Natanson, "Paul Cézanne," *La Revue blanche* 9, no. 50 (December 1, 1895): 499.

9.
Camille Mauclair, "M. Paul Cézanne," *Gil Blas* 17 (November 18, 1895): 2.

10.
Carol Armstrong, *Cézanne in the Studio: Still Life in Watercolors* (Los Angeles: J. Paul Getty Museum, 2004), 35. Lawrence Gowing described this watercolor as particularly "physical and sensual" in "The Logic of Organized Sensations," in William Rubin, ed., *Cézanne: The Late Work* (New York: The Museum of Modern Art, 1977), 65.

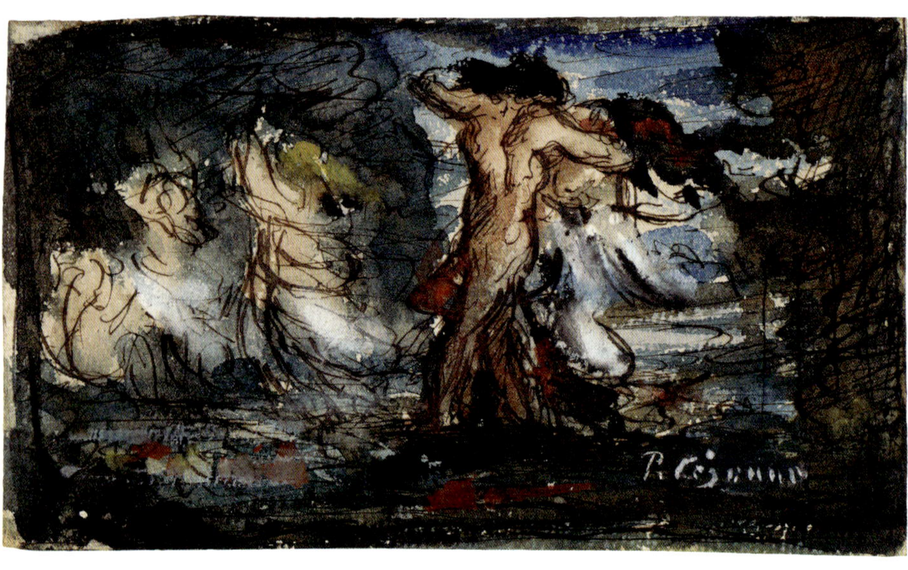

28. *The Abduction*. c. 1867. Ink, watercolor, and gouache on paper, 2 ¾ × 5" (7 × 12.7 cm)

29. *The Murder*. 1874–75. Pencil, watercolor, and gouache on paper, 5 ¾ × 6 ⅞" (14.6 × 17.5 cm)

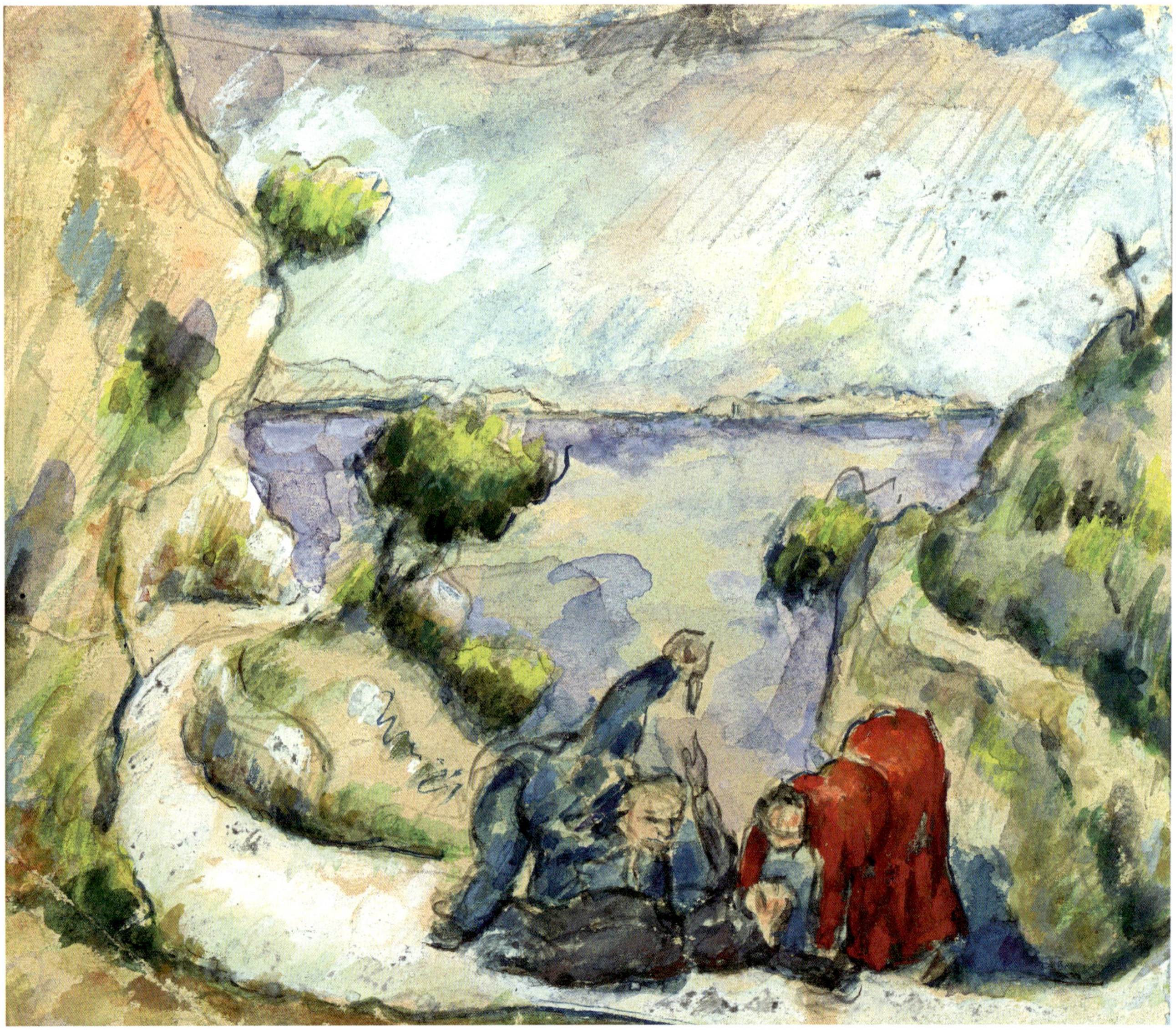

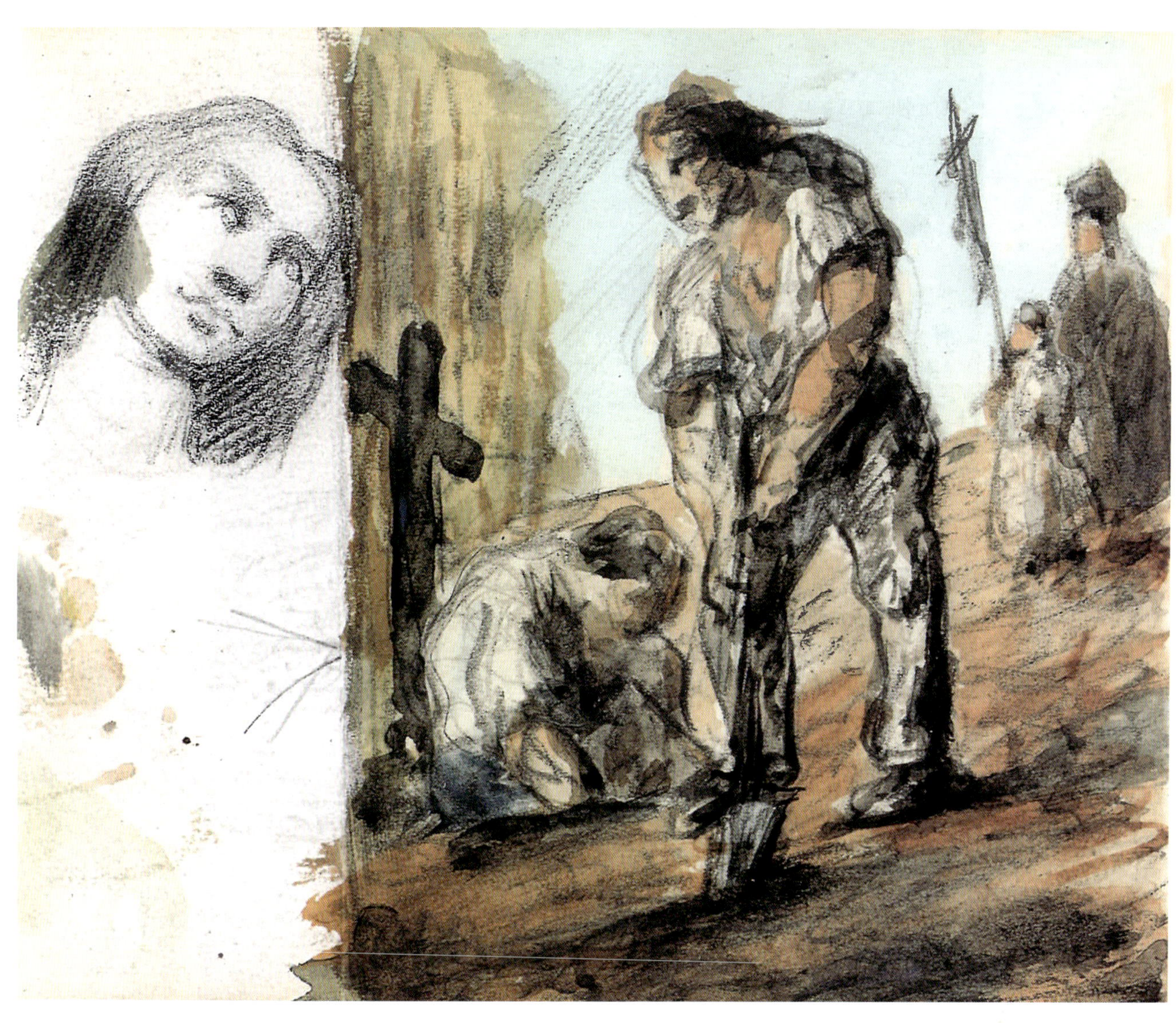

30. *The Gravediggers and a Study of a Head*. 1868–72. Pencil and watercolor on paper, 4 15/16 × 7 7/8" (12.5 × 20 cm)

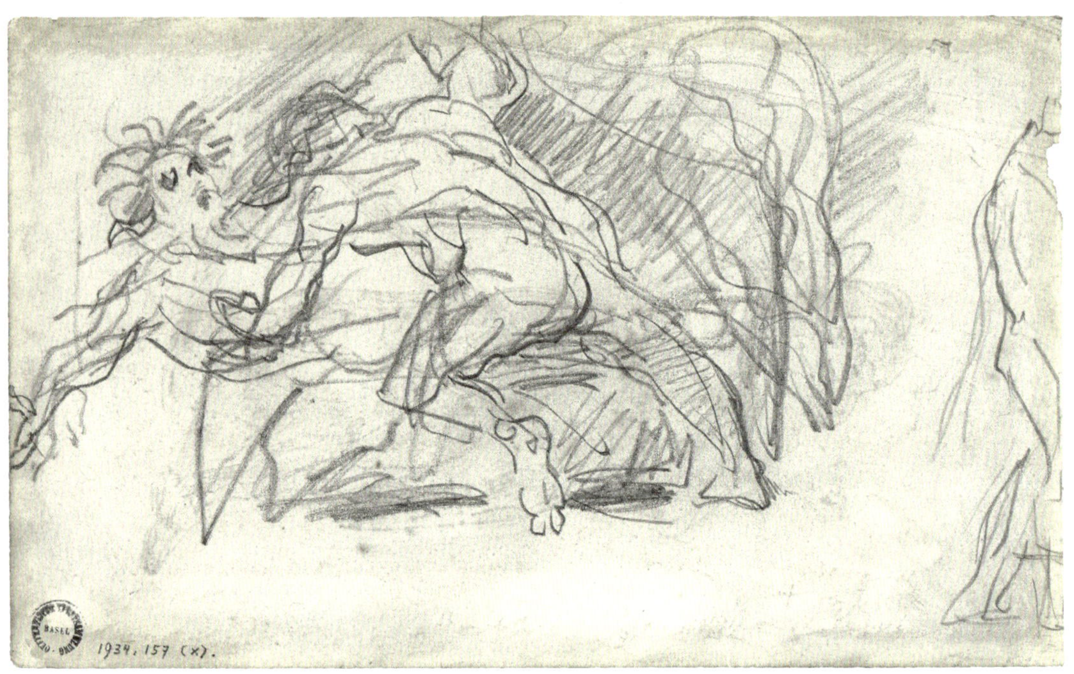

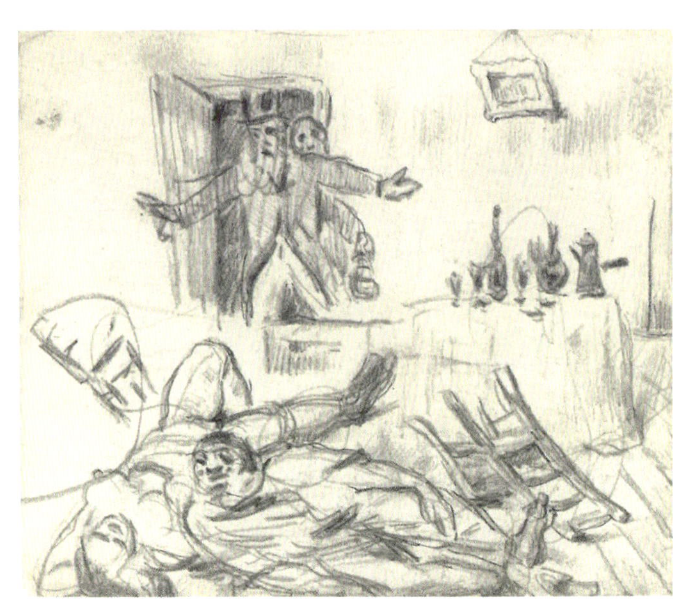

31. *The Rape*. 1868–70. Pencil on wove paper, 4 1/16 × 6 3/4" (10.3 × 17.1 cm)

32. *The Murder*. 1868–71. Pencil on paper, 5 1/4 × 6" (13.3 × 15.2 cm)

33. *Study of a Head and Hands*. 1867–69. Charcoal on laid paper, 12 3/8 × 19 5/16" (31.5 × 49 cm)

34. *Scene of Rape, Study of a Hand*. n.d. Pencil and ink on wove paper, 4 13/16 × 8 1/4" (12.3 × 20.9 cm)

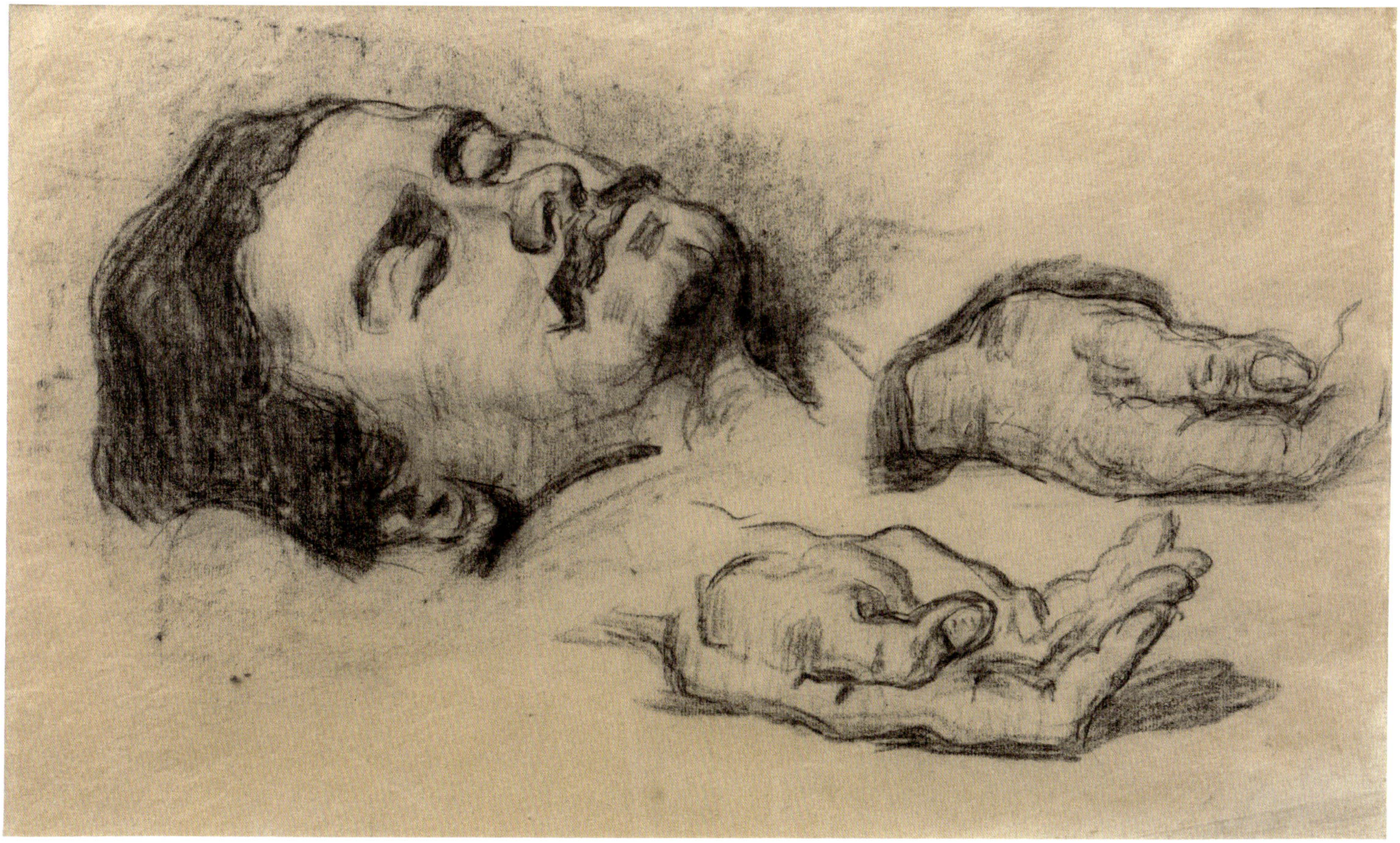

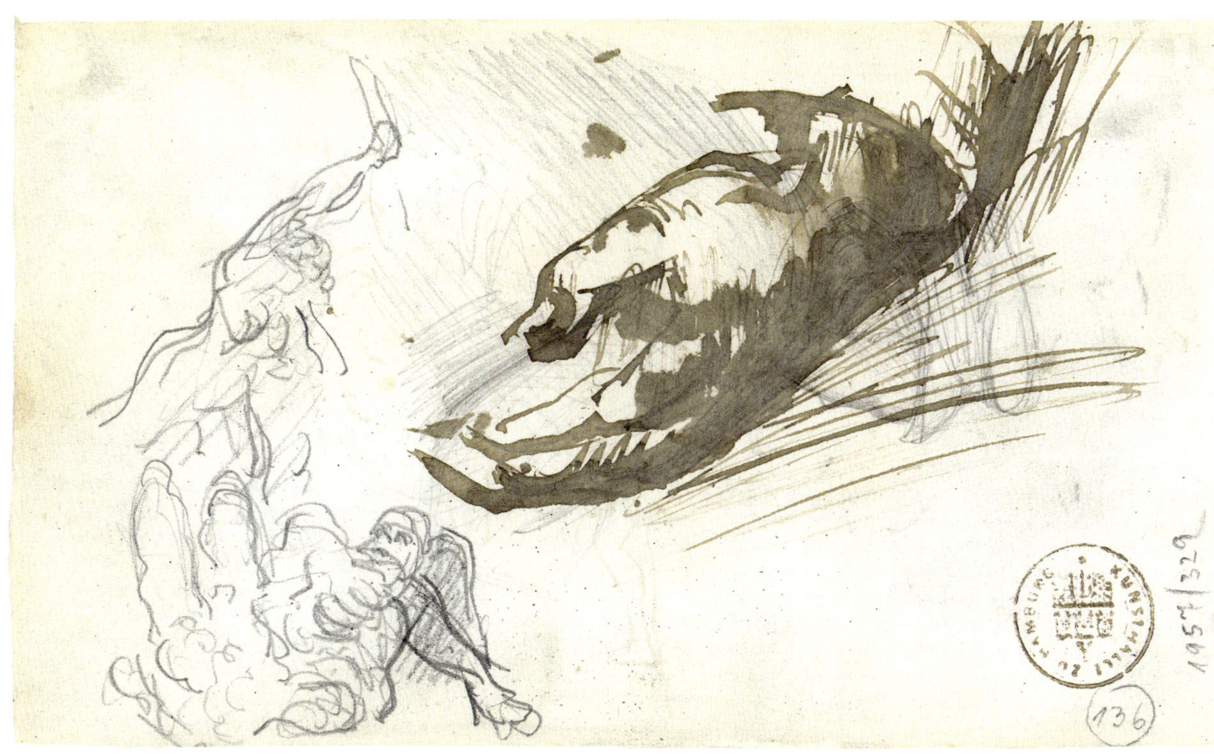
KUNSTHALLE ZU HAMBURG
1957/329
136

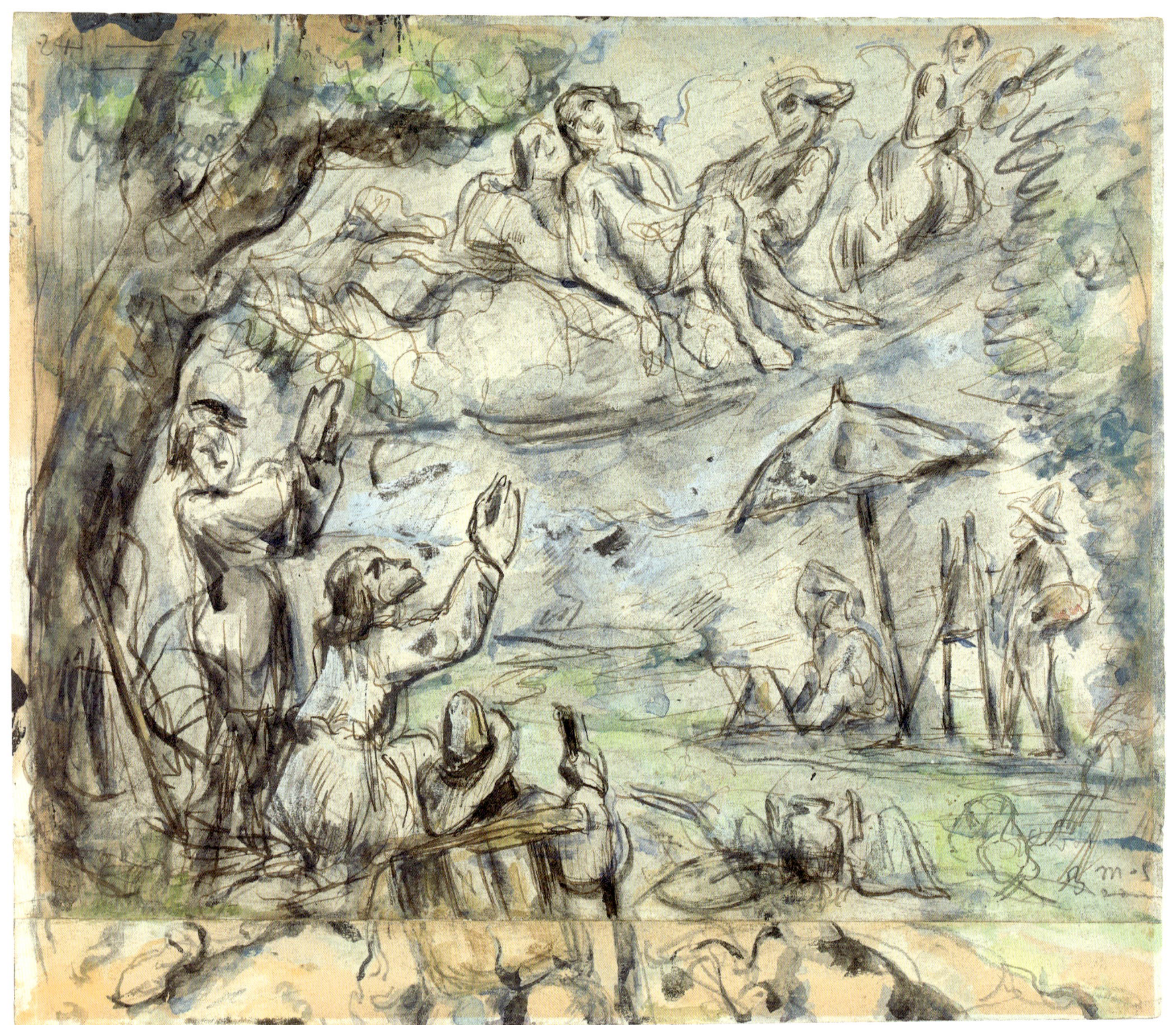

35. *The Apotheosis of Delacroix*. 1878–80 (completed later). Pencil, ink, and watercolor on wove paper, with a strip added at bottom, 7⅞ × 9 3⁄16" (20 × 23.3 cm)

36. *Pastoral Study*. c. 1870. Pencil on paper, 4 × 5¼" (10.2 × 13.3 cm)

37. *Aeneas Meeting Dido at Carthage*. c. 1875. Watercolor, gouache, and pencil on laid paper, 4¾ × 7¼" (12 × 18.4 cm)

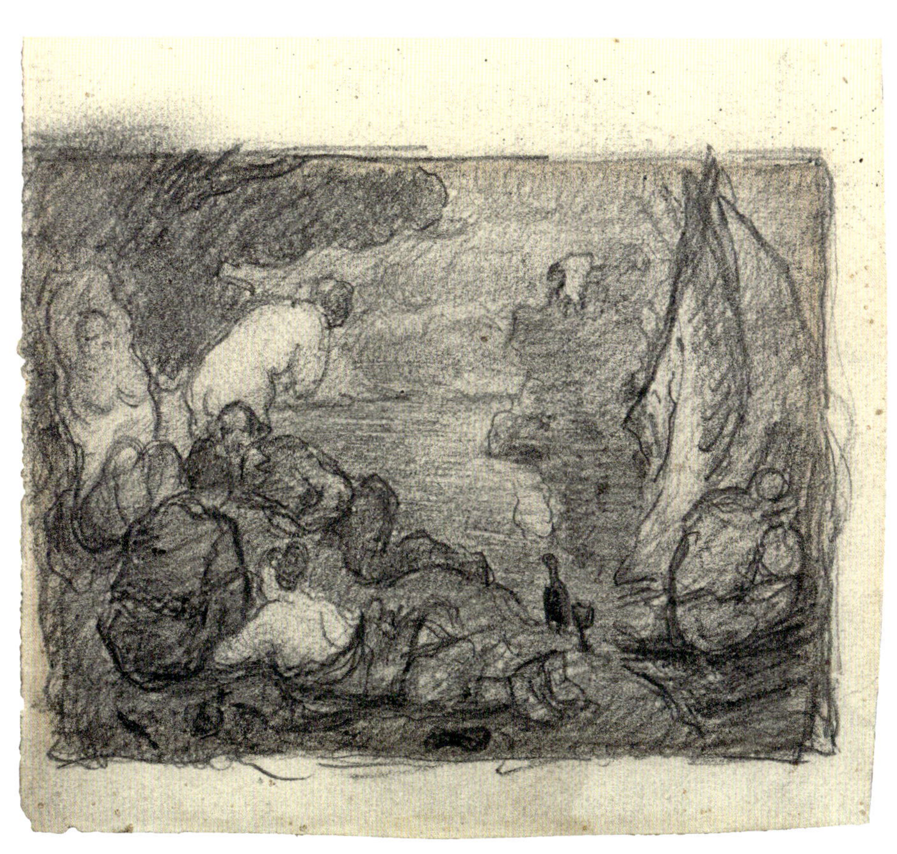

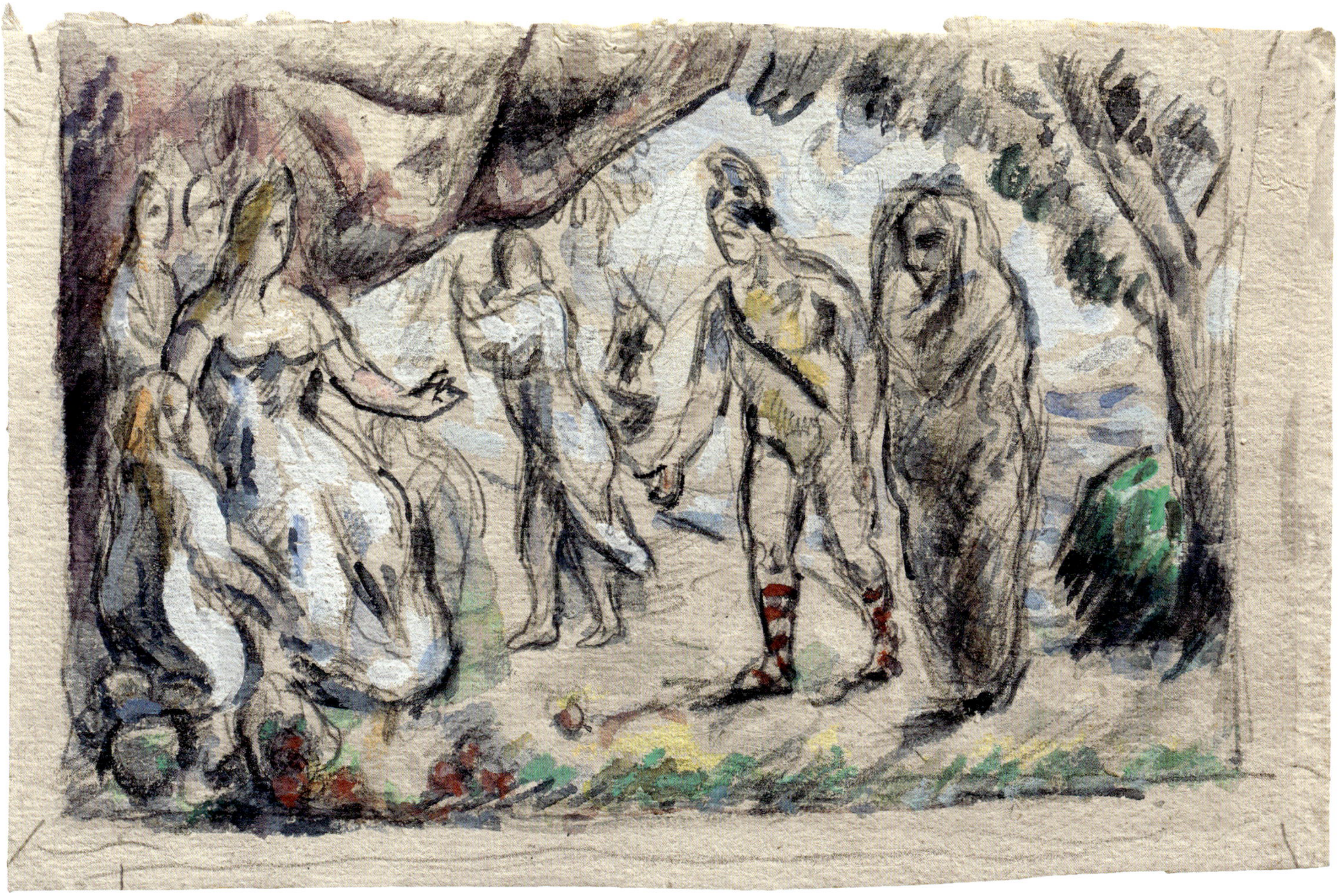

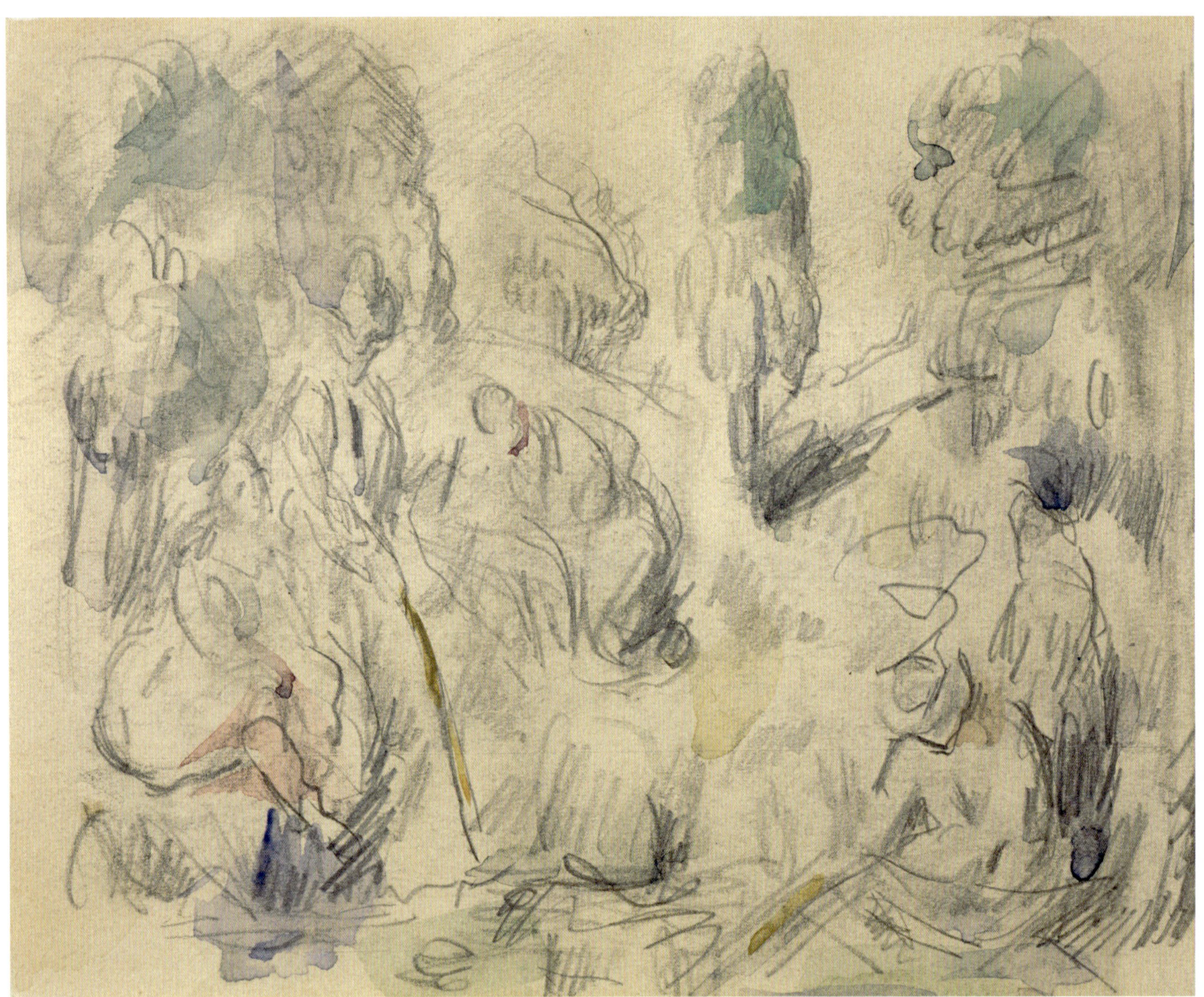

38. *At the Edge of the Pond*. 1875–80. Pencil and watercolor on paper, 4 13/16 × 6 1/8" (12.3 × 15.5 cm)

39. *Eternal Feminine*. c. 1877. Pencil, watercolor, and gouache on laid paper, 6 7/8 × 9" (17.4 × 22.8 cm)

40. *The Eternal Feminine*. 1890–95 (possibly later). Pencil and watercolor on wove paper, 8 1/4 × 10 5/8" (21 × 27 cm)

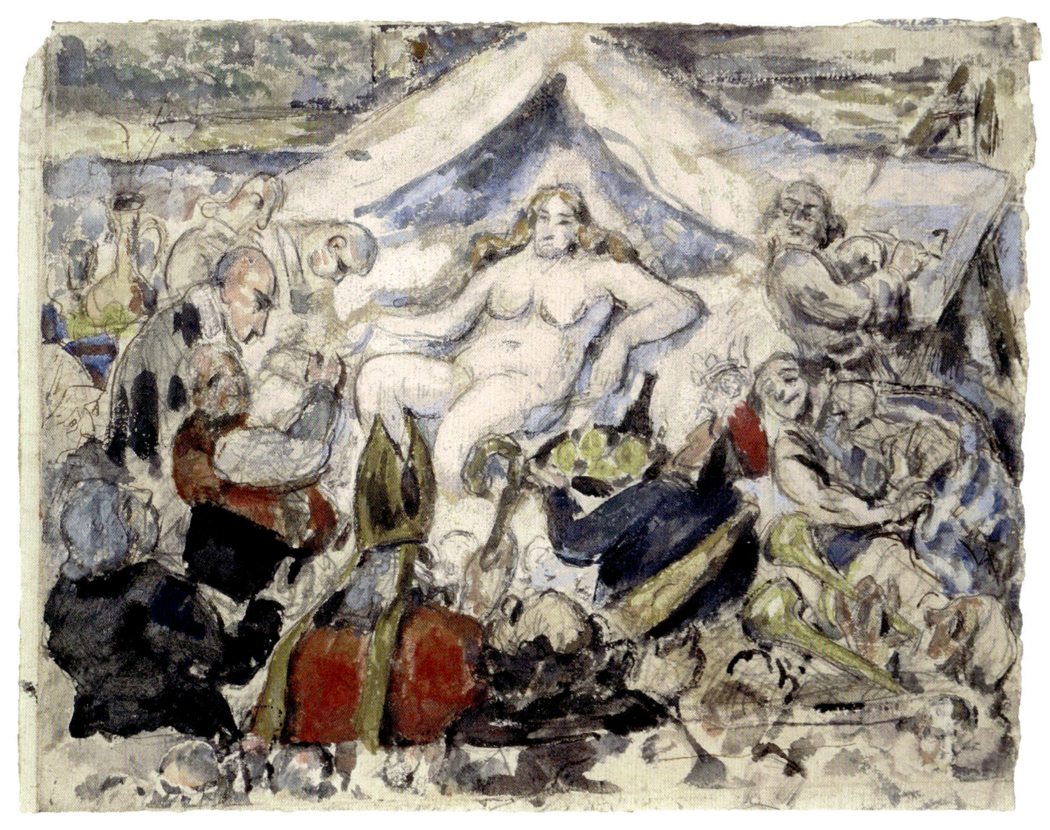

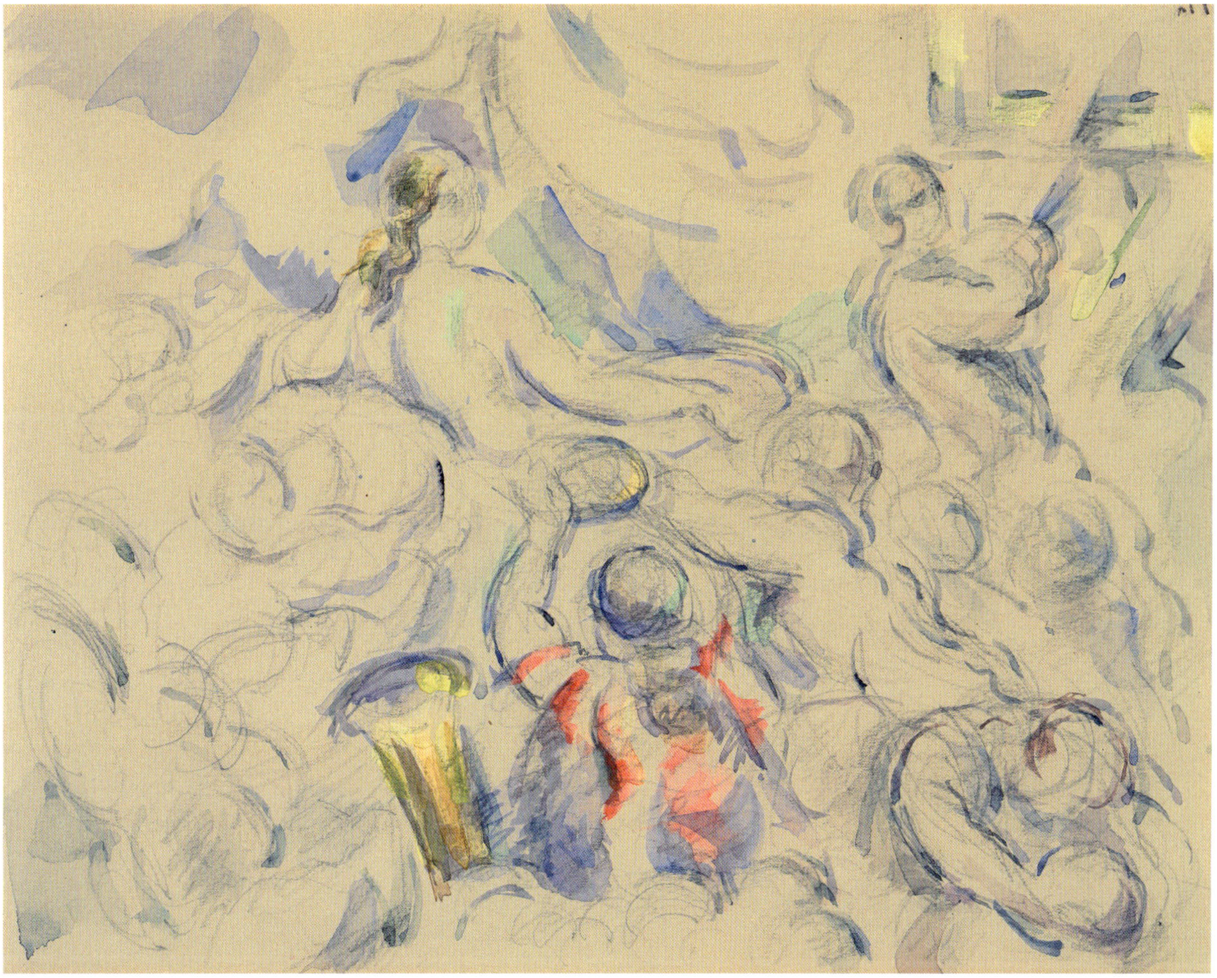

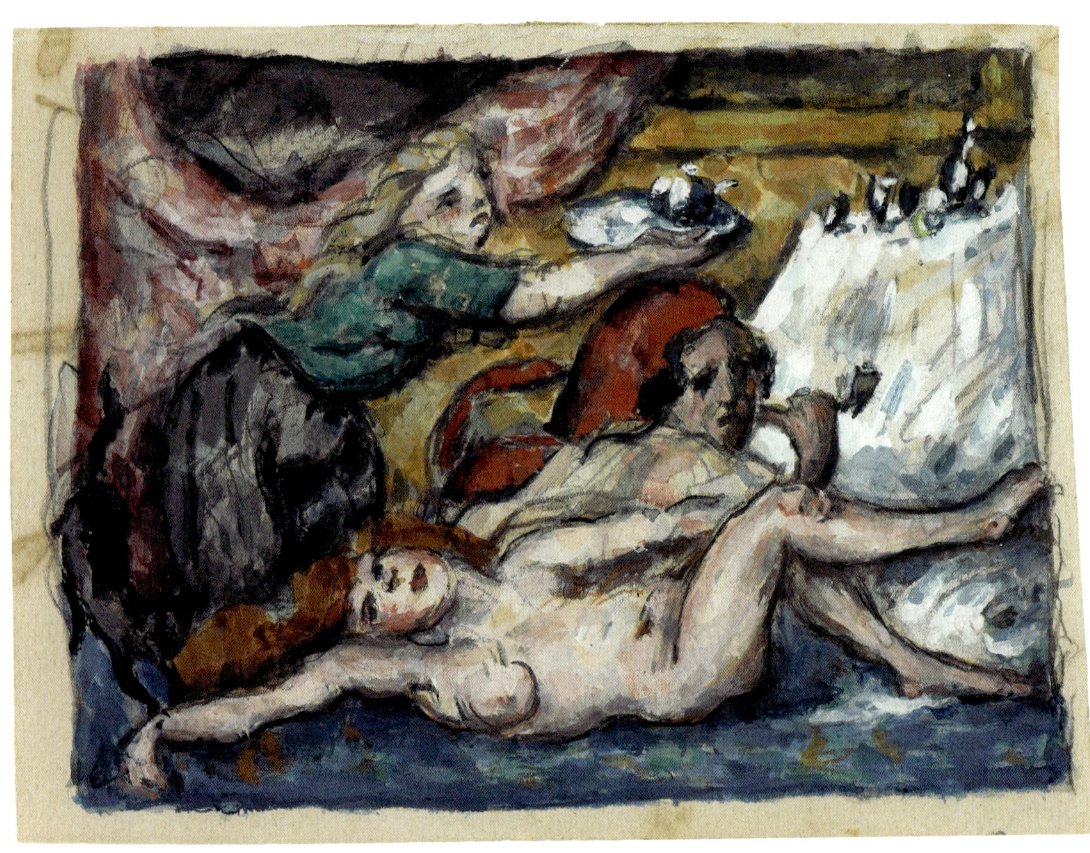

41. *The Wine Grog*. 1866–67. Pencil, watercolor, gouache, and ink on cardboard, 4 5/16 × 5 13/16" (11 × 14.8 cm)

42. *Man with a Female Nude*. 1867–70. Pencil, ink, and watercolor on paper, 3 9/16 × 6 5/16" (9 × 16 cm)

43. *The Temptation of St. Anthony*. 1873–75. Pencil, watercolor, ink, and gouache on paper, 4 3/4 × 7 11/16" (12 × 19.5 cm)

44. *Study for The Eternal Feminine*. c. 1870–75. Pencil on wove paper, 7 1/16 × 9 1/2" (18 × 24.1 cm)

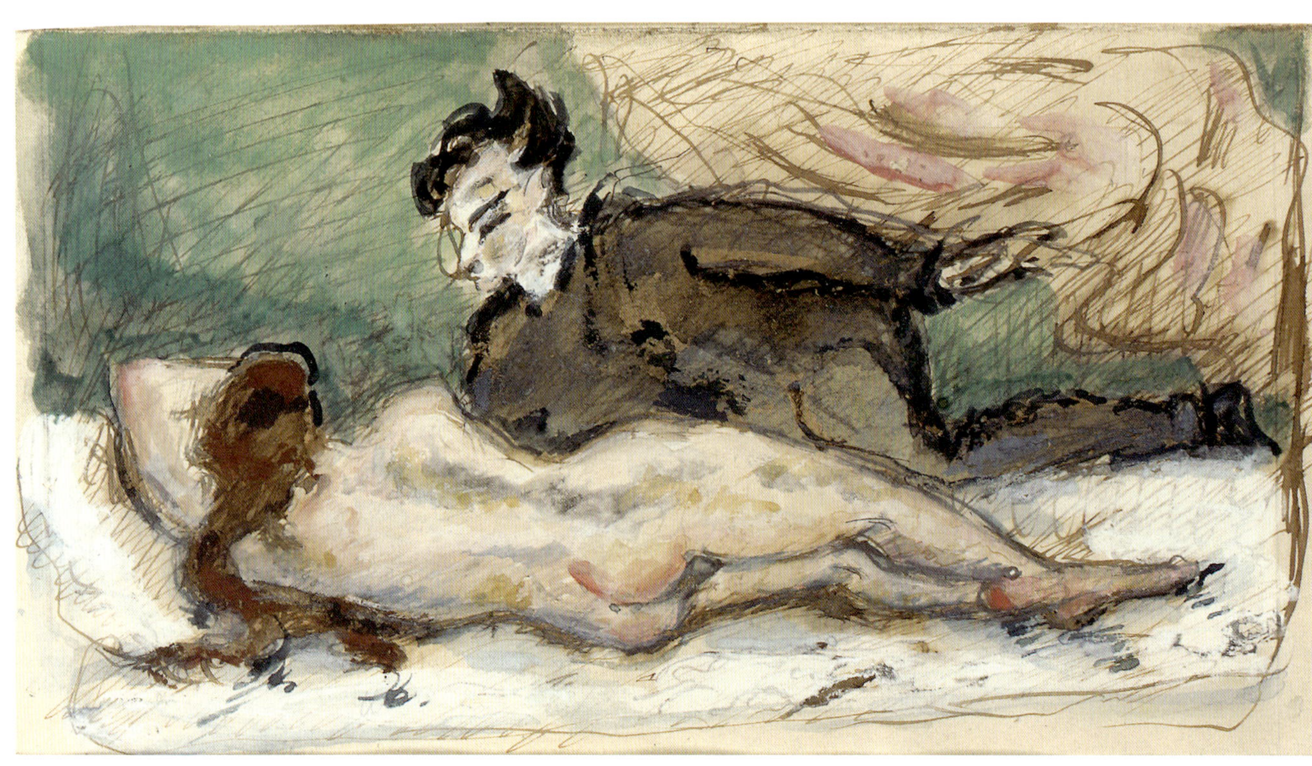

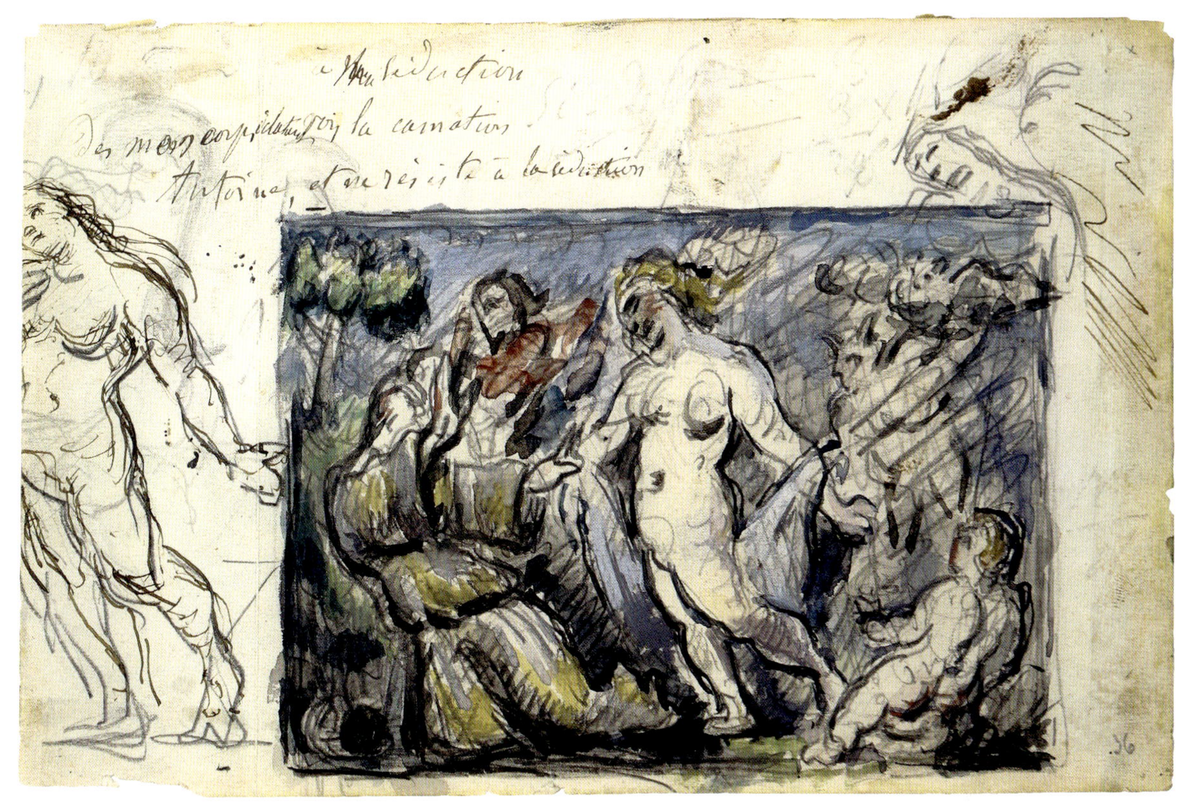

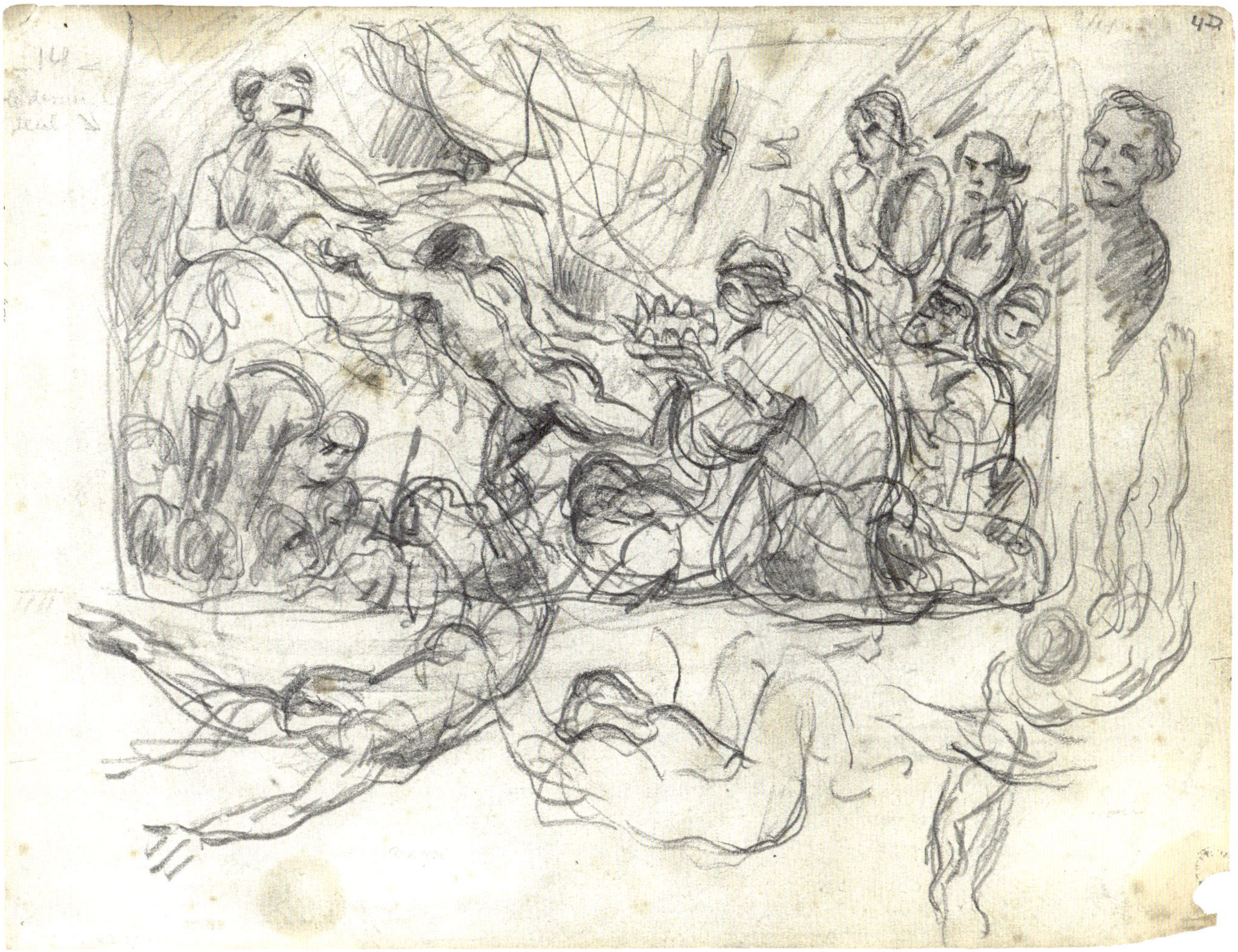

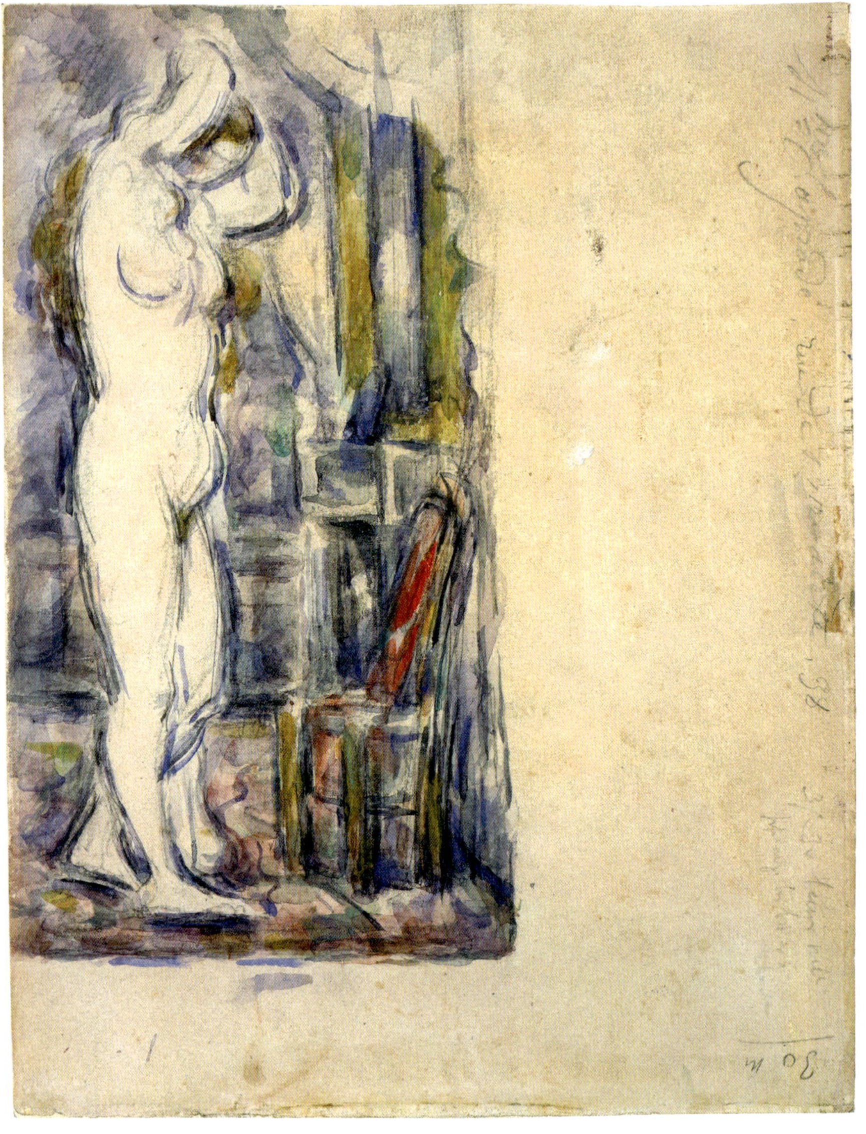

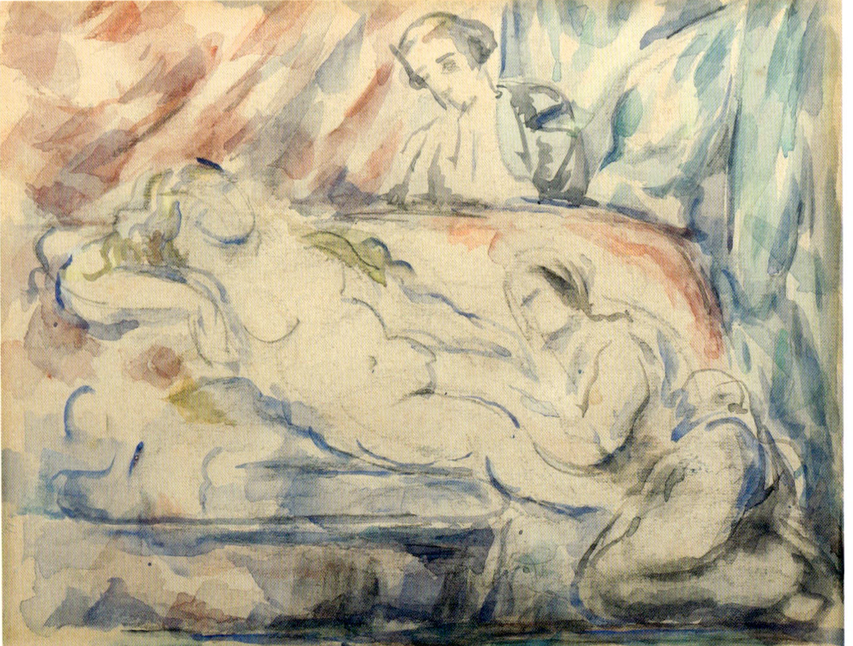

45. *Female Nude*. 1895–1900. Pencil and watercolor on wove paper, 10 ½ × 8" (26.6 × 20.3 cm)

46. *The Bath of the Courtesan*. c. 1880. Pencil and watercolor on paper, 7 ½ × 8 ¼" (19 × 21 cm)

47. *Olympia*. c. 1877. Pencil and watercolor on laid paper, 9 ½ × 10 ⅝" (24.1 × 27 cm)

48. *Waking Up*. c. 1880. Pencil and watercolor on wove paper, 17 ¼ × 12 ¼" (43.8 × 31.1 cm)

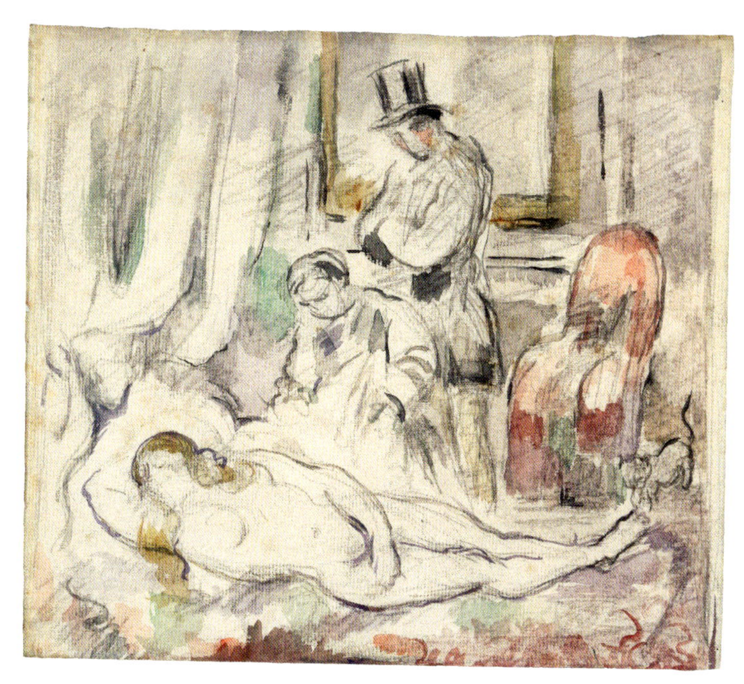

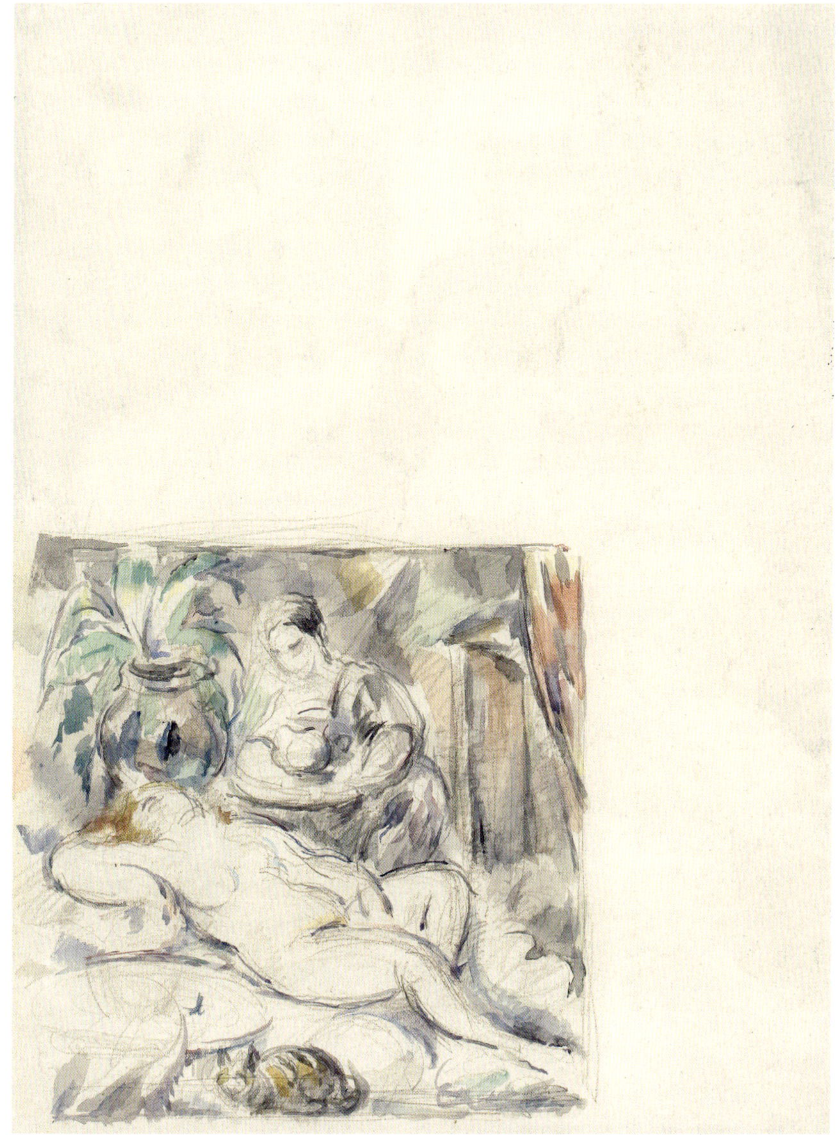

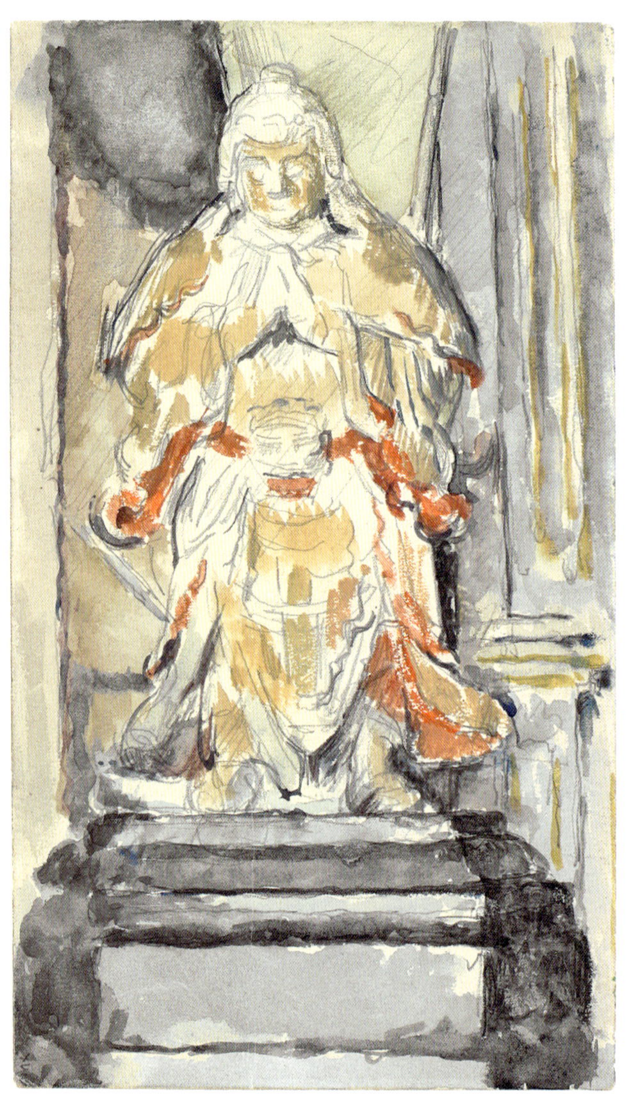

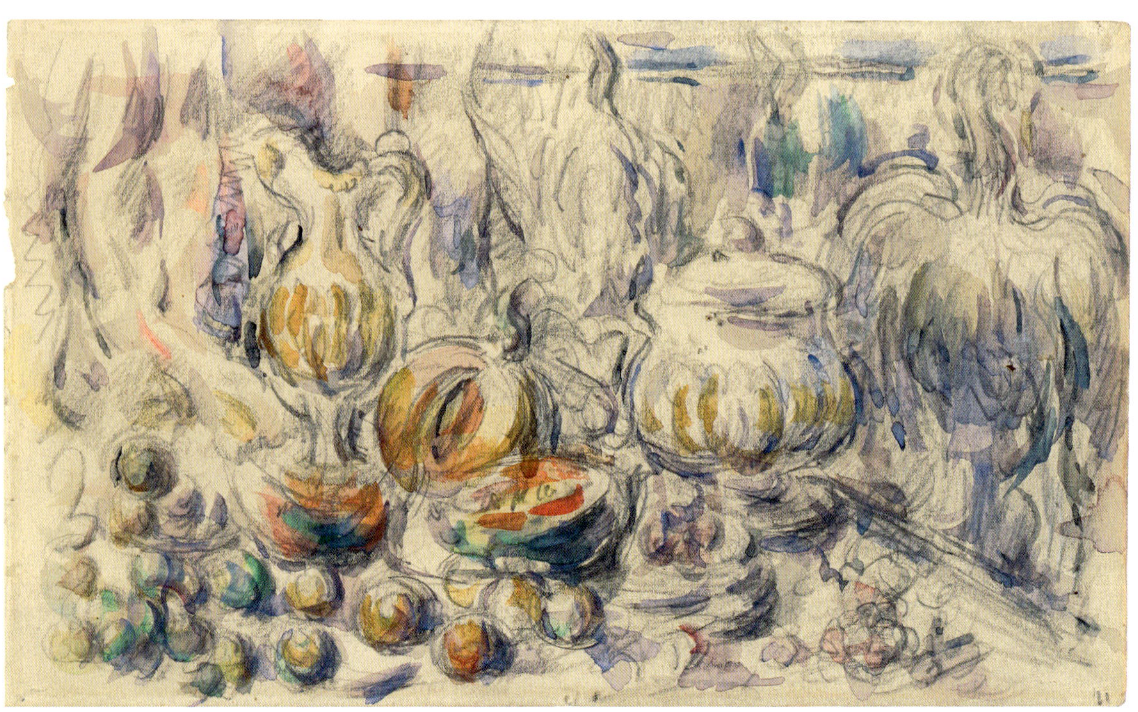

49. *Study of a Monument*. 1878–80. Pencil, ink, and watercolor on wove paper, 8 9/16 × 4 15/16" (21.7 × 12.6 cm)

50. *Pot and Soup Tureen*. 1888–90 (possibly later). Pencil and watercolor on wove paper, 4 13/16 × 8 7/16" (12.3 × 21.5 cm)

51. *The Banquet*. c. 1867. Gouache, pastel, and pencil on cardboard, with added rectangle pasted at lower edge, 12 3/4 × 9 1/8" (32.4 × 23.1 cm)

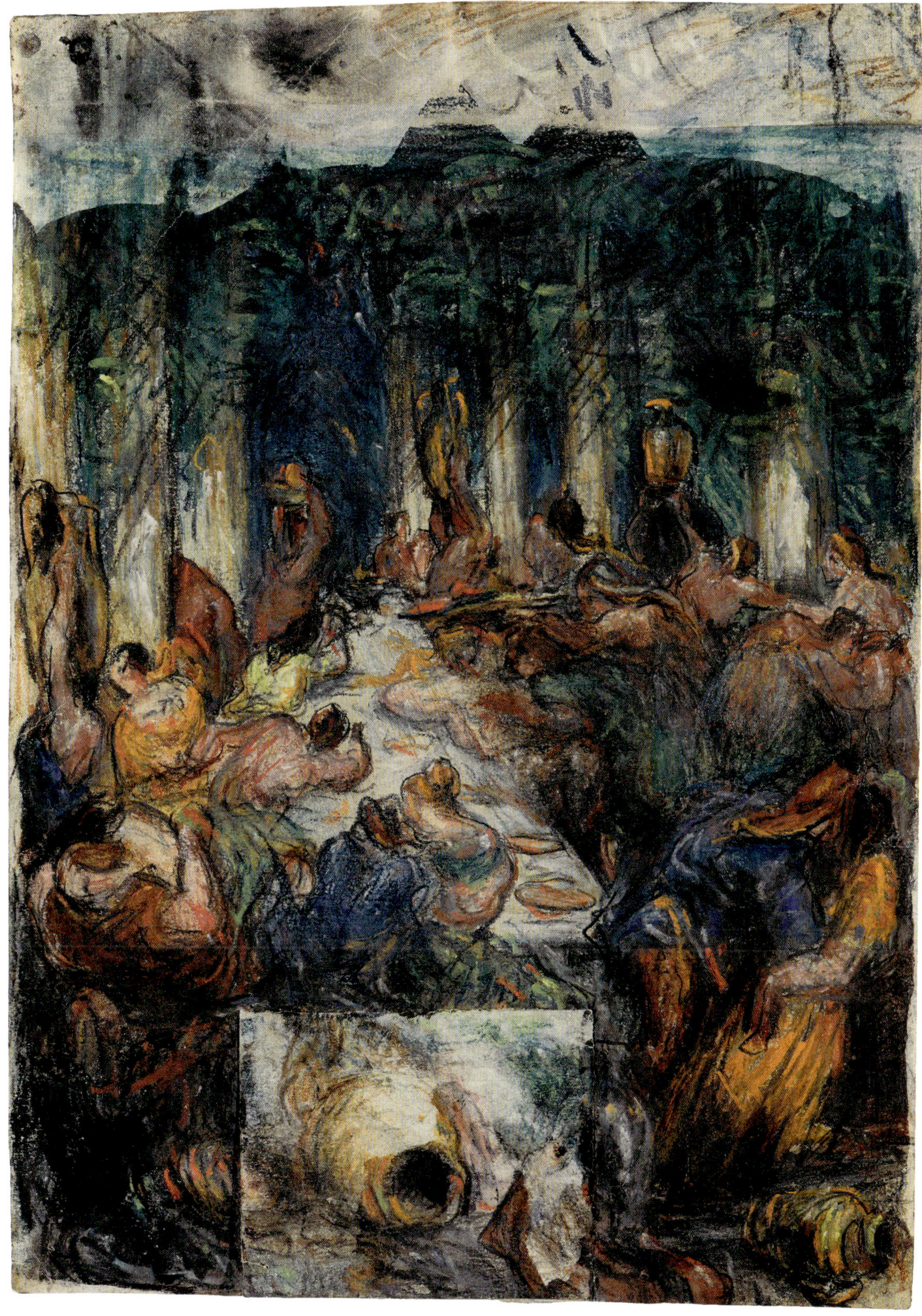

Samantha Friedman

"Time and contemplation gradually modify our vision."
—Paul Cézanne, in a letter to Émile Bernard (Aix-en-Provence, 1905)

"Threshold magic." This evocative phrase appears in *The Arcades Project*, Walter Benjamin's catalogue of nineteenth-century Parisian life, in the section called "The Interior, The Trace," suggesting the special frisson of passing into an unknown world. Although mysterious thresholds are most conspicuous in the public sphere—"at the entrance to the skating rink, to the pub, to the tennis court"—Benjamin submitted that "this same magic prevails more covertly in the interior of the bourgeois dwelling."[1] Unique in his oeuvre, Cézanne's watercolor *The Curtains* (c. 1885; plate 52) is replete with this enigmatic quality.[2] Here, an elaborately ornamental drapery is drawn back with tassled ties to reveal a darkened chamber with a doorway and a wall veiled in shadow. Formally extravagant—the fabric's intricate, likely North African pattern is rendered with a rare congruence between graphite and watercolor—the work seems to evade an ultimate subject. What private realm, we wonder, lies unseen beyond this double portal?[3]

Unlike the Nabis, his younger Parisian contemporaries, the Provençal Cézanne is more readily associated with the accoutrements of the kitchen and the studio—apples and oranges, pitchers, pots, and plaster casts—than with the secluded quarters of *intimisme*. Apart from imagined genre scenes of courtesans or mythological characters, Cézanne pictured bedrooms and toilet tables very rarely in his canvases, yet on paper they not only appear but recur—a testament to a shared intimacy between subject and medium. Throughout his work, motifs migrate freely from one support to another, but interior subjects—the unmade beds, empty chairs, or sleeping figures beyond the curtain—seem to prefer the intrinsic privacy of paper.

If, as Lawrence Gowing wrote, "the private cahiers were indispensable" for fostering Cézanne's "connected habits of drawing and dreaming," it seems fitting that beds appear on four pages of a now-dispersed sketchbook (plates 69–72).[4] Heaped with soft fabric and bounded by decorative frames or posts, each bed is subject to a close framing—zoomed-in, cropped—that accentuates its somatic associations. We can imagine climbing in, and, indeed, all signs point to someone having just climbed out. "To dwell means to leave traces," Benjamin observed, emphasizing the "coverlets and antimacassars, cases and containers" that lent a pliancy to nineteenth-century interiors.[5] While Cézanne's spaces are decidedly distinct from the bourgeois parlors to which Benjamin was referring, his behind-the-curtain drawings offer something beyond the spartan quarters with which the artist is most often associated. To borrow Bridget Alsdorf's useful taxonomy of interiors, they represent neither the studio—"much more sparse in its comforts" and with "domestic details minimized or stripped away"—seen in the late still lifes nor the "weighted down . . . interior space . . . with overflowing shelves, hangings, furniture, wallpaper and moldings" of the late figure paintings.[6] Rather, these works on paper hew to what she has described as "the faithfully transcribed presence of proximate things."[7]

The proximate things offer, in turn, traces of Cézanne and his intimates, not only in the beds, with their indexically rumpled sheets, but also in several depictions of the artist's sleeping son—a subject Cézanne sketched at least eleven times but never committed to canvas.[8] In *The Artist's Son Asleep* (c. 1886; plate 60), young Paul's head sinks into an object whose context says pillow but whose materiality evokes rock. The forceful proximity of head and cushion suggests that each might equally leave its impression on the other.

Of course, if "to dwell means to leave traces," to draw does too. These sheets of paper received Cézanne's marks just as a creased towel did his hands (plate 67). And the suggestion of human presence is as evident in the artist's watercolor touches or graphite hatches as it is in the folds of a jacket apparently so recently tossed on a chair that it retains the volume of its erstwhile inhabitant (plate 68). The literature on this watercolor, made in the early 1890s, is filled with persuasive reflections on its genre dysmorphia—its mountainous volume, its status as a still life object or surrogate portrait—but considerably less attention has been paid to its subject's character as a cast-off garment, a second skin lately shed.[9] Worn outside and removed upon entering the comfort of an interior, a jacket is undoubtedly a threshold article.

After kitchen vessels and their contents, the interior objects Cézanne most often depicted are those that measure time: a florid Rococo clock (plate 55), a humbler mantelpiece version (penciled on the verso of plate 25), and the often-revisited Louis XVI model (p. 21, fig. 2; plates 22, 54, 56, 57) bearing a decorative figure propped against the central clockface with an interdependence that recalls Paul and his pillow.[10] The absence of hour and minute hands in many of these works suggests that Cézanne may have sympathized with Kant's assessment (relatable for many in the pandemic year of this essay) that "to be at home is to recognize life's slow pace."[11] Additional gauges of domestic temporality turn up in drawings of candlesticks (plate 59) and oil lamps—which signal that the artist was working into the night, even as their connotations as vanitas objects suggest a more symbolic hour.

The direst warnings of time's passage, meanwhile, are also the ultimate human traces: the skulls that made tentative appearances in Cézanne's early drawings (plate 7) and persisted through his later years (plates 53, 73–76). Yet the artist often rendered them tracelessly, suspending mark-making to convey their bony whiteness through untouched paper. In *Skull on a Drapery* (1902–06; plate 53), the cranium achieves its materiality through absence. Not unlike a sleeping child, it is nestled in folds of cloth—here a replacement for absent skin. The fabric's elaborate pattern is a softer version of the curtains' sharp geometries; the skull's hollowed eyes are another shadowy threshold.

1.
Walter Benjamin, "The Interior, The Trace," Convolute I in *The Arcades Project*, trans. Howard Eiland and Kevin McLaughlin (Cambridge, Mass.: Belknap Press of Harvard University Press, 1999), 214.

2.
Most often compared to the painting *The Curtain* (*Le Rideau*, 1888–90; Abegg Stiftung, Riggisberg, Switzerland) and the related watercolor *Study of a Curtain* (*Étude de rideau*, 1888–90; Ulmer Museum, Ulm, Germany), *The Curtains* is itself a fully realized composition, while those works, blank beyond their patterned fabrics, are studies for drapery in other compositions.

3.
Carol Armstrong has envisioned this curtain as "the threshold of a world beyond the studio: the house and family of Cézanne." See *Cézanne in the Studio: Still Life in Watercolors* (Los Angeles: J. Paul Getty Museum, 2004), 31.

4.
Lawrence Gowing, *Paul Cézanne: The Basel Sketchbooks* (New York: The Museum of Modern Art, 1988), 11.

5.
Benjamin, "Paris, the Capital of the Nineteenth Century (1935)," in *Arcades Project*, 9.

6.
Bridget Alsdorf, "Interior Landscapes: Metaphor and Meaning in Cézanne's Late Still Lifes," *Word & Image* 26, no. 4 (October–December 2010): 320–21.

7.
Ibid., 316.

8.
Paul's eyes appear to be closed in two paintings, but his clothing and posture suggest that he was not asleep but rather caught in an introspective moment. See *Portrait of the Artist's Son* (*Portrait du fils de l'artiste*, 1881–82; private collection), and *Study for a Portrait of the Artist's Son* (*Esquisse pour un portrait du fils de l'artiste*, c. 1882; Wadsworth Atheneum, Hartford, Conn.).

9.
For Christopher Lloyd, it "rises up like a mountain range," while Alexander Eiling has seen rocklike "hollows and grottos," the rippling "muscle groups of his sculpture studies," and the triangular form of a Medea, after Delacroix, in its folds. Lloyd, *Paul Cézanne Drawings and Watercolors* (London: Thames & Hudson, 2015), 270; and Eiling, ed., *Cézanne: Metamorphoses* (Munich: Prestel/Staatliche Kunsthalle Karlsruhe, 2017), 318–21. For a discussion of this coat as the "skin of an organism stirring with inner life," see Inken Freudenberg, "And the Picture, Once Left, Torments Us and Pursues Us: Cézanne and Delacroix," in Judit Geskó, ed., *Cézanne and the Past: Tradition and Creativity* (Budapest: Museum of Fine Arts, 2012), 57.

10.
Theodore Reff has proposed that these drawings "represent a Louis XVI clock, probably by Gille l'Ainée." See his review of *Cézanne und die alten Meister*, *Art Bulletin* 42, no. 2 (June 1960): 148.

11.
Immanuel Kant, *A History of Private Life*, vol. 4, *From the Fires of Revolution to the Great War*, ed. Michelle Perrot, trans. Arthur Goldhammer (Cambridge, Mass.: Belknap Press of Harvard University Press, 1990), 342.

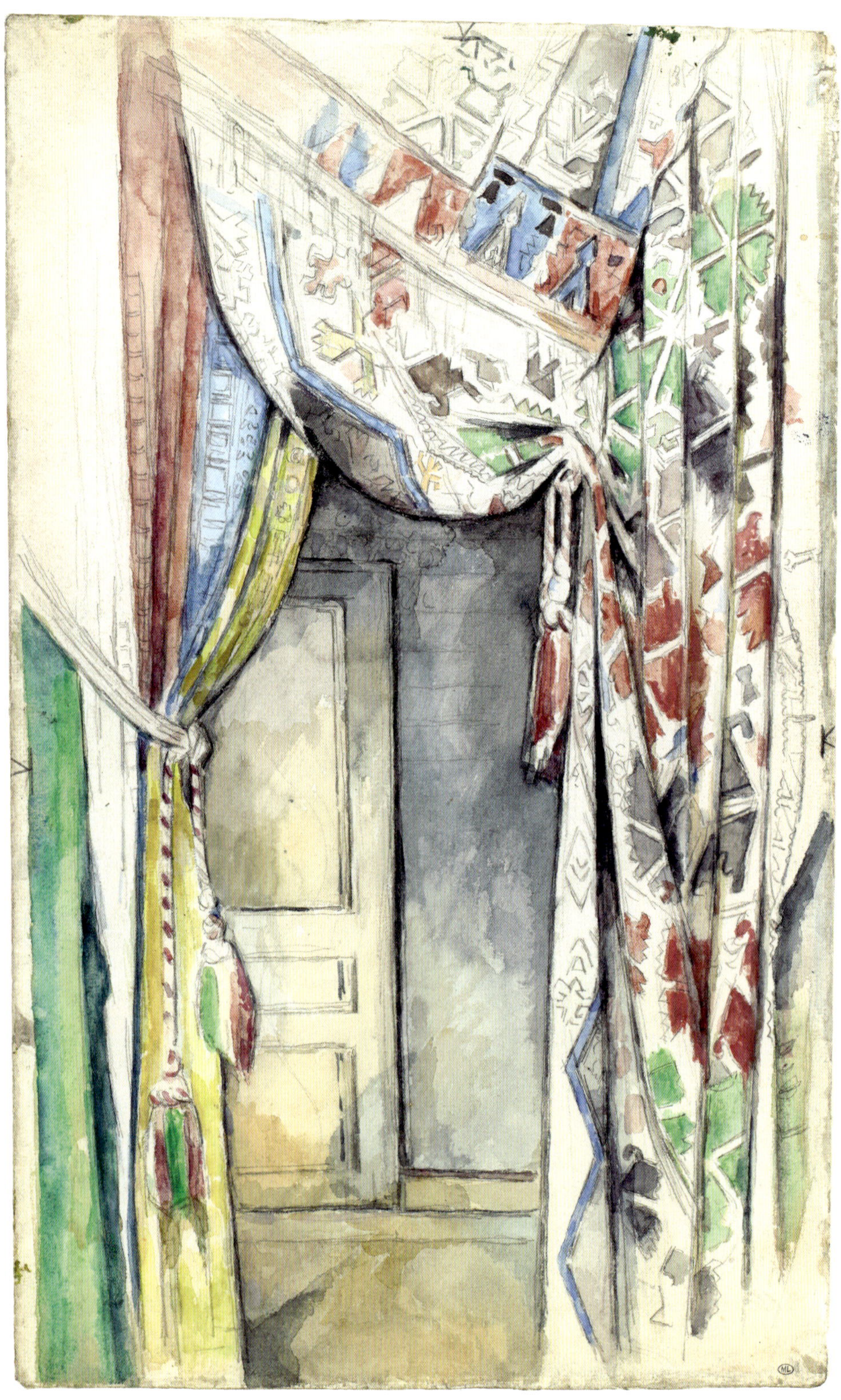

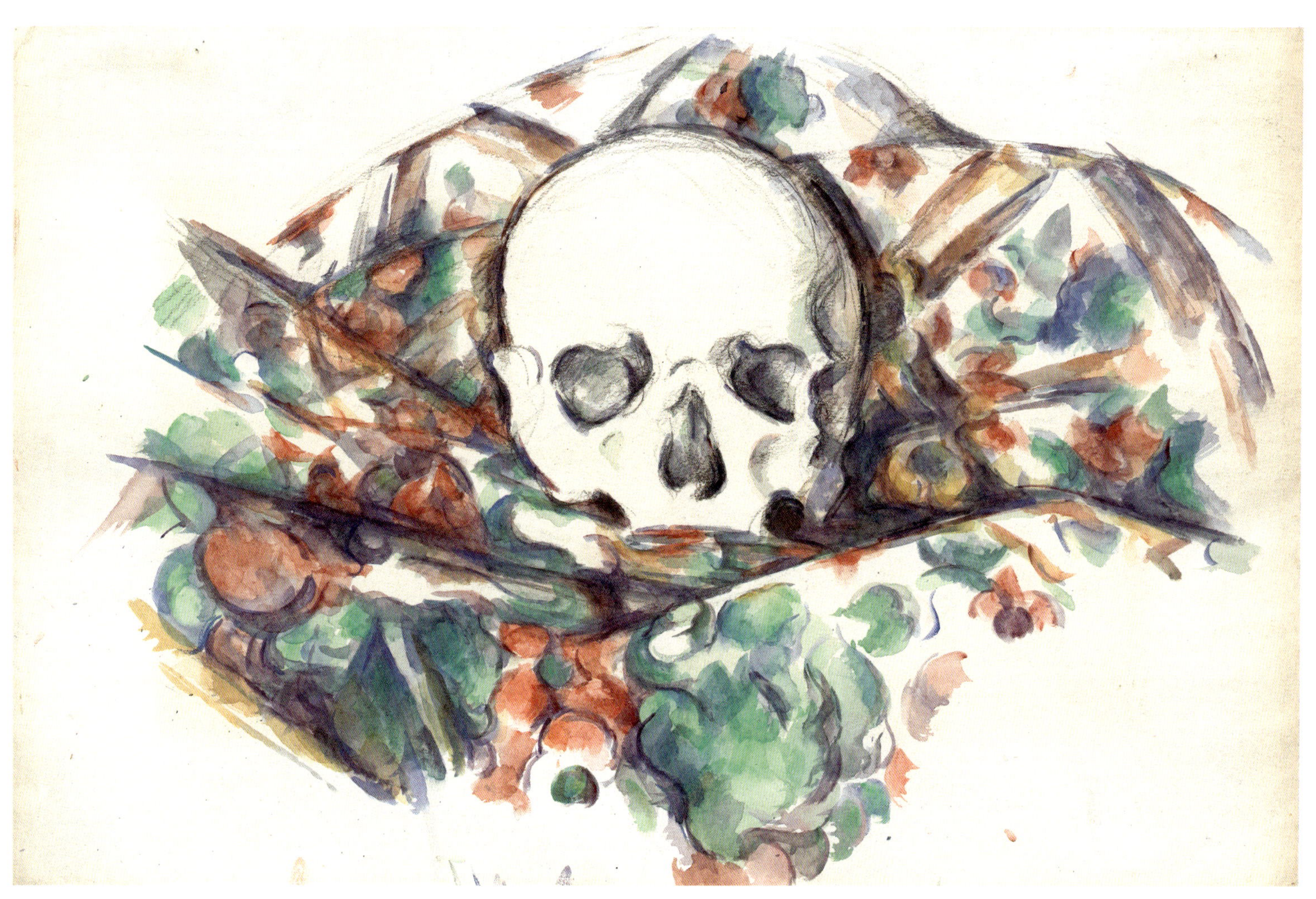

52. *The Curtains*. c. 1885. Pencil, watercolor, and gouache on wove paper, 19 5/16 × 12 1/16" (49 × 30.7 cm)

53. *Skull on a Drapery*. 1902–06. Pencil, gouache, and watercolor on wove paper, 12 ½ × 18 ¾" (31.7 × 47.6 cm)

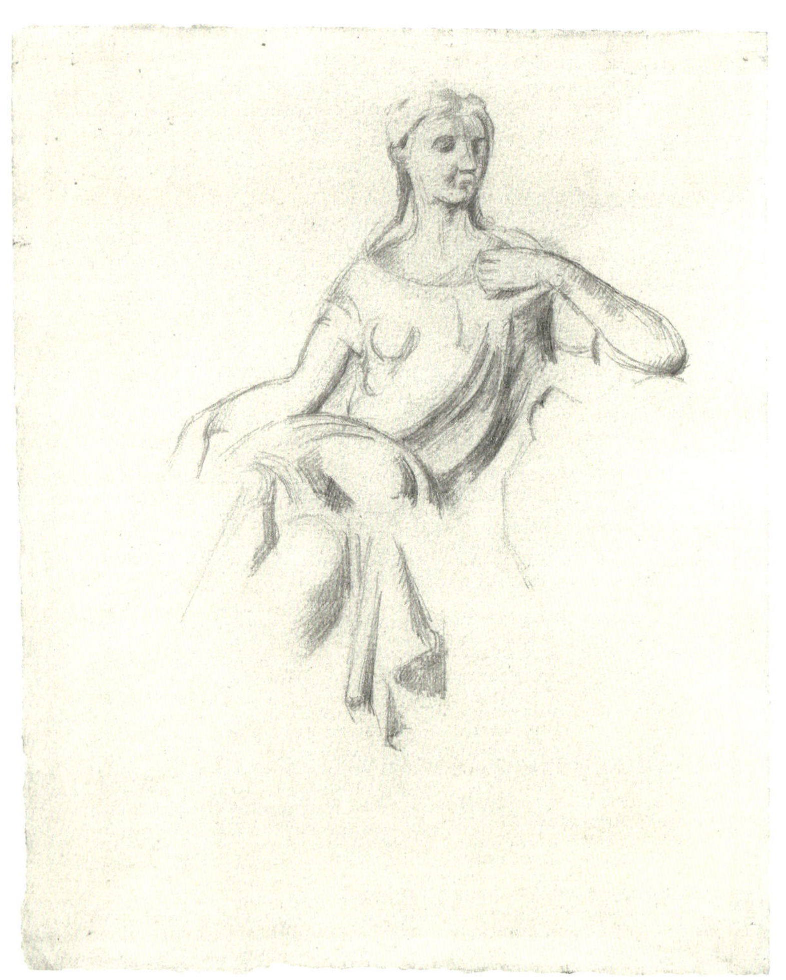

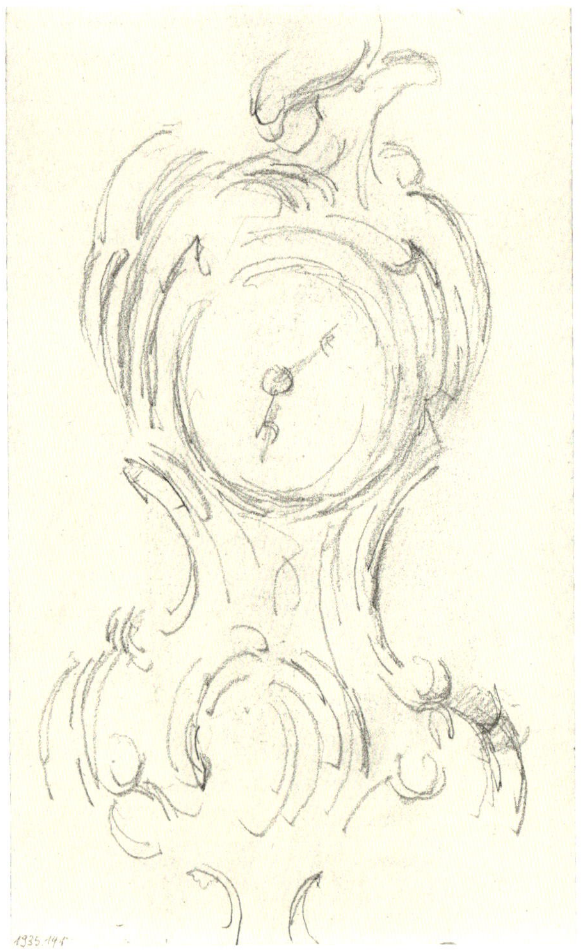

54. *Ornamental Clock Figure*. 1881–84. Pencil on paper, 11 13/16 × 9 13/16" (30 × 25 cm)

55. *Rococo Clock*. After 1900. Pencil on wove paper, 8 9/16 × 5 3/16" (21.8 × 13.1 cm)

56. *Study of a Mantel Clock*. 1895–98. Pencil on paper, 9 7/16 × 13 9/16" (23.9 × 34.5 cm)

57. *Page of Studies, Including a Clock and a Naiad*. 1876–79. Pencil on laid paper, 12 1/8 × 18 1/4" (30.8 × 46.3 cm)

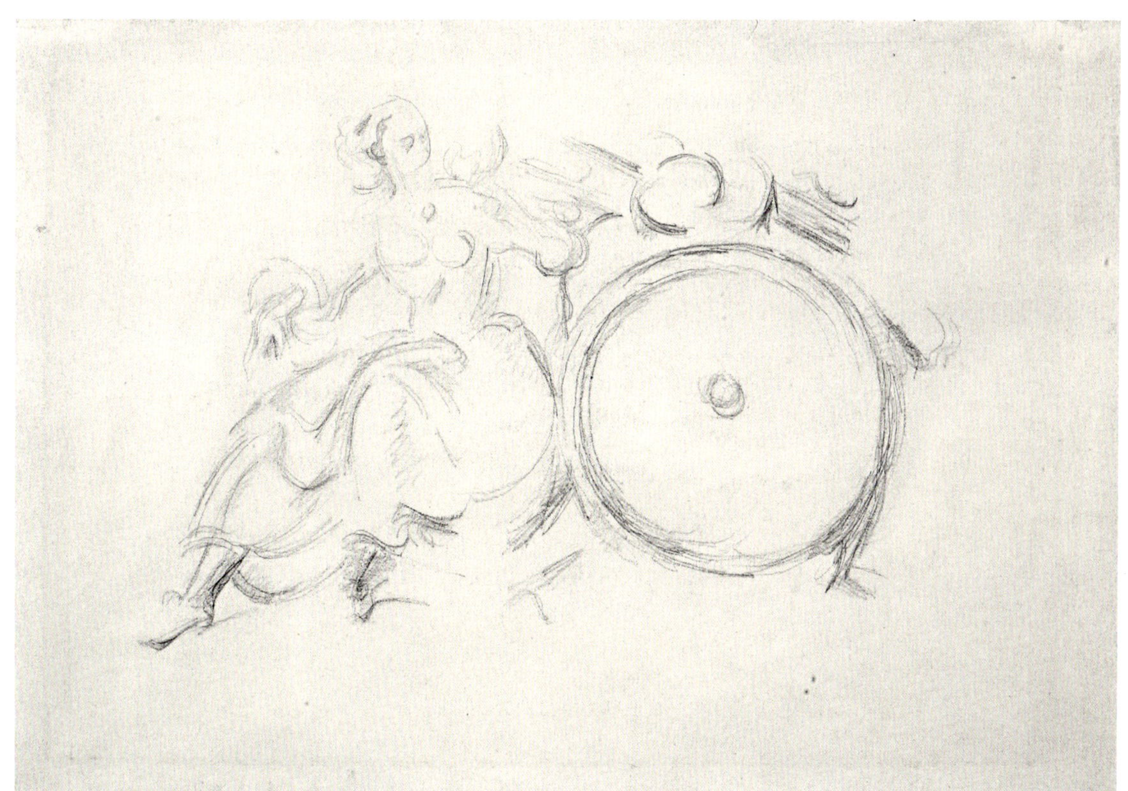

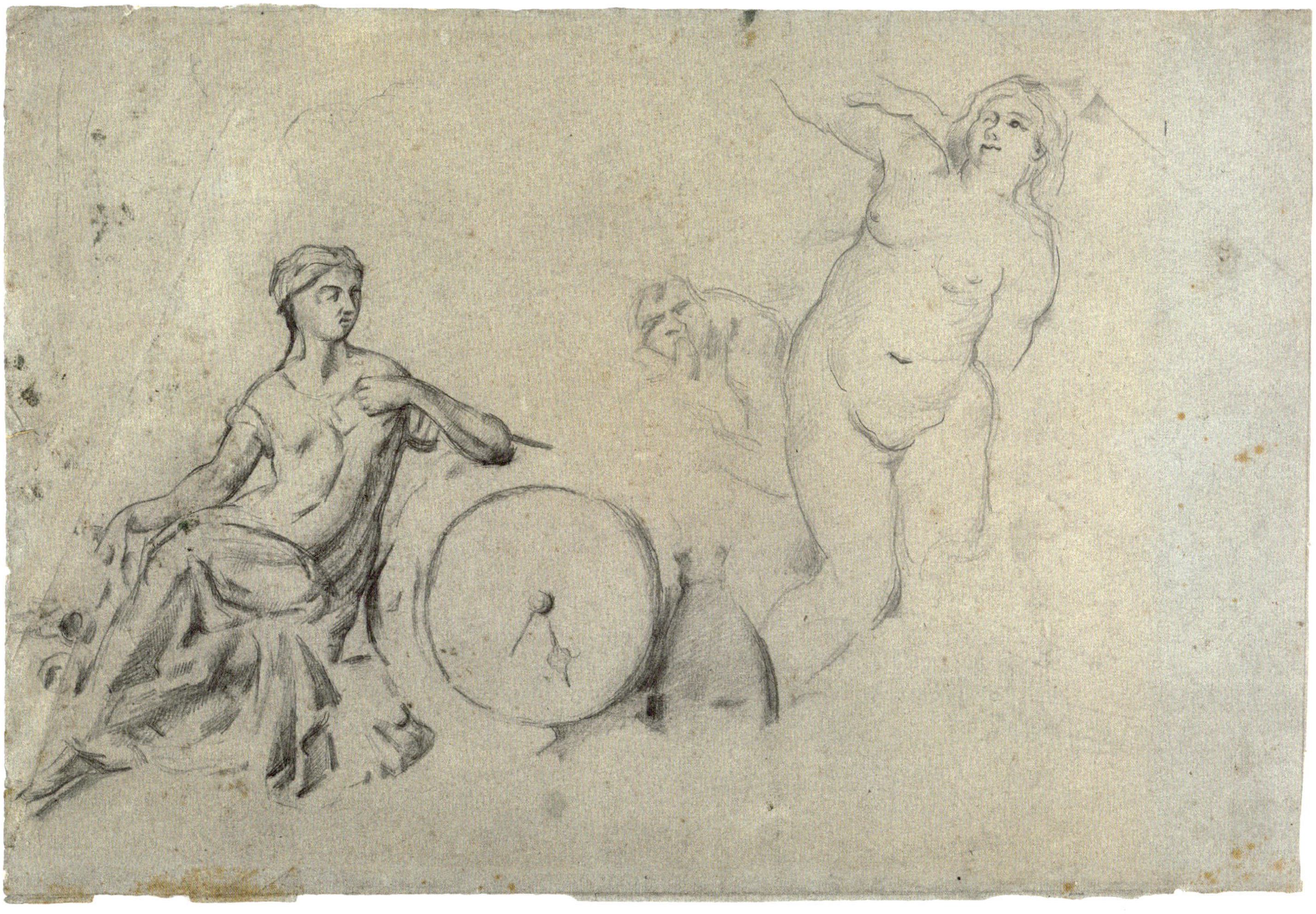

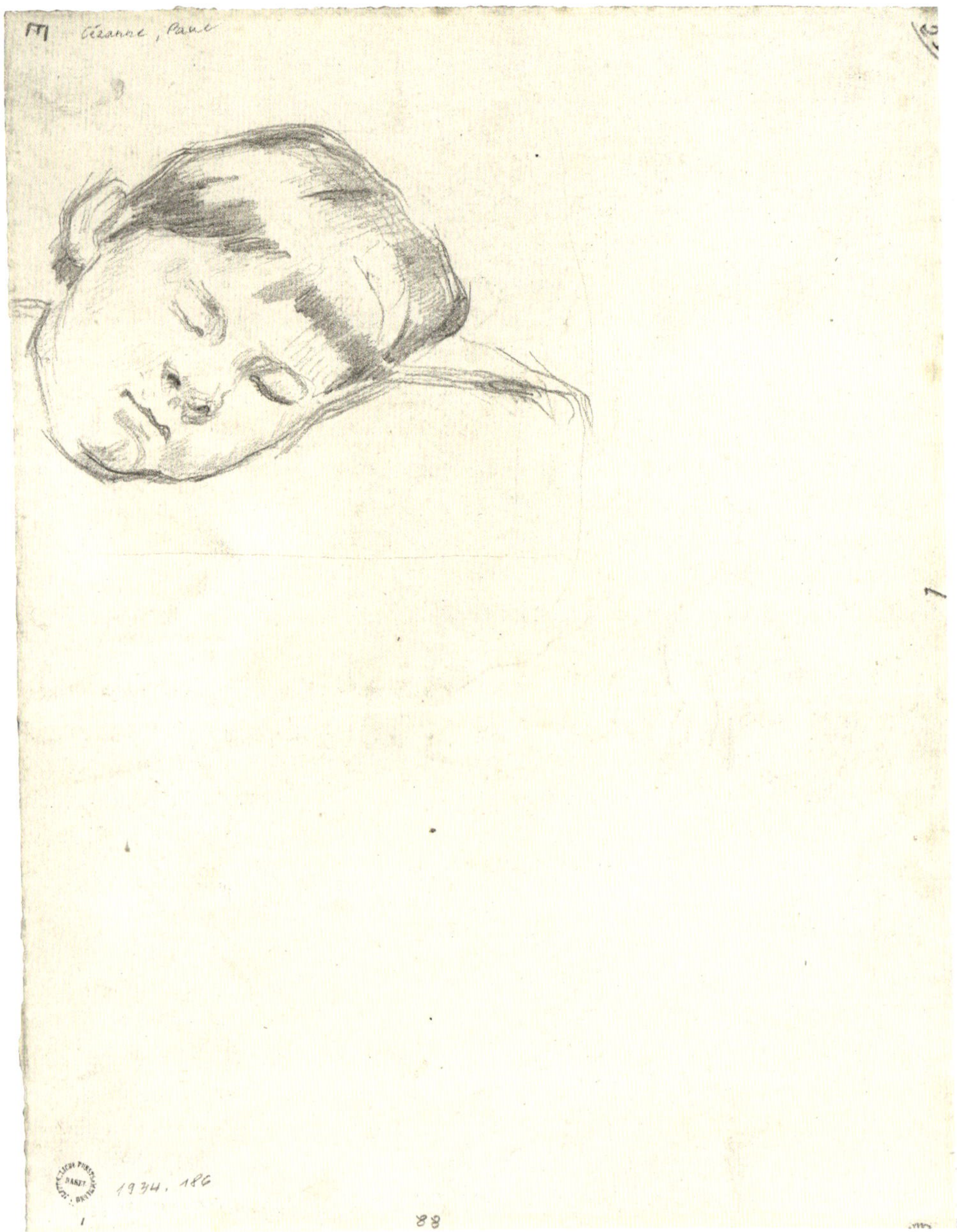

58. *Head of a Boy Asleep (The Artist's Son?)*. c. 1880. Pencil on laid paper, $8\frac{7}{8}$ × $7\frac{13}{16}$" (22.5 × 19.8 cm)

59. *Studies with Paul Cézanne Fils and Candle Holder*. c. 1879. Pencil on laid paper, $5\frac{11}{16}$ × $8\frac{7}{8}$" (14.5 × 22.5 cm)

60. *The Artist's Son Asleep*. c. 1886. Pencil on wove paper, $4\frac{9}{16}$ × $7\frac{3}{16}$" (11.6 × 18.3 cm)

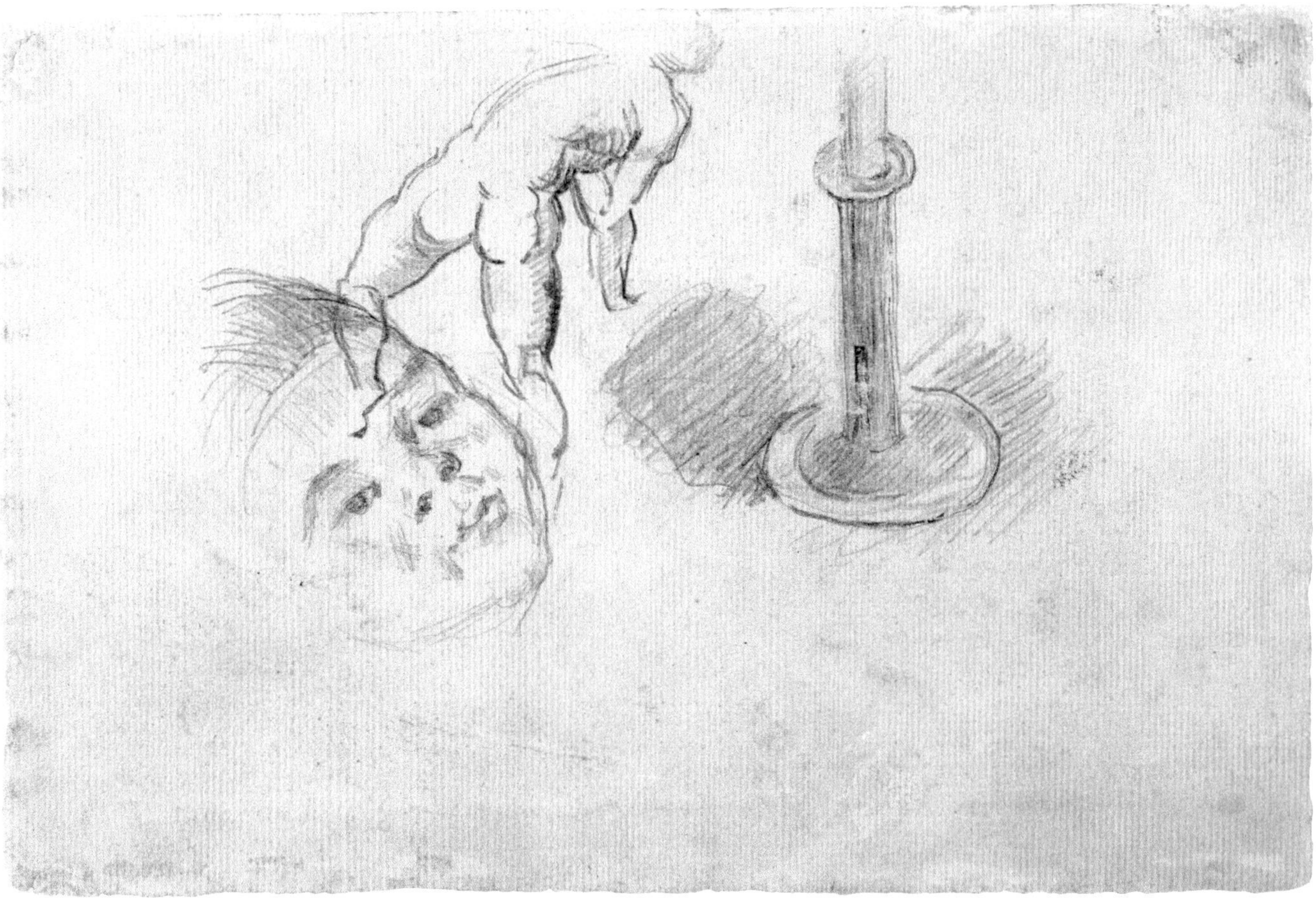

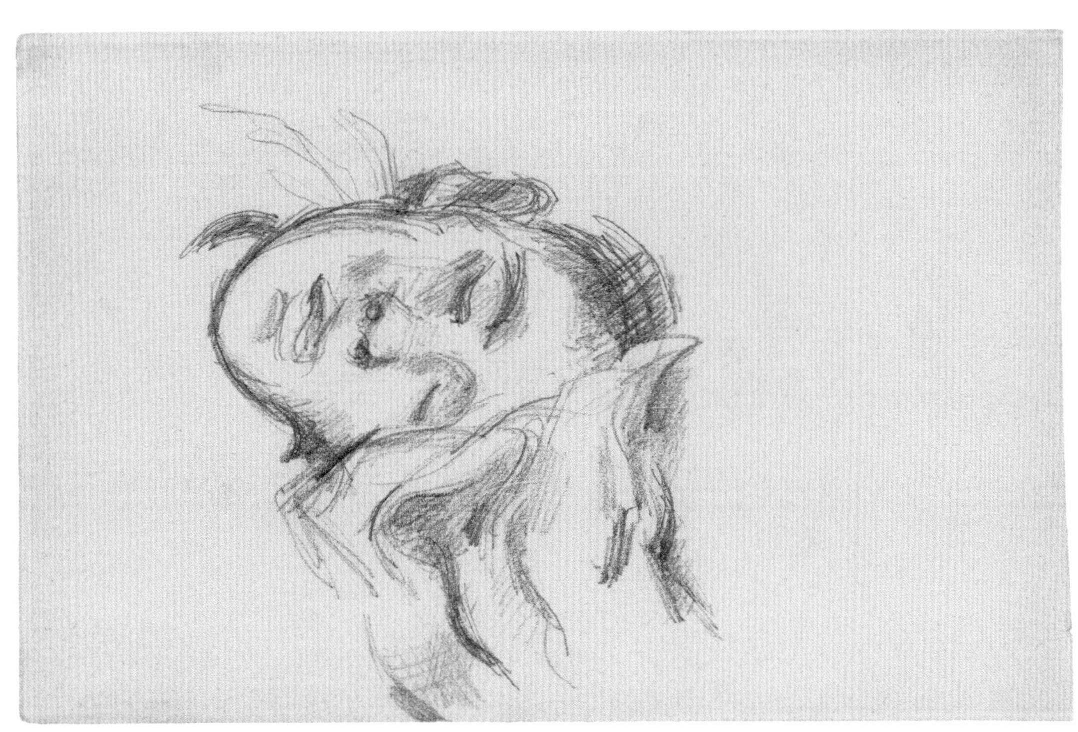

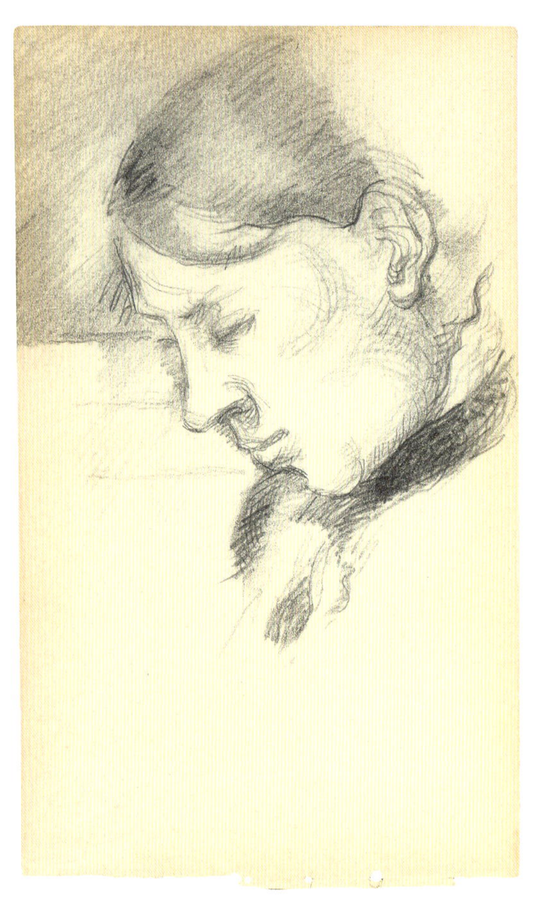

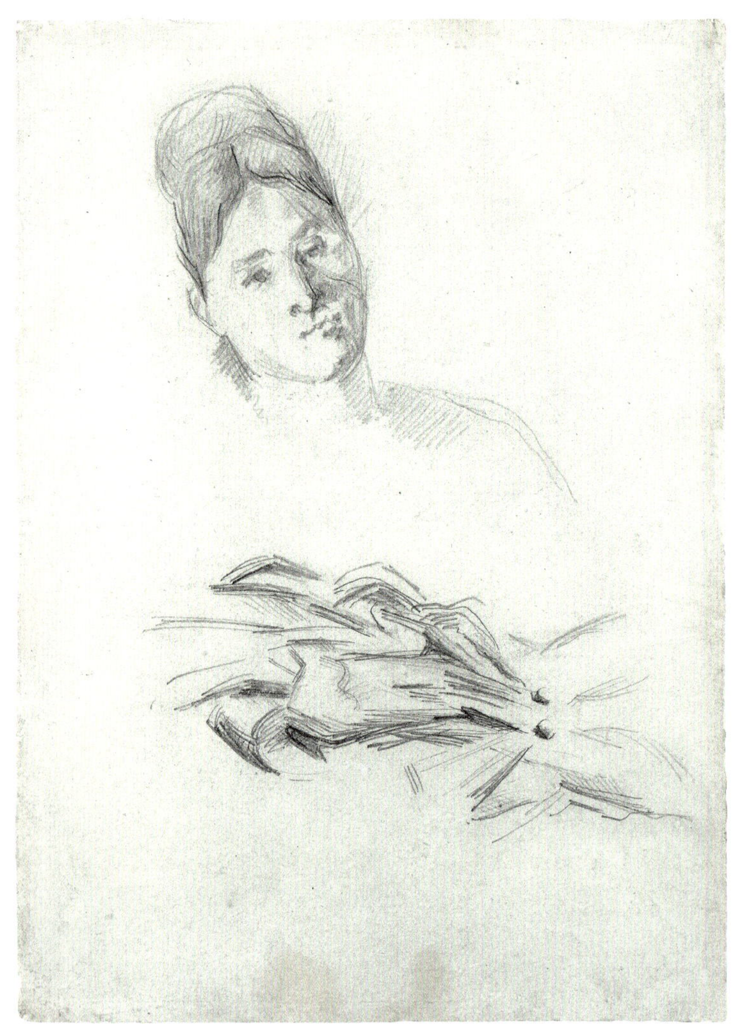

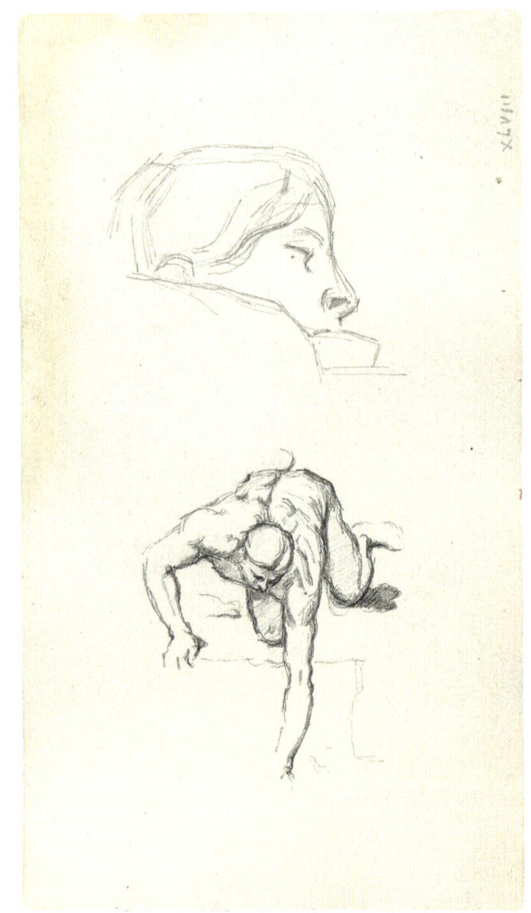

61. *Madame Cézanne.* c. 1884–87. Pencil on wove paper, 7 11/16 × 4 3/4" (19.5 × 12.1 cm)

62. *Page of Studies, Including One of Madame Cézanne.* c. 1874–76. Pencil on wove paper, 10 7/16 × 7 7/8" (26.5 × 20 cm)

63. *Head of a Woman Sleeping and Figure Sketch after Michelangelo.* c. 1875–79. Pencil on wove paper, 8 7/16 × 4 7/8" (21.5 × 12.4 cm)

64. *Hortense Fiquet (Madame Cézanne) Sewing.* c. 1880. Pencil on laid paper, 18 9/16 × 12 3/16" (47.2 × 30.9 cm)

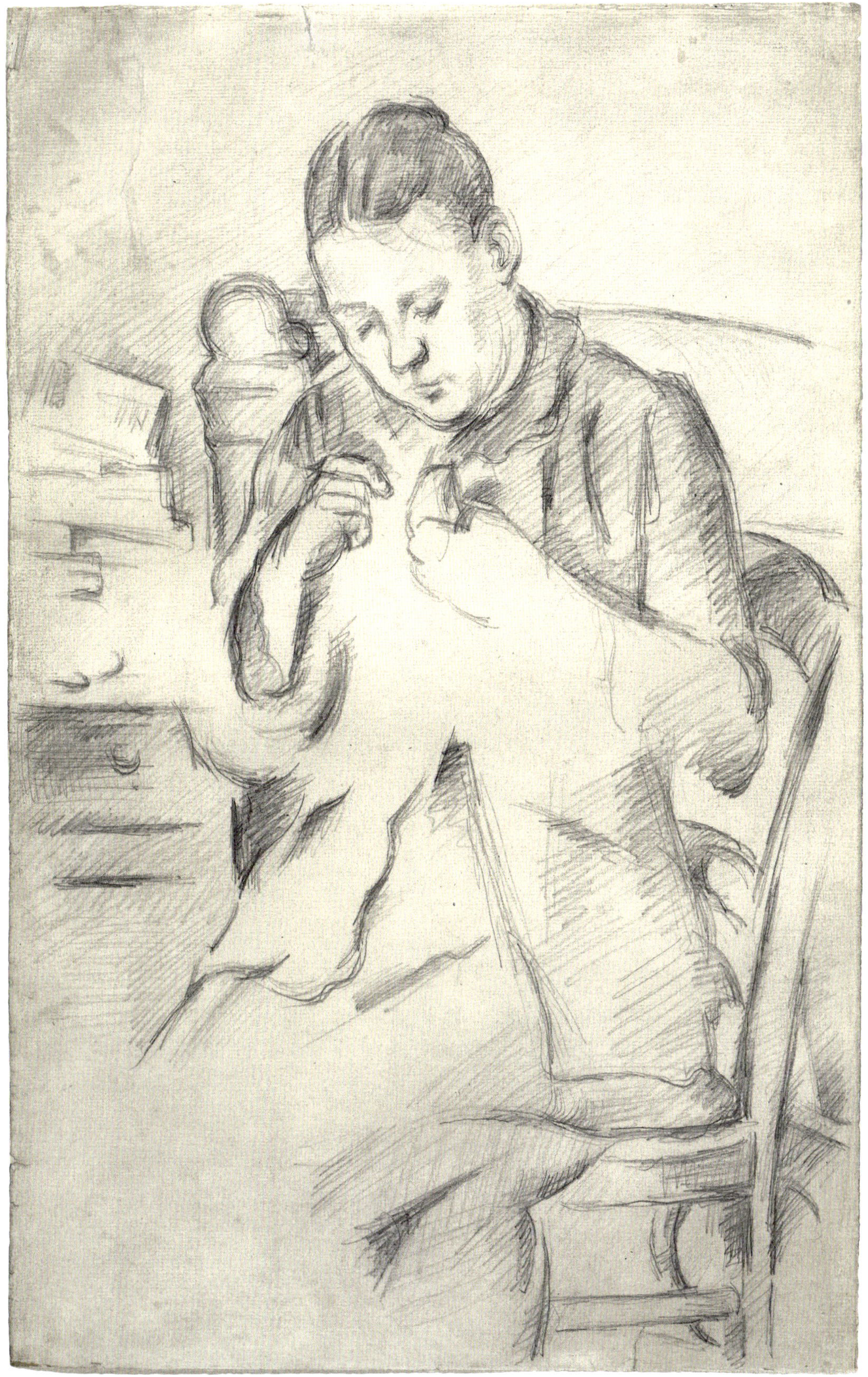

65. Spread from Sketchbook Chicago. Pages IIII verso and V

a. Child's drawing. n.d. Pencil on wove paper, 4⅞ × 8 9/16" (12.4 × 21.7 cm)

b. *House with Trees*. 1876–79. Pencil on wove paper, 4⅞ × 8 9/16" (12.4 × 21.7 cm)

66. Spread from Sketchbook Chicago. Pages XXI verso and XXII

a. *Study of Drapery*. 1881–84. Pencil on wove paper, 4⅞ × 8 9/16" (12.4 × 21.7 cm)

b. *Self-Portrait*. 1875–76. Pencil on wove paper, 4⅞ × 8 9/16" (12.4 × 21.7 cm)

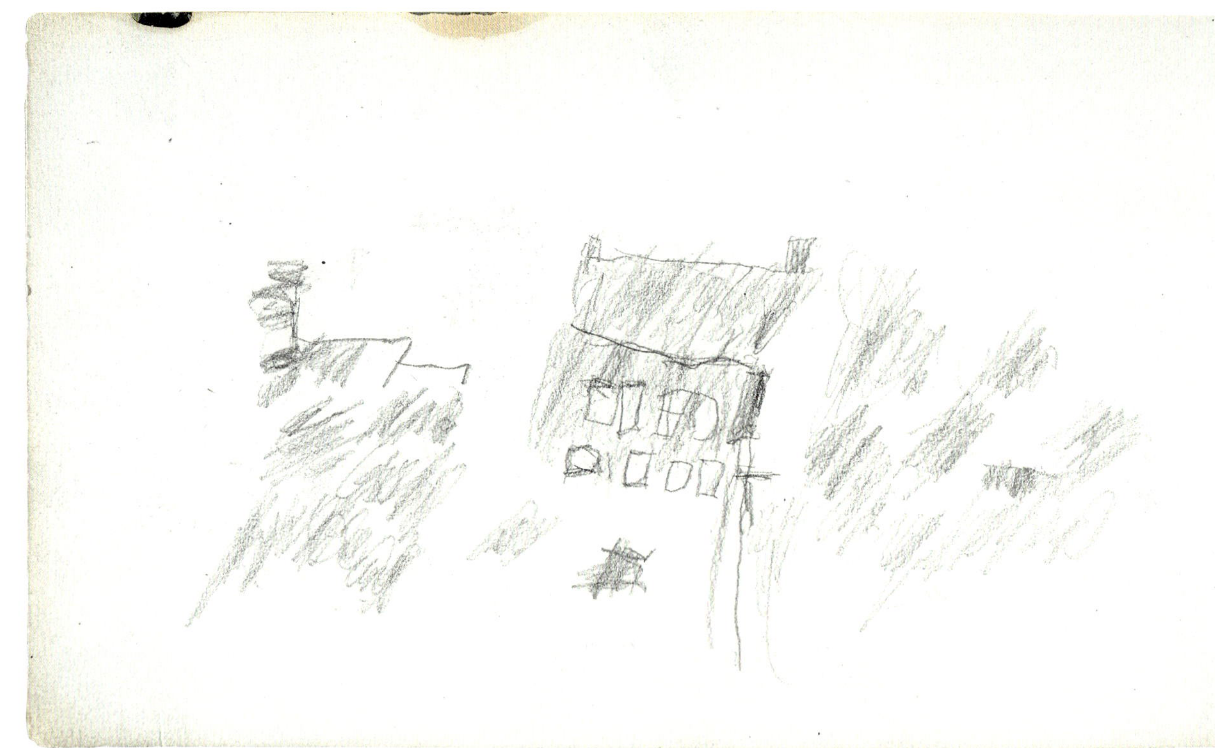

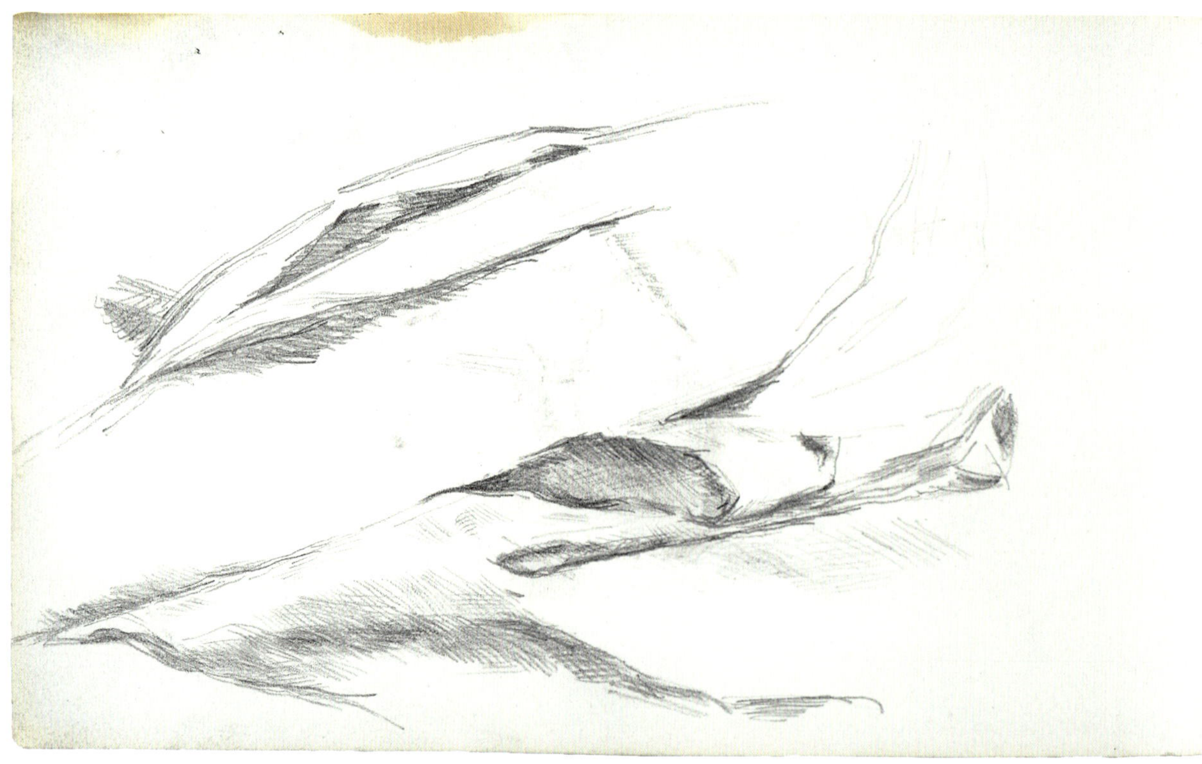

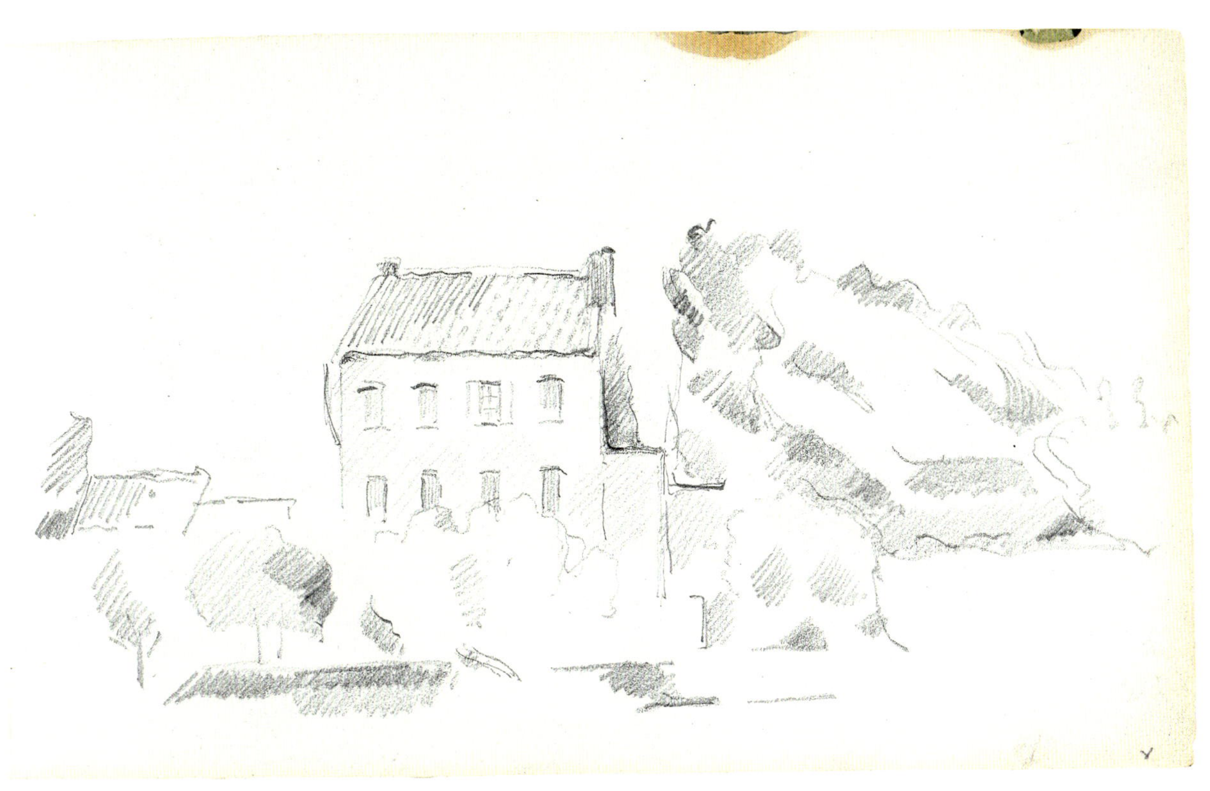

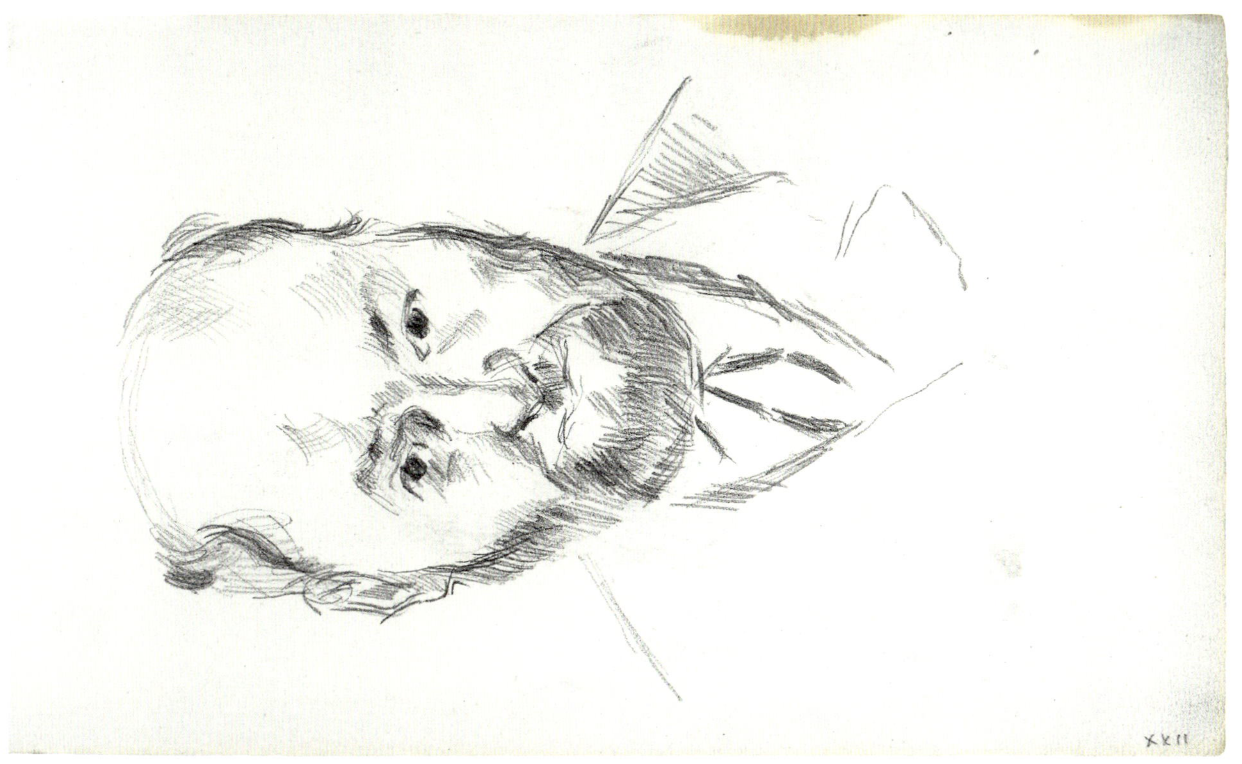

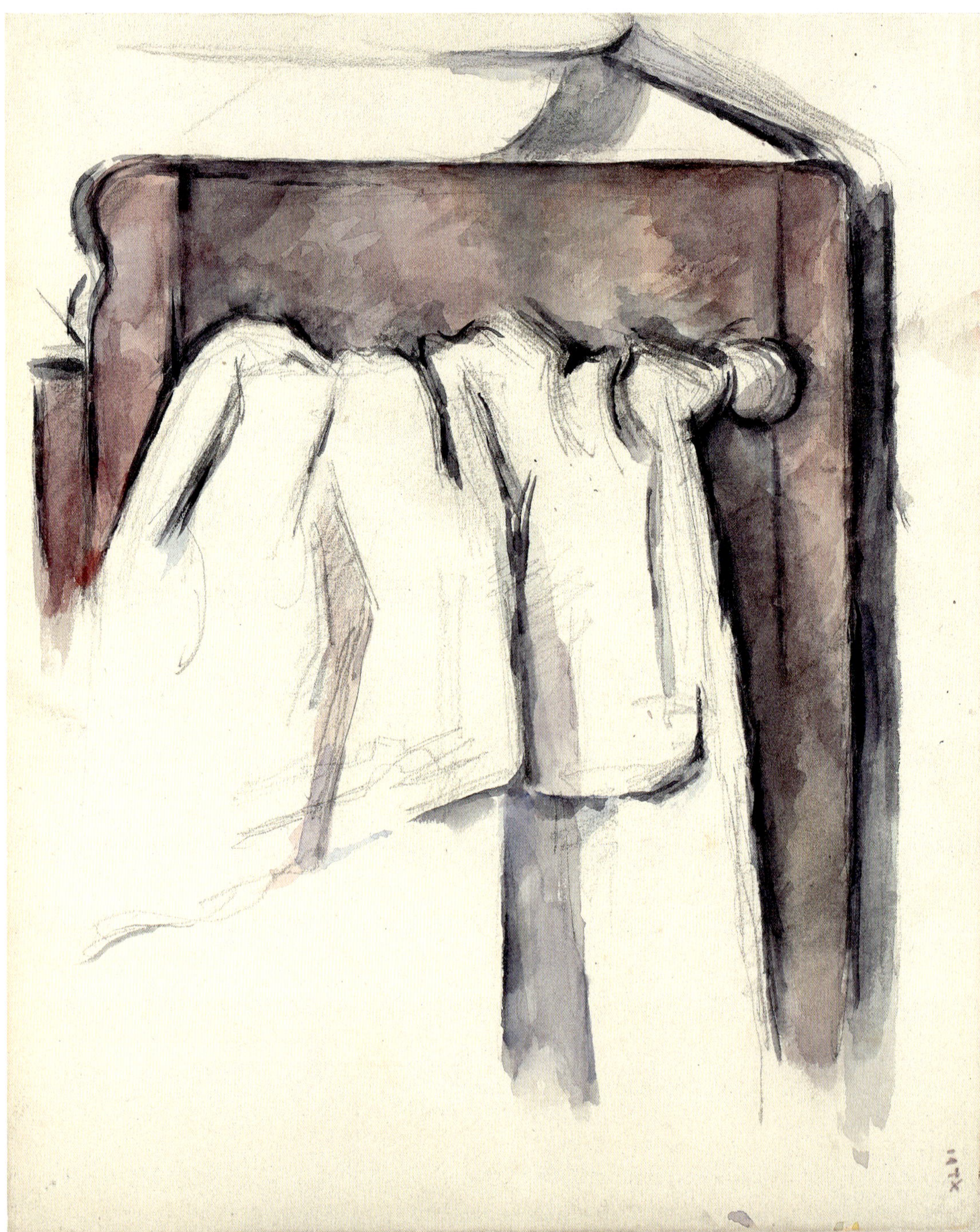

67. *Dressing Table with Towel and Basin*. 1890–95. Pencil and watercolor on wove paper, 10 1⁄16 × 8 1⁄4" (25.6 × 21 cm)

68. *Coat on a Chair*. 1890–92. Pencil and watercolor on laid paper, 18 11⁄16 × 12" (47.5 × 30.5 cm)

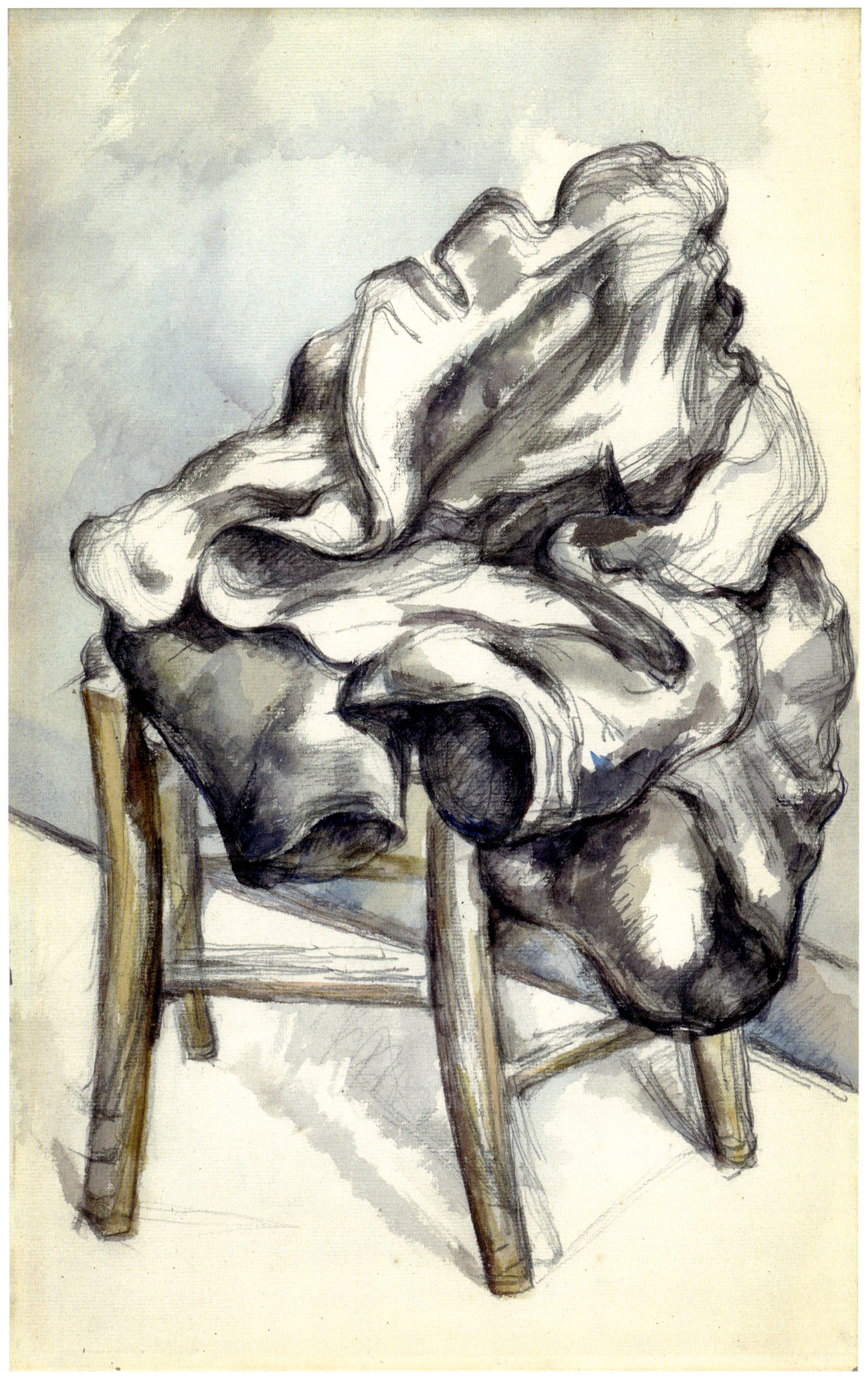

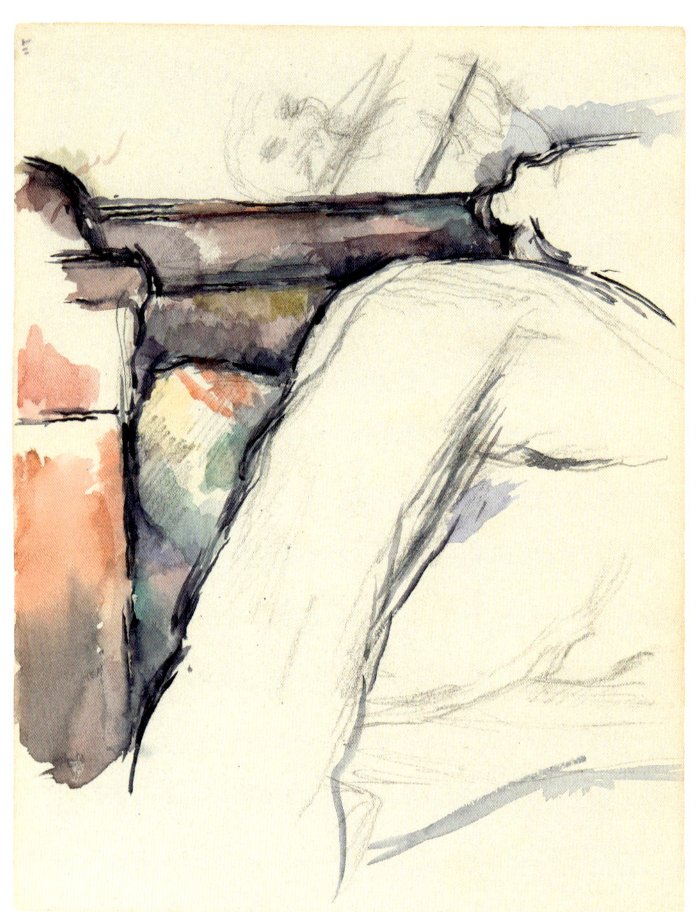

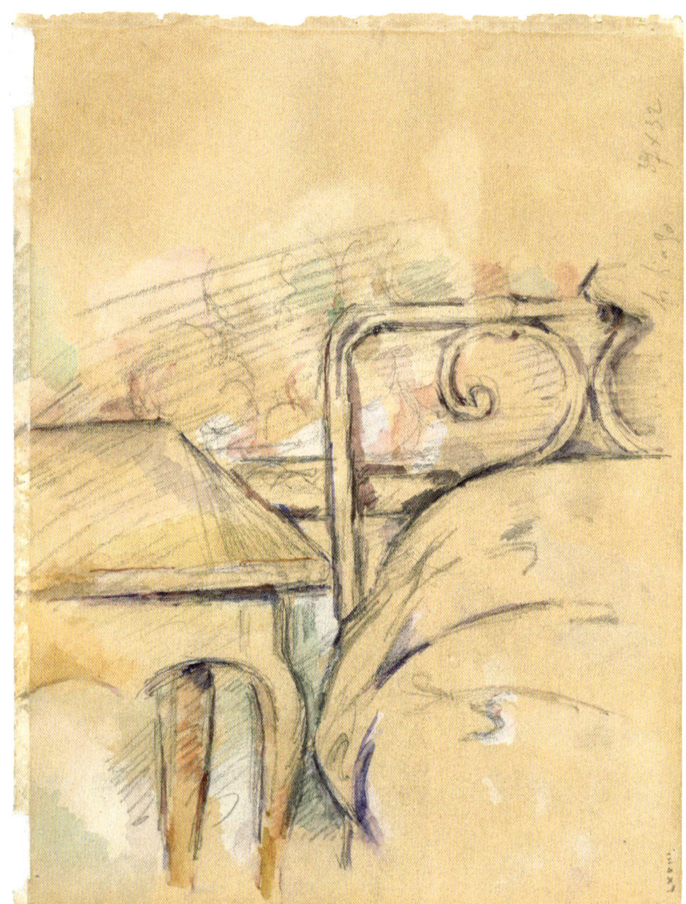

69. *Unmade Bed*. 1885–90. Pencil and watercolor on wove paper, 10 ¾ × 8 ¼" (27.3 × 21 cm)

70. *Bed and Table*. 1885–87. Pencil and watercolor on wove paper, 10 ¾ × 8 ¼" (27.3 × 21 cm)

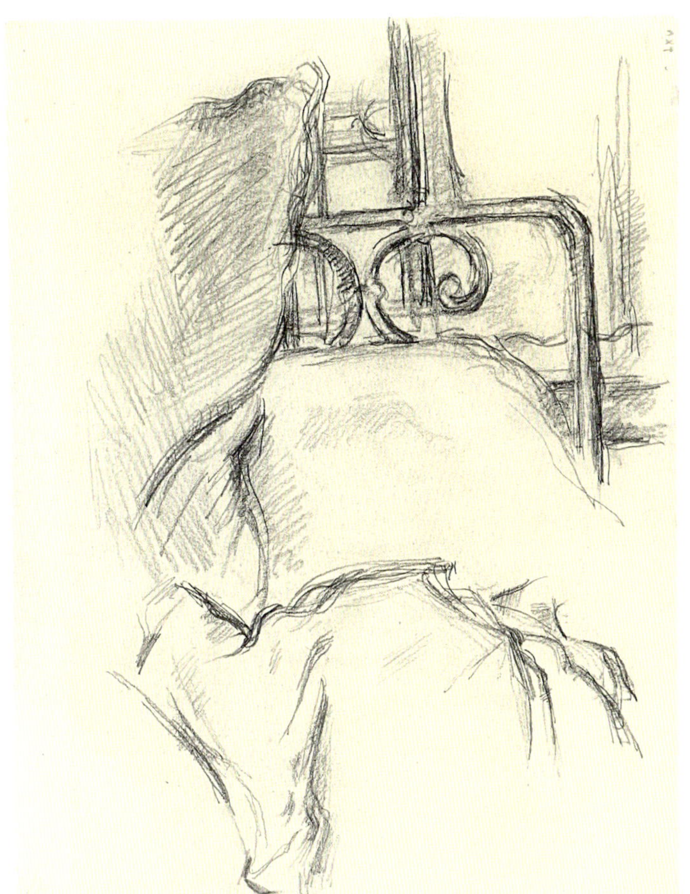

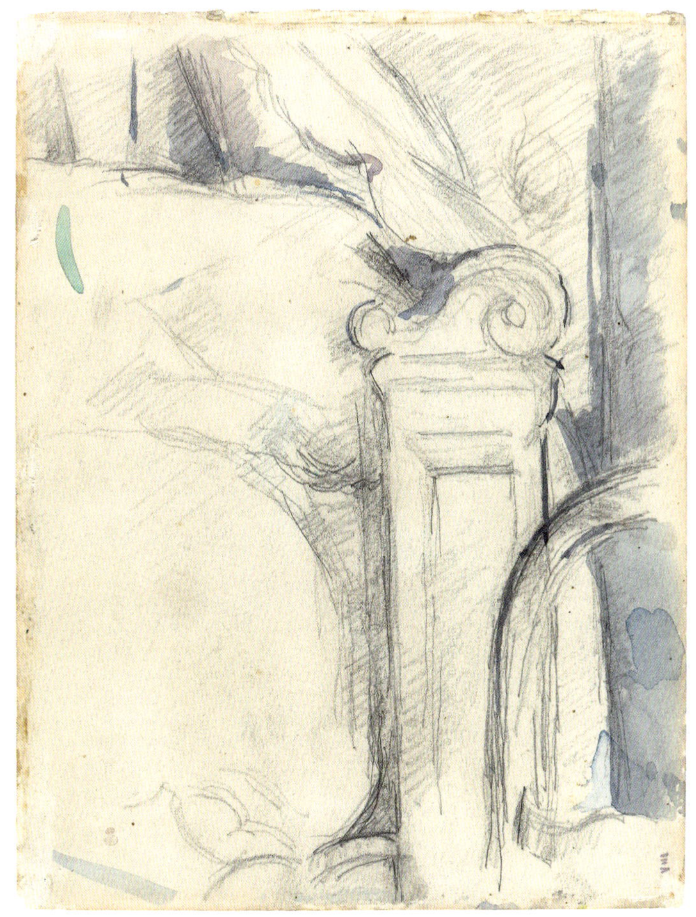

71. *Unmade Bed*. c. 1887. Pencil on wove paper, 10 ⅝ × 8 ¼" (27 × 21 cm)

72. *Bedpost*. c. 1886. Pencil and watercolor on wove paper, 10 ¹³⁄₁₆ × 8 ⁵⁄₁₆" (27.4 × 21.1 cm)

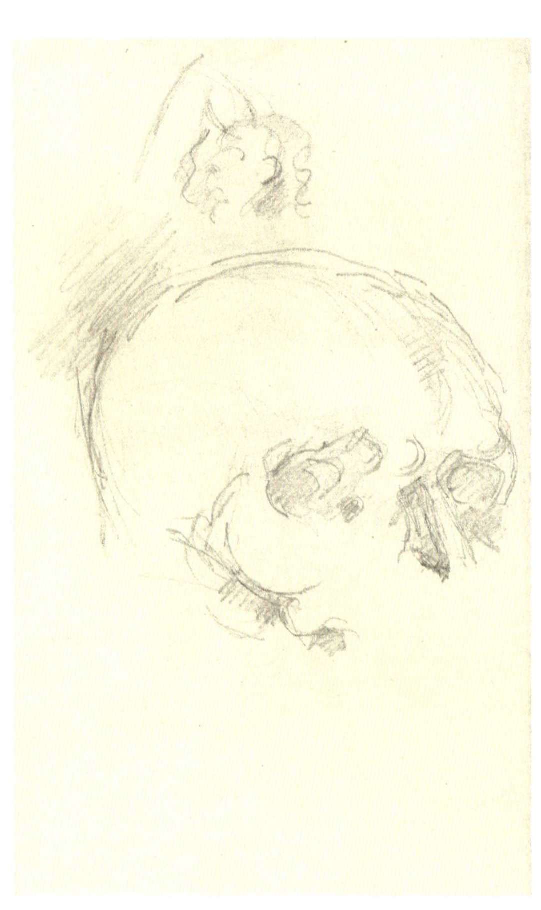

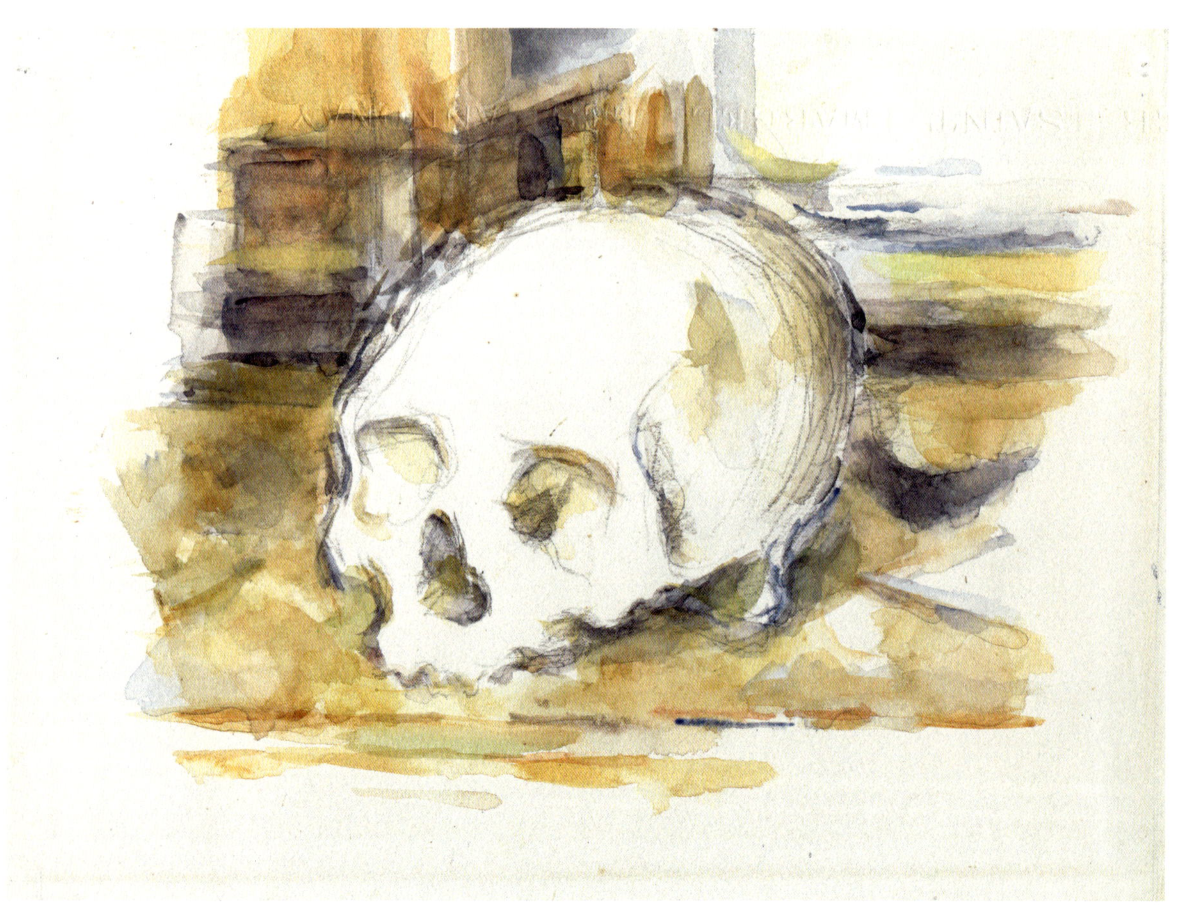

73. *Page of Studies, Including a Skull*. c. 1900. Pencil on wove paper, 8 3/8 × 4 7/8" (21.2 × 12.4 cm)

74. *Study of a Skull*. 1902–04. Pencil and watercolor on paper, 9 × 12 3/16" (22.9 × 31 cm)

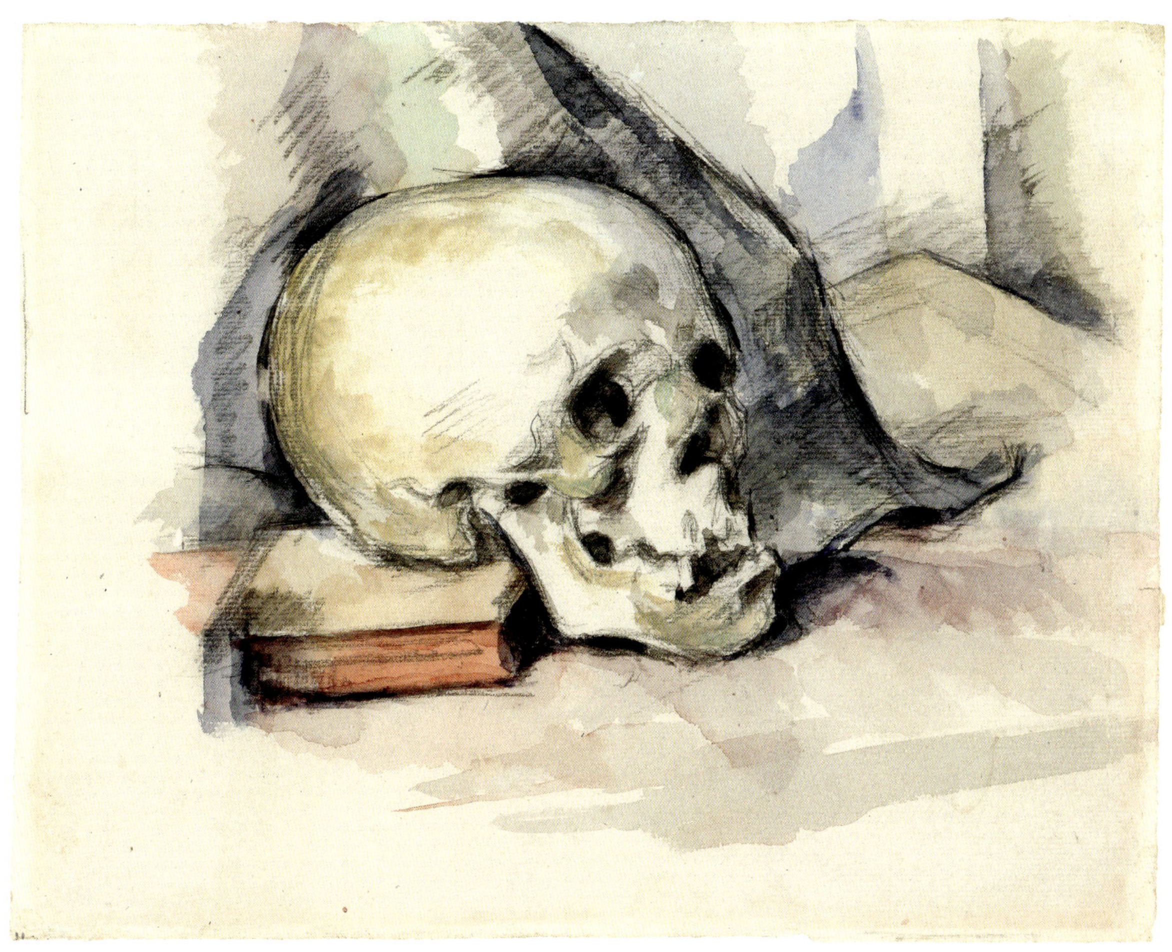

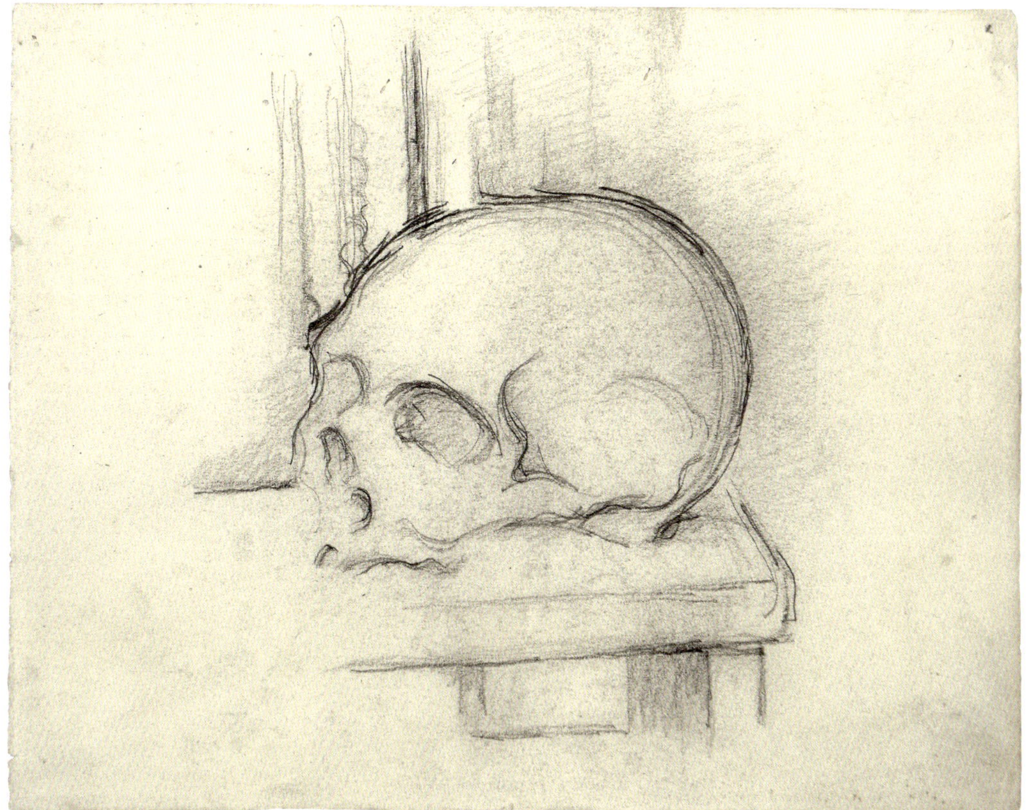

75. *Skull and Book*. c. 1885. Pencil and watercolor on laid paper, 9 ¼ × 12 3/16" (23.5 × 31 cm)

76. *Skull on a Table*. 1900 or later. Pencil on wove paper, 8 ¼ × 10 11/16" (21 × 27.2 cm)

Annemarie Iker

"There are two things . . . the eye for the vision of nature and the brain for the logic of organized sensations."
—Paul Cézanne, quoted in Émile Bernard, "Paul Cézanne" (1904)

Eye and brain: according to Cézanne, these were the essential attributes of an artist, "the eye for the vision of nature and the brain for the logic of organized sensations."[1] Eye and brain, vision and logic come together in a figure Cézanne returned to persistently throughout his life—a standing bather seen from behind, alone and with other bathers, variously rendered in graphite, ink, watercolor, and oil paint, on paper, lithographic stone, and canvas.[2]

Early iterations of the figure appear in a sketchbook the artist first opened in the late 1870s. On one page, the bather is delineated in repeated strokes of ink (plate 81); some twenty pages away, a similar figure is described in curving lines of graphite (plate 82). To shape the gestures and postures of these two bathers and others, beginning in the 1860s Cézanne undertook close, careful studies of artworks at the Louvre.[3] As in his sketchbook drawings of two ancient marble statues—including one of Marcellus, nephew of the Roman emperor Augustus (plate 78)—both bathers have distinctly sculptural builds. And as in his study of a preparatory drawing made by Luca Signorelli around the turn of the sixteenth century (plate 80), they are pictured from behind, with firmly rendered shading along their torsos and limbs.[4] Together these two figures attest to Cézanne's observant eye.

Yet vision, for Cézanne, had its limits. "One should not be too scrupulous, too sincere, nor too submissive to nature," he cautioned.[5] Rather than copy his sources, Cézanne turned to the "logic of organized sensation" to reconceive them for his standing bather, deploying new materials, settings, and poses. Experiments abound in a graphite, watercolor, and gouache drawing from around 1885 (plate 84), in which the figure shares the same rough outline as its late-'70s predecessors but stands, feet planted, amid a landscape conjured by transparent patches of brilliant pigment. A fresh element, moreover, is appended to its frame: the cloth that hangs from the crook of the arm, similar to that carried by Marcellus but shifted from the Roman's left side to the bather's right and expanded with billows and folds heightened by white gouache.

Equally striking are this bather's splayed feet and jaunty stance, both of which correspond to Signorelli's nude (itself informed by antique sculpture). Cézanne may have drawn these Signorelli-inflected legs at the Louvre, or he may have made them in his studio, based on his own studies of the Renaissance drawing. There is, however, an additional possibility, as the artist owned both a lithograph and a photograph of the Signorelli drawing, two of dozens of commercial images of paintings, sculptures, and works on paper found in his studio after his death.[6] The uneven quality of these reproductions surprised Cézanne's associates, as did his acknowledgment of using them as sources. "Cézanne was not, to my great astonishment, opposed to a painter making use of [photographs]," recalled the younger artist Émile Bernard, "but for him it was necessary to interpret this exact reproduction as one interpreted nature."[7] Acquaintances of the artist related that it was not only photographs he "interpreted," but illustrations from books and journals as well.[8]

Among Cézanne's reproductions was a framed photograph of Thomas Couture's *Romans of the Decadence* (1847), a monumental history painting set in ancient Rome and centered on a marble sculpture that resembles the Louvre's Marcellus.[9] Notably, Couture's Marcellus look-alike adopts a more animated pose than the marble statue, his right leg flexed as though midstride and his right arm raised toward the revelers ranged below him. Cézanne's later, loose-limbed treatments of the standing bather, such as the graphite and watercolor drawing *Bathers* (1885–90; plate 87), share this dynamism. In *Bathers*, short bursts of graphite define the figure's supple body, from his sloping shoulders to his spritely back heel, while pencil lines and stripes and splotches of blue pigment dart toward and away from each other. As in Couture's bacchanal, the standing bather now crowds beside other figures.

Although likely sources for the standing bather include a painting by Couture, ancient Roman sculptures, and an Italian Renaissance drawing, the manner in which Cézanne at times encountered these works—mediated by lithographs and photographs—was decidedly modern. In turn, this modernity galvanized the standing bather in ways that go beyond the bend of a leg or the angle of an elbow. Like nineteenth-century photographers composing images of sculpture, Cézanne explored varied backgrounds and selective cropping. Furthermore, he embraced the search for a single, salient perspective—a search that also absorbed period photographers of three-dimensional artworks.[10] While his numerous drawings of sculptures at the Louvre—most notably, of works by the French Baroque artist Pierre Puget (plates 106–15)—indicate that Cézanne scrutinized the objects from various vantage points, his treatments of the standing bather over many years embody the refinement of a single point of view.

Aruna D'Souza has observed that this figure is a "recurring character" in Cézanne's many bathers compositions.[11] "The circularity of Cézanne's practice, the constant return to the same set of resonant images, poses, and sites," she has written, "all of these things suggest a potentially limitless repetition without a clear and fixed result."[12] "Potentially limitless repetition" is also a characteristic of lithography and photography, the modern reproductive technologies that produced the objects the artist collected and interpreted as he elaborated his standing bather. If the many iterations of this figure are the products of eye and brain, Cézanne's were organs honed by modernity.

1.
Cézanne, in Émile Bernard, "Paul Cézanne," *L'Occident* 6 (July 1904): 23. Translations in this essay are by the author.

2.
In addition to the works discussed below, see, for example, plates 79, 83, 86, and 88.

3.
For Cézanne's sources, see Adrien Chappuis, *The Drawings of Paul Cézanne: A Catalogue Raisonné* (Greenwich, Conn.: New York Graphic Society, 1973); and John Rewald, *The Paintings of Paul Cézanne: A Catalogue Raisonné* (New York: Abrams, 1986). Cézanne also drew and painted from models and sitters; see, for example, plates 77, 119, 123, and 227.

4.
At the Louvre, see *Statue of Marcellus* (c. 20 BCE) and Luca Signorelli, *Nude Man, Standing, Seen from Behind, Carrying a Corpse on His Shoulders* (1499–1506).

5.
Cézanne, in Bernard, "Paul Cézanne," 25.

6.
Theodore Reff, "Reproductions and Books in Cézanne's Studio," *Gazette des beaux-arts* 102, no. 56 (1960): 303–09.

7.
Bernard, "Souvenirs sur Paul Cézanne et lettres inédites," *Mercure de France* 248 (October 15, 1907): 609.

8.
See, for example, ibid., 606–07; Ambroise Vollard, *Paul Cézanne* (Paris: Vollard Éditeur, 1915), 62 and 102; and Joachim Gasquet, *Cézanne* (Paris: Éditions Bernheim-Jeune, 1921), 65.

9.
Albert Boime proposed that this sculpture is a composite of two ancient Roman statues at the Louvre then thought to represent Germanicus, one being the marble Marcellus from c. 20 BCE. See *Thomas Couture and the Eclectic Vision* (New Haven, Conn.: Yale University Press, 1980), 139–41, 152–53.

10.
For recent scholarship on the photography of sculpture, see Roxana Marcoci, ed., *The Original Copy: Photography of Sculpture, 1893 to Today* (New York: The Museum of Modern Art, 2010); and Sarah Hamill and Megan R. Luke, eds., *Photography and Sculpture: The Art Object in Reproduction* (Los Angeles: Getty Research Center, 2018).

11.
Aruna D'Souza, *Cézanne's Bathers: Biography and the Erotics of Paint* (University Park: Pennsylvania State University Press, 2008), 95–96.

12.
Ibid., 26.

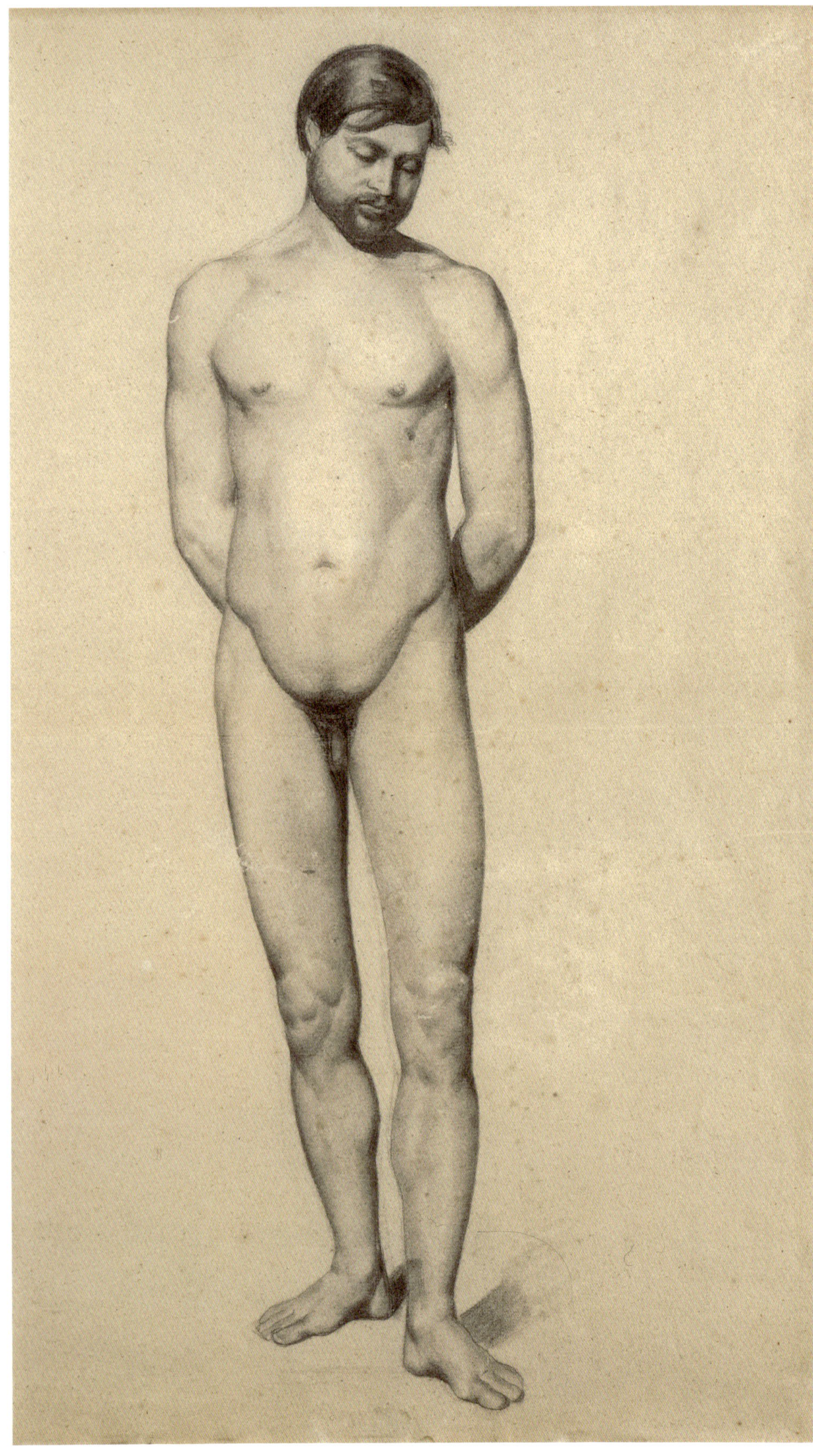

77. *Standing Male Nude: Academic Study*. 1862. Pencil on paper, 24 × 18 ½" (61 × 47 cm)

78. *After the Antique Statue of a Roman Orator*. 1887–90. Pencil on wove paper, 8 ¼ × 4 ¹³⁄₁₆" (20.9 × 12.3 cm)

79. *Bather Seen from the Back*. 1875–78. Pencil on colored wove paper, 8 ⁹⁄₁₆ × 4 ⅞" (21.8 × 12.4 cm)

80. *After Luca Signorelli: Buttocks and Legs*. 1877–80. Pencil on wove paper, 7 ¹¹⁄₁₆ × 4 ¾" (19.5 × 12 cm)

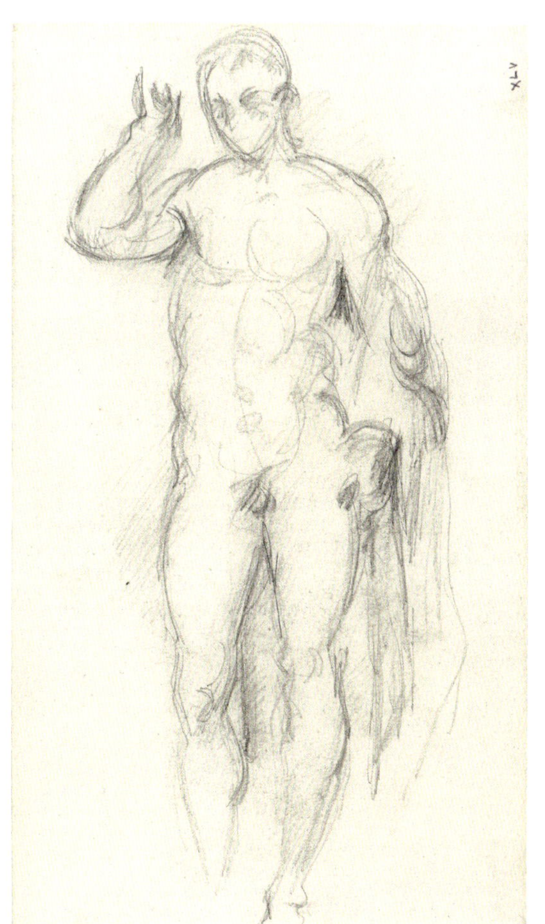

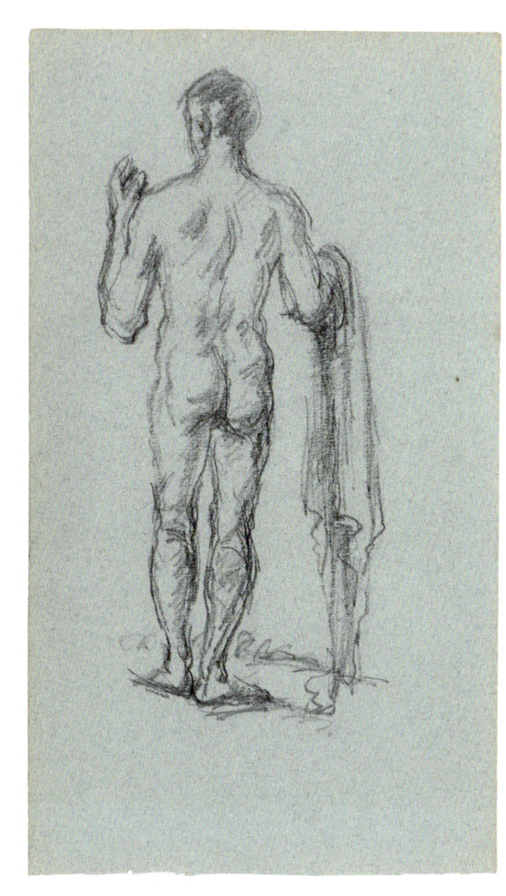

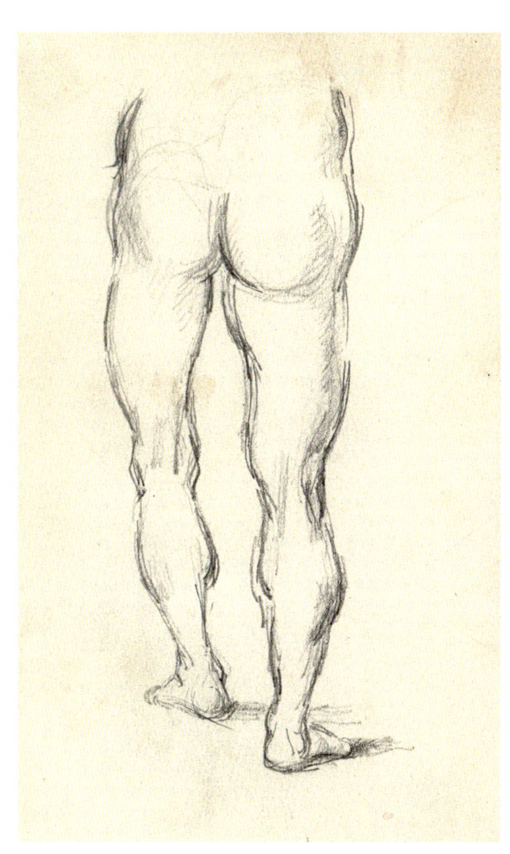

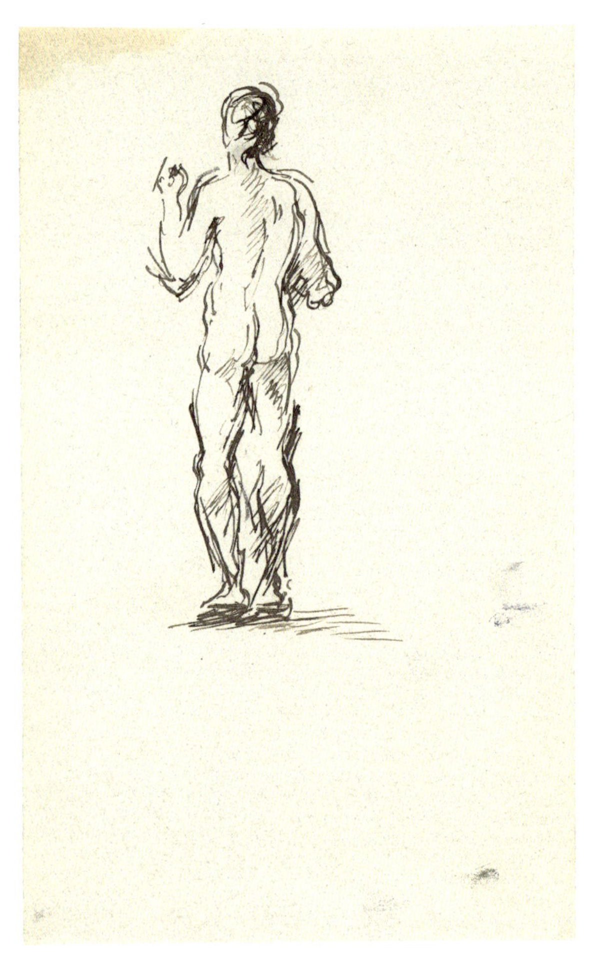

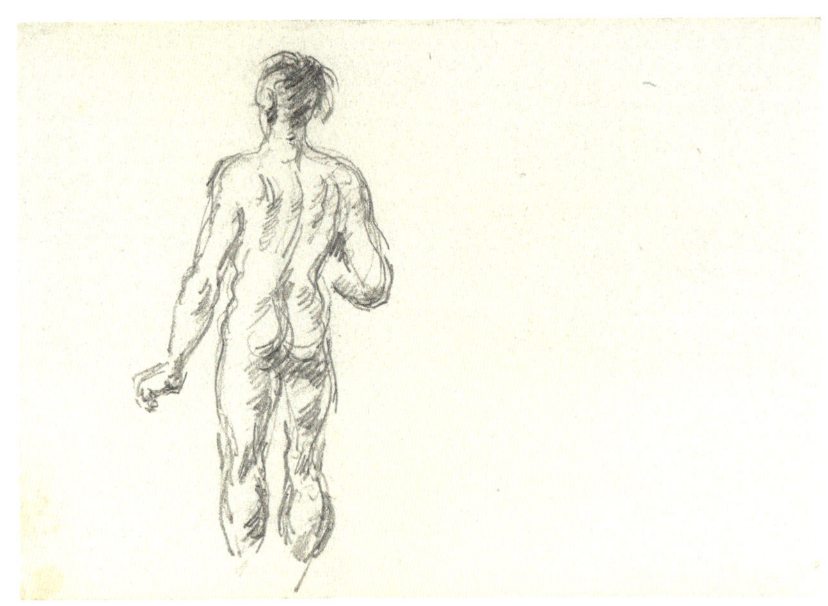

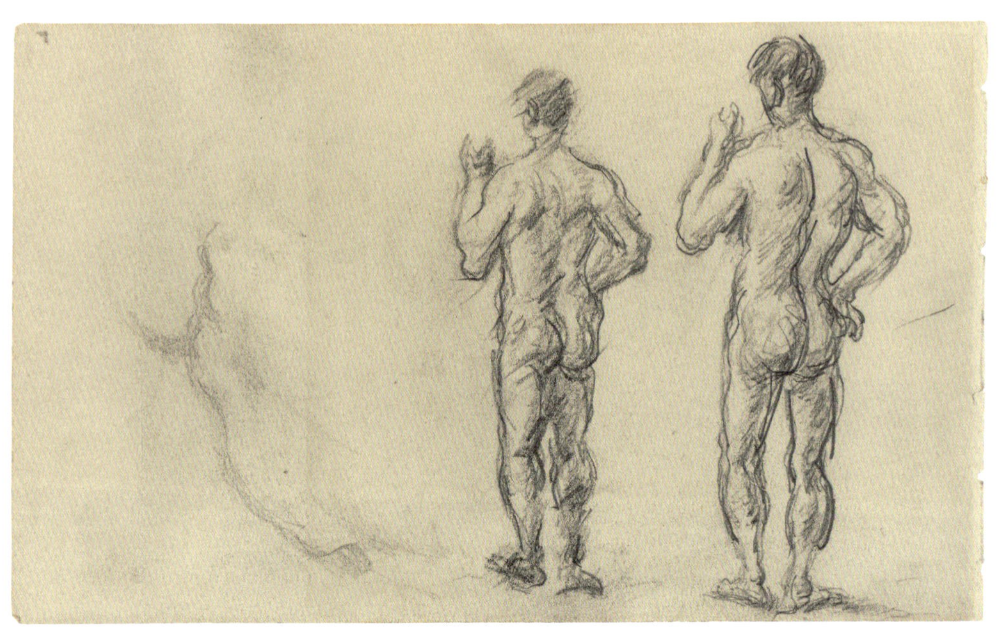

81. *Bather Seen from the Back*. 1877–80. Pencil and ink on wove paper, 7 15⁄16 × 4 7⁄8" (20.1 × 12.4 cm)

82. *Bather Seen from the Back*. 1877–80. Pencil on wove paper, 4 15⁄16 × 8 3⁄16" (12.5 × 20.8 cm)

83. *Two Standing Bathers*. 1876–79. Page L from Sketchbook Philadelphia II. Pencil on wove paper, 5 × 8 1⁄2" (12.7 × 21.6 cm)

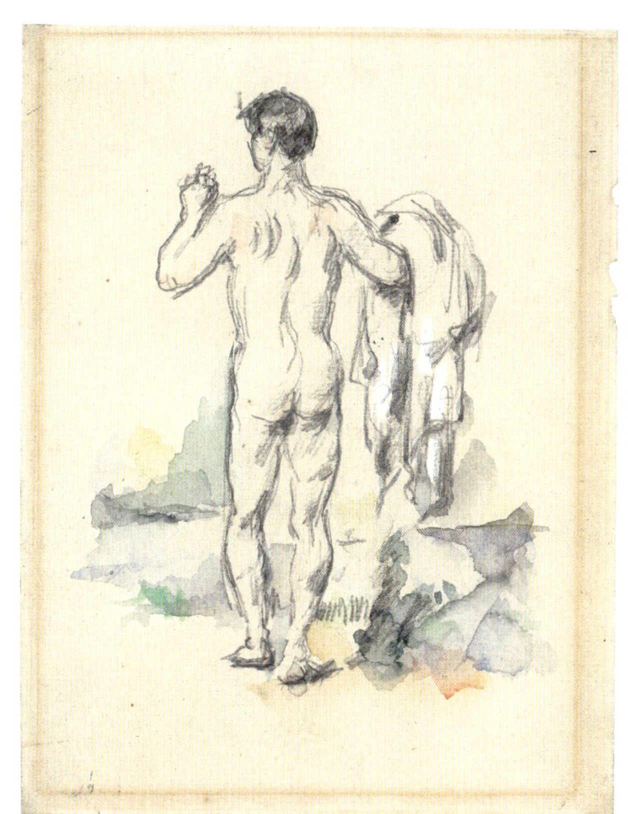

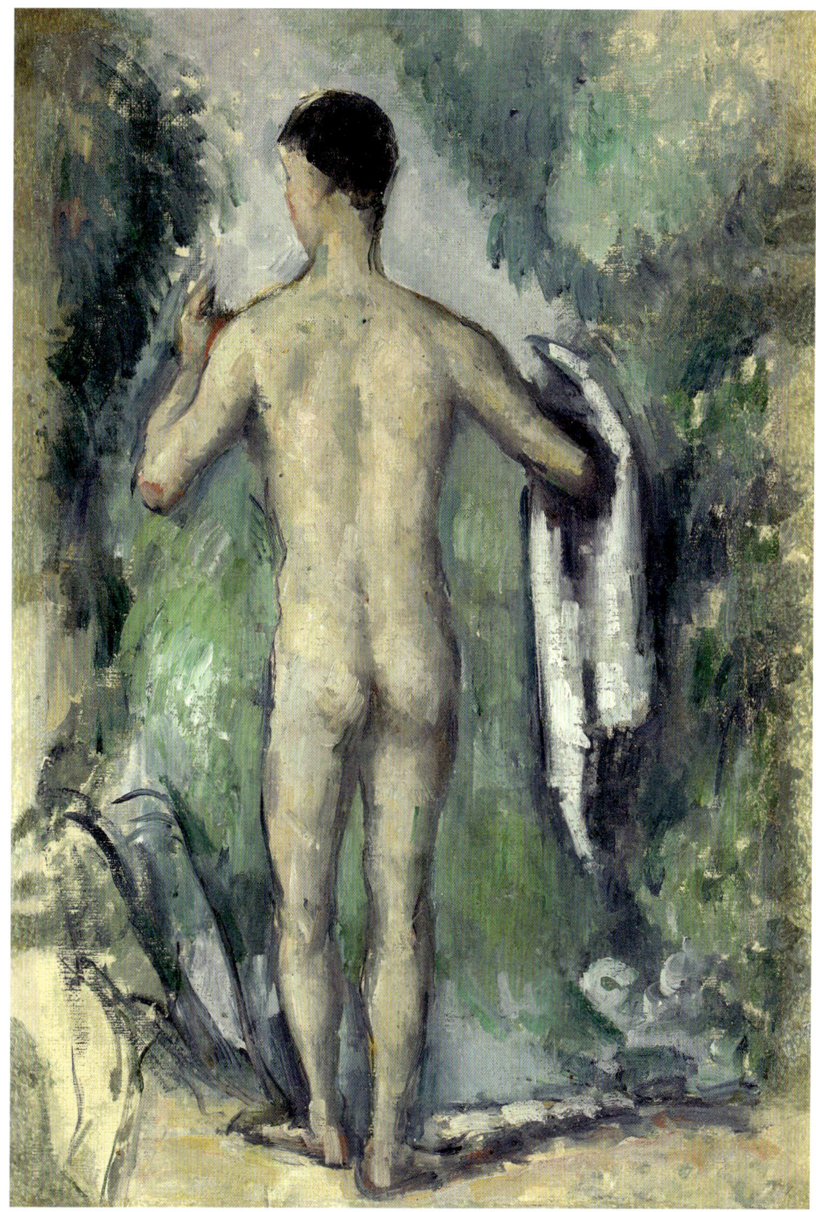

84. *The Bather*. c. 1885.
Pencil, watercolor, and gouache on laid paper, 8 ¾ × 6 ¾" (22.3 × 17.1 cm)

85. *Standing Bather, Seen from the Back*. 1879–82.
Oil on canvas, 12 ½ × 8 ½" (31.7 × 21.6 cm)

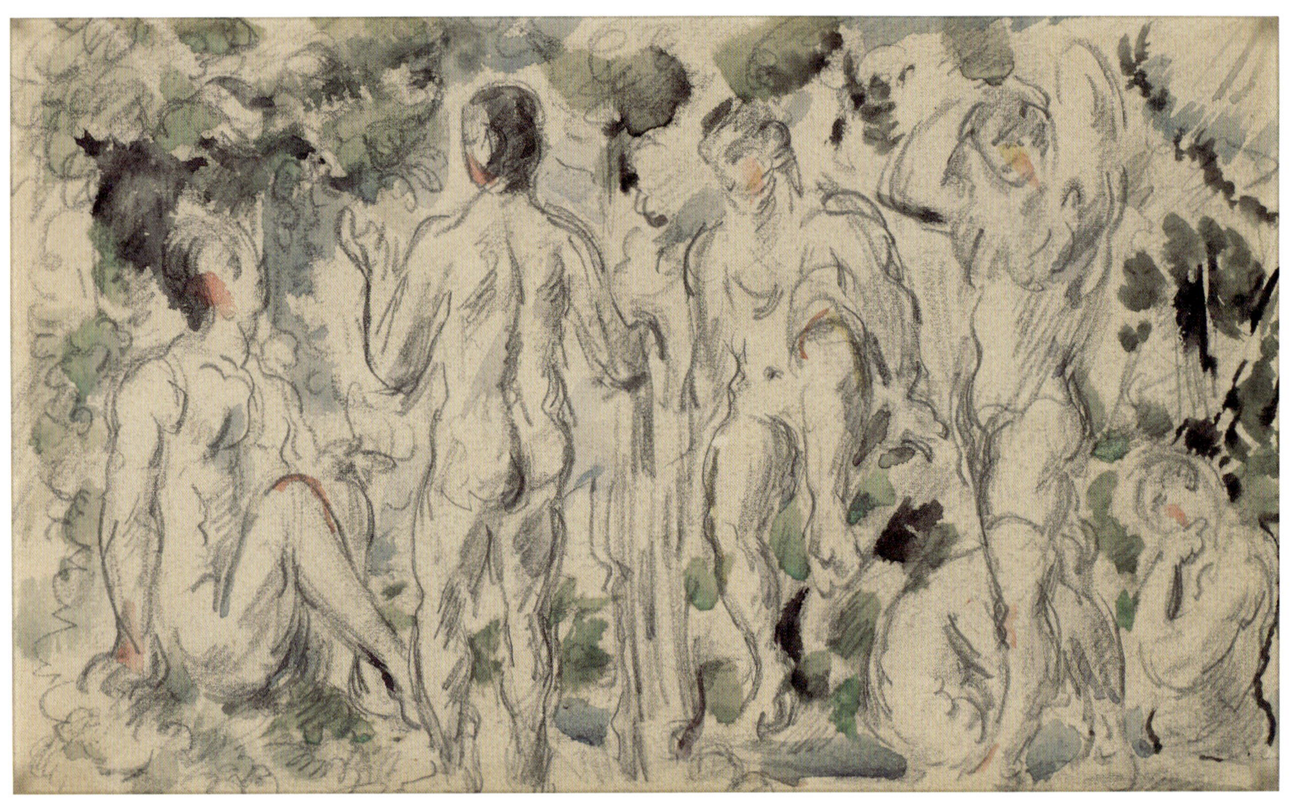

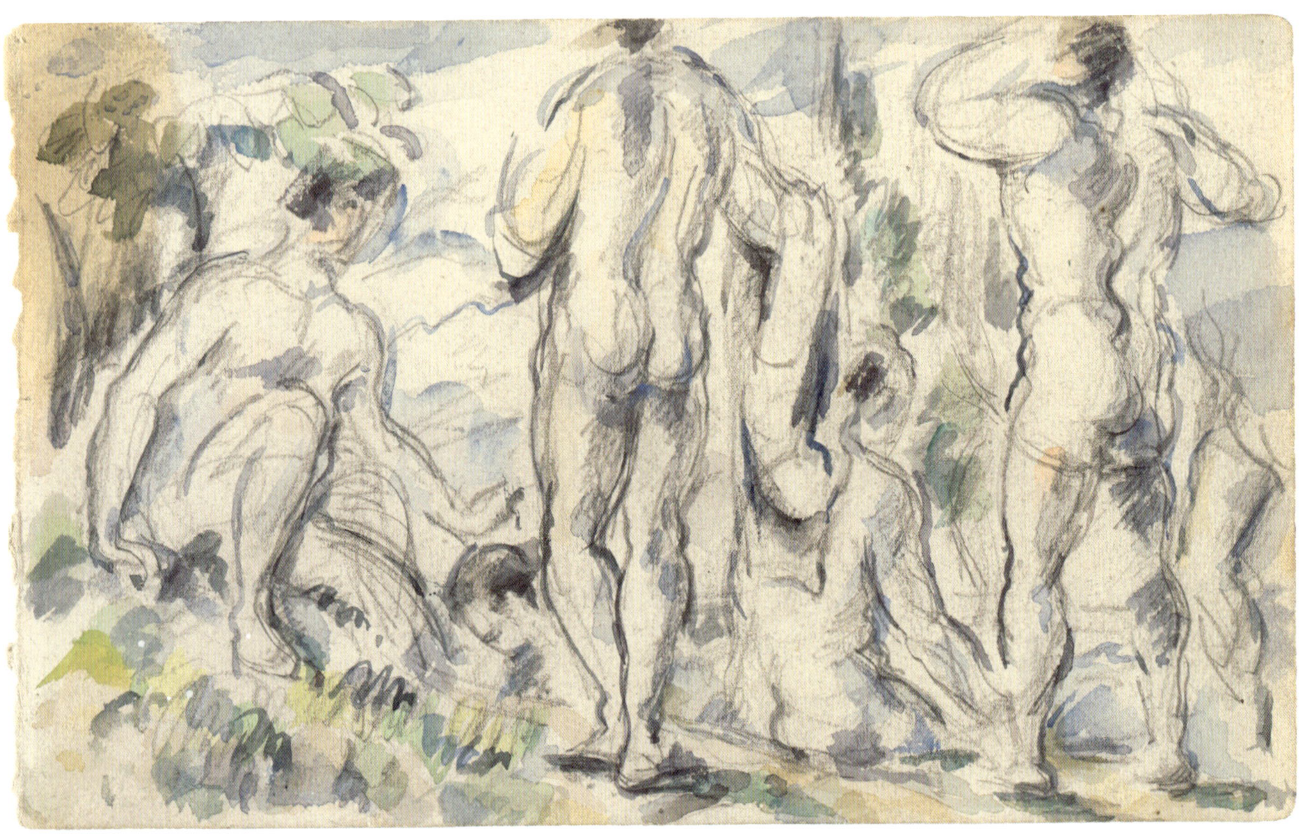

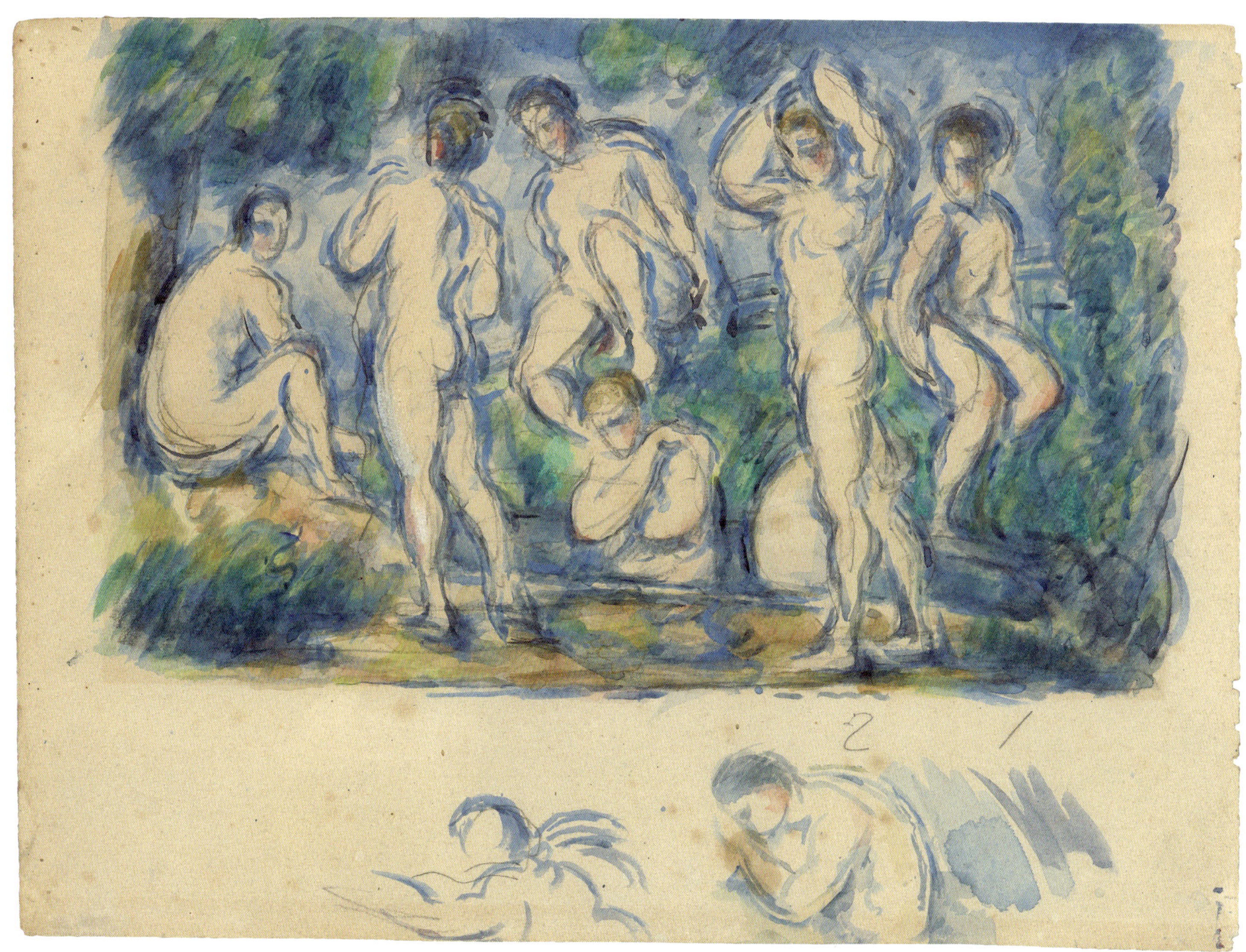

86. *Group of Male Bathers*. c. 1880. Pencil and watercolor on wove paper, 4 5/8 × 7 3/4" (11.8 × 19.7 cm)

87. *Bathers*. 1885–90. Watercolor and pencil on wove paper, 5 × 8 1/8" (12.7 × 20.6 cm)

88. *The Bathers*. c. 1900. Pencil and watercolor on wove paper, 7 15/16 × 10 13/16" (20.2 × 27.5 cm)

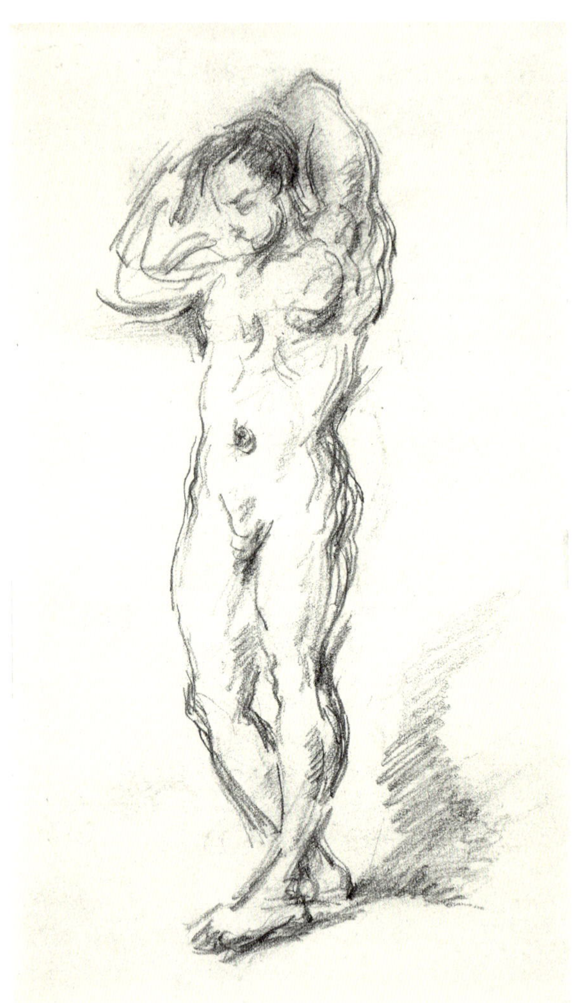

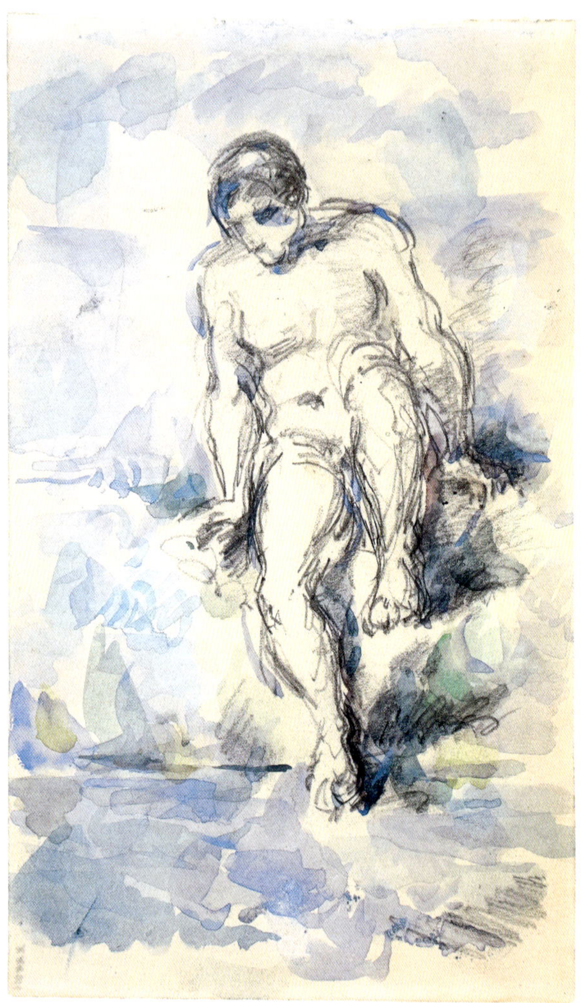

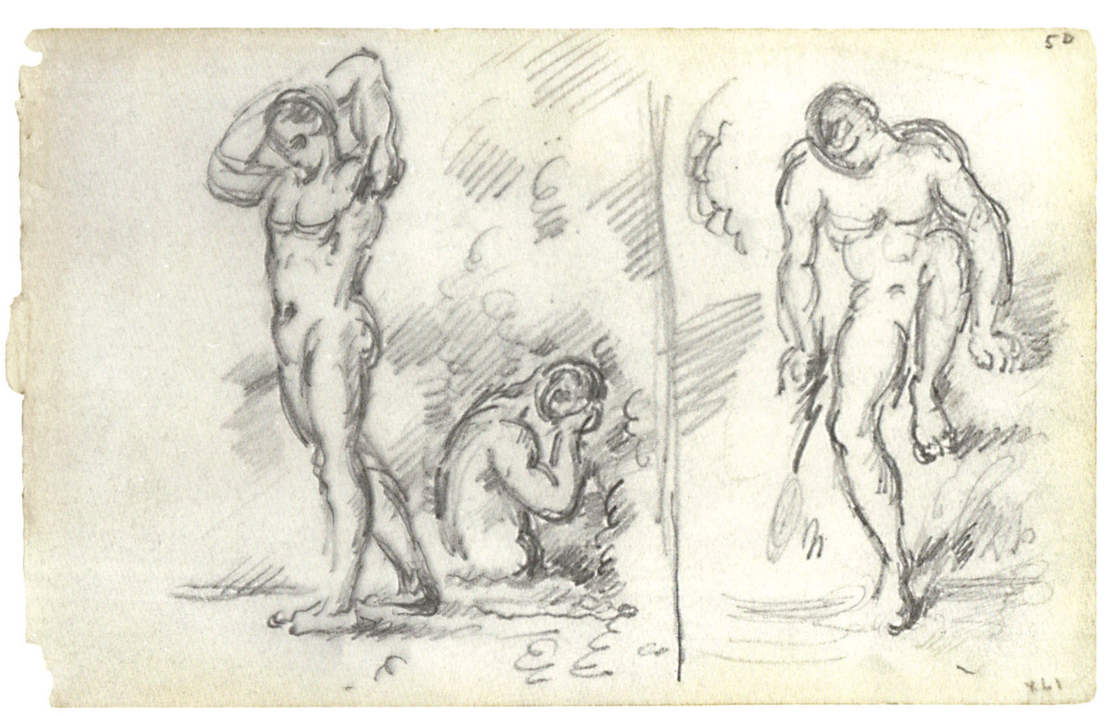

89. *Standing Bather* (verso); *Bather* (recto). 1879–82 (verso); c. 1885 (recto). Pencil on wove paper (verso); pencil and watercolor on wove paper (recto), 8 ¼ × 5 ⅛" (21 × 13 cm)

90. *Two Studies of Bathers*. 1872–75. Pencil and ink on wove paper, 4 ¾ × 7 ¹¹⁄₁₆" (12 × 19.5 cm)

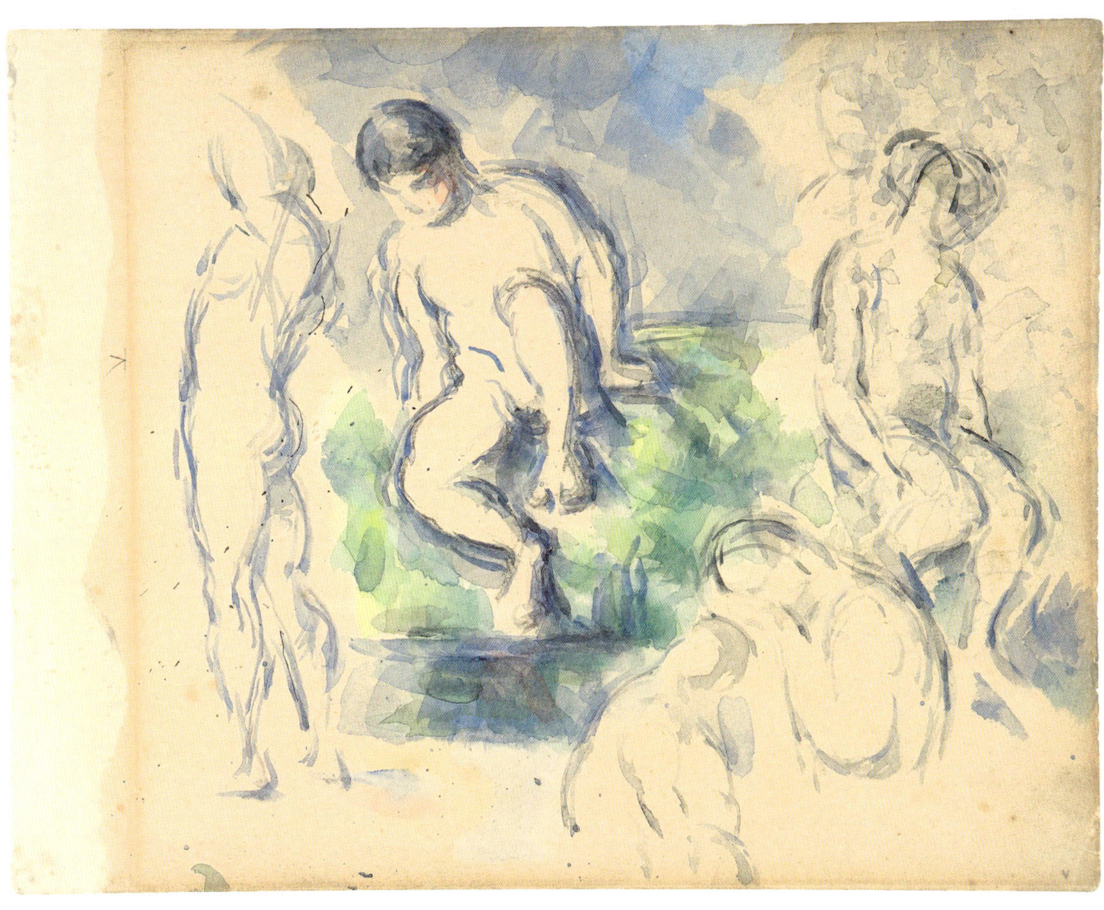

91. *Bathers*. c. 1890 (possibly later). Pencil and watercolor on wove paper, 8 5⁄16 × 10 11⁄16" (21.1 × 27.2 cm)

92. *Three Bathers*. c. 1881. Pencil and watercolor on wove paper, 7 1⁄16 × 4 5⁄16" (18 × 11 cm)

93. *Bather Stepping Down into the Water*. c. 1886–89. Pencil and ink on colored wove paper, 7 7⁄8 × 4 3⁄4" (20 × 12 cm)

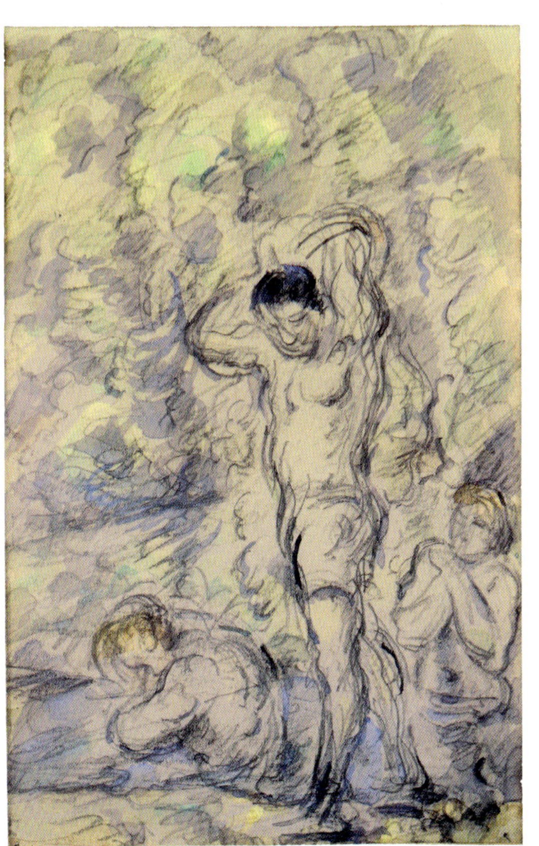

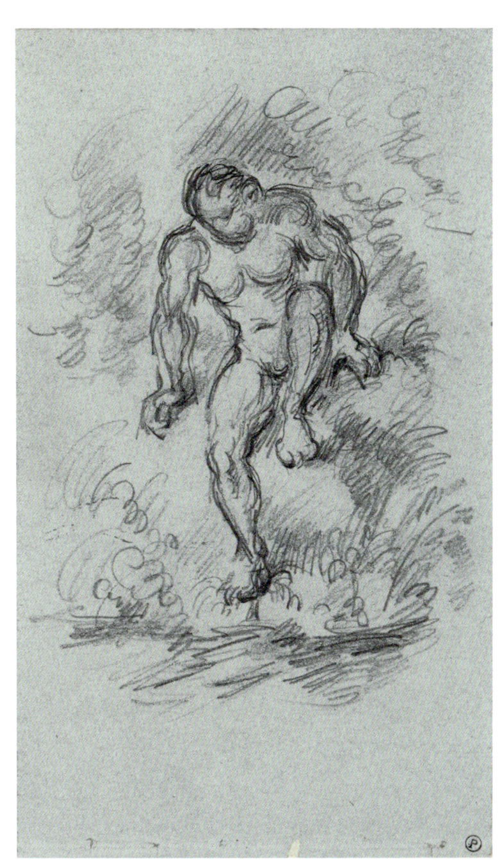

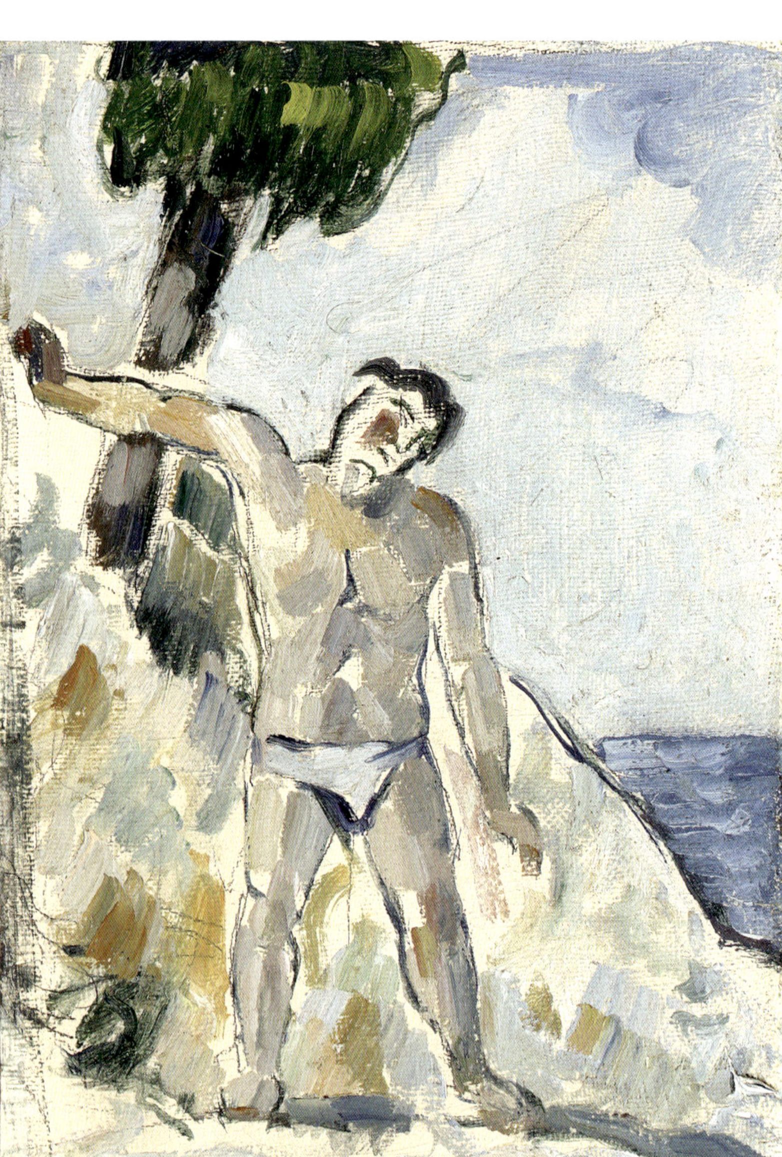

94. *Bather with Outstretched Arms*. c. 1876. Oil on canvas, 9 7/16 × 6 5/16" (24 × 16 cm)

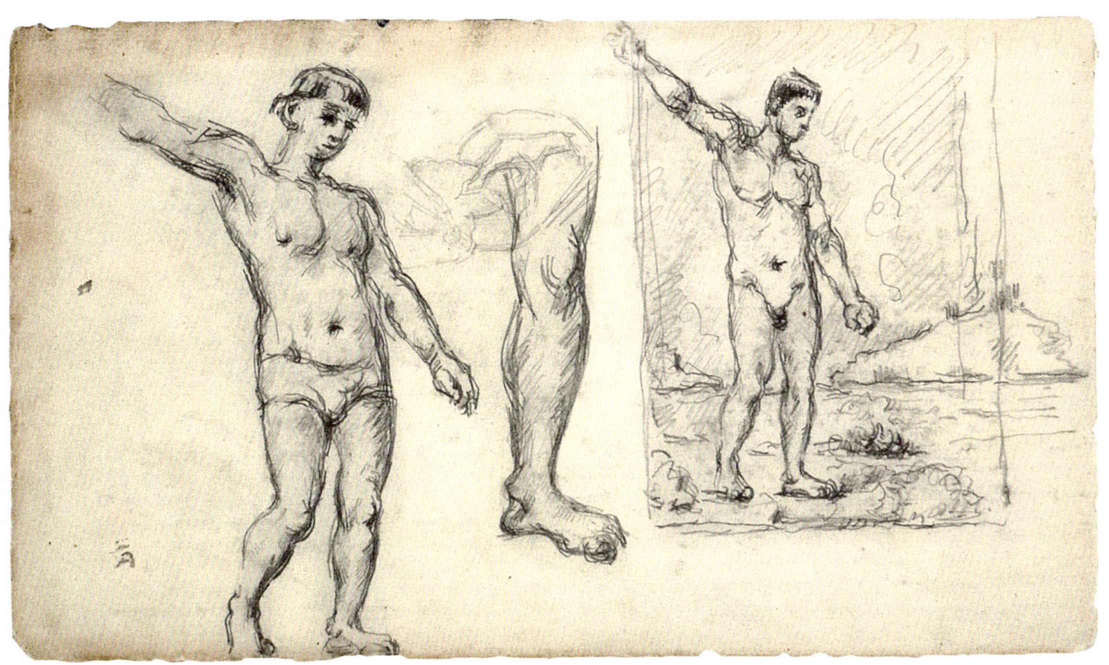

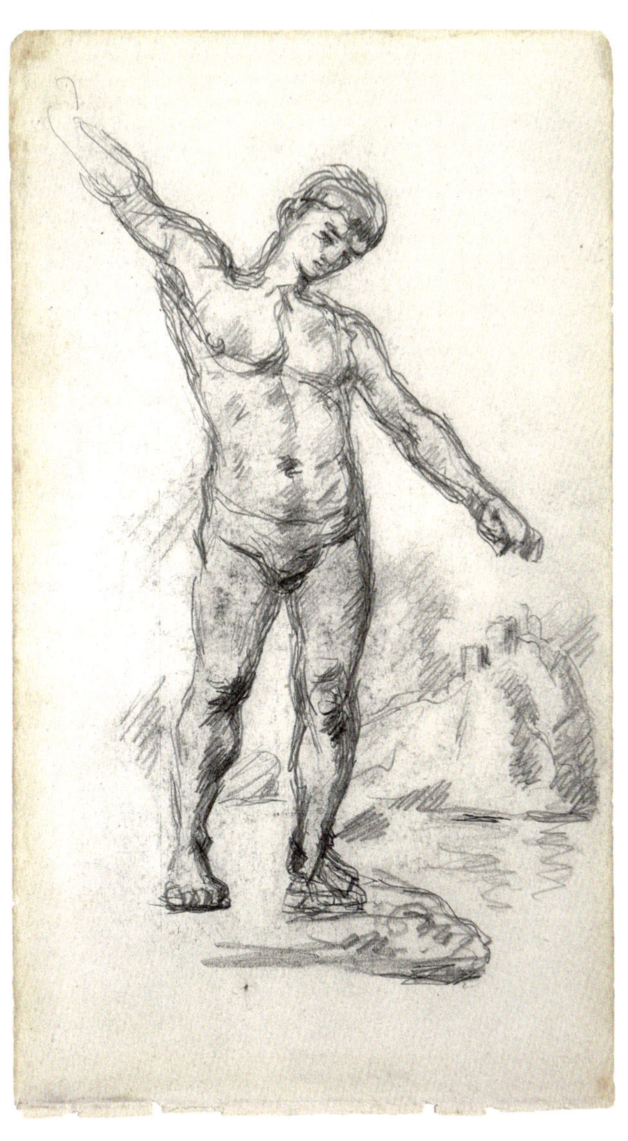

95. *Bathers, Caryatid*. c. 1883–86. Pencil on wove paper, 4 15⁄16 × 8 1⁄2" (12.5 × 21.6 cm)

96. *Bather with Outstretched Arms*. c. 1883–86. Pencil on wove paper, 8 11⁄16 × 4 15⁄16" (22 × 12.5 cm)

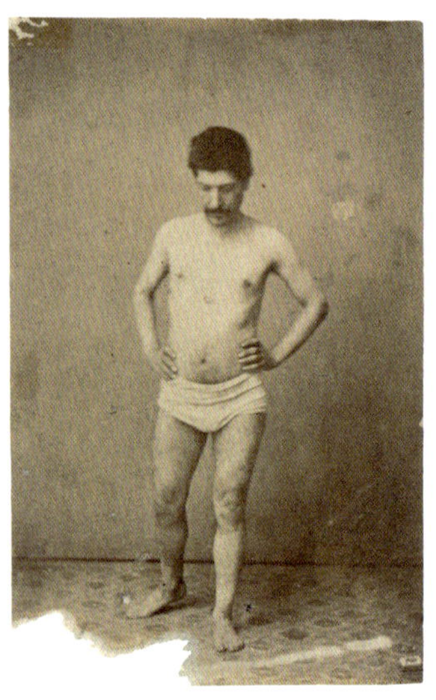

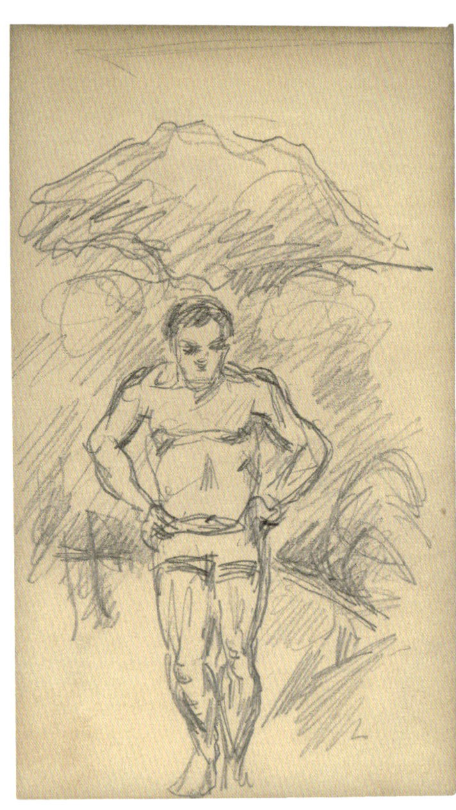

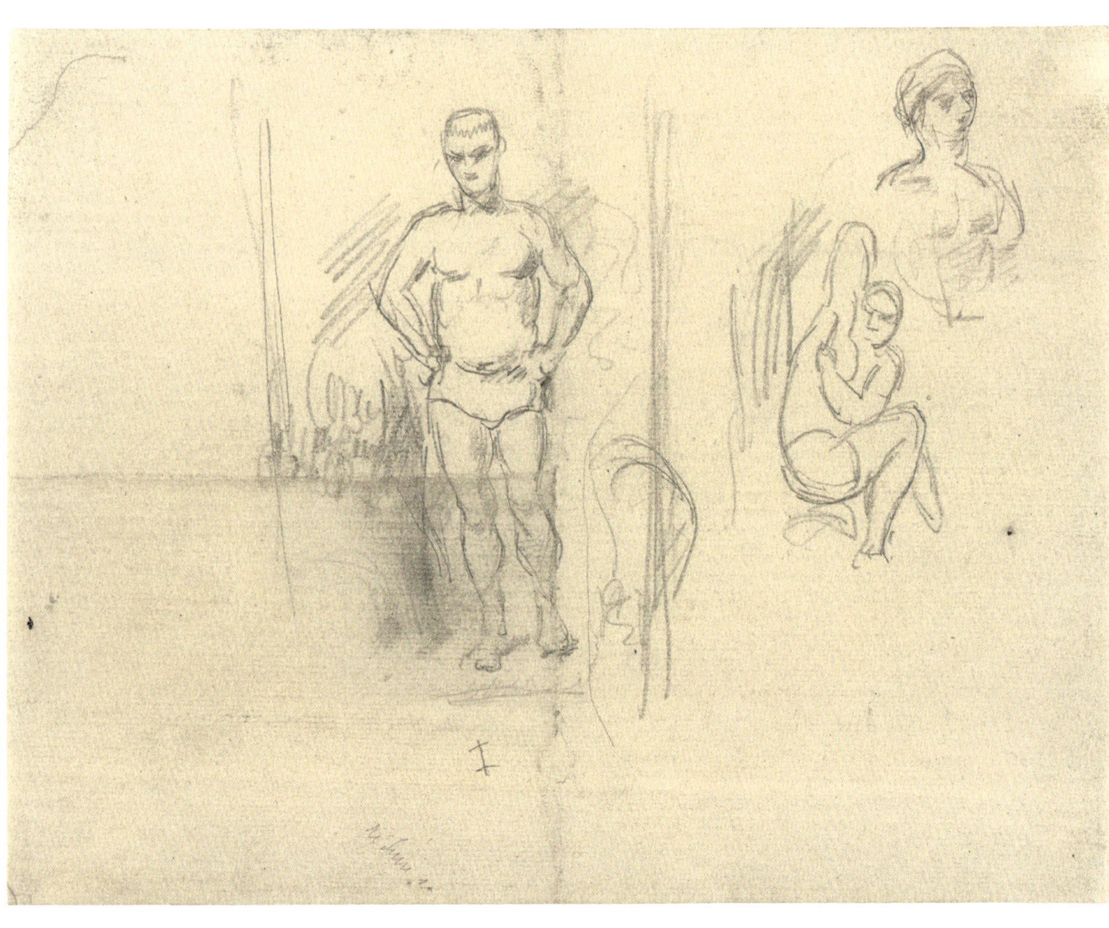

97. Unknown photographer. Untitled (Portrait of the Model for *The Bather*). c. 1885. Albumen silver print, 5 1/2 × 3 7/16" (13.9 × 8.8 cm)

98. *Standing Bather, in front of Mont Sainte-Victoire*. c. 1883–85. Page 27 verso from Sketchbook New York. Pencil on wove paper, 8 9/16 × 4 15/16" (21.7 × 12.6 cm)

99. *Study of Bathers*. 1886–89. Pencil on paper, 8 15/16 × 11 5/8" (22.7 × 29.5 cm)

100. *The Bather*. c. 1885. Oil on canvas, 50 × 38 1/8" (127 × 96.8 cm)

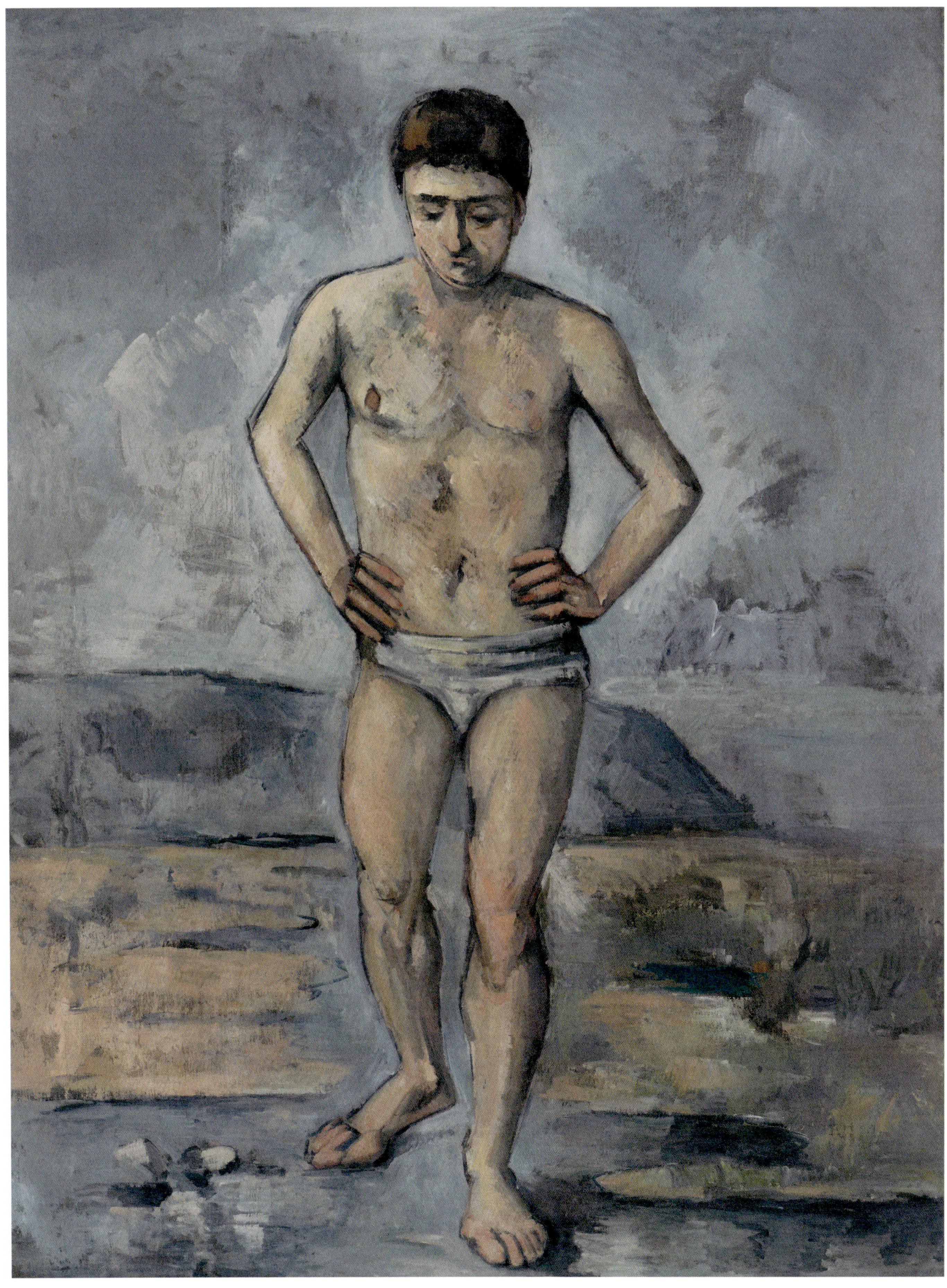

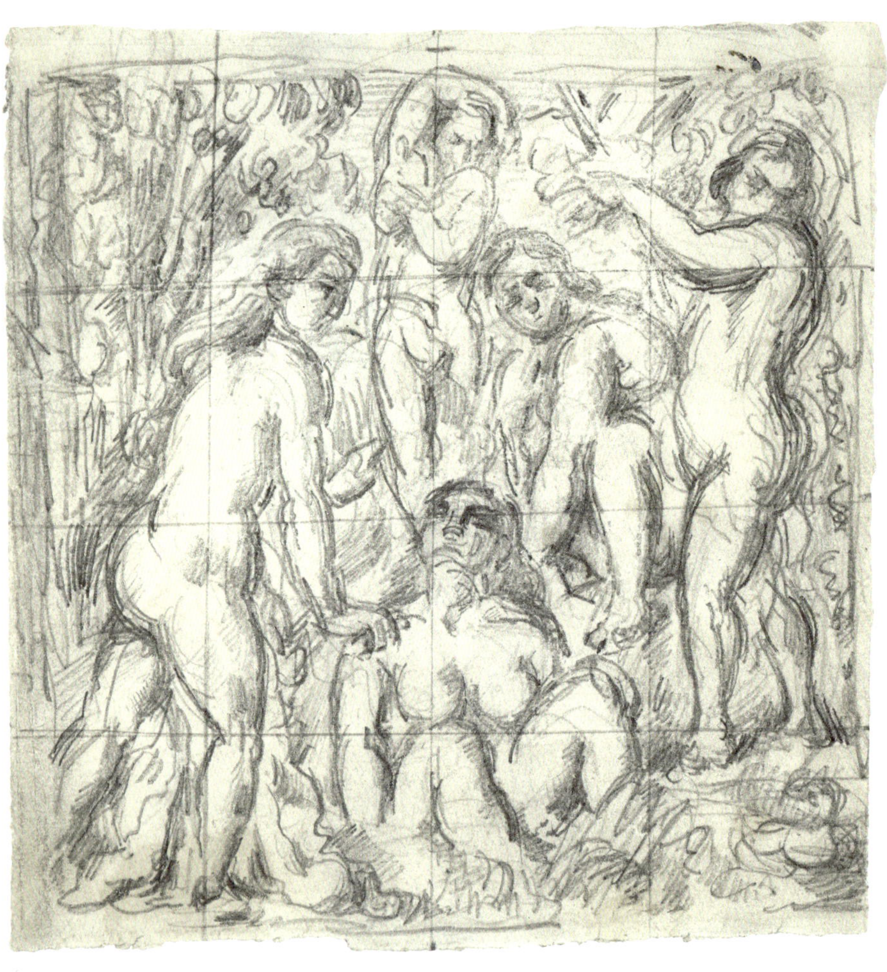

101. *Five Bathers*. 1879–82. Pencil on paper, 5 ¾ × 5 ¼" (14.6 × 13.3 cm)

102. *Bathers*. 1870–75. Pencil and watercolor on paper, 4 ½ × 9 ½" (11.4 × 24.2 cm)

103. *Bathers under a Bridge*. 1900–06. Pencil and watercolor on wove paper, 8 ¼ × 10 ¹¹⁄₁₆" (21 × 27.2 cm)

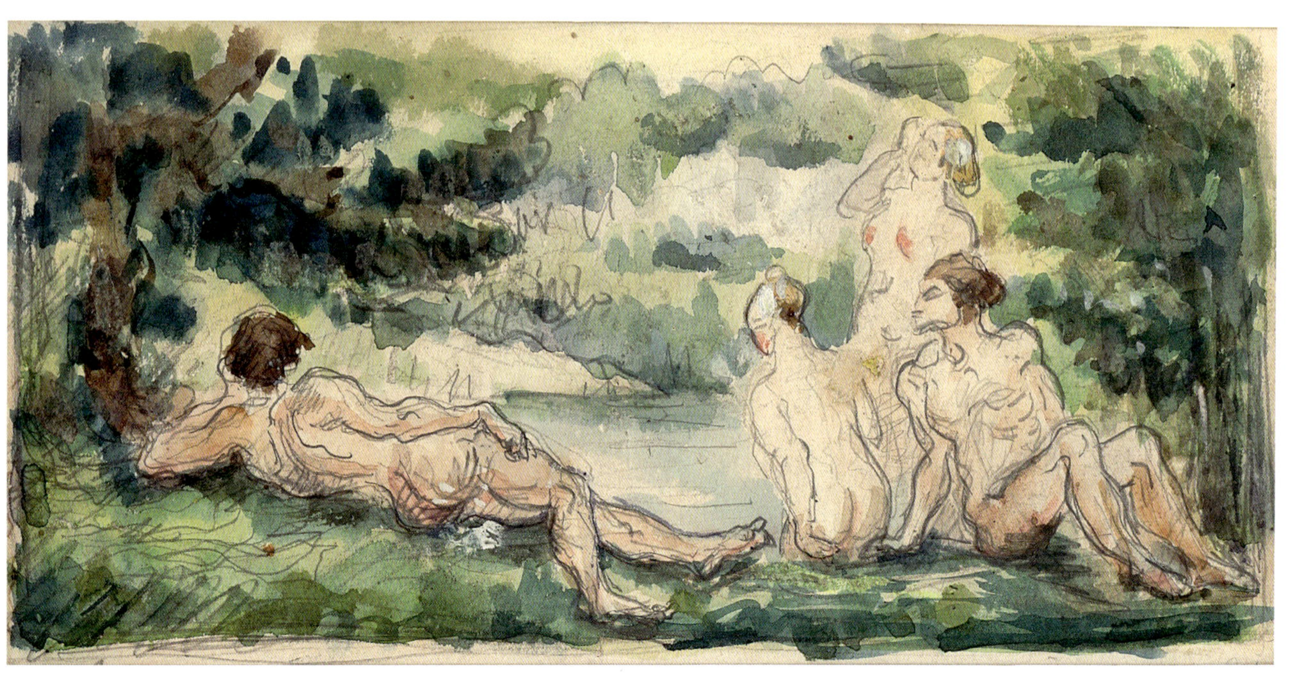

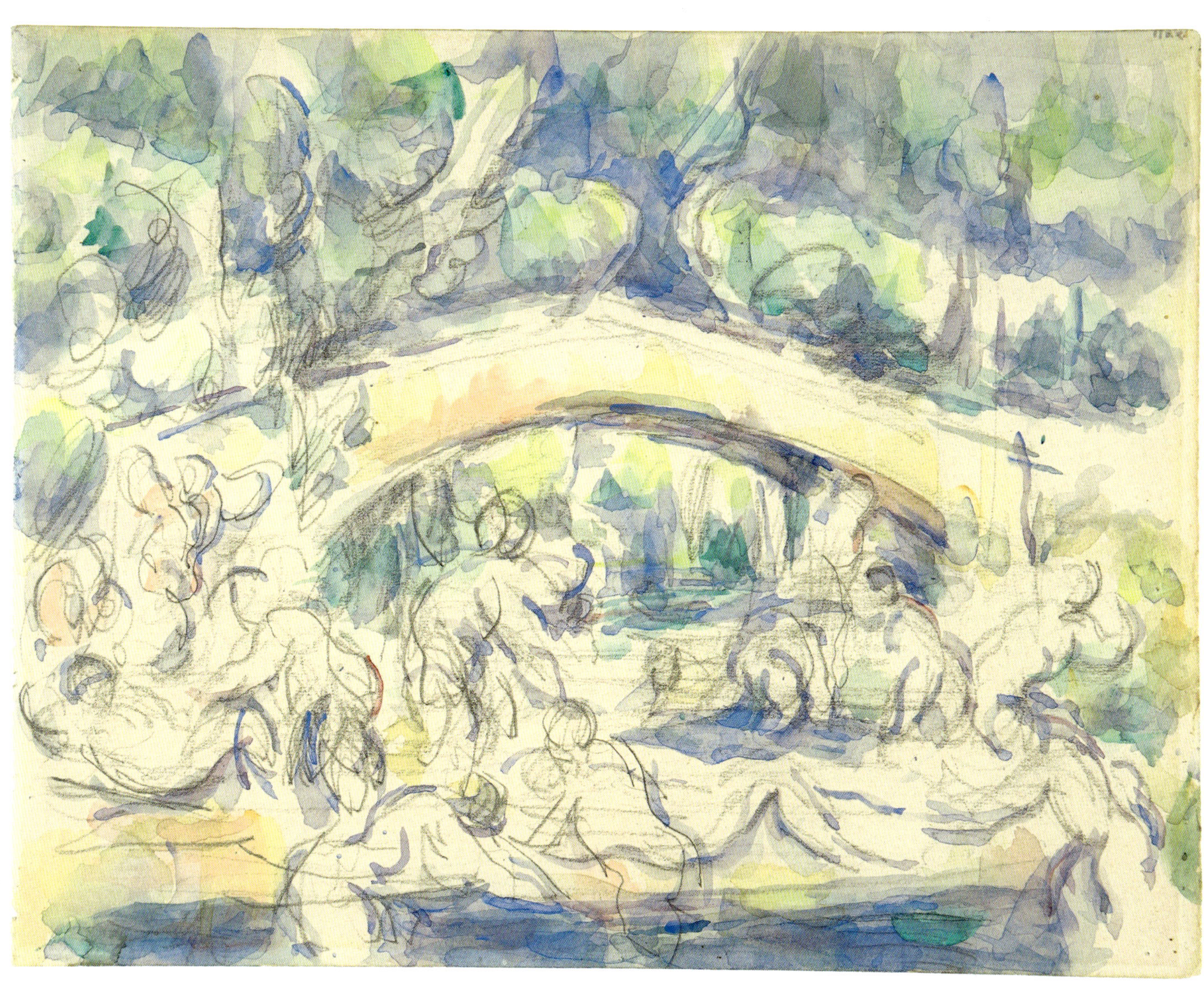

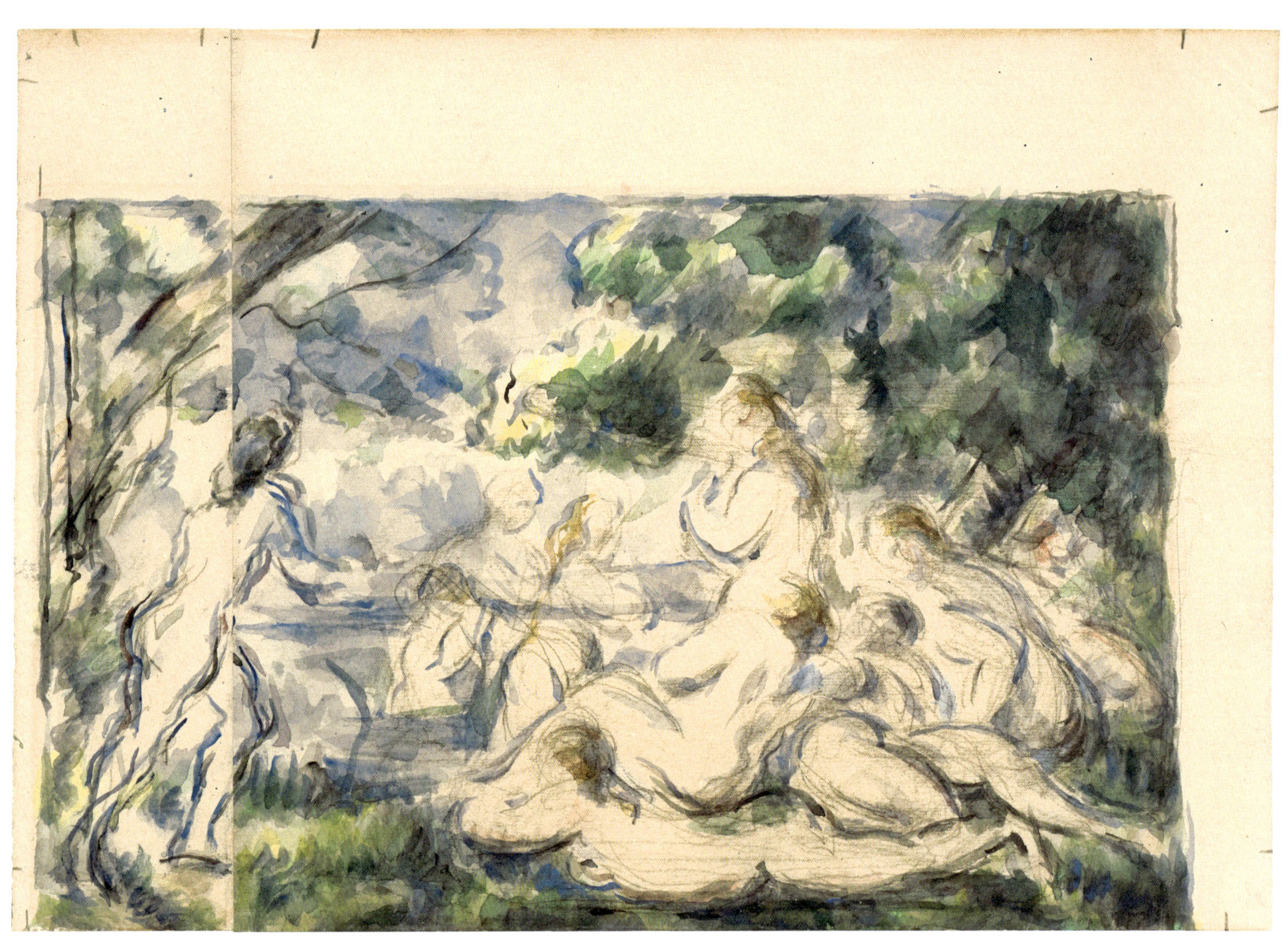

104. *Female Bathers.*
1900–06. Pencil and watercolor on laid paper, with strip added at left, 6 11⁄16 × 10 5⁄8" (17 × 27 cm)

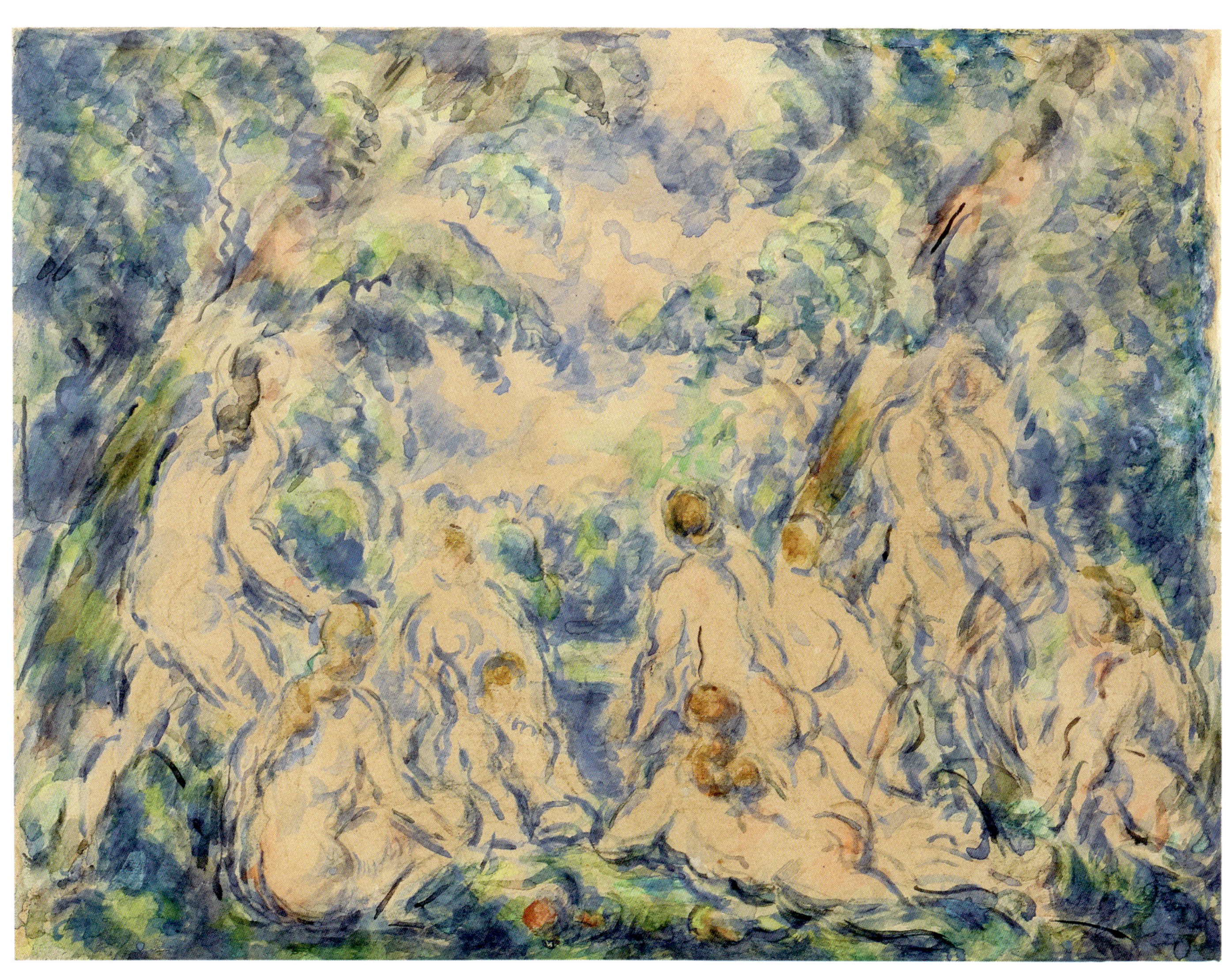

105. *Bathers*. 1900–06.
Watercolor on wove
paper, 7 1/16 × 9 13/16"
(18 × 25 cm)

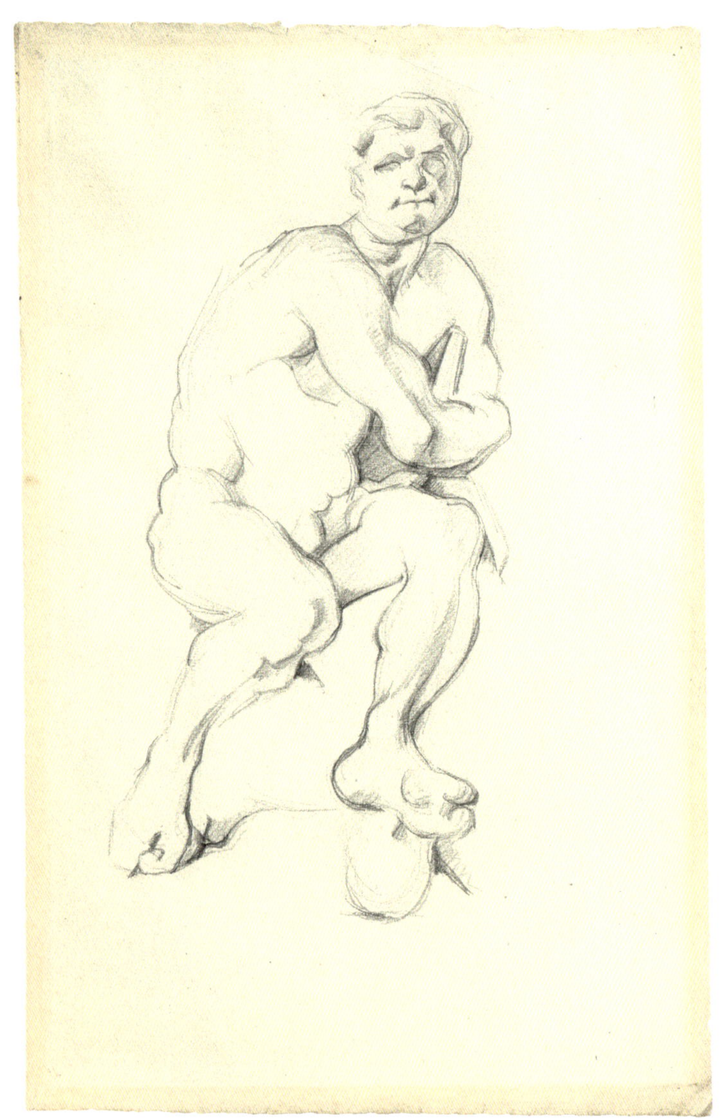

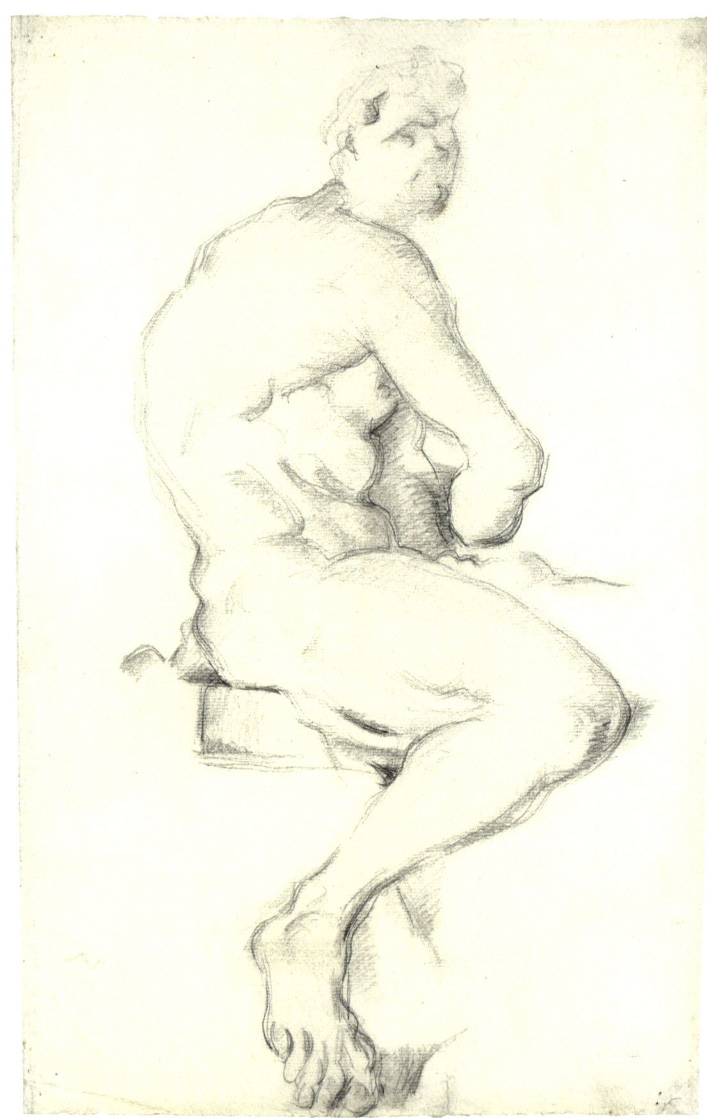

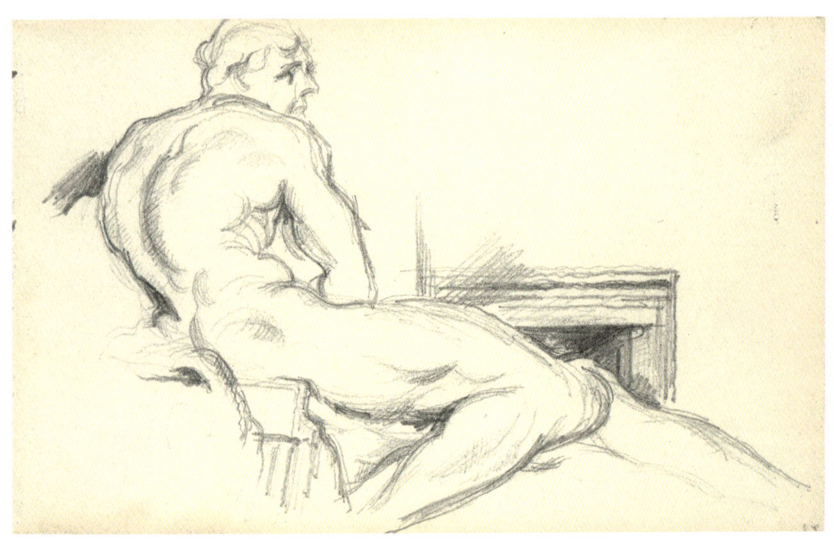

106. *Study after the Hercules Sculpture by Pierre Puget in the Louvre*. 1884–87. Pencil on laid paper, 18 ⅝ × 12 5⁄16" (47.3 × 31.3 cm)

107. *After Puget: Hercules Resting*. 1887–90. Pencil on paper, 19 × 12 ⅜" (48.3 × 31.5 cm)

108. *Hercules Resting*. 1884–87. Pencil on wove paper, 4 ⅝ × 7 ⅝" (11.8 × 19.4 cm)

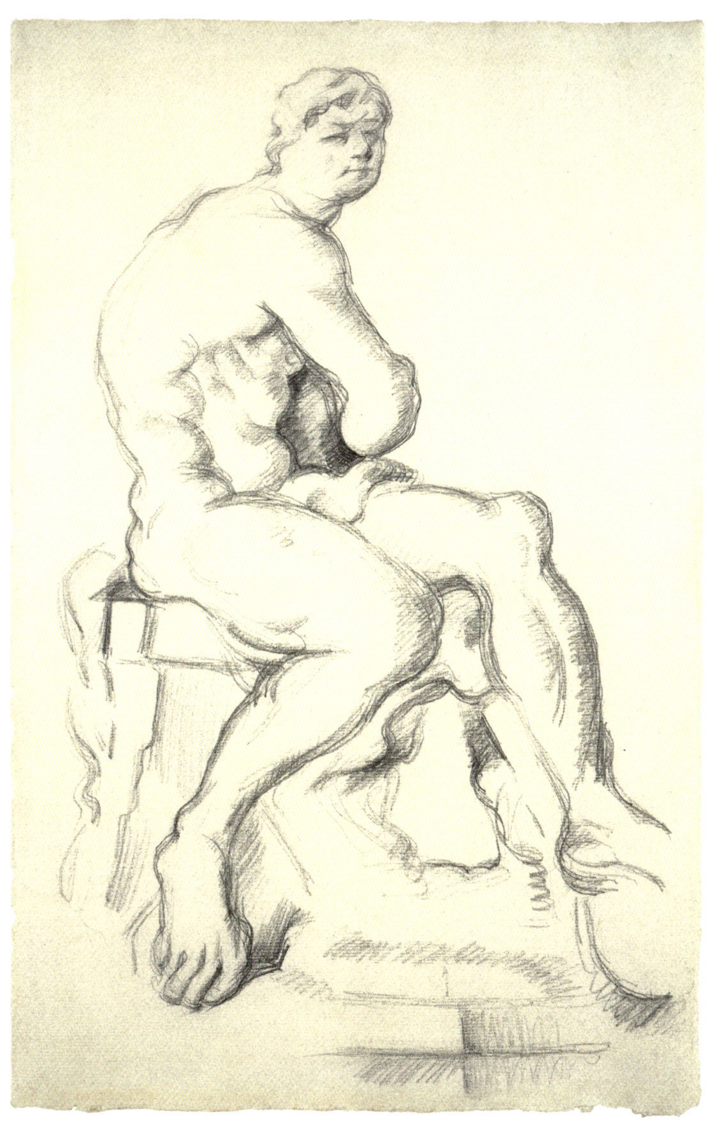

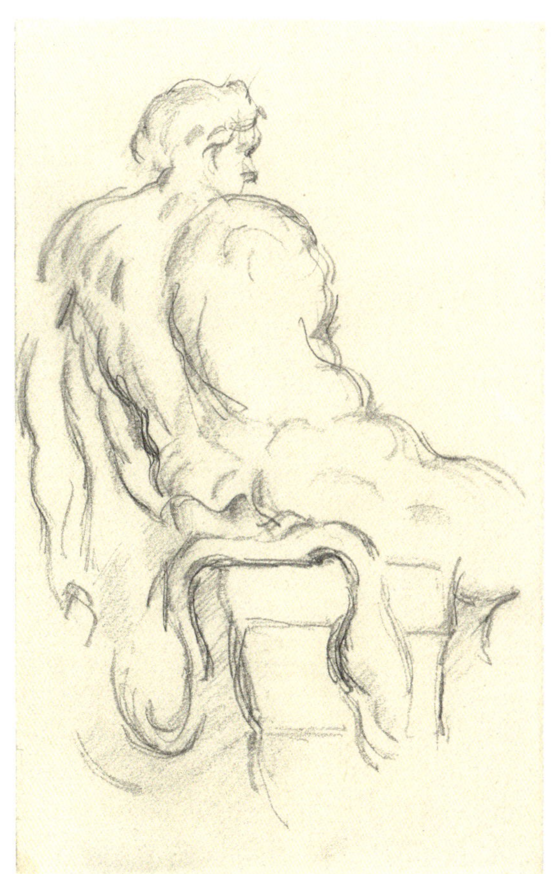

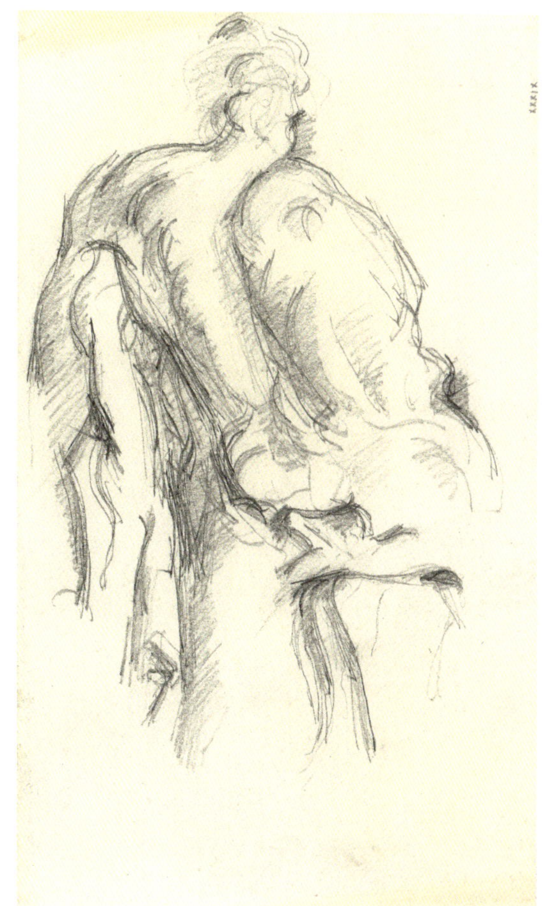

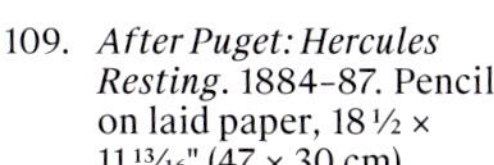

109. *After Puget: Hercules Resting*. 1884–87. Pencil on laid paper, 18½ × 11 13/16" (47 × 30 cm)

110. *After Puget: Hercules Resting*. 1894–97. Pencil on wove paper, 8 3/16 × 4 15/16" (20.8 × 12.5 cm)

111. *After Puget: Hercules Resting*. 1890–94. Pencil on wove paper, 8 × 4 13/16" (20.3 × 12.2 cm)

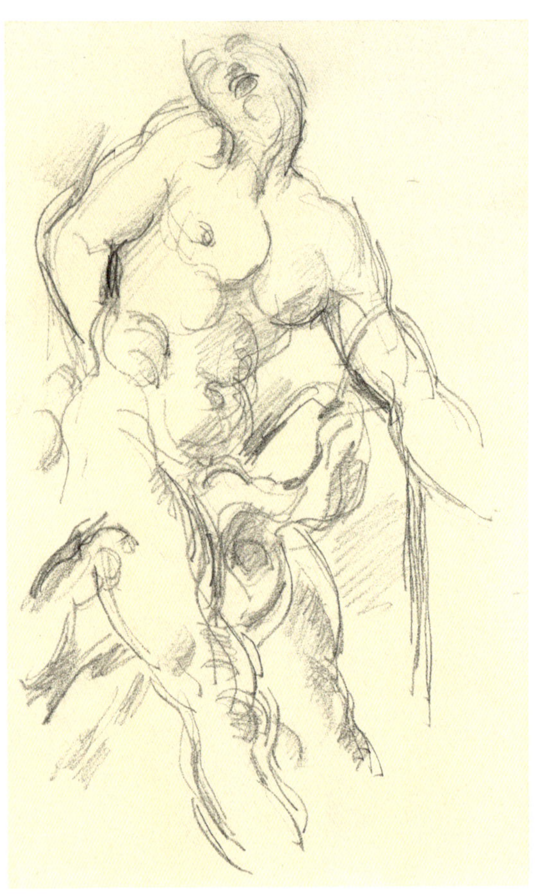

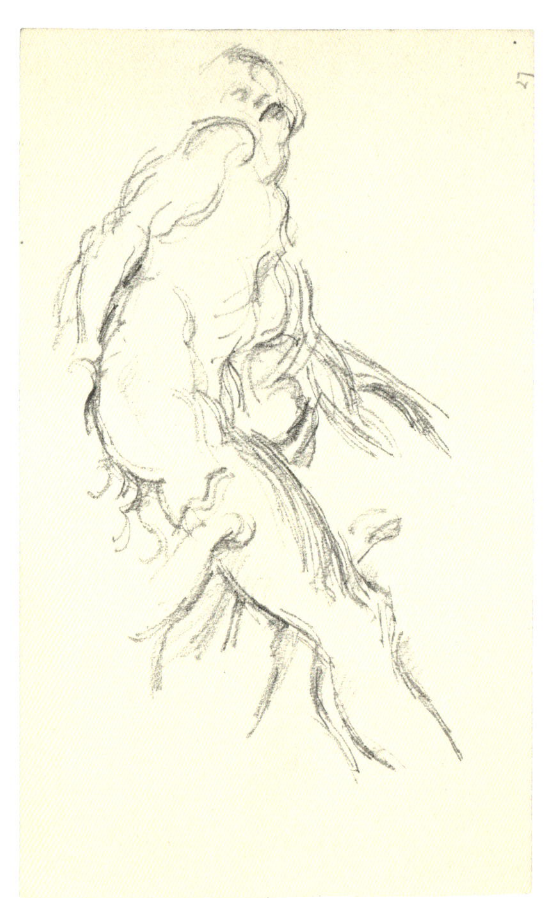

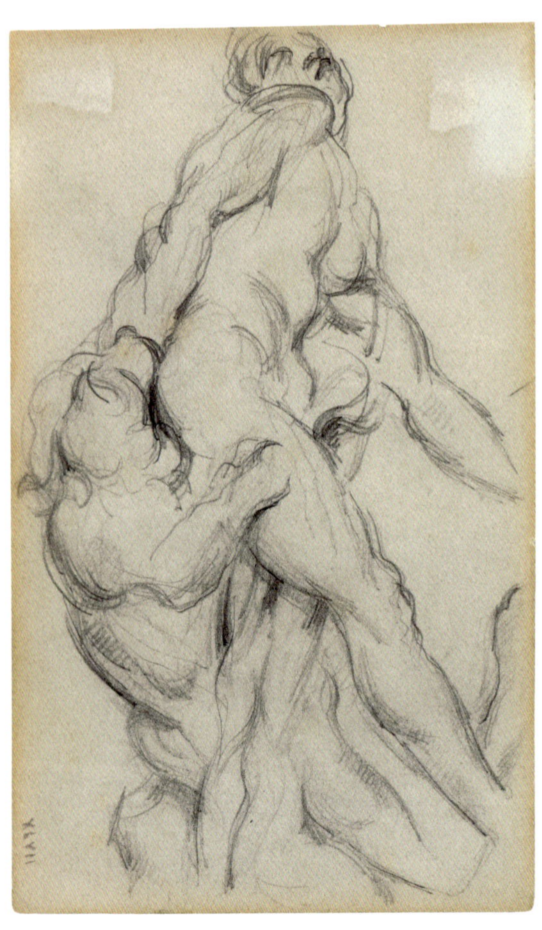

112. *After Puget: Milo of Crotona*. 1897–1900. Pencil on wove paper, 8 9/16 × 5 3/16" (21.8 × 13.1 cm)

113. *After Puget: Milo of Crotona*. 1880–83. Pencil on wove paper, 8 9/16 × 5 3/16" (21.8 × 13.2 cm)

114. *After Pierre Puget: Milo of Crotona*. c. 1882–85. Pencil on paper, 7 11/16 × 4 11/16" (19.6 × 11.9 cm)

115. *After Puget: Milo of Crotona*. c. 1890. Pencil on laid paper, 18 13/16 × 12 3/8" (47.8 × 31.4 cm)

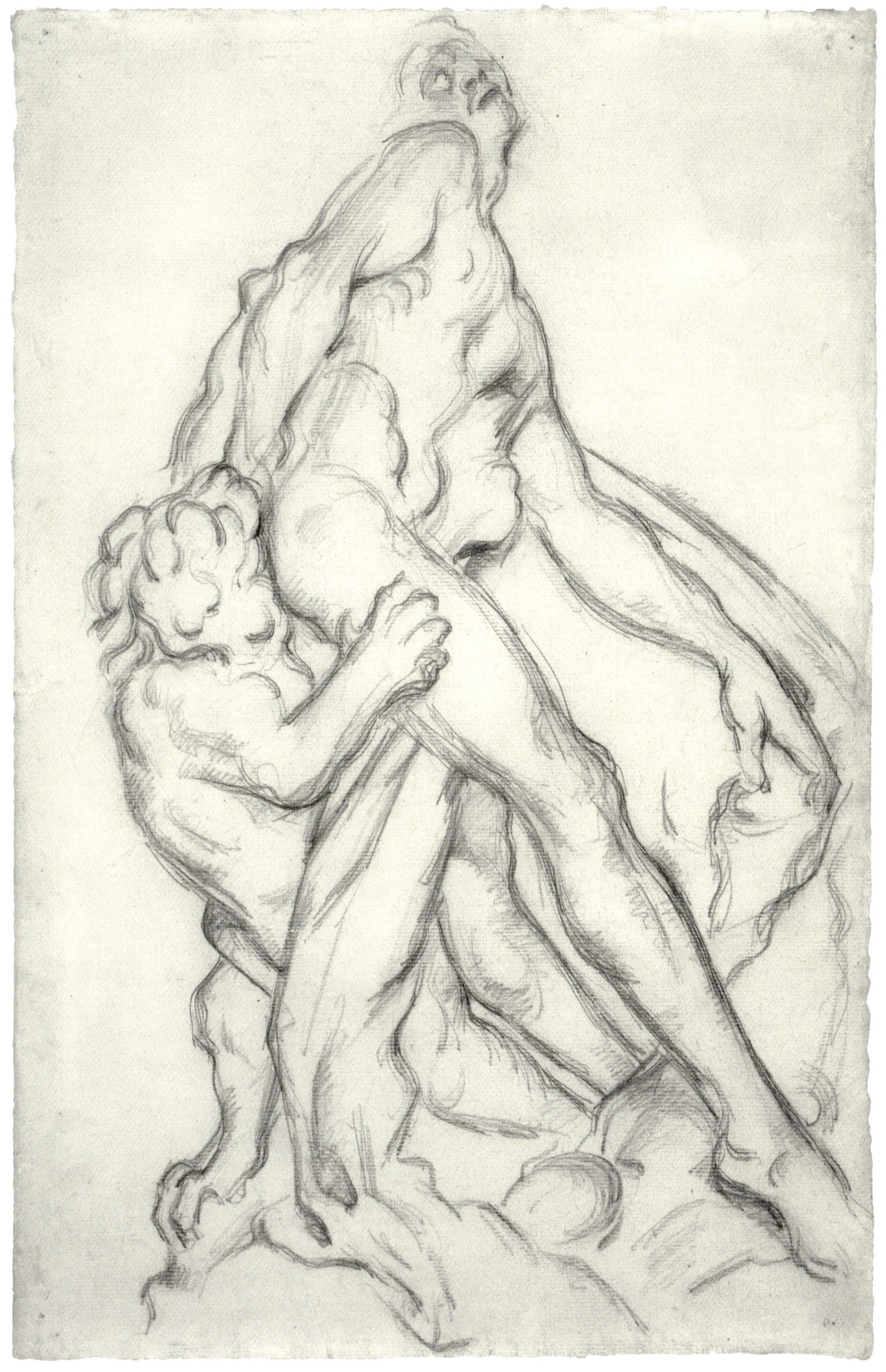

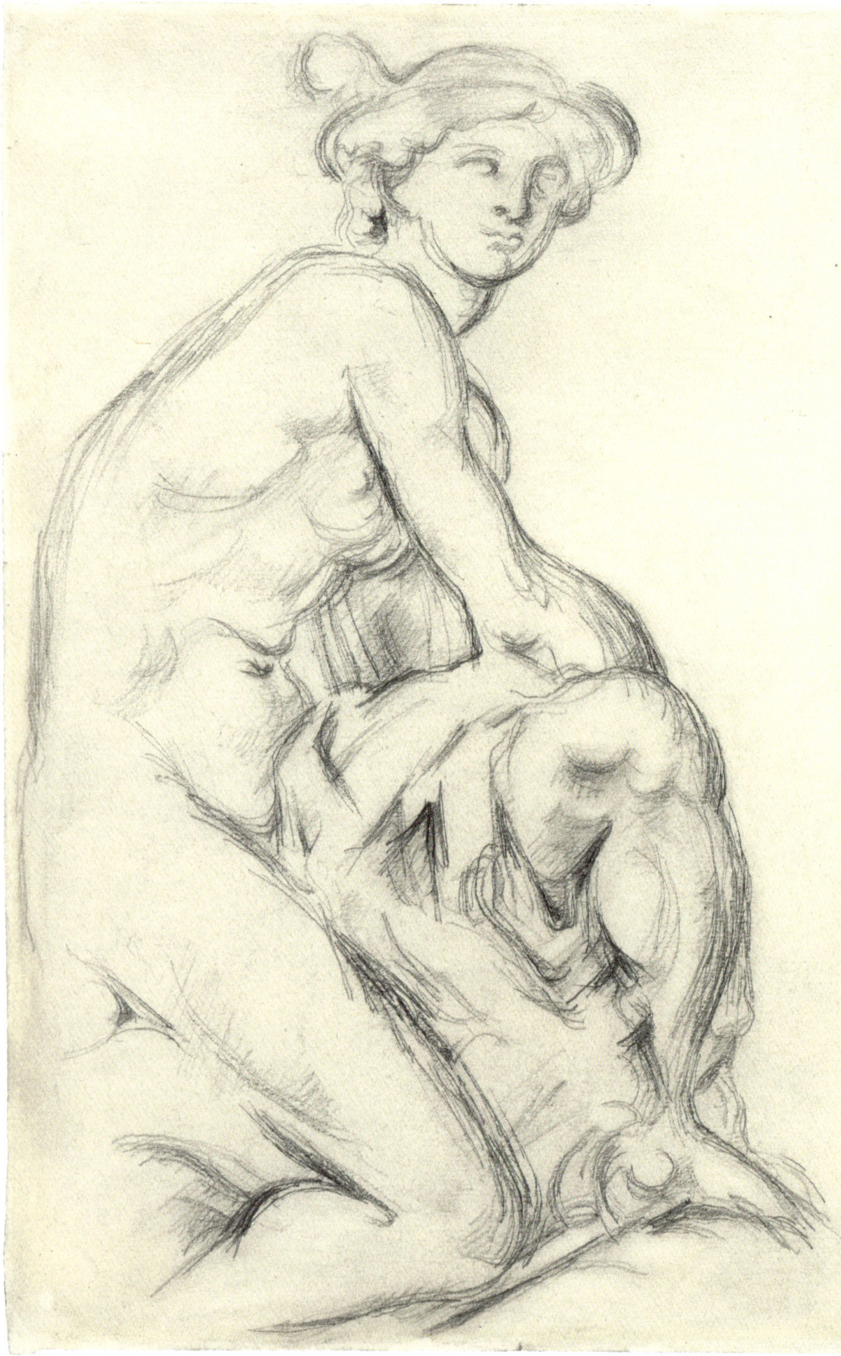

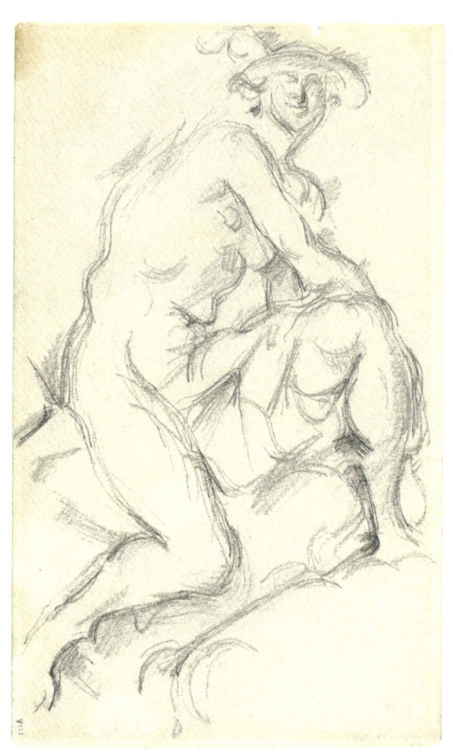

116. *Mercury after Pigalle.* c. 1890. Pencil on wove paper, 15 × 11" (38.1 × 27.9 cm)

117. *After Pigalle: Mercury.* c. 1890. Pencil on wove paper, 8 1/16 × 4 15/16" (20.5 × 12.5 cm)

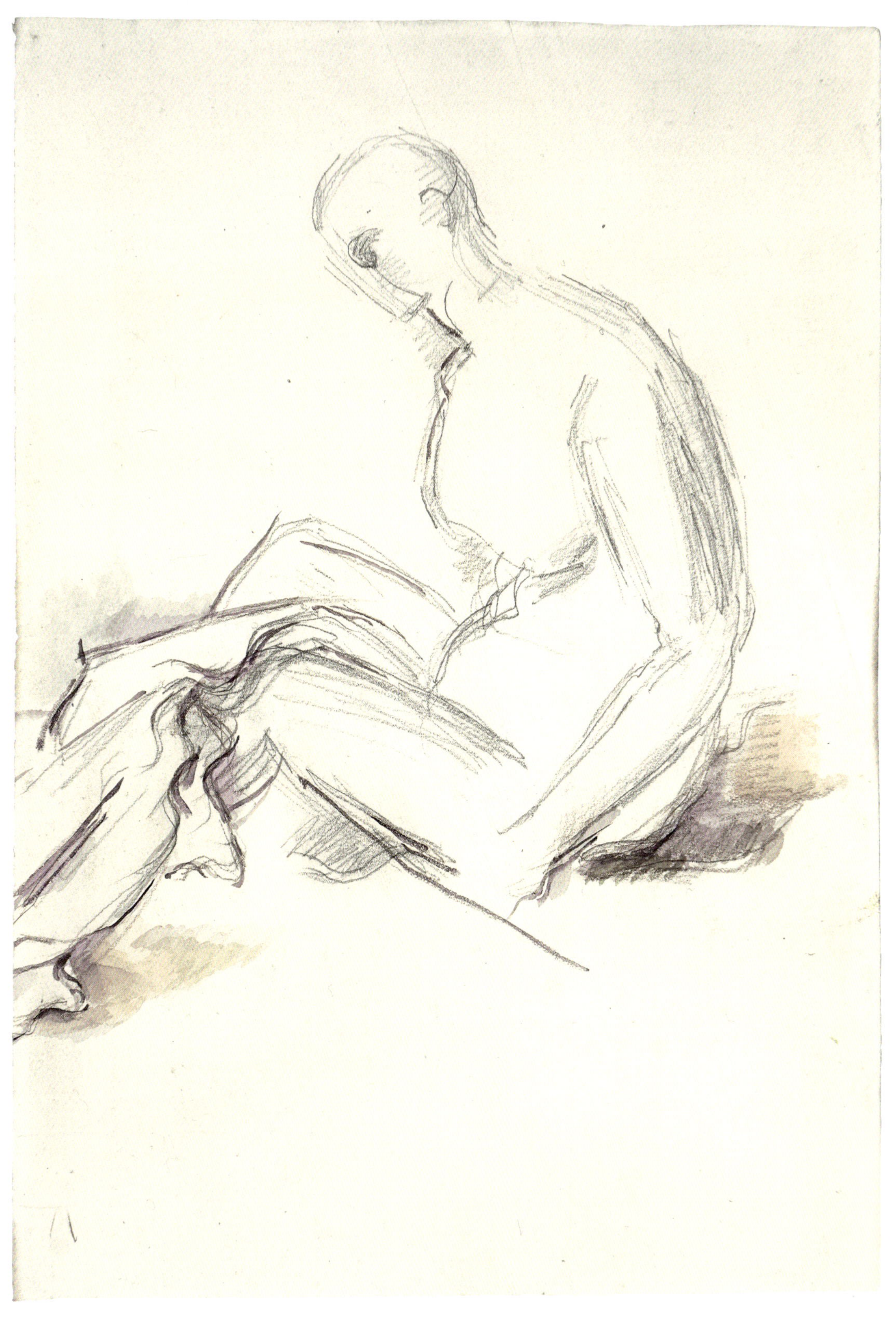

118. *Seated Nude*. 1882–85. Pencil and watercolor on paper, 17 ½ × 12 ½" (44.5 × 31.8 cm)

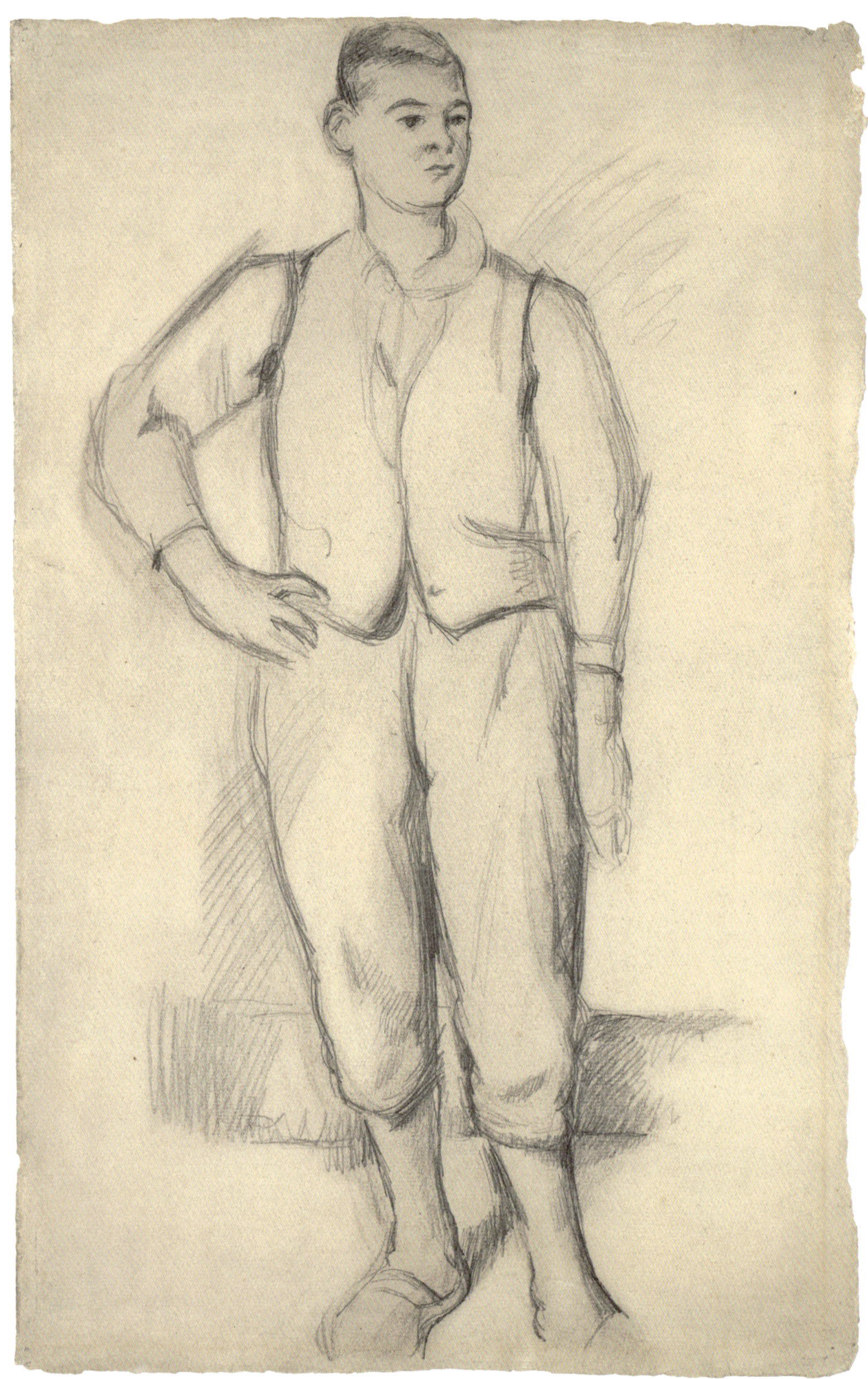

119. *Full-Length Portrait of the Artist's Son Paul.* c. 1885. Pencil on laid paper, 19 5/16 × 12 3/16" (49 × 31 cm)

120. *Paul Cézanne Fils as a Harlequin, Studies for Mardi Gras.* c. 1888. Pencil on paper, 7 15/16 × 10 11/16" (20.1 × 27.2 cm)

121. *Study of a Harlequin.* c. 1888. Pencil on laid paper, 18 13/16 × 12 1/2" (47.8 × 31.7 cm)

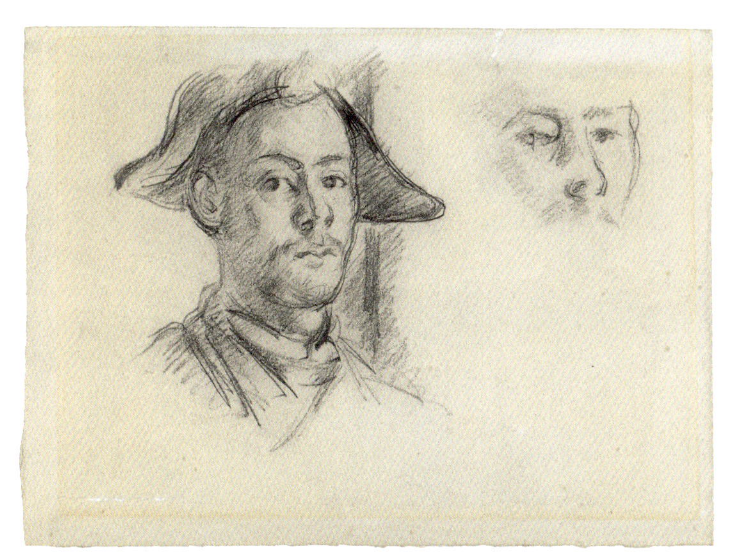

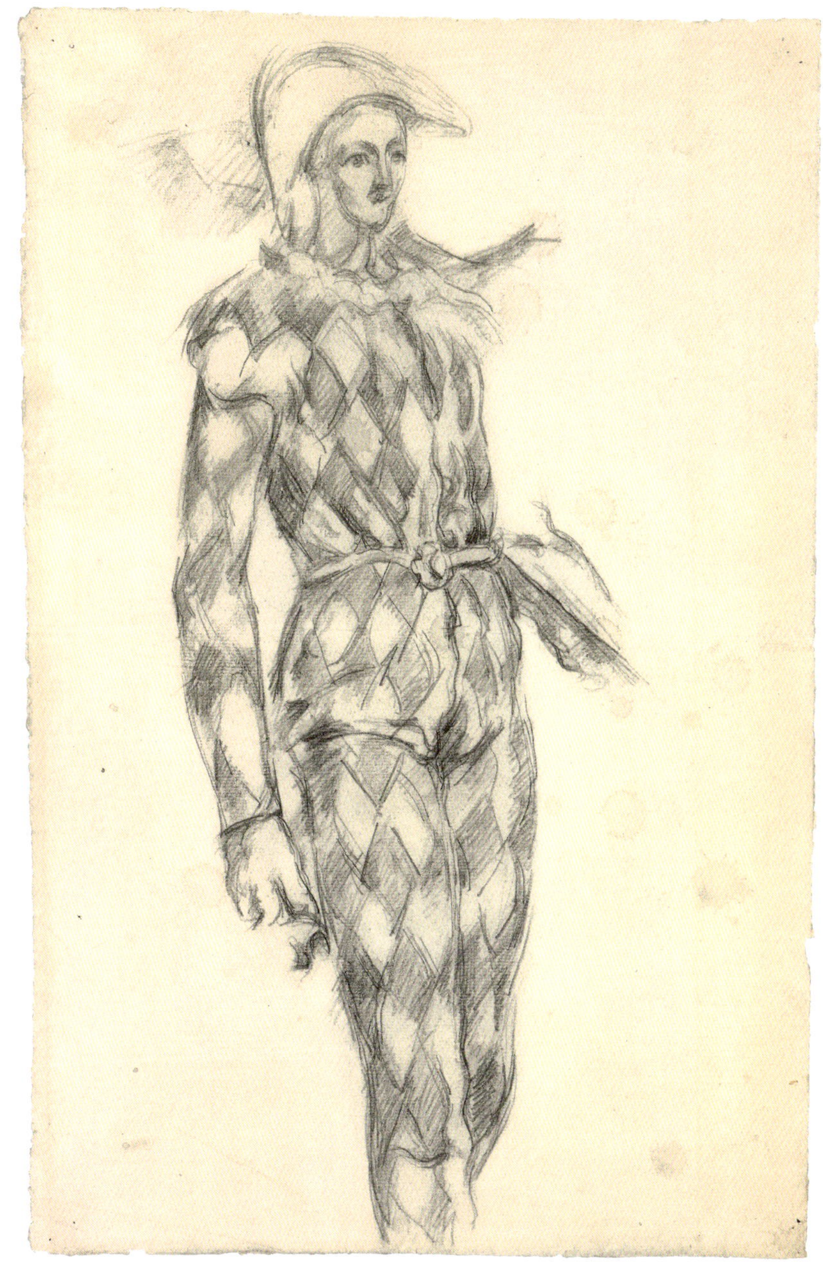

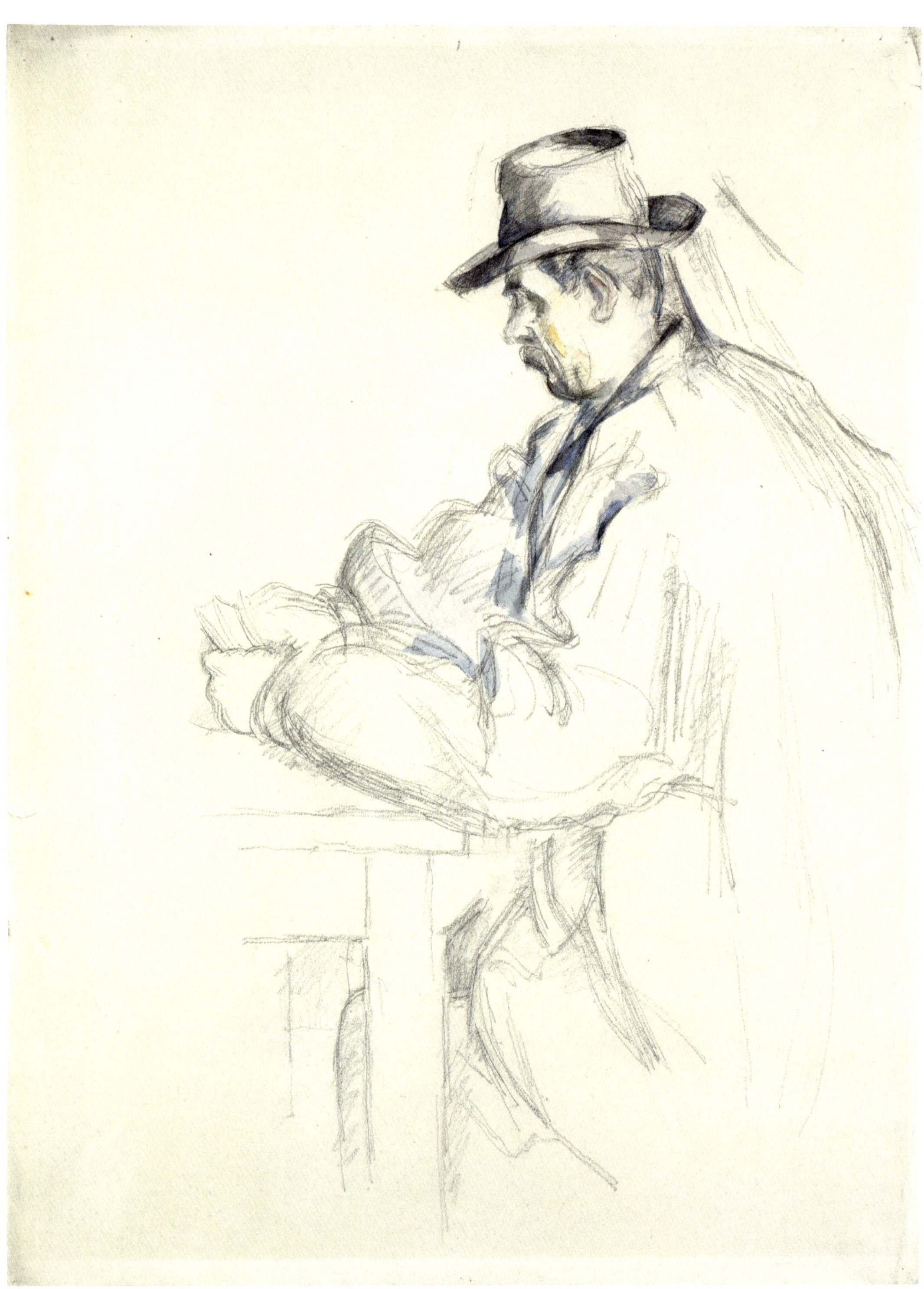

122. *The Card Player*. 1890–92. Pencil and watercolor on laid paper, 19 ⅛ × 14 ¼" (48.6 × 36.2 cm)

123. *Seated Peasant*. c. 1900 (possibly later). Watercolor on paper, 18 1/16 × 12 3/16" (45.8 × 31 cm)

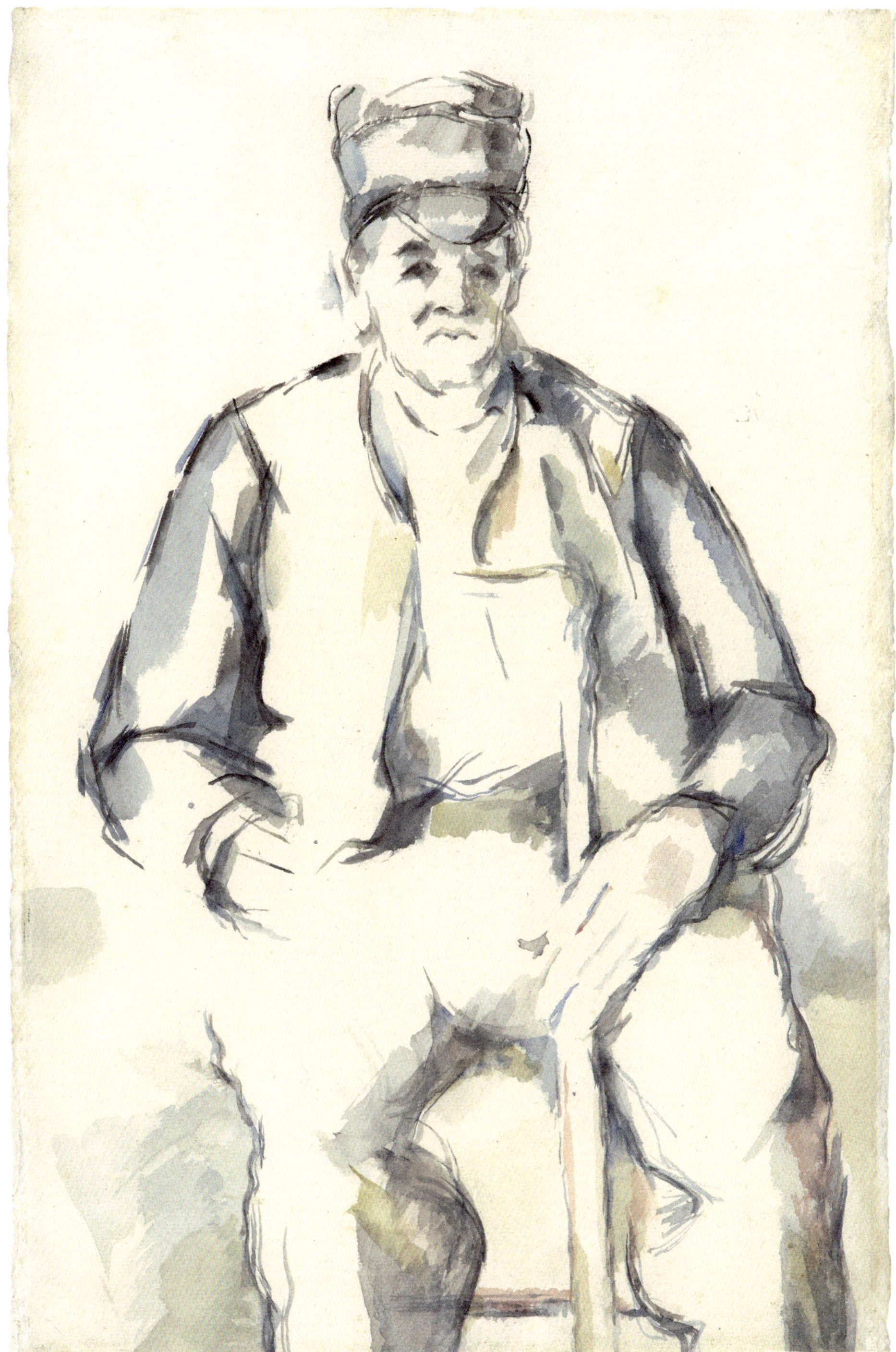

Kiko Aebi

"The real, prodigious study to undertake is the diversity of the scene offered by nature."
—Paul Cézanne, in a letter to Émile Bernard (Aix-en-Provence, 1904)

"The real, prodigious study to undertake," Cézanne wrote, "is the diversity of the scene offered by nature."[1] Throughout his career, painting and drawing the landscape *en plein air*, he examined this diversity through a rigorous process that proceeded from slow, attentive observation. In 1868 the natural scientist Antoine-Fortuné Marion, Cézanne's friend and occasional painting companion, remarked of his efforts, "He has now reached a surprising degree of scientific accuracy," alluding to the correspondence—in process and aim—between the artist and his contemporaries in the sciences.[2]

Cézanne's interest in science began in his youth. His dealer Ambroise Vollard wrote that as a schoolboy Cézanne was drawn especially to chemistry, "repeating the experiments at home, much to the agitation of the entire household."[3] In maturity the artist kept abreast of scientific advancements through periodicals like *Le Magasin pittoresque*, which regularly reported on the sciences (and to which his mother subscribed), and through conversations with his scientist friends.[4] When he began developing his landscape practice, in the 1860s, field-based observation had become a defining feature of scientific research in France.[5] A compulsory data-gathering step for any empirically driven inquiry, it was predicated on sustained, close looking within a delimited area. Cézanne's approach was analogous: he repeatedly stated his resolve "to stand firmly on the ground of observation" and "see beneath the veil of interpretation"[6] as he pursued what he referred to in his letters as his "research" and "studies" after nature.[7] Like his scientist counterparts, he investigated his subjects over long periods of time. The depth and persistence of his observational approach is demonstrated, in particular, in his forty-six watercolors and thirty-nine paintings of Mont Sainte-Victoire, a peak in southern France.

The diversity of this group—made over forty years—is exemplified by three watercolors from around the turn of the century, all picturing the view of Mont Sainte-Victoire from the artist's studio, overlooking Aix-en-Provence. In one, Cézanne layered loose graphite lines with abbreviated touches of translucent blue, green, rose, and yellow, producing a composition whose spareness approaches abstraction (plate 176). The same restrained handling is on display in another work, but Cézanne's brushstrokes are more opaque and heavily pigmented, scattered across uncovered paper to represent various features of the landscape: fields, farmhouses, and craggy peak (plate 175). By contrast, a third rendering coalesces into a vibrating field of color; a sense of dynamism pervades the composition, as if the observer is in motion (plate 180).

Cézanne's repetition of this motif suggests that Mont Sainte-Victoire served as a kind of control subject, a constant backdrop before which he might observe the environmental fluctuations that endlessly modify perception. Grappling with these fluctuations, the artist developed a disciplined process by which to transcribe his observations onto paper and canvas, revealing another commonality between his art-making and scientific inquiry: both require consistent parameters in order to yield epistemically meaningful evidence. Cézanne himself acknowledged this requisite, asking the archaeologist Jules Borély, during a visit in 1902, "Would you believe, I have almost completed formulating principles and a method for my profession?"[8] Cézanne's uncharacteristic candor with this unannounced visitor suggests that he felt an affinity with Borély, a scientist, and trusted that he would sympathize with the artist's methodological aims. Illustrating the uniformity of his approach, Cézanne's Mont Sainte-Victoire works almost invariably feature primary colors plus green, and all but four are oriented horizontally. They also represent a very limited selection of viewpoints: he depicted the peak as seen from his studio and just a handful of other sites.[9]

The parallels between Cézanne's artistic process and the scientific method attest to the shaping influence of what the writer Émile Zola, his confidant, called their "century of science."[10] No one played a more significant role in his immersion in these novel currents than Marion, who was renowned, Faya Causey has written, for his "ability to communicate complex ideas, current scientific research and theories, and his own scholarly explorations."[11] Their shared interests are expressed in notations Marion made in one of Cézanne's early sketchbooks: stratigraphic diagrams of Aix and Mont Sainte-Victoire; a phylogenetic tree; and a detailed illustration of a fossilized trilobite, which may have accompanied a discussion of evolution and mass extinction.[12]

These contributions, informed by Marion's own field observations in Aix, show the scientist lending Cézanne a lens through which to observe a kind of cohesion in the natural world even as he modeled an attention to concrete details. Cézanne's explorations of both the long view (plates 184–87) and the close-up (plates 139–42, 146) seem to respond to this formulation of nature, a correspondence noted by artists R. P. Rivière and Jacques Schnerb in 1905. Cézanne's landscapes, they wrote, represent "a part of nature both embraced and isolated by the gaze, a whole of that which is a fragment."[13] This tension between whole and part is foregrounded in a group of studies of nature observed in close proximity, featuring patches of vegetation, twisting vines, and solitary branches. In *Foliage* (1900–04; plate 142) the artist zoomed in on a tangle of vines and leaves, rendering a mosaic of transparent geometric facets evocative of plant cells as viewed under a microscope. In this and similar works, made over thirty years, Cézanne isolated the subject on the page, often flattening it in order to meticulously record its structure, as in a scientific illustration. But he also intimated its relationship to a larger environment, extending elements of the composition to the sheet's edges to indicate its continuation (plates 127, 128, 139, 140). Thus these works show him examining nature's own order of construction through a process consistent with the science of his day. And like his scientific contemporaries, Cézanne pursued his observations of nature's diversity determinedly, endeavoring, he wrote, to one day find "proof of [his] theories."[14]

1.
Cézanne, letter to Émile Bernard, May 12, 1904, in *The Letters of Paul Cézanne*, ed. and trans. Alex Danchev (Los Angeles: J. Paul Getty Museum, 2013), no. 234.

2.
Antoine-Fortuné Marion, letter to Heinrich Morstatt, April 1868, reprinted in Alfred Barr, "Cézanne d'après les lettres de Marion à Morstatt, 1865–1868," *Gazette des beaux-arts* 17, no. 883 (1937): 48. Trans. by the author.

3.
Ambroise Vollard, *En écoutant Cézanne, Degas, Renoir* (Paris: B. Grasset, 1994), 10, trans. Bruno Ely in Philip Conisbee and Denis Coutagne, *Cézanne in Provence* (New Haven, Conn.: Yale University Press/ National Gallery of Art, Washington, D.C., 2006), 34.

4.
Faya Causey, "Finds," in John Elderfield, ed., *Cézanne: The Rock and Quarry Paintings* (Princeton, N.J.: Princeton University Press, 2020), 42–57. In addition to Marion, Cézanne's close friends Émile Zola and Jean-Baptistin Baille were deeply engaged with the sciences; Baille became a noted author of both scholarly and popular science.

5.
Promoted earlier in the century by British scientist Charles Lyell, field observation had been quickly adopted by researchers in all fields, including Marion, who referred to himself as "an observational scientist." Ibid., 44–46.

6.
Cézanne, in Bernard, "Paul Cézanne" (1904), in Michael Doran, ed., *Conversations with Cézanne*, trans. Julie Lawrence Cochran (Berkeley: University of California Press, 2001), 38.

7.
See, for example, letters to Zola, Ambroise Vollard, and Bernard, in *Letters of Paul Cézanne*, nos. 80, 214, and 269.

8.
Cézanne, in Jules Borély, "Cézanne at Aix" (1902), in Doran, *Conversations*, 20.

9.
Nina Athanassoglou-Kallmyer, "Sainte-Victoire and the End of Time," in *Cézanne and Provence: The Painter in His Culture* (Chicago: University of Chicago Press, 2003), 149–50.

10.
Zola, "Causerie: À Frédéric Mistral," in *Œuvres complètes*, ed. Henri Mitterand (Paris: Le Cercle du Livre Précieux, 1966–69), 10:762, trans. in Conisbee and Coutagne, *Cézanne in Provence*, 3.

11.
Causey, "Appendix: Marion's Geological Drawings," in Elderfield, *Rock and Quarry Paintings*, 150.

12.
Ibid.

13.
R. P. Rivière and J. F. Schnerb, "The Studio of Cézanne" (1905), in Doran, *Conversations*, 89.

14.
Cézanne, letter to Bernard, September 21, 1909, no. 269.

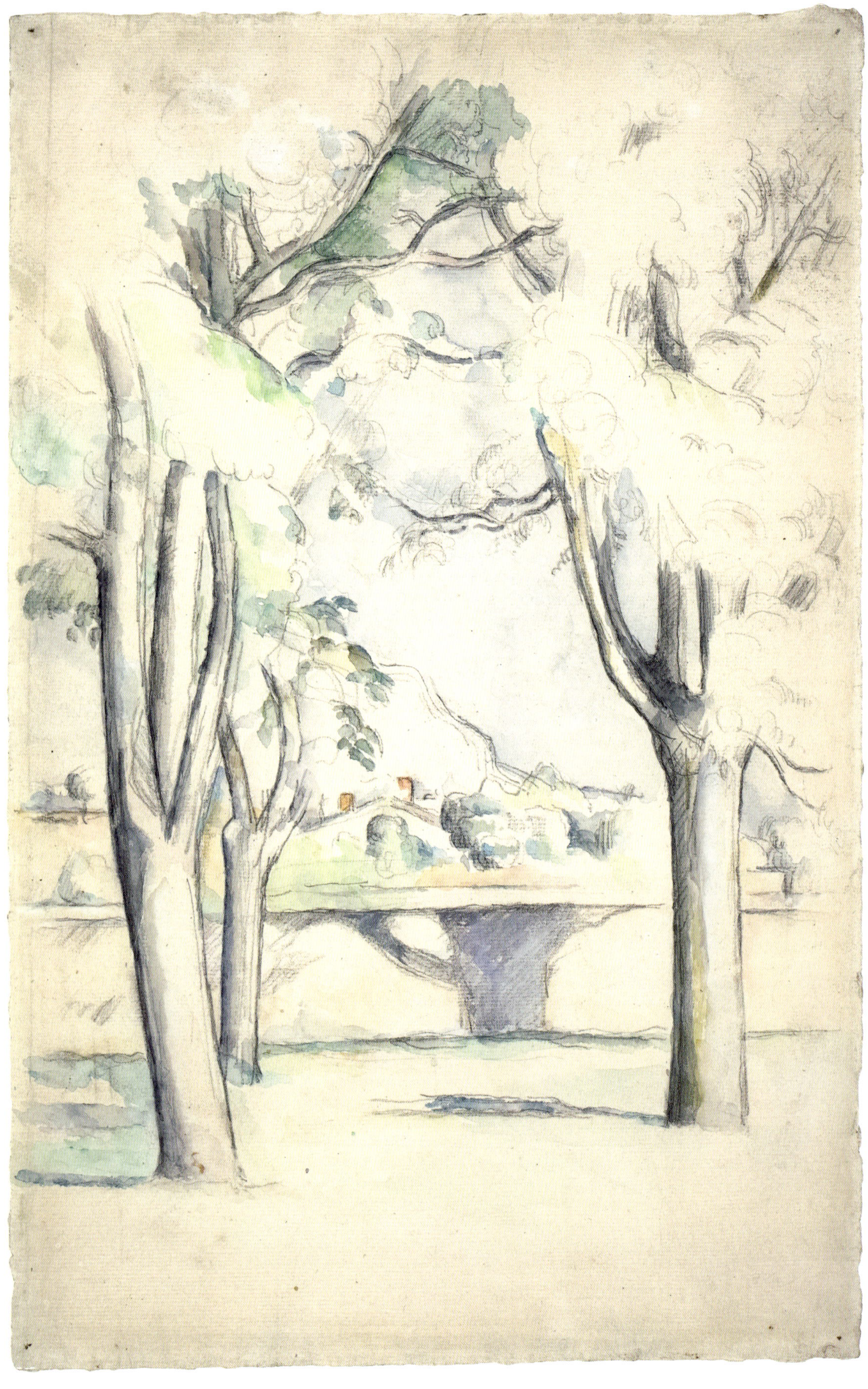

124. *Mont Sainte-Victoire Seen beyond the Wall of the Jas de Bouffan*. 1885–88. Pencil and watercolor on laid paper, 18 9⁄16 × 12" (47.2 × 30.5 cm)

125. *Trees at the Jas de Bouffan*. c. 1878. Pencil and watercolor on laid paper, 11 7⁄16 × 8 7⁄8" (29 × 22.5 cm)

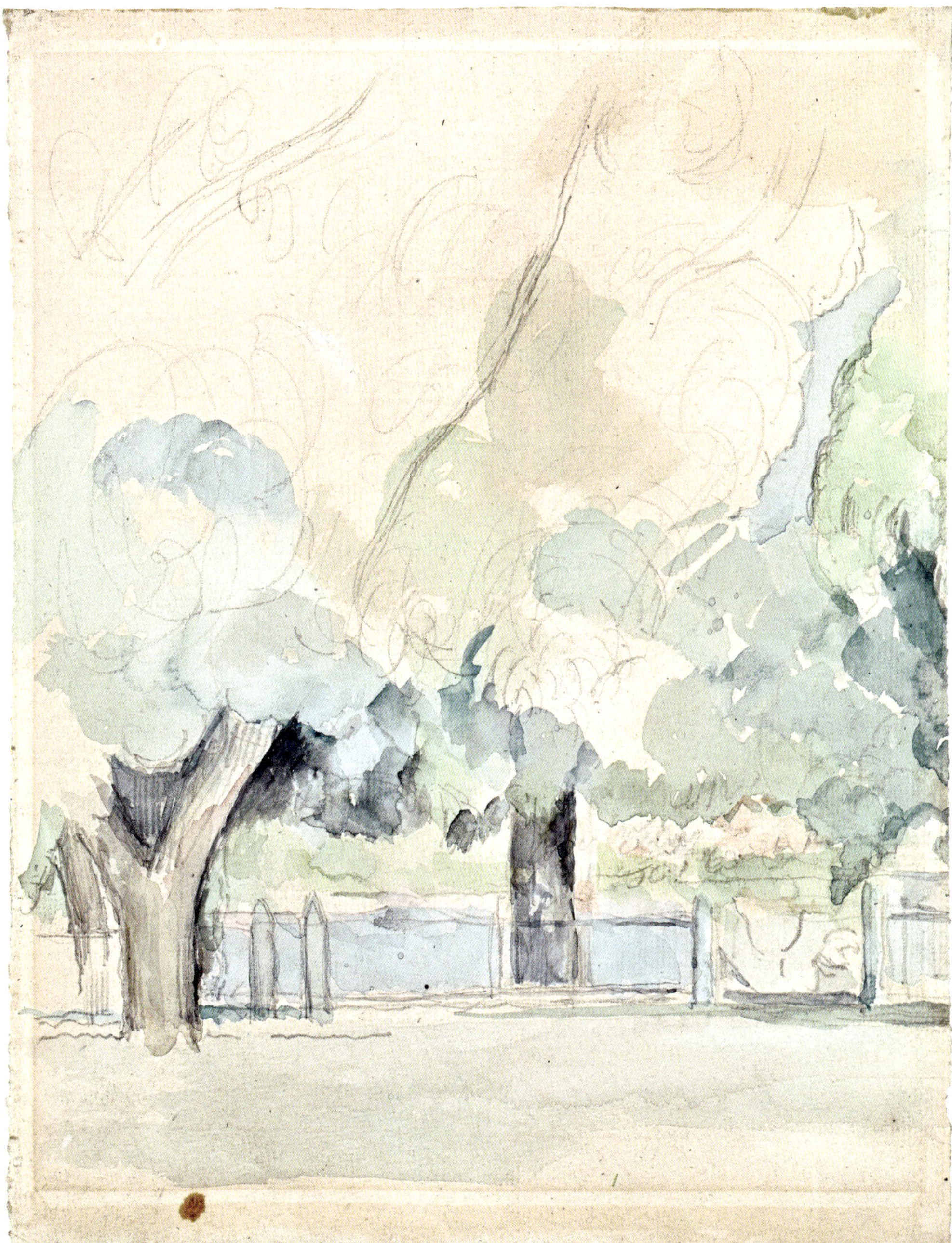

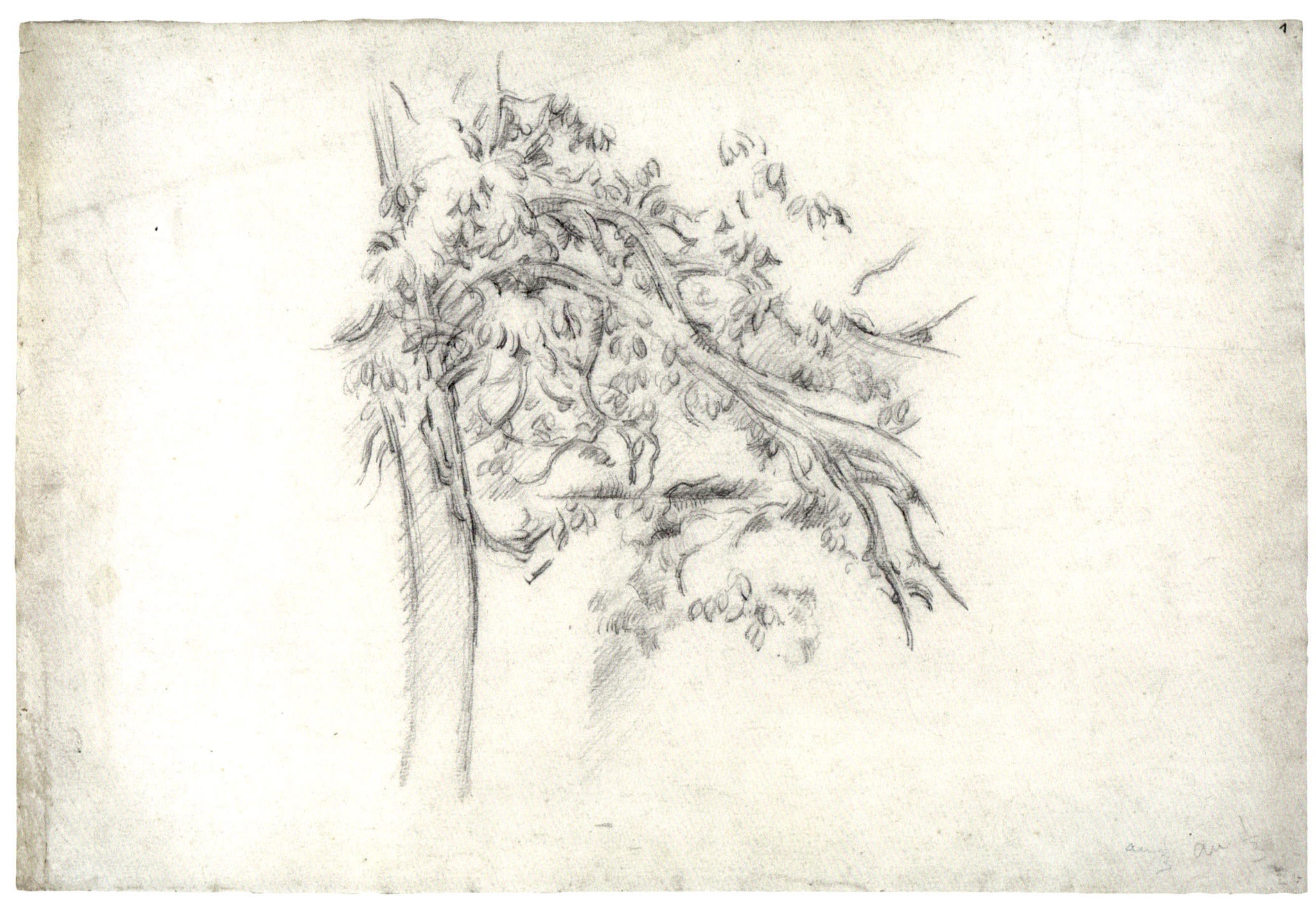

126. *Study of a Tree*. c. 1885–87. Pencil on wove paper, 12 ⅜ × 18 ⅝" (31.4 × 47.3 cm)

127. *Large Pine, Study*. 1885–90. Pencil and watercolor on laid paper, 12 $\frac{9}{16}$ × 19 ½" (31.9 × 49.5 cm)

128. *Large Pine, Study*. 1885–90. Pencil and watercolor on wove paper, 12 ¼ × 18 $\frac{13}{16}$" (31.1 × 47.8 cm)

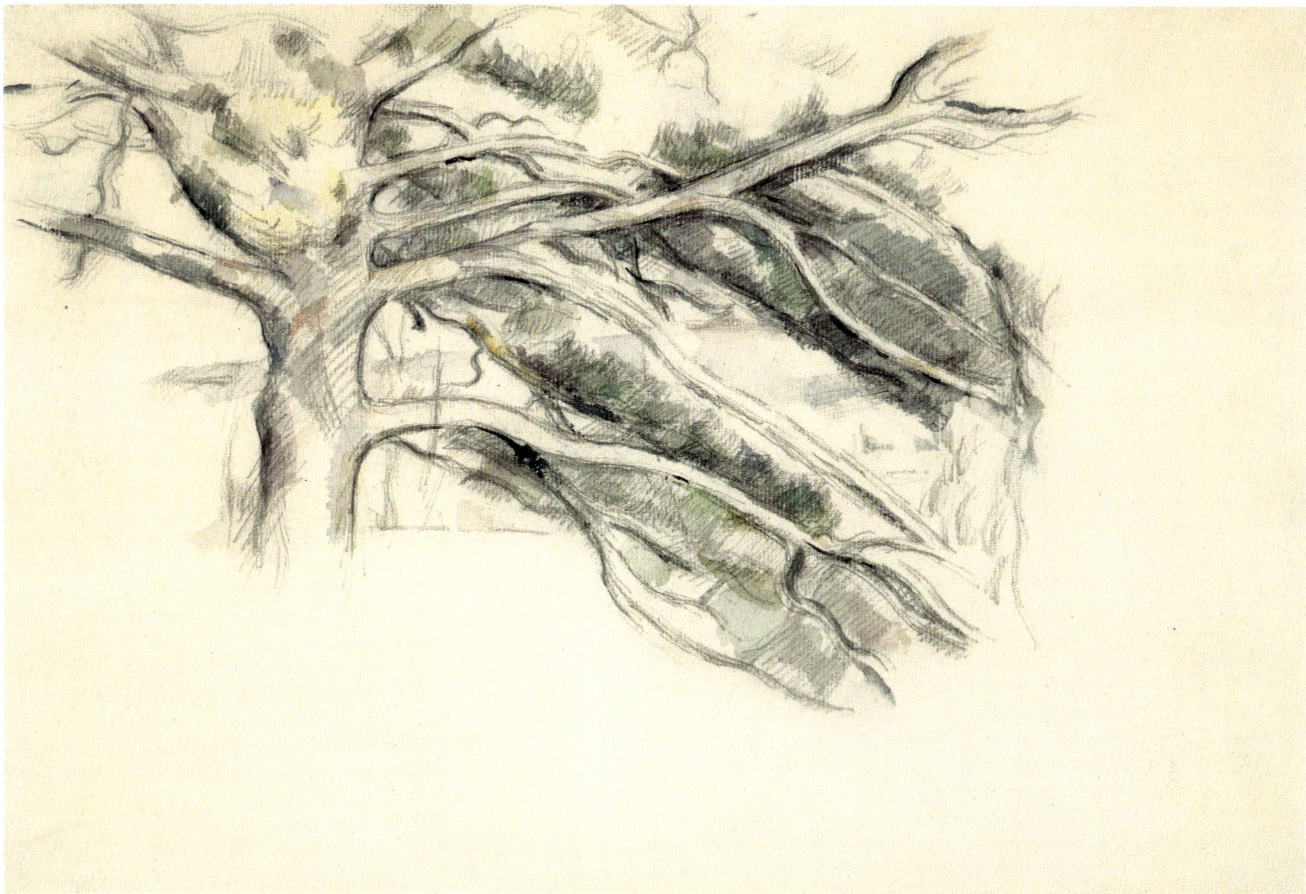

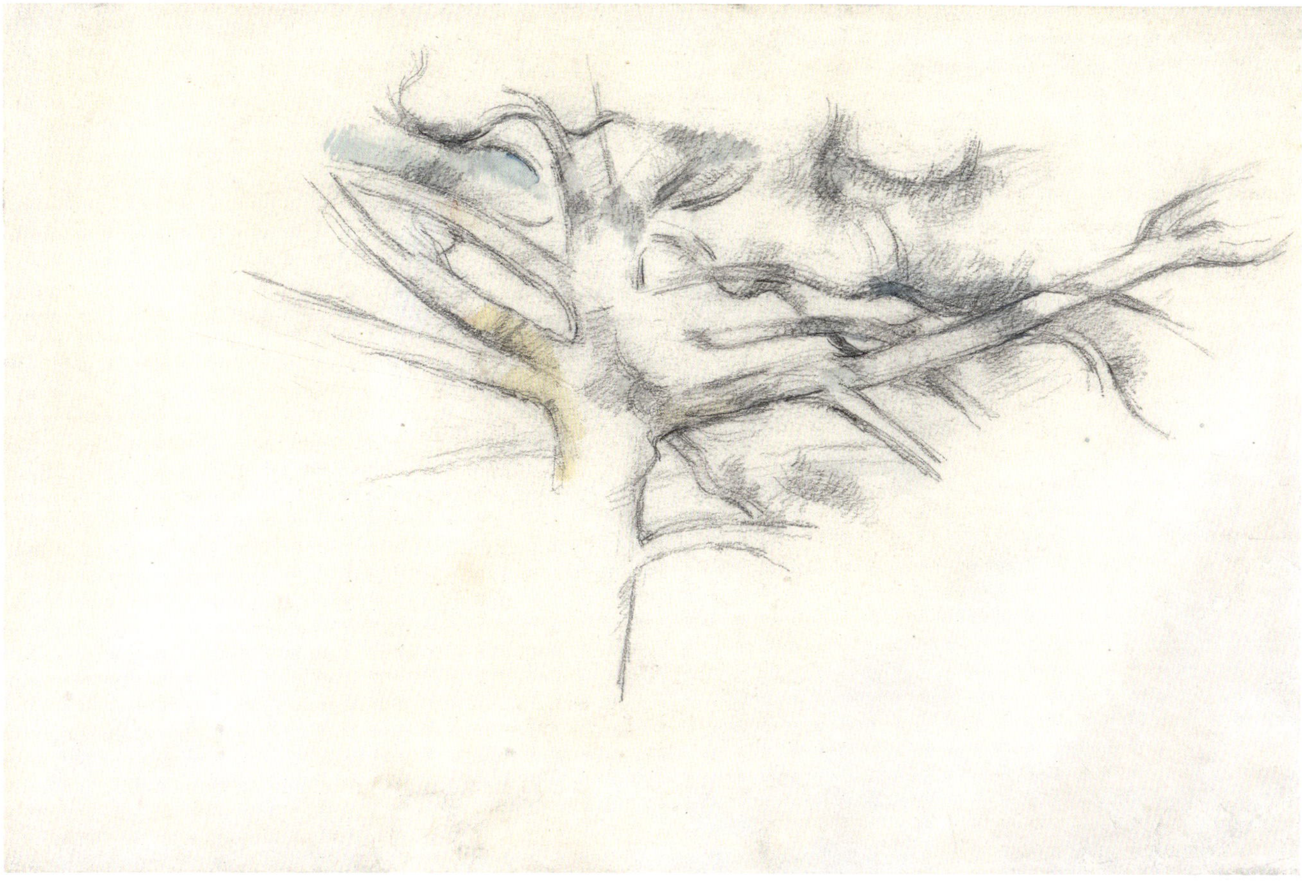

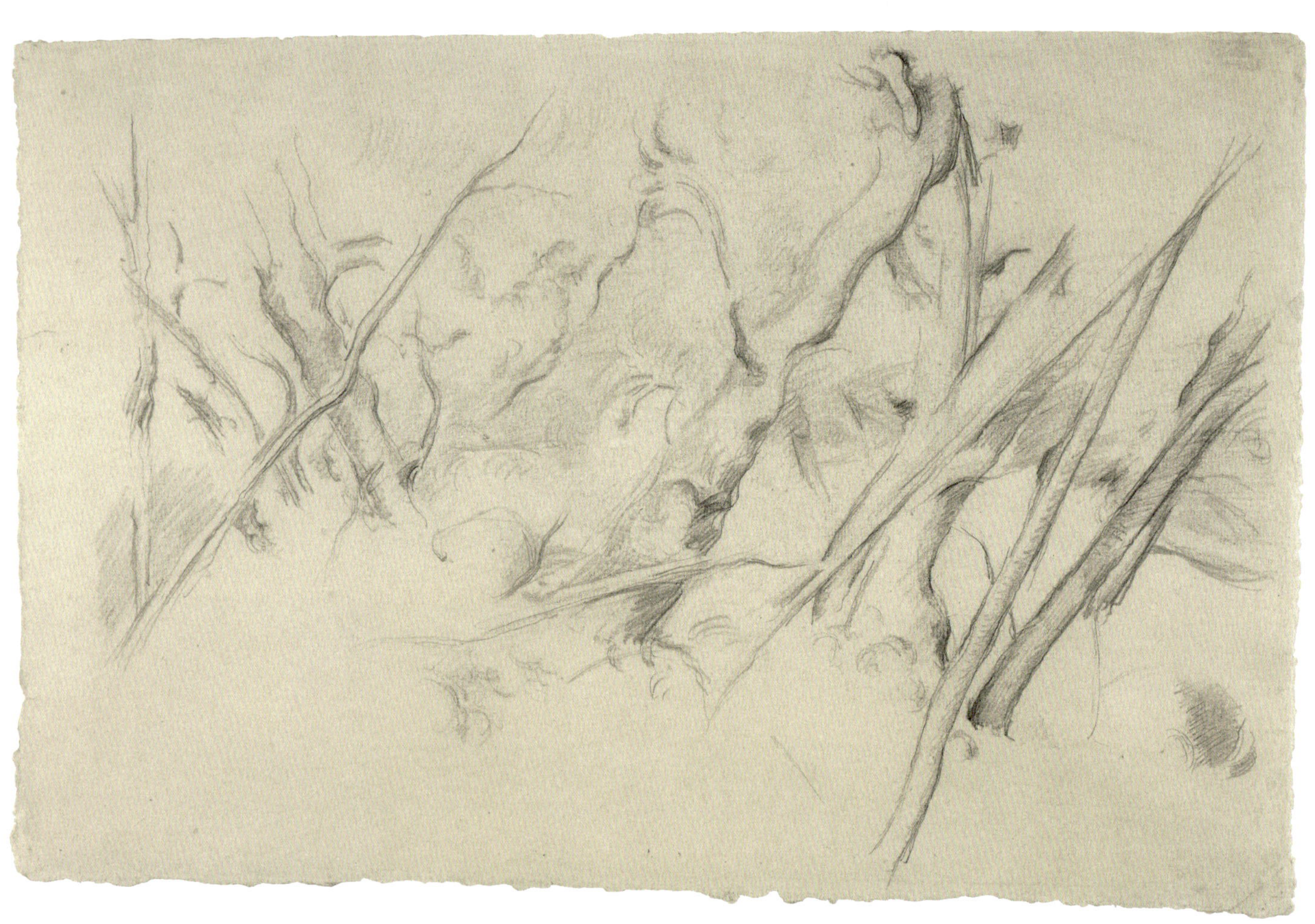

129. *Sloping Trees*. 1896–99.
Pencil on laid paper, 12 1/16 × 18 1/2" (30.6 × 47 cm)

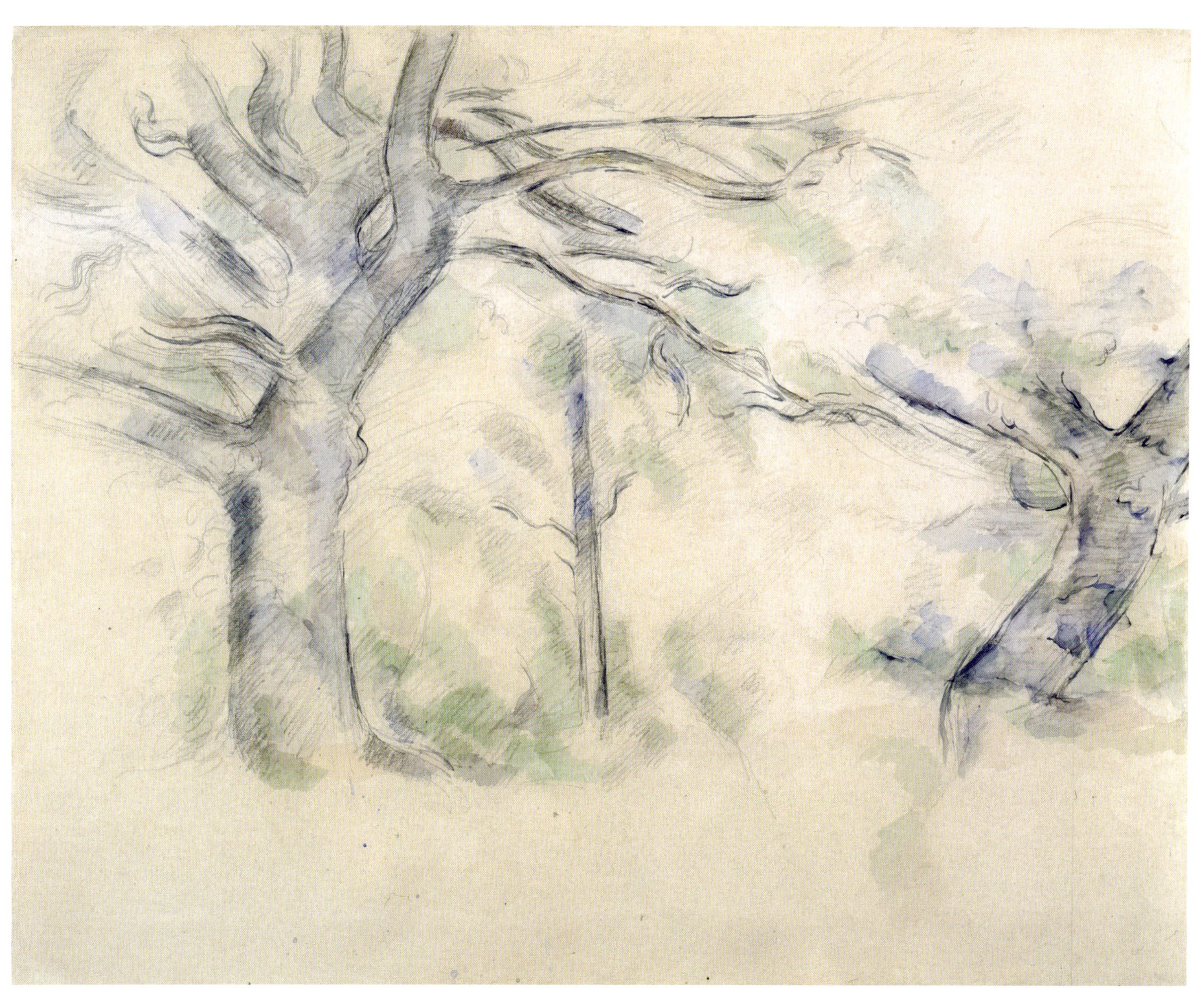

130. *The Large Trees*. 1902–04. Pencil and watercolor on paper, 18 ½ × 23 1⁄16" (47 × 58.5 cm)

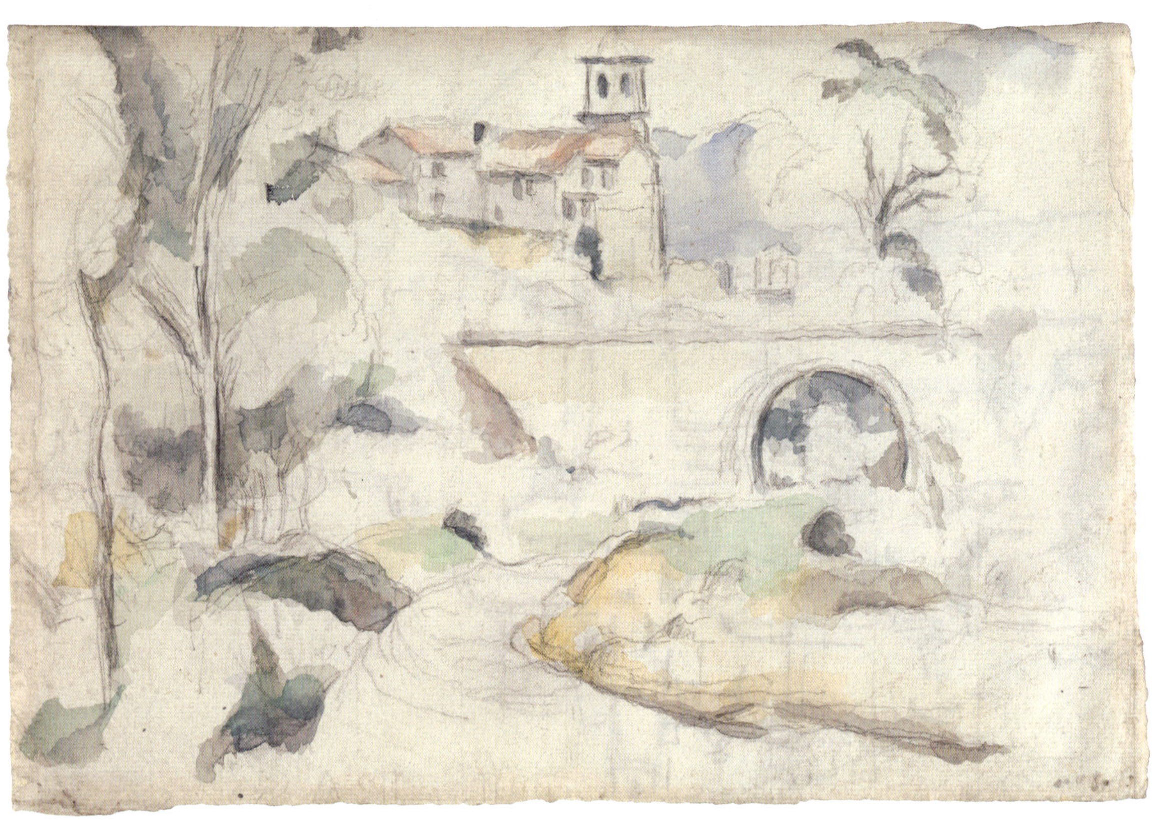

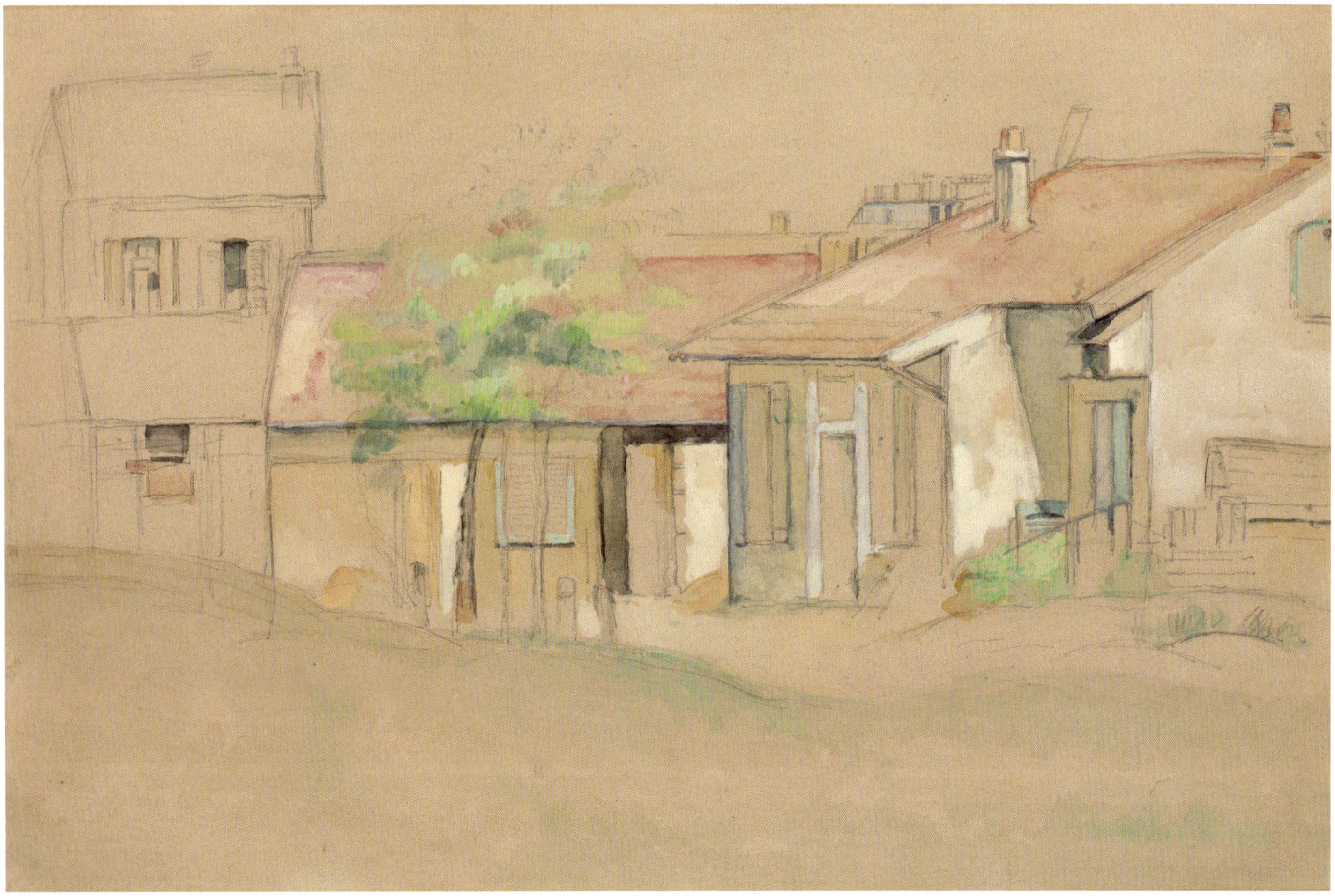

131. *The Bridge at Gardanne*. 1885–86. Watercolor and pencil on laid paper, 8 1/8 × 12 1/4" (20.6 × 31.1 cm)

132. *Village Houses*. 1880–85. Pencil, watercolor, and gouache on paper, 12 7/8 × 19 5/8" (32.7 × 49.9 cm)

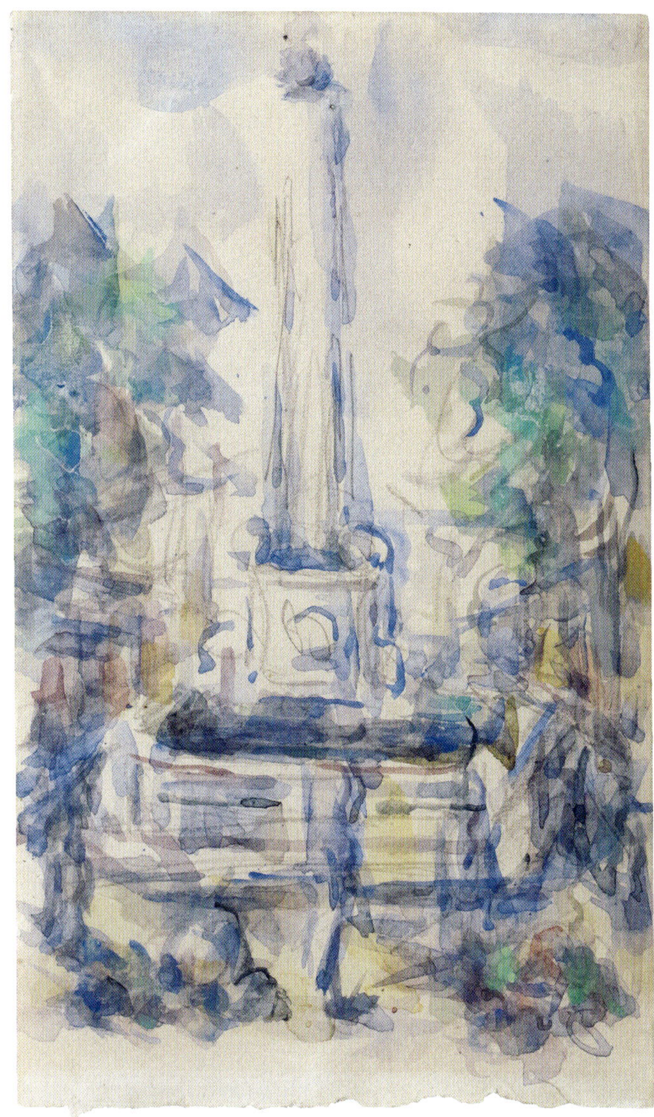

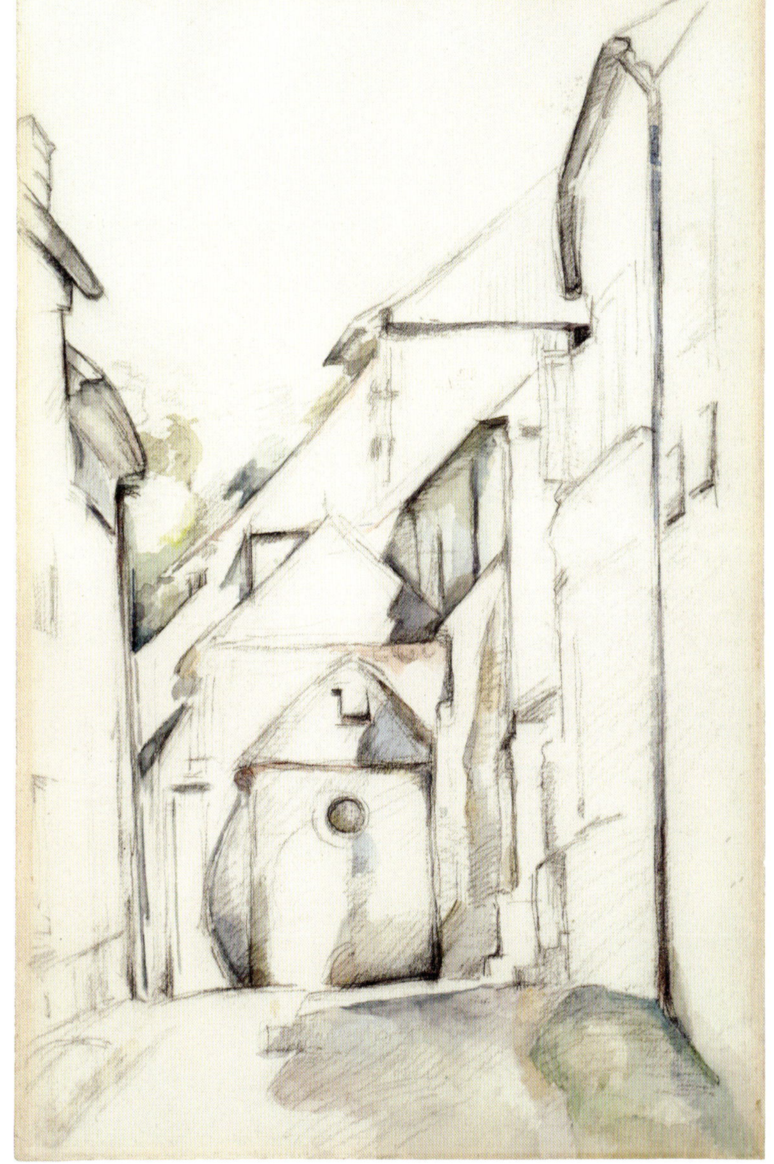

133. *Fountain, Place de la Mairie in Aix-en-Provence*. c. 1900. Pencil and watercolor on wove paper, 8 7⁄16 × 5" (21.5 × 12.7 cm)

134. *Saint Pierre Church in Avon*. 1892–94. Pencil and watercolor on paper, 18 ½ × 12 ⅛" (47 × 30.8 cm)

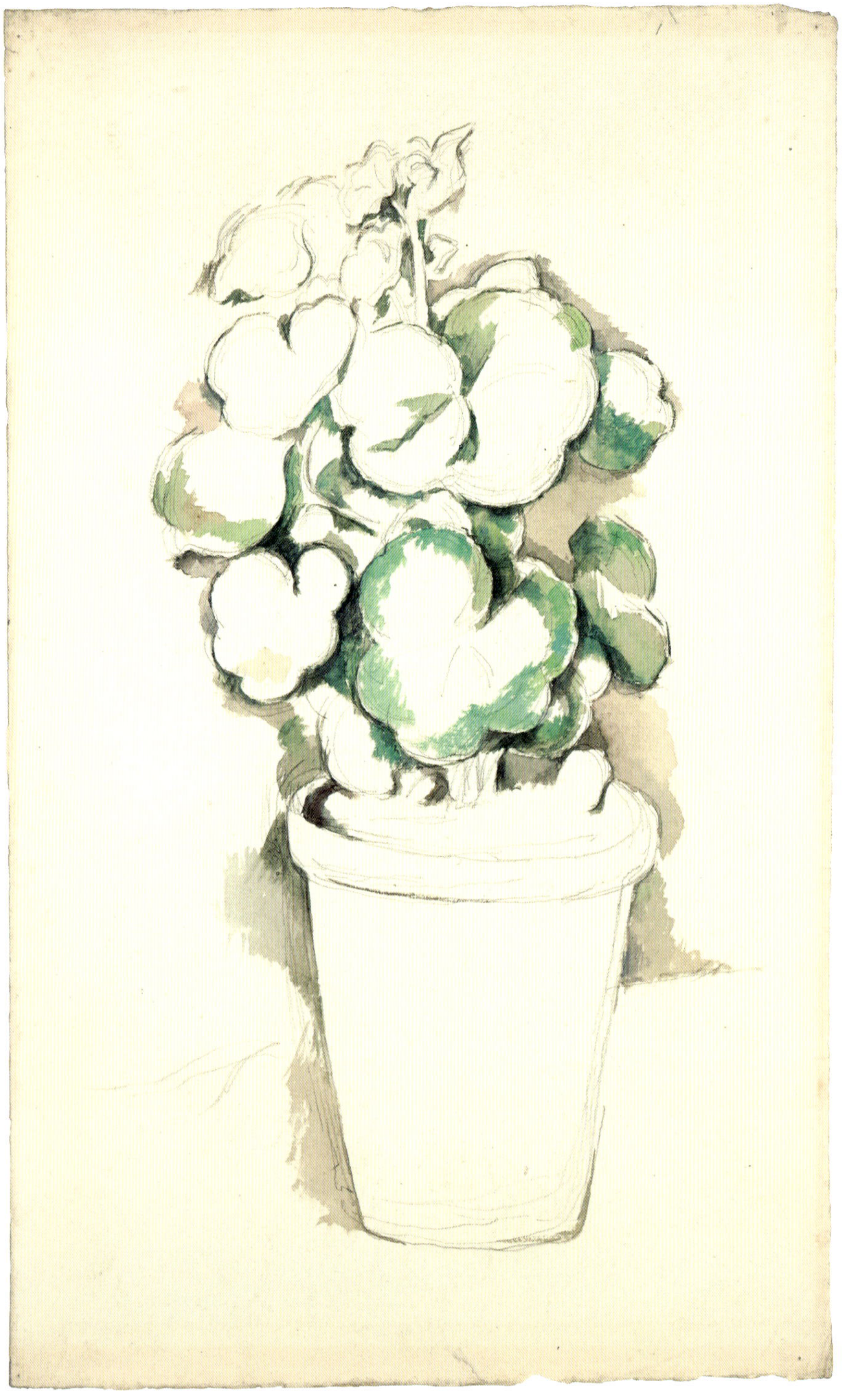

135. *Pot of Geraniums*. c. 1885. Pencil and watercolor on paper, 19 9/16 × 12 1/8" (49.7 × 30.8 cm)

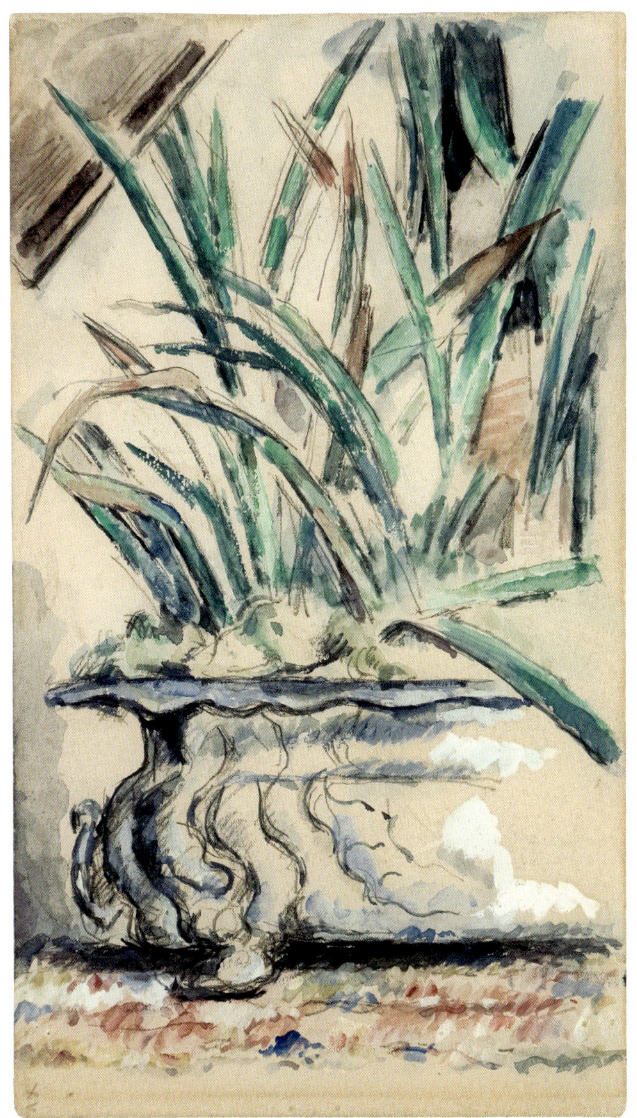

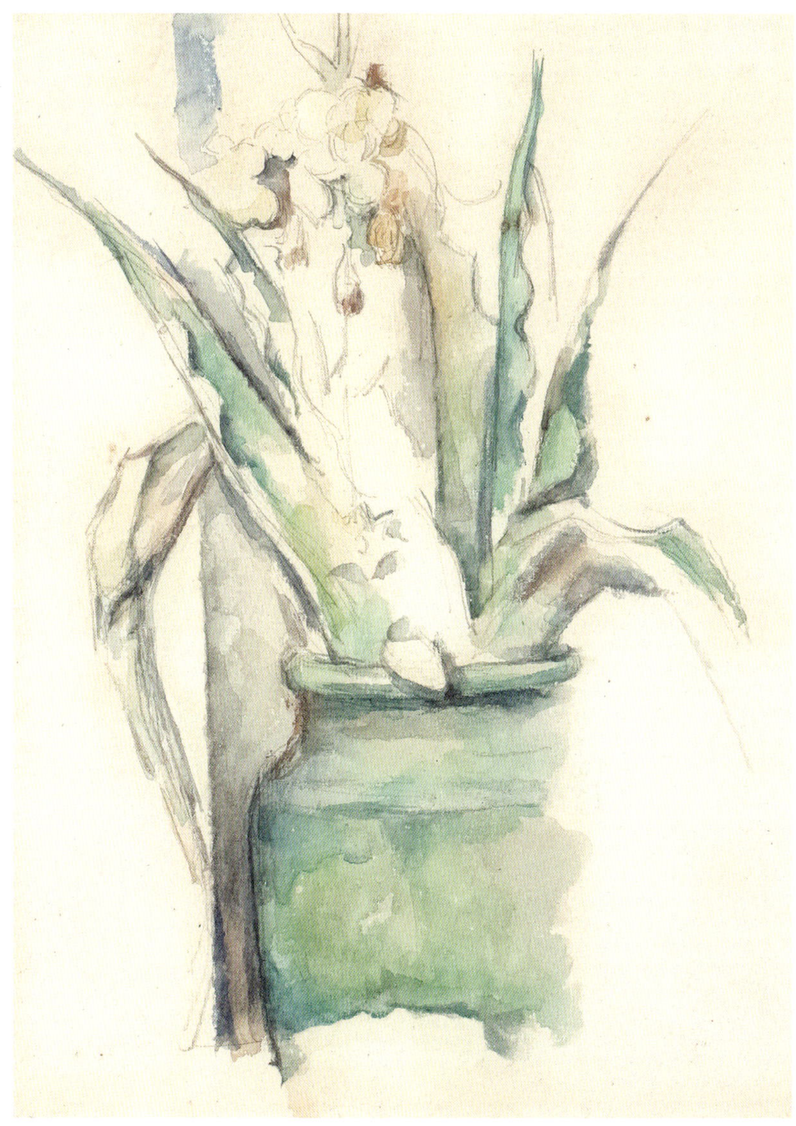

136. *The Blue Pot Warmer*. c. 1885. Pencil, watercolor, and gouache on wove paper, 8 7⁄16 × 4 15⁄16" (21.5 × 12.5 cm)

137. *The Vase and the Column*. c. 1890. Pencil and watercolor on paper, 11 13⁄16 × 9 1⁄16" (30 × 23 cm)

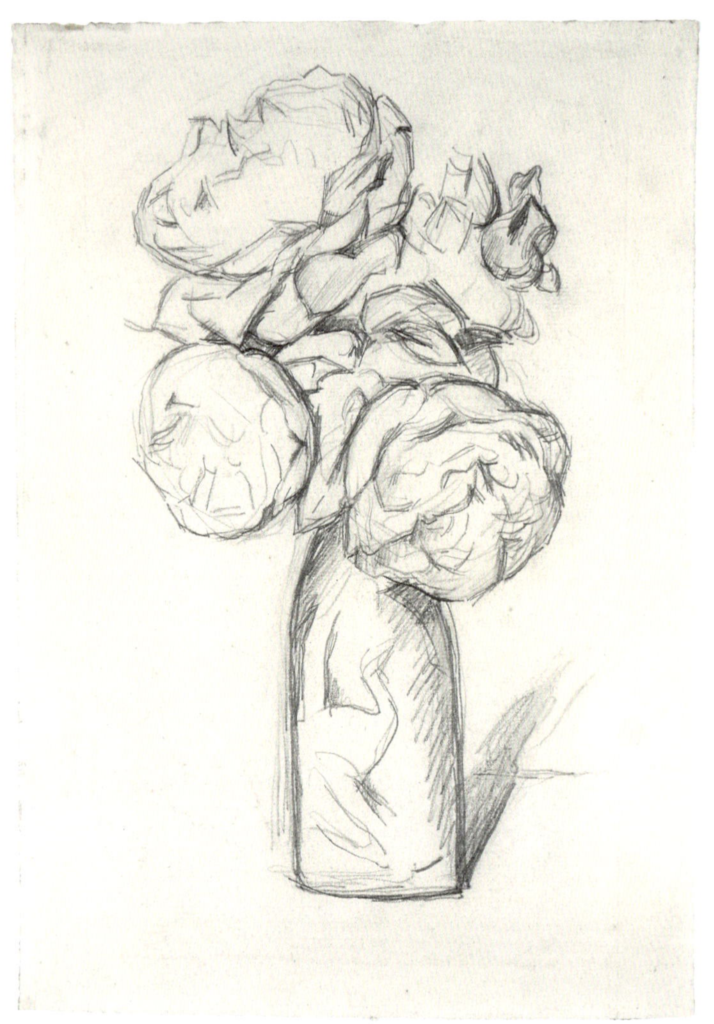

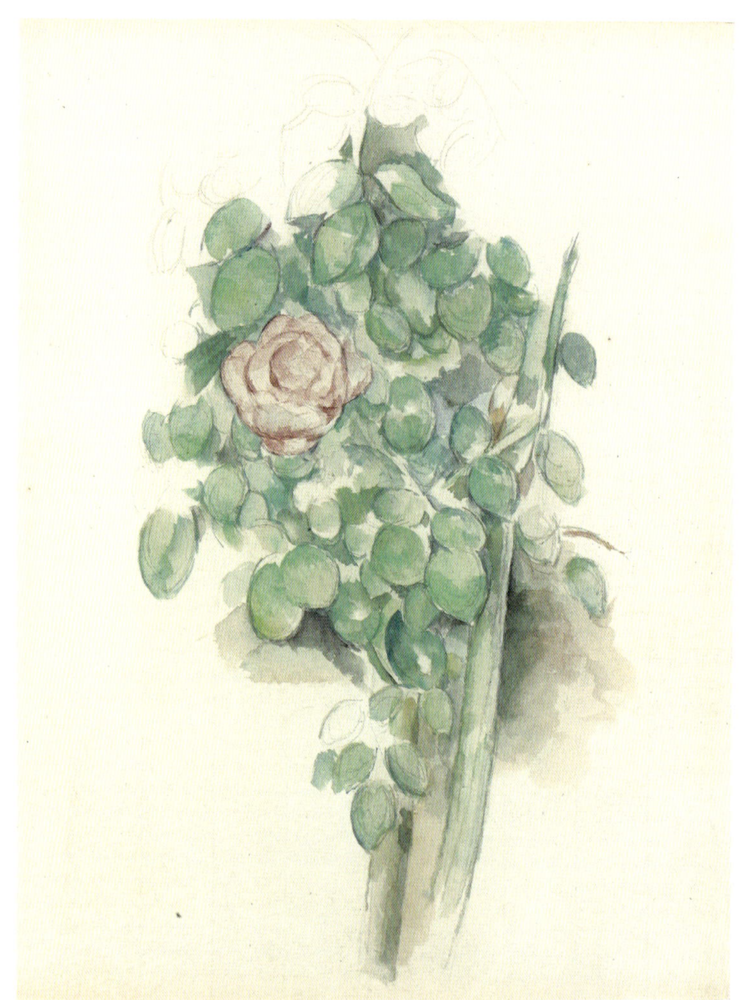

138. *Roses in a Vase*. 1883–86. Pencil on laid paper, 11 ½ × 8" (29.2 × 20.3 cm)

139. *Rose*. 1885–88. Pencil and watercolor on laid paper, 15 ½ × 11 ¾" (39.3 × 30 cm)

140. *Roses*. 1895–1900. Pencil and watercolor on paper, 18 ⅞ × 12 $^{3}/_{16}$" (48 × 31 cm)

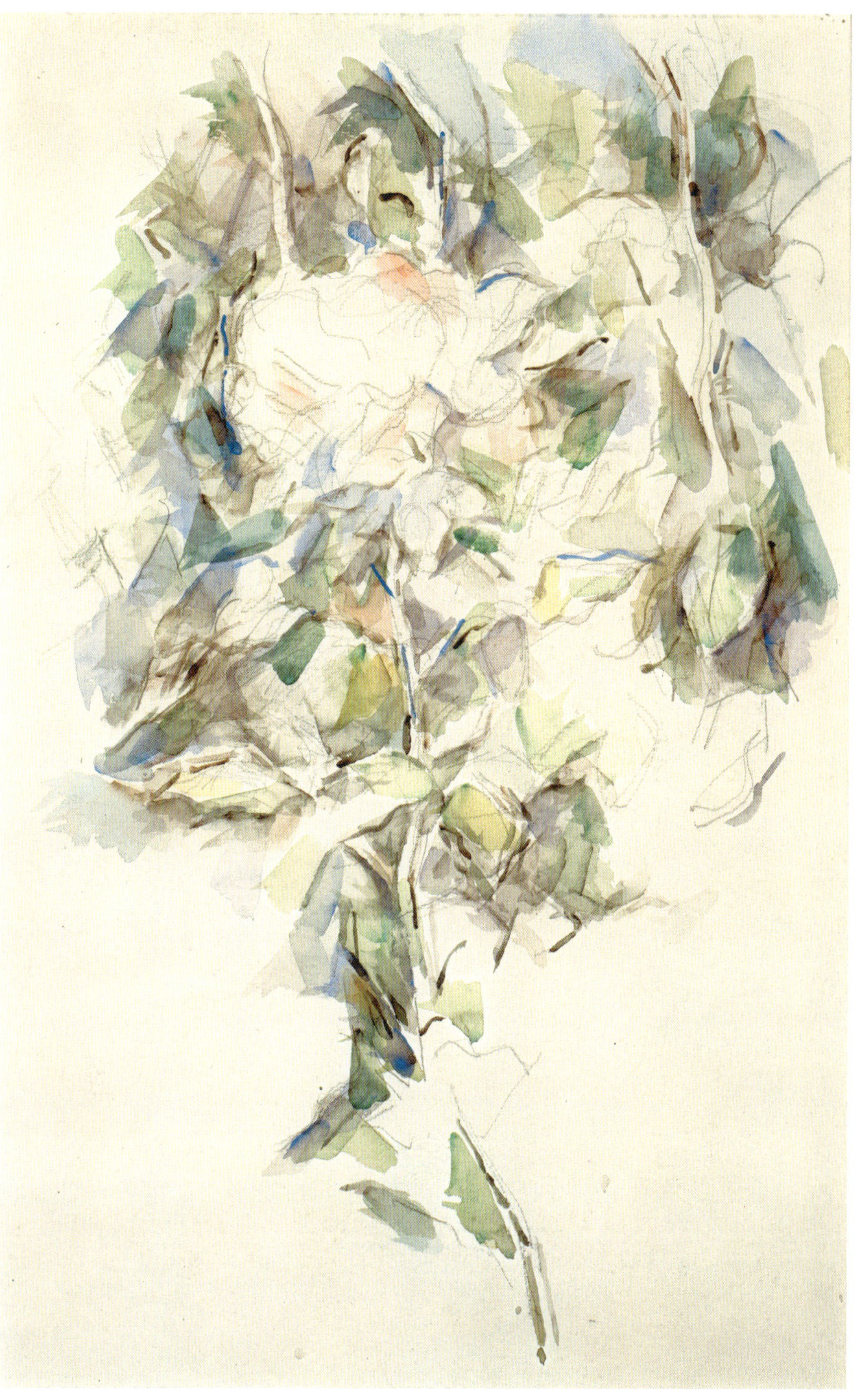

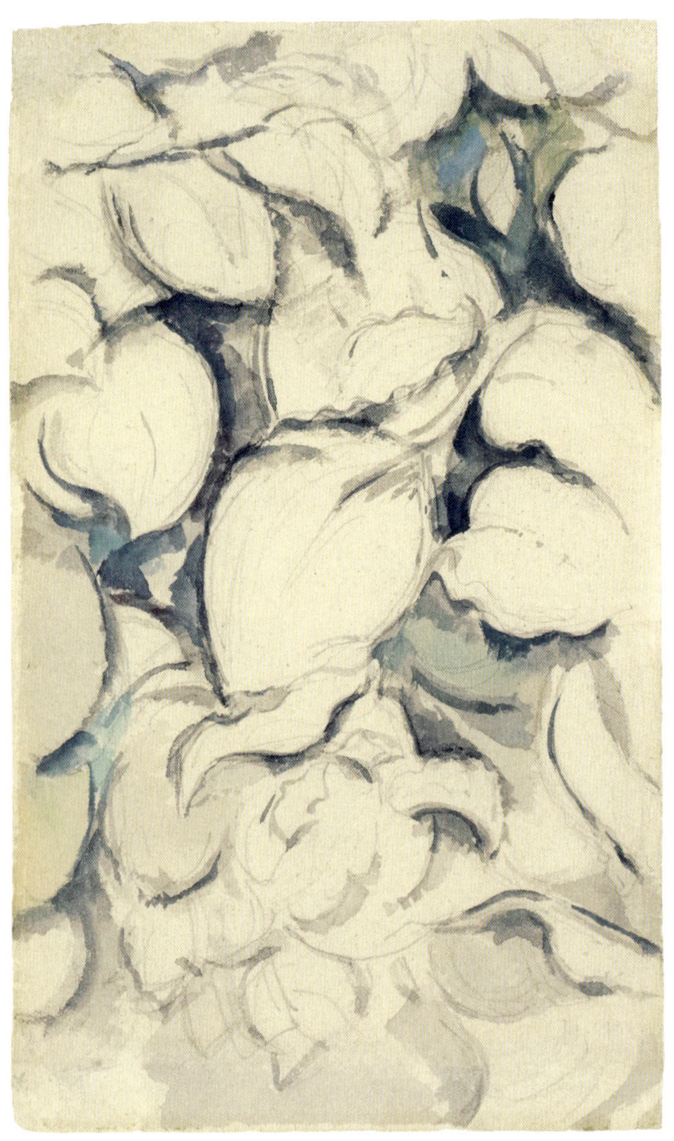

141. *Foliage and Flowers*. c. 1895. Pencil and watercolor on wove paper, 7 5/8 × 4 5/8" (19.4 × 11.7 cm)

142. *Foliage*. 1900–04. Watercolor and pencil on wove paper, 17 5/8 × 22 3/8" (44.8 × 56.8 cm)

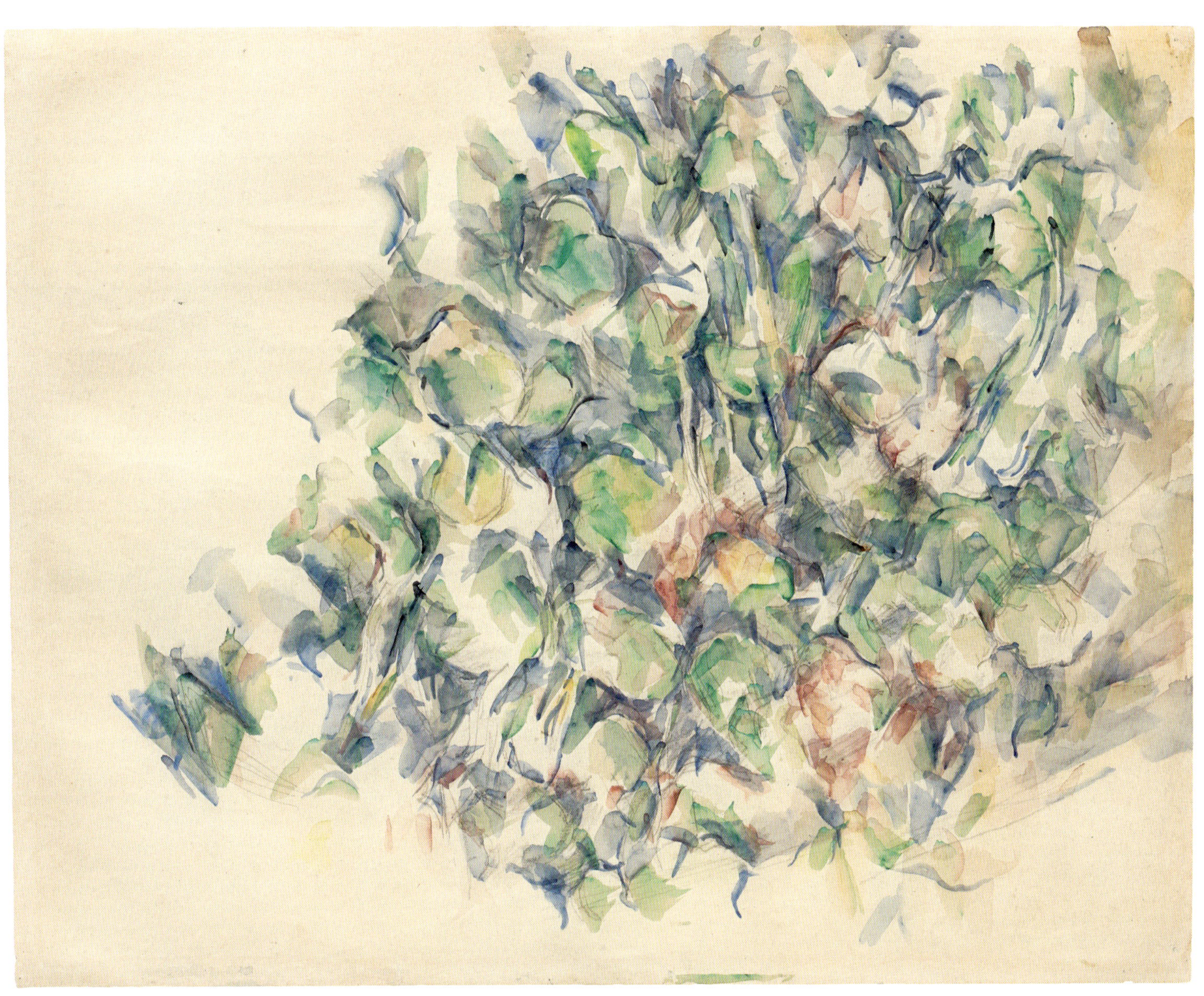

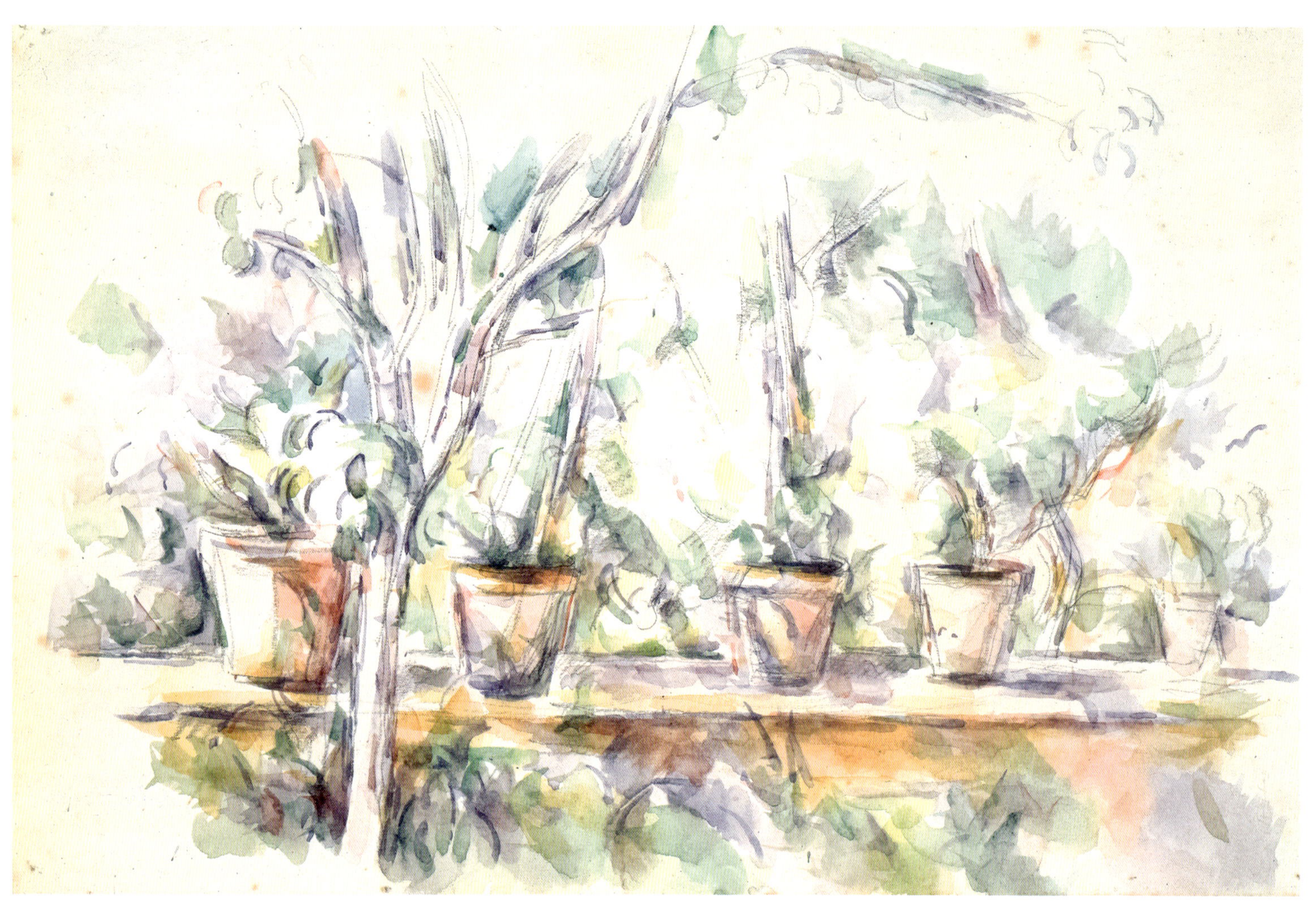

143. *Flowerpots*. 1902–06. Pencil and watercolor on paper, 12 3⁄16 × 18 1⁄2" (31 × 47 cm)

144. *Flowerpots on the Terrace of Les Lauves*. 1902–06. Pencil and watercolor on paper, 23 7⁄8 × 18 13⁄16" (60.7 × 47.8 cm)

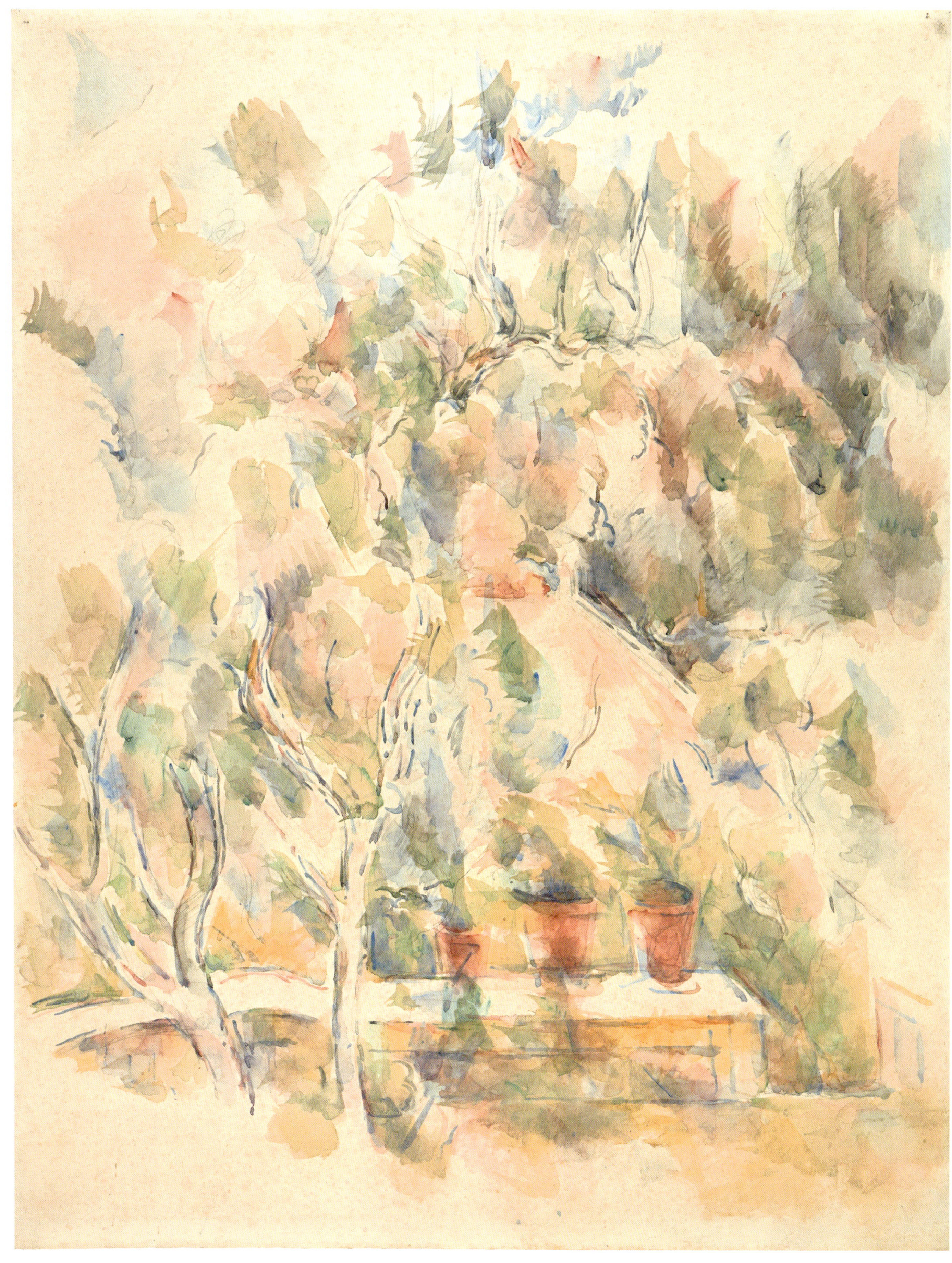

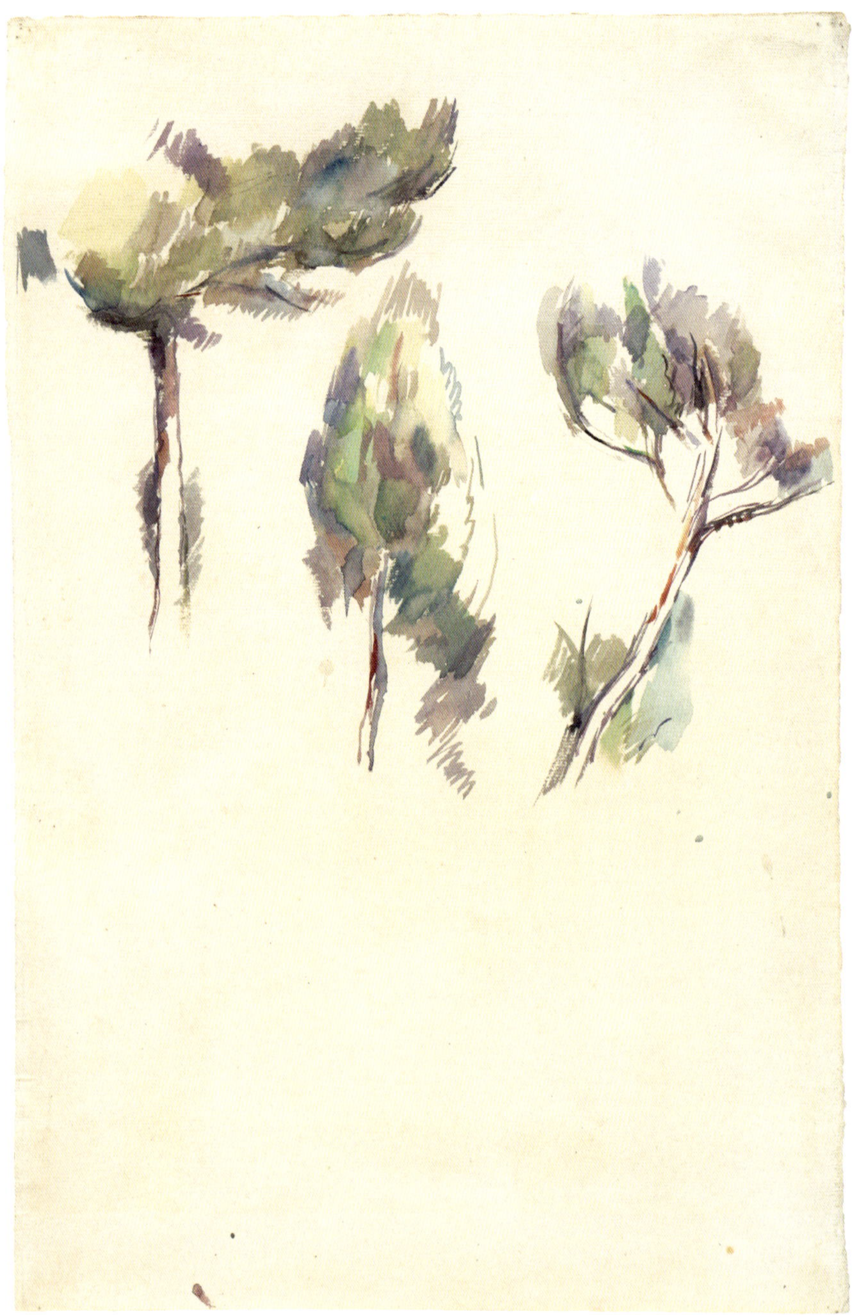

145. *Sketch of Three Pine Trees*. 1890–95. Watercolor on laid paper, 18 ⅞ × 12 3/16" (48 × 31 cm)

146. *Study of a Tree*. 1885–90. Watercolor on paper, 14 3/16 × 11⅛" (36 × 28.2 cm)

147. *Trees at the Water's Edge*. 1900–04. Watercolor on paper, 12 ⅝ × 19 5/16" (32 × 49 cm)

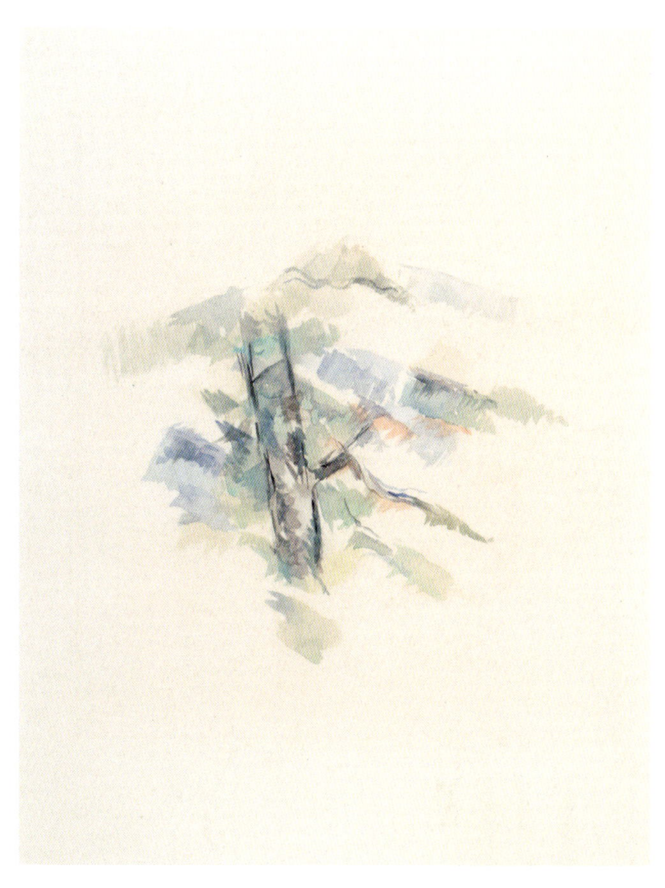

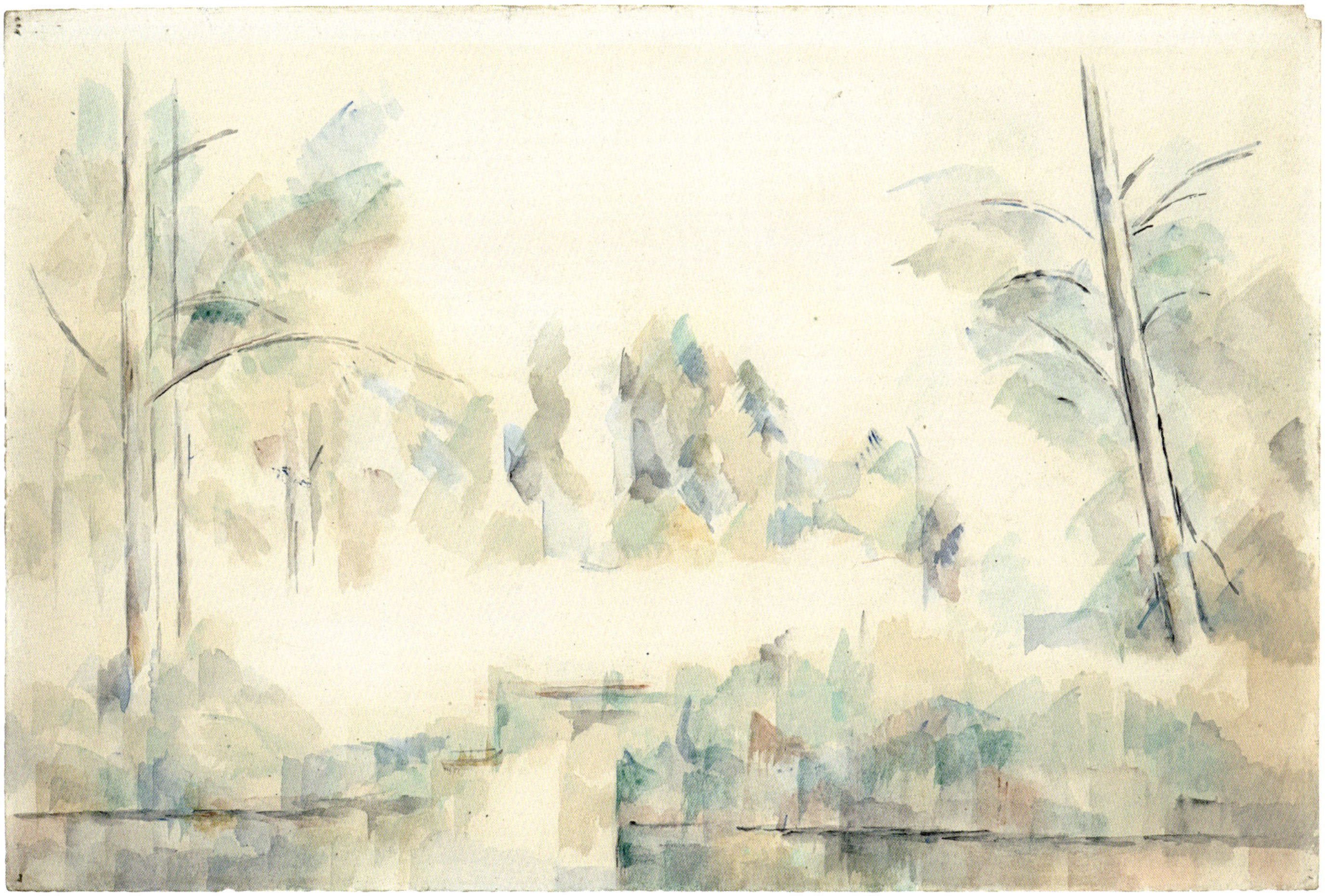

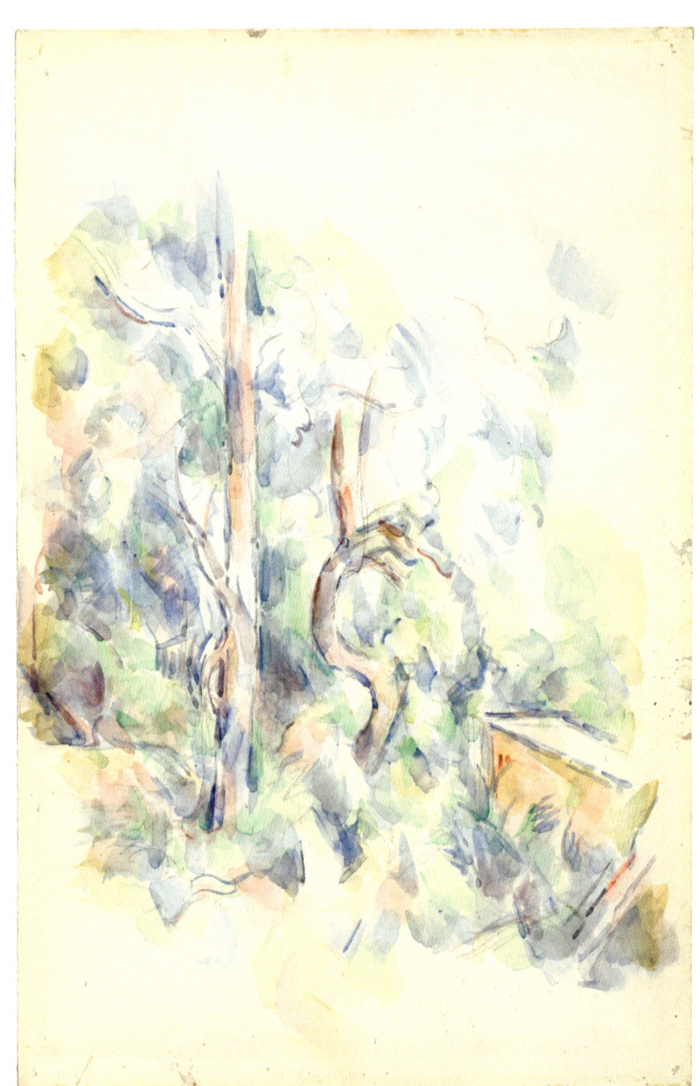

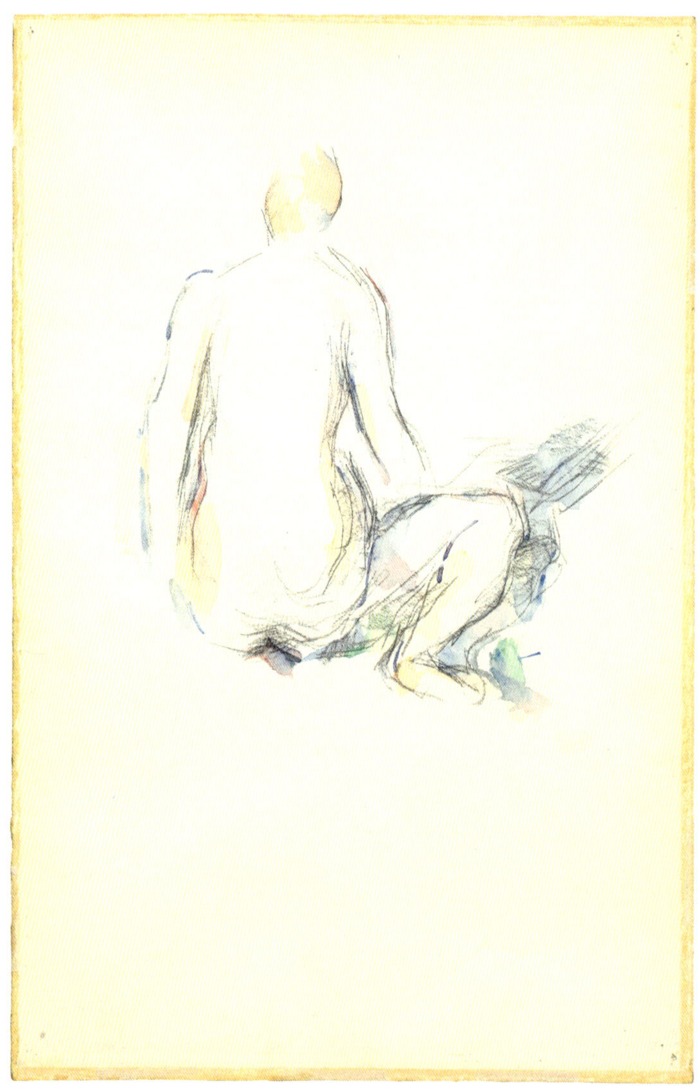

148. *Trees and Cistern in the Park of Château Noir* (recto); *Seated Bather* (verso). 1900–02 (recto); c. 1885 (verso). Pencil and watercolor on wove paper, 18 13⁄16 × 12 3⁄8" (47.8 × 31.4 cm)

149. *Study of Trees* (verso); *Vase of Flowers* (recto). 1887–90 (verso); 1885–88 (possibly later) (recto). Pencil and watercolor on paper, 18 ⅜ × 11 ¹³⁄₁₆" (46.6 × 30 cm)

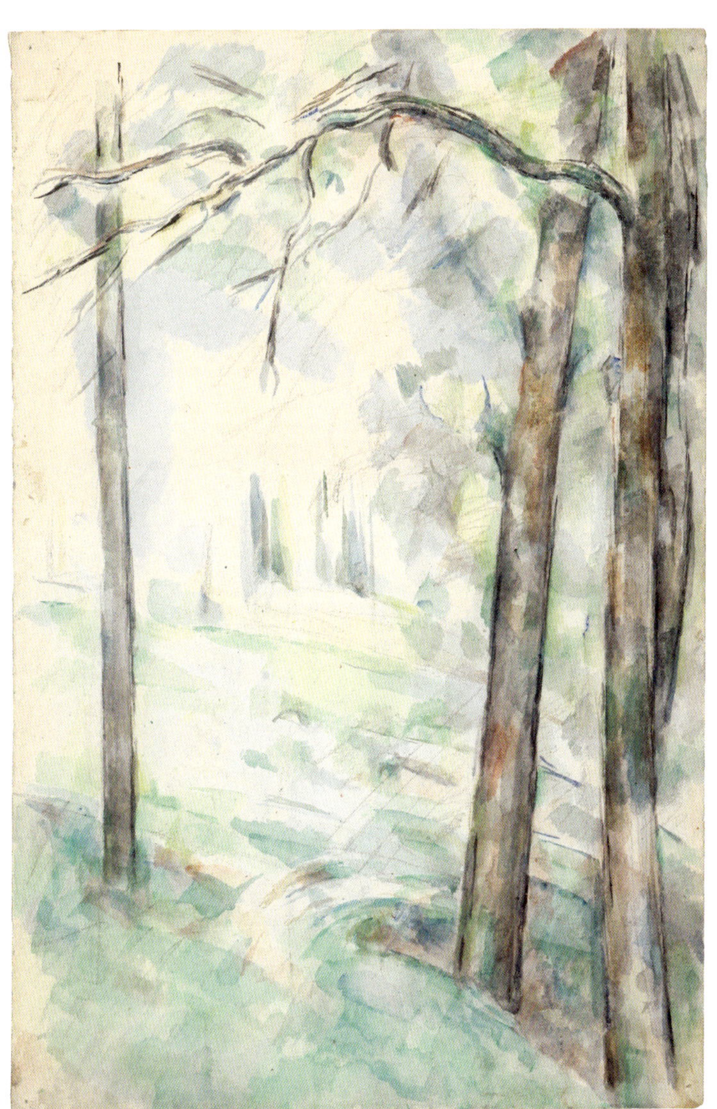

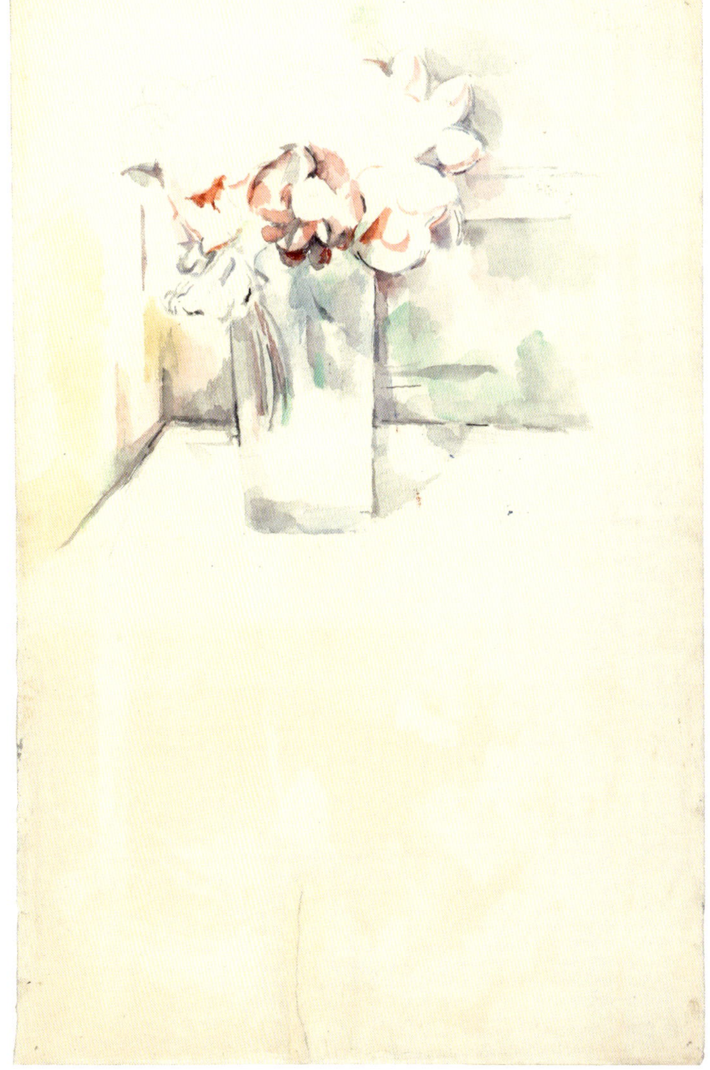

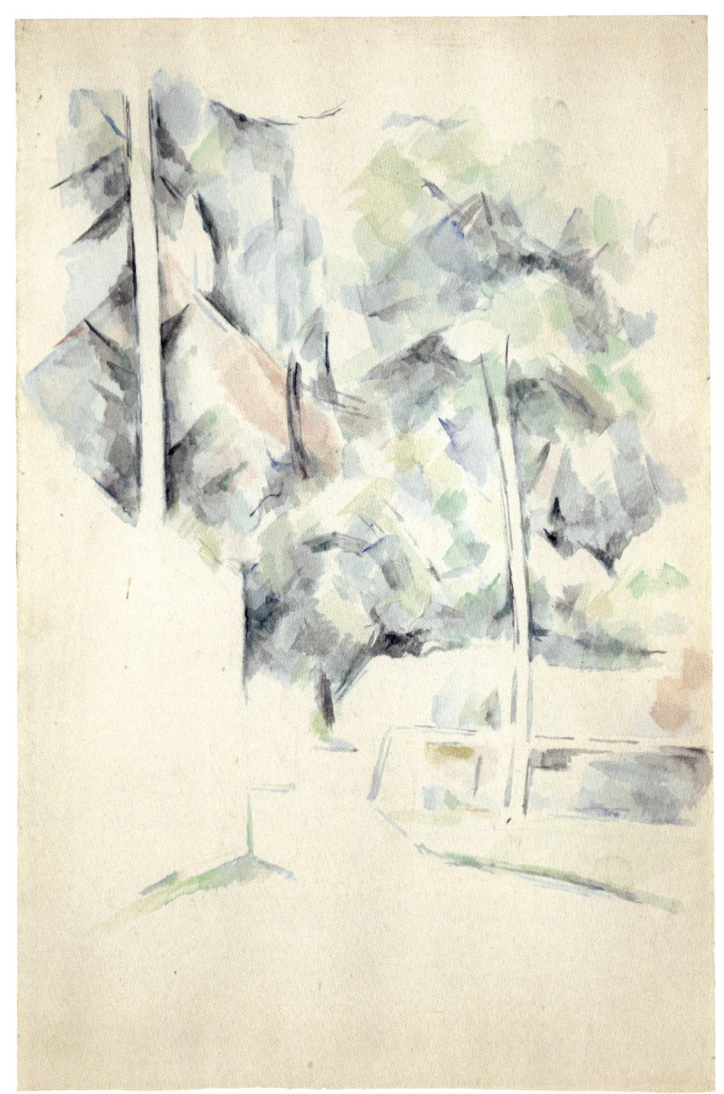

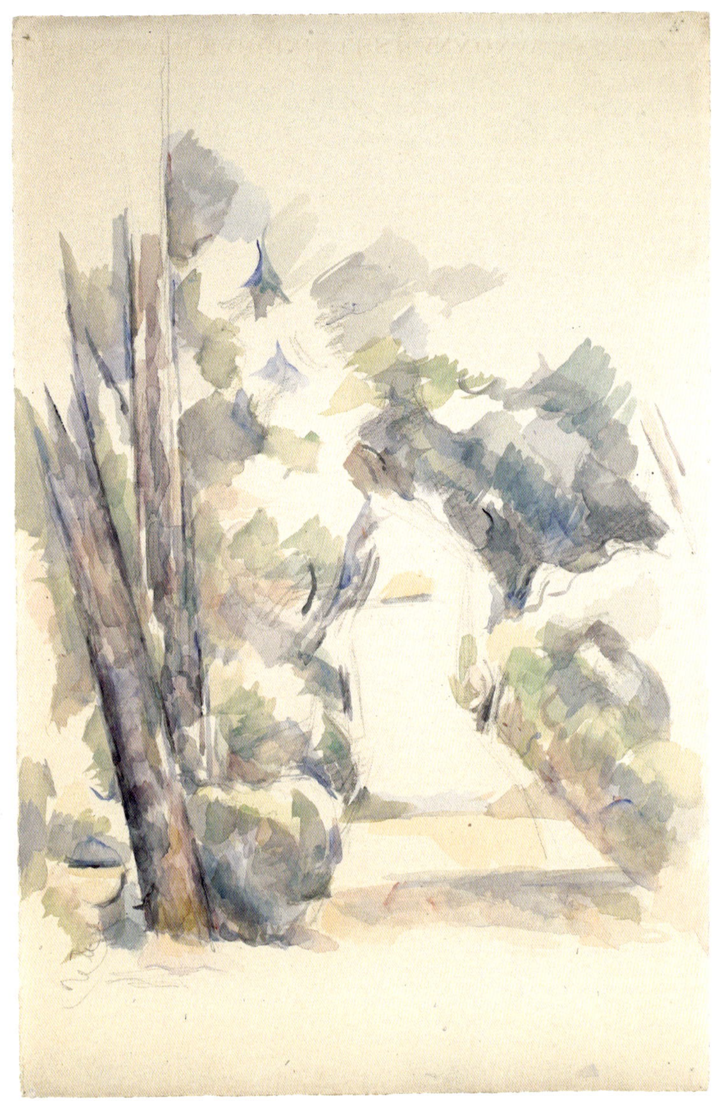

150. *Path, Trees, and Walls*. c. 1900. Watercolor on paper, 18 ⅜ × 12 ⅜" (46.7 × 31.4 cm)

151. *Forest Path*. c. 1890. Pencil and watercolor on paper, 19 × 12 ½" (48.3 × 31.8 cm)

152. *Winter Trees*. c. 1885. Pencil and watercolor on paper, 18 ⅞ × 12 3/16" (48 × 31 cm)

153. *In the Forest*. 1895–98. Pencil and watercolor on paper, 18 ⅞ × 12 3/16" (48 × 31 cm)

154. *In the Forest*. 1895–98. Pencil and watercolor on paper, 17 ⅝ × 11 ⅞" (44.8 × 30.1 cm)

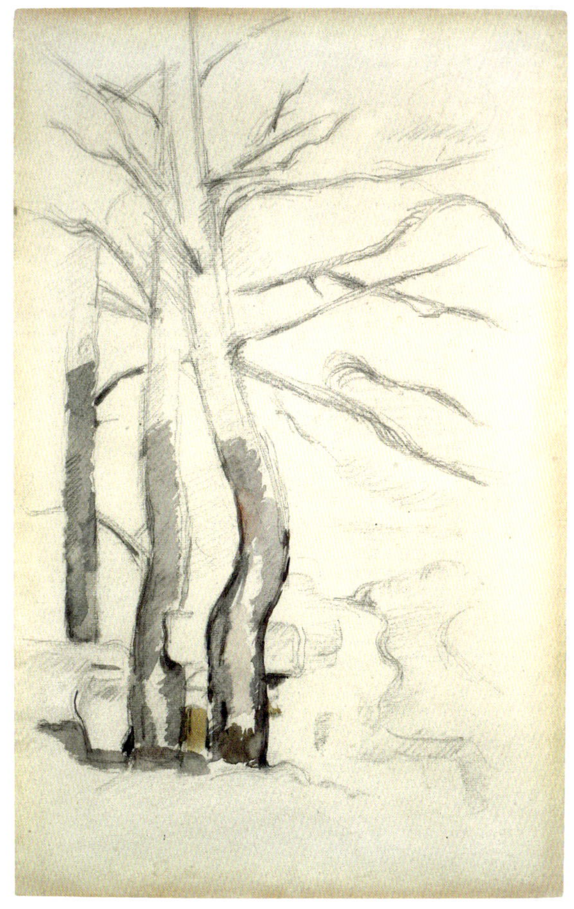

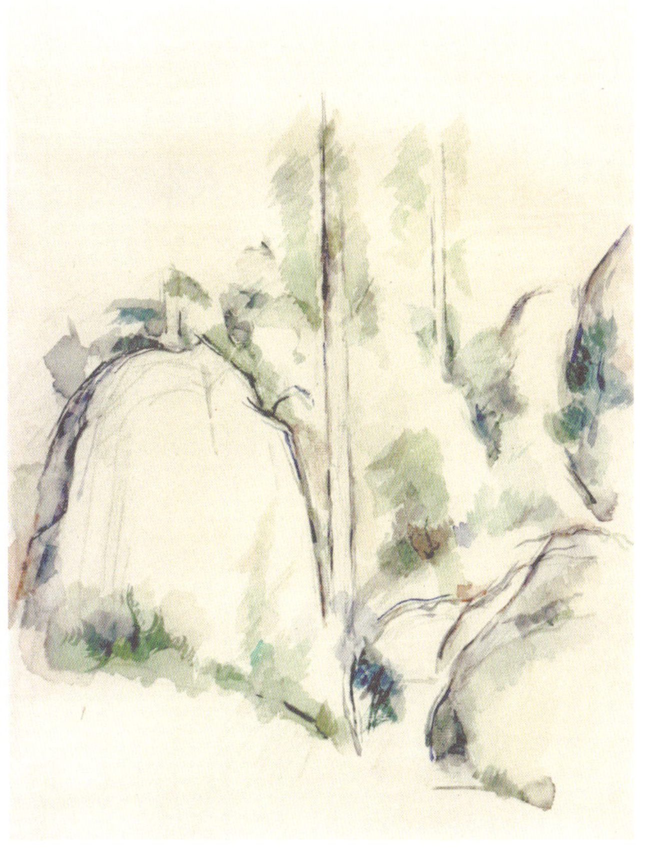

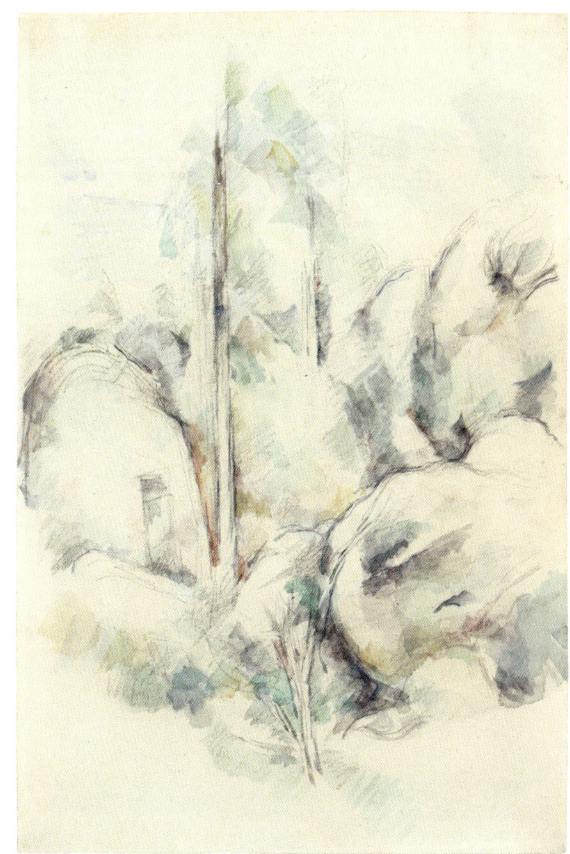

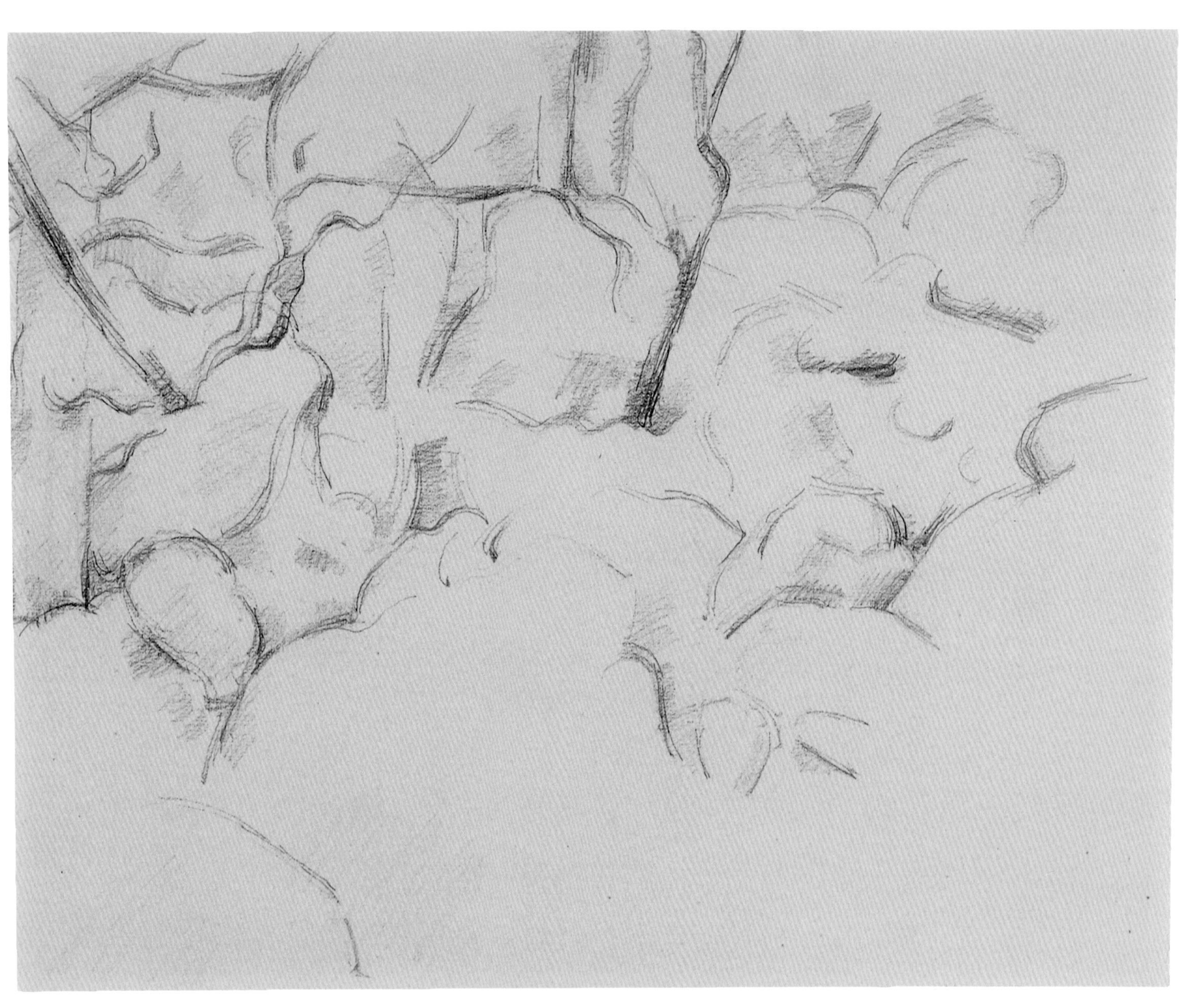

155. *Landscape with Boulders and Trees*. 1890–94. Pencil on wove paper, 8 ¼ × 10 ⅛" (21 × 25.7 cm)

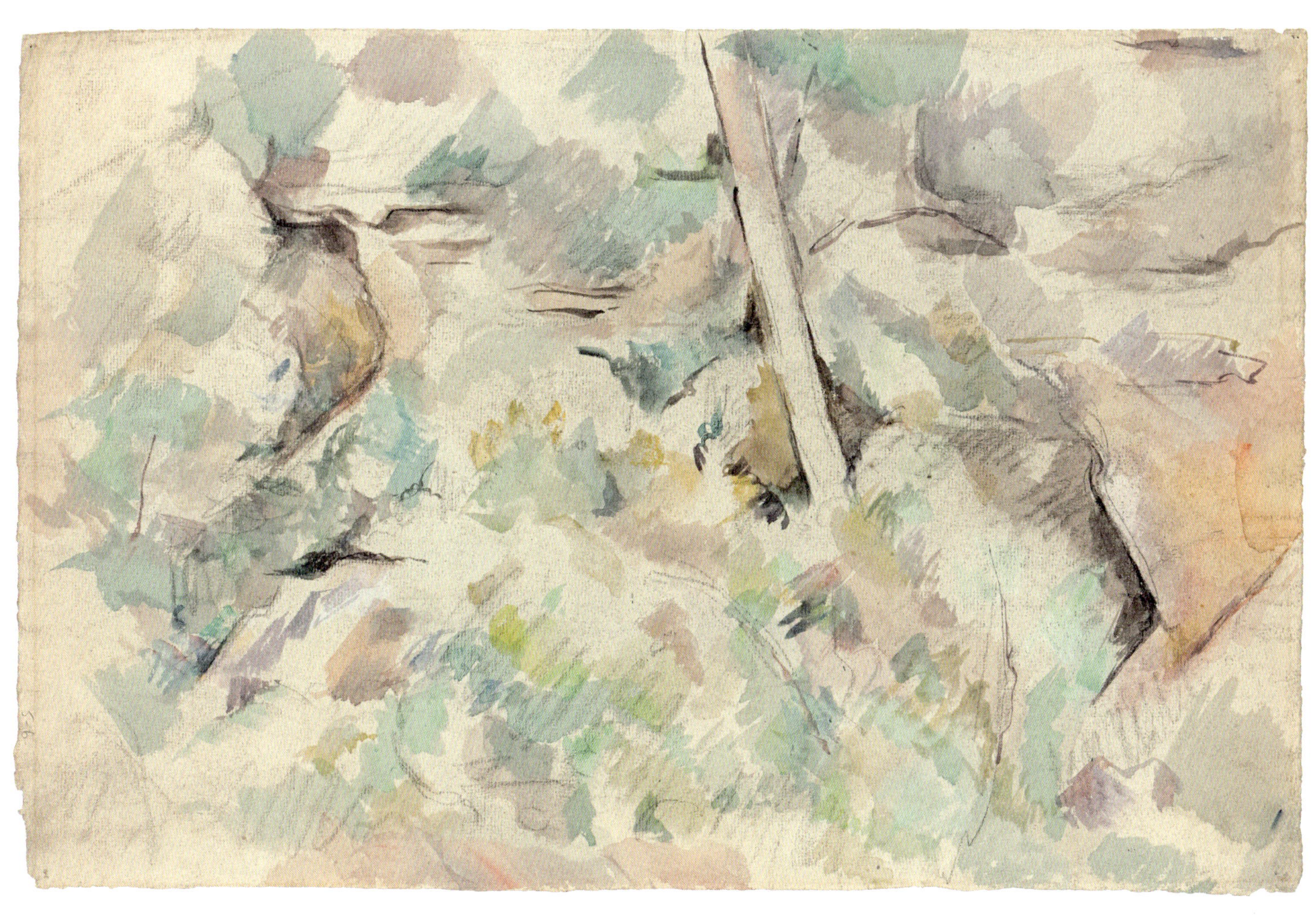

156. *Trees and Rocks*. c. 1895. Pencil and watercolor on laid paper, 12 3/8 × 19 1/8" (31.5 × 48.5 cm)

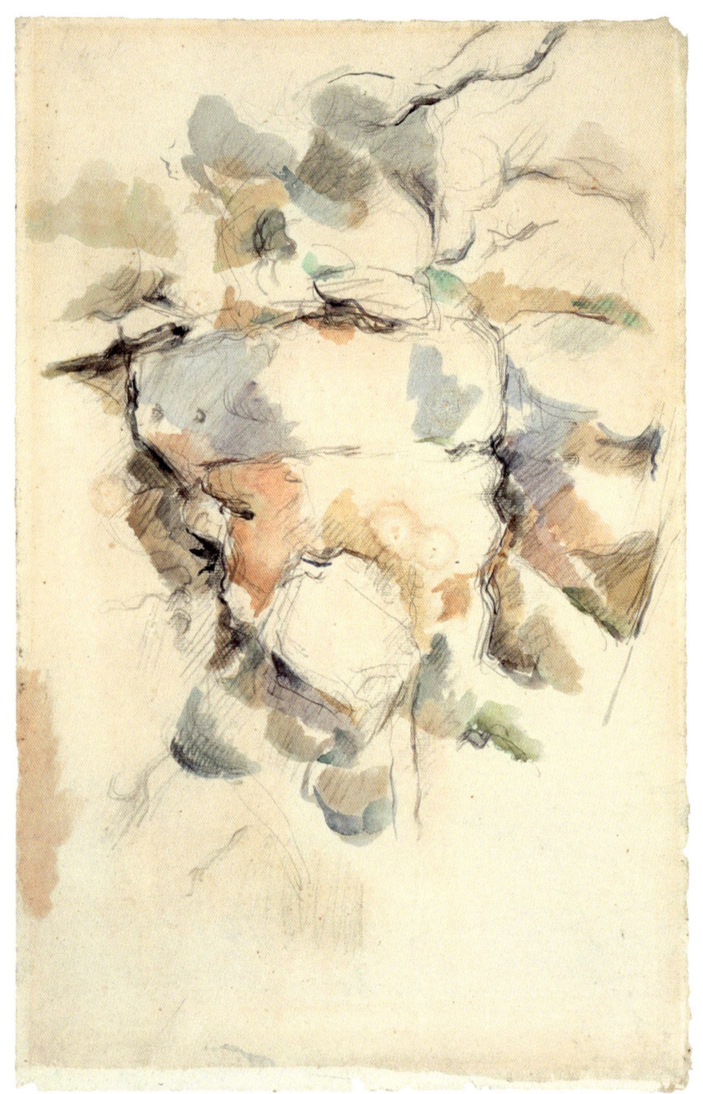

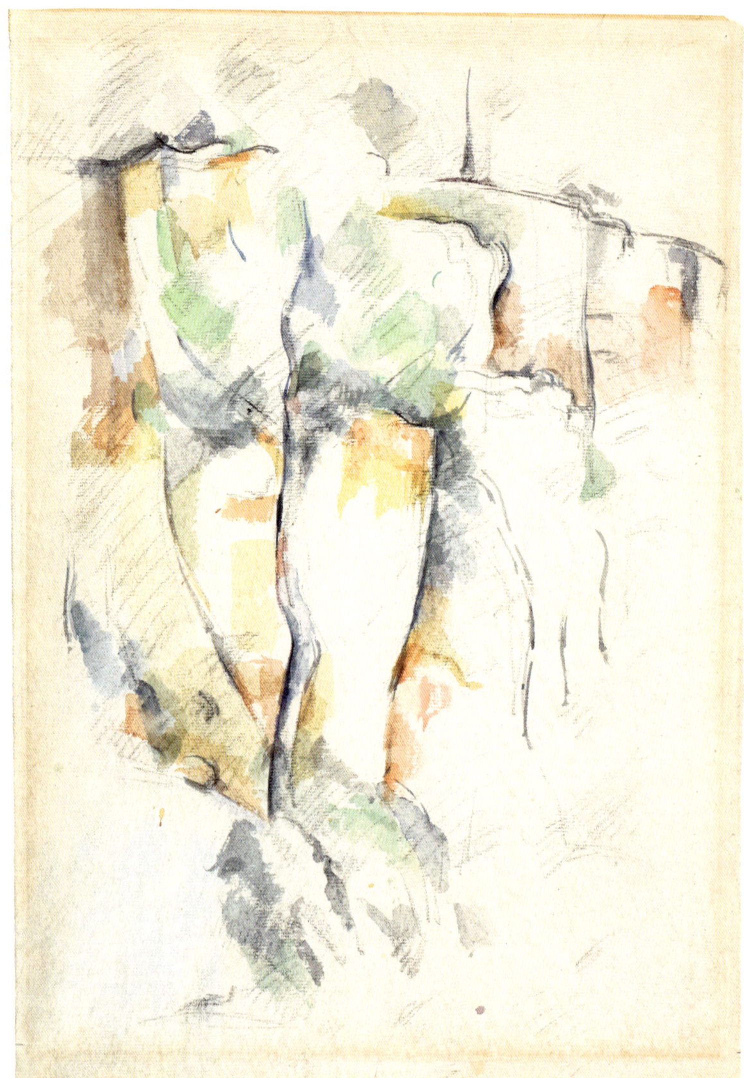

157. *Rocks near the Caves above Château Noir*. 1895–1900. Pencil and watercolor on paper, 18 11/16 × 11 13/16" (47.5 × 30 cm)

158. *Rocks at Bibémus*. 1887–90. Pencil and watercolor on laid paper, 18 1/16 × 12 1/2" (45.9 × 31.8 cm)

159. *Rocks near the Château Noir*. 1895–1900. Watercolor on paper, 19 1/4 × 11 7/16" (48.9 × 29 cm)

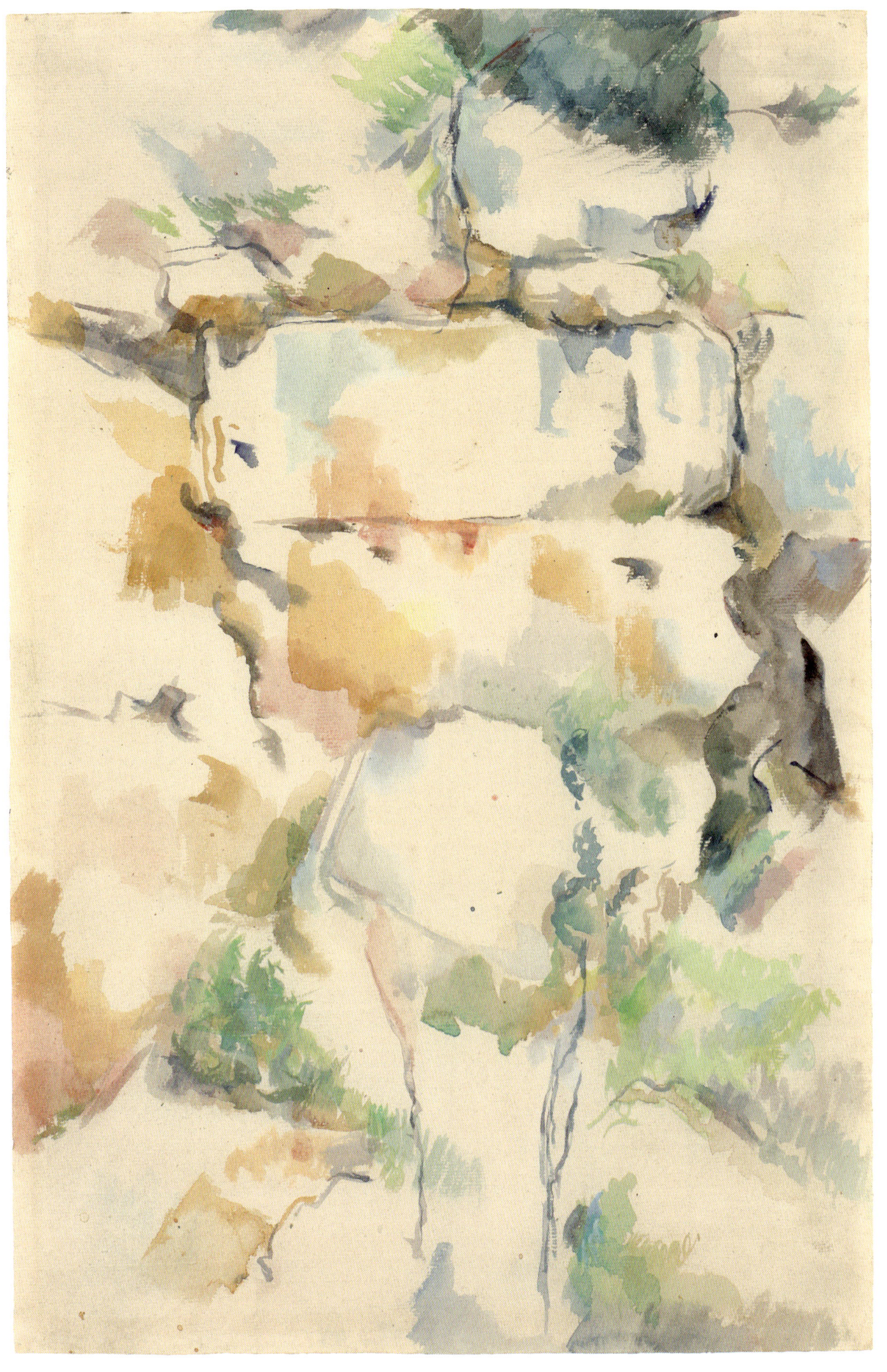

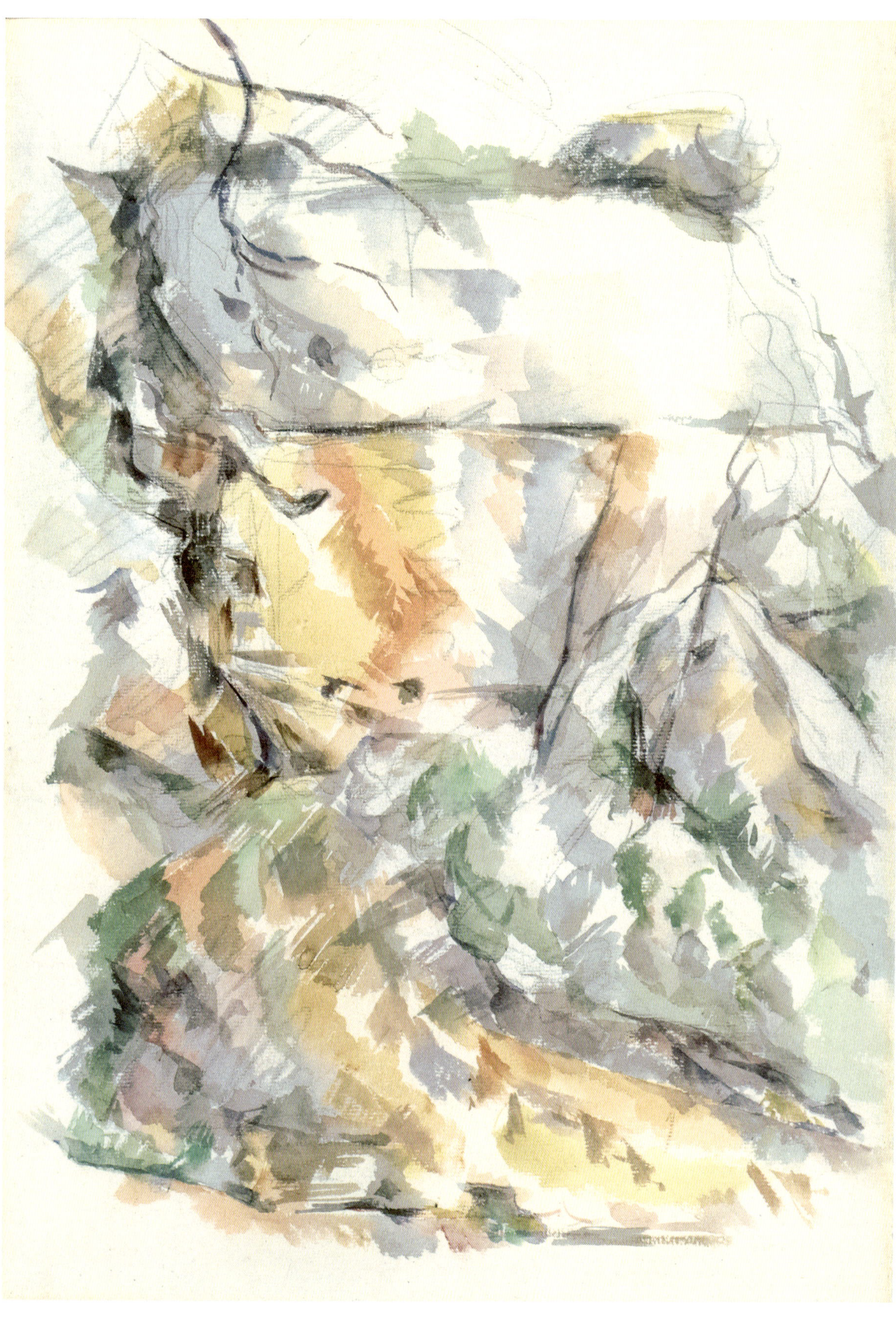

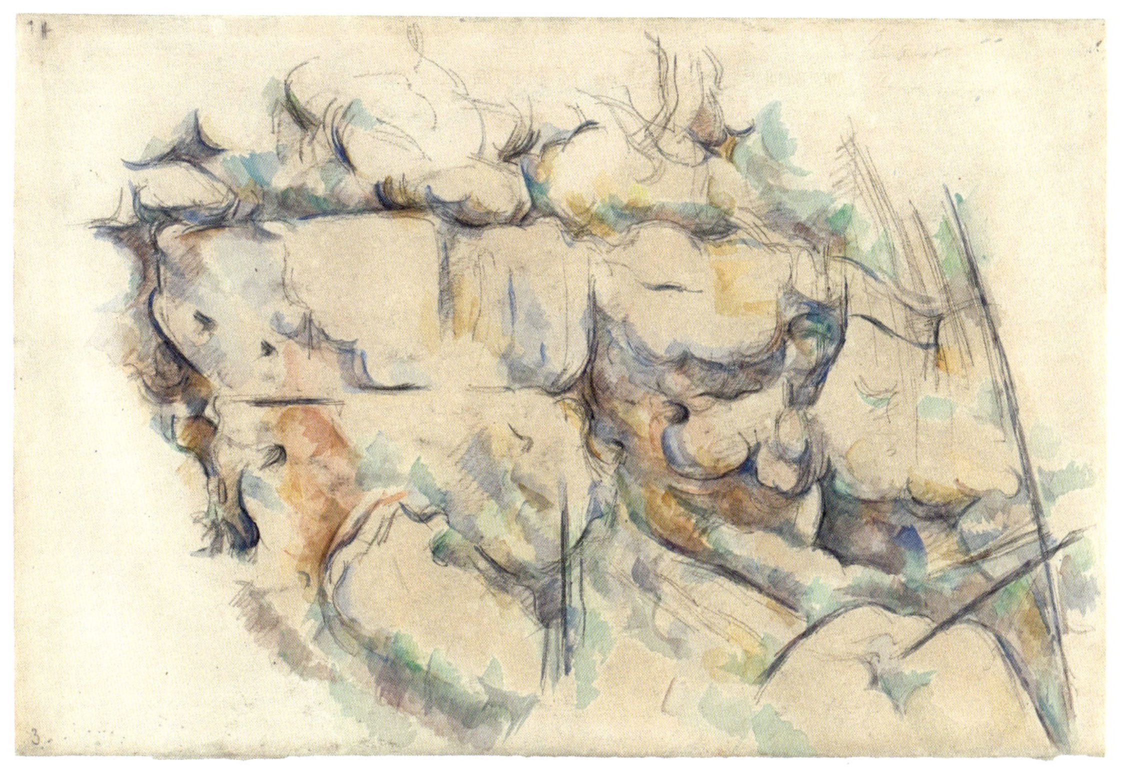

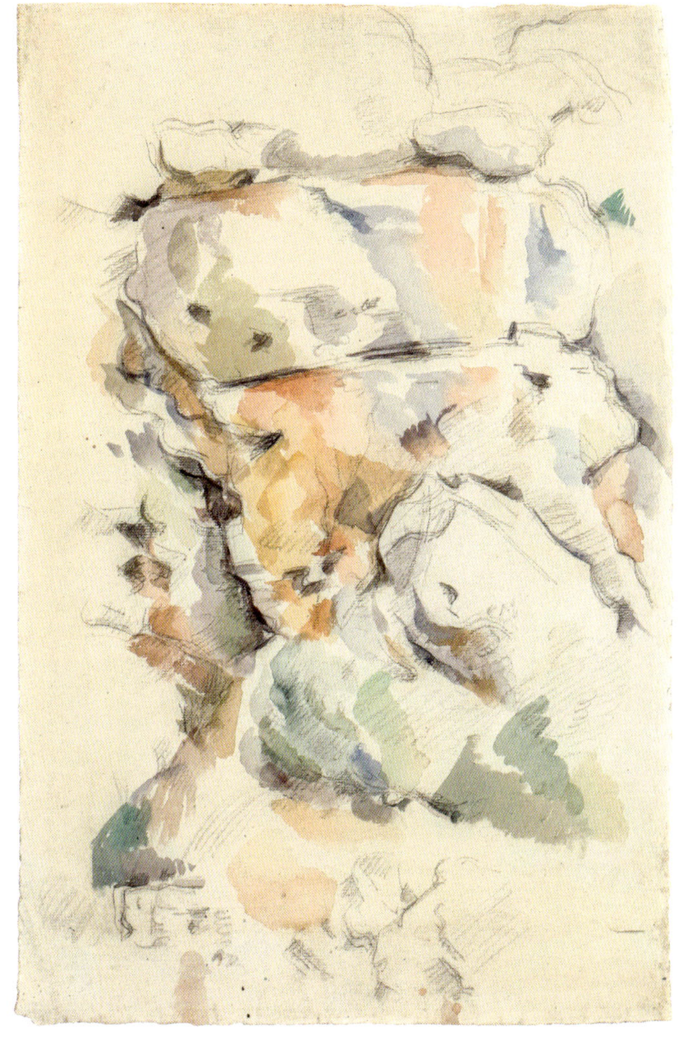

160. *Rocks near the Caves above Château Noir*. 1895–1901. Pencil and watercolor on paper, 17 ½ × 11 ¹³⁄₁₆" (44.5 × 30 cm)

161. *Rocks near the Caves above Château Noir*. 1895–1900. Watercolor and pencil on wove paper, 12 ½ × 18 ¾" (31.7 × 47.5 cm)

162. *Rocks near the Caves above Château Noir*. 1895–1900. Pencil and watercolor on laid paper, 18 × 11 ⅝" (45.7 × 29.6 cm)

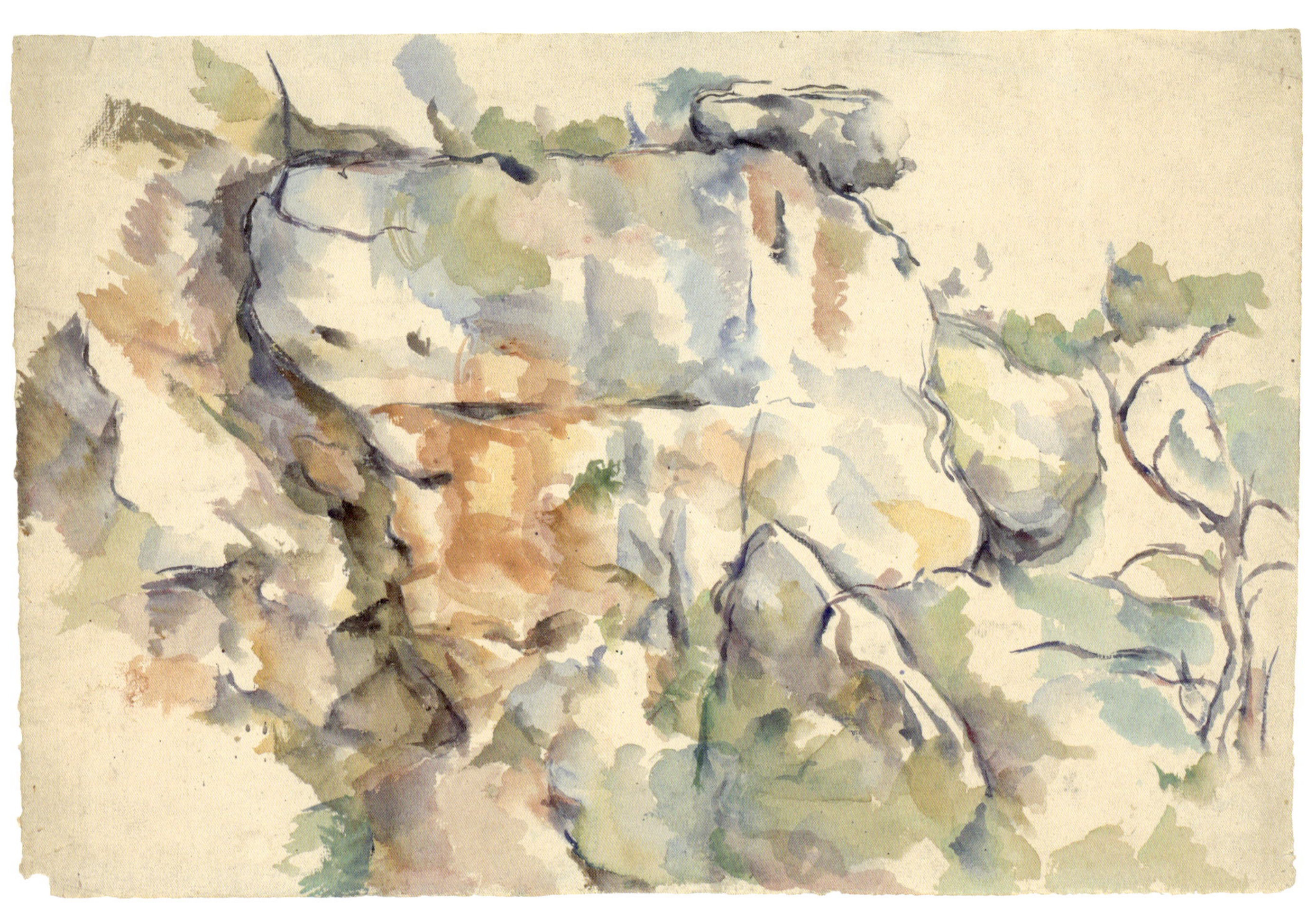

163. *Rocks near the Caves above Château Noir*. 1895–1900. Watercolor on paper, 12 3⁄16 × 18 ½" (31 × 47 cm)

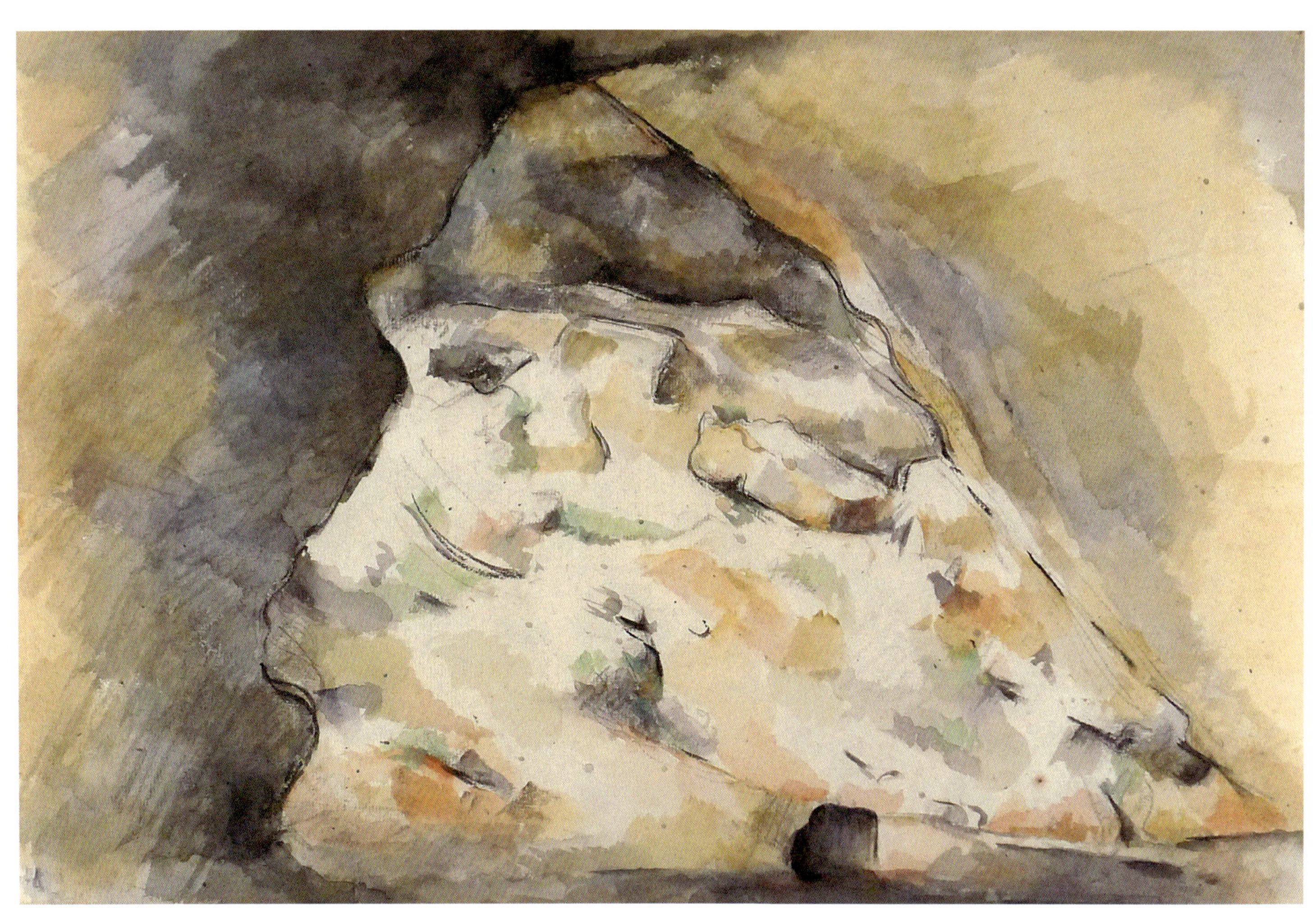

164. *The Quarry near Bibémus*. 1895–1900. Pencil and watercolor on laid paper, 12 $^{9}/_{16}$ × 20" (31.9 × 50.8 cm)

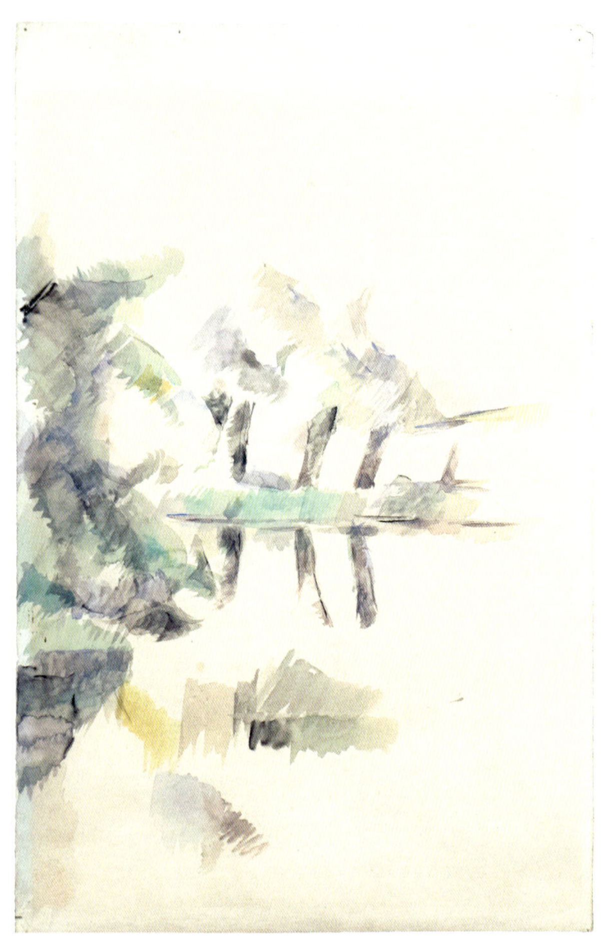

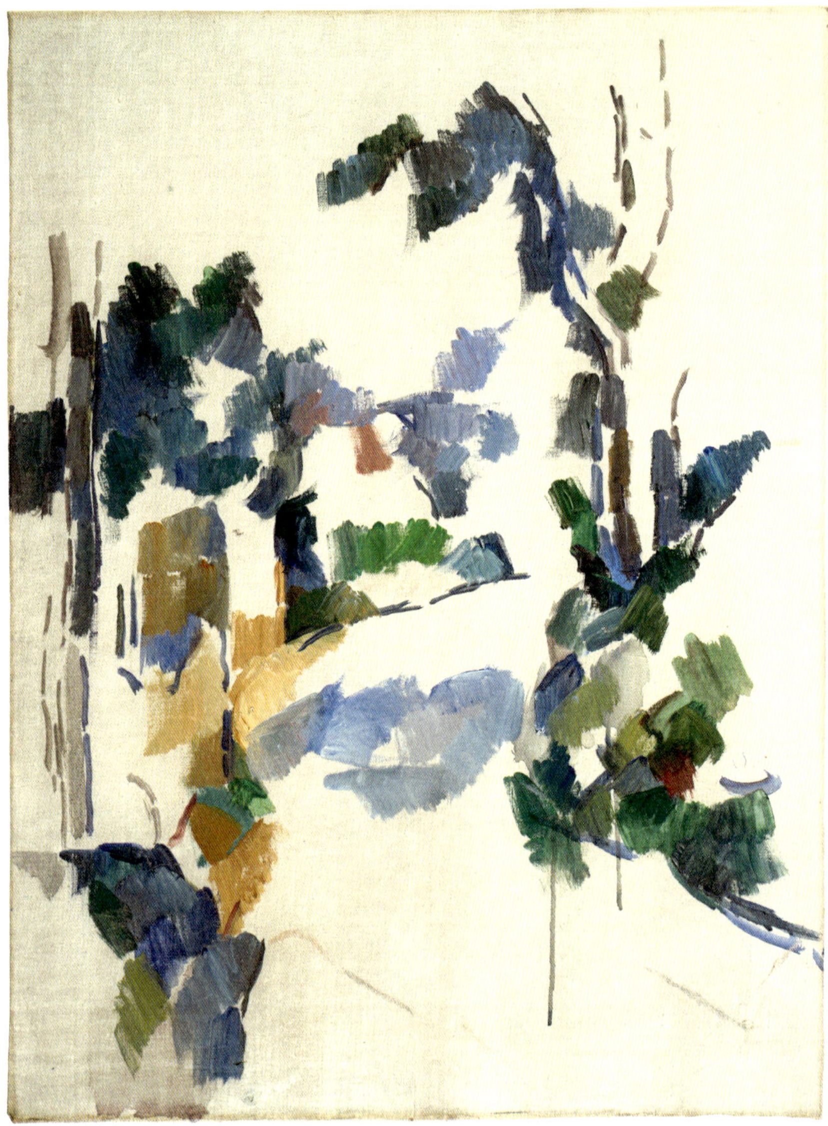

165. *Reflection in the Water, Lake Annecy*. 1896. Watercolor on paper, 19 ⅜ × 12 $^{11}/_{16}$" (49.2 × 32.2 cm)

166. *Study of Trees*. c. 1904. Oil on canvas, 25 $^{5}/_{16}$ × 19 ¼" (64.3 × 48.9 cm)

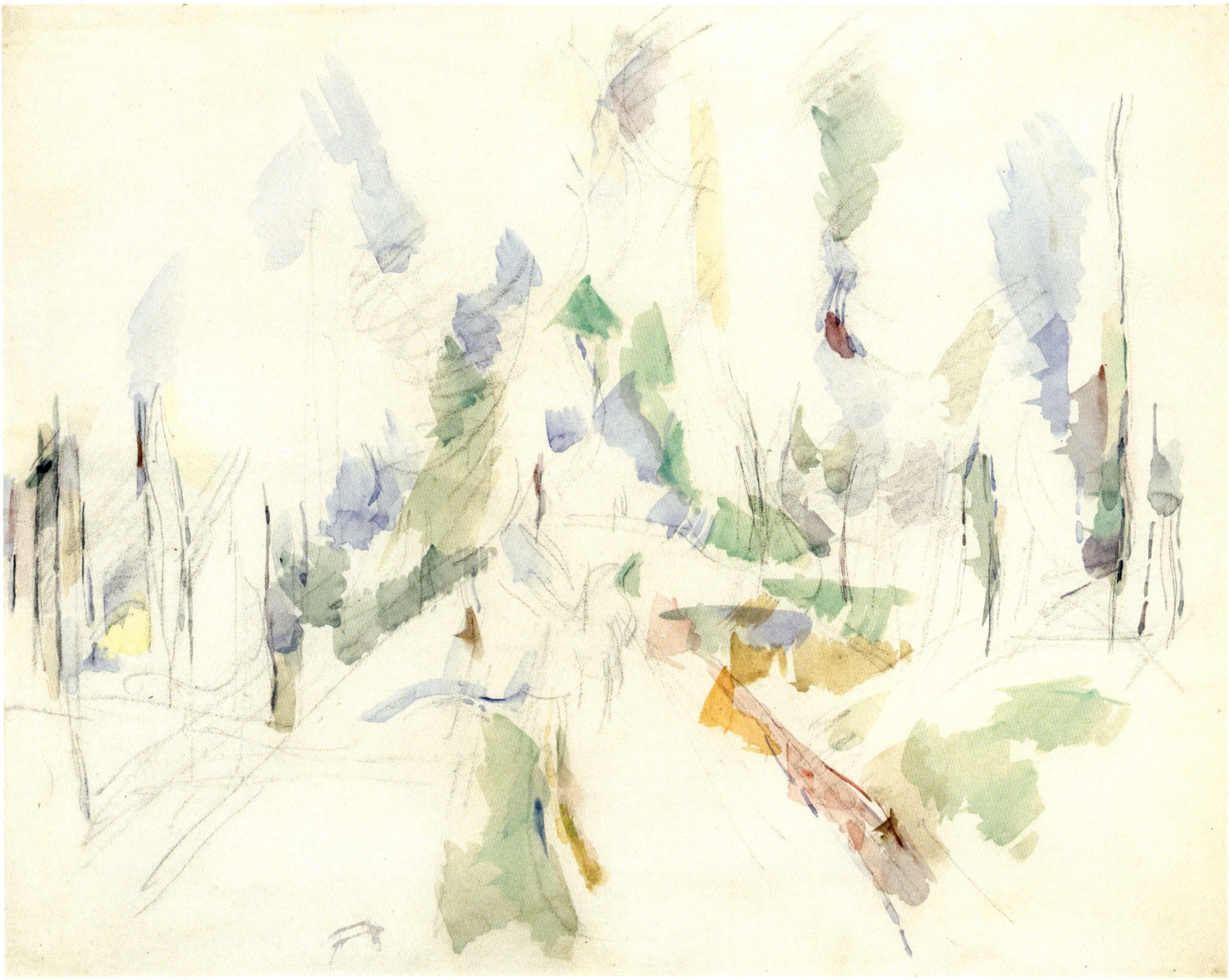

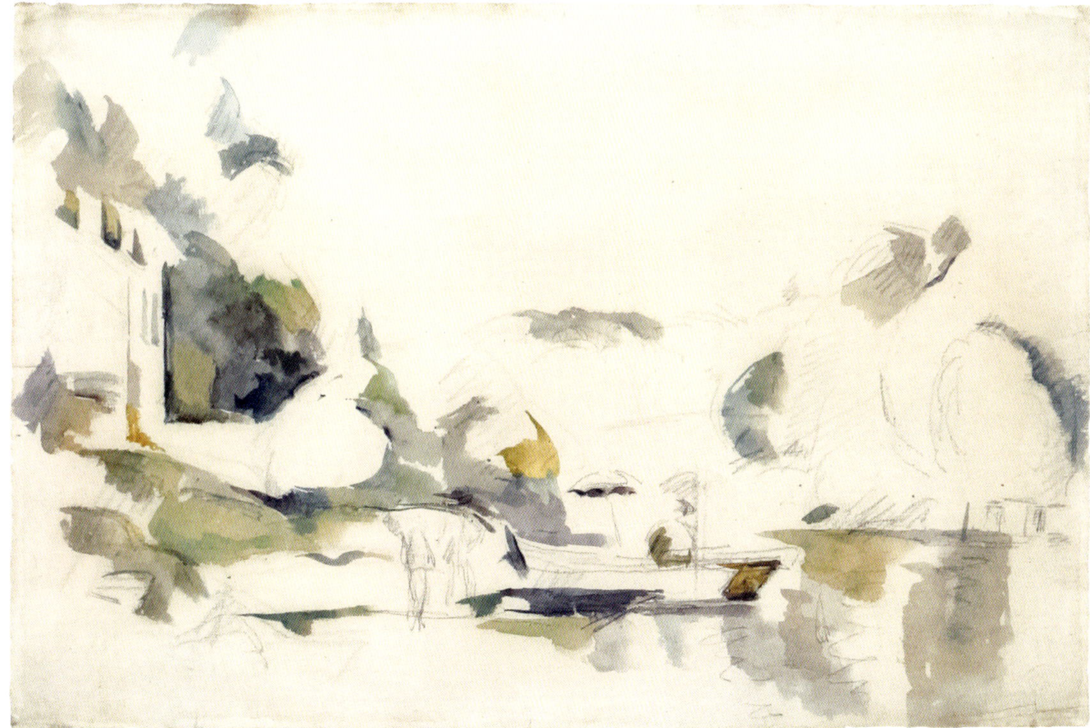

167. *Road through the Woods*. c. 1900. Pencil and watercolor on paper, 18 1/4 × 23 9/16" (46.3 × 59.8 cm)

168. *The Boat, Lake Annecy*. 1896. Pencil and watercolor on laid paper, 12 1/4 × 18 5/8" (31.1 × 47.3 cm)

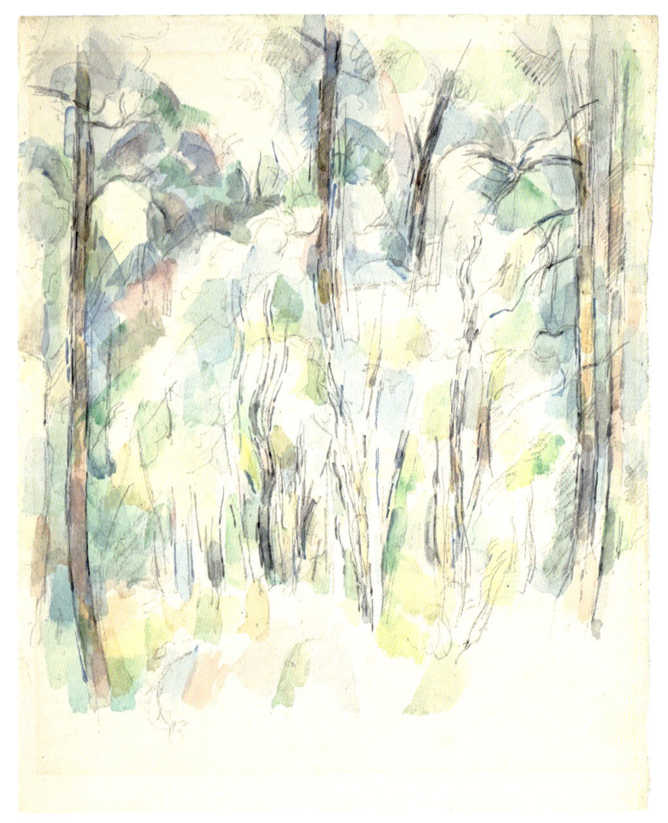

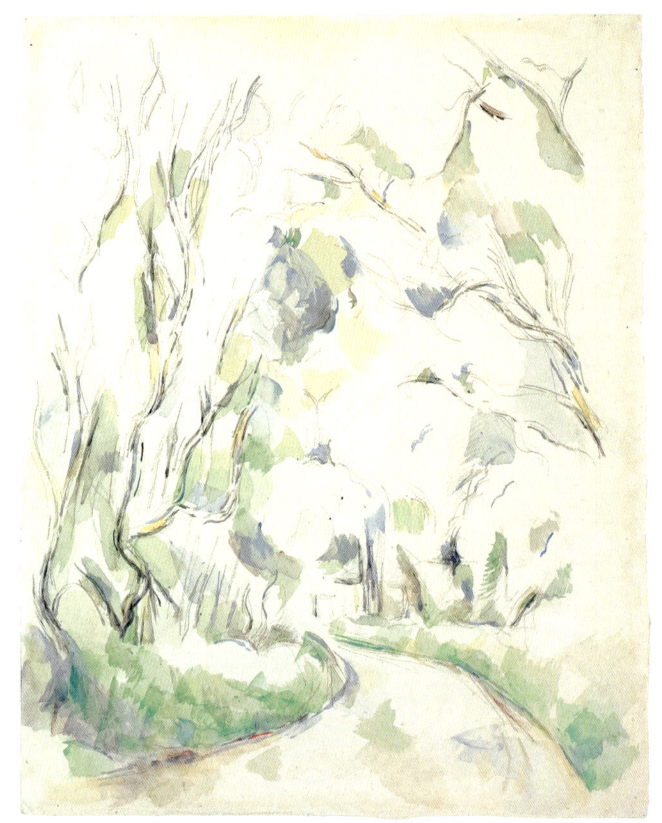

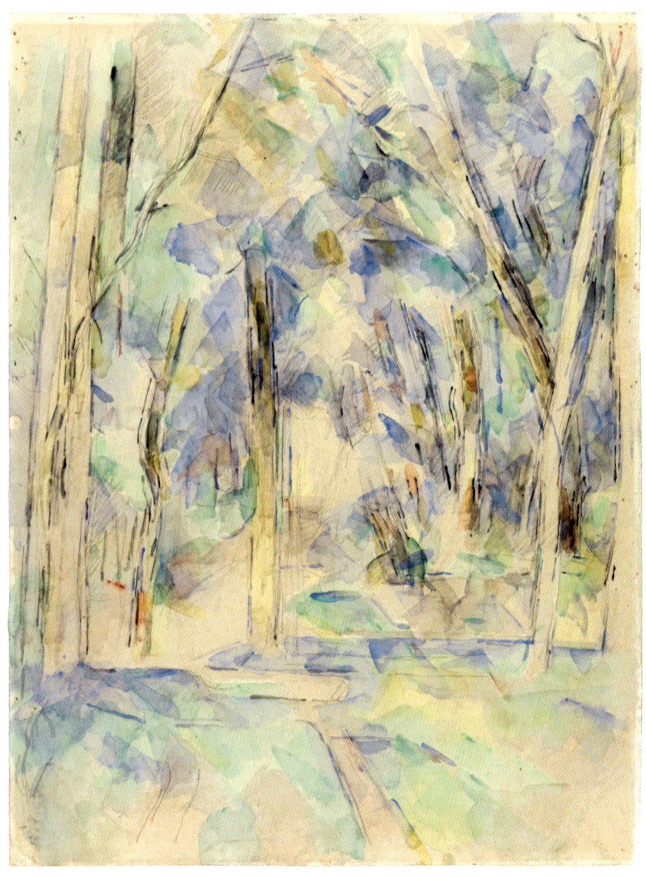

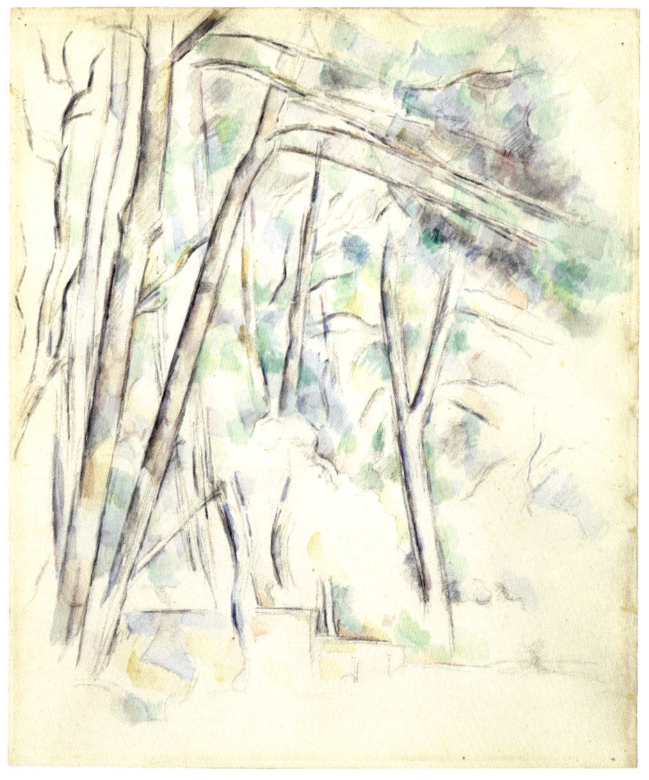

169. *Brushwood*. 1900–04. Pencil and watercolor on paper, 20 × 17" (50.8 × 43.2 cm)

170. *Well and Winding Road in the Park of the Château Noir*. c. 1900. Pencil and watercolor on paper, 21 × 16 ⅞" (53.3 × 42.9 cm)

171. *Trees Forming an Arch*. 1904–05. Pencil and watercolor on paper, 23 ¹¹⁄₁₆ × 18 ¹⁄₁₆" (60.2 × 45.8 cm)

172. *Cistern in the Park of Château Noir*. 1895–1900. Pencil and watercolor on wove paper, 19 ¹⁵⁄₁₆ × 17 ¹⁄₁₆" (50.6 × 43.4 cm)

173. *The Bend in the Road*. 1902–06. Pencil and watercolor on paper, 22 ¹⁄₁₆ × 16 ⁹⁄₁₆" (56 × 42 cm)

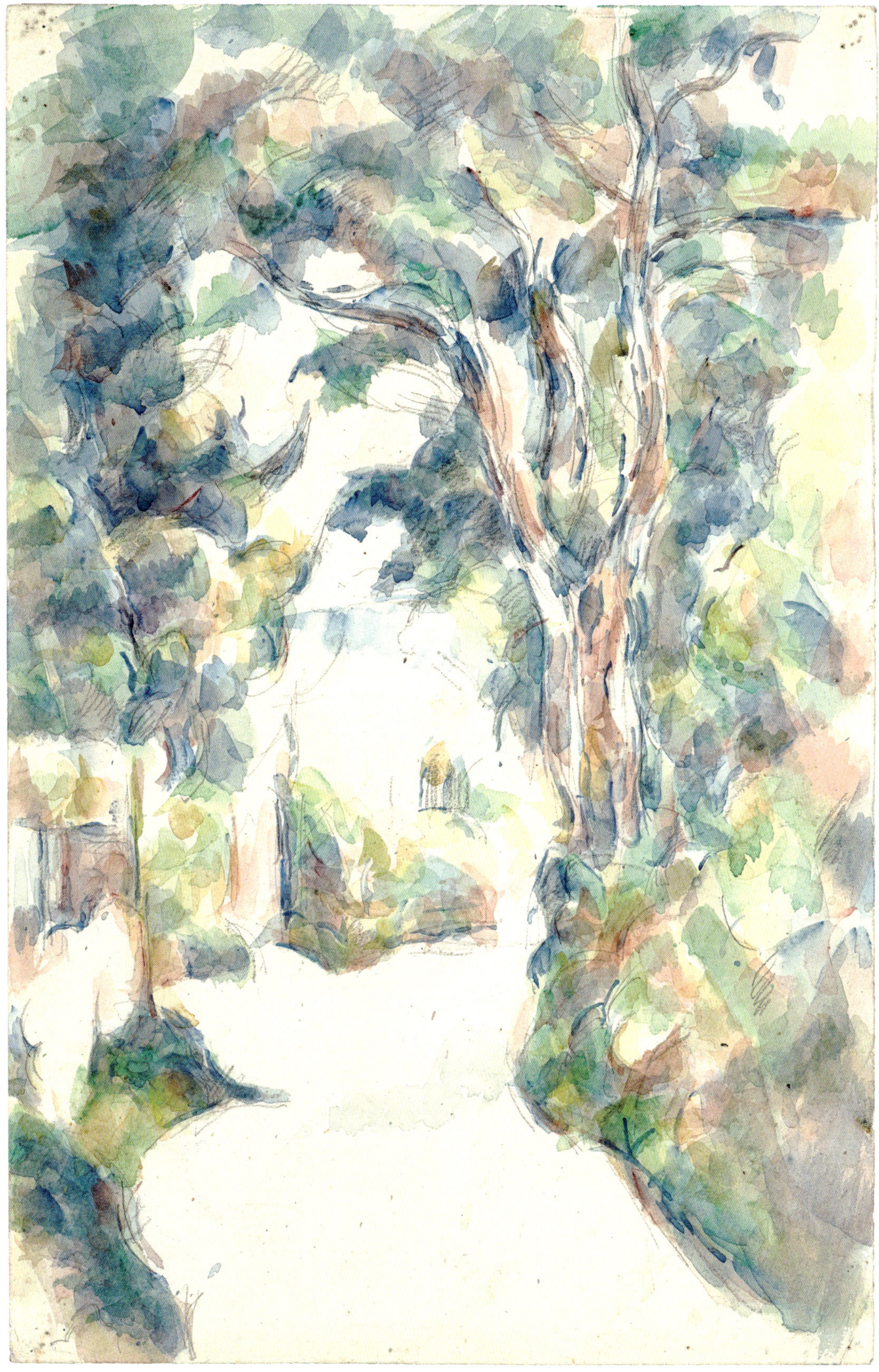

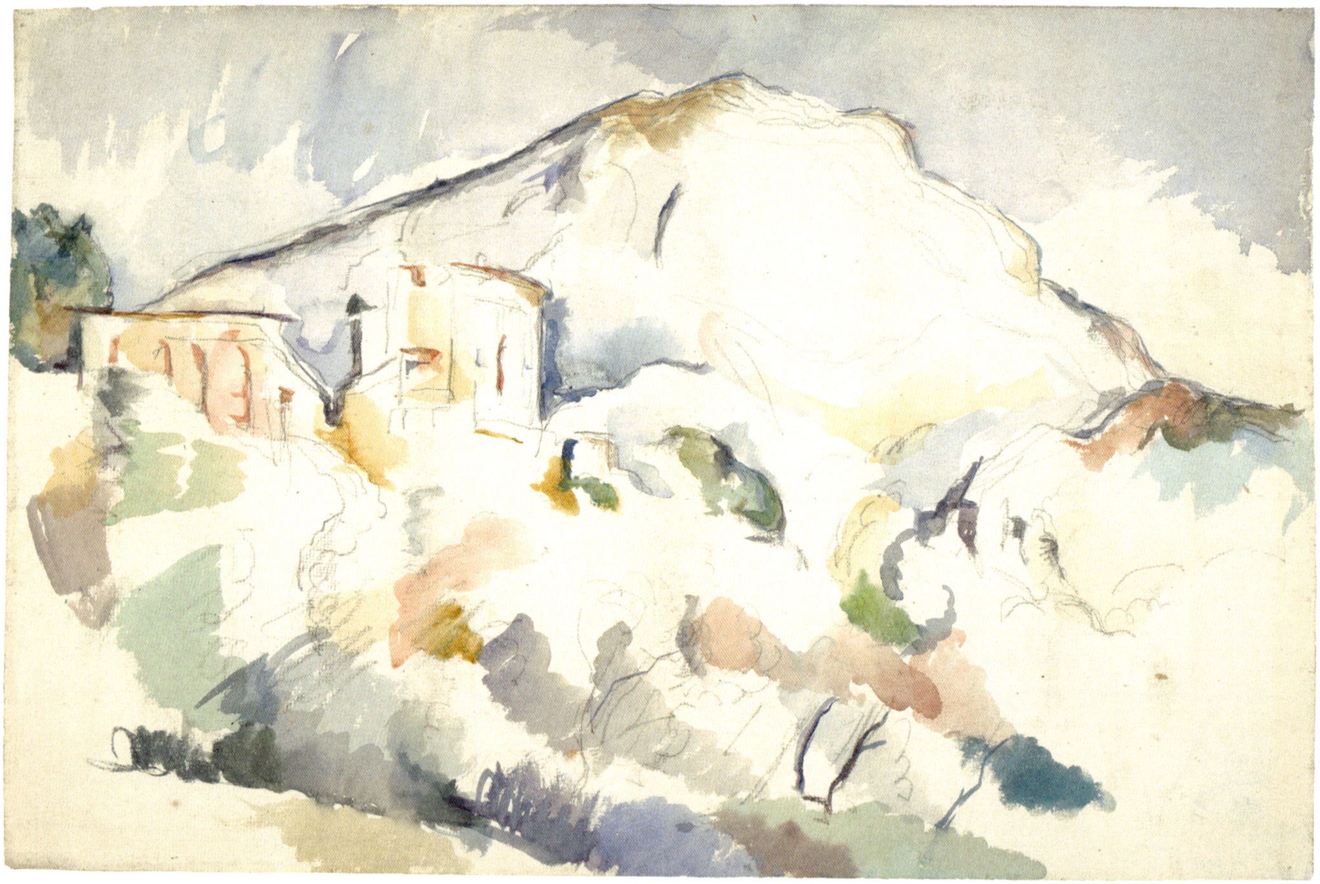

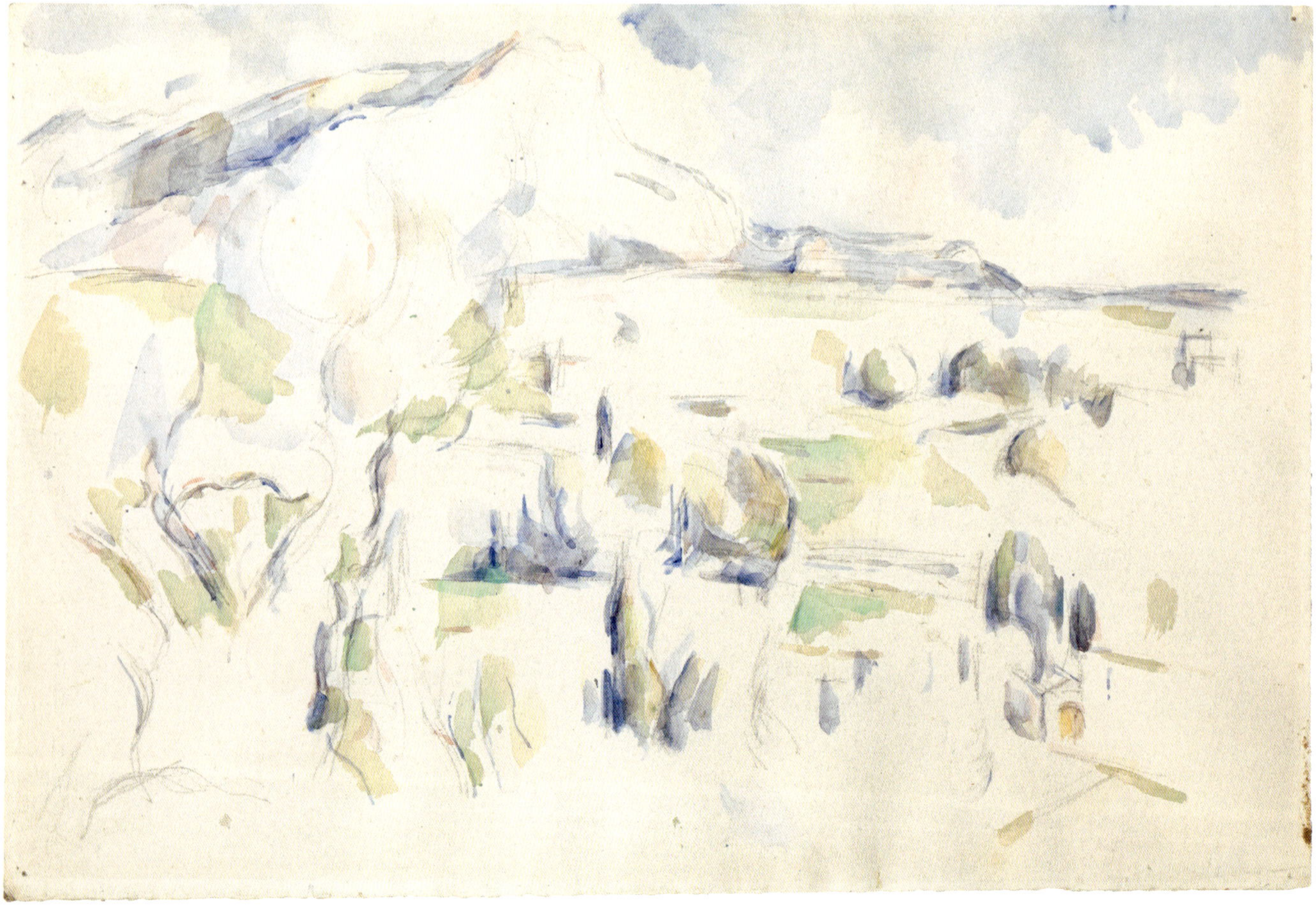

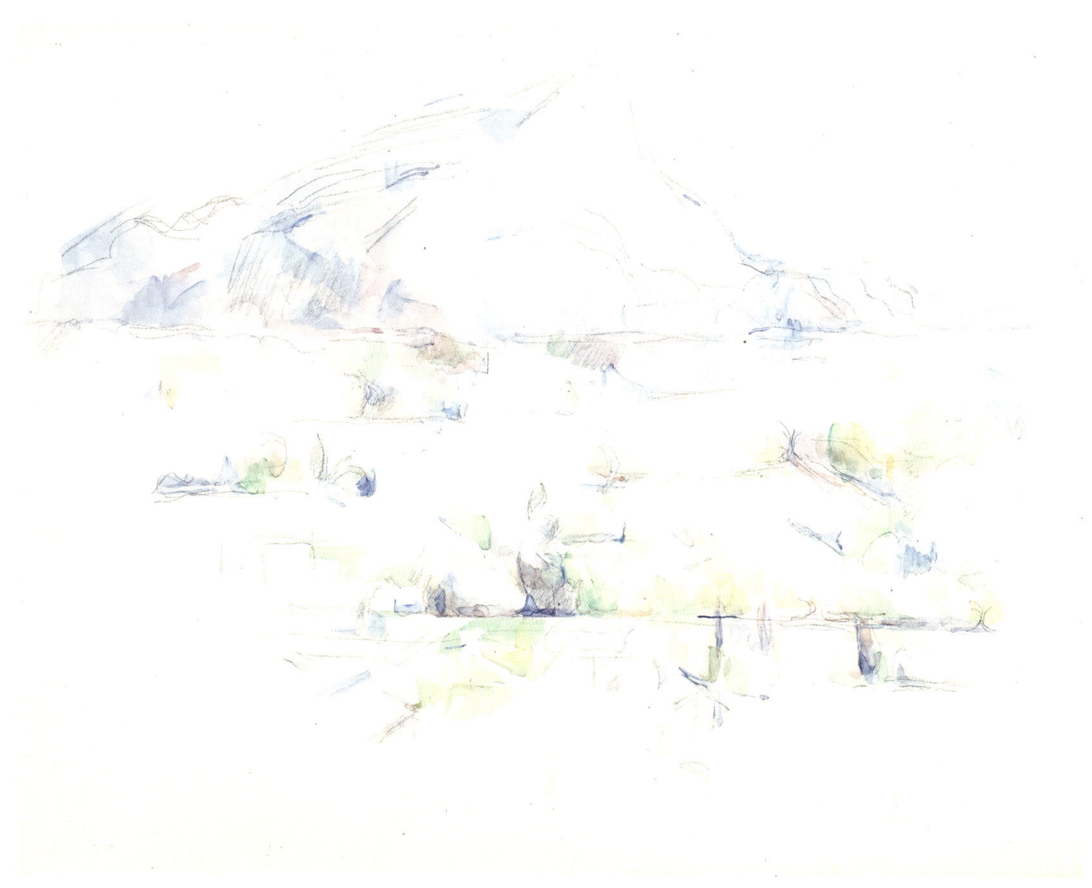

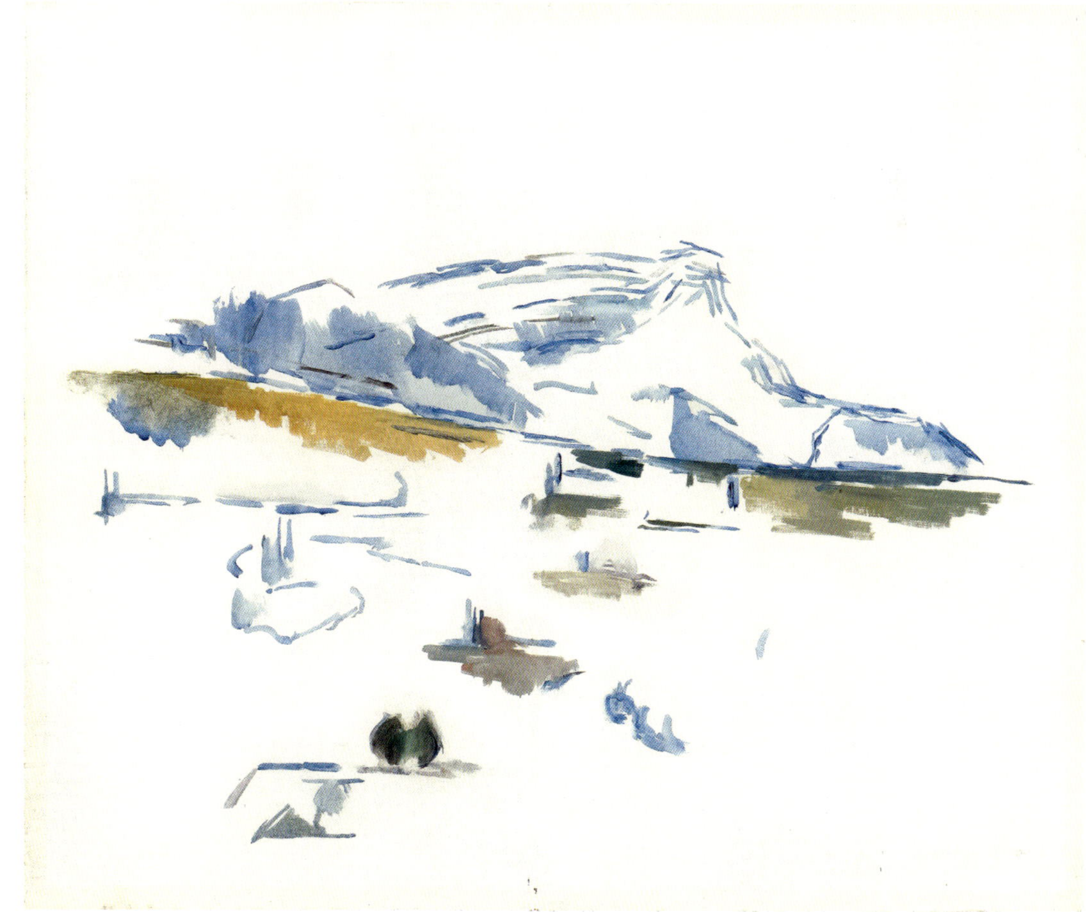

174. *The Château Noir with Mont Sainte-Victoire*. 1890–95. Watercolor and pencil on laid paper, 12 3/16 × 19" (31 × 48.3 cm)

175. *Mont Sainte-Victoire*. 1901–06. Pencil and watercolor on wove paper, 12 9/16 × 18 3/4" (31.9 × 47.6 cm)

176. *Mont Sainte-Victoire Seen from Les Lauves*. 1901–06. Pencil and watercolor on paper, 18 11/16 × 24 3/16" (47.5 × 61.5 cm)

177. *Mont Sainte-Victoire*. c. 1904. Oil on canvas, 21 1/4 × 25 9/16" (54 × 65 cm)

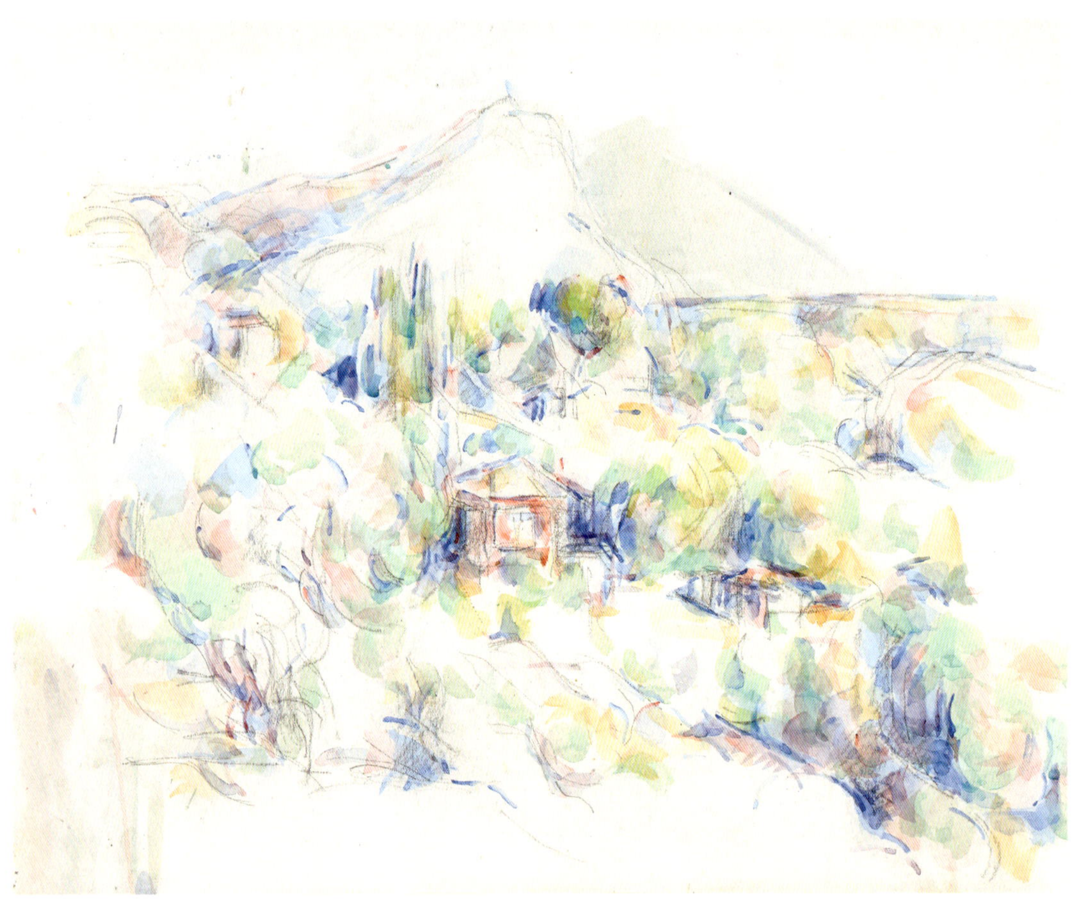

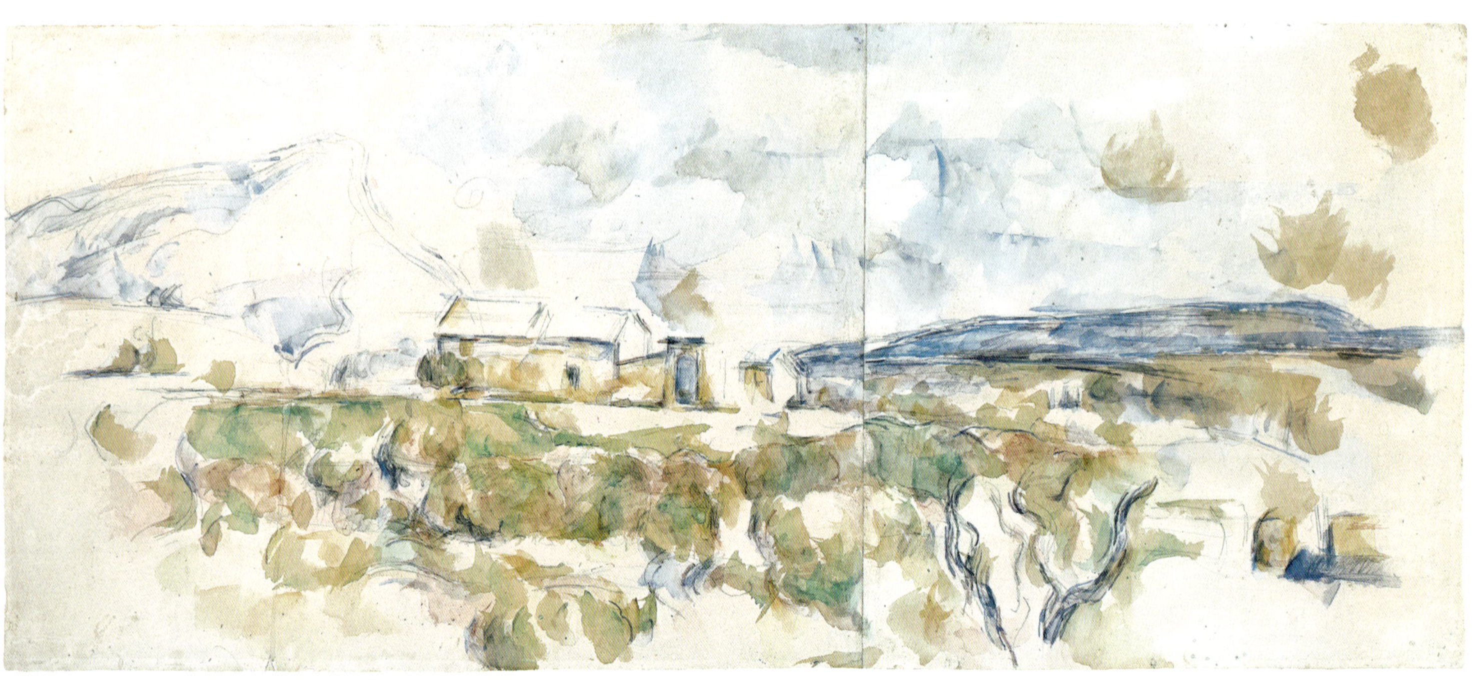

178. *Mont Sainte-Victoire.* c. 1906. Pencil and watercolor on paper, 16 1/16 × 21 1/4" (40.8 × 54 cm)

179. *Mont Sainte-Victoire Seen from Les Lauves.* 1902–06. Pencil and watercolor on two joined sheets of paper, 12 1/8 × 28 1/4" (30.8 × 71.8 cm)

180. *Mont Sainte-Victoire.* 1902–06. Watercolor and pencil on wove paper, 16 3/4 × 21 3/8" (42.5 × 54.2 cm)

181. *Mont Sainte-Victoire.* 1902–06. Pencil and watercolor on paper, 14 3/16 × 21 5/8" (36 × 55 cm)

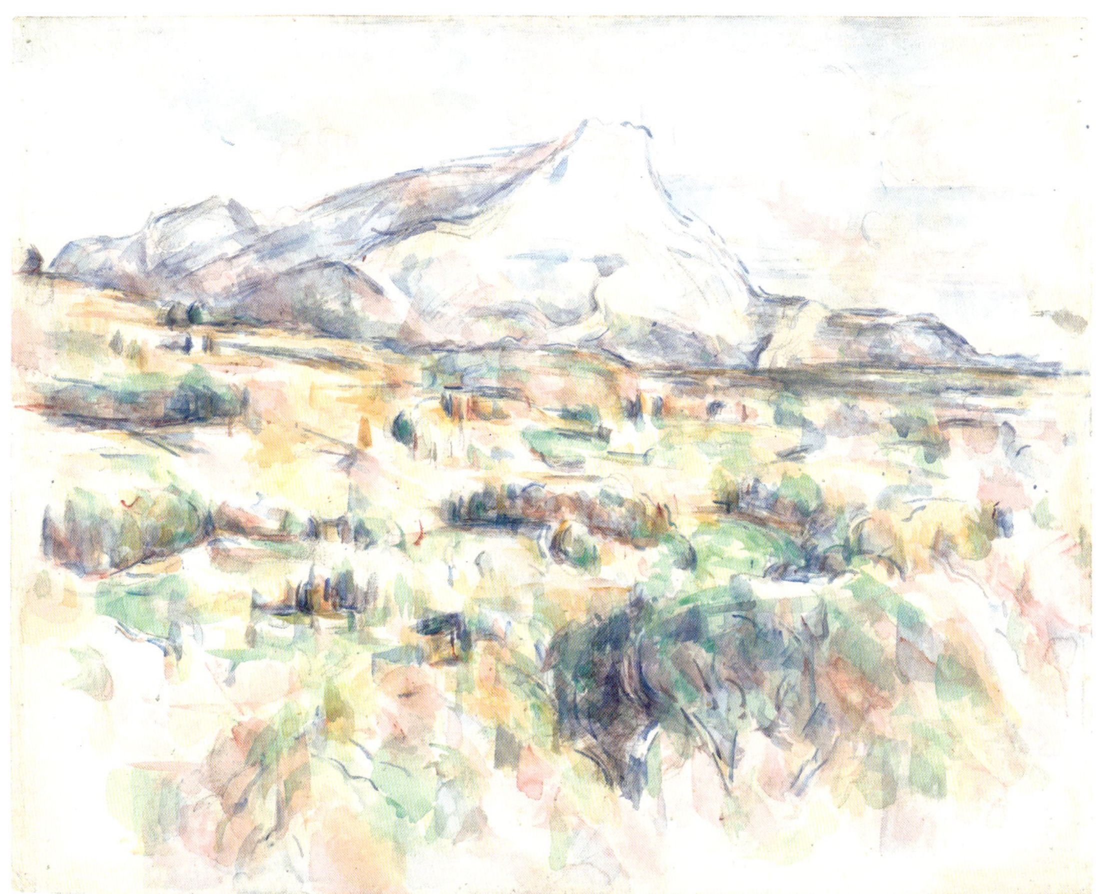

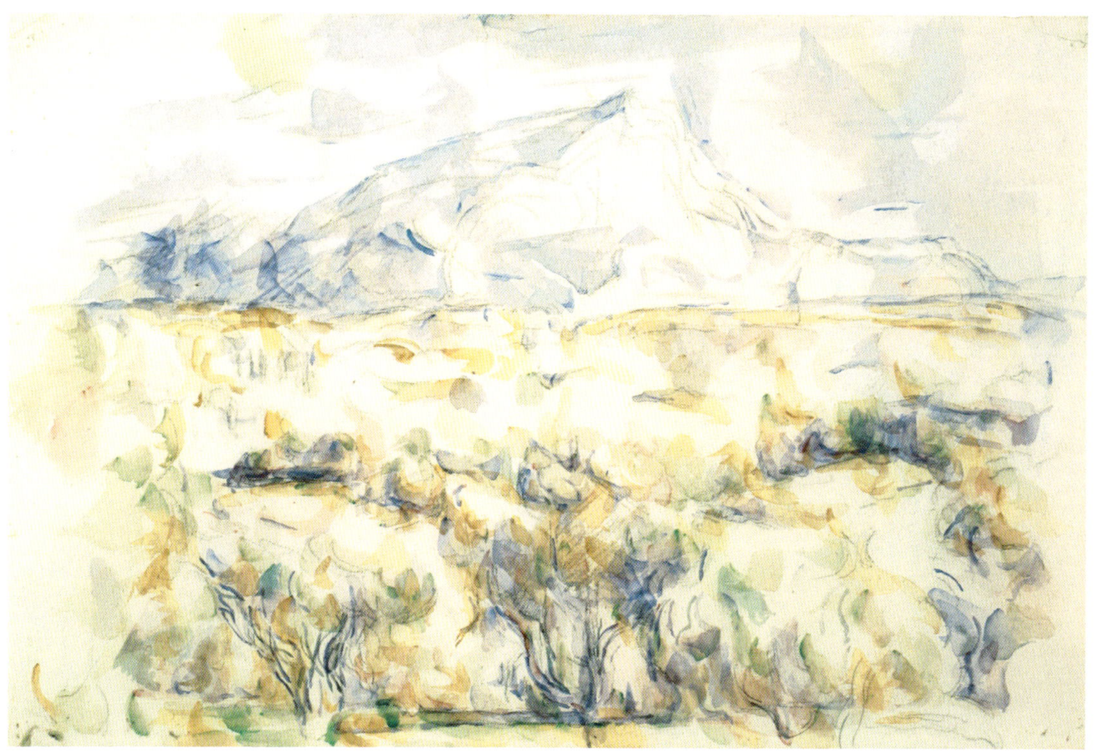

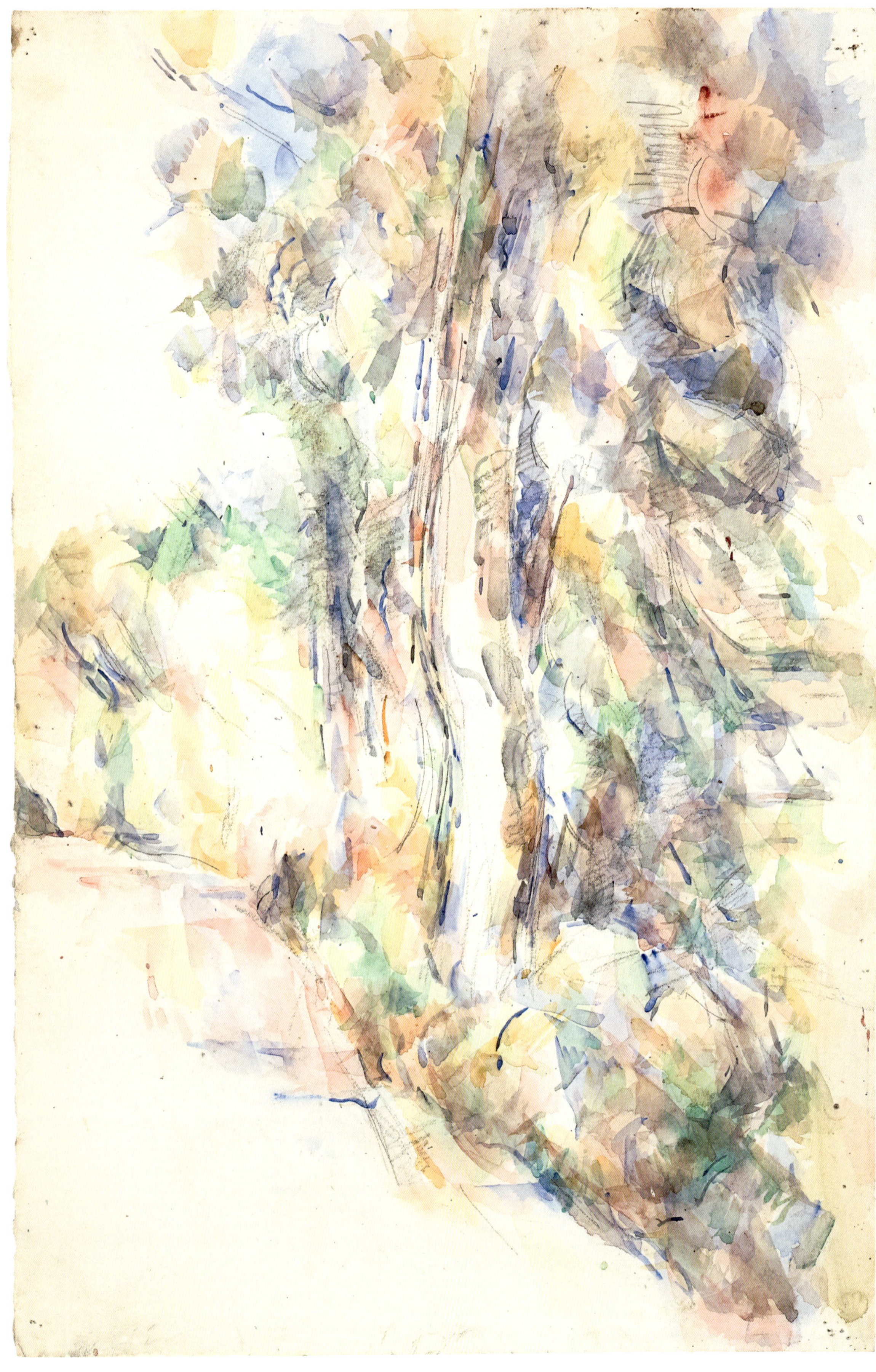

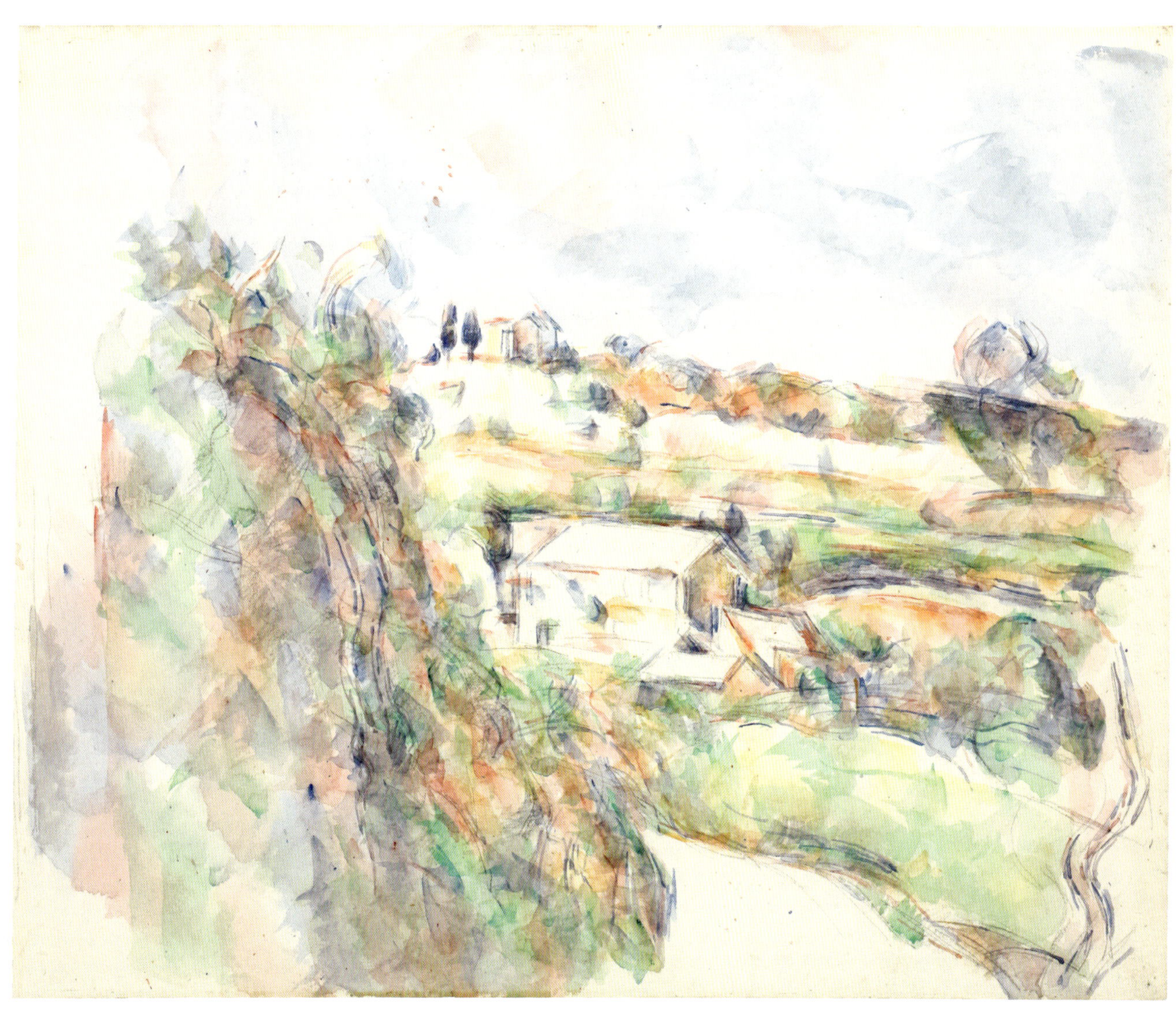

182. *Road with Trees on a Slope*. c. 1904. Watercolor and pencil on paper, 18 13⁄16 × 12 ½" (47.8 × 31.7 cm)

183. *Chemin des Lauves: The Turn in the Road*. 1904–06. Pencil and watercolor on paper, 18 7⁄8 × 23 1⁄16" (47.9 × 58.6 cm)

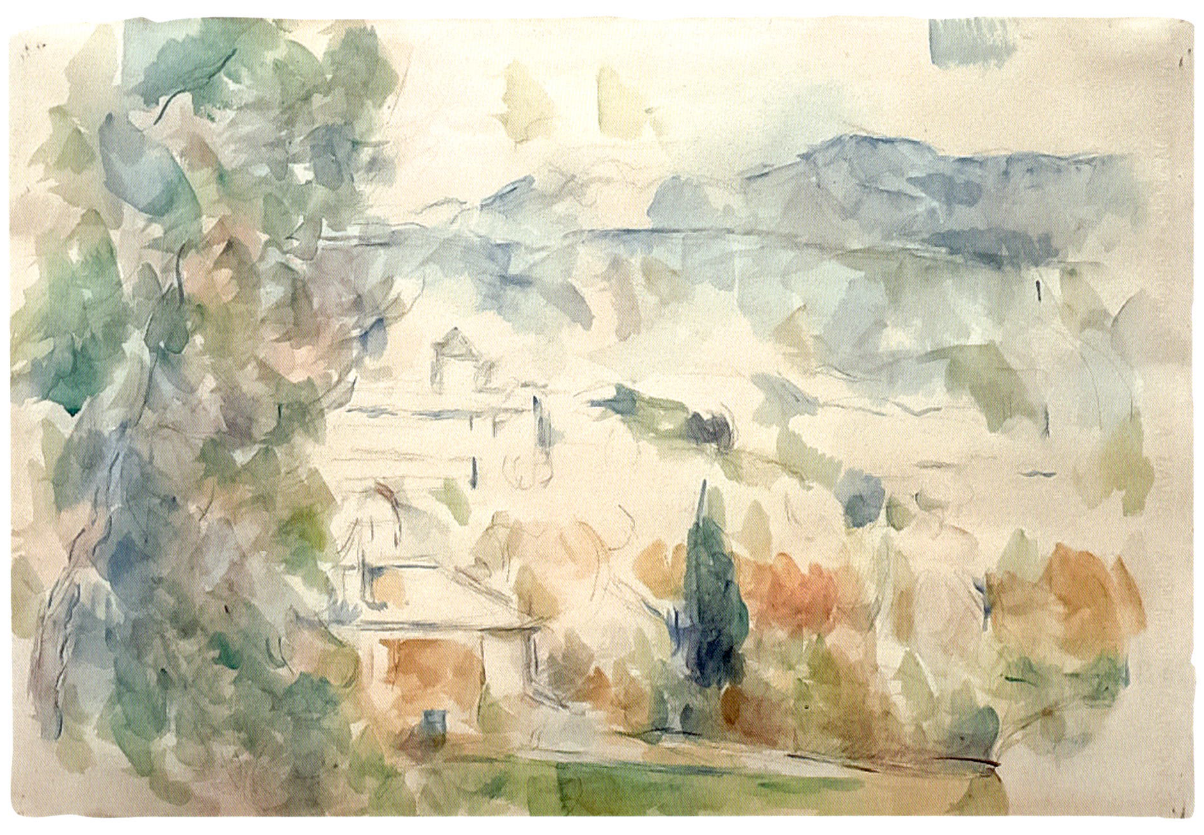

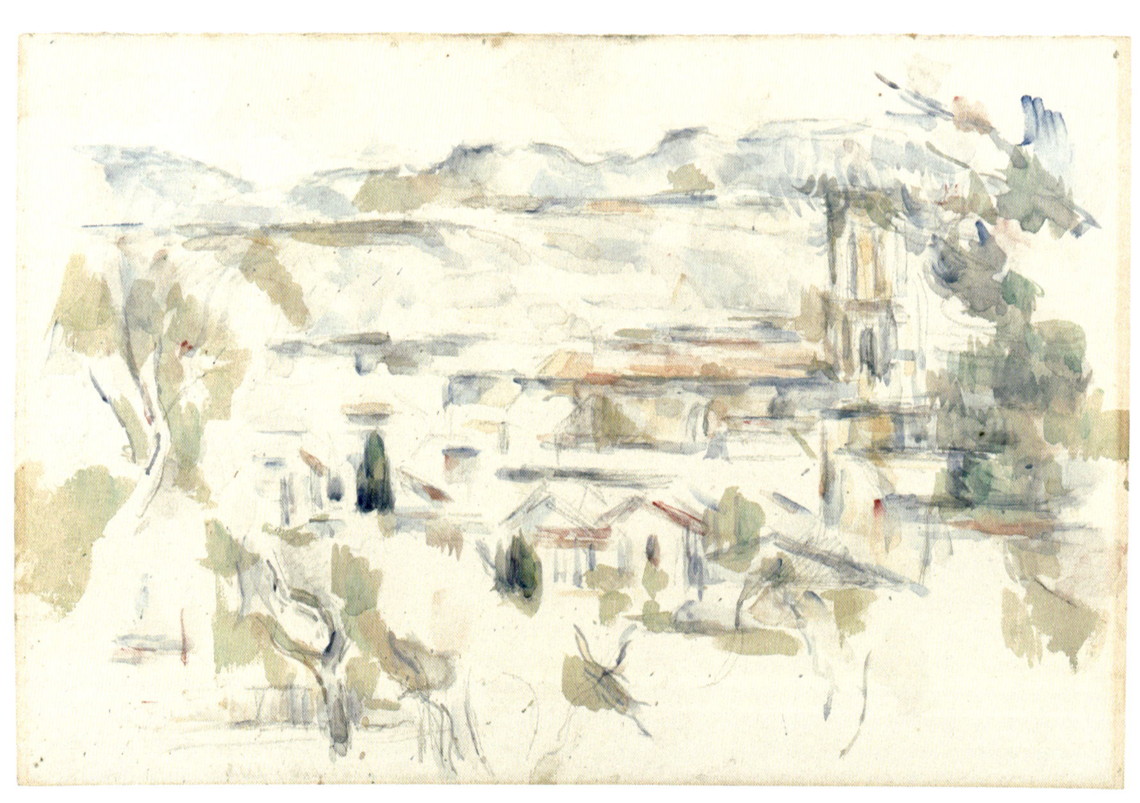

184. *Outskirts of Aix*. 1900–06. Pencil and watercolor on paper, 14 ½ × 21 ½" (36.8 × 54.6 cm)

185. *The Cathedral of Aix, Seen from the Studio at Les Lauves*. 1902–04. Pencil and watercolor on paper, 12 5⁄16 × 18 5⁄8" (31.2 × 47.3 cm)

186. *View from Les Lauves near Aix*. 1902–06. Watercolor on paper, 15 ¾ × 21 ¼" (40 × 54 cm)

187. *The Cathedral of Aix Seen from the Studio at Les Lauves*. 1904–06. Pencil, watercolor, and gouache on paper, 12 ½ × 18 ½" (31.8 × 47 cm)

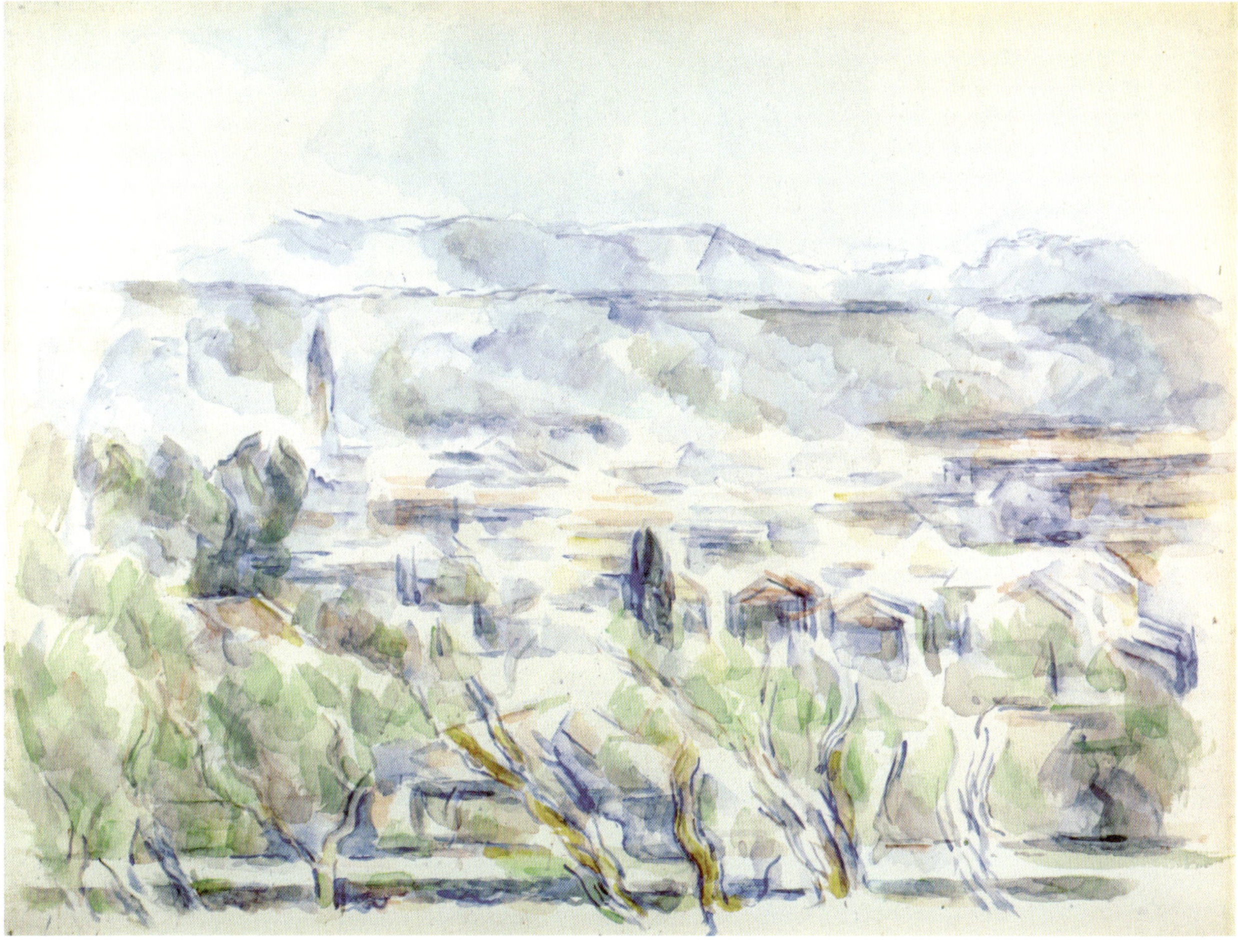

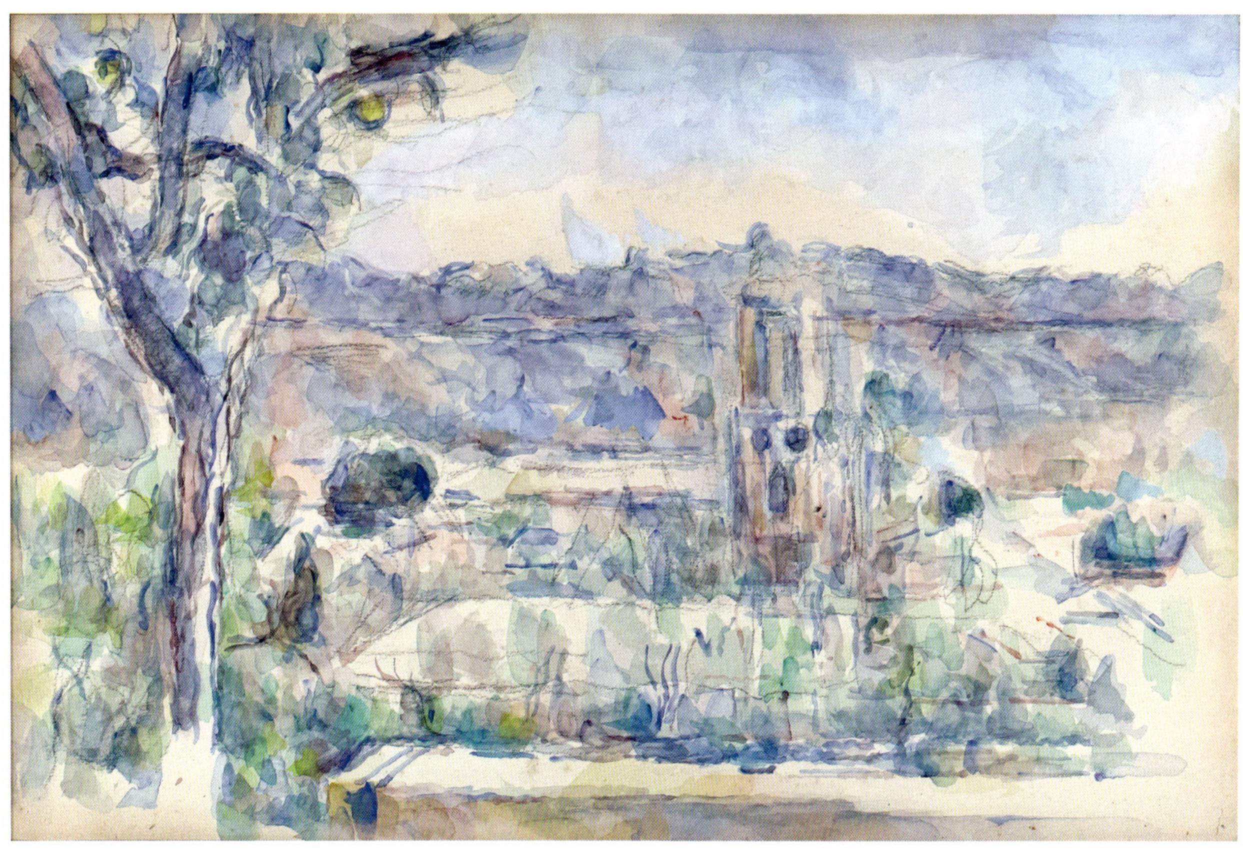

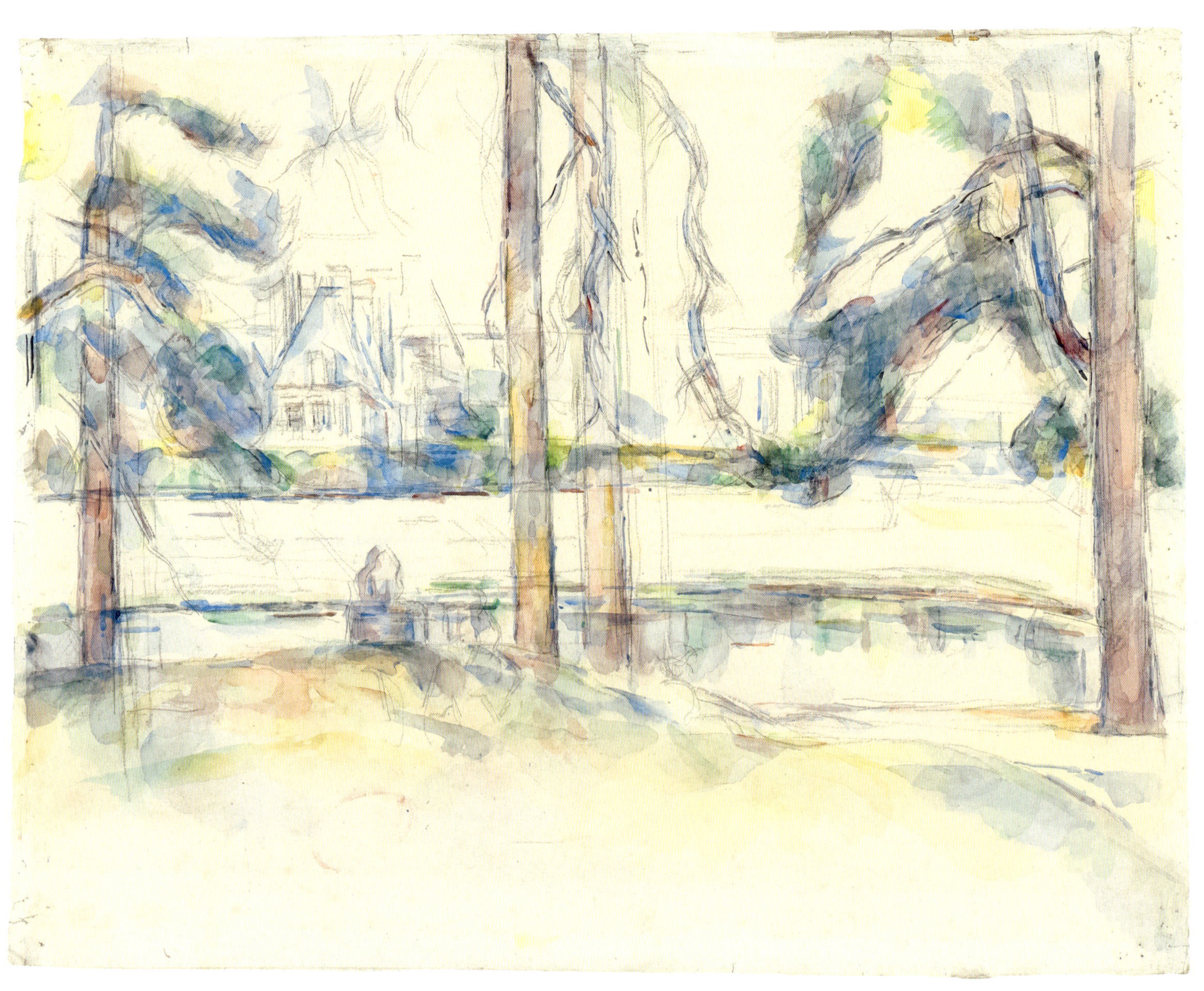

188. *The Château of Fontainebleau*. 1904–05. Pencil and watercolor on paper, 17 5/16 × 21 5/8" (44 × 55 cm)

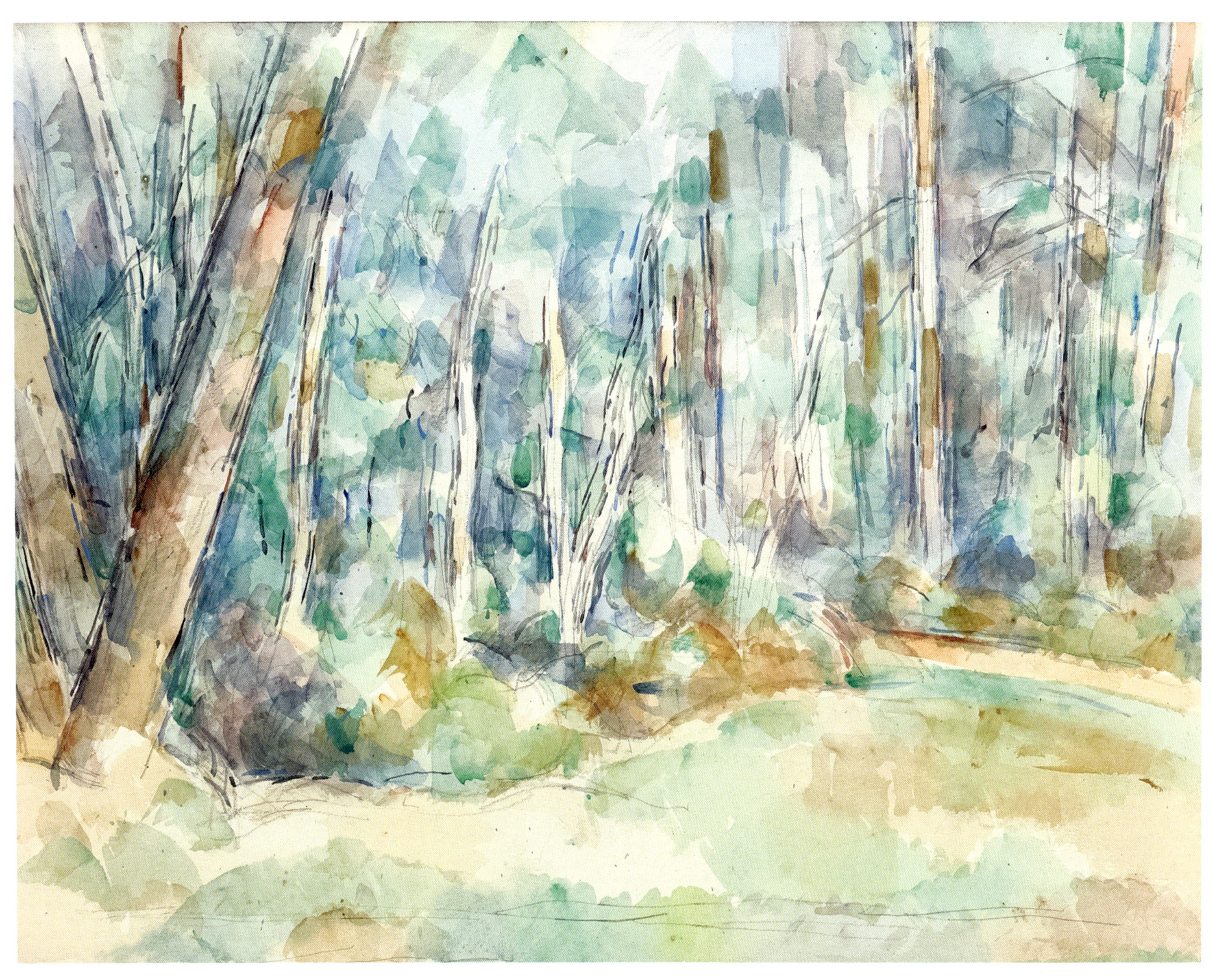

189. *Forest Landscape*.
1904–06. Pencil and watercolor on paper, 18 5/8 × 23 5/8" (47.3 × 60 cm)

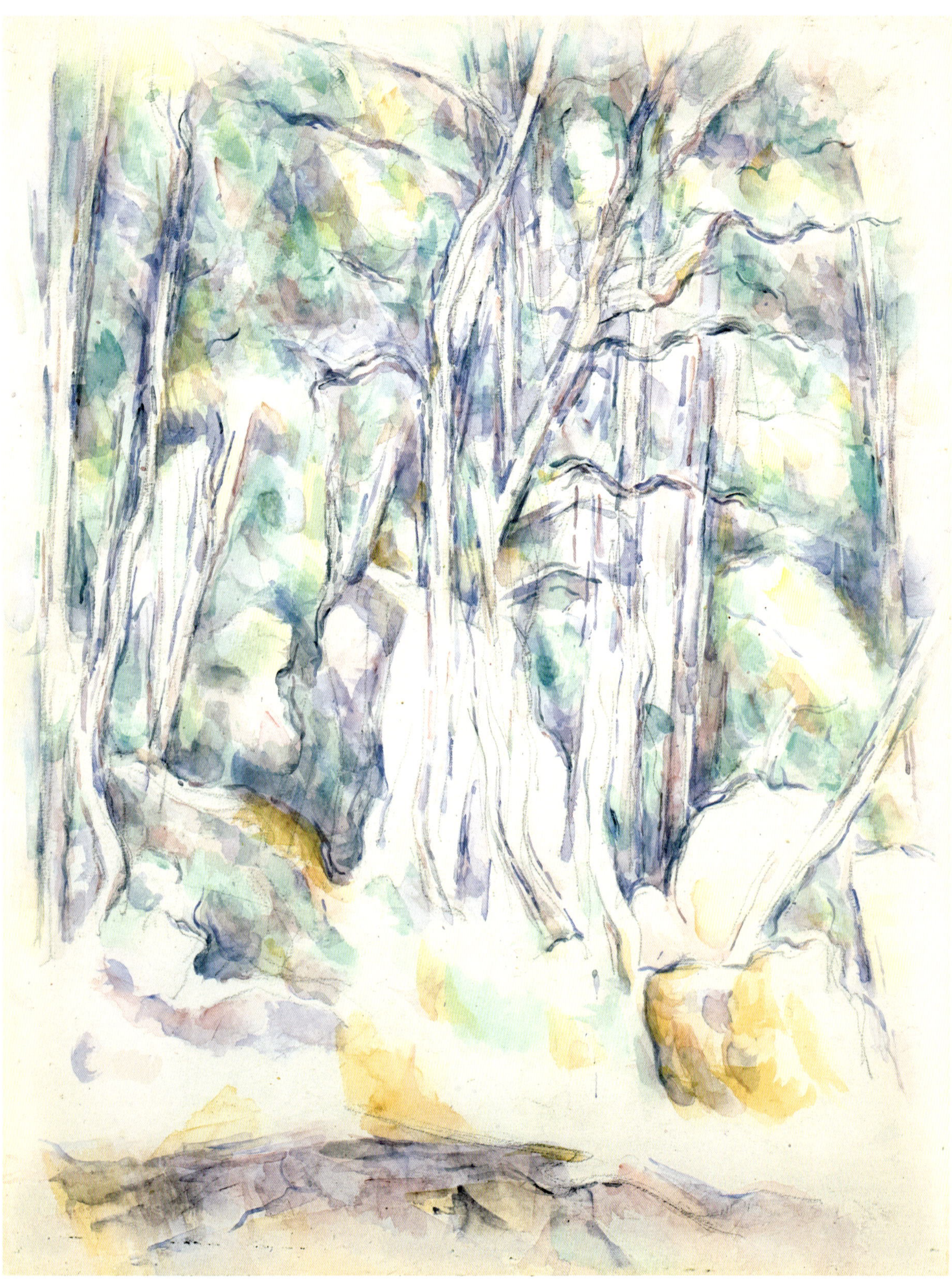

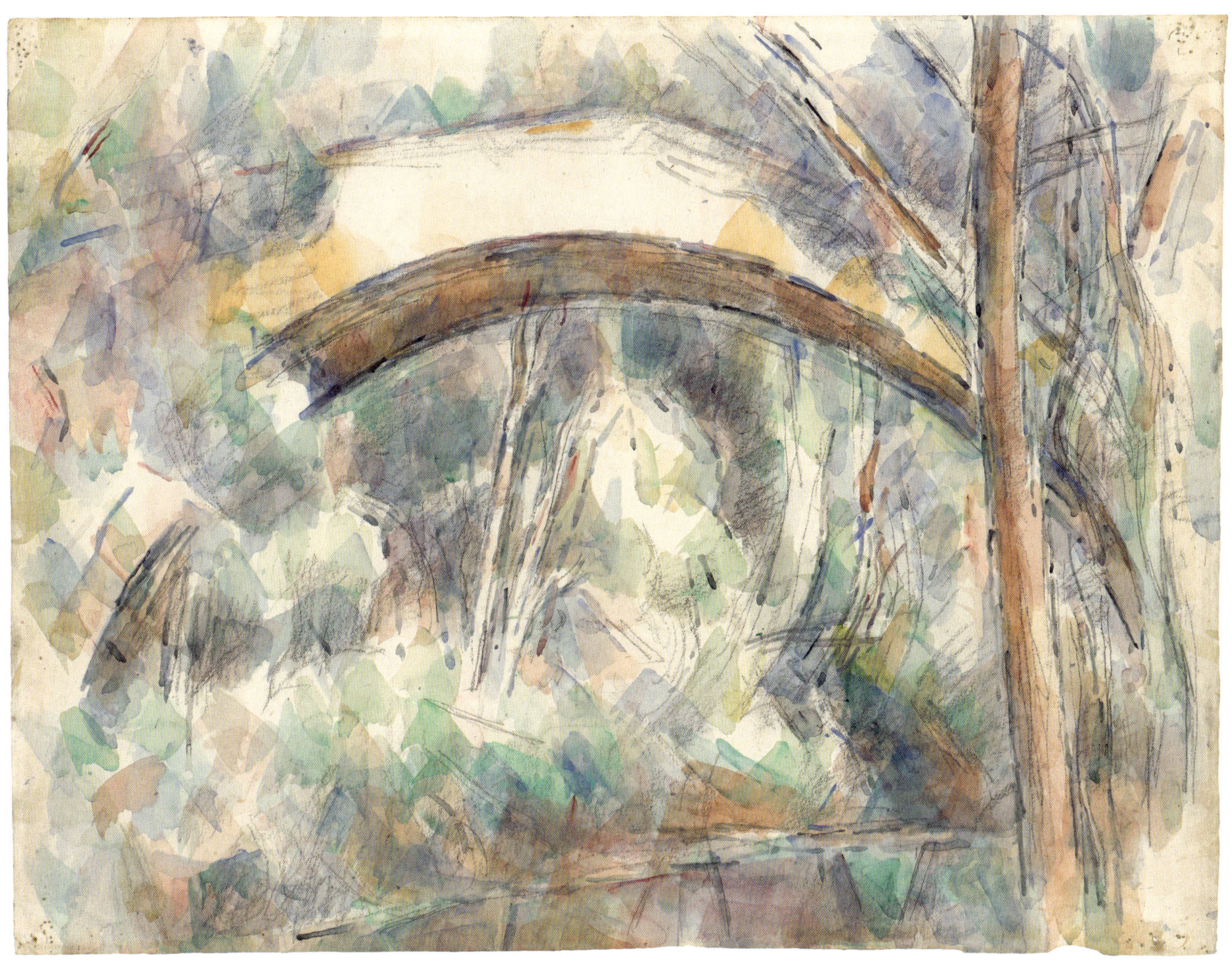

190. *Rocks and Trees near the Château Noir*. 1900–04. Pencil and watercolor on paper, 21 ¾ × 16 ¾" (55.3 × 42.6 cm)

191. *The Bridge of Trois-Sautets*. 1906. Pencil and watercolor on paper, 16 ¹⁄₁₆ × 21 ⅜" (40.8 × 54.3 cm)

Jodi Hauptman

"Objects penetrate one another.
They never cease to be alive."
—Paul Cézanne, as reported by
Joachim Gasquet in *Cézanne* (1921)

Does a teacup feel? Does a sugar bowl have a soul? Does an apple love? Joachim Gasquet recounts Cézanne's description of his fraught relationship with "those little fellows," his still life objects: "People think a sugar bowl has no physiognomy or soul. But that changes every day here. You have to take them, cajole them. . . . These glasses, these dishes, they talk among themselves. They whisper interminable secrets. . . . Fruits . . . love to have their portraits painted. They sit there and apologize for changing color."[1] Cézanne's interpreters have noticed that chatter—or, to the contrary, a resolute silence. Rainer Maria Rilke revels in the objects' quiet absorption, the way they are "so wonderfully occupied with themselves." Vasily Kandinsky tells us that Cézanne "made a living thing out of a teacup—or rather in a teacup he realized the existence of something alive." For Roger Ballu, Cézanne's *natures mortes* "are not dead enough." More recently, Carol Armstrong has compared the "physical and formal associations between objects" to "the social and affective ties between people . . . the play of dominion and submission that mark human relations."[2]

As pleasurable as it may be to imagine the curmudgeonly Cézanne communing with pots and pitchers, apples and onions, what most animates his still lifes are the materials of their making. Self-consciousness, Cézanne argues, is central to the labor of his art: "He becomes a painter through the very qualities of painting itself. By exploring its coarse materiality."[3] This material exploration, this self-conscious revelation of the possibilities and logic of common art supplies, results in a work that is "a repository of process," to borrow Ewa Lajer-Burcharth's words.[4] The papery-ness of his sheets, the liquidity and translucency of his watery pigment, the silver-gray strokes of pencil—it is in them, to return to Kandinsky, that Cézanne "realized the existence of something alive," achieved his self-professed aspiration to "astonish Paris with an apple."[5] By creating equivalences between means and subjects, calling out paper by not painting it at all, and staging analogies among approaches and forms,[6] Cézanne makes of his watercolor still lifes essays in the mechanics of seeing and creating.

Aqueous itself, watercolor perfectly represents liquid: washy blue and rose denote water in a half-filled carafe (plate 217), conjuring its moisture, clarity, luminosity; deeper reds and blues together suggest purply wine in a tall bottle, lighter and brighter at the surface (plate 216); deep indigo fills an inkpot (plate 206). Unlike opaque oil paint or gouache, watercolor is also an apt equivalent for translucent glass, and Cézanne deployed curving strokes in pencil and paint, and patches of color, to establish dimensionality (plate 210). Meanwhile, broken lines, often in blue, materialize the eyes' own skips and starts, especially around glassware—vision's part-by-part efforts of comprehension, made ever more challenging by reflections that move and change with shifting illumination (plate 217). Watercolor's transparent liquidity offers Cézanne an evocative way to describe shadow, letting it "bleed" across a surface, like the shade cast by a green jug on a table (plate 197).

For Cézanne, paper equals paper. Mostly unpainted areas of creamy sheets form the paper labels on wine and liquor bottles (plates 215, 217). Arcs of color or pencil indicate how these paper rectangles bow to adhere to a rounded form; as the "uppermost surface" in the composition, the label is, Armstrong points out, paradoxically "represented by the undermost surface."[7] Cézanne gives myriad other responsibilities to unpigmented paper in his still lifes, from representing the texture of those objects he so carefully composes on tables and sideboards (the bright white of a cloth [plate 212]; the shiny surface of porcelain [plate 203]; the glassy finish of enamel [plate 213]; the smooth burnish of bone [plate 53]) to emphasizing shape (an unpainted patch indicating the "culminating point" closest to the spectator[8] [plate 197]; the hard edge of a tabletop delimiting space [plate 216]); from proposing analogies between items and thus transformations (rounded fruits allude to bodies [plate 205]; double oval highlights on a melon suggest a skull's blank sockets [plate 212]) to isolating subjects in an unpainted void (whether a branch with a single rose or an assembly of apples and pears [plates 139, 201]). In this way, "unfinish" generates a back-and-forth between what we understand as paper's materiality and its contingent function in the composition.

Usually relegated to a supporting, or background, role—indeed the very terms for paper are "support" and "ground"—paper is instead the central protagonist in Cézanne's still lifes. The nomenclature "work on paper" is similarly misleading. The work is not on paper, it is paper. Watercolor's luminosity—its very being—is wholly dependent on the sheet on which it is painted; its tone, its brilliance, a balance between transparent pigment and the bright paper seen through.

And this is where the productive tensions—what in fact seem like brainteasers—complicating these works may be found. As a medium, paper is both opaque and not opaque. Not transparent itself, it creates transparency. As an actor in Cézanne's compositions, paper represents both opaque surfaces (from paper to cloth to porcelain) and translucent ones—those of glasses, carafes, and bottles. Contradictory terms like opacity and transparency, then, "stand in relation to each other," as T. J. Clark has explained, "doubting and qualifying each other's truth."[9] While in *Still Life with Apples on a Sideboard* (1900–06; plate 215) the white paper straightforwardly signifies only smooth, nontransparent surfaces—the paper label, the porcelain pitcher, the ceramic plate—in *Bottles, Pot, Alcohol Stove, and Apples* (1900–06; plate 214) paper represents variously textured materials: wine bottle label, glass tumblers (filled with sugar?), bread, straw cord weaving around a liquor bottle. As we move from object to object, from one unpainted area to another, we must recalibrate our understanding of that creamy white. A similar contradictory analogy is made in *Still Life with Carafe, Bottle, and Fruit* (1906; plate 217), where the shape of the label echoes that of a nearby glass. The grapes, at center, meanwhile, are dense enough to block our view of the bottom of the wine bottle, yet are only scarcely defined by arcs of blue. In *Still Life with Green Melon* (1902–06; plate 208) Cézanne imbues the spherical surface of a melon with the shine and glimmer of the adjacent glass through the multiple patches of green that form its skin (not at all the thick rind that we know, but a luminous, verdant light source); with a culminating point of brightness that focuses our eye on the fruit's roundness; and with repeated, agitated, and broken strokes, which simultaneously describe and doubt its circumference, making the melon appear to shudder and quake.

Thus we see that as much as Cézanne attends to the material logic of paper, watercolor, and pencil, he also, Émile Bernard writes with admiration, "transforms his means, bending them forcefully to his use."[10]

The title of this essay is borrowed from Roger Marx, "Le Salon d'Automne," *Gazette des beaux-arts* 32 (December 1, 1904): "From Cézanne has come the tendency, so prevalent today, to express in all fullness the beauty and life of materiality" (464).

1.
Cézanne, as reported by Joachim Gasquet in *Cézanne* (Paris: Les Éditions Bernheim-Jeune, 1921). Trans. in Michael Doran, ed., *Conversations with Cézanne*, trans. Julie Lawrence Cochran (Berkeley: University of California Press, 2001), 156.

2.
Rainer Maria Rilke, *Letters on Cézanne*, ed. Clara Rilke, trans. Joel Agee (New York: North Point, 1985, 2002), 77; letter dated October 14, 1907. Vasily Kandinsky, in Alex Danchev, *Cézanne: A Life* (New York: Pantheon, 2012), 109. Roger Ballu, "L'Exposition des peintres impressionnistes," *Le Chronique des arts et de la curiosité*, April 14, 1877, quoted in Benedict Leca, "'The Painter of Apples': Cézanne, Still Life, and Self-Fashioning," in Leca, ed., *The World Is an Apple: The Still Lifes of Paul Cézanne* (Hamilton, Canada: Art Gallery of Hamilton, 2014), 37. Carol Armstrong, *Cézanne in the Studio: Still Life in Watercolors* (Los Angeles: J. Paul Getty Museum, 2004), 31.

3.
Cézanne, in Émile Bernard, "Paul Cézanne," *L'Occident* 6 (July 1904). Trans. in Doran, *Conversations*, 39.

4.
See Ewa Lajer-Burcharth, *The Painter's Touch: Boucher, Chardin, Fragonard* (Princeton, N.J.: Princeton University Press, 2018), 89. This idea is central to Armstrong's argument in *Cézanne in the Studio*, an indispensable exploration of Cézanne's still lifes.

5.
Related by Gustave Geffroy in *Claude Monet: Sa vie, son temps, son œuvre* (Paris: G. Crès et cie, 1922), 197.

6.
On the topic of analogy, see Bridget Alsdorf, "Interior Landscapes: Metaphor and Meaning in Cézanne's Late Still Lifes," *Word and Image* 26, no. 4 (October–December 2010): 314–23, and Richard Shiff, "Cézanne's Physicality: The Politics of Touch," in Salim Kemal and Ivan Gaskell, eds., *The Language of Art History* (New York: Cambridge University Press, 1991). Shiff writes, "The general principle at work in [Cézanne's] art is analogy: one thing is made to look like, or somehow be like, another, despite the differences and dissimilarities that otherwise obtain" (142).

7.
Armstrong, *Cézanne in the Studio*, 133.

8.
In a letter to Bernard, Cézanne wrote, "I mean that in an orange, an apple, a ball, a head, there is a culminating point, and this point is always the closest to our eye, the edges of objects recede towards a centre placed at eye level." *The Letters of Paul Cézanne*, ed. and trans. Alex Danchev (Los Angeles: J. Paul Getty Museum, 2013), July 25, 1904, no. 237. The culminating point is often, but not only, this area of unpainted paper. See Lawrence Gowing, "The Logic of Organized Sensations," in William Rubin, ed., *Cézanne: The Late Work* (New York: The Museum of Modern Art, 1977), esp. 57–59.

9.
T. J. Clark, "Phenomenality and Materiality in Cézanne," in Tom Cohen et al., eds., *Material Events: Paul de Man and the Afterlife of Theory* (Minneapolis: University of Minnesota Press, 2000), 94. He continues: "They *exemplify* the other's account of matter—by showing it at the point it encounters paradox, and begins to follow a contrary logic." [Emphasis in original.]

10.
Émile Bernard, "Les Aquarelles de Cézanne," *L'Amour de l'art* 5 (February 1924): 36. Trans. Annemarie Iker.

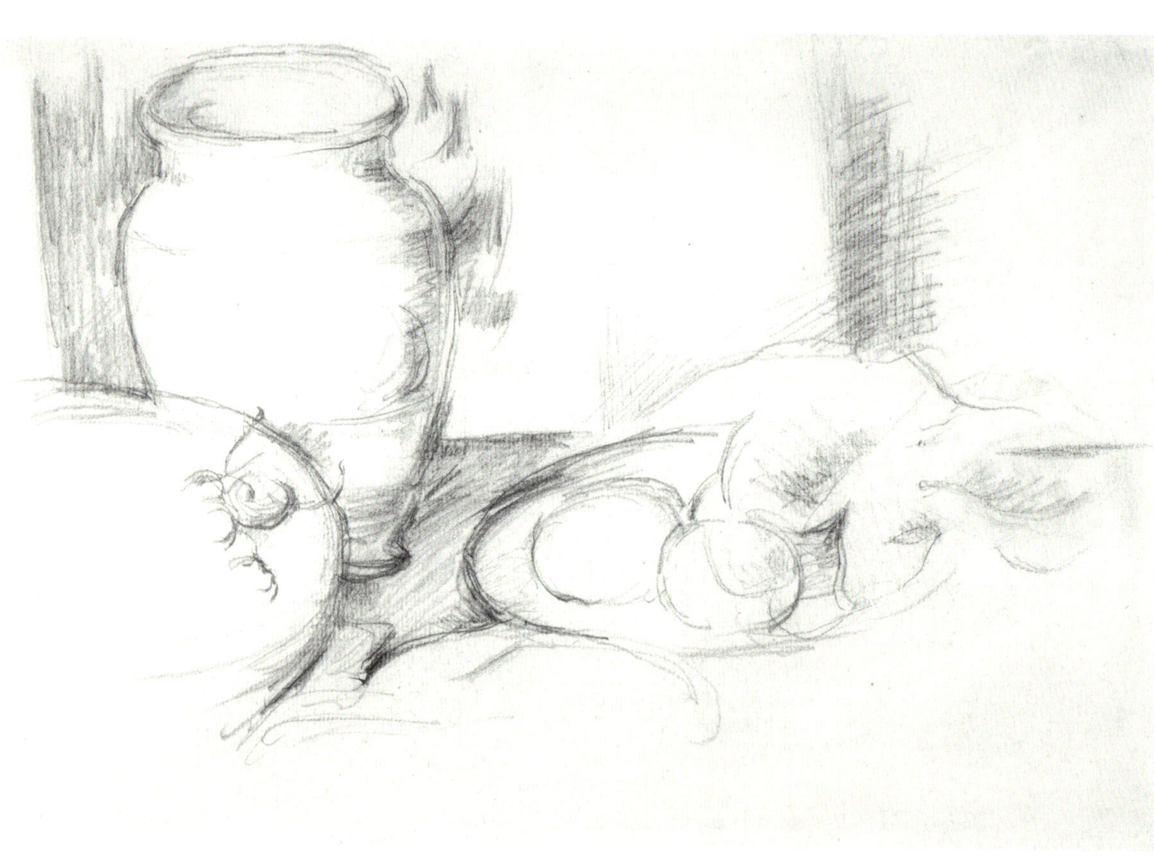

192. *Still Life*. 1881–84. Pencil on laid paper, 10 7/8 × 16 1/2" (27.6 × 41.9 cm)

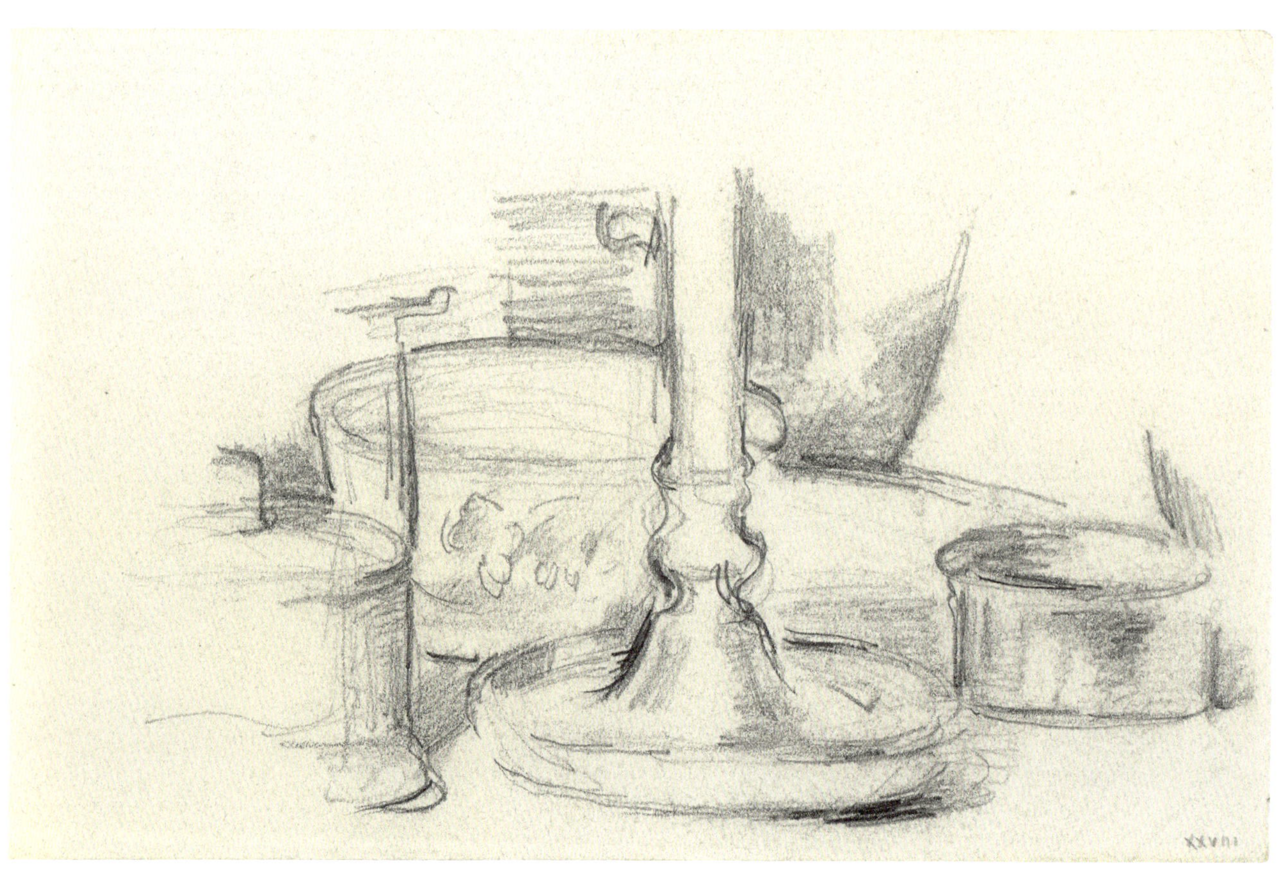

193. *Still Life with a Candlestick*. 1881–84. Pencil on wove paper, 4 15/16 × 8 3/16" (12.5 × 20.8 cm)

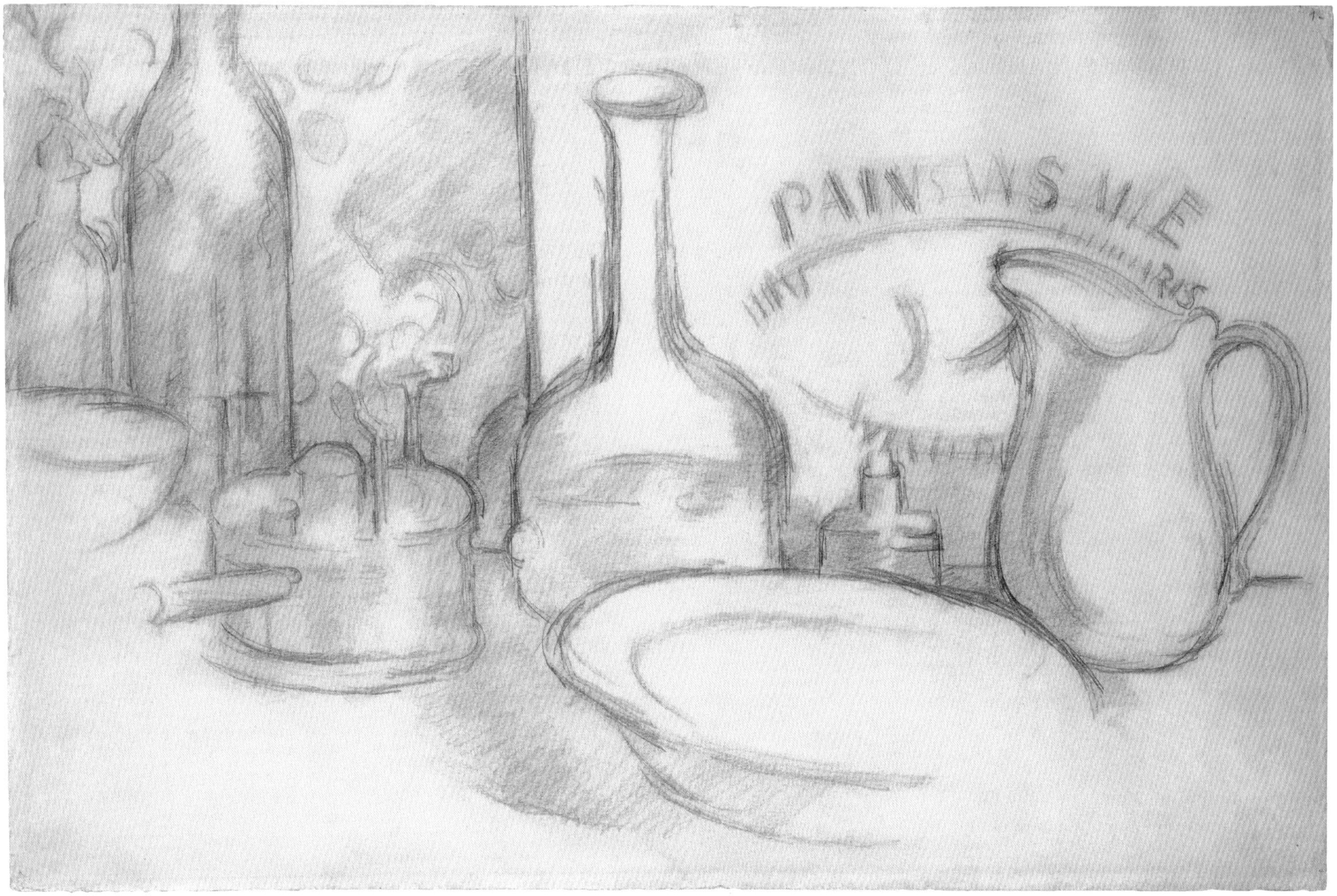

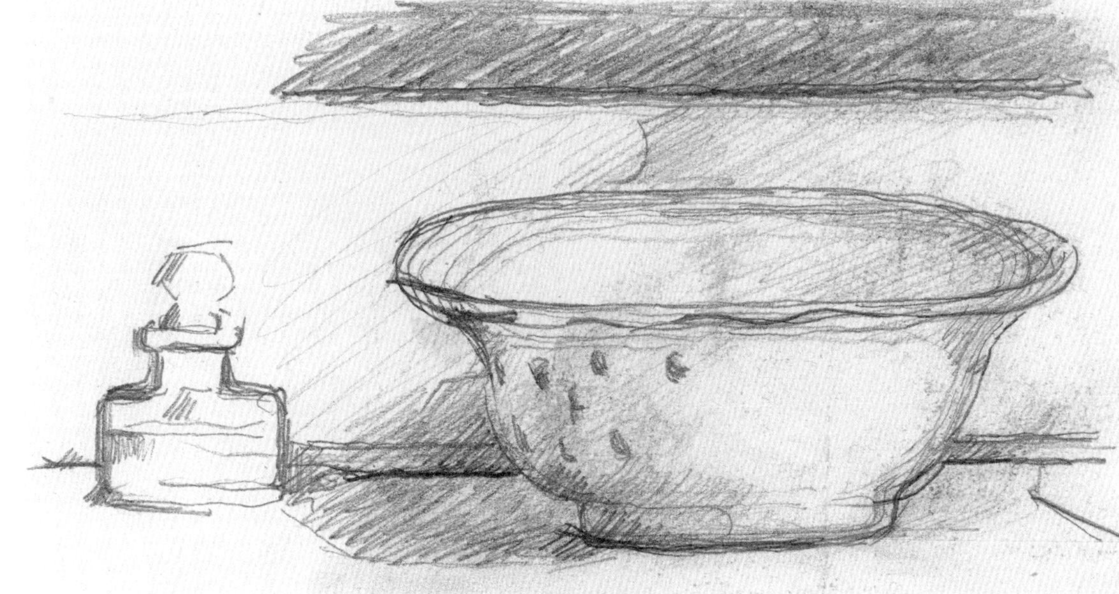

194. *Still Life with Spirit Lamp*. c. 1887–90. Pencil on paper, 12½ × 19⅜" (31.8 × 49.2 cm)

195. *Wash Basin and Scent Bottle*. 1877–81. Pencil on wove paper, 4 15/16 × 8 9/16" (12.5 × 21.7 cm)

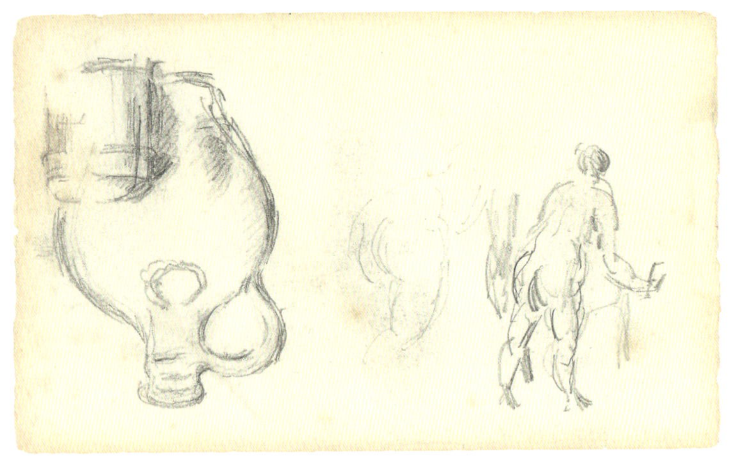

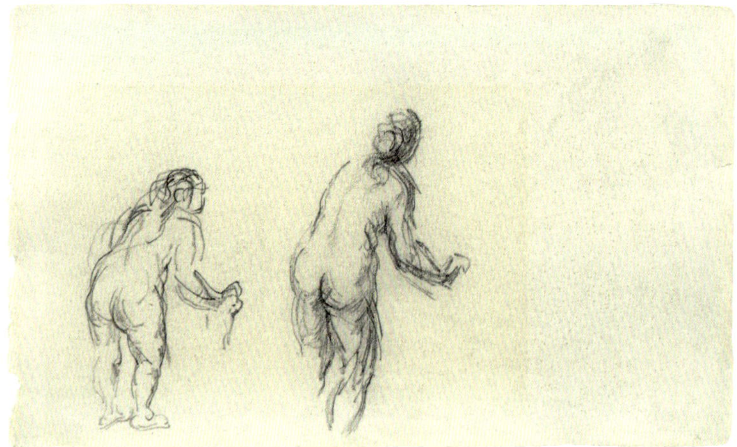

196. Spread from Sketchbook Chappuis I

a. *Earthenware Pitcher, Pot, Woman Bather*. c. 1891–92. Pencil on wove paper, 4 ¾ × 7 ⅝" (12 × 19.4 cm)

b. *Two Studies of a Bather*. Left: 1876–79, right: 1879–82. Pencil on wove paper, 4 ⅝ × 7 ¾" (11.8 × 19.7 cm)

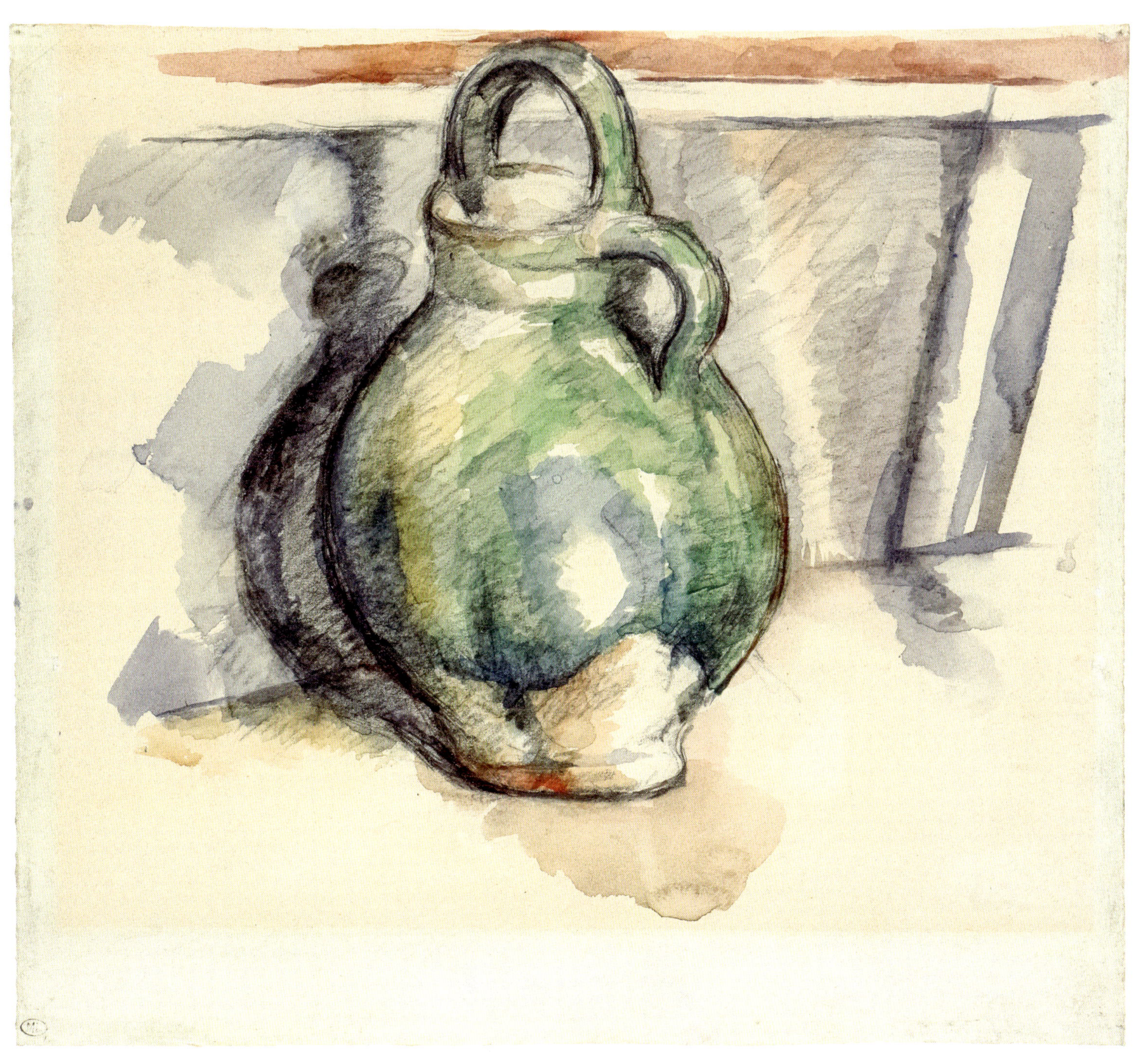

197. *The Green Jug*. 1885–87. Pencil and watercolor on paper, 8 11⁄16 × 9 3⁄4" (22 × 24.7 cm)

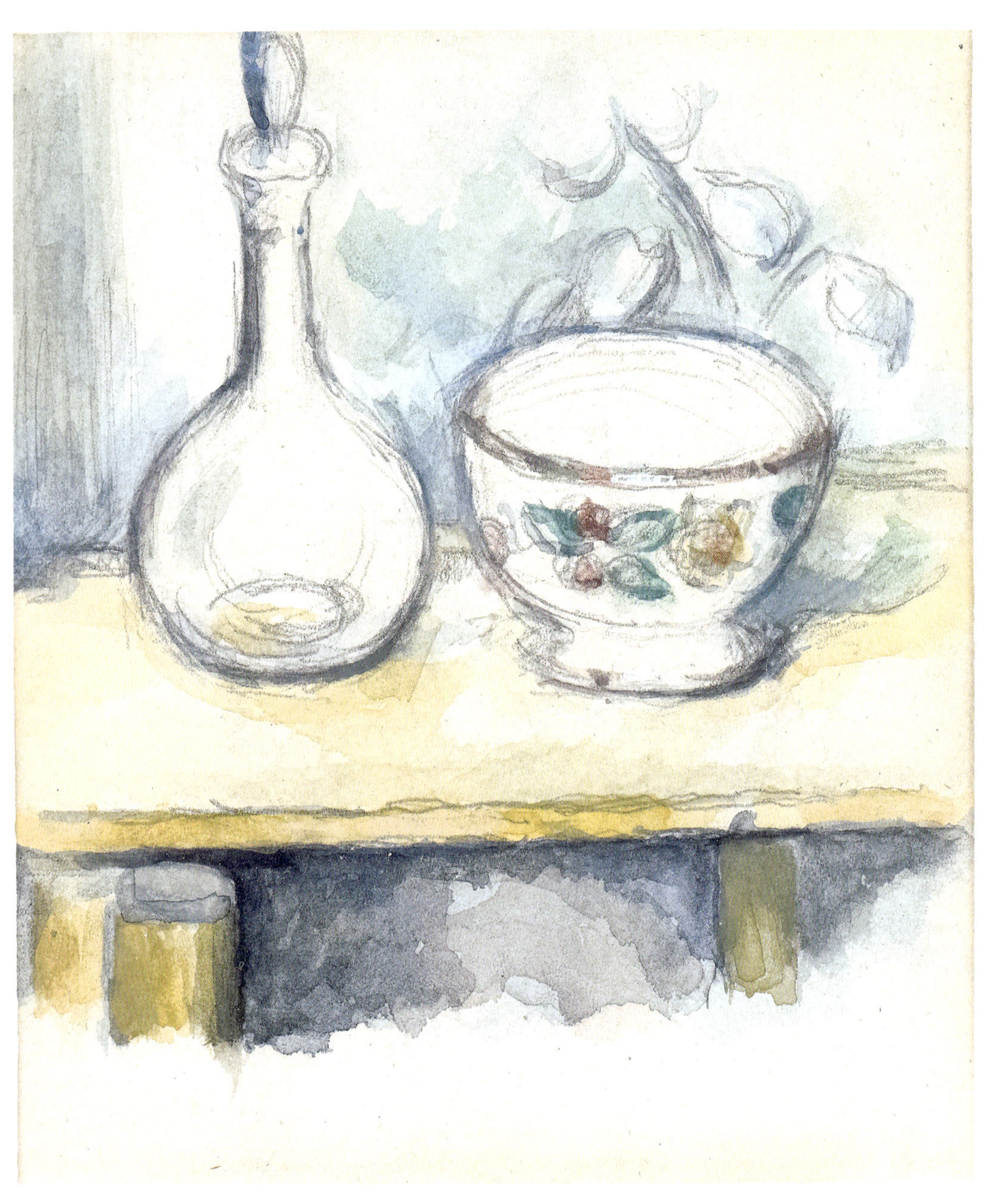

198. *Decanter and Bowl*. 1878–80. Pencil and watercolor on paper, 6 ⅞ × 4 ½" (17.5 × 11.4 cm)

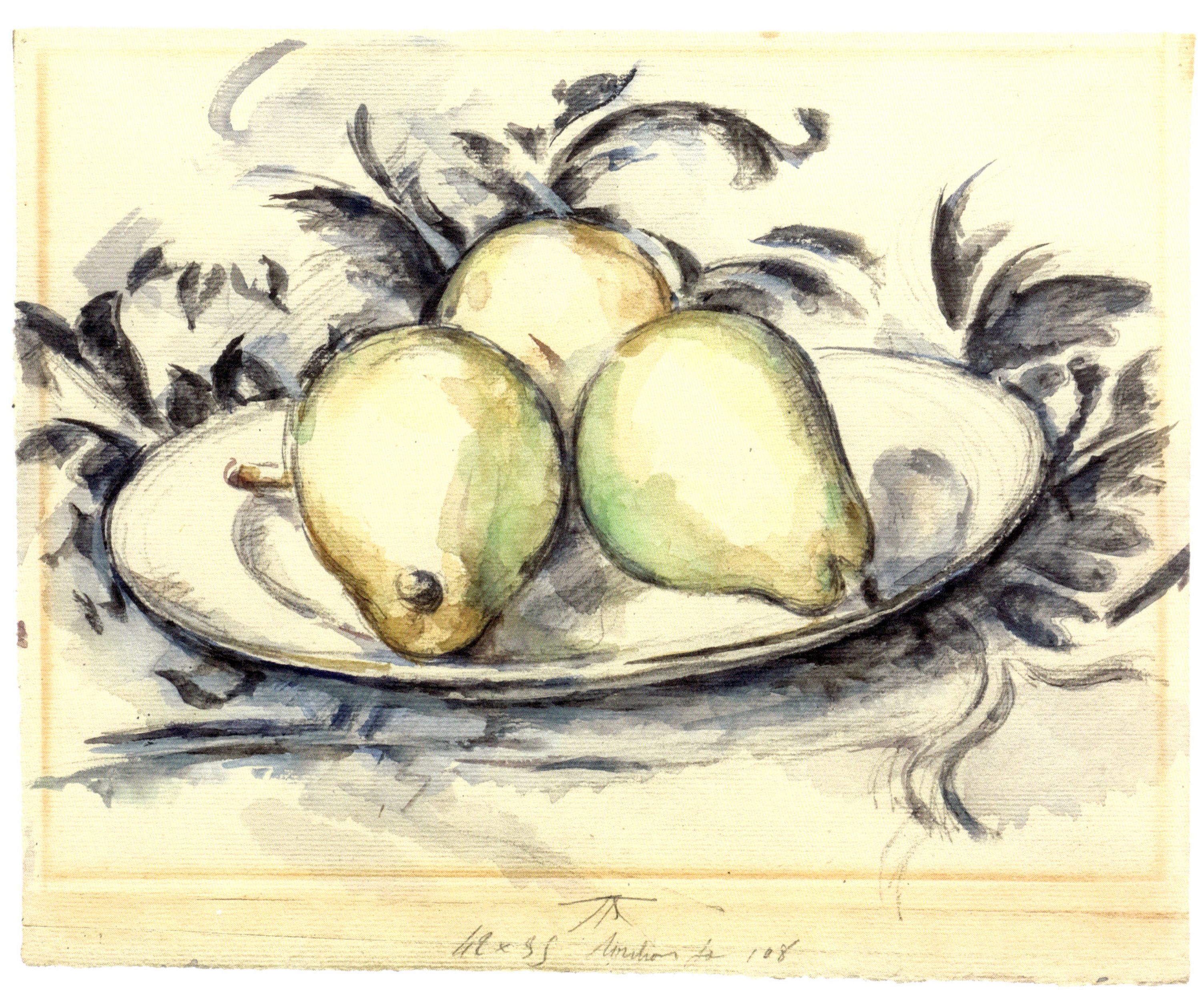

199. *Three Pears*. 1888–90. Pencil and watercolor on laid paper, 9 ½ × 12 3/16" (24.2 × 31 cm)

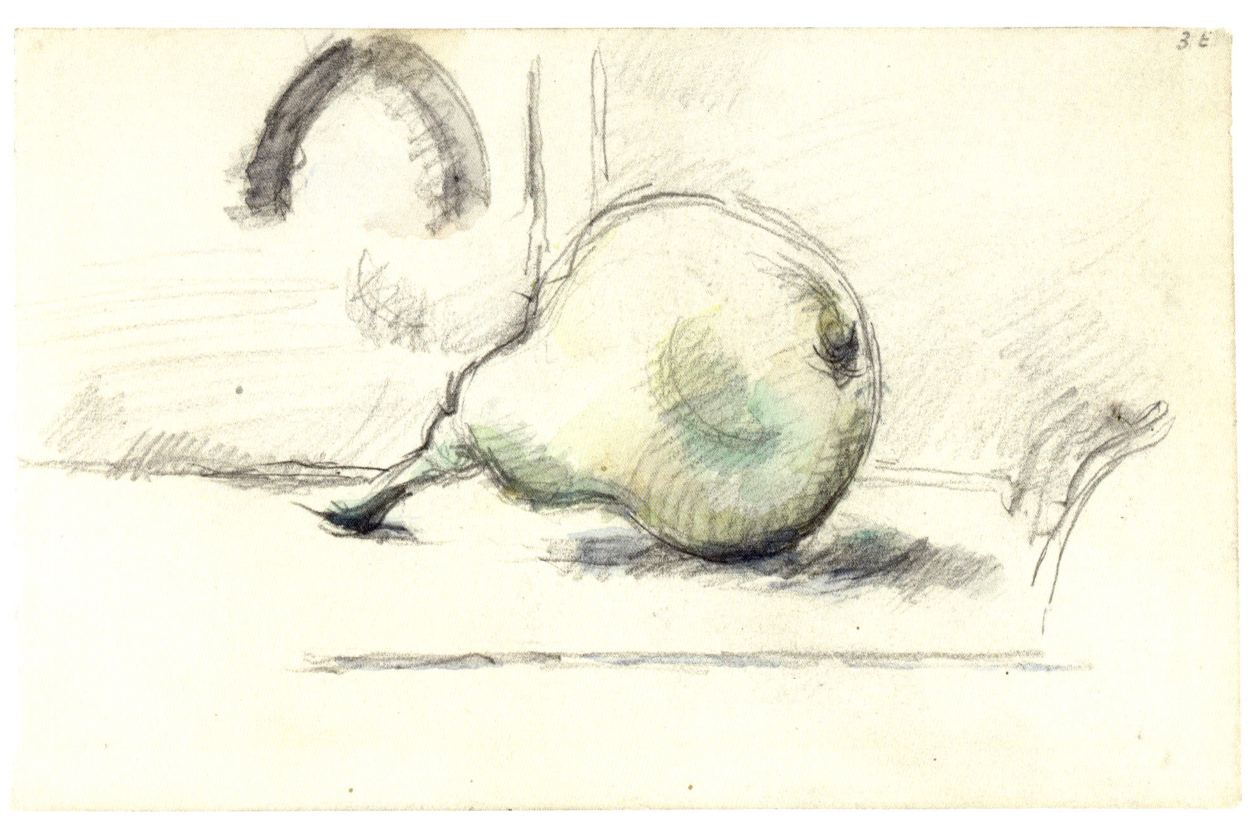

200. *Pear*. c. 1882 (possibly later). Pencil and watercolor on wove paper, 5 × 8 3/16" (12.7 × 20.8 cm)

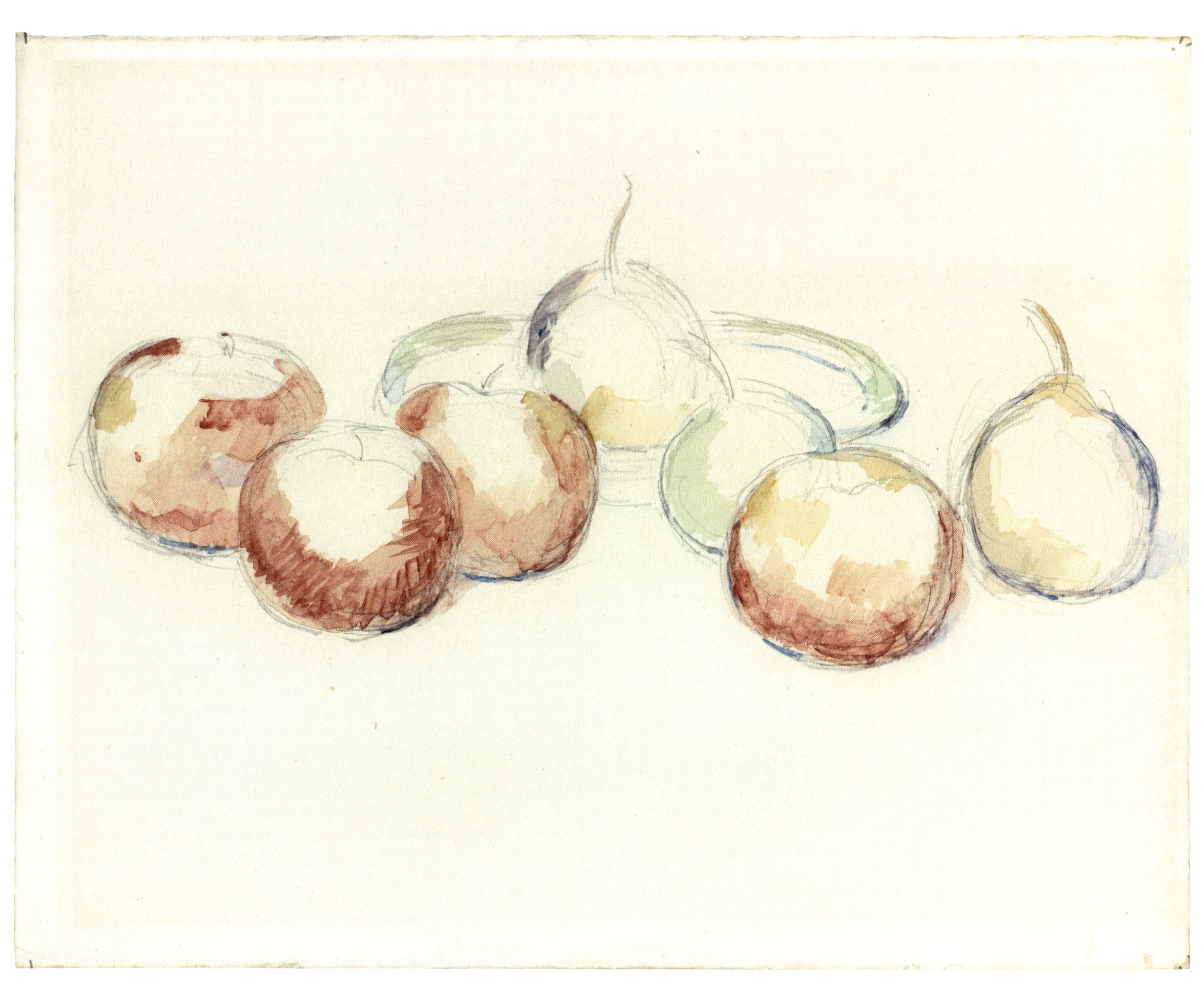

201. *Apples and Pears*. 1882–85. Pencil and watercolor on paper, 8 7/16 × 12 5/8" (21.5 × 32 cm)

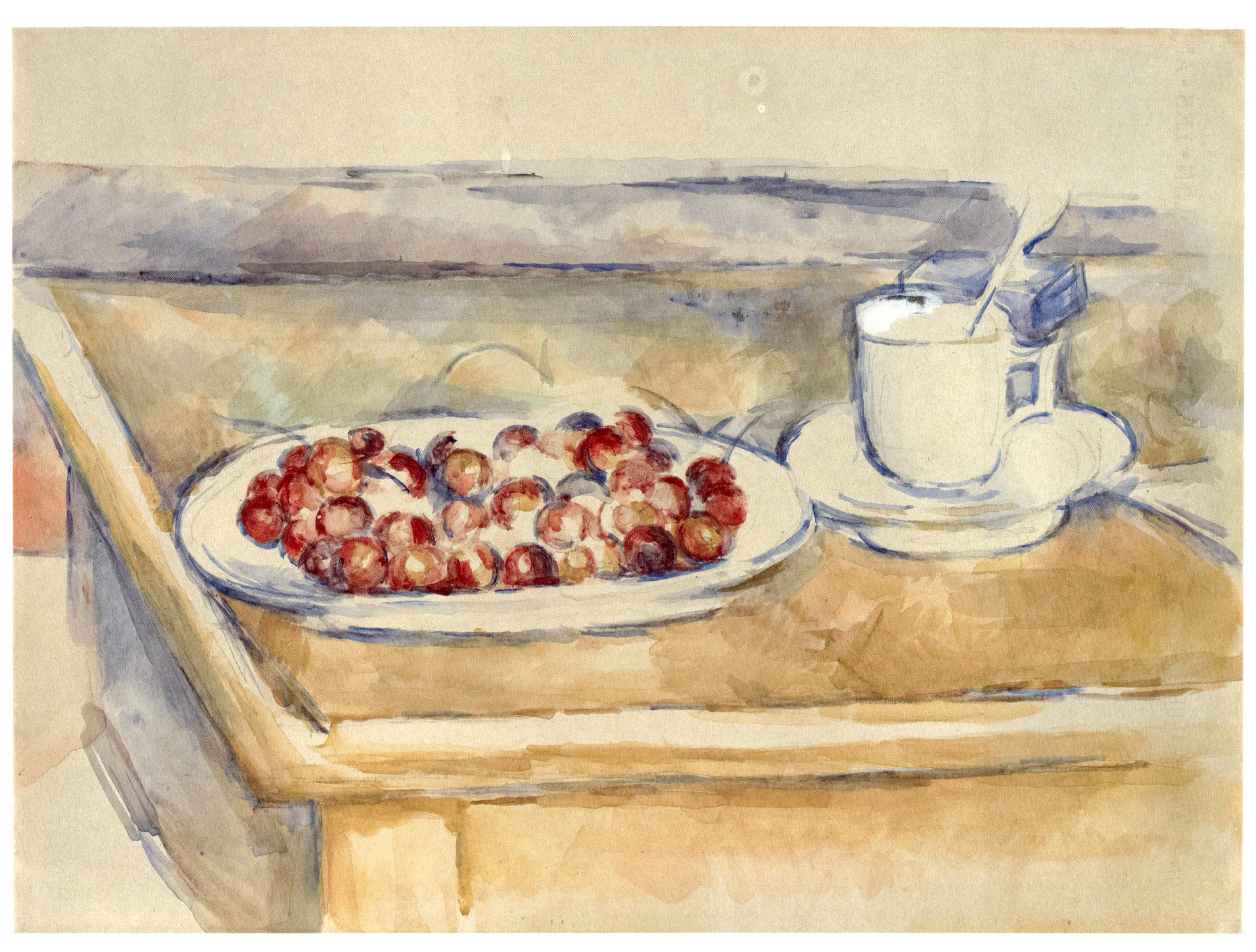

202. *Still Life: Cup and Cherries*. c. 1890 (possibly later). Pencil and watercolor on paper, 14 15⁄16 × 19 5⁄16" (38 × 49 cm)

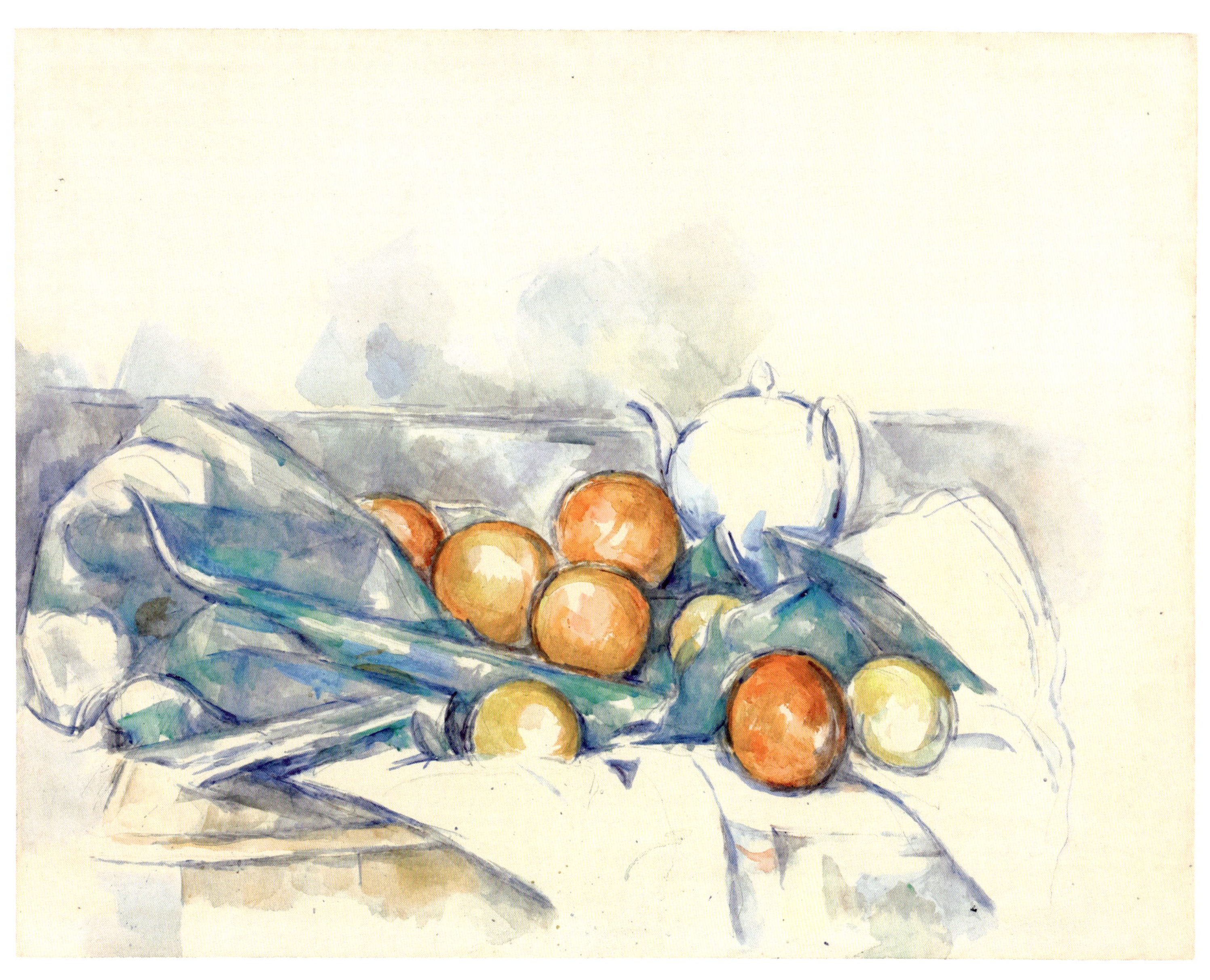

203. *Teapot and Fruit*. 1895–1900. Pencil and watercolor on paper, 18 ⅞ × 24 ⅝" (47.9 × 62.5 cm)

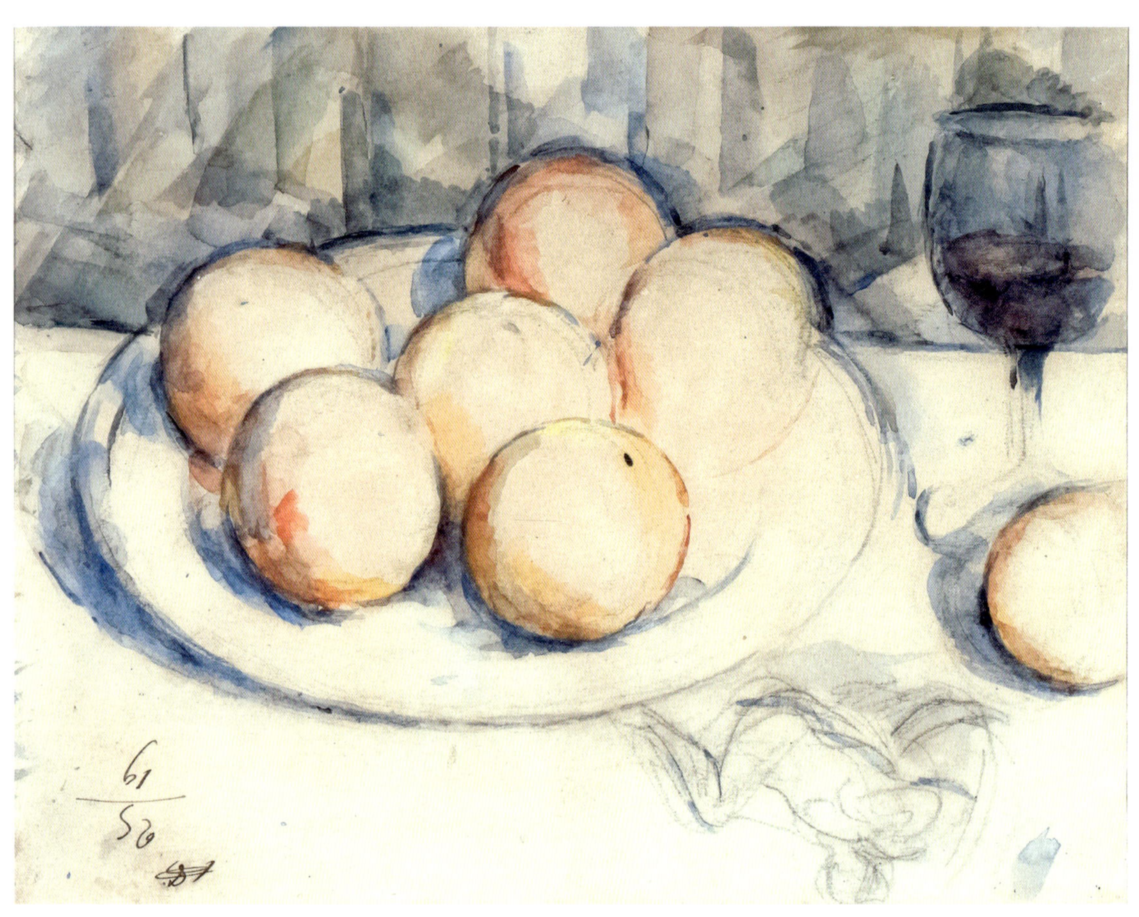

204. *Oranges and Glass*. c. 1900. Pencil and watercolor on wove paper, 8 ¼ × 10 ¾" (21 × 27.3 cm)

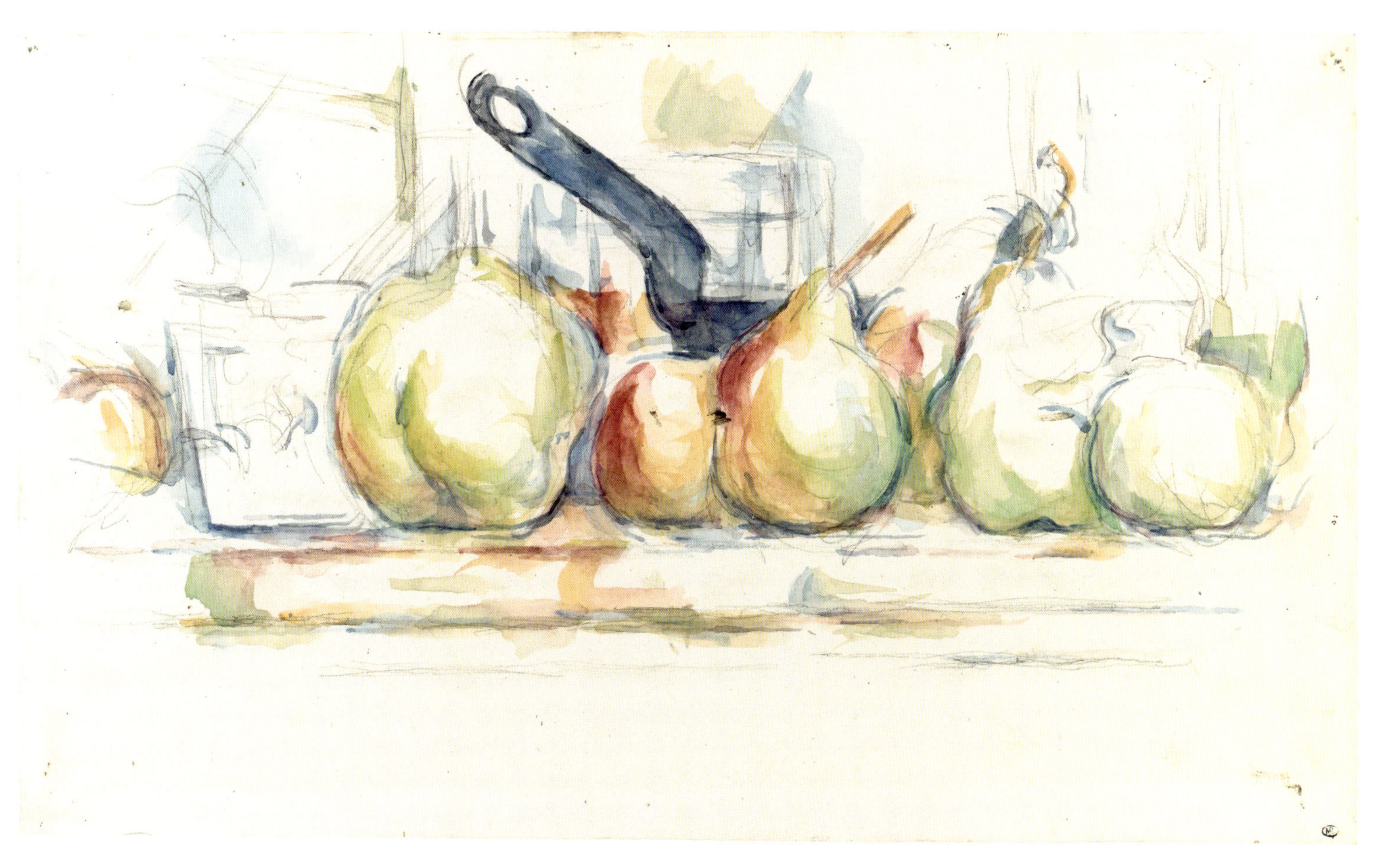

205. *Still Life with Apples, Pears, and a Pot*. 1900–04. Pencil and watercolor on paper, 10 ¼ × 17 ¹¹⁄₁₆" (26 × 45 cm)

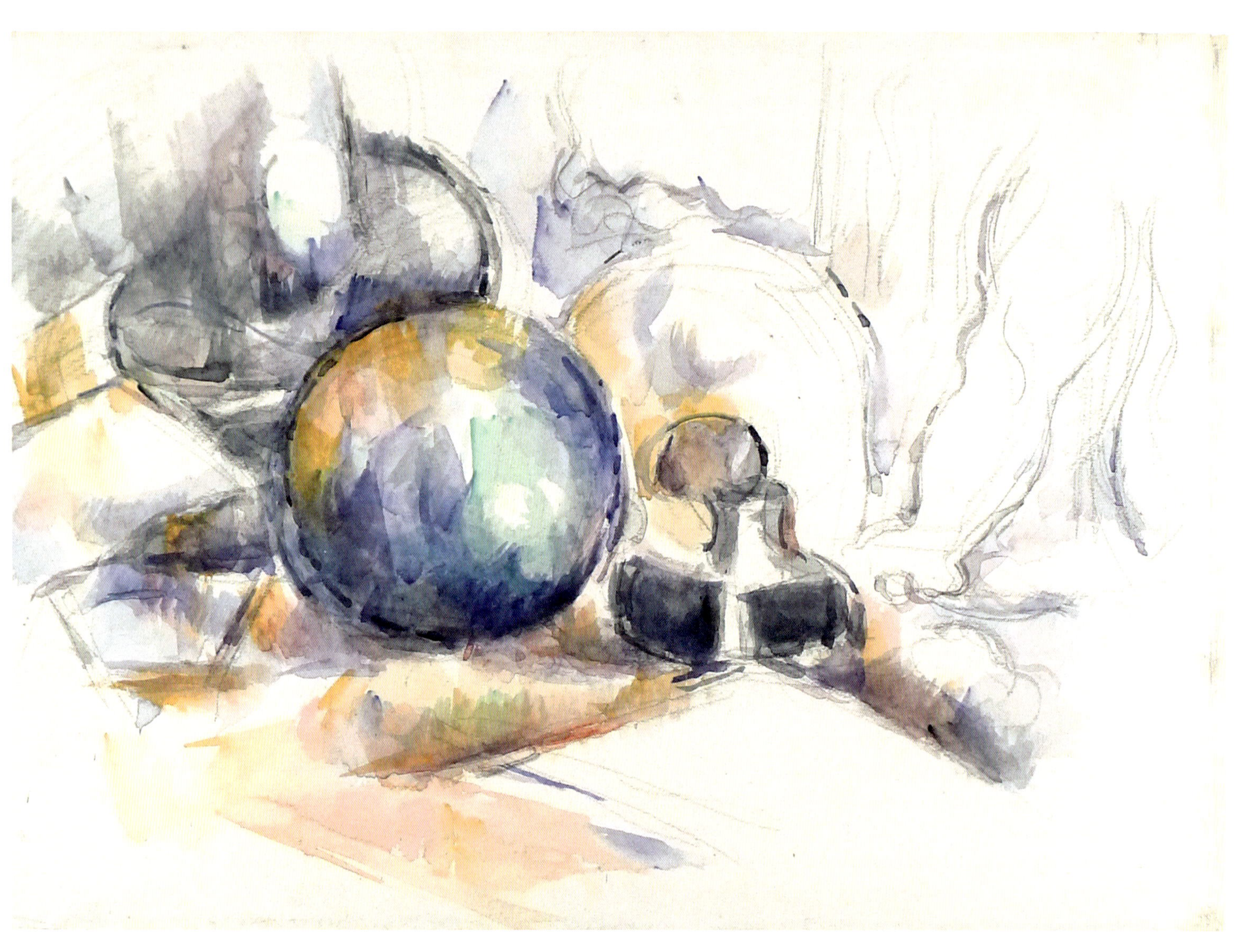

206. *Still Life with Inkpot.* 1900–04. Pencil and watercolor on paper, 12 3⁄16 × 18 7⁄8" (31 × 48 cm)

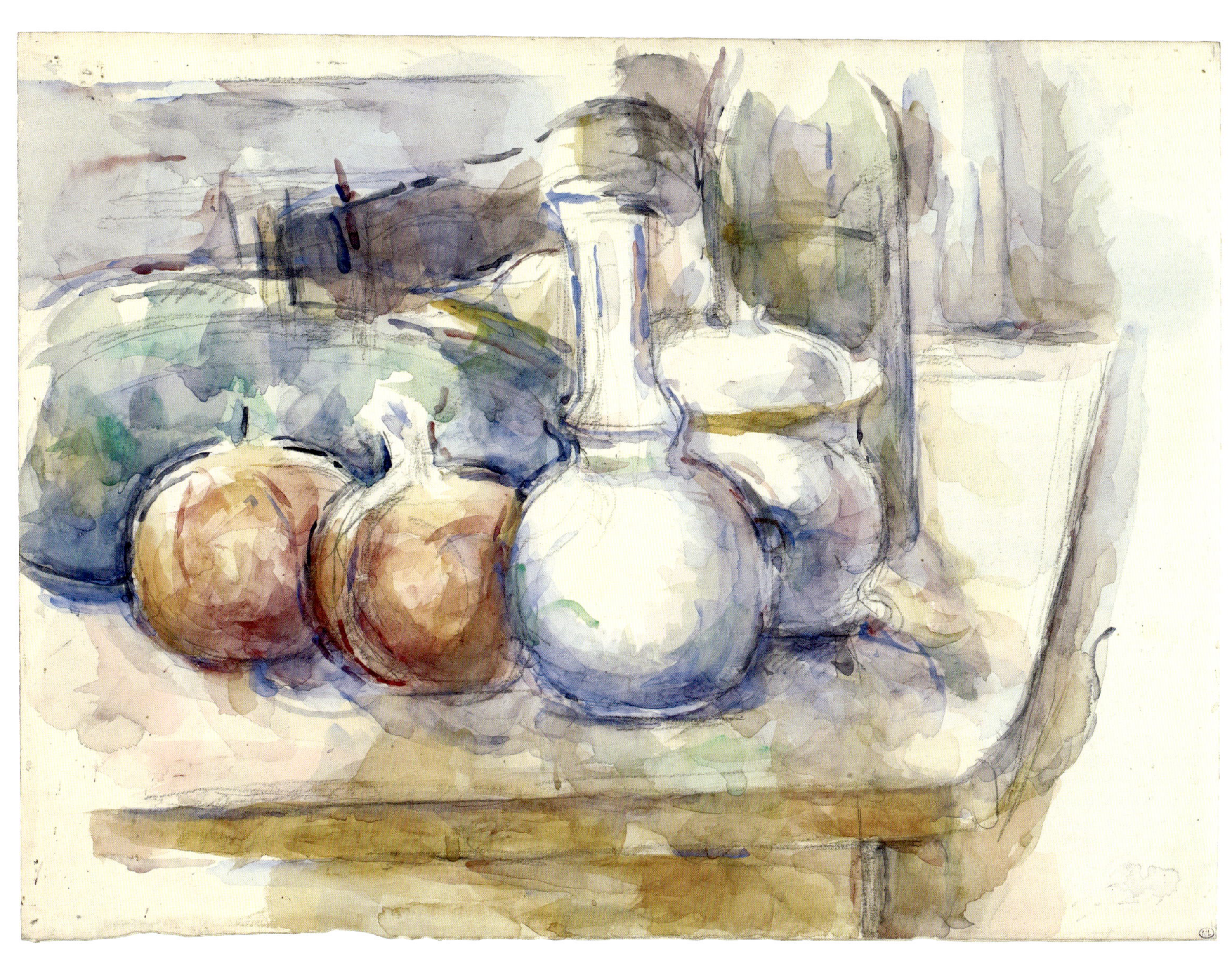

207. *Still Life with Fruit, Carafe, Sugar Bowl, and Bottle*. 1900–06. Pencil and watercolor on paper, 12 ½ × 17 1/16" (31.8 × 43.4 cm)

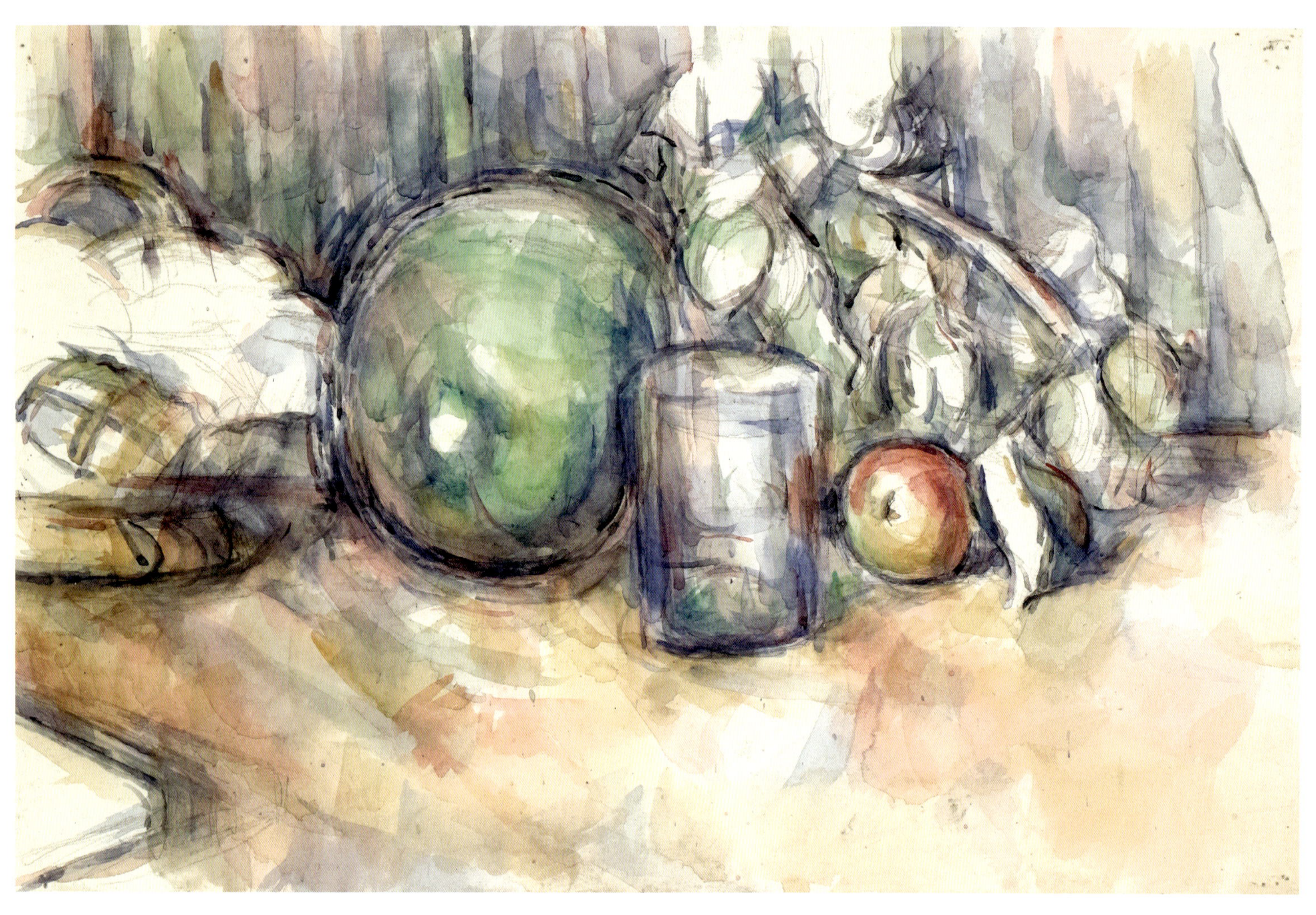

208. *Still Life with Green Melon*. 1902–06. Watercolor and pencil on paper, 12 ⅜ × 18 ¹¹⁄₁₆" (31.5 × 47.5 cm)

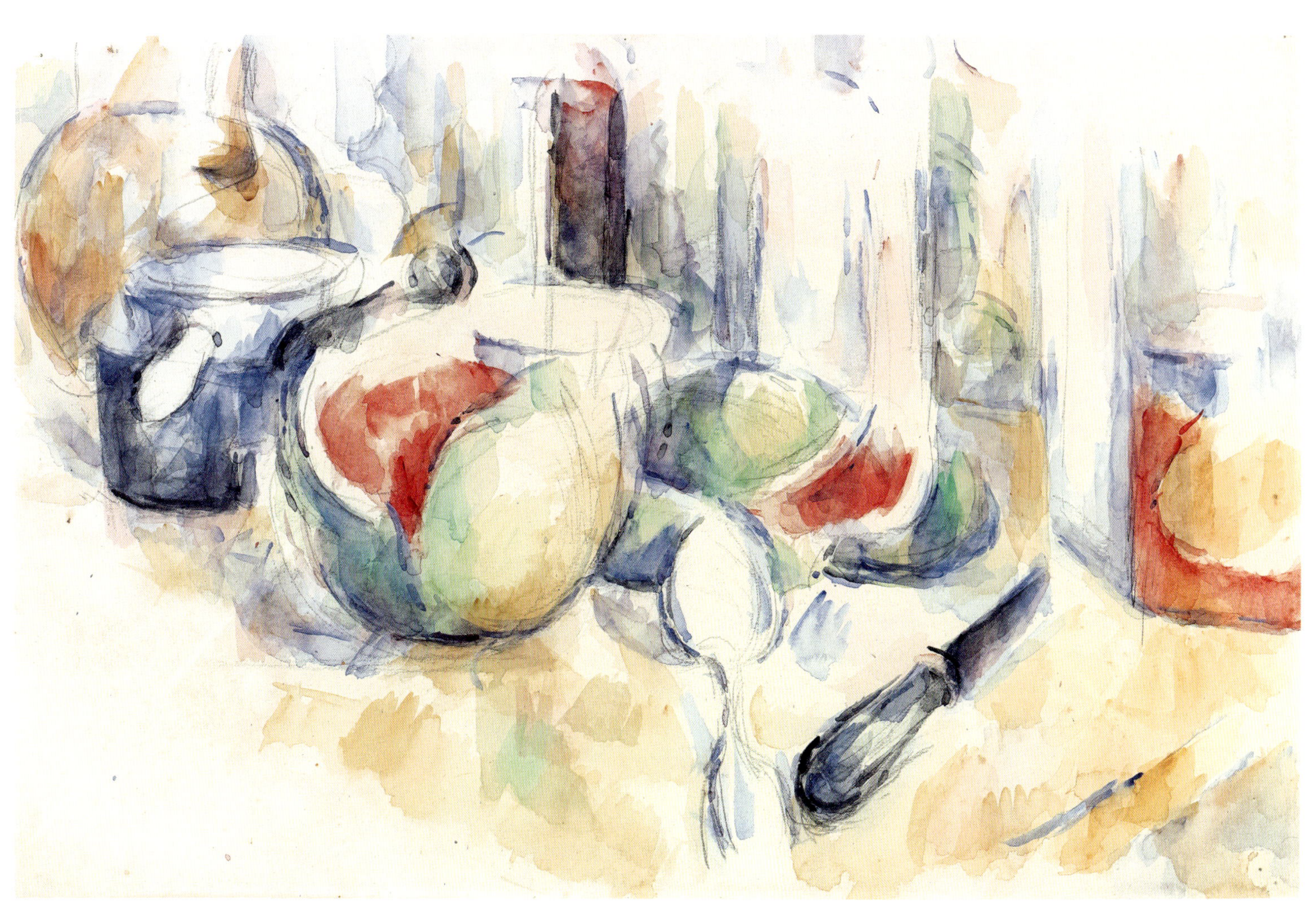

209. *Still Life with Cut Watermelon*. c. 1900. Pencil and watercolor on paper, 12 3/8 × 19 1/8" (31.5 × 48.5 cm)

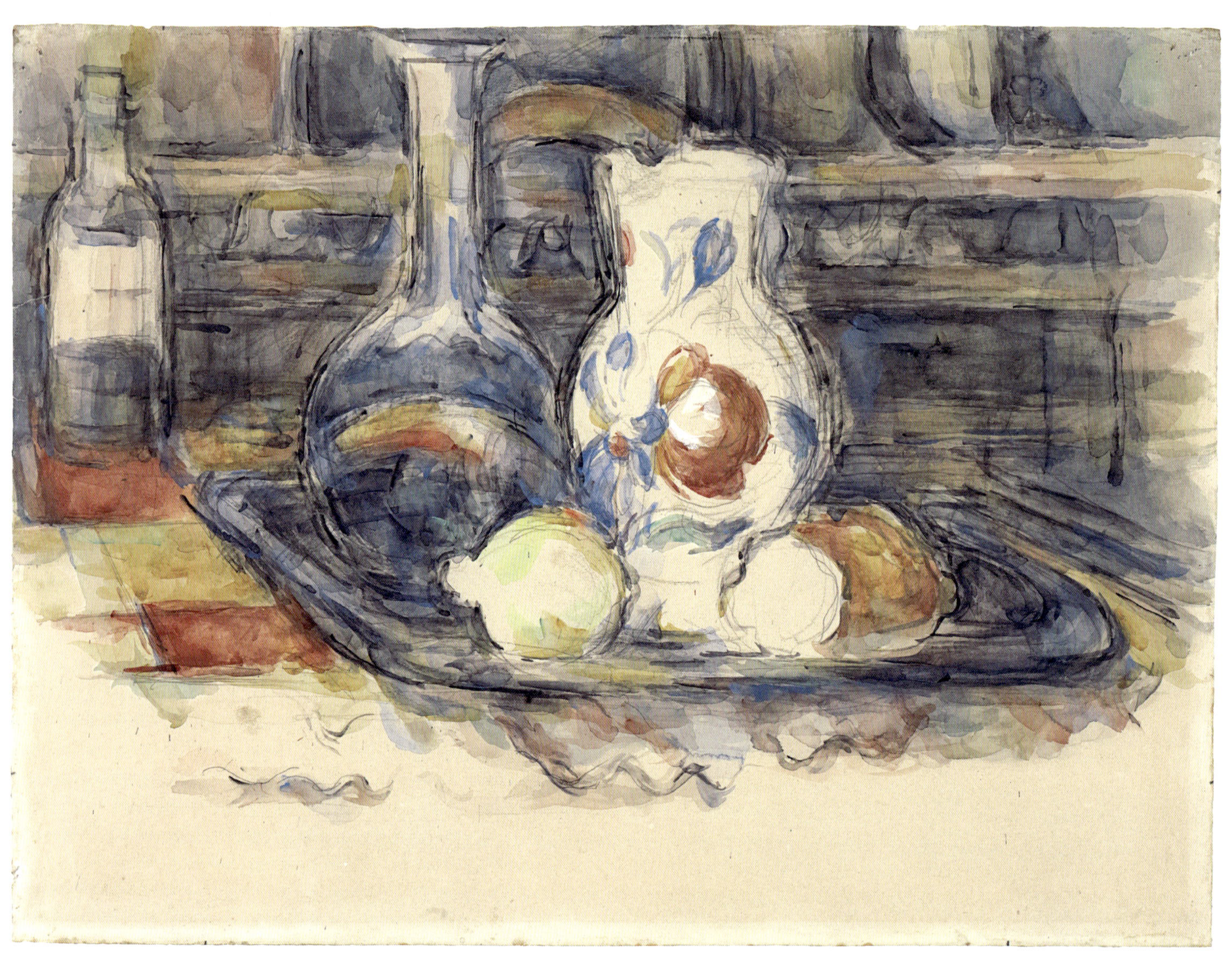

210. *Bottle, Carafe, Jug, and Lemons*. 1902–06. Pencil, watercolor, and gouache on paper, 17 ½ × 23 ⅝" (44.5 × 60 cm)

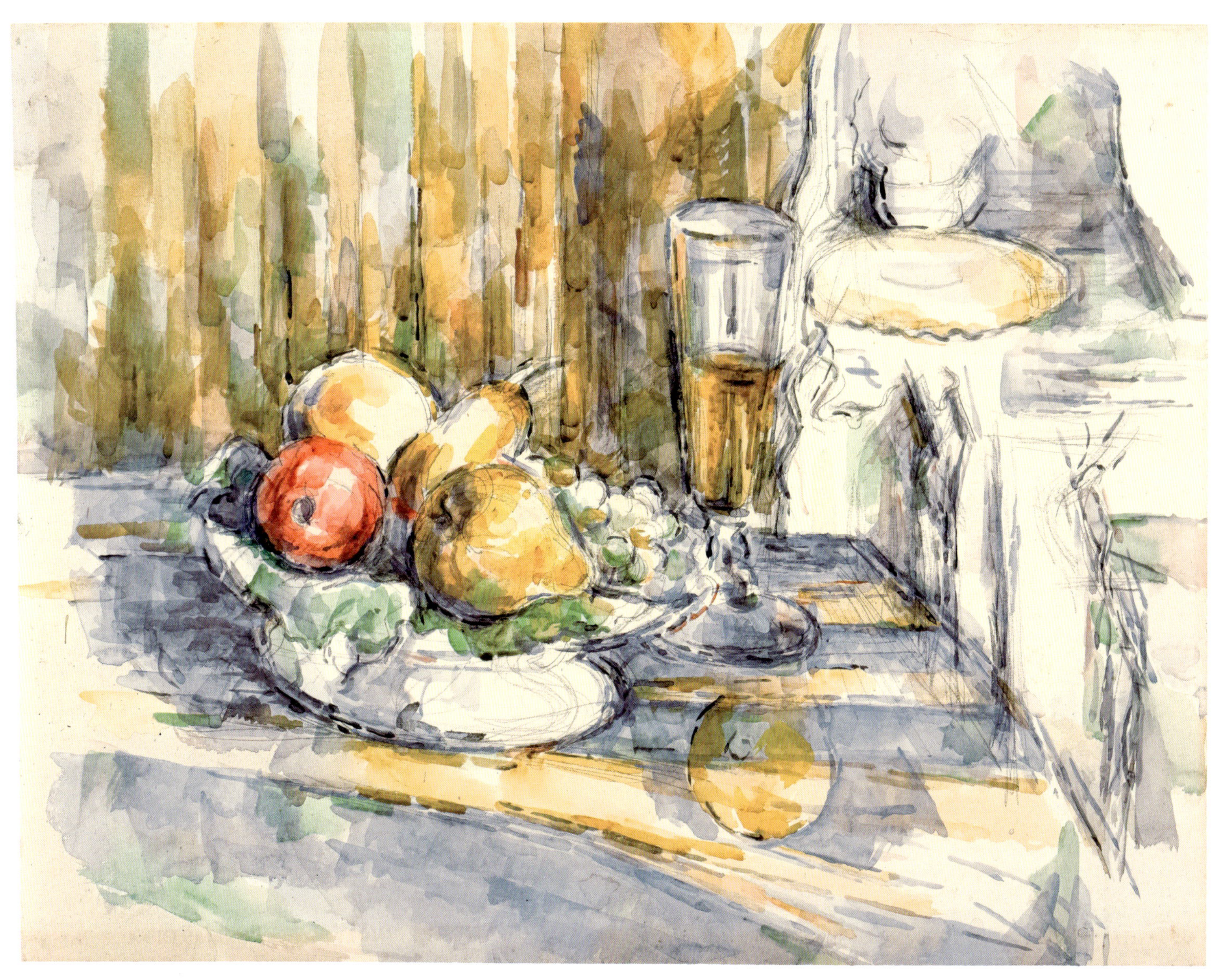

211. *The Dessert*. c. 1900–06.
Pencil and watercolor
on paper, 18 ½ × 24"
(47 × 61 cm)

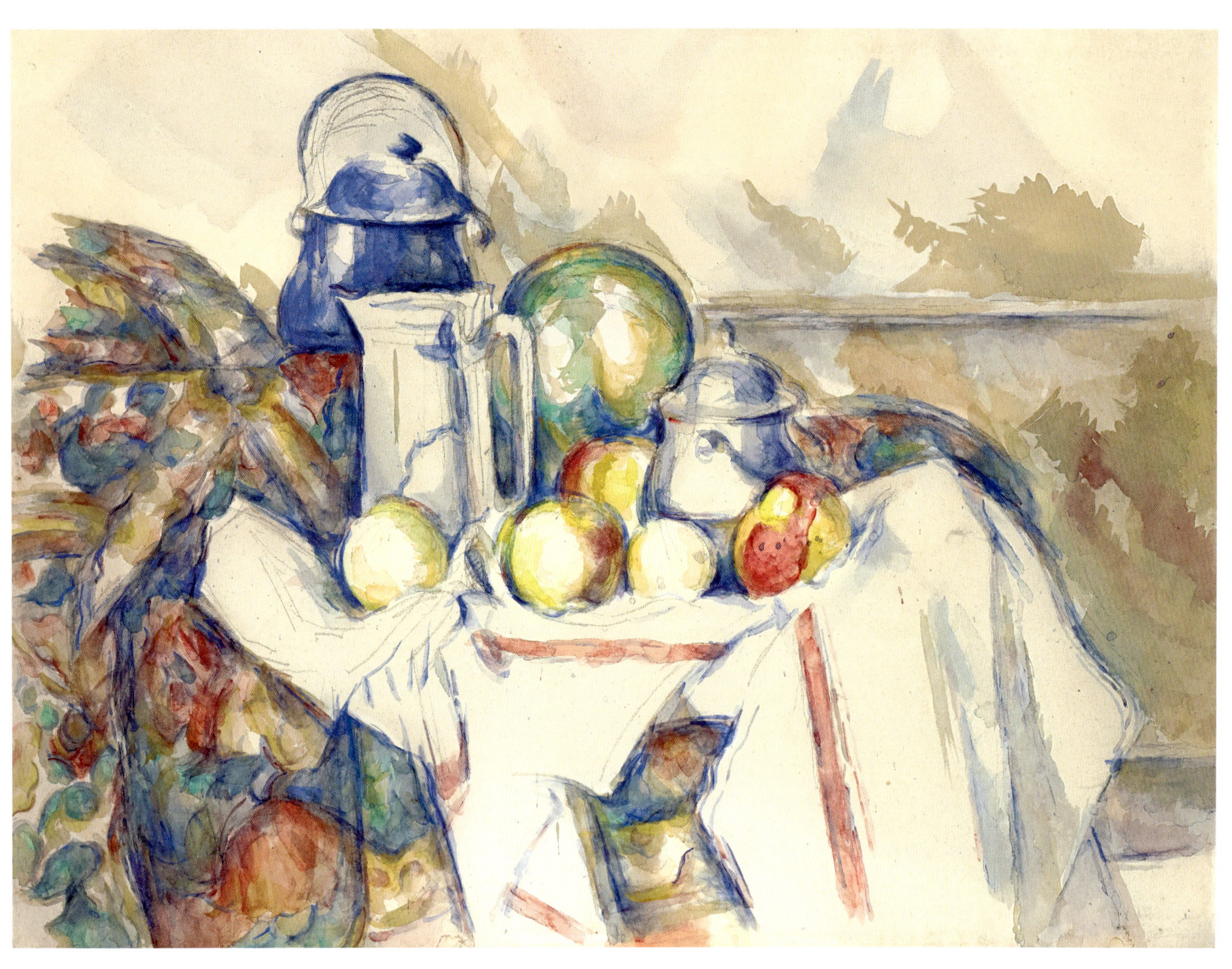

212. *Still Life with Milk Pot, Melon, and Sugar Bowl*. 1900–06. Pencil and watercolor on paper, 19 × 24 ½" (48.2 × 62.2 cm)

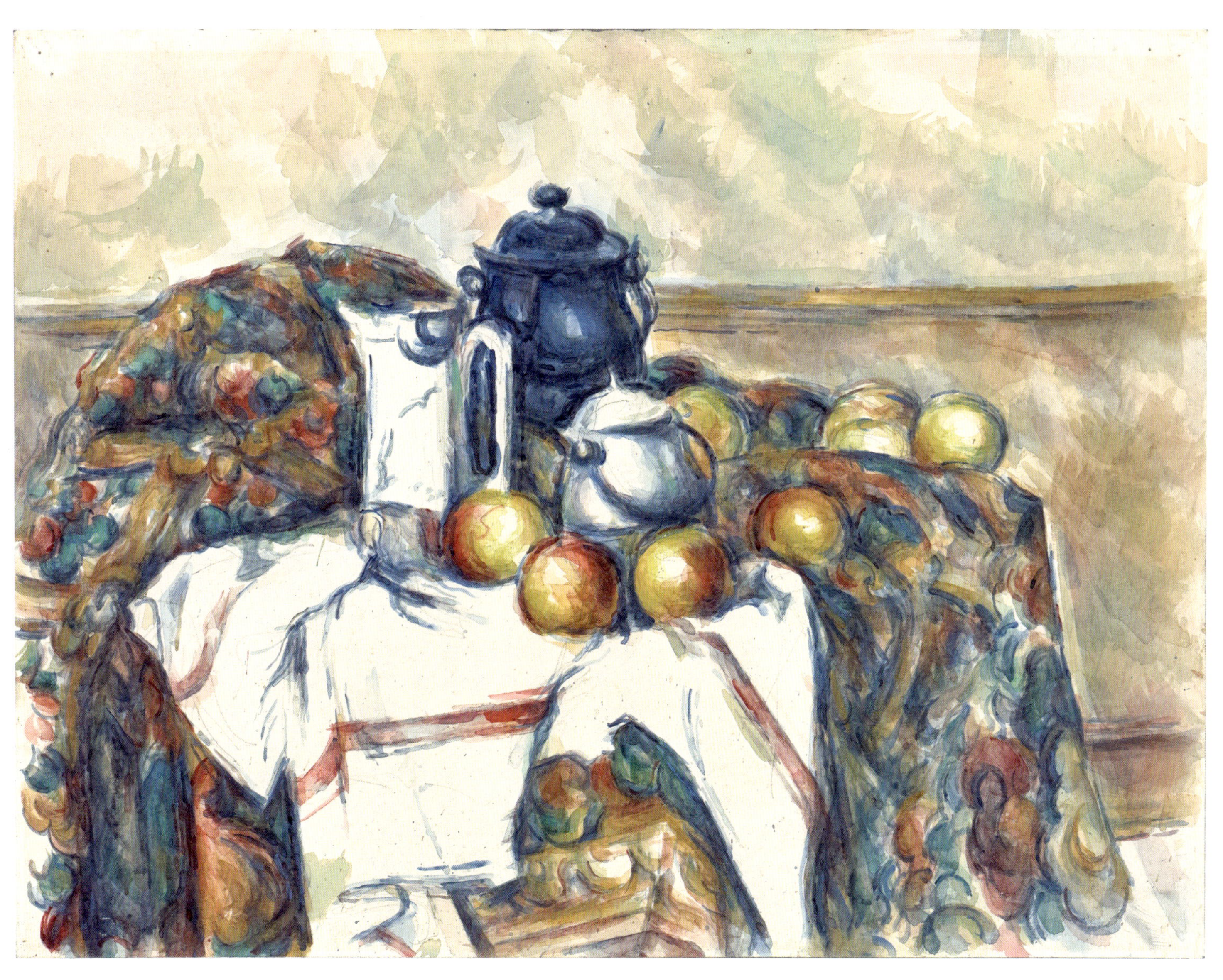

213. *Still Life with Blue Pot*. 1900–06. Pencil and watercolor on paper, 18 15/16 × 24 7/8" (48.1 × 63.2 cm)

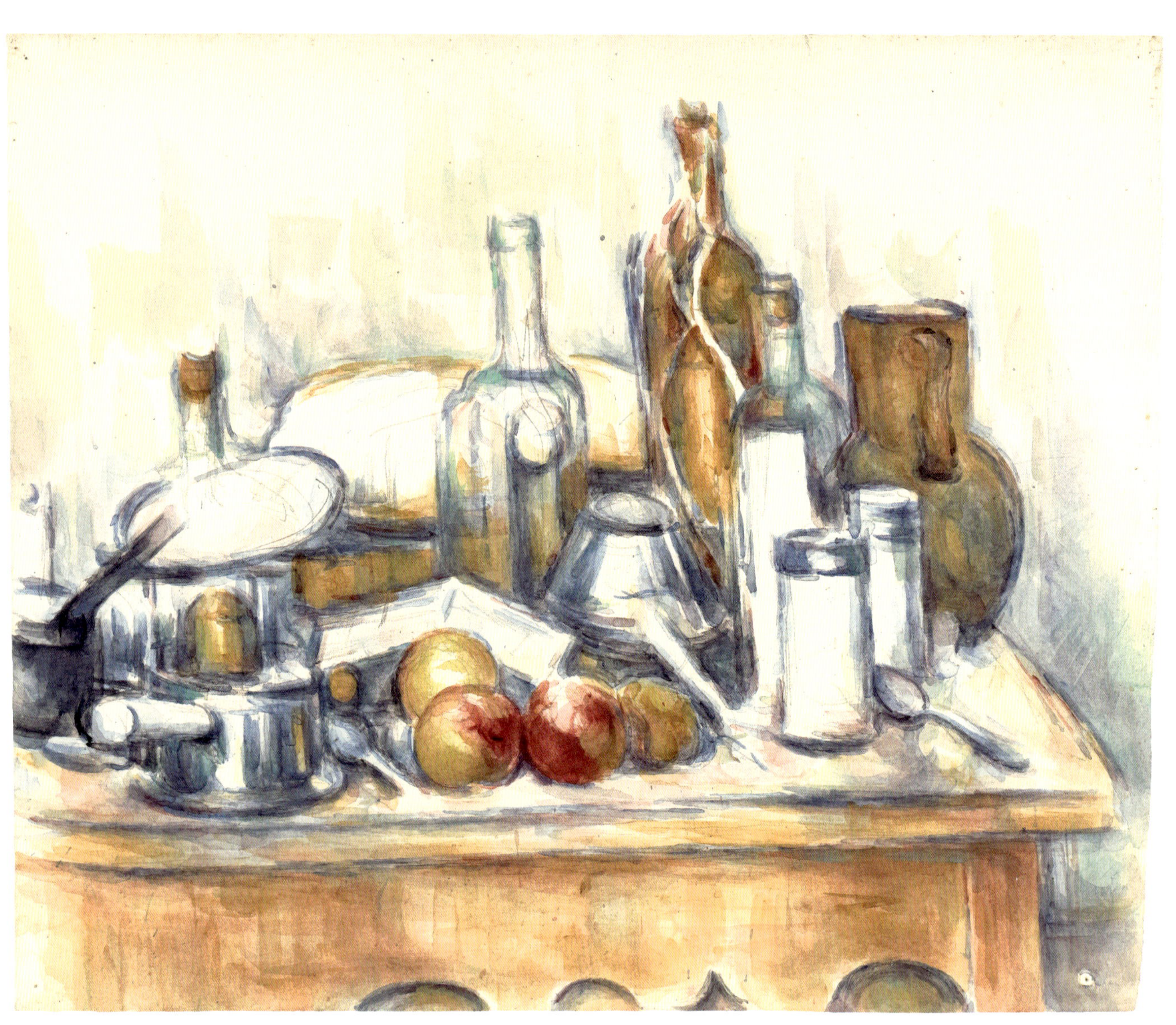

214. *Bottles, Pot, Alcohol Stove, and Apples.* 1900–06. Pencil and watercolor on paper, 18 ½ × 22 ¹⁄₁₆" (47 × 56 cm)

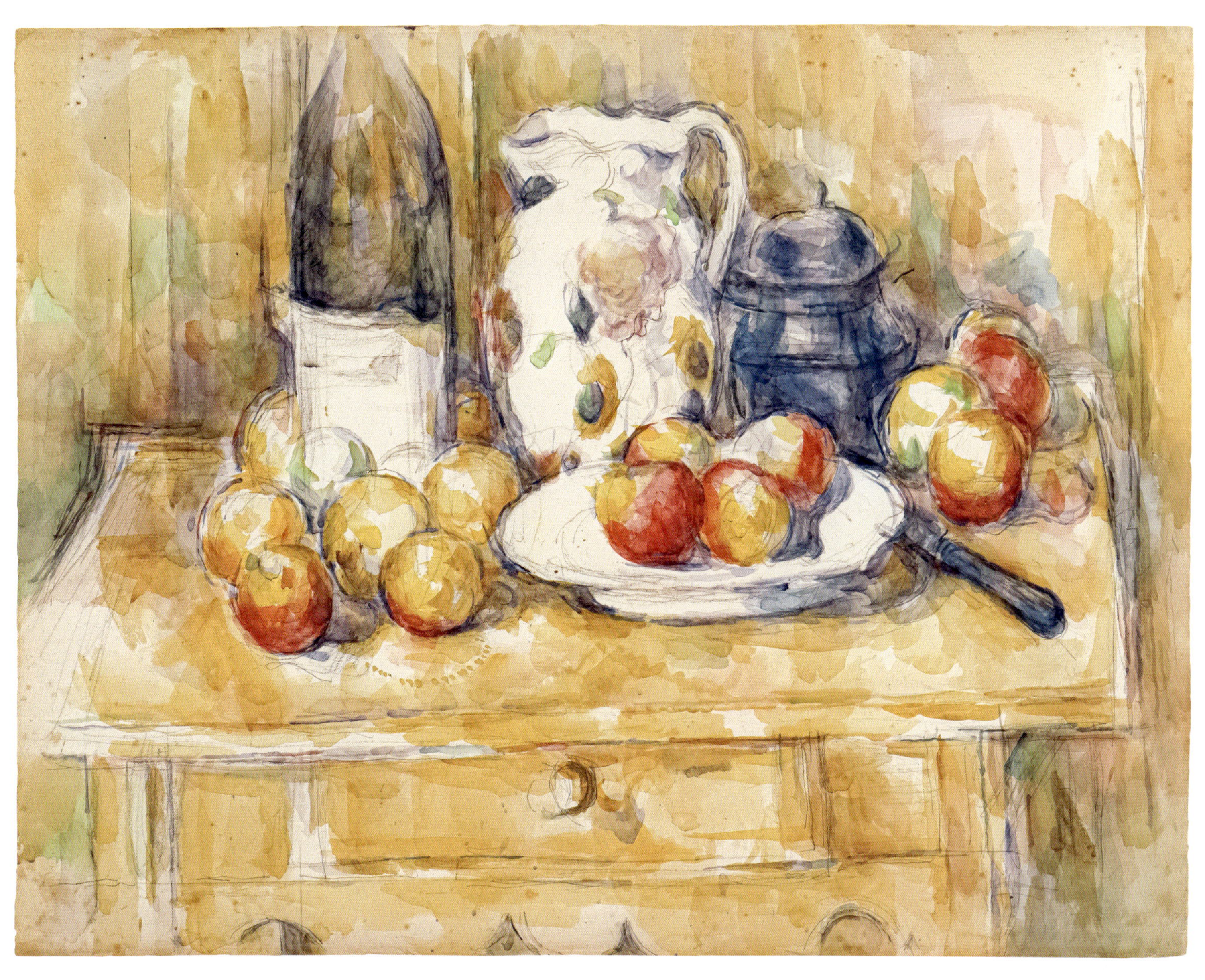

215. *Still Life with Apples on a Sideboard*. 1900–06. Pencil and watercolor on paper, 19 ⅛ × 24 ⅞" (48.6 × 63.2 cm)

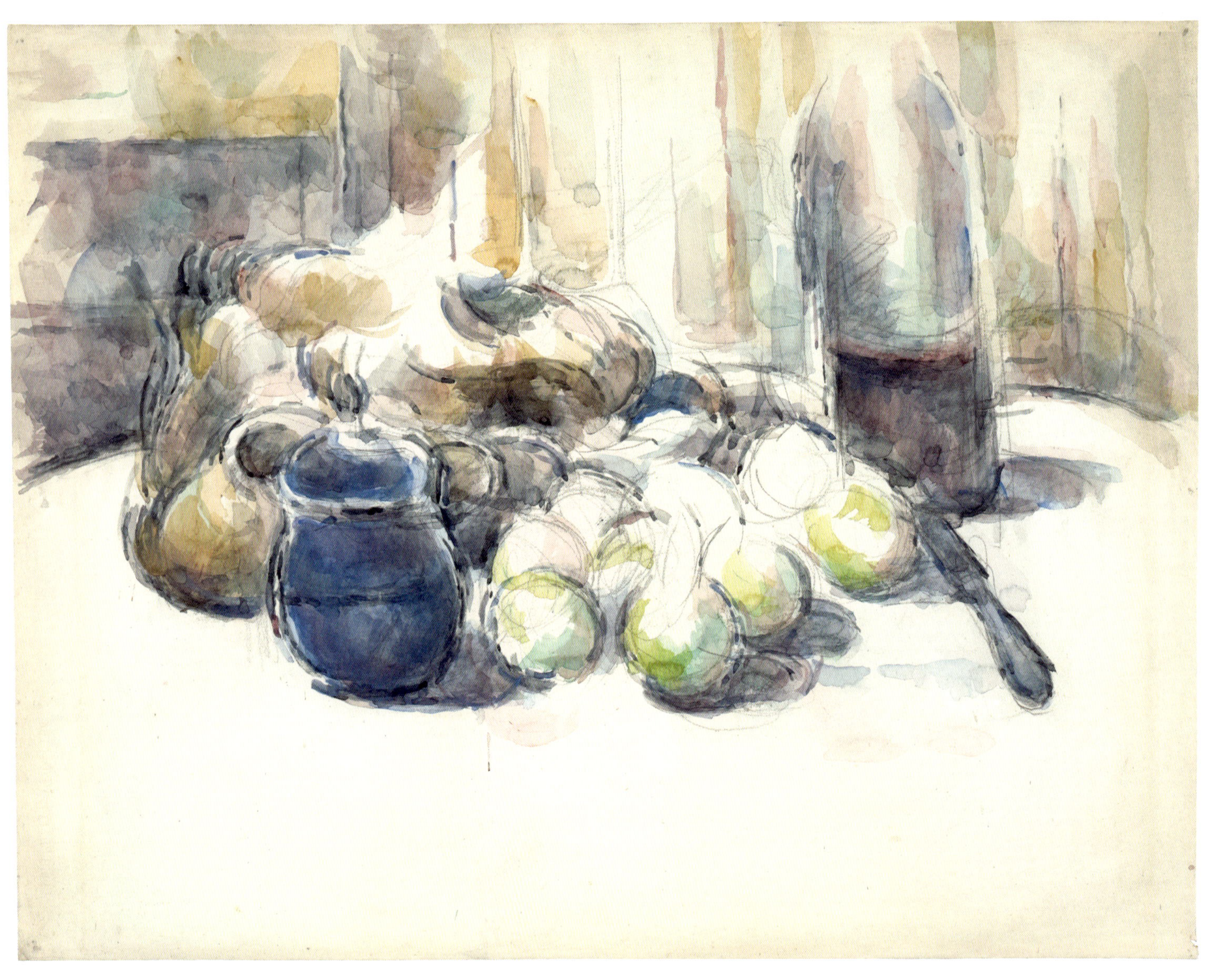

216. *Still Life with Pears and Apples, Covered Blue Jar, and a Bottle of Wine.* 1902–06. Watercolor and pencil on paper, 18 ¾ × 24 15/16" (47.6 × 63.3 cm)

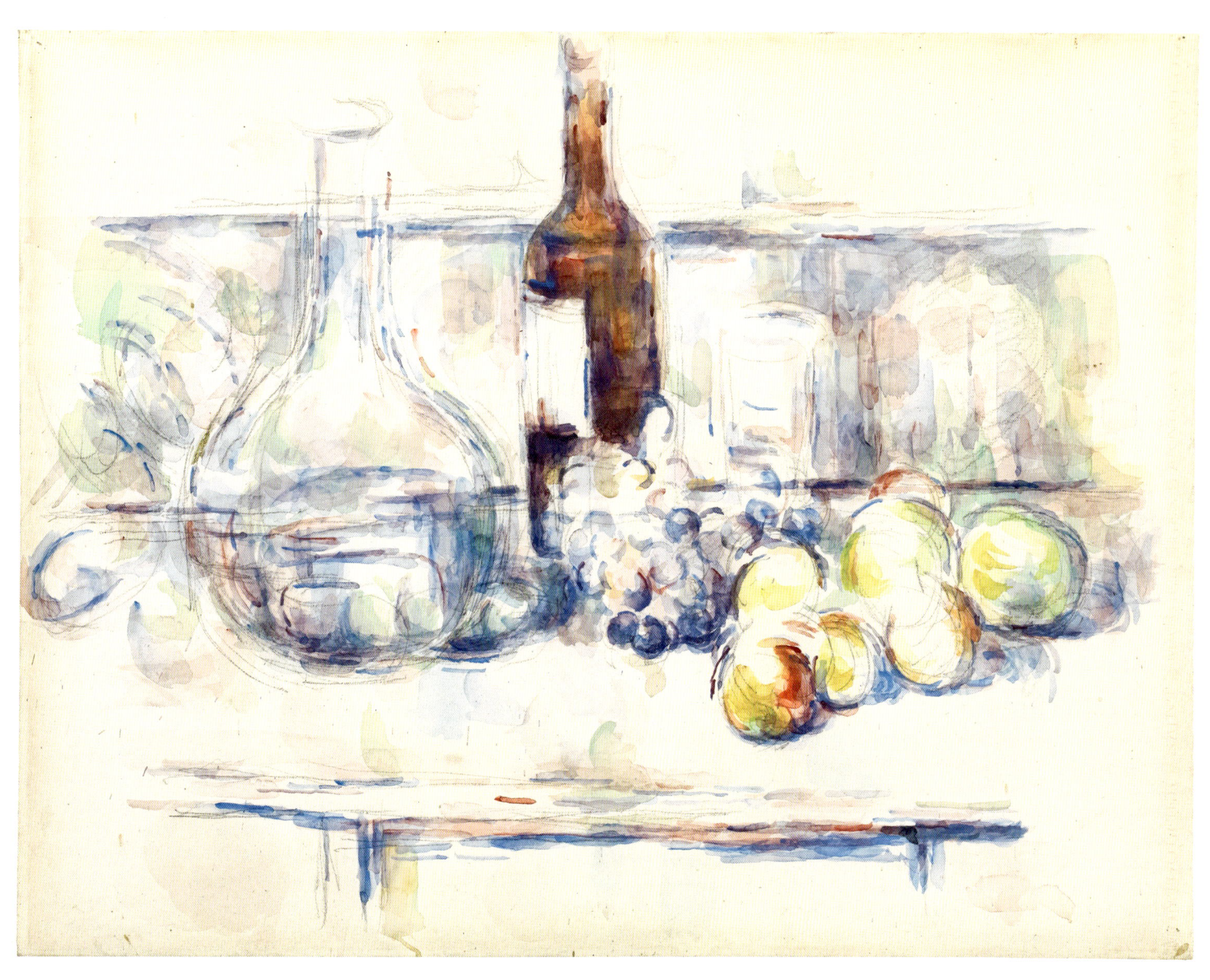

217. *Still Life with Carafe, Bottle, and Fruit*. 1906. Pencil and watercolor on paper, 18 ⅞ × 24 ⅝" (48 × 62.5 cm)

Kiko Aebi

"Gradually as one paints, one draws."
—Paul Cézanne, quoted in Émile Bernard, "Souvenirs sur Paul Cézanne" (1907)

Cézanne's originality lies, in part, in his experimentation across mediums, and relationships are readily evident among his drawings and paintings of the same subject. In his oil-on-canvas portrait of his gardener, for example, Cézanne constructed Vallier and the foliage around him through thick brushstrokes, generating opacity and solidity, while allowing small patches of canvas to peek through (plate 229). On paper, depicting his subject in an identical pose, Cézanne used veils of watercolor and tangles of pencil that imbue the composition with a sense of dynamism, as though, paradoxically, the sitter is in motion (plates 227, 228). A similar dynamism is on display in a seated watercolor portrait of Madame Cézanne, with its repeated, multicolored, jittery designations of dress and chair (plate 223); in the related painting, Cézanne retained those broken lines while also constructing his composition with patches of color, effacing distinctions between subject and ground (plate 224). Here, spurred by our interest in the artist's multi-image study-sheet drawings (see, for example, plates 13, 14, 23, 24), we explore an additional, underexamined link between his practices on paper and on canvas.[1] Close investigation, in collaboration with conservators, has led to the hypothesis that Cézanne, more often than previously understood, may have used his canvases as he did his study sheets: to explore multiple motifs, overlapping and rotating them around the support.

Only one such composite painting by Cézanne is widely known. *Female Nude (Leda)* (*Femme nu [Léda]*, c. 1887) features two distinct compositions in a fascinatingly unresolved conflation. At the center of the canvas, a naked woman reclines on a divan, her right arm raised languidly. A rumpled white tablecloth bearing two upside-down pears encroaches on her from the upper left, covering her outstretched hand. The still life and the boudoir scene relate formally: the pears' fleshy bodies visually rhyme with the woman's pear-shaped figure.[2]

X-rays have revealed that, at some point, the canvas was cut and the two compositions separated.[3] While it is not known when or by whom the excision (or the subsequent rejoining of the pieces) was performed, recent research on the fragmentation of Cézanne's works on paper offers an important parallel. Fabienne Ruppen has reconstructed a number of study sheets and other drawings by Cézanne, piecing together works that, she suggests, were cut apart during his lifetime or immediately following his death, likely by family members or dealers.[4] Her research has shown that the practice of dividing Cézanne's works on paper was more extensive than previously known.[5] Until now, the possibility that this practice extended to canvases has not been extensively investigated.[6]

In his 1915 monograph on Cézanne, the dealer Ambroise Vollard recounted that the artist habitually made canvases with "several little studies of various subjects," which he left with Julien Tanguy, a paint supplier and informal dealer of Cézanne's work, to cut up for collectors who could not afford larger works. "One might have seen Tanguy," Vollard wrote, "scissors in hand, disposing of tiny 'motifs,' while some poor *Mycaenas* paid him a louis and marched off with three *Apples* by Cézanne!"[7] Suggesting that the artist did not cut his own canvases (although implying, perhaps dubiously, that he permitted the practice), this anecdote points to the existence of multiple composite paintings.

In 1996 the conservator Gillian McMillan discovered a group of oil sketches on the verso of a painting possibly by Cézanne. A conversation with McMillan, in conjunction with documentary and material evidence, led us to begin searching for other paintings that may once have been part of a composite canvas.[8] In one possible pairing, a study of a pipe-smoking card player (plate 241) seems to have originally abutted a painting of the plaster cupid Cézanne kept in his studio (plate 242), a favorite subject. Flipped upside down, *Man with Pipe* fits like a puzzle piece to the left of the cupid, near its head and upper torso, replacing a section of newer canvas that had been added later to square off the work (note the seam running vertically alongside the statue) (p. 199 B).[9] Passages from one canvas carry over to the other, most notably where the vigorously worked backgrounds converge. As in the study sheets, where analogies of form and content proliferate, a comparison of the rendering of the card player and the cupid intimates Cézanne's interest in the relationship between surface and depth, planarity and volume: while the cupid steps forward in space, the man, shown in profile, is comparatively flattened, the taut angularity of his face accentuating, by contrast, the cupid's plump curves. Cézanne likely painted the cupid before rotating the canvas to begin the pipe smoker, since a portion of the latter's back overlaps the cupid's head.

A similar rotation is evident in another potential composite canvas (p. 199 C), this one featuring two still lifes in vertically mirrored orientations, executed with similar brushstrokes and representing seven apples in dispersed and condensed arrangements.[10] An ocher area at right in the larger composition (plate 244) is contiguous with the smaller work (plate 243), comprising part of its background and the shadow of an apple.[11] In another possible composite (p. 199 D), two still lifes (plates 245, 247) may once have bordered a portrait of the artist's son (plate 246) at left and below—with a corner of the sideboard in one and an expanse of the background in the other continuing across the cuts that now separate the compositions. Although the two still lifes are conventionally dated to the late 1870s or 1880 and the portrait to 1881–82, it is likely—based on the visible overlapping of paint—that the portrait was made before the two still lifes.[12]

Why would Cézanne paint in this manner? Vollard's narrative suggests that he did so for financial reasons, but this seems doubtful, especially in light of an account provided by Joachim Gasquet, Cézanne's younger friend, who reported that the artist resolved "to tear up or burn his unfinished studies" once he learned "that people were beginning to make money out of all his works, including unconsidered scraps which he despised particularly."[13] It is likely that these paintings were never intended for sale or public viewing as composites. Executed in the privacy of his studio, they were, like his study-sheet drawings, personal investigations—means of grappling with surface and depth, the condensation of unrelated motifs, and formal and conceptual relationships among genres. While additional research remains to be done—including further in-person study, imaging, thread counting to match canvas-weave densities, and pigment analysis—the potential relationships among these canvases offer new insight into the affinities between Cézanne's drawing and painting practices, expanding our understanding of his working methods.

1.
For a discussion of these multi-image works, see, in this volume, Samantha Friedman, "Condensation: Cézanne's Study Sheets."

2.
Fabienne Ruppen discusses this painting and suggests that Cézanne may have made other composite compositions on canvas in her essay "On Margins and Versos: The Hidden Relationships among Cézanne's Works on Paper," in Alexander Eiling, ed., *Cézanne: Metamorphoses* (Munich: Prestel/Staatliche Kunsthalle Karlsruhe, 2017), 91.

3.
The painting is in the collection of the Von der Heydt-Museum, Wuppertal, Germany. I am grateful to Kateryna Kostiuchenko, Researcher, for ultraviolet and X-ray images of this painting.

4.
See p. 32 for an example of a study sheet that was separated into three parts. This particular reconstruction was identified by Adrien Chappuis. See *The Drawings of Paul Cézanne: A Catalogue Raisonné* (Greenwich, Conn.: New York Graphic Society, 1973), 1:77.

5.
Ruppen, "Tackling Cézanne's Paper: On the Reconstruction of Loose Sheets," in *Reconstructing Cézanne* (London: Ridinghouse/Luxembourg & Dayan, 2019), 17–22.

6.
Divided canvases were not unknown, however. Curator Michel Hoog reconstructed a still life that had been cut in half sometime before 1914 to form two smaller works. See Hoog, "Une nature morte de Cézanne reconstituée," *Revue du Louvre*, no. 3 (1992): 64–66.

7.
Ambroise Vollard, *Paul Cézanne: His Life and Art*, trans. Harold L. Van Doren (New York: Nicholas Brown, 1923), 72–73. First published in French, in 1915. Intriguingly, none of the paintings we have identified here passed through Tanguy, and all but one in our study were at one point in Vollard's possession.

8.
See Gillian McMillan, "The Discovery of Oil Sketches on the Reverse of 'Le Bassin de Jas de Bouffan,'" in *ICOM Committee for Conservation, 11th Triennial Meeting, Preprints*, vol. 1 (1996), 282–87. I identified the potential composite canvases at MoMA in 2019–20, through visual examination of photographs of the paintings, following a February 2019 conversation among our team, McMillan, and her colleagues.

9.
In this and other visual reconstructions, sections of the original supports are not accounted for (still to be discovered, perhaps, or discarded when the canvases were divided).

10.
Both still lifes were owned by Edgar Degas, who bought them months apart from Vollard.

11.
We are especially grateful to Markus Gross, Chief Conservator, with Friederike Steckling, Conservator, Fondation Beyeler, and Rupert Featherstone, Director, with Rowan Frame, Postgraduate Student in the Conservation of Easel Paintings, the Hamilton Kerr Institute, Cambridge, UK, for sharing X-rays of each still life. Jane Munro, Keeper of Paintings, Drawings, and Prints, at the Fitzwilliam Museum, University of Cambridge, and Ulf Küster, Curator, Fondation Beyeler, also contributed invaluable insight on still lifes and on our research.

12.
Bowl and Milk Can (*Bol et boîte à lait*, c. 1879, possibly earlier; Artizon Museum, Tokyo) and *Portrait of Paul, the Artist's Son* (*Portrait du fils de l'artiste*, c. 1880; Henry and Rose Pearlman Foundation [on extended loan to the Princeton University Art Museum]) may constitute two sections of canvas from another composite painting.

13.
Joachim Gasquet, *Cézanne: A Memoir with Conversations*, trans. Christopher Pemberton (London: Thames & Hudson, 1991), 122.

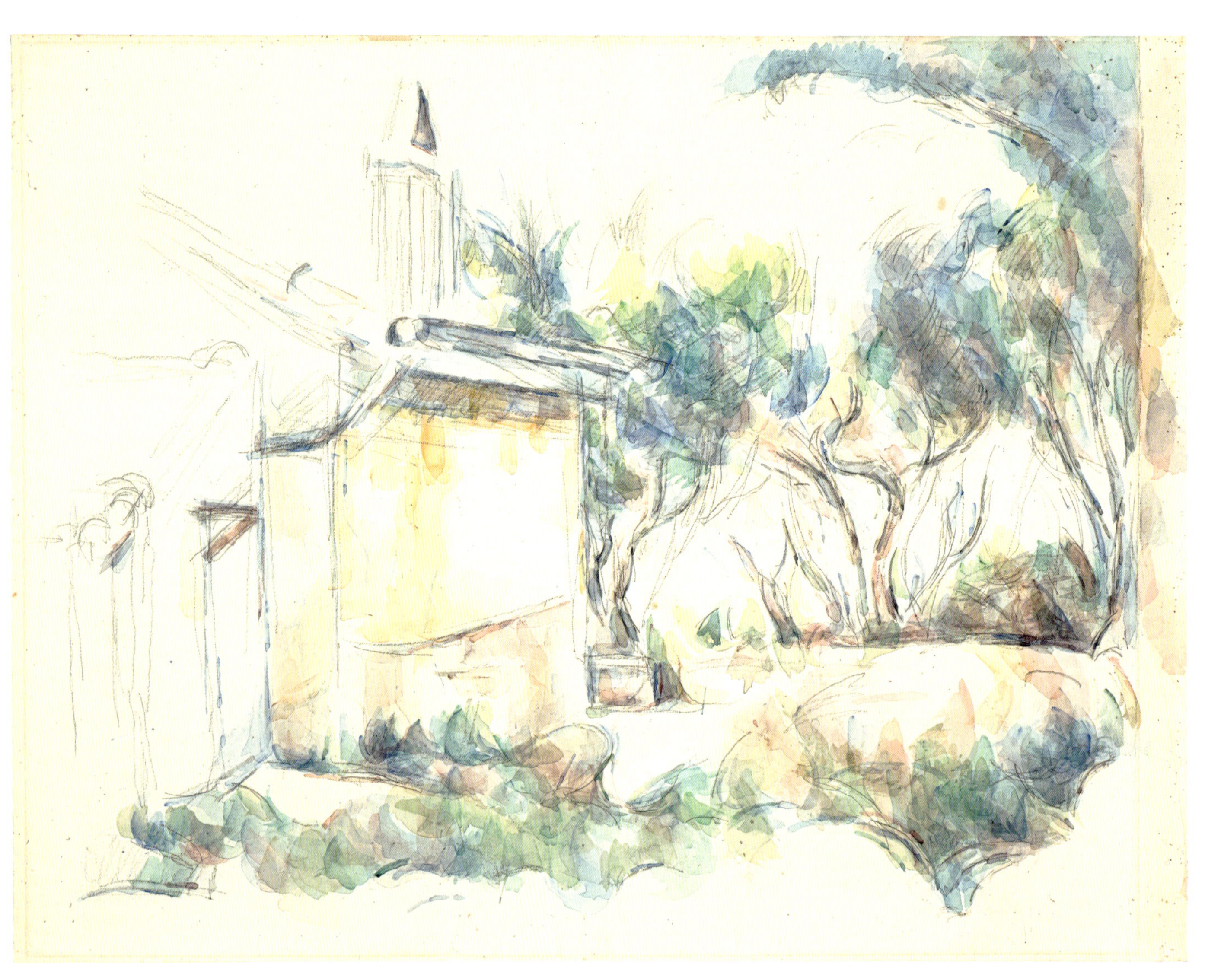

218. *The Cabin of Jourdan*. 1906. Pencil and watercolor on paper, 18 ⅞ × 24 ¾" (48 × 62.8 cm)

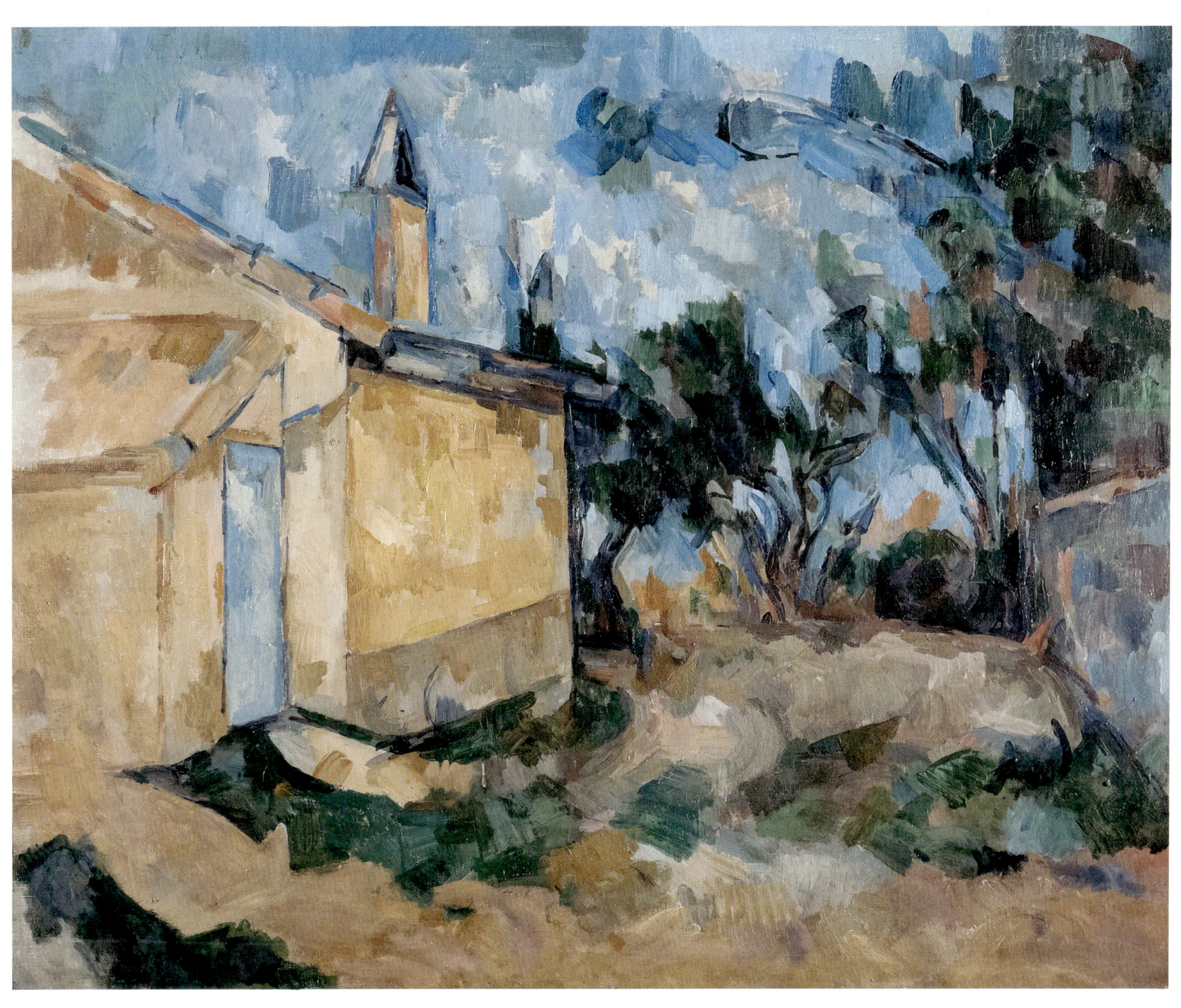

219. *The Cabin of Jourdan*.
1906. Oil on canvas,
$25\frac{9}{16} \times 31\frac{7}{8}$" (65 × 81 cm)

220. *Portrait of Mme Cézanne.* c. 1877–80. Pencil on wove paper, 7⅛ × 7½" (18.1 × 19.1 cm)

221. *Madame Cézanne.* 1885–86. Oil on canvas with traces of pencil, 21⅞ × 18" (55.6 × 45.7 cm)

222. *Madame Cézanne in the Conservatory.* 1891–92. Oil and probably soft graphite pencil on canvas, 36¼ × 28¾" (92.1 × 73 cm)

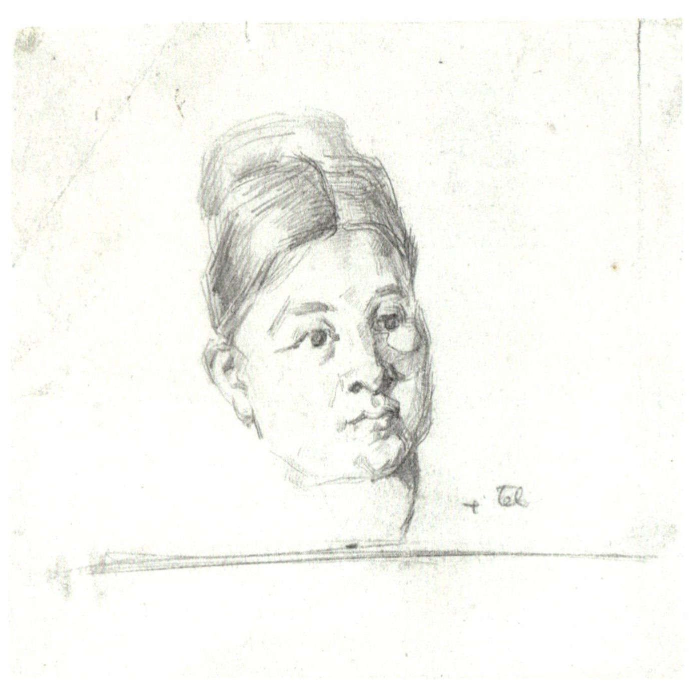

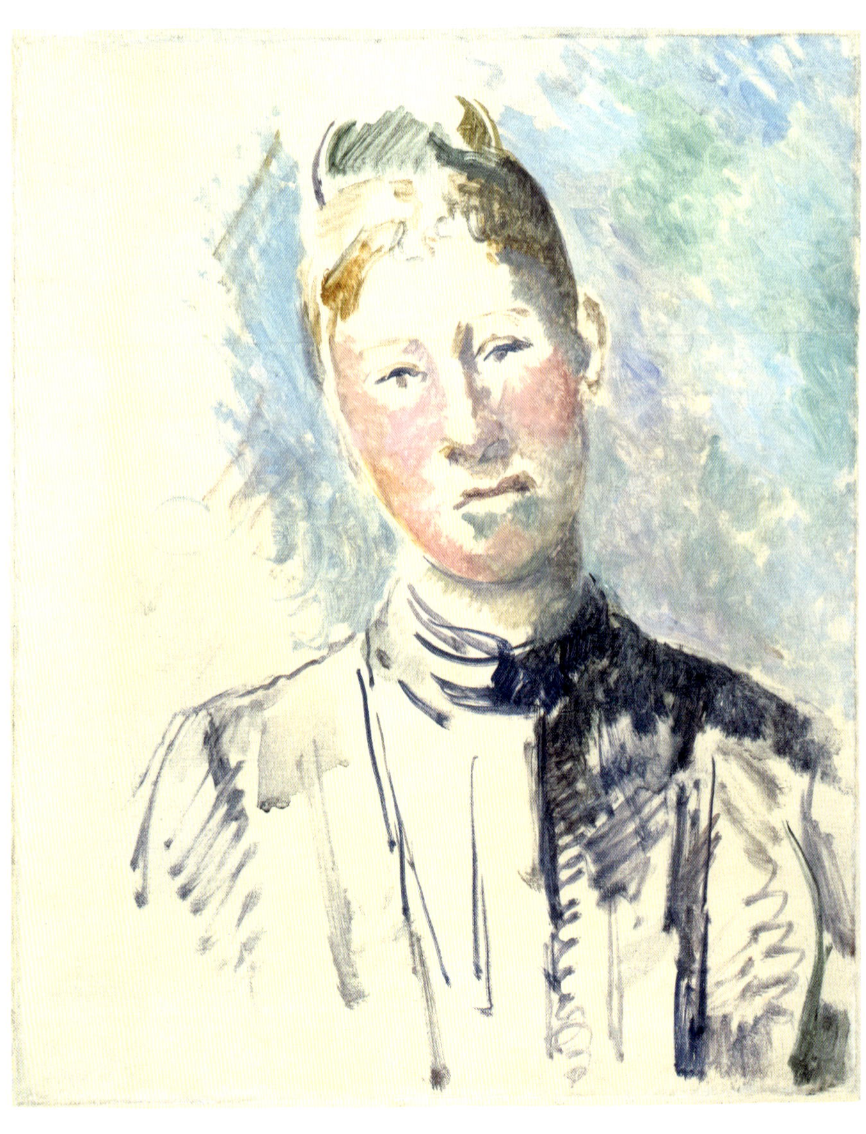

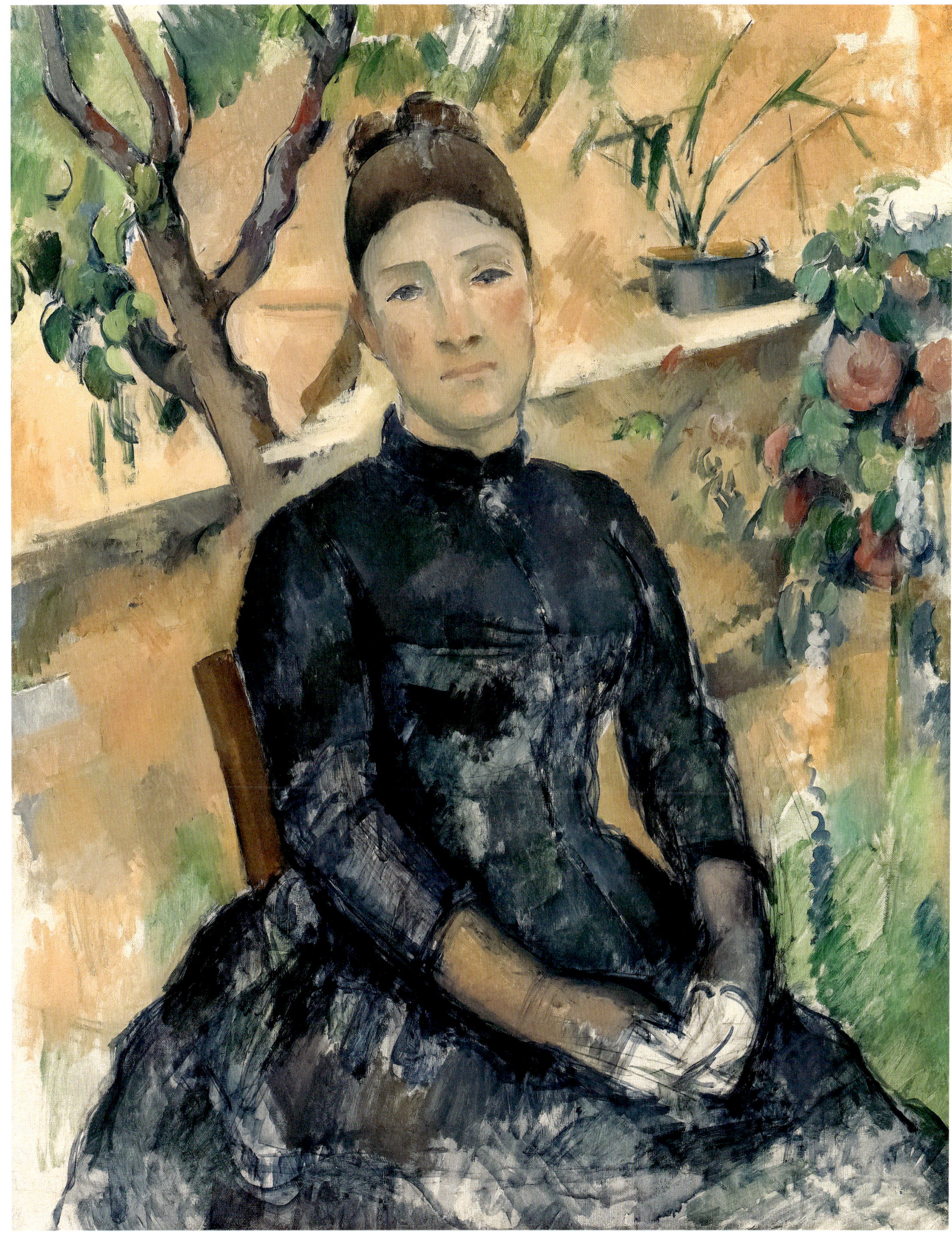

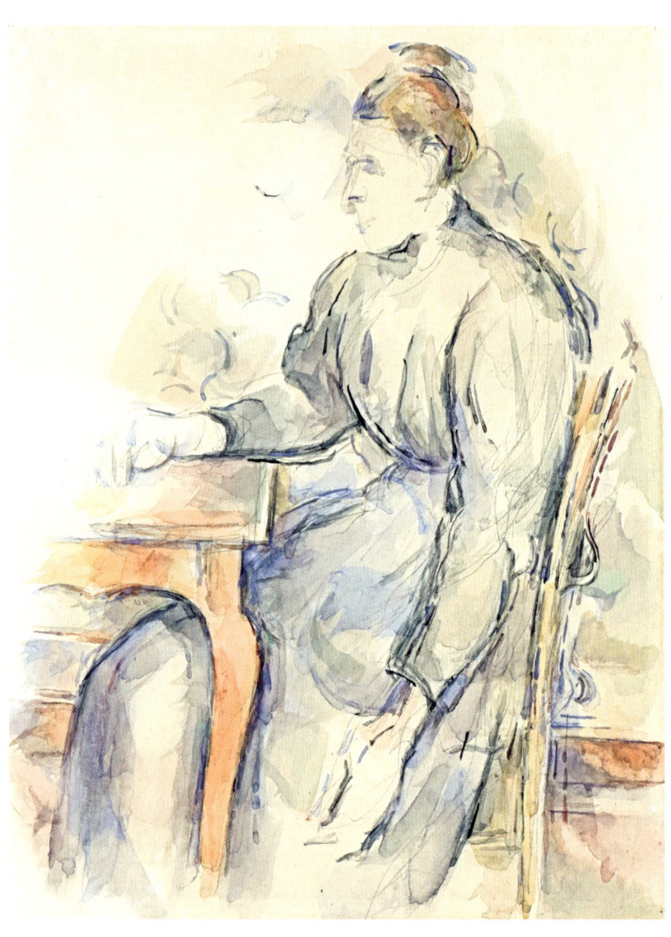

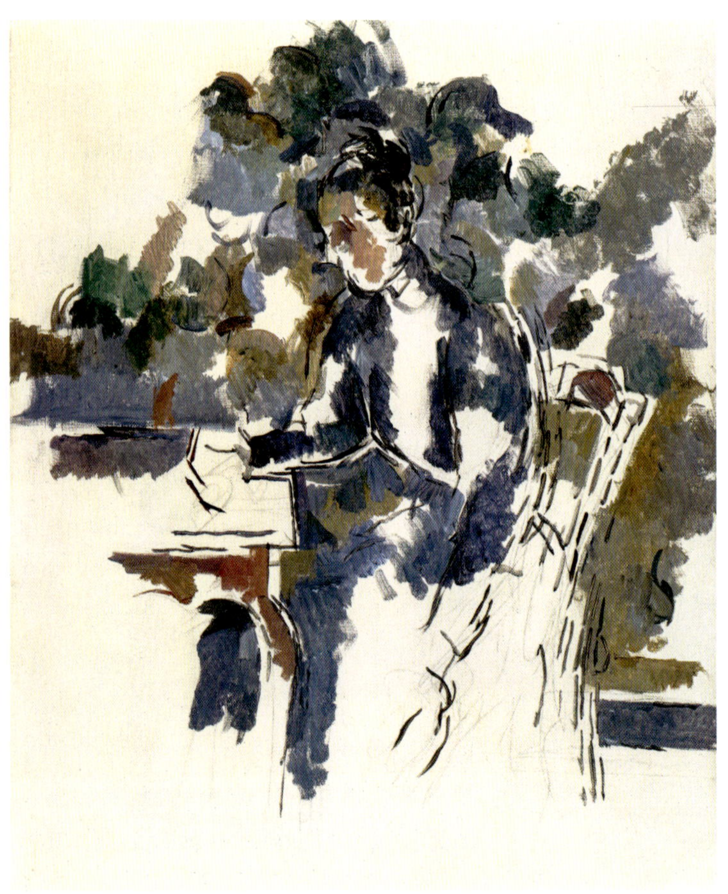

223. *Seated Woman (Madame Cézanne).* 1902–04. Pencil and watercolor on paper, 18 7/8 × 14 3/16" (48 × 36 cm)

224. *Portrait of a Woman (Madame Cézanne?).* 1902–06. Oil on canvas, 25 3/4 × 21 1/2" (65.4 × 54.6 cm)

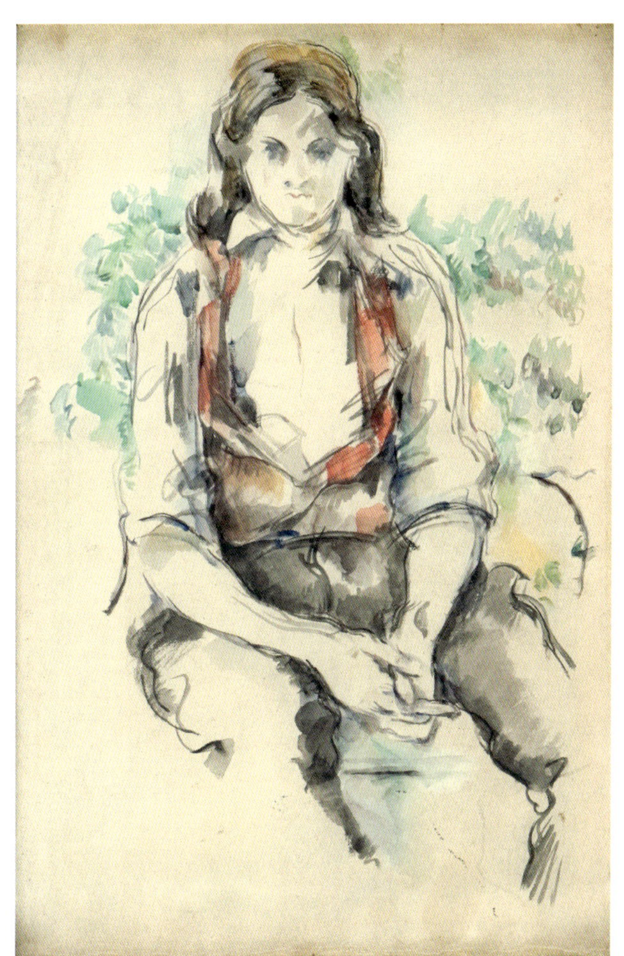

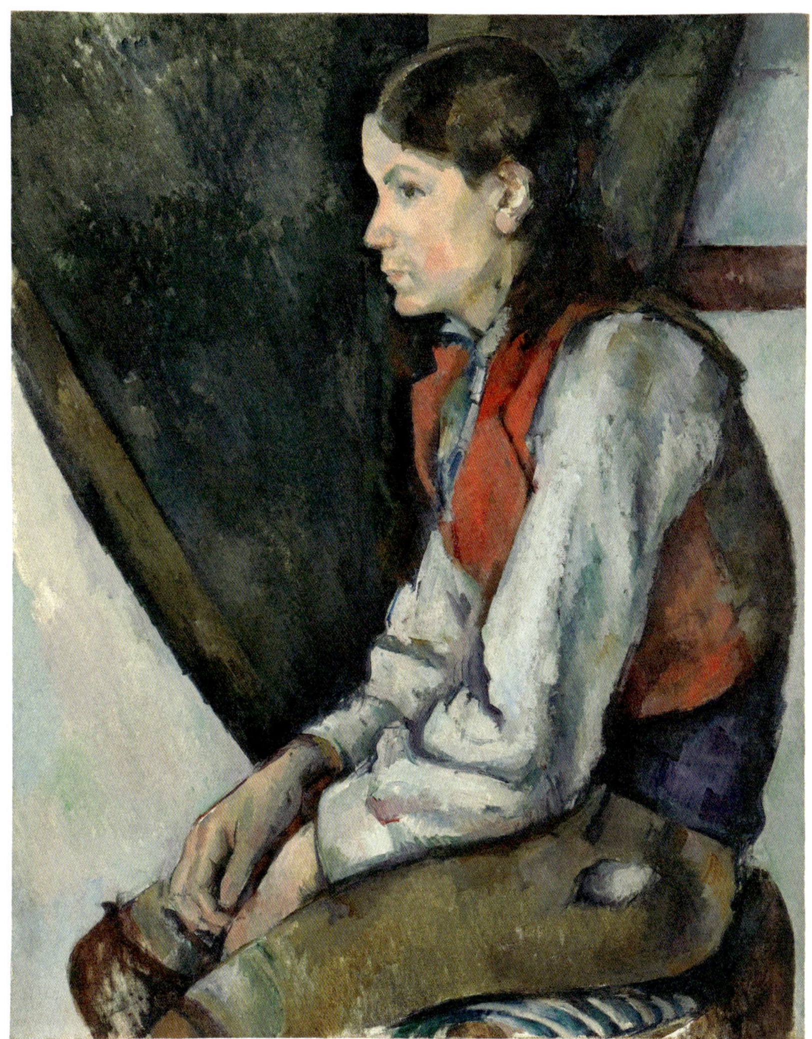

225. *Boy with a Red Waistcoat*. 1889–90. Watercolor on laid paper, 18 ⅛ × 12 $^{3}/_{16}$" (46 × 31 cm)

226. *Boy in a Red Vest*. 1888–90. Oil on canvas, 32 × 25 ⅝" (81.2 × 65 cm)

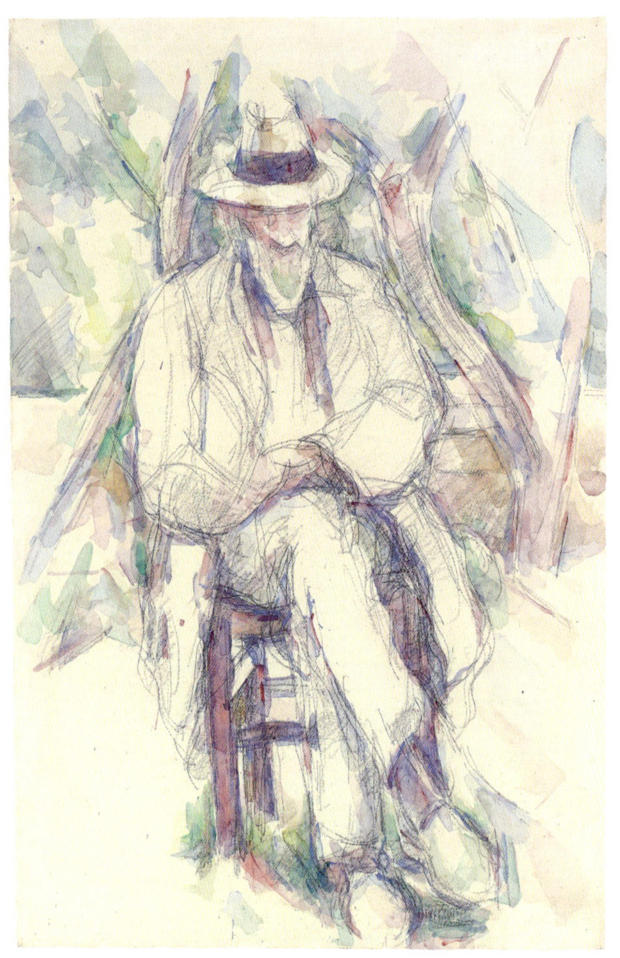
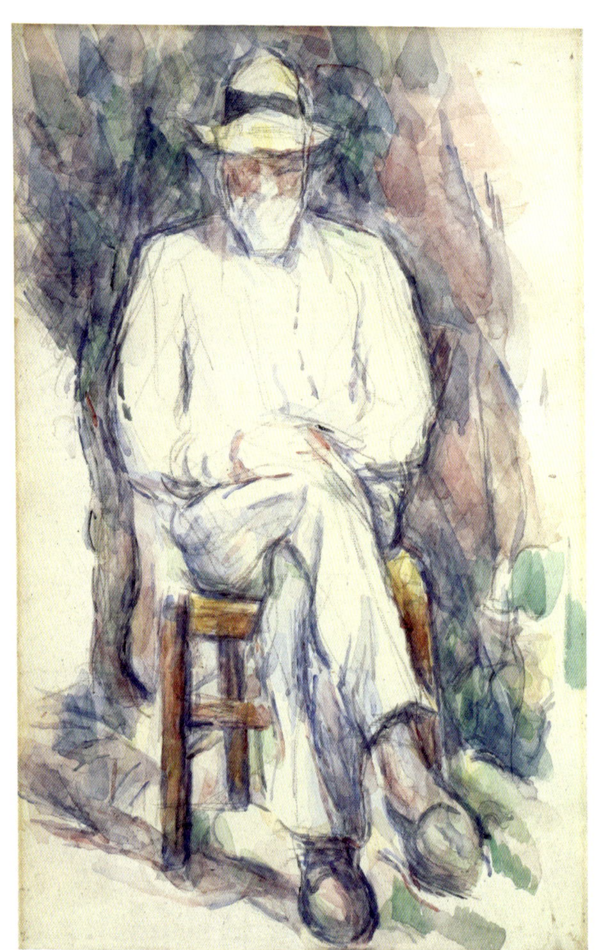
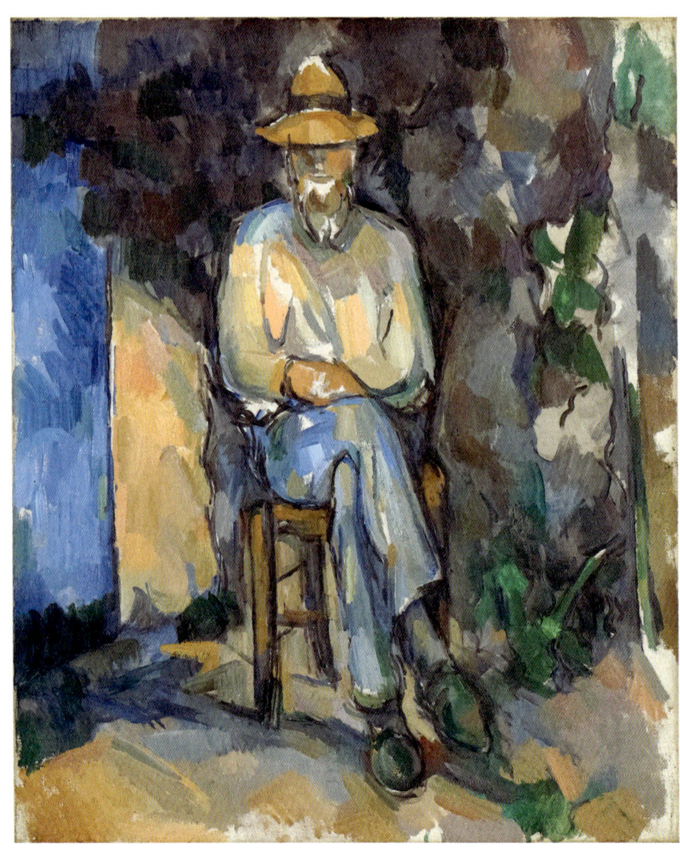

227. *Portrait of Vallier.* 1904–06. Pencil and watercolor on paper, 18 ¹¹⁄₁₆ × 12 ³⁄₁₆" (47.5 × 31 cm)

228. *Portrait of Vallier.* c. 1906. Pencil and watercolor on paper, 18 ⅞ × 12 ⅜" (48 × 31.5 cm)

229. *The Gardener Vallier.* 1905–06. Oil on canvas, 25 ¹³⁄₁₆ × 21 ⅝" (65.5 × 55 cm)

230. *Portrait of Vallier.* 1906. Pencil and watercolor on paper, 18 ⅞ × 12 ⅝" (48 × 32 cm)

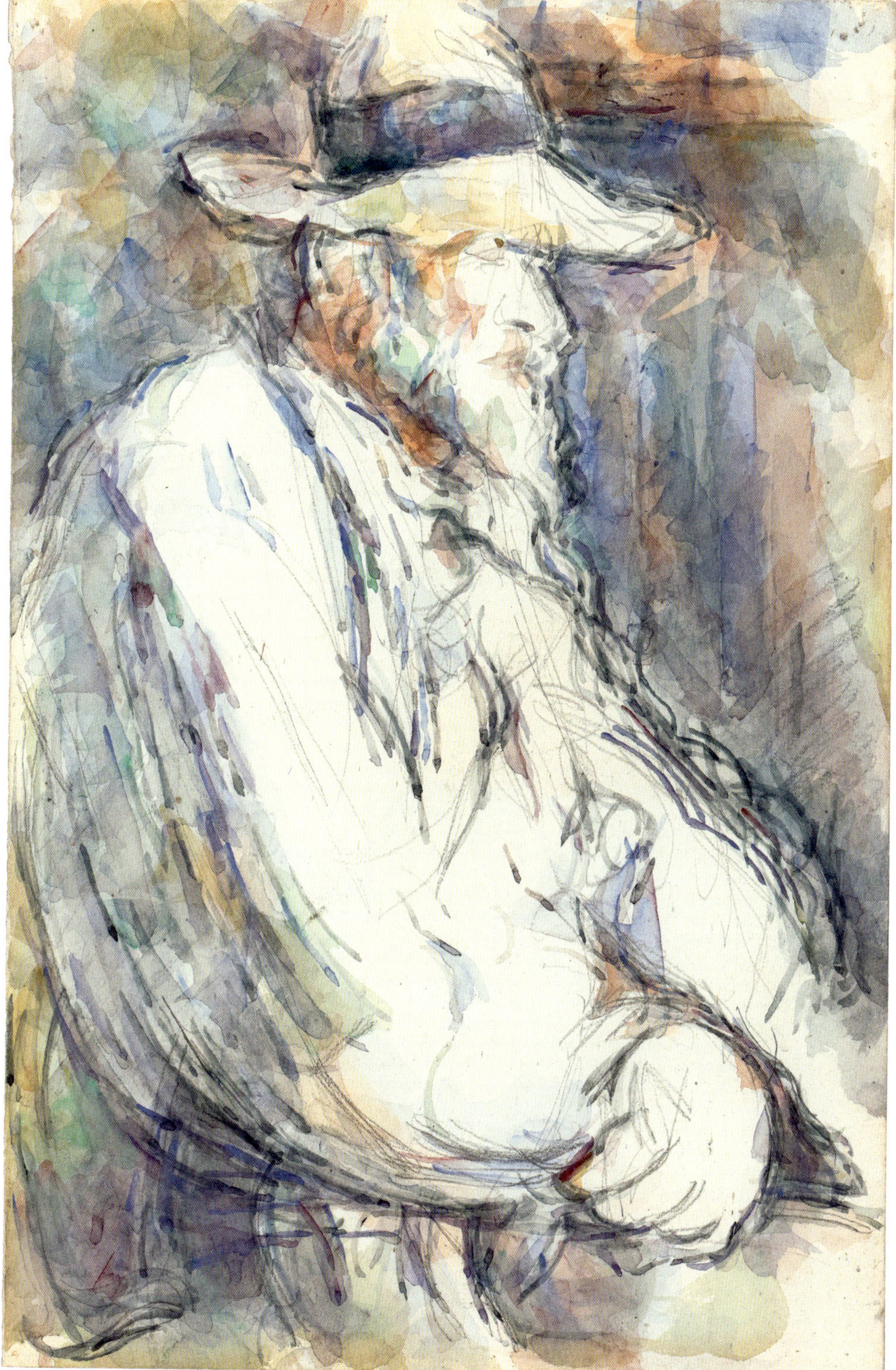

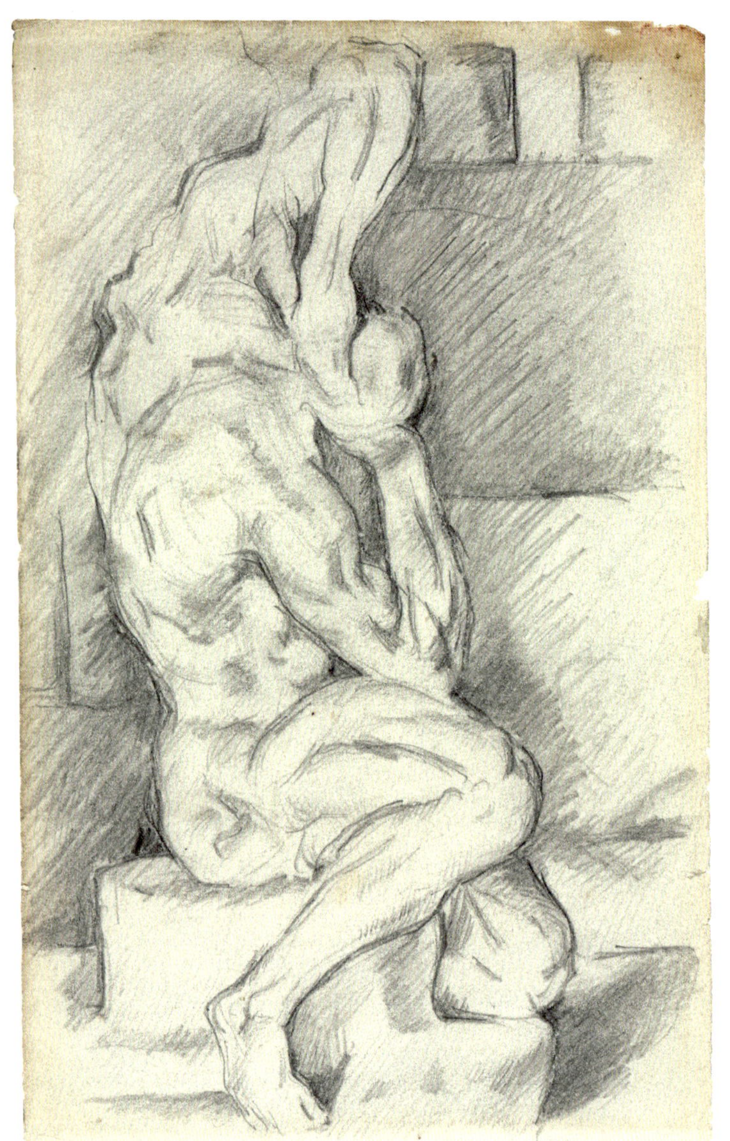

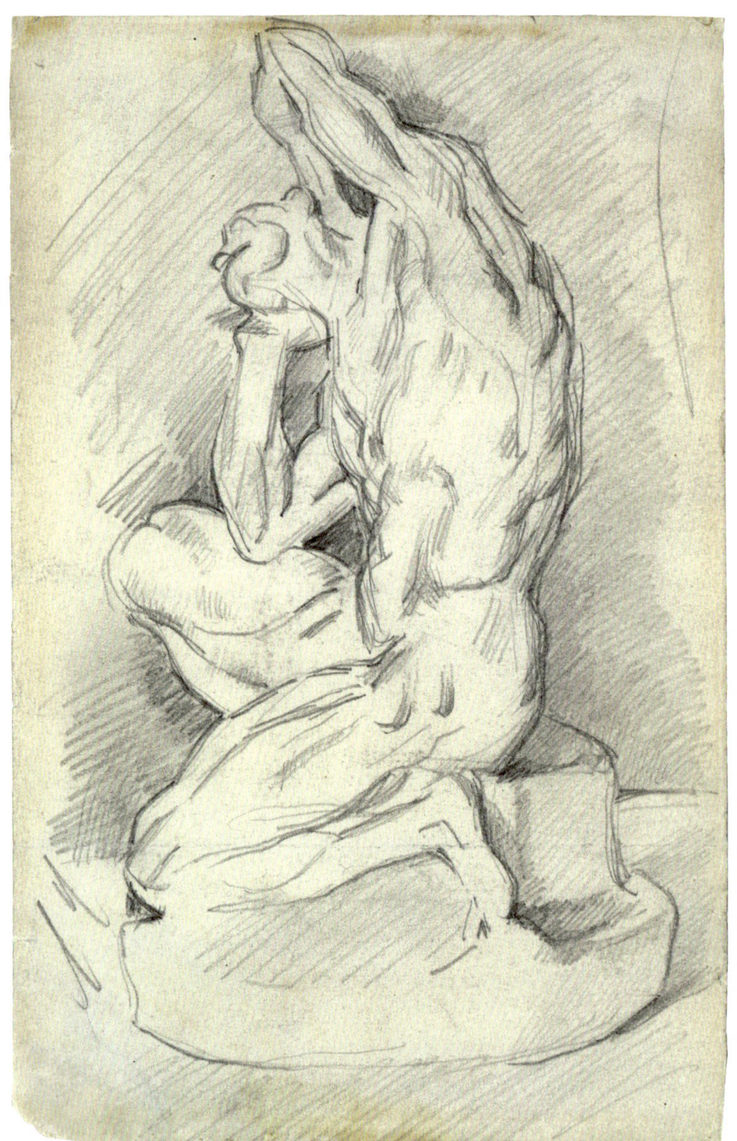

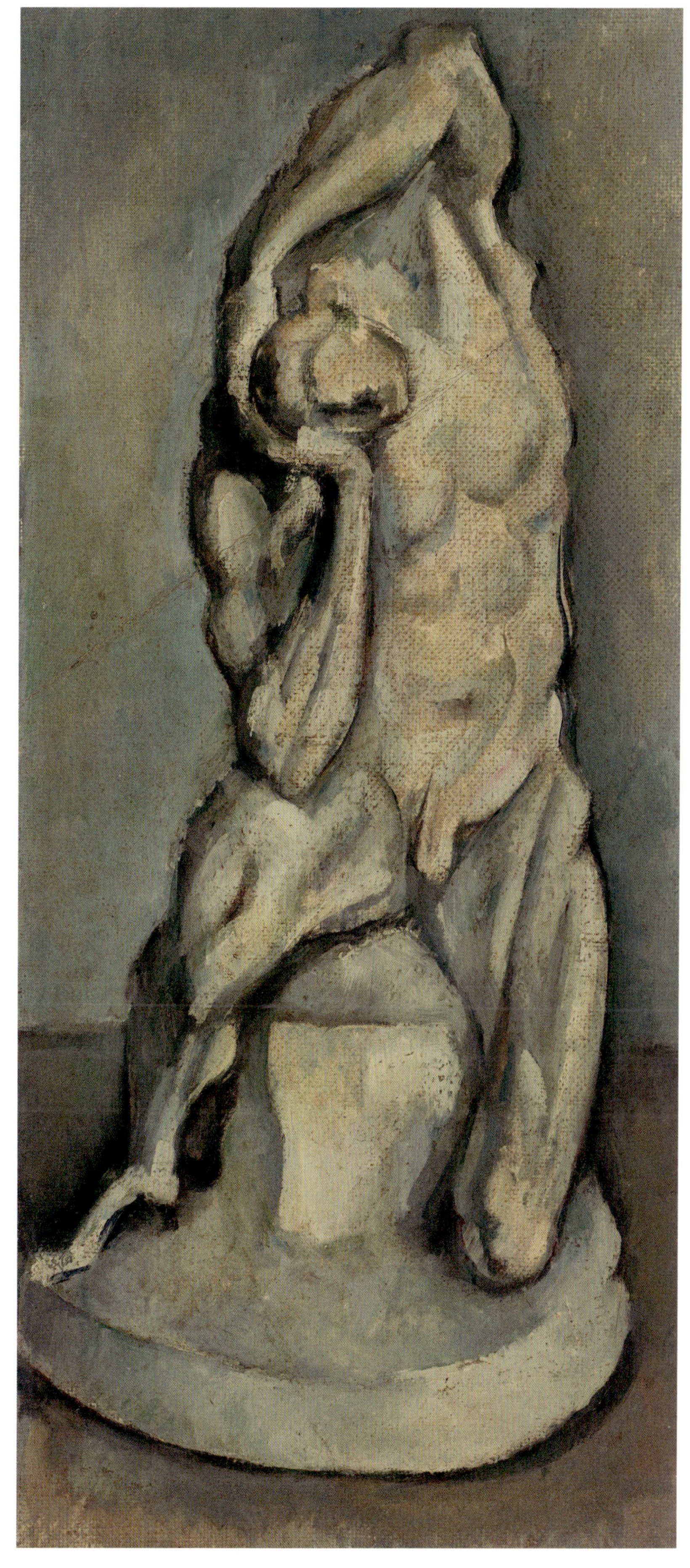

231. *After the Écorché*. 1881–84. Pencil on wove paper, 8 5⁄16 × 5 1⁄4" (21.1 × 13.3 cm)

232. *After the Écorché*. 1893–96. Pencil on wove paper, 8 1⁄4 × 5 1⁄4" (21 × 13.3 cm)

233. *After the Écorché*. c. 1892. Oil on canvas, 13 5⁄8 × 6 1⁄2" (34.6 × 16.5 cm)

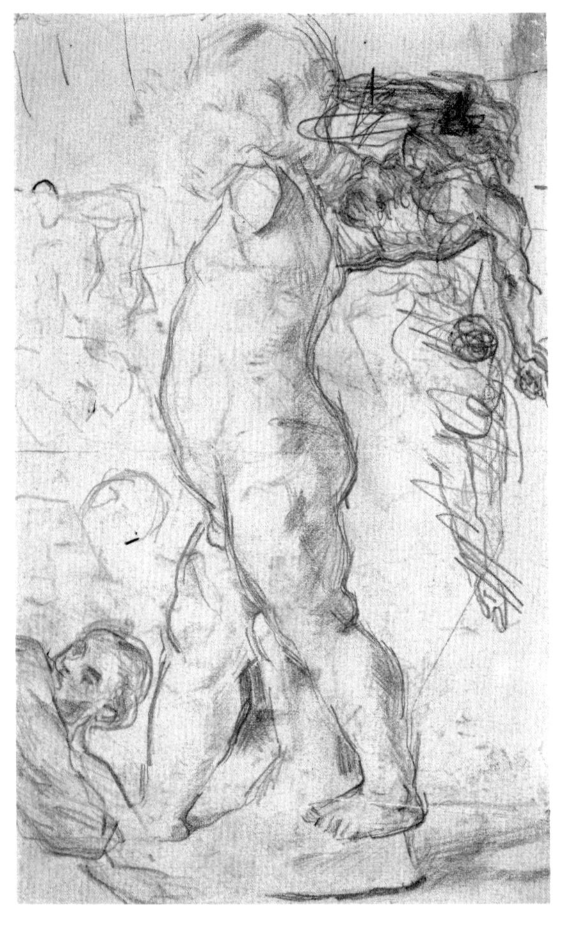

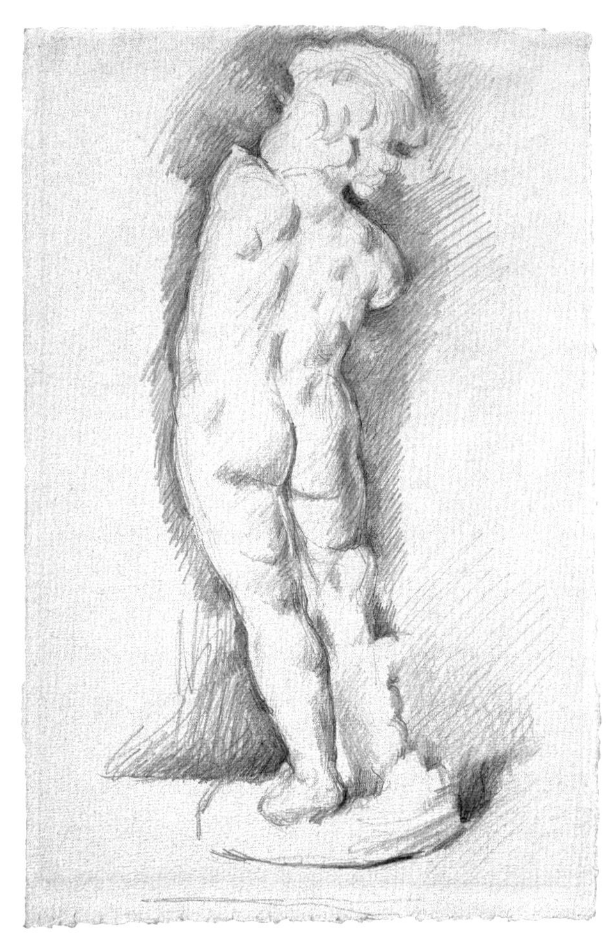

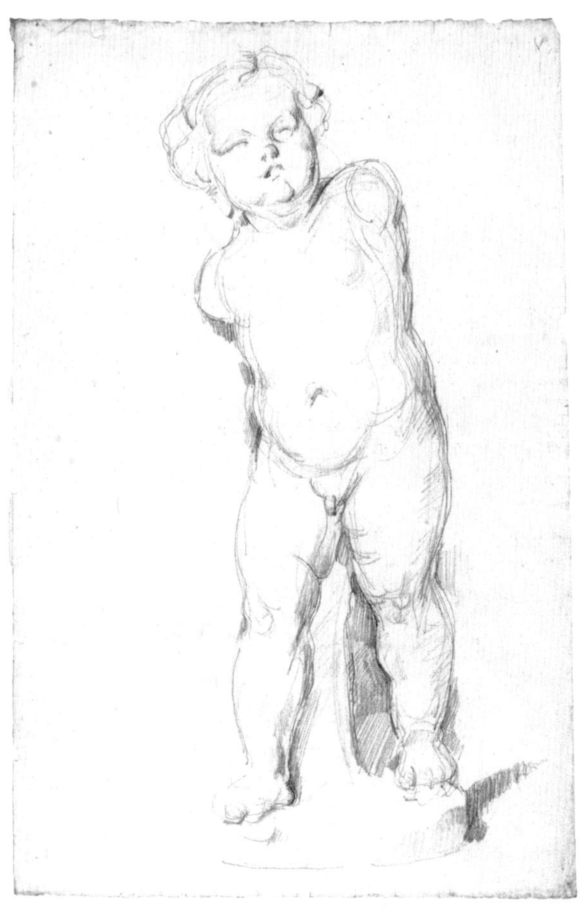

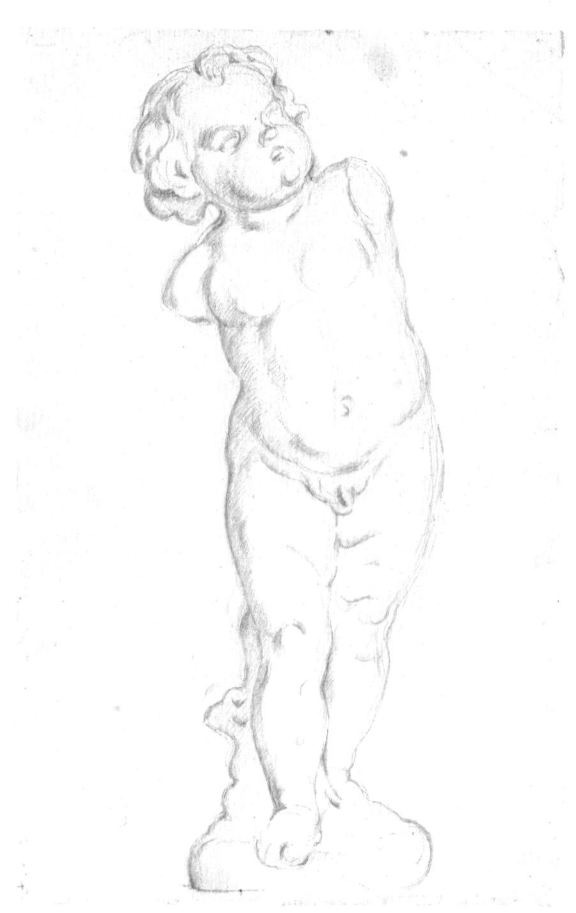

234. *After the Cupid Attributed to Puget*. 1875–78. Pencil on wove paper, 8 ¼ × 5 ¼" (21 × 13.3 cm)

235. *After the Cupid Attributed to Puget*. 1879–82. Pencil on laid paper, 19 3/16 × 12 ½" (48.7 × 31.8 cm)

236. *Study from a Statuette of a Cupid*. c. 1890. Pencil on laid paper, 19 ¼ × 12 ¾" (48.9 × 32.4 cm)

237. *Study after a Plaster Cast of a Putto Sculpture Attributed to Pierre Puget*. c. 1890. Pencil on paper, 19 × 12 3/16" (48.2 × 31 cm)

238. *Plaster Cupid*. c. 1900. Pencil and watercolor on paper, 24 13/16 × 19 5/16" (63 × 49 cm)

239. *The Plaster Cupid*. 1900–04. Pencil and watercolor on paper, 18 15/16 × 8 15/16" (48.1 × 22.7 cm)

240. *Plaster Cupid*. 1900–04. Pencil and watercolor on paper, 18 ⅞ × 12 ⅜" (48 × 31.5 cm)

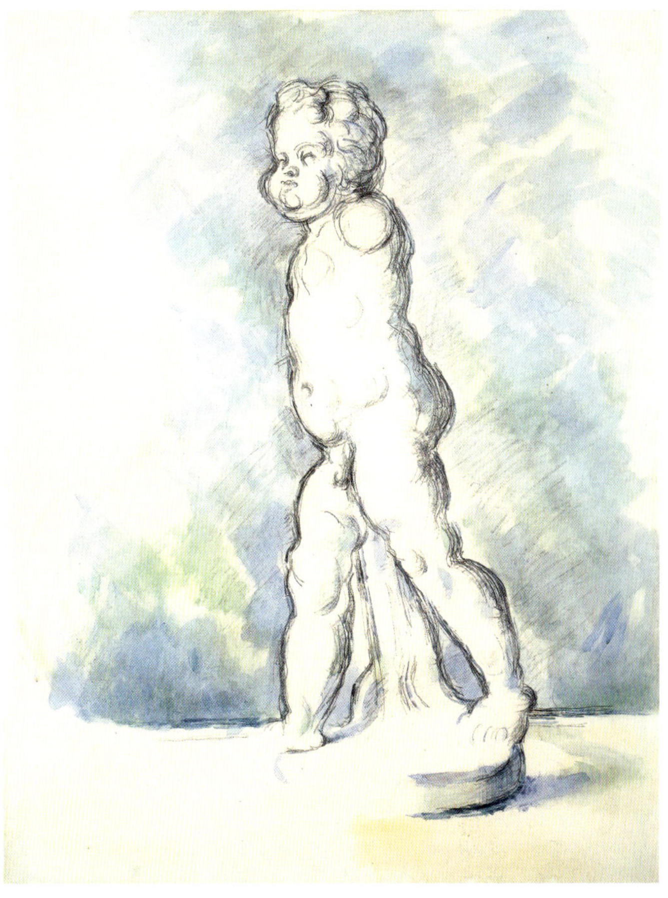

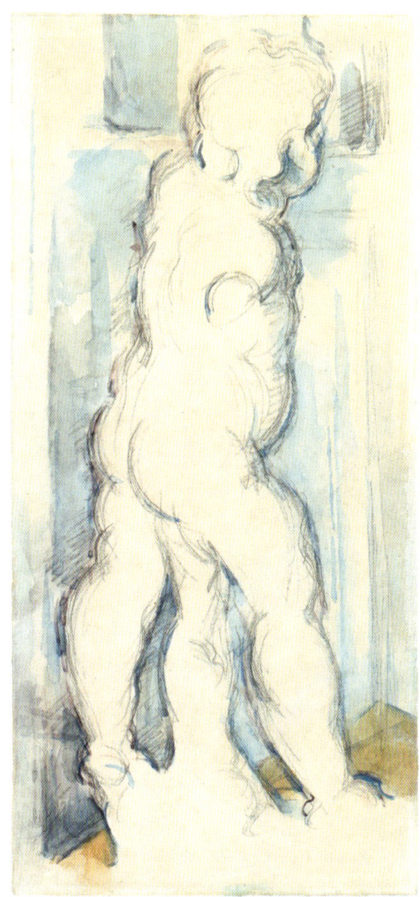

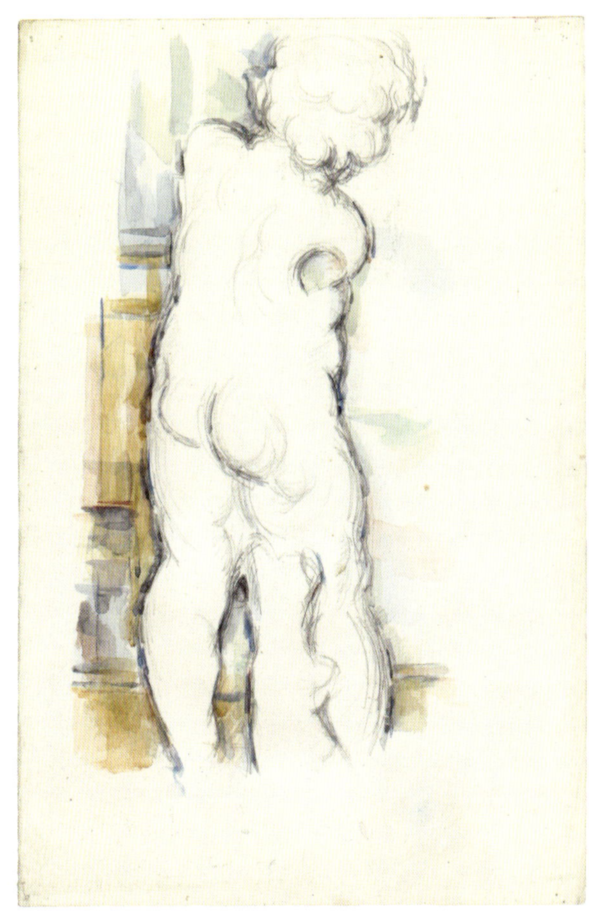

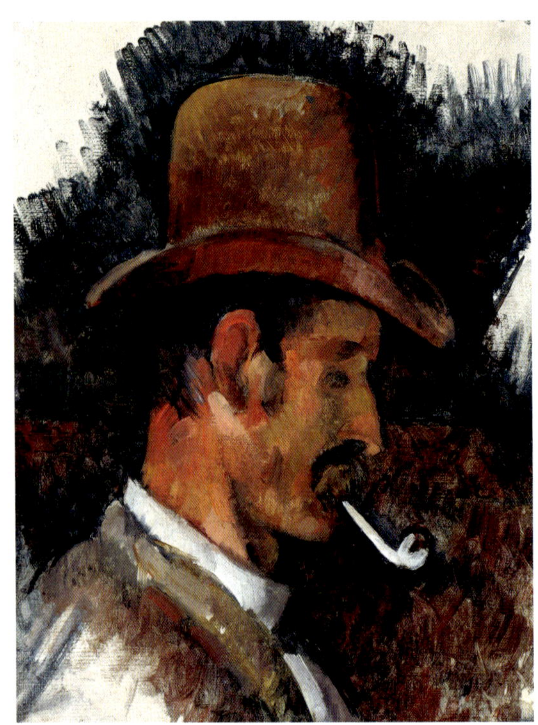

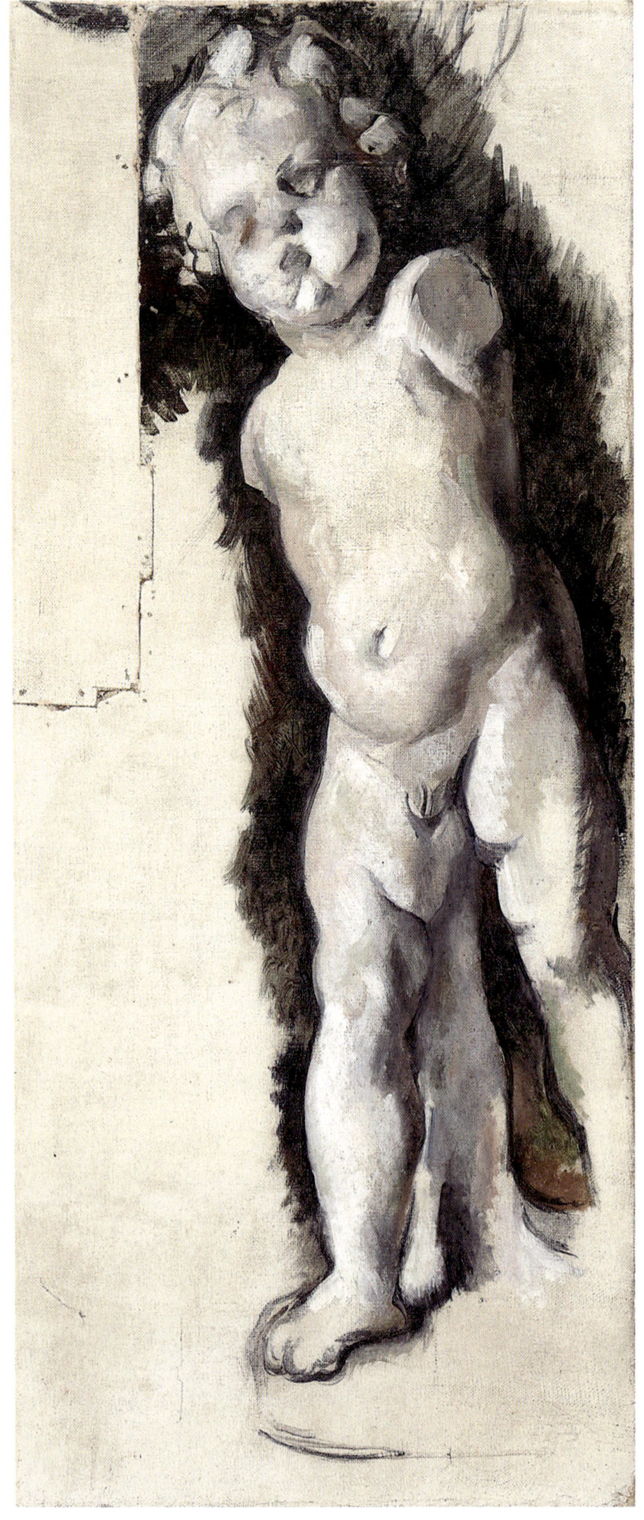

241. *Man with Pipe*. 1892–96. Oil on canvas, 10 ¼ × 7 15/16" (26.1 × 20.2 cm)

242. *After the Cupid Attributed to Puget*. 1894–95. Oil on canvas, 22 ½ × 9 ¾" (57.2 × 24.8 cm)

243. *Still Life with Apples.* c. 1878. Oil on canvas, 7 ½ × 10 ½" (19 × 26.7 cm)

244. *Glass and Apples.* 1879–80. Oil on canvas, 12 ⅜ × 15 ¾" (31.5 × 40 cm)

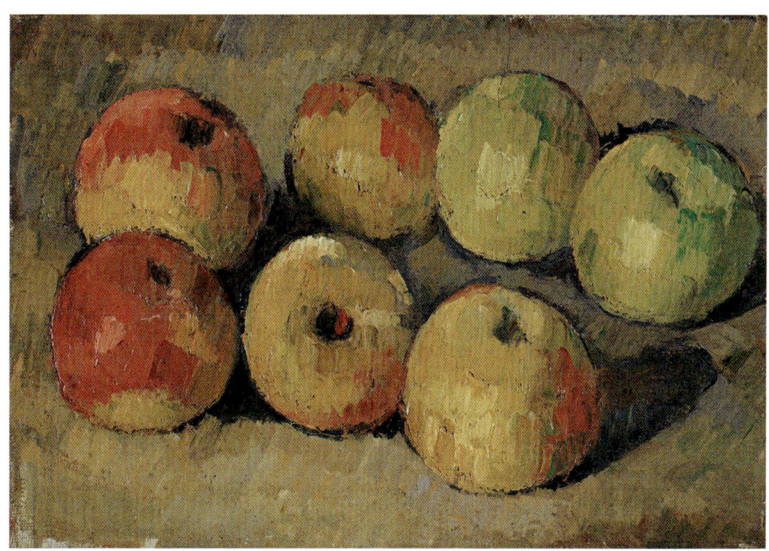

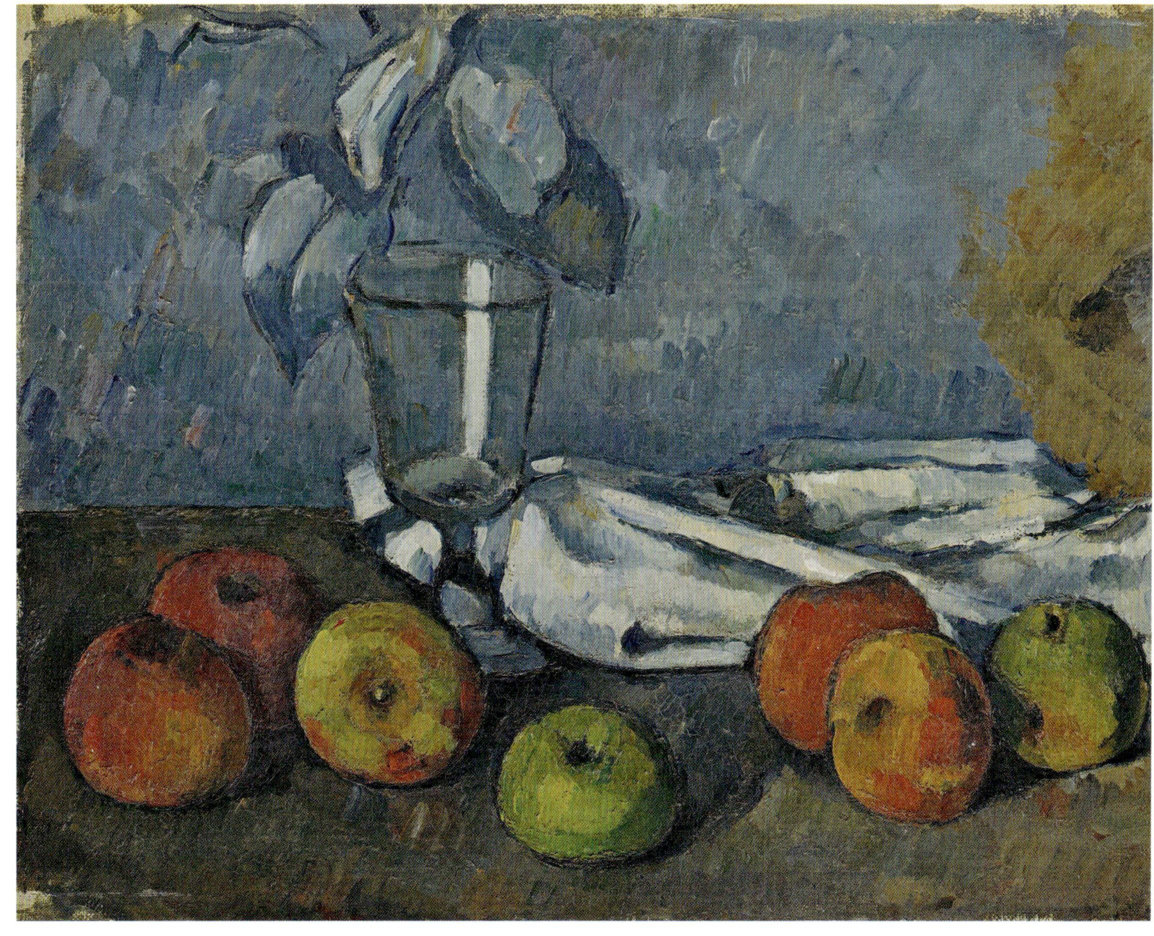

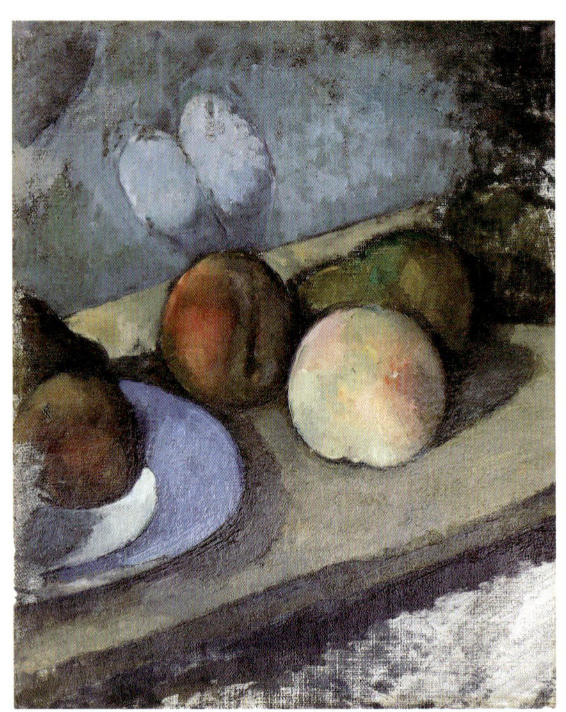

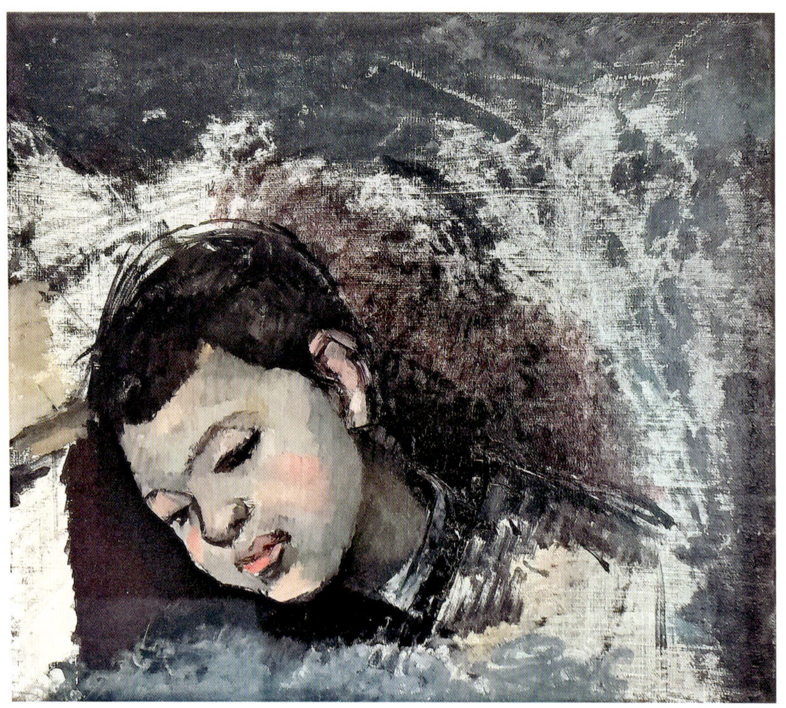

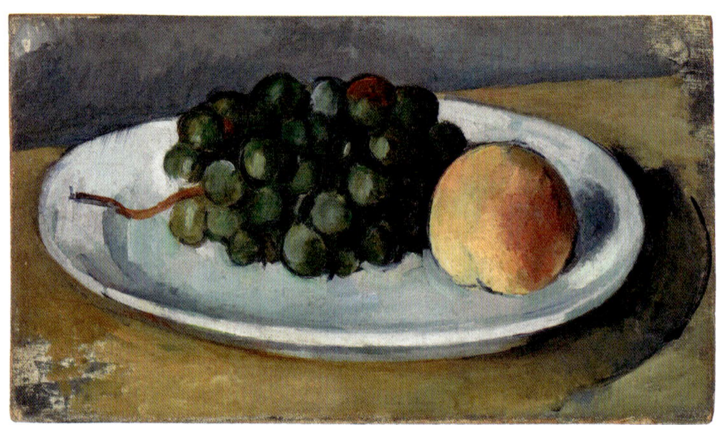

245. *The Blue Plate*. 1879–80. Oil on canvas, 11 × 8 15/16" (28 × 22.7 cm)

246. *Portrait of Paul, the Artist's Son*. 1881–82. Oil on canvas, 11 1/4 × 12 13/16" (28.6 × 32.6 cm)

247. *Grapes and Peach on a Plate*. 1877–79. Oil on canvas, 6 9/16 × 11 5/8" (16.6 × 29.5 cm)

B. Proposed reconstruction of plates 241, 242

C. Proposed reconstruction of plates 243, 244

D. Proposed reconstruction of plates 245–47

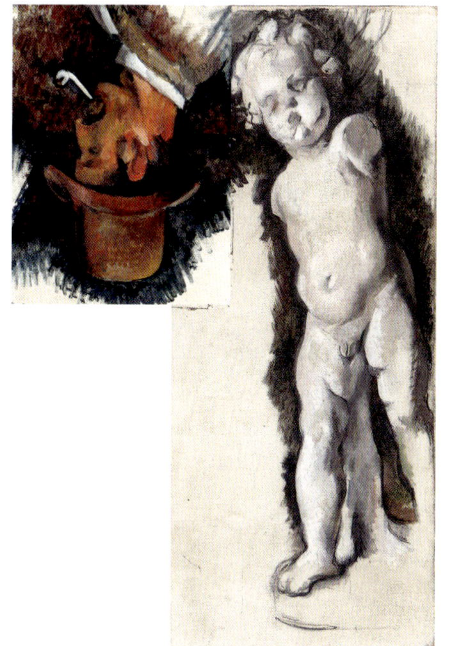

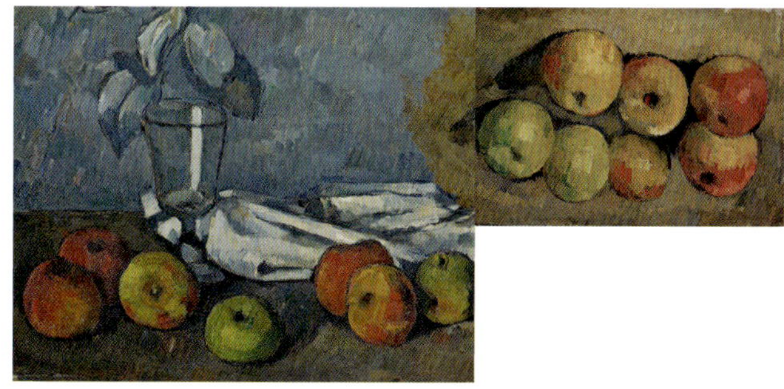

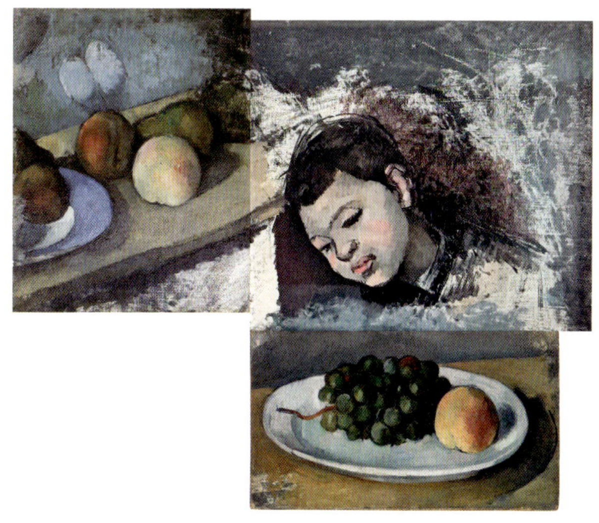

Laura Neufeld

BELLE FORMULE: MATERIALS AND METHODS IN CÉZANNE'S WATERCOLORS

fig. 1

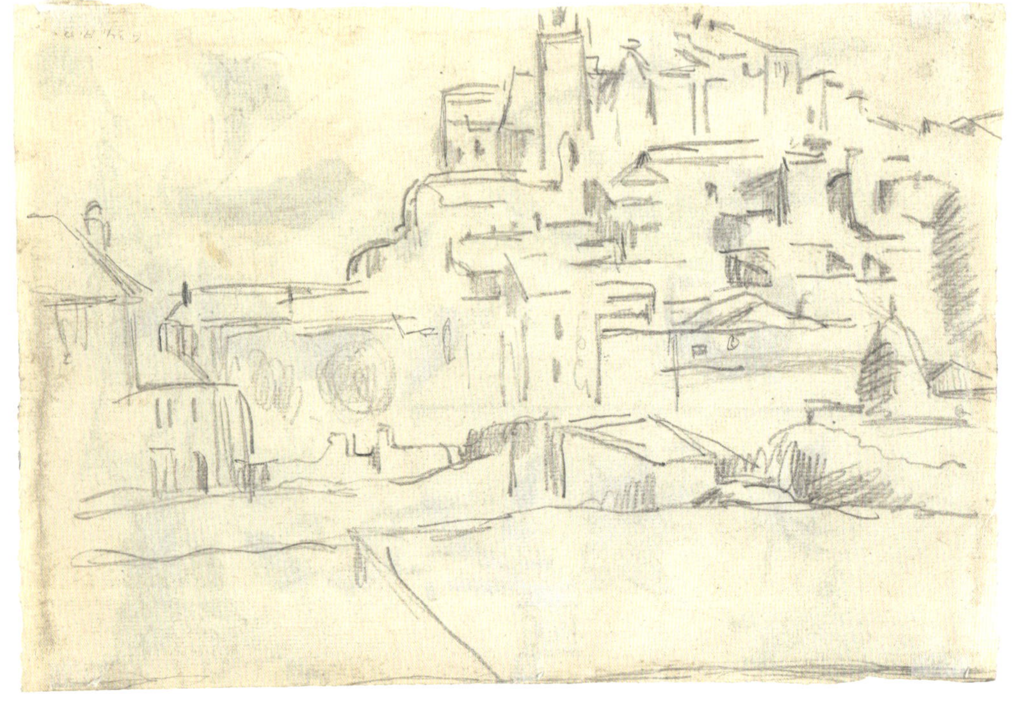

fig. 1 Paul Cézanne (French, 1839–1906). *View of Gardanne* (*Vue de Gardanne*). 1885–86. Pencil on laid paper, 8 ⅛ × 12 ¼" (20.8 × 30.8 cm). The Museum of Modern Art, New York. Lillie P. Bliss Collection

In the late 1890s, in a parlor-game-style interview, Cézanne was asked a series of pithy questions. When queried as to his "ideal of earthly happiness," he responded, "To have my own *belle formule*," or "beautiful way of painting."[1] The artist's watercolors, in their mutable mixture of graphite and paint, are ideal illustrations of his development of such a formula and of its radical results. Remaining today are more than two thousand drawings and watercolors made by Cézanne between the 1850s and his death in 1906.[2] His use of watercolor grew from his drawing practice, when he began adding color to his sketches, and over time it developed into a hybrid technique of line and color enriched by his skills as a draftsman and painter. The watercolors display a wide range of finish, from minimal brushstrokes to densely painted scenes, and together they elucidate the artist's distinctive approach to the construction of a composition. Cézanne's primary materials—paper, graphite pencil, and watercolor—were mass-produced and readily available from local suppliers around Paris and Aix. His watercolor palette and paper selection became more refined over time, as he strove to render his perceptions of light, color, and atmosphere.

PAPER

Cézanne made drawings and watercolors both on loose sheets of paper and in bound sketchbooks. As his technique evolved, he became more attuned to the physical qualities of paper, including its color, texture, thickness, and absorbency, and to the effects of these qualities on the media he was using. He experimented with watercolor on a wide variety of supports, including sheets produced for artists: thin laid papers, engineered for use with dry media or ink, and thicker wove papers, with a smoother texture, produced for use with both dry and wet media, including watercolor.[3]

Cézanne's early drawings and watercolors, from the 1850s, '60s, and '70s, were composed primarily on small fragments of paper and apparently without preference for laid or wove textures. Only the formal figure drawings the artist made as a student at the École Gratuite de Dessin, in Aix, and at the Académie Suisse, in Paris, occupy full sheets. During periods of financial struggle or limited access to materials, he also used alternative supports, including ruled writing paper, cardboard, and commercially printed sheets from books and magazines.[4] Compositions on printed supports typically occupy the unprinted side of the sheet, thus hiding its origin. *Portrait of Mme Cézanne* (c. 1877–80; plate 220) was executed in silvery graphite on the verso of an engraved book plate depicting a maritime scene.[5] While the portrait is unrelated to the original image, the drawing's narrow tonal range was dictated by the thick, spongy paper. Cézanne responded to the sheet's softness by reducing his pressure on the pencil; in the darker lines in the subject's eyes and nostrils, fibers were disrupted by the pencil's sharp tip.

As watercolor increasingly engaged Cézanne, in the late 1870s and '80s, he selected larger sheets of paper, making a material investment in the medium. He explored how watercolor flowed over the ribbed surface of laid supports and absorbed into the fibers, but as his practice developed he came to prefer less absorbent and smoother-textured wove papers. Cézanne most often used sheets produced by the French mill Canson et Montgolfier, renowned for its selection of artist's papers; beginning in the 1880s the mill's watermarks are prevalent on his laid and wove sheets.[6] The watermarks state the location of the mill and sometimes give a directive for the paper's use, such as *crayon* (pencil), for dry media, and *lavis* (wash) for wet—directives Cézanne did not closely follow.[7] Many watercolors from the artist's last years are on white or cream-colored Canson et Montgolfier wove papers, often full sheets. These works best display the artist's nuanced exploitation of the paper's color, smooth surface, and absorbency to maximize the vibrancy of the media.

Cézanne primarily selected full sheets in the French *raisin* format, which measures 24 13/16 by 18 7/8 inches (63 by 48 centimeters), and often halved or quartered the papers, extending his supply and creating smaller, portable sizes for working outdoors. Sometimes he divided the support after abandoning a composition on one part of the sheet. Trimmed edges on oddly proportioned artworks may indicate that the paper was cropped to center an image or that a sheet with multiple images was split into individual works—adjustments made either by the artist or by a later hand to facilitate sales or framing.[8]

Many of the sheets have compositions on both sides. The watercolor *The Bridge at Gardanne* and the pencil drawing *View of Gardanne* (both 1885–86)

1. Cézanne, "My Confidences" (c. 1896), in Michael Doran, ed., *Conversations with Cézanne*, trans. Julie Lawrence Cochran (Berkeley: University of California Press, 2001), 101.
2. See Walter Feilchenfeld, Jayne Warman, and David Nash, *The Paintings, Watercolors and Drawings of Paul Cézanne: An Online Catalogue Raisonné*, www.cezannecatalogue.com (FWN).
3. Laid papers have a distinctive grooved texture that is imparted by the wire screen on which the sheet is formed. Wove papers are cast on a finely woven wire mesh that produces an even surface texture.
4. Fabienne Ruppen, "Paul Cézanne's Loose Sheets in the Kupferstichkabinett of the Kunstmuseum Basel," in Anita Haldemann, ed., *The Hidden Cézanne: From Sketchbook to Canvas* (Basel: Kunstmuseum Basel, 2017), 17–46.
5. The print, titled *Les Contrebandiers*, was published in Amédée Gréhan, *La France maritime*, vol. 2 (Paris: Dutertre, 1855), 295. Cézanne likely removed the page from a copy of the book.
6. These observations are consistent with foundational technical research by Faith Zieske and Ruppen. See Zieske, "Paul Cézanne's Watercolors: His Choice of Pigments and Papers," in Harriet Stratis and Britt Salvesen, eds., *The Broad Spectrum* (London: Archetype, 2002), 89–100; and Ruppen, "On Margins and Versos: The Hidden Relationships among Cézanne's Works on Paper," in Alexander Eiling, ed., *Cézanne: Metamorphoses* (Munich: Prestel/Staatliche Kunsthalle Karlsruhe, 2017), 85–99.
7. Laid sheets bear the wire-formed watermark VIDALON (the location of the mill, in Ardèche, France) or an ornamental knot. Wove supports bear the impressed watermarks MONTGOLFIER SAINT MARCEL LES ANNONAY or ANCNE MANUFRE CANSON & MONTGOLFIER VIDALON-LES-ANNONAY.
8. See Kiko Aebi, "From Study Sheet to Composite Canvas," in this volume, for a discussion of Cézanne's divided works.

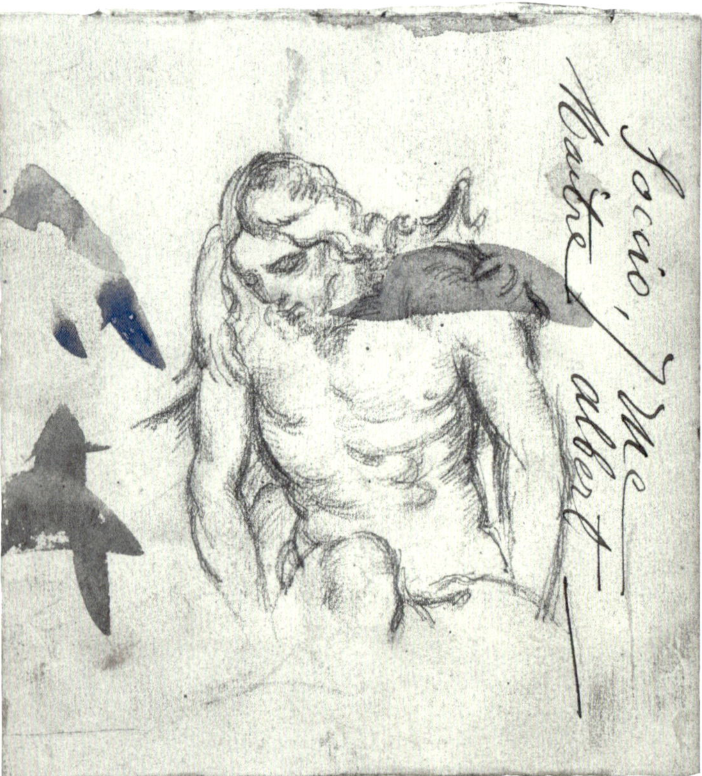

fig. 2

share a thin, half sheet of laid paper. In *The Bridge at Gardanne* (plate 131), washes of watercolor are applied over a lightly drawn pencil sketch. Heavily applied graphite marks are visible through the sheet from the drawing on the verso, in which bold lines simplify the hillside village into vertical and horizontal planes (fig. 1). Gardanne was an infrequent subject for the artist, and it is probable that the related scenes were made in consecutive working sessions. Where double-sided sheets feature unrelated subjects and stylistic differences, the timespan between compositions was likely longer, indicating that Cézanne sometimes kept his works on paper for years before using the sheets again (plate 148)—a practice that is mirrored in his sketchbooks.

Bound sketchbooks containing blank sheets of wove paper suitable for use with wet or dry media became widely available to artists in the mid-nineteenth century.[9] Cézanne used at least nineteen such sketchbooks during his career, and their pages offer intimate glimpses into his daily life and imagination. Repeated motifs, including portraits of the artist's son throughout his childhood, indicate that Cézanne used multiple sketchbooks at once, often making drawings in each over the course of several years. The varied orientation of the images on the page and the lack of logical sequential order suggests that he frequently opened a sketchbook to a random page and began drawing. While multiple images often share a single page, sometimes in witty visual rhymes of shape or subject, compositions rarely span facing pages. Watercolors often depict domestic interiors and small still lifes, compositions made, perhaps, in idle moments at home or in the studio and that were easily scaled to the intimate size of the page.[10]

GRAPHITE

Cézanne derived compositions from direct observation and from his imagination. To render these images on paper, graphite pencil was the drawing medium he most often used, alone or in conjunction with watercolor.[11] The simplicity of pencil suited the artist's direct, unmediated approach to drawing. He did not manipulate the graphite on the support by blending or erasing, and he incorporated corrections into the composition. Tonal range was achieved by varying the pressure on the pencil and by building up layers of medium. In works composed from close observation, such as portraits and self-portraits, the line quality is expressive but organized, simplifying forms to basic shapes and modelling the surface with parallel strokes and perpendicular cross-hatched lines (plate 26).

Cézanne's drawing style includes a lexicon of abbreviated marks, a graphic shorthand of gestural, fragmented outlines for figures and objects, loops and spirals designating foliage, and scribbled patches indicating shadows. These notations are visible in the loose underdrawings of many watercolors but are most evident in his bather sketches, which are unique in their transformation of directly observed figures into imagined compositions. Cézanne derived his bathers from multiple sources: classical sculptures, Renaissance paintings and drawings, printed images, and the observation of live models. As bathers are iterated

fig. 2 Paul Cézanne (French, 1839–1906). *Dead Christ* (*D'après Alonso Cano: Le Christ mort*). After 1882. Page 45 from Sketchbook Philadelphia I. Pencil on wove paper, 4 9/16 × 4 7/8" (11.6 × 12.4 cm). Philadelphia Museum of Art. Gift of Mr. and Mrs. Walter H. Annenberg

fig. 3 Detail of *Foliage* (1900–04; plate 142), showing layered strokes of watercolor with ridges of pigment along the edges, characteristic of wet-over-dry paint application

fig. 4 Detail of *Foliage*, showing diffuse mixing of watercolors applied wet-into-wet

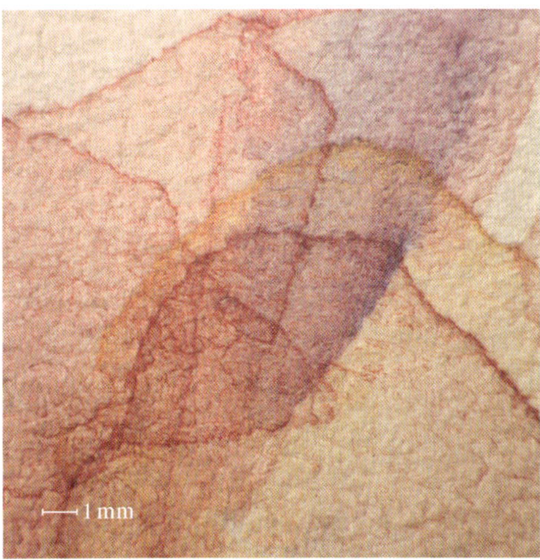

fig. 3

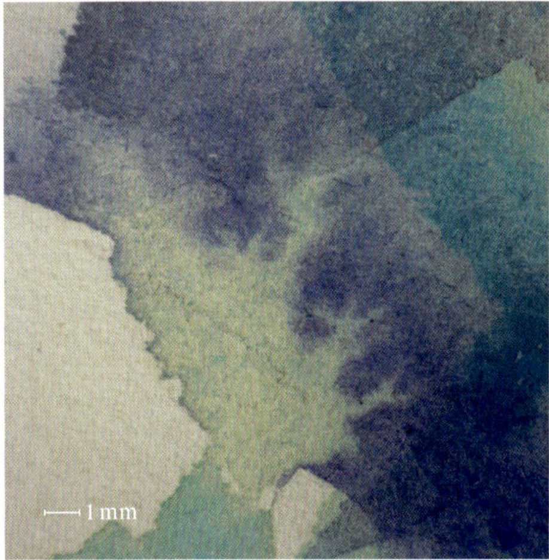

fig. 4

and reiterated in his sketches, they become increasingly removed from their sources, translated into a reflexive shorthand. This is illustrated by a figure the artist copied from a reproduction of the oil painting *The Dead Christ Supported by an Angel*, of 1646–52, by the Spanish artist Alonso Cano.[12] Cézanne copied Christ's torso with assured pencil strokes, emulating the engraved lines with subtle hatching (fig. 2). Making slight adjustments, including reversing the position of the legs, he then repeated the figure in at least twelve other compositions, spanning nearly a decade. In *Bather Stepping Down into the Water* (c. 1886–89; plate 93), its contours are rendered in jittery graphite and surrounded by scrawled vegetation. Pencil is augmented by fractured strokes of blue watercolor in *Bathers* (c. 1890, possibly later; plate 91), in which the figure perches on a lush bank of yellow and green watercolor and is joined by the ghostly painted outlines of other bathers.[13]

WATERCOLOR

Watercolor paint is primarily composed of ground pigment dispersed in an aqueous binder, traditionally gum arabic. When dissolved in water, the gum holds the pigment particles in suspension, allowing them to flow over the paper with the movement of the brush, and it adheres them to the surface as the paint dries.[14] The hallmark luminance of watercolor is created by the reflection of light through washes of pigment applied to white or cream-colored papers. The transparency of the medium varies based on the physical properties of the pigment and any fillers that might be added to increase opacity.

Cézanne's early watercolors, such as *The Abduction* (c. 1867; plate 28), were often studies for oil paintings and depicted imagined or allegorical motifs.[15] His initial handling of the medium derived from his oil technique: densely applied, the paint fills the underlying drawn outlines and covers the paper; white gouache renders the highlights. While working alongside the Impressionist Camille Pissarro in the 1870s, Cézanne adopted a brighter, prismatic oil and watercolor palette, limited to red, blue, yellow, green, and white, and he began to use thin, layered washes of watercolor and to incorporate reserves of blank paper into his compositions.[16] Most prevalent in his watercolors are emerald green, cobalt blue, iron oxide yellows

9. Marjorie Shelly, "Cézanne as Draftsman: Sketchbooks and Graphite Drawings," in Dita Amory, ed., *Madame Cézanne* (New York: Metropolitan Museum of Art, 2014), 107–27.
10. For Cézanne's multi-image drawings and his domestic interiors and still lifes, respectively, see, in this volume, Samantha Friedman, "Condensation: Cézanne's Study Sheets" and "To Leave Traces."
11. The appearance and physical characteristics of Cézanne's graphite marks suggest that he used semi-hard pencils, which produce dark lines but are less prone to smudging. Ibid., 118.
12. Adrien Chappuis, *The Drawings of Paul Cézanne: A Catalogue Raisonné* (Greenwich, Conn.: New York Graphic Society, 1973), 1:155.
13. For Cézanne's bathers drawings, see, in this volume, Annemarie Iker, "Eye and Brain."
14. For an overview of watercolor materials and techniques, see Marjorie B. Cohn, *Wash and Gouache: A Study of the Development of the Materials of Watercolor* (Cambridge, Mass.: Fogg Art Museum, 1977).
15. See Iker, "Scenes of Violence," in this volume, for Cézanne's early works with violent themes.
16. Matthew Simms, *Cézanne's Watercolors: Between Drawing and Painting* (New Haven, Conn.: Yale University Press, 2008), 43–52.
17. Elemental analysis of Cézanne's watercolor pigments was performed at The Museum of Modern Art by Abed Hadadd, David Booth Fellow in Conservation Science, and Ana Martins, Conservation Scientist, using X-ray fluorescence, Raman, and Fourier transform infrared spectroscopy. For more on the identification of pigments in Cézanne's watercolors, see Zieske, "Paul Cézanne's Watercolors"; and Elizabeth Reissner, "Transparency of Means," in *The Courtauld Cézannes* (London: Courtauld Gallery/Paul Holberton, 2008), 49–71.

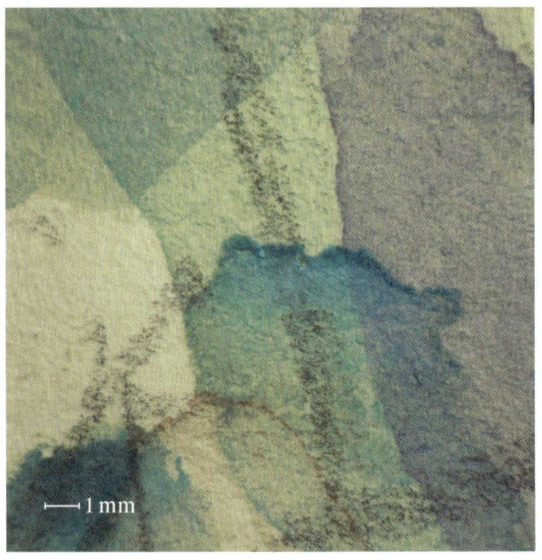

fig. 5

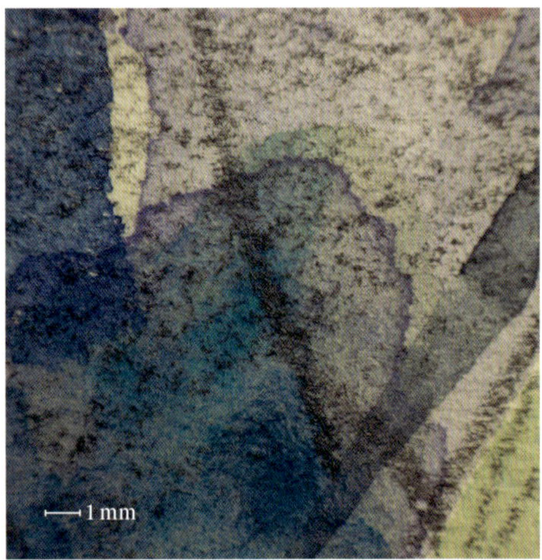

fig. 6

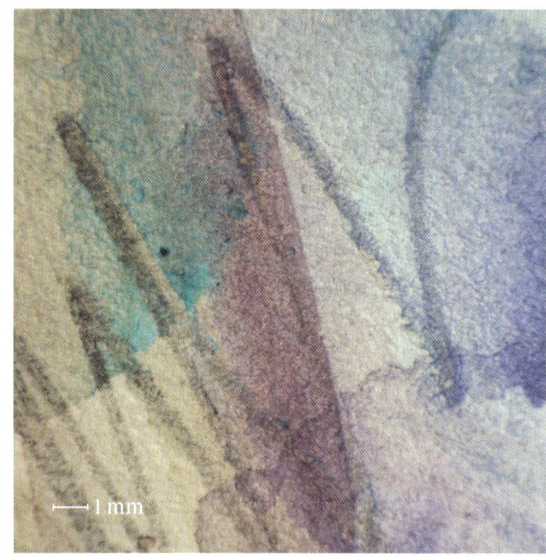

fig. 7

and reds, and reds derived from organic dyes.[17] These colors are abundant in many of Cézanne's watercolors and also correlate with pigments identified in Cézanne's oil palette and those listed in sketchbooks and letters.[18]

Cézanne mixed watercolors in three ways: on his palette before application, by superimposing layers of color on the paper, and by combining strokes of wet paint on the sheet. Palette mixing was for colors he did not purchase premade, such as purple, orange, and gray, or to adjust hues. Cézanne achieved the jewel tones in his late watercolors by applying discrete strokes of color to the paper and allowing each to dry before adding another layer. This method requires attentiveness to the rate of drying, which varies based on paint dilution, ambient heat and humidity, and the absorbency of the paper. Brushstrokes may have been layered after several minutes or several days: Cézanne was observed to be a slow and studious painter.[19] Measured application of watercolor also minimizes distortions in the paper, even on thin supports, since the moisture is localized. Pinholes in the corners of many works, some ringed with pigment, indicate that Cézanne painted with the paper simply tacked to a board. Compositions with elongated spatters and drips of watercolor were likely painted with the board propped upright.

Traditional watercolor brushes are soft and flexible and have a bulbous shape that tapers to a point, allowing the brush to hold a reserve of liquid that is released when pressure is exerted. Light pressure produces fine lines; firm pressure fans out the hairs and creates a broader mark. Flat watercolor brushes modeled on rectangular oil brushes were designed for applying large areas of wash to the paper. The shapes of the brushstrokes in Cézanne's watercolors suggest that he used both round, pointed brushes and wide, flat brushes. Some brushstrokes are defined at their edges by ridges of pigment, where particles collected as the paint dried. This is most visible in Cézanne's watercolors on wove supports, including sized, semi-absorbent Canson et Montgolfier papers. Sizing—such as gelatin, alum, and rosin, applied as a surface coating or incorporated into the pulp before the sheet is formed—prevents the watercolor from being immediately absorbed into the fibers, allowing pigment particles to settle instead on the surface of the paper. Layers of crisply defined brushstrokes indicate that the wet medium was applied to dry paper, a method known as wet-over-dry (fig. 3). Wet-into-wet mixing—brushstrokes overlapped in quick succession—can create unpredictable gradations of color and marbling effects as pigments swirl together (fig. 4). This technique is evident in many of Cézanne's watercolors and is used to striking effect in *Sketch of Three Pine Trees* (1890–95; plate 145), which is also notable for its lack of graphite.[20] The trees are rendered with dilute strokes of paint that feather together in pools of color linked by sinuous liner strokes that define the trunks and branches. Deposits of pigment in the grooves of the paper and brushstrokes that catch only the peaks of the laid lines add subtle texture to the image.

Cézanne's mature watercolor technique is characterized by vibrant juxtapositions of color and an intricate layering of media. In 1904 the painter Émile Bernard—a friend of the artist—observed of Cézanne's watercolor process that he began by painting his subject's shadow "with a single stroke, which he covered by a second stroke that extended beyond the first, then a third, until these colors, like folding screens, modeled and at the same time colored the object."[21] Oppositions of cool and warm hues and complementary colors are used to describe light and shadow, a technique that is evident in *Mont Sainte-Victoire* (1902–06; plate 180), in which the shaded side of the mountain is dappled with cool blue and warm red, while the vegetation in the middle ground and foreground is signified by adjacent or overlapping strokes of complementary colors. Cézanne diluted his paints to broaden the tonal range of his limited palette and made subtle additions to adjust their opacity. Elemental analysis suggests that the emerald-green watercolor in *Mont Sainte-Victoire* contains white pigment, which increases the opacity of the paint when it is more heavily applied—in areas of shadow, for example—but remains transparent in thin washes. Dense strokes of yellow ocher were enriched by the artist with vermillion, a naturally opaque pigment that also deepens the saturation of the color.

In many of Cézanne's mature compositions, pencil marks delineate the underdrawing and were applied between and over layers of watercolor. This usage deviates from traditional methods of watercolor painting, where pencil is employed only for preliminary sketches that guide the application of color. Here, instead, the graphite reinforces edges, enhances shadows, and connects shapes, adding depth to the images. *Foliage* (1900–04; plate 142) reveals this entwined relationship when the surface is viewed under magnification. Three types of layering are visible (figs. 5–7). In the first, graphite is partially obscured by a stroke of watercolor. In the second, it is drawn over the granular surface of dried paint. Finally, a zigzagging line threads between washes of watercolor: the pencil's blunt tip incised the damp paper and cut through a dried film of green paint; a section of the mark was then covered by purple and blue watercolor, which filled the depressions in the sheet, tinting the lines with pigment.

In a further melding of line and color, Cézanne frequently drew in watercolor with the pointed tip of his brush. "Lines parallel to the horizon give breadth," he explained, and perpendicular lines "give depth"; reds and yellows represent "vibrations of light," while blue tones provide "a sense of atmosphere."[22] In *Portrait of Vallier* (1906; plate 230), one of the artist's last compositions, the figure is defined by both looping graphite marks and segmented linear brushwork. At left, an accumulation of graphite and watercolor lines provides shadow and volume that contrast with the reserve of white paper. Wavy, dashed lines at right separate the sitter's body from the faceted washes of color in the background and suggest the glimmering effect of sunlight falling across his face and chest.

CONSERVATION OBSERVATIONS

The simplicity of watercolor—washes of pigment shimmering on white paper—makes the works vulnerable to change over time. Both paper and pigment are sensitive to discoloration from exposure to light and to acid, which is present in non-archival framing materials. While Cézanne most often used white or light-colored papers, the supports now display a range of tonalities. This is due in part to the presence of chemically processed grass and wood fibers, which were sometimes used in machine paper manufacturing as a cheaper alternative to cotton or linen rags: wood-pulp sheets are much more vulnerable to darkening from exposure to light or to acid. Analysis indicates that the Canson et Montgolfier wove papers Cézanne favored varied in their fiber content.[23] Though pure rag papers may have cost more, Cézanne was likely unaware of the material differences among the sheets when he made his selections.

The stability of watercolor paint is dependent on the physical and chemical properties of the pigments. Some pigments are prone to color change from exposure to light, while others are sensitive to atmospheric pollutants. Cézanne recognized the medium's sensitivity and reportedly kept a beloved Delacroix watercolor turned facing the wall of his studio to prevent its colors from fading.[24] However, his use of pigments known to discolor suggests that he prized the initial aesthetic properties of a color over its long-term stability. The most noticeable discolorations in his watercolors are thin washes of emerald green, a copper arsenate-based pigment, that have turned brown, and a dulling of rose and purple washes due to the fading of organic red lake pigments.

Both the visual harmony of colors and the dynamic relationship between painted passages and reserves of paper were essential to Cézanne's *belle formule*. Alteration of color in the paint or support can impact the aesthetic balance within a composition, but the vivid results of his methods remain evident in the watercolors, even those affected by color change.

Cézanne repeatedly returned to the same motifs, attempting to capture the subtle shifts and nuances of visual perception, and paper, graphite, and watercolor best synthesized the vivid, fleeting qualities of his sensations. Investigation into the artist's materials and methods shapes how his works are seen, interpreted, and preserved. Cézanne counseled that, in the study and rendering of nature, "time and reflection modify our vision"—an observation equally suited to the continued study of his art.[25]

figs. 5–7 Details of *Foliage*, showing graphite and watercolor layering. Left to right: Green watercolor over vertical stroke of graphite; graphite over washes of watercolor; graphite between layers of watercolor

18. Cézanne listed pigments in sketchbooks FWN 3000, 3002, 3005, 3007–10, 3015, and 3018. He also referred to pigments in letters to color merchants. See *The Letters of Paul Cézanne*, ed. and trans. Alex Danchev (Los Angeles: J. Paul Getty Museum, 2013), nos. 249, 251, 252, and 276.
19. Émile Bernard variously described Cézanne's application of watercolor and oil paint as slow, careful, and thoughtful. See Bernard, "Memories of Paul Cézanne" (1907), in Doran, *Conversations*, 50–79. Complex compositions with densely layered pencil and watercolor were likely developed over several working sessions. Landscapes made from observation may have required multiple treks to the site or later refinement in the studio.
20. Most of Cézanne's watercolors include graphite. Those that don't primarily date between 1890 and 1906, when Cézanne had full command of the watercolor technique.
21. Bernard, "Memories," 60.
22. Cézanne, letter to Bernard, April 15, 1904, no. 233.
23. Zieske, "Paul Cézanne's Watercolors," 96–99.
24. Bernard, "Memories," 67.
25. Cézanne, letter to Bernard, Friday [1905], no. 253.

Checklist of the Exhibition

The checklist is ordered chronologically. All works are by Paul Cézanne, with the exception of a single photograph by an unknown maker (c. 1885).

Titles
English and French titles are provided for each work. In many cases, these titles are not directly parallel but instead reflect the most widely known title of the work in each language. Most of the titles are drawn from *The Paintings, Watercolors and Drawings of Paul Cézanne: An Online Catalogue Raisonné*, organized under the direction of Walter Feilchenfeldt, Jayne Warman, and David Nash (FWN). For double-sided works, the side reproduced in the present catalogue or presented in the exhibition is listed first. Recto and verso are designated according to FWN, unless indicated differently by the owner or custodian of the work.

Dates
The dating of Cézanne's oeuvre is a notoriously complicated enterprise, as the artist seldom dated his work and rarely exhibited his drawings during his lifetime. For consistency, the dates used here are those given in FWN at the time of publication.

Dimensions
Measurements are given in inches and centimeters, with height preceding width. For works with multiple possible orientations—for example, some study sheets and double-sided drawings—the given dimensions reflect the orientation of the work as it is reproduced in this catalogue or presented in the exhibition.

Materials
Cézanne used sketchbooks of wove paper and loose sheets of both laid and wove paper. These descriptors are included when known.

Reference numbers
All works that appear in FWN are identified there by a reference number, which is given for each of the works by Cézanne listed here. Where the work is reproduced in this catalogue, its page, plate, or figure number is also given.

Sketchbooks
Of the nineteen known sketchbooks by Cézanne, only eight remain largely intact, including three in this exhibition: Sketchbook Chicago and Sketchbook New York (both bound), and Sketchbook Philadelphia II (unbound). These intact sketchbooks are treated as single entries here. Other sketchbooks have been separated, with individual sheets dispersed into public and private collections. Each separated sheet in this checklist is accompanied by an abbreviation (see below), referring to the sketchbook in which it originally belonged. Additionally, when known, a page number is included to indicate the sheet's original sequencing within the sketchbook. Some sketchbooks have alternative titles; the title given in FWN is listed first, below.

E
Early Sketchbook. 1857–75. FWN 3004

BSB
Sketchbook 18 × 24 (Carnet Basel). 1861–80. FWN 3017

BSA
Sketchbook 10.3 × 17 (Carnet Basel). 1863–65, 1869–73. FWN 3001

13.3 × 21.1
Sketchbook Fragment (13.3 × 21.1). 1866–95. FWN 3012

CP I
Sketchbook Chappuis I. 1871–92. FWN 3003

CP II
Sketchbook Chappuis II. 1871–98. FWN 3008

EH II
Sketchbook Philadelphia II (Carnet Enid Haupt II). 1872–95. FWN 3010

BS III
Sketchbook Basel III (Carnet Basel III). 1878–81, 1897–1900. FWN 3007

BS I
Sketchbook Basel I (Carnet Basel I). 1879–1900. FWN 3011

BS II
Sketchbook Basel II (Carnet Basel II). 1880–83, after 1900. FWN 3005

CP IV
Sketchbook Chappuis IV. 1881, 1884–1900. FWN 3018

EH I
Sketchbook Philadelphia I (Carnet Enid Haupt I). 1882–90. FWN 3002

Scene of Rape, Study of a Hand (*Études d'une scène de viol et d'une main*) (verso); *Scene from the Tannhäuser Saga* (*Étude d'une scène de Tannhäuser*) (recto). n.d. (verso); 1858–59 (recto)
Page 27 from the E sketchbook. Pencil and ink on wove paper, 4 13/16 × 8 1/4" (12.3 × 20.9 cm)
Hamburger Kunsthalle
FWN 3004-27b/a. Plate 34 (not in exhibition)

Standing Male Nude: Academic Study (*Académie d'homme*). 1862
Pencil on paper, 24 × 18 1/2" (61 × 47 cm)
Musée Granet, Aix-en-Provence
FWN 2077. Plate 77

Studies of a Rower (*Dessin académique: Nu à la rame*) (recto); *Man Lying on the Ground* (*Homme étendu sur le sol*) (verso). 1867–69 (recto); 1862–65 (verso)
Pencil on laid paper (recto); crayon on laid paper (verso), 8 15/16 × 11 3/4" (22.7 × 29.9 cm)
Museum Boijmans Van Beuningen, Rotterdam. Loan: Stichting Museum Boijmans Van Beuningen 1940 (former collection Koenigs)
FWN 2101r; FWN 2084v. Plate 3

Male Nude, Back View (*Homme nu vu de dos*) (recto); *Sheet of Studies for The Feast* (*Études pour L'Orgie*) (verso). 1863–65 (recto); n.d. (verso)
Page from the BSB sketchbook. Pencil on wove paper, 9 1/2 × 7" (24.1 × 17.8 cm)
Picker Art Gallery, Colgate University, Hamilton, New York. Gift of Mr. Joseph Katz
FWN 3017-05a/b. Plate 1

The Temptation of St. Anthony (*La Tentation de saint Antoine*) (recto); *Two Sketches* (*Deux Études*) (verso). 1873–75 (recto); 1863–66, 1868–71 (verso)
Pencil, watercolor, ink, and gouache on paper (recto); pencil on wove paper (verso), 4 3/4 × 7 11/16" (12 × 19.5 cm)
Collection Jasper Johns
FWN 3004-36a/b. Plate 43

After Fra Bartolommeo: Study of Christ (*D'après Fra Bartolomeo: Christ au tombeau*) (recto); *Studies for The Orgy* (*Études pour L'Orgie*) (verso). 1866–71 (recto); 1864–68 (verso)
Page from the BSB sketchbook. Pencil on wove paper, 7 1/16 × 9 1/2" (18 × 24.1 cm)
Kunstmuseum Basel, Kupferstichkabinett
FWN 3017-17a/b

Portrait of Delacroix and Various Studies (*Portrait de Delacroix et diverses études*) (recto); *After Paul Veronese: The Marriage at Cana* (*D'après Véronèse: Les Noces de Cana*) (verso). 1864–68 (recto); 1866–69 (verso)
Page from the BSB sketchbook. Pencil and ink on wove paper (recto); black crayon on wove paper (verso), 9 1/2 × 7 1/16" (24.1 × 18 cm)
Kunstmuseum Basel, Kupferstichkabinett
FWN 3017-13a/b

Study of Nudes Diving (*Études de nus plongeant*). 1865–66
Pencil on paper, 7 1/8 × 10 5/8" (18.1 × 27 cm)
Los Angeles County Museum of Art. Mr. and Mrs. William Preston Harrison Collection
FWN 2210. Plate 2

After Delacroix: Wild Animal, and Figure in Movement (*D'après Delacroix: Animal sauvage et figure en mouvement*) (recto); *Around a Table in the Garden* (*Autour d'une table dans le jardin*) (verso). 1865–68 (recto); c. 1868 (verso)
Page from the BSB sketchbook. Crayon on wove paper, 7 1/16 × 9 7/16" (18 × 24 cm)
Wallraf-Richartz Museum, Cologne
FWN 3017-26a/b. Plate 11 (not in exhibition)

Study after Pierre Puget's Sculpture the Milo of Croton, Composition Sketch of Figures in a Landscape around a Fire (*D'après Puget: Milon de Crotone et scène de genre, trois hommes allument un feu de bois*) (recto); *Sheet of Studies with Various Figures* (*Feuille d'études*) (verso). 1866–69, 1870–73 (recto); 1874–75, 1865–68 (verso)
Pencil on laid paper, 9 3/8 × 12 5/16" (23.8 × 31.3 cm)
Museum Boijmans Van Beuningen, Rotterdam. Loan: Stichting Museum Boijmans Van Beuningen 1940 (former collection Koenigs)
FWN 2220r; FWN 2255v. Plate 9

A Historical or Biblical Scene (*The Rape of Lucretia*) (*Femme prise au dépourvu*). 1865–69
Pencil and ink on paper, 4 5/8 × 6 7/8" (11.8 × 17.5 cm)
The Whitworth, The University of Manchester
FWN 1811. Plate 8

Study for The Eternal Feminine (*Étude pour L'Éternel féminin*) (recto); *Study for a Woman beside a Coffin* (*Femme agenouillée à côté d'un cercueil*) (verso). c. 1870–75 (recto); c. 1866 (verso)
Page from the BSB sketchbook. Pencil on wove paper (recto); pencil and crayon on wove paper (verso), 7 1/16 × 9 1/2" (18 × 24.1 cm)
Kunstmuseum Basel, Kupferstichkabinett
FWN 3017-22a/b. Plate 44

After Giulio Romano and an Unknown Work (*D'après Giulio Romano et une œuvre inconnue: Deux Figures*) (recto); *From an Undetermined Work: Mitred Bishop* (*Étude d'un évêque*) (verso). 1869–72 (recto); 1866–67 (verso)
Page from the BSB sketchbook. Pencil and ink on wove paper (recto); pencil on wove paper (verso), 9 7/16 × 6 15/16" (24 × 17.7 cm)
Kunstmuseum Basel, Kupferstichkabinett
FWN 3017-32a/b

Studies (*Études*) (verso); *The Entombment, after the Painting by Delacroix in Saint-Denis du Saint Sacrement, Paris* (*D'après Delacroix: La Pietà*) (recto). 1869–72 (verso); 1866–67 (recto)
Page from the BSB sketchbook. Pencil on wove paper, 7 1/16 × 9 7/16" (18 × 24 cm)
The British Museum, London
FWN 3017-14b/a. Plate 10

The Wine Grog (*Le Punch au rhum*). 1866–67
Pencil, watercolor, gouache, and ink on cardboard, 4 5/16 × 5 13/16" (11 × 14.8 cm)
Adriani Foundation
FWN 1812. Plate 41

Mother and Child, Ornamental Vase, Figure of a Woman (*Mère et enfant, vase d'ornement et figure de femme*) (recto); *Studies of a Female Figure* (*Études de figure de femme*) (verso). 1866–71 (recto); 1867–70 (verso)
Page from the BSB sketchbook. Pencil on wove paper, 7 × 9 7/16" (17.8 × 23.9 cm)
Kunstmuseum Basel, Kupferstichkabinett
FWN 3017-31a/b. Plate 6

The Banquet (*L'Orgie ou le banquet*). c. 1867
Gouache, pastel, and pencil on cardboard, with added rectangle pasted at lower edge, 12 3/4 × 9 1/8" (32.4 × 23.1 cm)
Adriani Foundation
FWN 1813. Plate 51

The Abduction (*L'Enlèvement*). c. 1867
Ink, watercolor, and gouache on wove paper, 2¾ × 5" (7 × 12.7 cm)
The Morgan Library and Museum, New York. Gift of Donald Oresman in honor of the 75th anniversary of the Morgan Library and the 50th anniversary of the Association of Fellows
FWN 1815. Plate 28

Study of a Head and Hands (*Étude de tête et de mains*). 1867–69
Charcoal on laid paper, 12⅜ × 19 5/16" (31.5 × 49 cm)
Collection Mr. and Mrs. Carroll L. Cartwright
FWN 2113. Plate 33

Man with a Female Nude (*Homme auprès d'une femme nue*). 1867–70
Pencil, ink, and watercolor on paper, 3 9/16 × 6 5/16" (9 × 16 cm)
Private collection
FWN 1816. Plate 42

Sheet of Studies: Still Life with Apples, Portrait of Fernand Navarrete, Bather, and Other Figures (*Feuilles d'études: Nature morte aux pommes, portrait de Fernand Navarrete, baigneur et d'autres figures*) (verso); *The Trench* (*La Tranchée*) (recto). 1873–77 (verso); 1867–70 (recto)
Pencil on laid paper (verso); watercolor, ink, and pencil on laid paper (recto), 12 1/16 × 10⅜" (30.7 × 26.3 cm)
Private collection
FWN 2254v; FWN 1015r. Plate 13

Studies after Passarotti, Domenichino, and an Unknown Master (*Études d'après Passarotti, le Dominiquin et un maître inconnu*) (recto); *Portrait of Fortuné Marion, and the Écorché* (*Portrait de Fortuné Marion et étude de l'écorché*) (verso). 1867–70 (recto); 1869–73 (verso)
Page from the BSB sketchbook. Pencil on wove paper (recto); pencil and ink on wove paper (verso), 7 1/16 × 9½" (18 × 24.1 cm)
Kunstmuseum Basel, Kupferstichkabinett
FWN 3017-29a/b. Plate 12

Eternal Feminine (*L'Éternel féminin*) (recto); *Man with a Wide-Brimmed Hat* (*Homme au chapeau à large bord*) (verso). c. 1877 (recto); 1867–72 (verso)
Pencil, watercolor, and gouache on laid paper (recto); pencil on laid paper (verso), 6⅞ × 9" (17.4 × 22.8 cm)
Collection Jasper Johns
FWN 1861r; FWN 1708v. Plate 39

Sheet of Studies, Including a Skull (*Feuille d'études dont un crâne*). c. 1868
Pencil with splatters of watercolor on wove paper, 4 13/16 × 9 1/16" (12.2 × 23 cm)
Harvard Art Museums/Fogg Museum, Cambridge, Massachusetts. Bequest of Richard B. Sisson and through the generosity of Anthony and Celeste Meier
FWN 2227. Plate 7

The Rape (*Le Viol, esquisse*) (verso); *Bearded Man, His Arms Crossed* (*Homme barbu aux bras croisés [Frenhofer]*) (recto). 1868–70 (verso); 1869–74 (recto)
Page from the BSA sketchbook. Pencil on wove paper, 4 1/16 × 6¾" (10.3 × 17.1 cm)
Kunstmuseum Basel, Kupferstichkabinett
FWN 3001-09b/a. Plate 31

The Murder (*Le Meurtre*). 1868–71
Pencil on paper, 5¼ × 6" (13.3 × 15.2 cm)
Private collection
FWN 1823. Plate 32

The Gravediggers and a Study of a Head (*Les Fossoyeurs et étude de tête*). 1868–72
Pencil and watercolor on paper, 4 15/16 × 7⅞" (12.5 × 20 cm)
Private collection
FWN 1825. Plate 30

After the Cupid Attributed to Puget (*L'Amour en plâtre et études pour La Tentation de saint Antoine*) (recto); *Studies for The Temptation of St. Anthony* (*Études pour La Tentation de saint Antoine*) (verso). 1875–78 (recto); 1869–72 (verso)
Possibly page from the 13.3 × 21.1 sketchbook. Pencil on wove paper, 8¼ × 5¼" (21 × 13.3 cm)
Collection Jasper Johns
FWN 3012-08a/b. Plate 234

Pastoral Study (*Étude pour pastorale ou idylle*). c. 1870
Pencil on paper, 4 × 5¼" (10.2 × 13.3 cm)
Henry and Rose Pearlman Foundation (on extended loan to the Princeton University Art Museum)
FWN 1829. Plate 36

Figure Studies around an Engraving of an Ornamental Vase (*Études autour d'une gravure décorative*) (verso); *L'Estaque* (*Paysage de l'Estaque*) (recto). c. 1878 (verso); 1870–72 (recto)
Pencil on found etching, 12 7/16 × 9 9/16" (31.6 × 24.3 cm)
The Art Institute of Chicago. Gift of Justin K. Thannhauser
FWN 2226v; FWN 1022r. Plate 4

Goblet, and Study for The Temptation of St. Anthony (*Verre à pied et étude pour La Tentation de saint Antoine*) (recto); *Left Ear and Fragment of an Etching* (*Oreille gauche et fragment d'une eau-forte*) (verso). 1870–73 (recto); 1874–76 (verso)
Pencil on paper (recto); pencil on found etching (verso), 6 × 8⅜" (15.3 × 21.2 cm)
Kunstmuseum Basel, Kupferstichkabinett
FWN 2262r; FWN 2239v. Plate 5

Bathers (*Baigneurs et baigneuses*). 1870–75
Pencil and watercolor on paper, 4½ × 9½" (11.4 × 24.2 cm)
Private collection
FWN 2002. Plate 102

Head of a Boy Asleep (The Artist's Son?) (*Tête de garçon endormi*) (verso); *Seated Man and Landscape with Two Figures* (*Homme assis et paysage avec figures*) (recto). c. 1880 (verso); 1871–74 (recto)
Pencil on laid paper (verso); pencil on laid paper (recto), 8⅞ × 7 13/16" (22.5 × 19.8 cm)
Kunstmuseum Basel, Kupferstichkabinett
FWN 1737v; FWN 2242r. Plate 58

Woman Bather, Two Men Wrestling, Boy's Head (*Baigneuses, deux lutteurs et tête de garçon*). 1871–78
Pencil on paper (verso of found lithograph), 7 3/16 × 10 5/16" (18.2 × 26.2 cm)
Kunstmuseum Basel, Kupferstichkabinett
FWN 2245. Plate 16

Two Studies of Bathers (*Deux Études de baigneurs*) (recto); *After the Antique: The Venus de Milo* (*D'après l'antique: Vénus de Milo*) (verso). 1872–75 (recto); 1877–80 (verso)
Page XLI from the CP I sketchbook. Pencil and ink on wove paper (recto); pencil on wove paper (verso), 4¾ × 7 11/16" (12 × 19.5 cm)
Collection Jasper Johns
FWN 3003-41a/b. Plate 90

Sketchbook Philadelphia II. 1872–95
Unbound sketchbook with forty-five sheets
Philadelphia Museum of Art. Gift of Mr. and Mrs. Walter H. Annenberg. Plate 83

The Murder (*Le Meurtre*). 1874–75
Pencil, watercolor, and gouache on paper (verso of found lithograph), 5¾ × 6⅞" (14.6 × 17.5 cm)
Collection Mr. Keith D. Stoltz, Wilson, Wyoming
FWN 1848. Plate 29

Page of Studies, Including One of Madame Cézanne (*Feuille d'études dont une de madame Cézanne*). c. 1874–76
Pencil on wove paper, 10 7/16 × 7⅞" (26.5 × 20 cm)
Museum Berggruen, Nationalgalerie–Staatliche Museen zu Berlin. On permanent loan by the Berggruen family
FWN 2256. Plate 62

Head of a Woman Sleeping and Figure Sketch after Michelangelo (*Tête de femme endormie et d'après Michel-Ange: Homme agenouillé*) (recto); *After Michelangelo: Two Soldiers* (*D'après Michel-Ange: Deux Soldats*) (verso). c. 1875–79 (recto); c. 1874–79 (verso)
Page XLVIII from the CP II sketchbook. Pencil on wove paper, 8 7/16 × 4⅞" (21.5 × 12.4 cm)
Private collection
FWN 3008-48a/b. Plate 63

Aeneas Meeting Dido at Carthage (*Énée recontrant Didon à Carthage*). c. 1875
Watercolor, gouache, and pencil on laid paper, 4¾ × 7¼" (12 × 18.4 cm)
Henry and Rose Pearlman Foundation (on extended loan to the Princeton University Art Museum)
FWN 1850. Plate 37

Bather Seen from the Back (*Baigneur vu de dos*). 1875–78
Page XXVIII from the CP II sketchbook. Pencil on colored wove paper, 8 9/16 × 4⅞" (21.8 × 12.4 cm)
Private collection
FWN 3008-28b. Plate 79

Page of Studies, Including Bathers and a Self-Portrait (*Feuille d'études avec baigneurs et autoportrait*). 1875–78
Pencil on laid paper, 11⅝ × 9⅛" (29.5 × 23.2 cm)
Henry and Rose Pearlman Foundation (on extended loan to the Princeton University Art Museum)
FWN 2264. Plate 23

At the Edge of the Pond (*Au bord de l'étang*). 1875–80
Pencil and watercolor on paper, 4 13/16 × 6⅛" (12.3 × 15.5 cm)
Private collection
FWN 1862. Plate 38

Sketchbook New York. 1875–85
Bound sketchbook, containing forty-eight sheets in pencil on wove paper, one with watercolor, 4 15/16 × 8½" (12.6 × 21.6 cm)
The Morgan Library and Museum, New York. Thaw Collection
FWN 3009. Plate 98

Sketchbook Chicago. 1875–86
Bound sketchbook, containing fifty sheets in pencil and ink on wove paper, 4⅞ × 8 9/16" (12.4 × 21.7 cm)
The Art Institute of Chicago. Arthur Heun Purchase Fund
FWN 3006. Plates 65, 66; p. 19, fig. 4

Bather with Outstretched Arms (*Baigneur aux bras écartés*). c. 1876
Oil on canvas, 9 7/16 × 6 5/16" (24 × 16 cm)
Bruce Barnes and Joseph Cunningham
FWN 912. Plate 94

Studies of Three Figures, Including a Self-Portrait (*Feuille d'études avec autoportrait et d'après Pajou: Psyché abandonee*). c. 1876, 1883, 1885
Pencil on laid paper, 19⅛ × 12⅝" (48.5 × 32 cm)
Museum Boijmans Van Beuningen, Rotterdam. Loan: Stichting Museum Boijmans Van Beuningen 1940 (former collection Koenigs)
FWN 2265. Plate 24

Page of Studies, Including a Clock and a Naiad (*Feuille d'études avec pendule et une naiade*). 1876–79
Pencil on laid paper, 12⅛ × 18¼" (30.8 × 46.3 cm)
Private collection
FWN 2271. Plate 57

Two Studies of a Bather (*Deux Études de baigneuses*) (recto); *Tree Trunks* (*Troncs d'arbres*) (verso). Left: 1876–79, right: 1879–82 (recto); 1885–87 (verso)
Page X from the CP I sketchbook. Pencil on wove paper, 4⅝ × 7¾" (11.8 × 19.7 cm)
Collection Jasper Johns
FWN 3003-10a/b. Plate 196b

Olympia. c. 1877
Pencil and watercolor on laid paper, 9½ × 10⅝" (24.1 × 27 cm)
Philadelphia Museum of Art. The Louis E. Stern Collection
FWN 1860. Plate 47

Studies and Portraits of the Artist's Son (*Études et portraits du fils de l'artiste*) (recto); *Studies, Including a Head and a Small Casserole* (*Études de têtes et petite casserole*) (verso). 1877–78 (recto); c. 1878 (verso)
Pencil on paper, 9¾ × 12⅛" (24.8 × 30.8 cm)
Albertina, Vienna
FWN 2276r; FWN 2285v. Plate 22

Grapes and Peach on a Plate (*Grappe de raisin et pêche sur une assiette*). 1877–79
Oil on canvas, 6 9/16 × 11⅝" (16.6 × 29.5 cm)
Barnes Foundation, Philadelphia
FWN 747. Plate 247 (not in exhibition)

After Luca Signorelli: Buttocks and Legs (*D'après Luca Signorelli: Étude de jambes*) (verso); *Studies: An Ear and a Male Figure* (*Études: Oreille et figure d'homme*) (recto). 1877–80
Page LIII from the CP I sketchbook. Pencil on wove paper, 7 11/16 × 4¾" (19.5 × 12 cm)
Private collection
FWN 3003-53b/a. Plate 80

Bathers, Caryatid (*Baigneurs, étude de jambe et caryatide*) (verso); *Still Life* (*Nature morte*) (recto). c. 1883–86 (verso); c. 1877–80 (recto)
Page L from the CP II sketchbook. Pencil on wove paper, 4 15/16 × 8½" (12.5 × 21.6 cm)
Ursula and R. Stanley Johnson Family Collection L.P.
FWN 3008-50b/a. Plate 95

Bather Seen from the Back (*Baigneur vu de dos*). 1877–80
Page V from the BS III sketchbook. Pencil and ink on wove paper, 7 15/16 × 4⅞" (20.1 × 12.4 cm)
Kunstmuseum Basel, Kupferstichkabinett
FWN 3007-05a. Plate 81

Bather Seen from the Back (*Baigneur vu de dos*). 1877–80
Possibly page XXVII from the BS III sketchbook. Pencil on wove paper, 4 15/16 × 8 3/16" (12.5 × 20.8 cm)
Kunstmuseum Basel, Kupferstichkabinett
FWN 3007-27a. Plate 82

Madame Cézanne and a Milk Can (*Madame Cézanne et pot à lait*). 1877–80
Pencil on laid paper, 9 1/16 × 5⅞" (23 × 15 cm)
Véronique and Louis-Antoine Prat Collection, Paris
FWN 2284. Plate 20

Page of Studies, Including a Portrait of Goya (*Feuille d'études dont un portrait de Goya*) (recto); *Page of Studies* (*Feuille d'études*) (verso). 1877–80 (recto); 1880–81 (verso)
Pencil on paper, 19 11/16 × 11 13/16" (50 × 30 cm)
Private collection, New York
FWN 2283r; FWN 2299v. P. 20, fig. 1; p. 21, fig. 2

Portrait of Mme Cézanne (*Portrait de madame Cézanne*). c. 1877–80
Pencil on wove paper (verso of found engraving), 7 1/8 × 7 1/2" (18.1 × 19.1 cm)
The Museum of Modern Art, New York. The William S. Paley Collection
FWN 1729. Plate 220

Self-Portrait (*Autoportrait*) (recto); *The Artist's Father and Object on a Mantel* (*Feuille d'études dont une pendule*) (verso). 1880–82 (recto); 1877–81 (verso)
Page XL from the CP II sketchbook. Pencil on wove paper, 8 11/16 × 4 15/16" (22 × 12.5 cm)
National Gallery of Art, Washington, D.C. Collection Mr. and Mrs. Paul Mellon, in Honor of the 50th Anniversary of the National Gallery of Art
FWN 3008-40a/b. Plate 25

Wash Basin and Scent Bottle (*Cuvette et flacon*) (recto); *Seated Bather* (*Baigneuse assise, études*) (verso). 1877–81 (recto); 1882–85 (verso)
Page XIIIbis from the CP II sketchbook. Pencil on wove paper, 4 15/16 × 8 9/16" (12.5 × 21.7 cm)
National Gallery of Art, Washington, D.C. Collection Mr. and Mrs. Paul Mellon
FWN 3008-13bisa/b. Plate 195

Still Life with Apples (*Pommes*). c. 1878
Oil on canvas, 7 1/2 × 10 1/2" (19 × 26.7 cm)
Fitzwilliam Museum, Cambridge, UK. Lent by the Provost and Fellows of King's College (Keynes Collection)
FWN 760. Plate 243

Trees at the Jas de Bouffan (*Arbres au Jas de Bouffan*). c. 1878
Pencil and watercolor on laid paper, 11 7/16 × 8 7/8" (29 × 22.5 cm)
Private collection
FWN 1045. Plate 125

Studies with Paul Cézanne Fils and Candle Holder (*Études avec Paul Cézanne fils et bougeoir*) (recto); *Heads of Paul Cézanne Fils and an Unknown Head* (*Têtes de Paul Cézanne fils et tête d'un inconnu*) (verso). c. 1879 (recto); c. 1878–79 (verso)
Pencil on laid paper, 5 11/16 × 8 7/8" (14.5 × 22.5 cm)
Private collection
FWN 2292r; FWN 2287v. Plate 59

The Apotheosis of Delacroix (*Apothéose de Delacroix*) (recto); *Some Baudelairian Verses* (*Esquisses de personnages et versets de Baudelaire*) (verso). 1878–80 (completed later)
Page from the BSB sketchbook. Pencil, ink, and watercolor on wove paper, with a strip added at bottom (recto); pencil on wove paper (verso), 7 7/8 × 9 3/16" (20 × 23.3 cm)
The British Museum, London
FWN 3017-02a/b. Plate 35

Decanter and Bowl (*Carafe et bol*). 1878–80
Pencil and watercolor on paper, 6 7/8 × 4 1/2" (17.5 × 11.4 cm)
Private collection, Switzerland
FWN 1902. Plate 198

Page of Studies: The Artist's Son; Head of Ceres (after Rubens); Female Bather (*Tête de Paul Cézanne fils, baigneuse et tête d'après Rubens: Cères*) (verso); *Landscape with Trees and Houses* (*Paysage avec arbres et maisons*) (recto). c. 1879, 1882–83, 1880 (verso); c. 1882–83, 1880 (recto)
Page XXXV from the CP II sketchbook. Pencil on wove paper, 8 11/16 × 4 15/16" (22 × 12.5 cm)
The Whitworth, The University of Manchester
FWN 3008-35b/a. Plate 15

Three Portraits of Paul and Studies after Pedro de Moya and Tintoretto (*Trois Portraits de Paul et études d'après Pedro de Moya et le Tintoret*) (verso); *Page of Studies* (*Feuille d'études*) (recto). 1879–80 (verso); c. 1879 (recto)
Pencil on paper, 9 7/16 × 12 3/16" (24 × 31 cm)
Phillips Family Collection
FWN 2297v; FWN 2293r. Plate 14

The Blue Plate (*L'Assiette bleue*). 1879–80
Oil on canvas, 11 × 8 15/16" (28 × 22.7 cm)
Ise Cultural Foundation, Japan
FWN 775. Plate 245 (not in exhibition)

Glass and Apples (*Verre et pommes*). 1879–80
Oil on canvas, 12 3/8 × 15 3/4" (31.5 × 40 cm)
Collection Rudolf Staechelin, Basel
FWN 779. Plate 244

Roses in a Vase (*Roses dans un vase*) (recto); *Landscape at Médan* (*Paysage à Médan*) (verso). 1883–86 (recto); 1879–80 (verso)
Pencil on laid paper, 11 1/2 × 8" (29.2 × 20.3 cm)
Collection Jasper Johns
FWN 1921r; FWN 1060v. Plate 138

After the Cupid Attributed to Puget (*L'Amour en plâtre*). 1879–82
Pencil on laid paper, 19 3/16 × 12 1/2" (48.7 × 31.8 cm)
Private collection
FWN 2141. Plate 235

Five Bathers (*Cinq Baigneuses*) (recto); *Study of Women Bathers* (*Études de baigneuse*) (verso). 1879–82
Pencil on paper, 5 3/4 × 5 1/4" (14.6 × 13.3 cm)
Collection Karsten Schubert Ltd.
FWN 2029r; FWN 2045v. Plate 101

Hercules Resting (*D'après Puget: Hercule au repos*) (recto); *Milk Jug and Spirit Stove* (*Réchaud à alcool et pot à lait*) (verso). 1884–87 (recto); 1879–82 (verso)
Page IV from the CP I sketchbook. Pencil on wove paper, 4 5/8 × 7 5/8" (11.8 × 19.4 cm)
The Art Institute of Chicago. Gift of Dorothy Braude Edinburg to the Harry B. and Bessie K. Braude Memorial Collection
FWN 3003-04a/b. Plate 108

Page of Studies, Including a Centaur after the Antique (*Feuille d'études dont un centaure d'après l'antique*). 1879–82
Pencil on laid paper, 14 15/16 × 12 5/16" (37.9 × 31.3 cm)
Albertina, Vienna
FWN 2301. Plate 17

Standing Bather (*Baigneur debout*) (verso); *Bather* (*Baigneur descendant dans l'eau*) (recto). 1879–82 (verso); c. 1885 (recto)
Page XXXIII from the EH II sketchbook. Pencil on wove paper (verso); pencil and watercolor on wove paper (recto), 8 1/4 × 5 1/8" (21 × 13 cm)
Collection Jasper Johns
FWN 3010-33b/a. Plate 89

Standing Bather, Seen from the Back (*Baigneur debout, vu de dos*). 1897–82
Oil on canvas, 12 1/2 × 8 1/2" (31.7 × 21.6 cm)
The Art Institute of Chicago. Bequest of Brooks McCormick
FWN 932. Plate 85

The Bath of the Courtesan (*La Toilette de la courtisane*) (recto); *Nude Female with Attendants* (*Femme nue entourée d'amirateurs*) (verso). c. 1880 (recto); c. 1885 (possibly later) (verso)
Pencil and watercolor on paper, 7 1/2 × 8 1/4" (19 × 21 cm)
Arkansas Museum of Fine Arts. Purchase
FWN 1873r; FWN 1874v. Plate 46

Dressing Table with Towel and Basin (*Table de toilette avec essuie-mains et cuvette*) (verso); *Landscape* (*Paysage*) (recto). 1890–95 (verso); c. 1880 (recto)
Page XLV from the CP IV sketchbook. Pencil and watercolor on wove paper (verso), pencil on wove paper (recto), 10 1/16 × 8 1/4" (25.6 × 21 cm)
Collection David Lachenmann, Zurich
FWN 3018-23b/a. Plate 67

Group of Male Bathers (*Groupe de baigneurs*) (recto); *After Coysevox: Faun Playing a Flute* (*D'après Coysevox: Faune jouant de la flûte*) (verso). c. 1880 (recto); n.d. (verso)
Page XLV from the CP I sketchbook. Pencil and watercolor on wove paper, 4 5/8 × 7 3/4" (11.8 × 19.7 cm)
Private collection. Courtesy Nukaga Gallery, Tokyo
FWN 3003-45a/b. Plate 86

Hortense Fiquet (Madame Cézanne) Sewing (*Madame Cézanne cousant*). c. 1880
Pencil on laid paper, 18 9/16 × 12 3/16" (47.2 × 30.9 cm)
The Samuel Courtauld Trust, The Courtauld Gallery, London. Princes Gate Bequest
FWN 1735. Plate 64

Bust of Madame Cézanne (*Tête et épaules de madame Cézanne et fruit rond*) (verso); *The Little Bridge* (*Paysage avec un petit pont*) (recto). c. 1880 (verso); 1884–85 (recto)
Page XXXIII from the CP II sketchbook. Pencil on wove paper, 8 9/16 × 4 7/8" (21.8 × 12.4 cm)
National Gallery of Art, Washington, D.C. Collection Mr. and Mrs. Paul Mellon, in Honor of the 50th Anniversary of the National Gallery of Art
FWN 3008-33b/a. Plate 19

Portrait of the Artist (*Autoportrait*) (recto); *Fragment of a Landscape Study* (*Étude de paysage*) (verso). 1880 (recto); n.d. (verso)
Pencil on laid paper, 13 7/16 × 11 3/16" (34.1 × 28.4 cm)
The Metropolitan Museum of Art, New York. Bequest of Walter C. Baker
FWN 1733r; FWN 1076v. Plate 27

Self-Portrait (*Autoportrait*) (recto); *Fragment of a Landscape* (*Fragment d'un paysage*) (verso). c. 1880 (recto); 1897–1900 (verso)
Pencil on laid paper, 12 5/8 × 5 3/4" (32.1 × 14.6 cm)
Collection Jasper Johns
FWN 1734r; FWN 1421v. Plate 26

Waking Up (*La Réveil*) (verso); *Roses in a Bottle* (*Roses dans une bouteille*) (recto). c. 1880 (verso); 1900–04 (recto)
Pencil and watercolor on wove paper, 17 1/4 × 12 1/4" (43.8 × 31.1 cm)
National Gallery of Art, Washington, D.C. Collection Mr. and Mrs. Paul Mellon
FWN 1965v; FWN 1872r. Plate 48

After Puget: Milo of Crotona (*D'après Puget: Milon de Crotone*). 1880–83
Page 27 from the BS I sketchbook. Pencil on wove paper, 8 9/16 × 5 3/16" (21.8 × 13.2 cm)
Kunsthalle Bremen–Der Kunstverein in Bremen, Department of Prints and Drawings
FWN 3011-27a. Plate 113

Bather with Outstretched Arms (*Baigneur aux bras écartés*) (recto); *Landscape* (*Paysage*) (verso). c. 1883–86 (recto); c. 1880–83 (verso)
Page IX from the CP II sketchbook. Pencil on wove paper, 8 11/16 × 4 15/16" (22 × 12.5 cm)
Collection Jasper Johns
FWN 3008-09a/b. Plate 96

Self-Portrait and Apple (*Autoportrait et pomme*). 1880–84
Pencil on paper, 6 13/16 × 9 1/16" (17.3 × 23 cm)
Cincinnati Art Museum. Gift of Miss Emily Poole
FWN 2306. Plate 21

Village Houses (*Maisonnettes*) (recto); *Study of a Piece of Upholstered Furniture* (*Esquisse d'un fauteuil*) (verso). 1880–85 (recto); n.d. (verso)
Pencil, watercolor, and gouache on paper, 12 7/8 × 19 5/8" (32.7 × 49.9 cm)
Smith College Museum of Art, Northampton, Massachusetts. Bequest of Charles C. Cunningham in memory of Eleanor Lamont Cunningham, class of 1932, through the kindness of Priscilla Cunningham, class of 1958
FWN 1100r; FWN 1934v. Plate 132

Corner of a Studio (*Coin d'atelier*) (verso); *Heads of Mme Cézanne and Louis-Auguste Cézanne* (*Feuille d'études avec têtes de madame Cézanne et de Louis-Auguste Cézanne*) (recto). 1881
Page XLI from the CP II sketchbook. Pencil on wove paper, 8 9/16 × 4 7/8" (21.8 × 12.4 cm)
Harvard Art Museums/Fogg Museum, Cambridge, Massachusetts. Bequest of Marian H. Phinney
FWN 3008-41b/a. P. 214

Three Bathers (*Trois Baigneurs*) (recto); *The Dinner* (*Le Dîner*) (verso). c. 1881 (recto); 1896–99 (verso)
Page 46 from the EH I sketchbook. Pencil and watercolor on wove paper (recto); pencil on wove paper (verso), 7 1/16 × 4 5/16" (18 × 11 cm)
Collection Jasper Johns
FWN 3002-46a/b. Plate 92

Portrait of Paul, the Artist's Son (*Portrait du fils de l'artiste*). 1881–82
Oil on canvas, 11 1/4 × 12 13/16" (28.6 × 32.5 cm)
Private collection, Derbyshire
FWN 459. Plate 246 (not in exhibition)

After the Écorché (*D'après l'écorché*) (recto); *Sketch of a Person and Scribbles of a Child* (*Esquisse de personnage et gribouillages d'enfant*) (verso). 1881–84 (recto); n.d. (verso)
Page from the 13.3 × 21.1 sketchbook. Pencil on wove paper, 8 5/16 × 5 1/4" (21.1 × 13.3 cm)
The Cleveland Museum of Art. Bequest of Leonard C. Hanna, Jr.
FWN 3012-06a/b. Plate 231

Madame Cézanne (*Portrait de Madame Cézanne, profil gauche*) (verso); *After Michelangelo: Slave* (*D'après Michel-Ange: L'Esclave rebelle*) (recto). c. 1884–87 (verso); 1881–84 (recto)
Page XLVIII from the CP I sketchbook. Pencil on wove paper, 7 11/16 × 4 3/4" (19.5 × 12.1 cm)
Private collection
FWN 3003-48b/a. Plate 61

Ornamental Clock Figure (*Figure d'ornement d'une pendule de cheminée*). 1881–84
Pencil on paper, 11 13/16 × 9 13/16" (30 × 25 cm)
Private collection
FWN 2147. Plate 54

Still Life (*Nature morte*). 1881–84
Pencil on laid paper, 10 7/8 × 16 1/2" (27.6 × 41.9 cm)
Fondation Marie Anne Poniatowski Krugier
FWN 1903. Plate 192

Still Life with a Candlestick (*Nature morte au bougeoir*). 1881–84
Page XXVIII from the BS III sketchbook. Pencil on wove paper, 4 15/16 × 8 3/16" (12.5 × 20.8 cm)
Kunstmuseum Basel, Kupferstichkabinett
FWN 3007-28a. Plate 193

Bed and Table (*Lit et table*) (verso); *Carafe and Knife* (*Carafe et couteau*) (recto). 1885–87 (verso); c. 1882 (recto)
Page LXVII from the CP IV sketchbook. Pencil and watercolor on wove paper, 10 3/4 × 8 1/4" (27.3 × 21 cm)
Philadelphia Museum of Art. A. E. Gallatin Collection
FWN 3018-34b/a. Plate 70 (not in exhibition)

Three Male Bathers; Pitcher (*Trois Baigneurs et annotations*) (verso); *Notes and figures* (*Notes et chiffres*) (recto). c. 1882 (verso); n.d. (recto)
Page 47 from the EH I sketchbook. Pencil on wove paper, 7 3/16 × 4 9/16" (18.2 × 11.6 cm)
Philadelphia Museum of Art. Gift of Mr. and Mrs. Walter H. Annenberg
FWN 3002-47b/a

Pear (*Une poire*) (recto); *Sketches of Figures* (*Esquisses de personnages*) (verso). c. 1882 (possibly later) (recto); n.d. (verso)
Possibly page from the EH II sketchbook. Pencil and watercolor on wove paper (recto); pencil on wove paper (verso), 5 × 8 3/16" (12.7 × 20.8 cm)
Nationalmuseum, Stockholm. Kersti Richthoffs Fund
FWN 3010-x1a/b. Plate 200

Standing Female Bather (*Baigneuse debout*) (recto); *Landscape with Donkey* (*Paysage avec un âne*) (verso). n.d. (recto); 1882 or later (verso)
Page 17 from the EH I sketchbook. Pencil and watercolor on wove paper (recto); pencil on wove paper (verso), 7 3/16 × 4 9/16" (18.3 × 11.6 cm)
Philadelphia Museum of Art. Gift of Mr. and Mrs. Walter H. Annenberg
FWN 3002-17a/b. P. 14, fig. 1

After Pierre Puget: Milo of Crotona (*D'après Pierre Puget: Milon de Crotone*). c. 1882–85
Page XLVII from the CP I sketchbook. Pencil on wove paper, 7 11/16 × 4 11/16" (19.6 × 11.9 cm)
The Whitworth, The University of Manchester
FWN 3003-47a. Plate 114

Apples and Pears (*Pommes et poires*). 1882–85
Pencil and watercolor on paper, 8 7/16 × 12 5/8" (21.5 × 32 cm)
Private collection
FWN 1908. Plate 201

Seated Nude (*Nu assis*). 1882–85
Pencil and watercolor on paper, 17 1/2 × 12 1/2" (44.5 × 31.8 cm)
Collection Jasper Johns
FWN 2033. Plate 118

Study of a Monument (*Étude d'après un monument*) (verso); *Landscape at the Jas de Bouffan and Portrait of a Young Man* (*Paysage au Jas de Bouffan et d'après Parmigianino: Portrait de jeune homme*) (recto). 1878–80 (verso); 1882–85 (recto)
Page XVI from the CP II sketchbook. Pencil, ink, and watercolor on wove paper (verso); pencil on wove paper (recto), 8 9/16 × 4 15/16" (21.7 × 12.6 cm)
Museum Boijmans Van Beuningen, Rotterdam. Loan: Stichting Museum Boijmans Van Beuningen 1940 (former collection Koenigs)
FWN 3008-16b/a. Plate 49

Dead Christ (*D'après Alonso Cano: Le Christ mort*) (verso); *Standing Male Bather (Baigneur débout et annotations)* (recto). After 1882
Page 45 from the EH I sketchbook. Pencil on wove paper, 4 9/16 × 4 7/8" (11.6 × 12.4 cm)
Philadelphia Museum of Art. Gift of Mr. and Mrs. Walter H. Annenberg
FWN 3002-45b/a. P. 202, fig. 2

Foliage and Flowers (*Feuilles et fleurs*) (recto); *After an Antique Sculpture: Faun and Child* (*D'après l'antique: Silène portant Dionysos*) (verso). c. 1895 (recto); after 1882 (verso)
Possibly page 5 from the EH I sketchbook. Pencil and watercolor on wove paper (recto); pencil on wove paper (verso), 7 5/8 × 4 5/8" (19.4 × 11.7 cm)
Collection Kate Ganz
FWN 3002-05a/b. Plate 141

Seated Man; Legs of a Bather (*Annotations, homme assis et jambes de baigneur*) (recto); *Still Life* (*Nature morte*) (verso). n.d. (recto); after 1882 (verso)
Page 43–44 from the EH I sketchbook. Pencil on wove paper, 7 3/16 × 4 9/16" (18.2 × 11.6 cm)
Philadelphia Museum of Art. Gift of Mr. and Mrs. Walter H. Annenberg
FWN 3002-43a/b; FWN 3002-44a/b

Small Tree; Person Asleep (*Le Fils de l'artiste endormi et étude de feuillage*) (recto); *Antique Crouching Venus* (*D'après l'antique: Vénus accroupie*) (verso). After 1882 (recto); 1892–96 (verso)
Page 11 from the EH I sketchbook. Pencil on wove paper, 4 9/16 × 7 3/16" (11.6 × 18.2 cm)
Philadelphia Museum of Art. Gift of Mr. and Mrs. Walter H. Annenberg
FWN 3002-11a/b. Plate 18

Study after a Plaster Cast of a Putto Sculpture Attributed to Pierre Puget (*L'Amour en plâtre*) (verso); *Study of the Sainte-Victoire Mountain, with a Tree and an Aqueduct* (*Pin et montagne Sainte-Victoire*) (recto). c. 1890 (verso); 1883–85 (recto)
Pencil on paper, 19 × 12 3/16" (48.2 × 31 cm)
Museum Boijmans Van Beuningen, Rotterdam. Loan: Stichting Museum Boijmans Van Beuningen 1940 (former collection Koenigs)
FWN 2160v; FWN 1131r. Plate 237

Pair of Scissors (*Ciseaux*) (recto); *Monument to Henry II; Head* (*D'après G. Pilon: Les Trois Grâces et étude de tête*) (verso). n.d. (recto); 1883–86 (verso)
Page 24 from the EH I sketchbook. Pencil on wove paper, 4 9/16 × 7 3/16" (11.6 × 18.3 cm)
Philadelphia Museum of Art. Gift of Mr. and Mrs. Walter H. Annenberg
FWN 3002-24a/b

Sketch with Louis-Auguste Cézanne Reading, a Mantelpiece, and a Man Looking Downward (*Louis-Auguste Cézanne lisant et cheminée*). c. 1883–86
Page XXXIV verso from the CP II sketchbook. Pencil on wove paper, 8 7/16 × 4 7/8" (21.5 × 12.4 cm)
Private collection
FWN 3008-34b

Earthenware Pitcher, Pot, Woman Bather (*Pichet en grès, boite et baigneuse*) (verso); *Young Man Asleep* (*Jeune Homme assoupi*) (recto). c. 1891–92 (verso); c. 1884 (recto)
Page IX from the CP I sketchbook. Pencil on wove paper (verso); ink on wove paper (recto), 4 3/4 × 7 5/8" (12 × 19.4 cm)
Private collection
FWN 3003-09b/a. Plate 196a

After Puget: Hercules Resting (*D'après Puget: Hercule au repos*). 1884–87
Pencil on laid paper, 18 1/2 × 11 13/16" (47 × 30 cm)
Städel Museum, Graphische Sammlung, Frankfurt am Main
FWN 2152. Plate 109

Rococo Clock (*Pendule rococo*) (verso); *After the Antique: African Fisherman* (*D'après l'antique: Vieux pêcheur*) (recto). After 1900 (verso); 1884–87 (recto)
Page 6 from the BS I sketchbook. Pencil on wove paper, 8 9/16 × 5 3/16" (21.8 × 13.1 cm)
Kunstmuseum Basel, Kupferstichkabinett
FWN 3011-06b/a. Plate 55

Study after the Hercules Sculpture by Pierre Puget in the Louvre (*D'après Puget: Hercule au repos*). 1884–87
Pencil on laid paper, 18 5/8 × 12 5/16" (47.3 × 31.3 cm)
Museum Boijmans Van Beuningen, Rotterdam. Loan: Stichting Museum Boijmans Van Beuningen 1940 (former collection Koenigs)
FWN 2150. Plate 107

After Puget: Hercules Resting (*D'après Puget: Hercule au repos*) (verso); *Landscape Sketch* (*Sentier dans la forêt*) (recto). 1894–97 (verso); c. 1885 (recto)
Page XII from the BS III sketchbook. Pencil on wove paper (verso); pencil and watercolor on wove paper (recto), 8 3/16 × 4 15/16" (20.8 × 12.5 cm)
Kunstmuseum Basel, Kupferstichkabinett
FWN 3007-12b/a. Plate 110

The Bather (*Baigneur debout vu de dos*). c. 1885
Pencil, watercolor, and gouache on laid paper, 8 3/4 × 6 3/4" (22.3 × 17.1 cm)
Wadsworth Atheneum, Hartford, Connecticut. The Ella Gallup Sumner and Marty Catlin Sumner Collection Fund
FWN 2032. Plate 84

The Bather (*Le Grand Baigneur*). c. 1885
Oil on canvas, 50 × 38 1/8" (127 × 96.8 cm)
The Museum of Modern Art, New York. Lillie P. Bliss Collection. Conservation was made possible by the Bank of America Art Conservation Project
FWN 915. Plate 100

The Blue Pot Warmer (*Le Cache-pot bleu*) (recto); *Sketch of the Artist's Son* (*Esquisse du fils de l'artiste*) (verso). c. 1885 (recto); n.d. (verso)
Page XV from the CP II sketchbook. Pencil, watercolor, and gouache on wove paper (recto); pencil on wove paper (verso), 8 7/16 × 4 15/16" (21.5 × 12.5 cm)
Collection Kate Ganz
FWN 3008-15a/b. Plate 136

The Curtains (*Les Rideaux*). c. 1885
Pencil, watercolor, and gouache on wove paper, 19 5/16 × 12 1/16" (49 × 30.7 cm)
Musée d'Orsay, held in the Musée du Louvre, département des arts graphiques, Paris
FWN 1923. Plate 52

Full-Length Portrait of the Artist's Son Paul (*Portrait du fils de l'artiste, Paul*). c. 1885
Pencil on laid paper, 19 5/16 × 12 3/16" (49 × 31 cm)
Private collection
FWN 1745. Plate 119

Mont Sainte-Victoire (*La Montagne Sainte-Victoire*) (recto); *Fruits and Foliage* (*Fruits et feuillage*) (verso). 1900–02 (recto); c. 1885 (possibly later) (verso)
Pencil and watercolor on paper, 12 3/16 × 18 7/8" (31 × 48 cm)
Private collection
FWN 1460r; FWN 1915v. P. 12

Pot of Geraniums (*Pot de geranium*). c. 1885
Pencil and watercolor on paper, 19 9/16 × 12 1/8" (49.7 × 30.8 cm)
Collezione Marco Brunelli, Milan
FWN 1917. Plate 135

Skull and Book (*Un crâne*). c. 1885
Pencil and watercolor on laid paper, 9 1/4 × 12 3/16" (23.5 × 31 cm)
Detroit Institute of Arts. Bequest of John S. Newberry
FWN 1913. Plate 75

Trees and Cistern in the Park of Château Noir (*Arbre tordu et citerne dans le parc de Château Noir*) (recto); *Seated Bather* (*Baigneuse assise vue de dos*) (verso). 1900–02 (recto); c. 1885 (verso)
Pencil and watercolor on wove paper, 18 13/16 × 12 3/8" (47.8 × 31.4 cm)
Henry and Rose Pearlman Foundation (on extended loan to the Princeton University Art Museum)
FWN 1453r; FWN 2034v. Plate 148

Unknown photographer
Untitled (Portrait of the Model for *The Bather*). c. 1885
Albumen silver print, 5 1/2 × 3 7/16" (13.9 × 8.8 cm)
The Museum of Modern Art, New York. Gift of Curt Valentin
Plate 97

Winter Trees (*Arbres*). c. 1885
Pencil and watercolor on paper, 18 7/8 × 12 3/16" (48 × 31 cm)
Private collection
FWN 1141. Plate 152

The Artist's Son Asleep (*Esquisse du fils de l'artiste endormi sur un lit*) (verso); *The Artist's Leg and Bedding; His Son Asleep* (*Le Fils de l'artiste endormi*) (recto). c. 1886 (verso); 1885–86 (recto)
Page 2 from the EH I sketchbook. Pencil on wove paper (verso); pencil and traces of oil paint on wove paper (recto), 4 9/16 × 7 3/16" (11.6 × 18.3 cm)
Philadelphia Museum of Art. Gift of Mr. and Mrs. Walter H. Annenberg
FWN 3002-02b/a. Plate 60

The Bridge at Gardanne (*Gardanne, le vieux pont*) (recto); *View of Gardanne* (*Vue de Gardanne*) (verso). 1885–86
Watercolor and pencil on laid paper (recto); pencil on laid paper (verso), 8 1/8 × 12 1/4" (20.6 × 31.1 cm)
The Museum of Modern Art, New York. Lillie P. Bliss Collection
FWN 1156r; FWN 1157v. Plate 131; p. 200, fig. 1

Madame Cézanne (*Portrait de madame Cézanne*). 1885–86
Oil on canvas with traces of pencil, 21⅞ × 18" (55.6 × 45.7 cm)
Solomon R. Guggenheim Museum, New York. Thannhauser Collection, Gift, Justin K. Thannhauser
FWN 481. Plate 221

The Green Jug (*Le Cruchon vert*) (recto); *Two Apples* (*Deux Pommes*) (verso). 1885–87 (recto); n.d. (verso)
Pencil and watercolor on paper (recto); watercolor on paper (verso), 8 11/16 × 9¾" (22 × 24.7 cm)
Musée d'Orsay, held in the Musée du Louvre, département des arts graphiques, Paris
FWN 1924r; FWN 1938v. Plate 197

Study of a Tree (*Étude d'arbre*). c. 1885–87
Pencil on wove paper, 12⅜ × 18⅝" (31.4 × 47.3 cm)
The Samuel Courtauld Trust. The Courtauld Gallery, London.
FWN 1173. Plate 126

Mont Sainte-Victoire Seen beyond the Wall of the Jas de Bouffan (*La Montagne Sainte-Victoire vue par delà le mur du Jas de Bouffan*). 1885–88
Pencil and watercolor on laid paper, 18 9/16 × 12" (47.2 × 30.5 cm)
National Gallery of Art, Washington, D.C. Collection Mr. and Mrs. Paul Mellon
FWN 1180. Plate 124

Rose (*Rosier*). 1885–88
Pencil and watercolor on laid paper, 15½ × 11¾" (39.3 × 30 cm)
Private collection. Courtesy Laurie Rubin Fine Art
FWN 1930. Plate 139

Study of Trees (*Clairière*) (verso); *Vase of Flowers* (*Vase de fleurs*) (recto). 1887–90 (verso); 1885–88 (possibly later) (recto)
Pencil and watercolor on paper, 18⅜ × 11 13/16" (46.6 × 30 cm)
Fitzwilliam Museum, Cambridge, UK. Bequest of Captain Stanley W. Sykes
FWN 1225v; FWN 1932r. Plate 149

Bathers (*Baigneurs*). 1885–90
Page XLVI verso from the BS III sketchbook. Watercolor and pencil on wove paper, 5 × 8⅛" (12.7 × 20.6 cm)
The Museum of Modern Art, New York. Lillie P. Bliss Collection
FWN 3007-46b. Plate 87

Large Pine, Study (*Étude d'arbre [Le Grand Pin]*). 1885–90
Pencil and watercolor on laid paper, 12 9/16 × 19½" (31.9 × 49.5 cm)
Harvard Art Museums/Fogg Museum, Cambridge, Massachusetts. Bequest of Theodore Rousseau; jointly owned by The Metropolitan Museum of Art, New York, and the Fogg Art Museum, Harvard University
FWN 1187. Plate 127

Large Pine, Study (*Étude d'arbre [Le Grand pin]*). 1885–90
Pencil and watercolor on wove paper, 12¼ × 18 13/16" (31.1 × 47.8 cm)
Virginia Museum of Fine Arts, Richmond. Collection Mr. and Mrs. Paul Mellon
FWN 1188. Plate 128

Study of a Tree (*Étude d'arbre*) (recto); *Studies of Trees* (*Études d'arbres*) (verso). 1885–90
Watercolor on paper (recto); pencil on paper (verso), 14 3/16 × 11⅛" (36 × 28.2 cm)
Fondation Marie Anne Poniatowski Krugier
FWN 1191r; FWN 1175v. Plate 146

Unmade Bed (*Lit défait*) (verso); *Trees Crossing over a Stretch of Water* (*Ruisseau sous une voûte d'arbres*) (recto). 1885–90 (verso); 1892–95 (recto)
Page LII from the CP IV sketchbook. Pencil and watercolor on wove paper (verso); pencil on wove paper (recto), 10¾ × 8¼" (27.3 × 21 cm)
Private collection, New York
FWN 3018-26b/a. Plate 69

Bedpost (*Pied de lit, montant sculpté et rideau*) (verso); *Mont Sainte-Victoire* (*Bords du lac d'Annecy*) (recto). c. 1886 (verso); c. 1895 (recto)
Page XLVIII from the CP IV sketchbook. Pencil and watercolor on wove paper (verso), watercolor on wove paper (recto), 10 13/16 × 8 5/16" (27.4 × 21.1 cm)
National Gallery of Art, Washington, D.C. Armand Hammer Collection
FWN 3018-24b/a. Plate 72

After Pigalle: Mercury (*D'après Pigalle: Mercure*) (recto); *Poplar Tree, Study* (*Étude de peuplier*) (verso). c. 1890 (recto); 1886–89 (verso)
Page VIII from the BS III sketchbook. Pencil on wove paper, 8 1/16 × 4 15/16" (20.5 × 12.5 cm)
Kunstmuseum Basel, Kupferstichkabinett
FWN 3007-08a/b. Plate 117

Bather Crossing His Arms behind His Neck (*Baigneur se croisant les bras derrière la nuque*) (recto); *Spectators* (*Spectateurs*) (verso). c. 1900 (recto); 1886–89 (verso)
Page XLVIII from the BS III sketchbook. Pencil on wove paper, 8 3/16 × 4 15/16" (20.8 × 12.5 cm)
Kunstmuseum Basel, Kupferstichkabinett
FWN 3007-48a/b

Bather Stepping Down into the Water (*Baigneur descendant dans l'eau*). c. 1886–89
Page XXXI from the CP I sketchbook. Pencil and ink on colored wove paper, 7⅞ × 4¾" (20 × 12 cm)
Véronique and Louis-Antoine Prat Collection, Paris
FWN 3003-31a. Plate 93

Study of Bathers (*Étude de baigneurs*). 1886–89
Pencil on paper, 8 15/16 × 11⅝" (22.7 × 29.5 cm)
Kunstmuseum Basel, Kupferstichkabinett
FWN 2038. Plate 99

Unmade Bed (*Lit défait*) (recto); *Unmade Bed, Sketch* (*Lit défait, esquisse*) (verso). c. 1887 (recto); n.d. (verso)
Page LXV from the CP IV sketchbook. Pencil on wove paper, 10⅝ × 8¼" (27 × 21 cm)
Private collection, Boston
FWN 3018-33a/b. Plate 71

After the Antique Statue of a Roman Orator (*D'après l'antique: Orateur romain [Statue de Marcellus]*). 1887–90
Page XLV from the BS II sketchbook. Pencil on wove paper, 8¼ × 4 13/16" (20.9 × 12.3 cm)
Kunstmuseum Basel, Kupferstichkabinett
FWN 3005-45a. Plate 78

After Pierre Puget, Hercules Resting (*D'après Puget: Hercule au repos*) (recto); *Study of a Head* (*Étude de tête*) (verso). 1887–90 (recto), n.d. (verso)
Page XL from the BS II sketchbook. Pencil on wove paper, 8 × 4¾" (20.3 × 12.1 cm)
Kunstmuseum Basel, Kupferstichkabinett
FWN 3005-40a/b

After Puget: Hercules Resting (*D'après Puget: Hercule au repos*). 1887–90
Pencil on paper, 19 × 12⅜" (48.3 × 31.5 cm)
Private collection
FWN 2167. Plate 106

Rocks at Bibémus (*Rochers à Bibémus*). 1887–90
Pencil and watercolor on laid paper, 18 1/16 × 12½" (45.9 × 31.8 cm)
Henry and Rose Pearlman Foundation (on extended loan to the Princeton University Art Museum)
FWN 1232. Plate 158

Still Life with Spirit Lamp (*Nature morte: Pain sans mie*). c. 1887–90
Pencil on paper, 12½ × 19⅜" (31.8 × 49.2 cm)
Private collection
FWN 1941. Plate 194

Paul Cézanne Fils as a Harlequin, Studies for Mardi Gras (*Étude pour Mardi gras*). c. 1888
Pencil on paper, 7 15/16 × 10 11/16" (20.1 × 27.2 cm)
Kunstmuseum Basel, Kupferstichkabinett
FWN 1748. Plate 120

Study of a Harlequin (*Arlequin*). c. 1888
Pencil on laid paper, 18 13/16 × 12½" (47.8 × 31.7 cm)
The Art Institute of Chicago. Margaret Day Blake Collection
FWN 1750. Plate 121

Boy in a Red Vest (*Le Garçon au gilet rouge*). 1888–90
Oil on canvas, 32 × 25⅝" (81.2 × 65 cm)
The Museum of Modern Art, New York. Gift of Mr. and Mrs. David Rockefeller. Conservation was made possible by the Bank of America Art Conservation Project
FWN 495. Plate 226

Pot and Soup Tureen (*La Buire et la soupière*). 1888–90 (possibly later)
Page II from the EH II sketchbook. Pencil and watercolor on wove paper, 4 13/16 × 8 7/16" (12.3 × 21.5 cm)
The National Museum of Western Art, Tokyo. Matsukata Collection
FWN 3010-02a. Plate 50

Three Pears (*Trois Poires*). 1888–90
Pencil and watercolor on laid paper, 9½ × 12 3/16" (24.2 × 31 cm)
Henry and Rose Pearlman Foundation (on extended loan to the Princeton University Art Museum)
FWN 1944. Plate 199

Boy with a Red Waistcoat (*Le Garçon au gilet rouge, II*). 1889–90
Watercolor on laid paper, 18⅛ × 12 3/16" (46 × 31 cm)
Private collection
FWN 1755. Plate 225

Skull on a Drapery (*Crâne sur une draperie*) (recto); *Trees and Rocks at Bibémus* (*Arbres et rochers à Bibémus*) (verso). 1902–06 (recto); 1889–92 (verso)
Pencil, gouache, and watercolor on wove paper, 12½ × 18¾" (31.7 × 47.6 cm)
Private collection
FWN 1986r; FWN 1249v. Plate 53

After Puget: Milo of Crotona (*D'après Puget: Milon de Crotone*). c. 1890
Pencil on laid paper, 18 13/16 × 12⅜" (47.8 × 31.4 cm)
Baltimore Museum of Art. Bequest of Etta Cone, from the Collection of Frederic W. Cone
FWN 2168. Plate 115

Basket of Fruit (*Corbeille de fruits*). c. 1890 (possibly later)
Pencil and watercolor on paper, 11 13/16 × 17 11/16" (30 × 45 cm)
Fondazione Magnani-Rocca, Mamiano di Traversetolo, Parma
FWN 1945. P. 16, fig. 3

Bathers (*Baigneurs*) (recto); *Still Life* (*Nature morte*) (verso). c. 1890 (possibly later) (recto); c. 1900 (verso)
Page V from the CP IV sketchbook. Pencil and watercolor on wove paper, 8 5/16 × 10 11/16" (21.1 × 27.2 cm)
The Metropolitan Museum of Art, New York. Gift of Mrs. Mabel Rossbach
FWN 3018-03a/b. Plate 91

Forest Path (*Route en sous-bois*). c. 1890
Pencil and watercolor on paper, 19 × 12½" (48.3 × 31.8 cm)
Private collection. Courtesy Jill Newhouse
FWN 1287. Plate 151

Mercury after Pigalle (*D'après Pigalle: Mercure*). c. 1890
Pencil on wove paper, 15 × 11" (38.1 × 27.9 cm)
The Museum of Modern Art, New York. The Joan and Lester Avnet Fund
FWN 2166. Plate 116

Still Life: Cup and Cherries (*Tasse et plat de cerises*). c. 1890 (possibly later)
Pencil and watercolor on paper, 14 15/16 × 19 5/16" (38 × 49 cm)
Fondazione Magnani-Rocca, Mamiano di Traversetolo, Parma
FWN 1949. Plate 202

Study from a Statuette of a Cupid (*L'Amour en plâtre*) (recto); *Drapery Study* (*Études de draperie*) (verso). c. 1890
Pencil on laid paper, 19¼ × 12¾" (48.9 × 32.4 cm)
Brooklyn Museum of Art. Frank L. Babbott Fund
FWN 2164r; FWN 1955v. Plate 236

Trees and Rocks (*Arbres et rochers*) (verso); *Tree* (*Arbre*) (recto). c. 1895 (verso); c. 1890 (recto)
Pencil and watercolor on laid paper, 12⅜ × 19⅛" (31.5 × 48.5 cm)
Private collection
FWN 1345v; FWN 1269r. Plate 156

The Vase and the Column (*Le Vase et la colonne*). c. 1890
Pencil and watercolor on paper, 11 13/16 × 9 1/16" (30 × 23 cm)
Private collection
FWN 1953. Plate 137

The Card Player (*Joueur de cartes à la blouse bleue*). 1890–92
Pencil and watercolor on laid paper, 19⅛ × 14¼" (48.6 × 36.2 cm)
Museum of Art, Rhode Island School of Design, Providence. Gift of Mrs. Murray S. Danforth
FWN 1761. Plate 122 (not in exhibition)

Coat on a Chair (*Veste sur une chaise*). 1890–92
Pencil and watercolor on laid paper, 18 11/16 × 12" (47.5 × 30.5 cm)
Private collection
FWN 1954. Plate 68

After Puget: Hercules Resting (*D'après Puget: Hercule au repos*). 1890–94
Page XXXIX from the BS II sketchbook. Pencil on wove paper, 8 × 4 13/16" (20.3 × 12.2 cm)
Kunstmuseum Basel, Kupferstichkabinett
FWN 3005-39a. Plate 111

Landscape with Boulders and Trees (Paysage avec rochers et arbres, Bibémus) (verso); *Page of Studies, Mainly Horses (Feuille d'études avec chevaux et personnage)* (recto). 1890–94 (verso); 1891–94 (recto)
Page LXXXIII from the CP IV sketchbook. Pencil on wove paper, 8 1/4 × 10 1/8" (21 × 25.7 cm)
Private collection
FWN 3018-42b/a. Plate 155

The Château Noir with Mont Sainte-Victoire (Château Noir devant la montagne Sainte-Victoire). 1890–95
Watercolor and pencil on laid paper, 12 3/16 × 19" (31 × 48.3 cm)
Albertina, Vienna
FWN 1330. Plate 174

The Eternal Feminine (L'Éternel féminin). 1890–95 (possibly later)
Possibly page LIV from the CP IV sketchbook. Pencil and watercolor on wove paper, 8 1/4 × 10 5/8" (21 × 27 cm)
National Museum of Western Art, Tokyo. Matsukata Collection
FWN 3018-27b. Plate 40

Sketch of Three Pine Trees (Esquisse de trois pins). 1890–95
Watercolor on laid paper, 18 7/8 × 12 3/16" (48 × 31 cm)
Collection Kate Ganz
FWN 1307. Plate 145

Madame Cézanne in the Conservatory (Madame Cézanne dans la serre). 1891–92
Oil and probably soft graphite pencil on canvas, 36 1/4 × 28 3/4" (92.1 × 73 cm)
The Metropolitan Museum of Art, New York. Bequest of Stephen C. Clark
FWN 509. Plate 222

After the Écorché (L'Écorché de Michel-Ange). c. 1892
Oil on canvas, 13 5/8 × 6 1/2" (34.6 × 16.5 cm)
Private collection, New York
FWN 690. Plate 233

Saint Pierre Church in Avon (L'Église Saint-Pierre à Avon). 1892–94
Pencil and watercolor on paper, 18 1/2 × 12 1/8" (47 × 30.8 cm)
Phyllis Lambert Collection
FWN 1328. Plate 134

Skull on a Table (Crâne sur une table) (verso); *Bare Tree (Arbre denudé)* (recto). 1900 or later (verso); c. 1892–95 (recto)
Page IX from the CP IV sketchbook. Pencil on wove paper, 8 1/4 × 10 11/16" (21 × 27.2 cm)
Collection Jasper Johns
FWN 3018-05b/a. Plate 76

Man with Pipe (L'Homme à la pipe). 1892–96
Oil on canvas, 10 1/4 × 7 15/16" (26.1 × 20.2 cm)
National Gallery of Art, Washington, D.C. Gift of the W. Averell Harriman Foundation in memory of Marie N. Harriman
FWN 683. Plate 241

After the Écorché (D'après l'écorché) (recto); *Woman's Head and Drawings of a Child (Tête de femme et gribouillage d'enfant)* (verso). 1893–96 (recto); n.d. (verso)
Possibly page VIII verso from the 13.3 × 21.1 sketchbook. Pencil on wove paper, 8 1/4 × 5 1/4" (21 × 13.3 cm)
Private collection, New York
FWN 3012-04a/b. Plate 232

After the Cupid Attributed to Puget (L'Amour en plâtre). 1894–95
Oil on canvas, 22 1/2 × 9 3/4" (57.2 × 24.8 cm)
Private collection
FWN 688. Plate 242

Bathers under a Bridge (Baigneuses sous un pont) (recto); *Study after Houdon's Écorché (D'après Houdon: L'Écorché)* (verso). 1900–06 (recto); 1894–98 (verso)
Page XXII from the CP IV sketchbook. Pencil and watercolor on wove paper (recto); pencil on wove paper (verso), 8 1/4 × 10 11/16" (21 × 27.2 cm)
The Metropolitan Museum of Art, New York. Maria De Witt Jessup Fund, acquired from The Museum of Modern Art, Lillie P. Bliss Collection
FWN 3018-11a/b. Plate 103

In the Forest (Dans la forêt, I). 1895–98
Pencil and watercolor on paper, 18 7/8 × 12 3/16" (48 × 31 cm)
Musée Granet, Aix-en-Provence. Charles Bain Hoyt Bequest
FWN 1364. Plate 153

In the Forest (Dans la forêt, II) (recto); *Study of Trees (Étude d'arbres)* (verso). 1895–98
Pencil and watercolor on paper, 17 5/8 × 11 7/8" (44.8 × 30.1 cm)
Private collection. Courtesy Luxembourg and Dayan
FWN 1365r; FWN 1360v. Plate 154

Study of a Mantel Clock (Étude de pendule). 1895–98
Pencil on paper, 9 7/16 × 13 9/16" (23.9 × 34.5 cm)
Snite Museum of Art at the University of Notre Dame
FWN 2315. Plate 56

Cistern in the Park of Château Noir (La Citerne au parc Château Noir). 1895–1900
Pencil and watercolor on wove paper, 19 15/16 × 17 1/16" (50.6 × 43.4 cm)
Henry and Rose Pearlman Foundation (on extended loan to the Princeton University Art Museum)
FWN 1368. Plate 172

Female Nude (La Toilette). 1895–1900
Possibly page from the CP IV sketchbook. Pencil and watercolor on wove paper, 10 1/2 × 8" (26.6 × 20.3 cm)
Private collection, New York
FWN 3018-x4a. Plate 45

Foliage (Étude de feuillage) (recto); *Study of Trees (Troncs d'arbres)* (verso). 1900–04 (recto); 1895–1900 (verso)
Watercolor and pencil on wove paper, 17 5/8 × 22 3/8" (44.8 × 56.8 cm)
The Museum of Modern Art, New York. Lillie P. Bliss Collection
FWN 1980; FWN 1405. Plate 142; pp. 203–04, figs. 3–7

The Quarry near Bibémus (Rochers et caverne, II). 1895–1900
Pencil and watercolor on laid paper, 12 9/16 × 20" (31.9 × 50.8 cm)
Private collection
FWN 1387. Plate 164

Rocks near the Caves above Château Noir (Rochers près des grottes au-dessus de Château Noir). 1895–1900
Pencil and watercolor on paper, 18 11/16 × 11 13/16" (47.5 × 30 cm)
Private collection
FWN 1389. Plate 157

Rocks near the Caves above Château Noir (Rochers près des grottes au-dessus de Château Noir). 1895–1900
Watercolor and pencil on wove paper, 12 1/2 × 18 3/4" (31.7 × 47.5 cm)
The Museum of Modern Art, New York. Lillie P. Bliss Collection
FWN 1390. Plate 161

Rocks near the Caves above Château Noir (Rochers près des grottes au-dessus de Château Noir). 1895–1900
Pencil and watercolor on laid paper, 18 × 11 5/8" (45.7 × 29.6 cm)
Collection Kate Ganz
FWN 1391. Plate 162

Rocks near the Caves above Château Noir (Rochers près des grottes au-dessus de Château Noir). 1895–1900
Watercolor on paper, 12 3/16 × 18 1/2" (31 × 47 cm)
Private collection
FWN 1392. Plate 163

Rocks near the Caves above Château Noir (Rochers près des grottes au-dessus de Château Noir). 1895–1901
Pencil and watercolor on paper, 19 11/16 × 17 1/2" (50 × 44.5 cm)
Private collection
FWN 1394. Plate 160

Rocks near the Château Noir (Rochers près des grottes au-dessus de Château Noir). 1895–1900
Watercolor on paper, 19 1/4 × 11 7/16" (48.9 × 29 cm)
Private collection
FWN 1388. Plate 159

Roses (Rose dans la verdure). 1895–1900
Pencil and watercolor on paper, 18 7/8 × 12 3/16" (48 × 31 cm)
Anonymous, New York
FWN 1957. Plate 140

Teapot and Fruit (Théière et oranges [La Nappe]). 1895–1900
Pencil and watercolor on paper, 18 7/8 × 24 5/8" (47.9 × 62.5 cm)
Private collection
FWN 1959. Plate 203

The Boat, Lake Annecy (La Barque, le lac d'Annecy). 1896
Pencil and watercolor on laid paper, 12 1/4 × 18 5/8" (31.1 × 47.3 cm)
Private collection. Courtesy Jacobson Space, London, and Jill Newhouse Gallery, New York
FWN 1398. Plate 168

Reflection in the Water, Lake Annecy (Reflets dans l'eau, lac d'Annecy). 1896
Watercolor on paper, 19 3/8 × 12 11/16" (49.2 × 32.2 cm)
Von der Heydt-Museum, Wuppertal
FWN 1411. Plate 165 (not in exhibition)

Trees at the Water's Edge (Arbres au bord de l'eau) (recto); *Sketch of a Landscape (Annecy?) (Étude de paysage [Annecy?])* (verso). 1900–04 (recto); c. 1896 (verso)
Watercolor on paper, 12 5/8 × 19 5/16" (32 × 49 cm)
Esther Grether Family Collection
FWN 1413r; FWN 1461v. Plate 147

Sloping Trees (Arbres penchés). 1896–99
Pencil on laid paper, 12 1/16 × 18 1/2" (30.6 × 47 cm)
Private collection, New York
FWN 1419. Plate 129

After Puget: Milo of Crotona (D'après Puget: Milon de Crotone). 1897–1900
Page 23 from the BS I sketchbook. Pencil on wove paper, 8 9/16 × 5 3/16" (21.8 × 13.1 cm)
Kunstmuseum Basel, Kupferstichkabinett
FWN 3011-23b. Plate 112

The Bathers (Groupe de baigneurs) (recto); *Head of a Boy and a Male Nude (Tête d'un garçon et homme nu)* (verso). c. 1900
Possibly page from the CP IV sketchbook. Pencil and watercolor on wove paper (recto); pencil on wove paper (verso), 7 15/16 × 10 13/16" (20.2 × 27.5 cm)
The Morgan Library and Museum, New York. Thaw Collection
FWN 3018-x2a/b. Plate 88

Fountain, Place de la Mairie in Aix-en-Provence (La Fontaine sur la place de la mairie à Aix-en-Provence). c. 1900
Possibly page XXII from the EH II sketchbook. Pencil and watercolor on wove paper, 8 7/16 × 5" (21.5 × 12.7 cm)
Henry and Rose Pearlman Foundation (on extended loan to the Princeton University Art Museum)
FWN 3010-22a. Plate 133

Oranges and Glass (Oranges et verre) (verso); *Cézanne Fils Reading (Cézanne fils lisant)* (recto). c. 1900 (verso); n.d. (recto)
Page XXIX from the CP IV sketchbook. Pencil and watercolor on wove paper (verso); pencil on wove paper (recto), 8 1/4 × 10 3/4" (21 × 27.3 cm)
Private collection
FWN 3018-15b/a. Plate 204 (not in exhibition)

Page of Studies, Including a Skull (Feuille d'études avec crâne et figure de Bellone). c. 1900
Page VIII from the BS II sketchbook. Pencil on wove paper, 8 3/8 × 4 7/8" (21.2 × 12.4 cm)
Kunstmuseum Basel, Kupferstichkabinett
FWN 3005-08b. Plate 73

Path, Trees, and Walls (Chemin, arbres et murs). c. 1900
Watercolor on paper, 18 3/8 × 12 3/8" (46.7 × 31.4 cm)
Henry and Rose Pearlman Foundation (on extended loan to the Princeton University Art Museum)
FWN 1434. Plate 150

Plaster Cupid (L'Amour en plâtre). c. 1900
Pencil and watercolor on paper, 24 13/16 × 19 5/16" (63 × 49 cm)
Private collection
FWN 2179. Plate 238

Road through the Woods (Route à travers bois) (recto); *Road, Trees, and Building (Route, arbres et bâtiment)* (verso). c. 1900
Pencil and watercolor on paper, 18 1/4 × 23 9/16" (46.3 × 59.8 cm)
Galerie Rosengart, Lucerne
FWN 1454r; FWN 1456v. Plate 167

Seated Peasant (Paysan assis). c. 1900 (possibly later)
Watercolor on paper, 18 1/16 × 12 3/16" (45.8 × 31 cm)
Kunsthaus Zürich. Collection of Prints and Drawings
FWN 1776. Plate 123

Still Life with Cut Watermelon (Nature morte avec pastèque entamée) (recto); *Study (Étude)* (verso). c. 1900
Pencil and watercolor on paper (recto); watercolor on paper (verso), 12 3/8 × 19 1/8" (31.5 × 48.5 cm)
Fondation Beyeler, Riehen/Basel. Beyeler Collection
FWN 1962r; FWN 1422v. Plate 209

Trees Forming an Arch (*Toits vus par une fenêtre ouverte*) (recto); *Roofs Seen through an Open Window* (*Arbres formant une voûte [Fontainebleau?]*) (verso). 1904–05 (recto); c. 1900 (possibly later) (verso)
Pencil and watercolor on paper, 23 11/16 × 18 1/16" (60.2 × 45.8 cm)
Henry and Rose Pearlman Foundation (on extended loan to the Princeton University Art Museum)
FWN 1428r; FWN 1510v. Plate 171

Well and Winding Road in the Park of the Château Noir (*Puits et route tournante dans le parc de Château Noir*). c. 1900
Pencil and watercolor on paper, 21 × 16 7/8" (53.3 × 42.9 cm)
The Claudio and Doriana Marzocco Collection. Courtesy Stephenson Art, London
FWN 1451. Plate 170

Women Bathers (*Groupe de baigneuses*). c. 1900
Pencil and watercolor on paper, 4 ¾ × 7 ⅛" (12.1 × 18.1 cm)
Fondation Socindec
FWN 2040

Brushwood (*Sous-bois*). 1900–04
Pencil and watercolor on paper, 20 × 17" (50.8 × 43.2 cm)
Esther Grether Family Collection
FWN 1465. Plate 169

Plaster Cupid (*L'Amour en plâtre*). 1900–04
Pencil and watercolor on paper, 18 7/8 × 12 3/8" (48 × 31.5 cm)
Museum of Fine Arts, Budapest. P. Majovszky Bequest
FWN 2180. Plate 240

The Plaster Cupid (*L'Amour en plâtre*). 1900–04
Pencil and watercolor on paper, 18 15/16 × 8 15/16" (48.1 × 22.7 cm)
The Morgan Library and Museum, New York. Thaw Collection
FWN 2181. Plate 239

Rocks and Trees near the Château Noir (*Le Parc du Château Noir avec la citerne*). 1900–04
Pencil and watercolor on paper, 21 ¾ × 16 ¾" (55.3 × 42.6 cm)
Kravis Collection
FWN 1452. Plate 190

Still Life with Apples, Pears, and a Pot (*Pommes, poires et casserole [La Table de cuisine]*). 1900–04
Pencil and watercolor on paper, 10 ¼ × 17 11/16" (26 × 45 cm)
Musée d'Orsay, held in the Musée du Louvre, département des arts graphiques, Paris
FWN 1963. Plate 205

Still Life with Inkpot (*Nature morte avec encrier*). 1900–04
Pencil and watercolor on paper, 12 3/16 × 18 7/8" (31 × 48 cm)
Private collection
FWN 1964. Plate 206

Bathers (*Baigneuses*) (recto); *Study of Bathers* (*Étude de baigneuses*) (verso). 1900–06
Possibly page LXXXI from the CP IV sketchbook. Watercolor on wove paper, 7 1/16 × 9 13/16" (18 × 25 cm)
Private collection
FWN 3018-x1a. Plate 105

Bottles, Pot, Alcohol Stove, and Apples (*Bouteilles, pots, réchaud à alcool, pommes*). 1900–06
Pencil and watercolor on paper, 18 ½ × 22 1/16" (47 × 56 cm)
Private collection
FWN 1967. Plate 214

The Dessert (*Le Dessert*). c. 1900–06
Pencil and watercolor on paper, 18 ½ × 24" (47 × 61 cm)
Private collection
FWN 1975. Plate 211

Female Bathers (*Baigneuses*). 1900–06
Pencil and watercolor on laid paper, with strip added at left, 6 11/16 × 10 5/8" (17 × 27 cm)
Private collection
FWN 2043. Plate 104

Outskirts of Aix (*Les Bastides Lou Deven et Barbaroux*). 1900–06
Pencil and watercolor on paper, 14 ½ × 21 ½" (36.8 × 54.6 cm)
Collection Mr. and Mrs. Barron U. Kidd, Dallas
FWN 1469. Plate 184

Portrait of Vallier (*Portrait de Vallier de profil*) (recto); *Study* (*Étude*) (verso). 1906 (recto); 1900–06 (verso)
Pencil and watercolor on paper, 18 7/8 × 12 5/8" (48 × 32 cm)
Private collection
FWN 1782r; FWN 1473v. Plate 230

Still Life with Apples on a Sideboard (*Pommes avec bouteille, pichet et pot bleu*). 1900–06
Pencil and watercolor on paper, 19 ⅛ × 24 7/8" (48.6 × 63.2 cm)
Dallas Museum of Art. The Wendy and Emery Reves Collection
FWN 1968. Plate 215

Still Life with Blue Pot (*Nature morte au pot au lait bleu*). 1900–06
Pencil and watercolor on paper, 18 15/16 × 24 7/8" (48.1 × 63.2 cm)
The J. Paul Getty Museum, Los Angeles
FWN 1970. Plate 213

Still Life with Fruit, Carafe, Sugar Bowl, and Bottle (*Nature morte avec grenades, carafe, sucrier, bouteille et pastèque*) (recto); *Flowerpots and Landscape* (*Pots de fleurs et paysage*) (verso). 1900–06 (recto); n.d. (verso)
Pencil and watercolor on paper, 12 ½ × 17 1/16" (31.8 × 43.4 cm)
Musée d'Orsay, held in the Musée du Louvre, département des arts graphiques, Paris
FWN 1972r; FWN 1981v. Plate 207

Still Life with Milk Pot, Melon, and Sugar Bowl (*Nature morte avec pot au lait, melon et sucrier*). 1900–06
Pencil and watercolor on paper, 19 × 24 ½" (48.2 × 62.2 cm)
Private European collection. Courtesy Christie's
FWN 1971. Plate 212

Mont Sainte-Victoire (*La Montagne Sainte-Victoire vue des Lauves en hiver*). 1901–06
Pencil and watercolor on wove paper, 12 9/16 × 18 ¾" (31.9 × 47.6 cm)
Henry and Rose Pearlman Foundation (on extended loan to the Princeton University Art Museum)
FWN 1476. Plate 175

Mont Sainte-Victoire Seen from Les Lauves (*La Montagne Sainte-Victoire vue des Lauves*). 1901–06
Pencil and watercolor on paper, 18 11/16 × 24 3/16" (47.5 × 61.5 cm)
National Gallery of Ireland, Dublin. Gift of Mrs. Chester Beatty
FWN 1480. Plate 176

The Cathedral of Aix, Seen from the Studio at Les Lauves (*La Cathédrale d'Aix, vue de l'atelier*). 1902–04
Pencil and watercolor on paper, 12 5/16 × 18 5/8" (31.2 × 47.3 cm)
Musée Picasso, Paris
FWN 1484. Plate 185

The Large Trees (*Les Grands Arbres*). 1902–04
Pencil and watercolor on paper, 18 ½ × 23 1/16" (47 × 58.5 cm)
Véronique and Louis-Antoine Prat Collection, Paris
FWN 1493. Plate 130

Seated Woman (*Madame Cézanne*) (*Femme assise*). 1902–04
Pencil and watercolor on paper, 18 7/8 × 14 3/16" (48 × 36 cm)
Anonymous, New York
FWN 1778. Plate 223

Study of a Skull (*Étude de crâne*). 1902–04
Pencil and watercolor on paper, 9 × 12 3/16" (22.9 × 31 cm)
Henry and Rose Pearlman Foundation (on extended loan to the Princeton University Art Museum)
FWN 1985. Plate 74

The Bend in the Road (*Route tournante*) (recto); *Mont Sainte-Victoire, View from Les Lauves* (*La Montagne Sainte-Victoire vue des Lauves*) (verso). 1902–06
Pencil and watercolor on paper, 22 1/16 × 16 9/16" (56 × 42 cm)
Esther Grether Family Collection
FWN 1498r; FWN 1495v. Plate 173

Bottle, Carafe, Jug, and Lemons (*Bouteille, carafe, cruche et cirtrons*). 1902–06
Pencil, watercolor, and gouache on paper, 17 ½ × 23 5/8" (44.5 × 60 cm)
Museo Nacional Thyssen-Bornemisza, Madrid
FWN 1976. Plate 210

Flowerpots on the Terrace of Les Lauves (*Pots de fleurs sur la terrasse de l'atelier des Lauves*). 1902–06
Pencil and watercolor on paper, 23 7/8 × 18 13/16" (60.7 × 47.8 cm)
David Lachenmann, Zurich
FWN 1982. Plate 144

Flowerpots (*Les Pots de fleurs*). 1902–06
Pencil and watercolor on paper, 12 3/16 × 18 ½" (31 × 47 cm)
Private collection
FWN 1983. Plate 143

Mont Sainte-Victoire (*La Montagne Sainte-Victoire vue des Lauves*). 1902–06
Pencil and watercolor on paper, 14 3/16 × 21 5/8" (36 × 55 cm)
Tate. Bequeathed by Sir Hugh Walpole
FWN 1496. Plate 181

Mont Sainte-Victoire (*La Montagne Sainte-Victoire vue des Lauves*). 1902–06
Watercolor and pencil on wove paper, 16 ¾ × 21 3/8" (42.5 × 54.2 cm)
The Museum of Modern Art, New York. Gift of Mr. and Mrs. David Rockefeller
FWN 1504. Plate 180

Mont Sainte-Victoire Seen from Les Lauves (*La Montagne Sainte-Victoire vue des Lauves*) (recto); *The Garden Terrace at Les Lauves* (*La Terrasse du jardin des Lauves*) (verso). 1902–06
Pencil and watercolor on two joined sheets of paper, 12 ⅛ × 28 ¼" (30.8 × 71.8 cm)
The Callimanopulos Collection
FWN 1503; FWN 1490. Plate 179

Portrait of a Woman (*Madame Cézanne?*) (*Portrait de femme [Madame Cézanne?]*). 1902–06
Oil on canvas, 25 ¾ × 21 ½" (65.4 × 54.6 cm)
Collection Stephen Mazoh and Martin Kline
FWN 539. Plate 224

Still Life with Green Melon (*Nature morte au melon vert*). 1902–06
Watercolor and pencil on paper, 12 3/8 × 18 11/16" (31.5 × 47.5 cm)
Private collection
FWN 1974. Plate 208

Still Life with Pears and Apples, Covered Blue Jar, and a Bottle of Wine (*Pot bleu et bouteille de vin*) (recto); *Landscape Sketch with Mont Sainte-Victoire and Trees* (*La Montagne Sainte-Victoire vue des Lauves*) (verso). 1902–06
Watercolor and pencil on paper, 18 ¾ × 24 15/16" (47.6 × 63.3 cm)
The Morgan Library and Museum, New York. Thaw Collection
FWN 1978r; FWN 1475v. Plate 216

View from Les Lauves near Aix (*Vue prise des Lauves vers Aix*). 1902–06
Watercolor on paper, 15 ¾ × 21 ¼" (40 × 54 cm)
Private collection
FWN 1491. Plate 186

Mont Sainte-Victoire (*La Montagne Sainte-Victoire vue des Lauves*). c. 1904
Oil on canvas, 21 ¼ × 25 9/16" (54 × 65 cm)
Private collection, Derbyshire
FWN 366. Plate 177 (not in exhibition)

Road with Trees on a Slope (*Route avec arbres sur une pente*). c. 1904
Watercolor and pencil on paper, 18 13/16 × 12 ½" (47.8 × 31.7 cm)
Fondation Beyeler, Riehen/Basel. Beyeler Collection
FWN 1509. Plate 182

Study of Trees (*La Route tournante*). c. 1904
Oil on canvas, 25 5/16 × 19 ¼" (64.3 × 48.9 cm)
Harvard Art Museums/Fogg Museum, Cambridge, Massachusetts. The Lois Orswell Collection
FWN 344. Plate 166

The Château of Fontainebleau (*Le Château de Fontainebleau*). 1904–05
Pencil and watercolor on paper, 17 5/16 × 21 5/8" (44 × 55 cm)
Private collection
FWN 1515. Plate 188

The Cathedral of Aix Seen from the Studio at Les Lauves (*La Cathédrale d'Aix vue de l'atelier des Lauves*). 1904–06
Pencil, watercolor, and gouache on paper, 12 ½ × 18 ½" (31.8 × 47 cm)
Collection Rita and Alex Hillman Foundation
FWN 1492. Plate 187

Chemin des Lauves: The Turn in the Road (*Maison près d'un tournant en haut du Chemin des Lauves*). 1904–06
Pencil and watercolor on paper, 18 7/8 × 23 1/16" (47.9 × 58.6 cm)
Henry and Rose Pearlman Foundation (on extended loan to the Princeton University Art Museum)
FWN 1520. Plate 183

Forest Landscape (*Intérieur de forêt*). 1904–06
Pencil and watercolor on paper, 18 5/8 × 23 5/8" (47.3 × 60 cm)
Private collection
FWN 1517; FWN 1490. Plate 189

Forest Path (*Chemin sous bois*). 1904–06
Pencil and watercolor on paper, 17 15/16 × 24 13/16" (45.5 × 63 cm)
Henry and Rose Pearlman Foundation (on extended loan to the Princeton University Art Museum)
FWN 1516. P. 16, fig. 2

Portrait of Vallier (*Portrait de Vallier*). 1904–06
Pencil and watercolor on paper, 18 11/16 × 12 3/16" (47.5 × 31 cm)
Private collection
FWN 1780. Plate 227

The Gardener Vallier (*Le Jardinier Vallier*). 1905–06
Oil on canvas, 25 13/16 × 21 5/8" (65.5 × 55 cm)
Tate. Bequeathed by C. Frank Stoop
FWN 547. Plate 229

The Bridge of Trois-Sautets (*Le Pont des Trois-Sautets*). 1906
Pencil and watercolor on paper, 16 1/16 × 21 3/8" (40.8 × 54.3 cm)
Cincinnati Art Museum. Gift of John J. Emery
FWN 1519. Plate 191

The Cabin of Jourdan (*Le Cabanon de Jourdan*). 1906
Pencil and watercolor on paper, 18 7/8 × 24 3/4" (48 × 62.8 cm)
Esther Grether Family Collection
FWN 1521. Plate 218

The Cabin of Jourdan (*Le Cabanon de Jourdan*). 1906
Oil on canvas, 25 9/16 × 31 7/8" (65 × 81 cm)
Galleria Nazionale d'Arte Moderna, Rome
FWN 380. Plate 219 (not in exhibition)

Mont Sainte-Victoire (*La Montagne Sainte-Victoire vue du nord d'Aix*). c. 1906
Pencil and watercolor on paper, 16 1/16 × 21 1/4" (40.8 × 54 cm)
Private collection
FWN 1507. Plate 178

Portrait of Vallier (*Portrait de Vallier*). c. 1906
Pencil and watercolor on paper, 18 7/8 × 12 3/8" (48 × 31.5 cm)
Museum Berggruen, Nationalgalerie–Staatliche Museen zu Berlin. On permanent loan by the Berggruen family
FWN 1781. Plate 228

Still Life with Carafe, Bottle, and Fruit (*La Bouteille de cognac*). 1906
Pencil and watercolor on paper, 18 7/8 × 24 5/8" (48 × 62.5 cm)
Henry and Rose Pearlman Foundation (on extended loan to the Princeton University Art Museum)
FWN 1988. Plate 217

Photograph credits

Individual works of art appearing in this book may be protected by copyright in the United States and in other countries and may not be reproduced without the permission of the rights holders. In reproducing the images contained in this publication, the Museum obtained the permission of the rights holders whenever possible. Should the Museum have been unable to locate a rights holder, notwithstanding good-faith efforts, it requests that any contact information concerning such rights holders be forwarded so that they may be contacted for future editions.

The credit lines listed below are in some instances provided at the request of the rights holders.

The Art Institute of Chicago/Art Resource, NY: page 72 above, 73 above. Photo Robert Bayer: 148, 197 below, 199 center left. Photo Robert Bayer/bildpunkt: 127 below, 142 above left, 143, 184. bpk Bildagentur/Nationalgalerie, Museum Berggruen, Staatliche Museen/Art Resource, NY: 70 above right, 190 above right. bpk/Staatsgalerie Stuttgart, ADRIANI FOUNDATION: 61. bpk/Staatsgalerie Stuttgart, Leihgabe der ADRIANI STIFTUNG seit 2020: 56 above. Kunsthalle Bremen–Karen Blindow–ARTOTHEK: 100 above right. Bridgeman Images: 41, 79 above, 155, back cover. © The Trustees of the British Museum: 34 above, 52. Courtesy James Butterwick Fine Art: 168. Courtesy François Chédeville: 32 below right. © 2021 Christie's Images Limited: front endpaper 2, 36, 56 below, 70 above left, 90, 118, 132, 142 above right, 160 left, 167, 176, 190 above left, back endpaper 1. Courtesy Thomas Colville Fine Art: 119 right. © The Samuel Courtauld Trust, The Courtauld Gallery, London/Bridgeman Images: 71, 112. Courtesy Dallas Museum of Art: 179. © Fitzwilliam Museum, Cambridge: 129 all. Photo Bob Goedewaagen: 43 right, 194 below right. Photo Damian Griffiths Photography: 131 below right, 141 above. The Solomon R. Guggenheim Foundation/Art Resource, NY: 186 below. © Hamburger Kunsthalle/bpk, photo Christoph Irrgang: 51 below. © President and Fellows of Harvard College: 32 above, 113 above, 140 right, 214. Photo Cecilia Heisser/Nationalmuseum, Stockholm: 164. Photo Mitro Hood: 101. © The Israel Museum, Jerusalem, photo Peter Lanyi: 22 above right. Courtesy Jacobson Space, London, and Jill Newhouse Gallery: 141. © The Provost and Scholars of King's College, Cambridge: 197 above, 199 center right. Courtesy Kislak Center for Special Collections, Rare Books and Manuscripts, University of Pennsylvania: 22 below left and right. By permission of Ministero dei Beni e delle Attività Culturali e per il Turismo: 185. The Morgan Library & Museum, New York: 24 above, 48 above, 87, 92 above right, 180, 195 below left. © Museum Associates/LACMA: 29 above. © 2021 The Museum of Modern Art, New York, Department of Imaging and Visual Resources, photo Peter Butler: 86 below, 102 left, 137 above, 186 above; Robert Gerhardt: front cover, 86 above, 104, 116 below, 135, 138, 147 above, 189 right, 193; John Wronn: 93, 123, 136 above, 200, back endpaper 2. © National Gallery of Ireland: 145 above. Photo Laura Neufeld: 125. Courtesy Jill Newhouse Gallery: 130 right. The Henry and Rose Pearlman Collection/Art Resource, NY, photo: Bruce M. White: 16 above, 43 left, 53 all, 78 below, 117 left, 128 all, 130 left, 134 right, 142 below left and right, 144 below, 149, 163, 181. Photo Robert Pettus: 134 left. Allen Phillips/Wadsworth Atheneum: 85 left. Courtesy Picker Art Gallery, Colgate University: 28. Photo © Michael Pollard: 32 below left, 38, 100 below. © Rheinisches Bildarchiv Köln: 34 below. Courtesy of the RISD Museum, Providence, RI: 106. © RMN-Grand Palais/Art Resource, NY: 27, 171; photo Tony Querrec: 64, 168; Jean-Gilles Berizzi: 150 below, 161. Klaus Ruland photography: 152. Scala/Art Resource, NY: 16 below, 164, 195 below right. Photo Peter Schibli: 173. Courtesy Sotheby's, New York: 49, 50 below, 120 right, 162, 164 below, 172, 188 above. Städel Museum–U. Edelmann–ARTOTHEK: 99 above left. Photo Jim Strong: 192 right. © Tate: 147 below, 190 below. © Bernard Terlay/Musée Granet, Ville d'Aix-en-Provence: 82, 131 below left. Photo Jerry Thompson: 122, 126. © Museo Nacional Thyssen-Bornemisza, Madrid: 174. Photo Jean Paul Torno: 131 above. Photo Studio Tromp: 33 all, 60 above, 98 above right. Troy Wilkinson © Virginia Museum of Fine Arts: 113 below. Photo Antje Zeis-Loi, Medienzentrum Wuppertal: 140 left.

Leadership support for the exhibition is provided by The International Council of The Museum of Modern Art, Ronald S. and Jo Carole Lauder, the Kate W. Cassidy Foundation, the Steven & Alexandra Cohen Foundation, The Halvorsen Family Foundation, and Monique M. Schoen Warshaw.

Generous funding is provided by the Eyal and Marilyn Ofer Family Foundation, the Robert Lehman Foundation, the Dian Woodner Exhibition Endowment Fund, and Emily Rauh Pulitzer.

Special thanks to William L. Bernhard and the late Catherine Cahill, Andreas Dracopoulos, Jack Shear, Anne Hendricks Bass Foundation, Ann R. Kinney in Memory of Gilbert H. Kinney, and John Wilmerding for their gifts to The International Council in support of the exhibition.

Major support for the publication is provided by The Museum of Modern Art's Research and Scholarly Publications endowment established through the generosity of The Andrew W. Mellon Foundation, the Edward John Noble Foundation, Mr. and Mrs. Perry R. Bass, and the National Endowment for the Humanities' Challenge Grant Program, and by the Jo Carole Lauder Publications Fund of The International Council of The Museum of Modern Art.

We are also deeply grateful to Ronald S. and Jo Carole Lauder for their generous support in making the reprint of this catalogue possible.

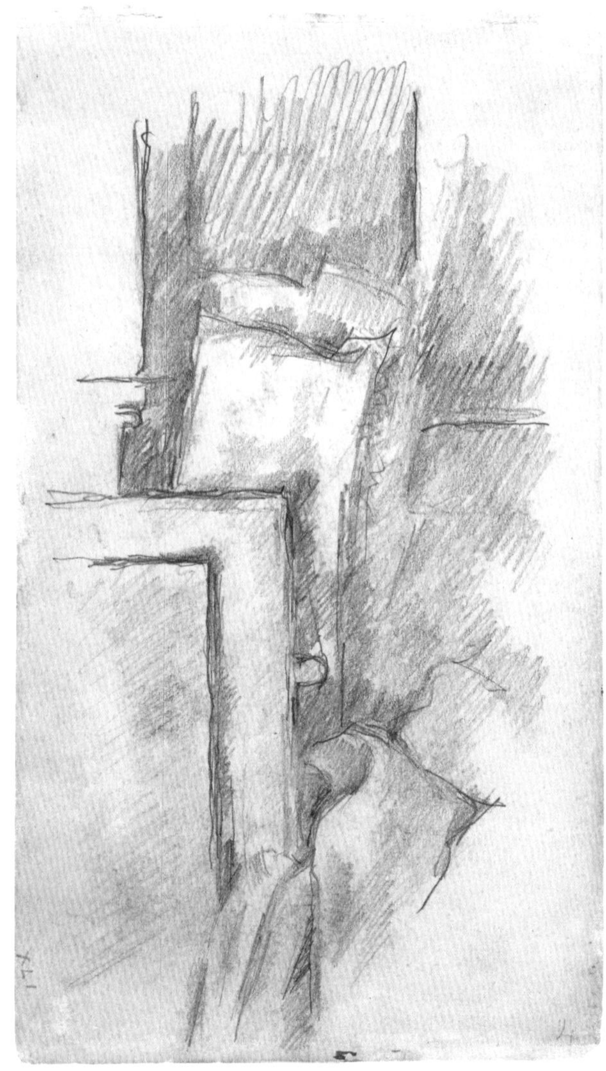

Corner of a Studio. 1881.
Pencil on wove paper,
8 9/16 × 4 7/8" (21.8 × 12.4 cm)

Published in conjunction with the exhibition *Cézanne Drawing* at The Museum of Modern Art, New York, June 6 to September 25, 2021. Organized by Jodi Hauptman, Senior Curator, and Samantha Friedman, Associate Curator, with Kiko Aebi, Curatorial Assistant, Department of Drawings and Prints.

Leadership support for the exhibition is provided by The International Council of The Museum of Modern Art, Ronald S. and Jo Carole Lauder, the Kate W. Cassidy Foundation, the Steven & Alexandra Cohen Foundation, The Halvorsen Family Foundation, and Monique M. Schoen Warshaw.

Generous funding is provided by the Eyal and Marilyn Ofer Family Foundation, the Robert Lehman Foundation, the Dian Woodner Exhibition Endowment Fund, and Emily Rauh Pulitzer.

Special thanks to William L. Bernhard and the late Catherine Cahill, Andreas Dracopoulos, Jack Shear, Anne Hendricks Bass Foundation, Ann R. Kinney in Memory of Gilbert H. Kinney, and John Wilmerding for their gifts to The International Council in support of the exhibition.

This exhibition is supported by an indemnity from the Federal Council on the Arts and the Humanities.

Major support for the publication is provided by The Museum of Modern Art's Research and Scholarly Publications endowment established through the generosity of The Andrew W. Mellon Foundation, the Edward John Noble Foundation, Mr. and Mrs. Perry R. Bass, and the National Endowment for the Humanities' Challenge Grant Program, and by the Jo Carole Lauder Publications Fund of The International Council of The Museum of Modern Art.

We are also deeply grateful to Ronald S. and Jo Carole Lauder for their generous support in making the reprint of this catalogue possible.

Produced by the Department of Publications, The Museum of Modern Art, New York

Hannah Kim, Business and Marketing Director
Don McMahon, Editorial Director
Marc Sapir, Production Director
Curtis R. Scott, Associate Publisher

Edited by Rebecca Roberts and Don McMahon
Designed by Damien Saatdjian and Prin Limphongpand
Production by Matthew Pimm
Proofread by Maria Marchenkova
Printed and bound by Trifolio s.r.l., Verona

This book is typeset in Suisse Works. The paper is 150 gsm Magno Volume.

Library of Congress Control Number: 2021933857
ISBN: 978-1-63345-126-1

Published by The Museum of Modern Art
11 West 53 Street
New York, New York 10019-5497
www.moma.org

Distributed in the United States and Canada by
Artbook | D.A.P.
75 Broad Street, Suite 630
New York, New York 10004
www.artbook.com

Distributed outside the United States and Canada by
Thames & Hudson
181A High Holborn, London WC1V 7QX
www.thamesandhudson.com

Printed in Italy

Front cover:
Forest Path (*Chemin sous bois*) (detail). 1904–06. Pencil and watercolor on paper, 17 15⁄16 × 24 13⁄16" (45.5 × 63 cm). Henry and Rose Pearlman Foundation (on extended loan to the Princeton University Art Museum). See p. 16, fig. 2

Front endpaper:
After the Écorché (*D'après l'écorché*) (detail). 1881–84. Pencil on wove paper, 8 5⁄16 × 5 1⁄4" (21.1 × 13.3 cm). The Cleveland Museum of Art. Bequest of Leonard C. Hanna, Jr. See plate 231

Teapot and Fruit (*Théière et oranges [La Nappe]*) (detail). 1895–1900. Pencil and watercolor on paper, 18 7⁄8 × 24 5⁄8" (47.9 × 62.5 cm). Private collection. See plate 203

Studies and Portraits of the Artist's Son (*Études et portraits du fils de l'artiste*) (detail). 1877–78. Pencil on paper, 9 3⁄4 × 12 1⁄8" (24.8 × 30.8 cm). Albertina, Vienna. See plate 22

Page 2:
Bathers under a Bridge (*Baigneuses sous un pont*) (detail). 1900–06. Pencil and watercolor on wove paper, 8 1⁄4 × 10 11⁄16" (21 × 27.2 cm). The Metropolitan Museum of Art, New York. Maria De Witt Jessup Fund, acquired from The Museum of Modern Art, Lillie P. Bliss Collection. See plate 103

Back endpaper:
Still Life with Milk Pot, Melon, and Sugar Bowl (*Nature morte avec pot au lait, melon et sucrier*) (detail). 1900–06. Pencil and watercolor on paper, 19 × 24 1⁄2" (48.2 × 62.2 cm). Private collection. See plate 212

Foliage (*Étude de feuillage*) (detail). 1900–04. Watercolor and pencil on wove paper, 17 5⁄8 × 22 3⁄8" (44.8 × 56.8 cm). The Museum of Modern Art, New York. Lillie P. Bliss Collection. See plate 142

Head of a Boy Asleep (The Artist's Son?) (*Tête de garçon endormi*) (detail). c. 1880. Pencil on laid paper, 8 7⁄8 × 7 13⁄16" (22.5 × 19.8 cm). Kunstmuseum Basel, Kupferstichkabinett. See plate 58

Back cover:
Self-Portrait and Apple (*Autoportrait et pomme*). 1880–84. Pencil on paper, 6 13⁄16 × 9 1⁄16" (17.3 × 23 cm). Cincinnati Art Museum. Gift of Miss Emily Poole. See plate 21

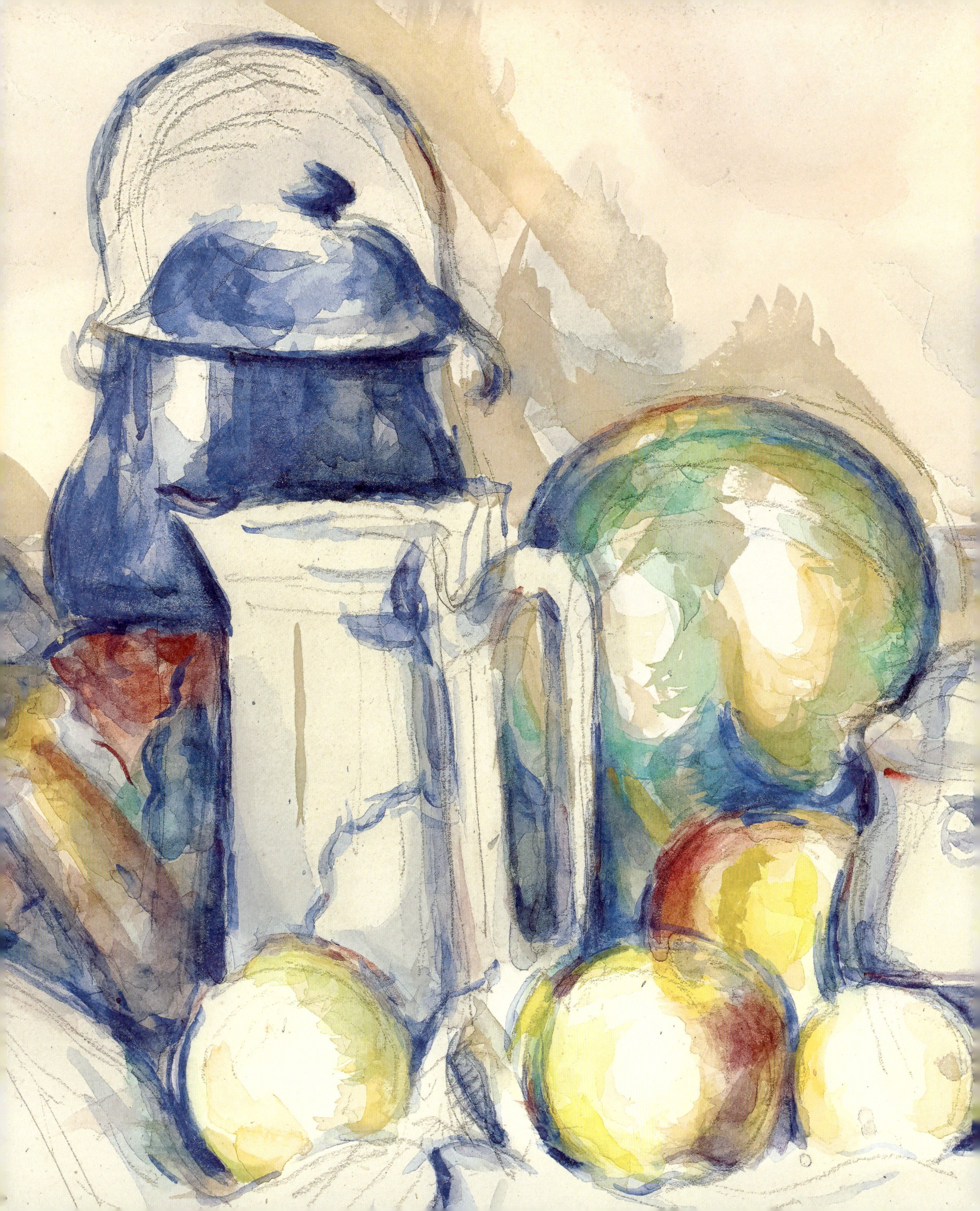

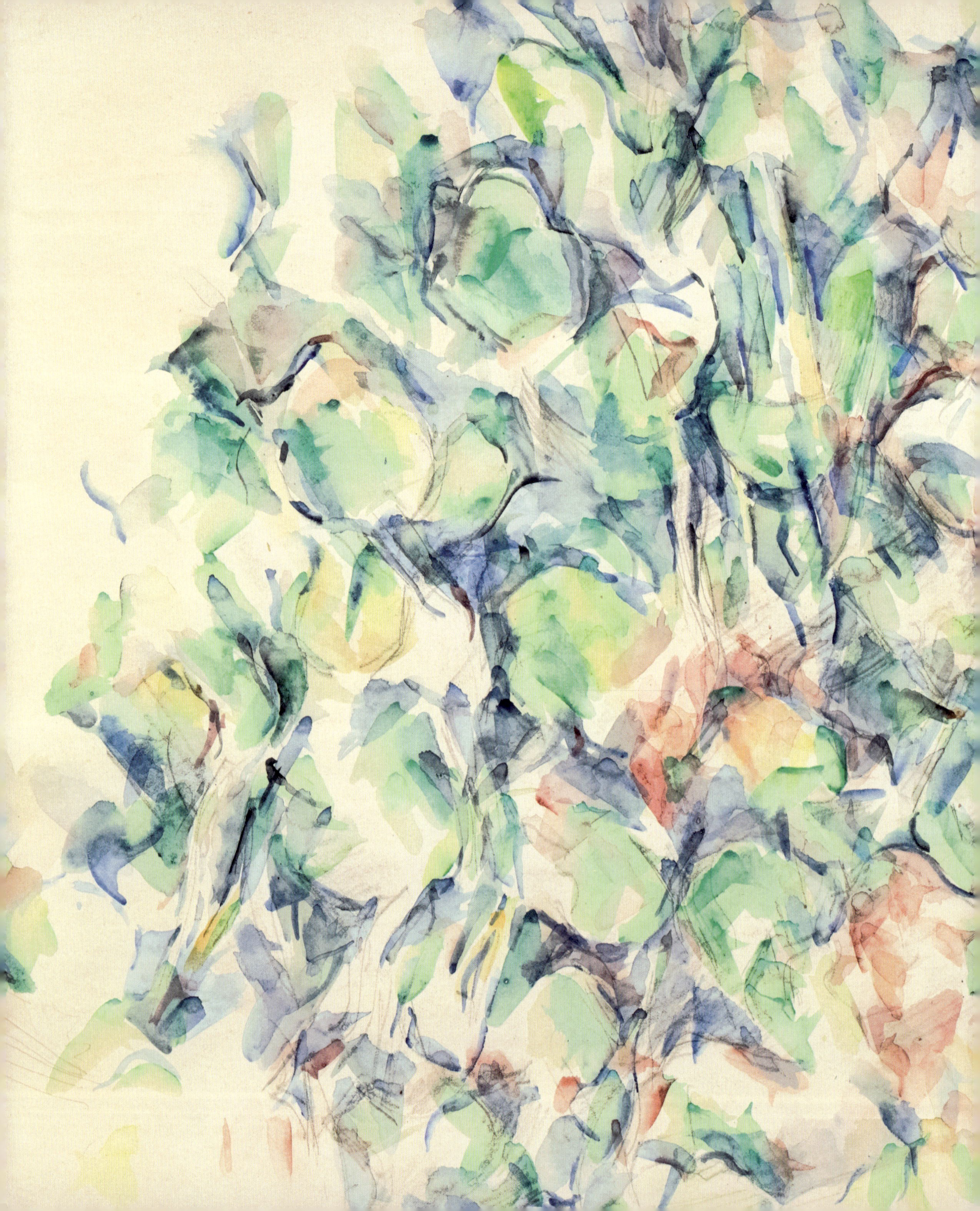